IMPROV NATION

IMPROV NATION

How We Made

a Great

American Art

SAM WASSON

AN EAMON DOLAN BOOK   HOUGHTON MIFFLIN HARCOURT   BOSTON   NEW YORK   2017

Library of Congress Cataloging-in-Publication Data is available.
ISBN 978-0-544-55720-8

Book design by Brian Moore

Printed in the United States of America
DOC 10 9 8 7 6 5 4 3 2 1

For
Jeffrey Wasson
Cindy Wasson
Sophie Wasson
Andrea Martin
Bob Dolman
Jack Dolman
Joe Dolman

Ours is the only modern country which is in a state of permanent revolution.

—Harold Clurman, *The Fervent Years:*
The Group Theatre and the Thirties

CONTENTS

Hi, How Are You?   xi

I

WE THE JEWS

1940–1968

1

II

WE THE PUNKS

1969–1984

135

III

WE THE NERDS

1984–

281

Goodnight, Everyone   377

Acknowledgments   380

Notes   384

Index   436

HI, HOW ARE YOU?

No one had any idea this would happen. Improvisational theater — as created in the early twentieth century by a young settlement worker, Viola Spolin, to foster self-expression and interaction among immigrant children; then developed by the young artists and intellectuals of the University of Chicago; then urged on by Mike Nichols and Elaine May into an expression of psychological healing and liberation; then urged on further into visionary presentational forms by director Paul Sills — was laughed into what we call improv comedy, or improv, for short, completely by accident. None of these giants set out for laughs, yet somehow we owe them Second City, Alan Arkin, Bill Murray, Tina Fey, *The Graduate, Saturday Night Live, Waiting for Guffman* — you name it.

The commerce, practice, and eventual art of improv comedy were themselves improvised. And why not? Many have surmised that improv's origins date back centuries, to commedia dell'arte. I don't agree. Nor do I believe it was "always there." Like anything else, improvisation had to be invented — and it was invented, in America, by young, mostly middle-class amateurs, performers, and producers who, in the true spirit of the form, were making it up as they went along. Sounds crazy at best, stupid at worst, and definitely not like the foundations of a sensible commercial or creative enterprise — let alone an entire industry and America's farthest-reaching indigenous art form, which is what improv comedy has become. As you'll soon see, no one in this story expected that to happen.

But I think that's partly why people went to see and be a part of it, returned for more, and keep coming back. They can't believe it. They can't believe anyone, sane or insane, would risk that kind of public humiliation. And when improv really hits the heights, they *really* can't believe it. "No way," you'll hear over your shoulder. "They must have written that. They couldn't have just made it up!" On those nights, it's like watching a magic trick, but while a magician always knows more than the audience, improv's magic is just as mysterious to its improvisers. It's a special form that says, *Even though you're down there and we're up here, we're discovering this together.*

We all of us can identify with the improviser's predicament, the terror of not knowing what to say or do when all eyes are on you. That right there is a human drama on its own, and it's really happening to real people, right in this moment.

And if you're there in the room, you'll likely realize that the deepest, most explosive laugh, the painful, blinding gasping for breath that has you physically bracing yourself on something solid so you don't fall over, is the laugh that erupts from the spontaneous materials of real time, in real life.

This is improvisation, the First Amendment in action. In improv venues across America, speech is, theoretically, as free as it's going to get; free of pop culture conventions and political correctness, free of the watch-what-you-do-because-it's-written-in-stone inhibitions of everything published in print or online. In improv, nothing is written in stone. "It's kind of like fireworks," Del Close, one of its foremost innovators, once said, "the most ephemeral of art forms. Once it's gone, it's gone, baby. There's the afterimage for a few seconds, but nobody will ever see anything like it again."

The impact this ephemeral art form has had on popular entertainment, beginning with the opening of Second City in 1959, is undeniable. Since then, the number of leading comedy artists who rely on improvisational techniques has grown exponentially. America in midcentury had only one, two, or three improv comedy theaters operating at a given moment, and only in Chicago, St. Louis, and New York. Today you can see improv in practically every big city and on every college campus in the country. Burgeoning and proliferating, meme-like, from a dingy avant-garde theater outside the University of Chicago all the way to *The Colbert Report*, improv has replaced jazz as America's most popular art.

This is the story of that proliferation, of improv comedy's fifty-year ascent from performance technique to popular entertainment to formally and emotionally complex art to philosophy of being — and all of it as American as democracy. For improvisation isn't merely an analogue for democracy, it *is* democracy, demanding that its individual players and audience members uphold the democratic ideal of total collaboration, of hearing and being heard, and rewarding both sides with the very good feeling of shared humanity.

This book about democracy in comedy is not in itself egalitarian, insofar as it does not consider the life and art of every single improviser who has ever improvised. Many — I hope not too many — have been left out or scaled down. A better strategy than holding up an all-encompassing mirror, I decided, would be to chart the high points, to tease out the grander story of improv's invention, cultural dissemination, and artistic development, and portray the changing circle of improvisers who kept making history happen.

Who knows what the next chapter will be? A significant change at this point in improv's history is that we know now there will be a next chapter. We didn't always. For its first decades, the Second City — the world's longest-running and most successful improv and comedy theater — was always on the verge of shutting down. Its founders, better intellectuals than businesspeople, struggled to negotiate the rough waters of changing tastes and commerce; its leading improvisers, once "discovered," were forever leaving for Hollywood and New York; its critics, thinking they had seen it all, got used to denigrating popular improv as on a level with mediocre sitcoms — or worse, as "jokey." It was only in the last decades of the twentieth century — after Del Close and Charna Halpern's iO (formerly ImprovOlympic) shook up the Chicago scene, Andrew Alexander and his team of producers re-improvised old standards of Second City comedy, and the new run of luminaries from Chris Farley to Tina Fey, the first generation to come of age in a culture made by improvisation, infiltrated the establishment — that improv's financial and creative stations, a half-century after Viola Spolin first asked for an audience suggestion, were finally secured. My book ends there, but its story is still a work in progress. I leave it to someone else — to you, to everyone, really — to write the next installment. And I do mean you, whoever you are. Because as any experienced improviser will tell you, every audience member watching the show is improvising too.

WE THE JEWS

1940–1968

1

1940–1955

Imagine Viola Spolin, the mother, the Jewish mother, Paul Sills's mother, Tina Fey's spiritual grandmother, the mother of theatrical improvisation. There was no radio in those days, in the early part of the century, and Viola's parents, Russian immigrants, didn't have a lot of money, so as kids Viola and her friends had to invent their own amusement. Instead of going to the theater, they played tag, jacks, marbles, hopscotch, changing the rules as it suited them, breaking the rules, inventing new ones, up and down the streets of Chicago and for as long as the day would let them. When it got dark, Viola joined her big, rollicking, Jewish socialist family — father, mother, and five siblings — for long and elaborate games of charades, dressing up together, falling down laughing, and singing impromptu, Yiddish-flavored operas.

Let's jump ahead to 1924, when Viola, now a pretty and adventurous eighteen-year-old with an interest in social work, enrolled at Hull House, a community center offering educational and cultural enrichment programs to Chicago's poor, immigrant populations. There she trained under sociologist Neva Boyd, a progressive educator and leading play theorist. Boyd's Recreation Training School at Hull House instructed participants in group games and other communal activities including theater arts. Viola called Boyd, who envisioned play as essential to emotional and physical well-being, her "inspirator." "Play means happiness," Boyd wrote. "It is characterized by feelings of pleasure which tend to break out in laughter." Boyd took her students out of the classroom to engage in "play behavior," learn, and remember why, as children, playing felt so good. "When we find ourselves in situations in which we are free to act as our 'feelings' prompt," Boyd wrote in "Play — A Unique Discipline," "there is no emotional conflict in the functioning of the organism. This is what happens in spontaneous play." When you play, you are free to be most *you*.

Viola began to think about play as a way into the unconscious, a means of unearthing, as she wrote to herself, "qualities which cannot be talked about."

Some years later, talk was a problem for the multiethnic, multilingual youth of the recreational theater Viola directed at Hull House. Participants were intensely inhibited onstage. As long as these children — divided by culture and self-censored by fear — were unable to communicate, they would stay locked in, isolated from one another and ultimately from themselves. Getting them to play together, Viola believed, would loosen them up onstage and maybe light a flame under the melting pot. To provide them "a non-authoritarian climate" necessary for freedom, she had them extemporize together. Imagine a world where adults did not exist, she prompted. What would you do? "The unfolding of the scene was quite a revelation," she wrote. "Never were boys and girls more charming, more courteous to one another. They were gentle and tender, they spoke in soft tones, they were concerned with each other's simplest problems — they loved one another!"

They were improvising. That's what happens when you improvise.

Now let's go six hundred miles southwest, to Manhattan, Kansas, where, in 1942, nine-year-old Del Close — chubby, with big glasses and crooked teeth — was sitting in a movie theater.

"To be or not to be?"

This was the question Jack Benny was asking in a film of the same name, as Del sat watching, riveted to the movie screen. When it ended, he drifted from the theater high on the film's title: *To Be or Not to Be*, "the first intelligent question," he said, "I'd heard a human being ask himself." Who was this Shakespeare and what was he up to and why would anyone *not* want to be? What did that mean, *not to be*? He needed more.

Had his father, Del Close senior, a depressive alcoholic jeweler, been at any way available to his son, instead of caught up in his work at Del Close Jewelers, or in his depression and his drinking, had Mr. Close been home the night Del discovered human beings had a choice, and therefore a very big problem, and *therefore* a lifelong pain no metaphoric tunnel of what-ifs could help them escape, Del would not have made the trip to his grandfather's bar in nearby Abilene. "My grandfather," Close would recall, "kind of caught on that I thought some kind of secret shit was going on." Stepping around the bar, the old man led Del — the incipient mad scientist of improvisation — to his first lesson in freedom. From inside a glass-door bookcase, Grandpa removed a leather-bound copy of *Hamlet,* and put it in the boy's hands.

Back now to Viola, the teacher, the social worker, the bringer-together. She met and married Ed Spolin in 1940, while they were at work for the Chicago WPA; he was a set designer, she a theater director at the WPA's Recreation Project, by that time divorced and with two teenage sons, Paul and William Sills (when they wed, her husband had taken her surname). Expanding on her earlier efforts at Hull House, Viola was formulating techniques to help disparate populations dramatize their shared problems. By then, she had developed a format. First she would split her players into two groups. The performing group would decide on a subject worthy of improvisation, play for two or three scenes for the second group, their audience, who in turn would respond to the scenes with feedback. Then they would improvise the scenes again. "Every few months, the cast would pick out the best scenes and perform them for an actual audience. There were about 150 people in [one] cast," Viola would say, "Italians, Greeks, Mexicans, Negroes, and I don't know of what other racial strains. They were of all ages and of both sexes." And they all played together.

In 1940, in Chicago, Viola introduced the notion of audience suggestions.

On a trip out West several years later, Viola and Ed fell in love with the brown and purple wilds of the Santa Monica Mountains, and bought a patch of raw hillside on the edge of Mulholland. Ed built them a cabin in the hills over the city, and Viola bought herself a lime-green convertible, in which she would curl down the mountain to a big red barn at 1745 North La Brea, just north of Hollywood Boulevard, that she named the Young Actors Company.

From the bus stop on Hollywood and La Brea, her charges trekked up an old road that led them, just behind the Hollywood Women's Club, to the clapping of a fountain and Viola's big red barn, nestled in a ring of tall oaks. "It was like stepping into paradise," said actor Paul Sand, who began studying improvisation with Viola at age nine. Kneeling to child height, Viola would hike up her sarong-like dress and meet her young actors face-to-face, booming with warmth. She gave off the homey scents of roast chicken, herbs, and cigarettes, and her skin was tan from being outside all day playing with children. But although she was always gentle, "Viola was a powerful woman with a very strong voice," said her student Ronnie Austin. "You would have cast her as a labor organizer."

Imagine them playing inside too, onstage, games Viola designed to release spontaneity. Games were for rehearsal, intended to help the players — Viola became weary of the term "actor" — apply their full selves to traditional scripted performances. "The games were really what the whole class was," said student Jackie Joseph, "although Viola didn't call them theater games at the time. She called them improvisations." Divesting herself of parental power and authority, Viola said it was the games, not the teacher, that instructed. That was important. Playing the role of "teacher" could introduce what she called approval/disapproval syndrome and inhibit spontaneity. Viola was careful then not to become a rule maker but rather a diagnostician, prescribing a specific game to each actor to address a specific interpersonal block. Was a player struggling to relate physically with the others? Have him play Contact! (in which the individual touches someone every time he says a line). Was a player thinking too much? Play Mirror! (Mirroring someone else, you stop thinking about yourself.) "We were guinea pigs for the games," Paul Sand said. "She was creating them on us, with us."

Sometimes Viola would give the players a Who, Where, and a What, and have them figure out the How, tossing out "some surprise little thing," as Joseph put it, from her folding chair in the back of the auditorium.

"The submarine window broke!"

"Your pants just fell off!"

"Paul, you're a fish — go!"

Or, when their commitment to the improvised reality broke: "Focus!"

Laughing focused them. Viola laughed all the time. Joseph said, "Viola gave me, by her laughter, the confidence I needed to keep my focus."

Focus on the game was essential. Actually *doing*, not thinking or feeling, was the way to freedom. Engaging with the imagined physical space

— the "Where," Viola called it — was the only way an improviser could van-quish his everyday anxieties and habitual pasts and emerge with new selves, reborn in the moment. Don't think, *do!* "Out of your head and into the space!" Viola would say. Need a glass of water in your scene? Reach out and grab one! Another player might pull up a chair and join you. Now you're at a table together. The two of you have communicated Where without speak-ing a word. You've collaborated. "The games really are a form of breaking the ego," said Ronnie Austin. "If you really get into full communication with others and start feeling their feelings, you really do find yourself letting go of yourself." When a roomful of improvisers has let go of themselves, they can be remade into an ensemble. "You can't play tag alone!" Viola would remind them.

In rehearsal for the two-act children's comedy *The Clown Who Ran Away,* they tried an improvisation for feet. Sand said, "We had to get a lot of safety pins and pin up this curtain so only our feet would show and convey what was happening to us only through our feet." Using a technique she called side coaching ("directing" was too close to tyranny), Viola would call out helpful reminders to focus the players as they played. "See each other with your toes!" "Cry with your feet!" It worked. Players played, and character relationships surfaced. The games freed truthful behaviors.

Paul Sand, Viola's freest, most buoyant young improviser, particularly impressed a twelve-year-old student in Viola's class. "I remember Sand was kind of a big shot," Alan Arkin said. "He was very tall and kind of ruled the roost there." The Arkins had only just moved from Brooklyn to Los Angeles. Arkin's father had come to Hollywood expecting to work as a set painter, but he arrived with his family just as the set decorators were about to strike. "We didn't have a lot of money for me to do anything," Arkin said, "and my aunt Helen knew I wanted to act, so she got me a scholarship to Viola's workshop."

Viola's teenage son, Paul Sills, was often present. He had been exposed to improvisation his whole life, since the days he tagged around after Viola at Hull House. "I grew up with a lot of these games," Sills said. "This is my family work." Visiting the Young Actors Company with his friend, a black-haired girl Viola introduced to the group as Elaine, Sills's interest in his mother's experiments deepened. Mother and son would sit together in the audience, rapt in discussion about improvisation, and how, if at all, they could be used to create a totally new kind of theater. A theater of personal liberation. For years he had watched improvisation create communities of players and audience, instantly bound together, in ways traditional theater rarely could, through this act of communal spontaneity. He watched his mother teach them to rediscover what they had lost — what had been buried under years and years of petrified behaviors mistaken for free will — the old roads to their intuition, "the diamonds," Paul Sand said, "that you have as a kid." Sills watched her teach them how to be themselves.

Meanwhile, in his Kansas basement, young Del Close was experimenting. "As a kid," he said, "I wanted to be a chemist."

The glass bottles, beakers, burners, droppers, and clamps of Del's beloved chemistry set would be tinkling there on the magic mixing table he loved like a best friend. But far more entertaining than a human friend, and far more compliant, Del's boys-only Gilbert Chemcraft was the greatest thing his parents ever gave him. Here was the joy of limitless discovery, the wild rainbow of escape. What happens when you mix sodium bicarbonate and tannic acid? What happens if you take a hammer to a packet of potassium permanganate and sulfur, a trick Del liked to perform for his friends? (*Ka-BOOM!*) What is dangerous?

To be or not to be? Yes! Yes to both!

The answer for Del, even if he ultimately discovered it was no, always started as yes.

And what about people? If you stirred together the right emotions and certain odd circumstances, would ancient and ferocious selves shoot out of their bodies? "Every kid assumes he has a secret identity," Close would say, "and if you could just find the magic word, the godlike powers would indeed burst forth."

Other people only sometimes listened; Mike Nichols could hear. Waiting for his moment, lingering on the edges of the University of Chicago coffee shop, absorbing the chorus of student dialogue around him, he could feel, beneath the words, people's real selves pouring into him. Conversation was just a public vessel, like good manners or clothing. Reality came to Nichols under cover of rhythm, silence, and volume — a secret knowledge he harvested from air. It was his superpower, honed over years of difference and estrangement. He did not always understand. But he heard. Pauses, panics, subtleties the literalness of language could not convey. Over there: He hears a man falling out of love with the girl sitting across from him. Another only pretends to hate Senator McCarthy; really, he is afraid not to. And there: one couple he's been observing sound ready to leave — the moment Nichols has been waiting for, his cue to hover, then swoop in just as they get up from the table and, before the busboy beats him to it, steal the unfinished food off their plates.

It was humiliating. Acutely so for Nichols, who had been born Mikhail Igor Peschkowsky, resplendent of Europe's cultural aristocracy, son of Dr. Nicholaeivitch Peschkowsky and Brigitte Landauer, herself the daughter of Hedwig Lachmann, poet, translator, and onetime librettist for Richard Strauss, and the estimable Gustav Landauer, philosopher, anarchist, magazine editor, and one of the first Jews — the very first, Nichols believed — to be killed by the Nazis ("pre-Nazis, really," Nichols said) in 1919, months after the provisional Bavarian Soviet Republic had declared Landauer their minister of public information. "Basically, they beat my grandfather to death over two days. Kicked him to death," Nichols said. "It took him forever to die."

Mikhail retained few details of Nazi violence from his early childhood in Berlin. Once, at school — a school for Jews — some Blackshirt kids stole his bicycle. He remembered that. But more formative than the scenes themselves were the intentions. Like the silence between words, what would linger years later was the panic that accompanied the Peschkowskys' mobilization. He was too young to understand what his parents were doing, pulling every string, meeting with consulates and diplomats who could help them pay, sign, and stamp their way out of Germany, fast. Looking back, he would understand how they got out. Their escape — which Nichols would come to regard, with the lifelong terror of a debt unpaid, as mere luck — owed itself to the Hitler-Stalin Pact, which permitted Russian Jews, briefly, to leave Germany. "I'm incredibly lucky," Nichols would say, "and getting on that boat was my first piece of luck because two weeks later, the next boat to America was turned away."

On April 28, 1939, Mikhail, seven, and his brother, three, boarded the *Bremen* with nothing but fifteen marks sewn into their shirts and eight words of the native language: "I don't speak English" and, to ward off the kindness of strangers, "Please don't kiss me." Neither parent accompanied them. Mrs. Peschkowsky was too sick to travel and their father was already in New York. He had gone a year earlier to set up a new medical practice.

The first thing Mikhail saw when he got to New York, to America, was a Jewish deli. "Is that allowed?" he asked his father.

"It is here."

His father said they could be Jews in America, but in his intuitiveness Mikhail heard something different: hiding wouldn't hurt. "I don't know what happened," he said, "but I must have, without knowing it, wanted to put Europe aside completely." He said "Europe," but you could hear "Jew."

No one would tell him how to be an American. The secrets of assimilation took figuring out, had to be gleaned. "I think there is an immigrant's ear that is particularly acute for 'How are they doing it here? What must I do to be noticeable, to be like them?'"

Five years later, more injustice: Nichols's father died of leukemia. It was his X-ray machines; in those days, few people knew the risks of radiation. Nichols's mother took a series of jobs (bakery, bookstore), but without her husband, money would be scarce. She grew angry. Nichols grew angrier.

Every young boy feels different, but unlike most of his classmates, Mikhail really was. He sounded like a Nazi to them and had no grip on their customs ("They fucked me on baseball"); he did not carry in him the freedom they took for granted, and perhaps most humiliating of all, he was bald. A bad reaction to a whooping cough vaccine rendered Mikhail completely hairless. "The kid was as far outside as an outsider can get," said one of his classmates at the Dalton School (and, like Nichols, a future titan of improvisation), Buck Henry.

Mikhail saw how they watched him, but assimilating, or trying to, was grasping at quicksand. "Nichols" — the new family name — made him a liar. Even if the goyim bought the disguise, the Mikhail Igor inside him never could. "He's the one," Nichols said of the enraged child. "He's somewhere saying, 'Don't fuck with me.' And I can't stop him." Which isn't to say he didn't make a beautiful "Mike Nichols." Consider — but not too closely — all that convincing blond hair and those thin, elegant eyebrows. Consider his grateful smile, his rich, rolling laugh, the three-pound diamond he had for a brain. They would never know Mike was a refugee for life. "That was cast in bronze," Nichols said. "That's where I was chained in the galaxy forever."

In self-defense, he learned to hear — or imagined he heard — what people thought. "It makes for being socially adept," Nichols said. He was too new to this business of hearing to understand that his exile's ear, all that sensing instead of seeing, would sharpen his powers of interpersonal acuity into an instinct verging on ESP, Mozart via Freud, but in time, he would learn that language and behavior were utterly distinct, one guarded truth and one revealed it, and that by mastering the secrets of human motivation, one could master one's enemies.

One day he would get back at them — or it: "I was motivated then," he said, "and for a long time afterwards by revenge."

His prodigious brain had earned him a scholarship to the University of Chicago in 1950, but all Mike Nichols knew, lurking in that coffee shop, was hunger. He had two choices. Either he could attempt the leftovers method or, for a full meal, walk into the student cafeteria backwards, through the exit, to give the impression he had already paid, and then grab a bowl of peas. What's the worst that could happen? If one of the busboys caught and hauled Nichols back to New York or Germany, at least then he'd stop feeling bad about feeling good and finally feel bad for good, which is what he, a survivor, deserved.

To hold your attention, Del would tell you about the time he ran away from home for the traveling geek and freak show carnivals he knew, or heard, were crammed with hoopla, string games, rat games, the Armless Wonder from Tulsa, Oklahoma ("See her dial a telephone! See her comb her hair!"), and Whitey the Albino, who taught him how to swallow swords. Or about the time someone strapped his fat body to the hood of a beat-up car and crashed it head-on through a brick (trick) wall. Dangerous? Of course it was dangerous! That was the point!! There was no miracle until Del, hundreds of eyes in the palm of his hand, got up off the dirt and gave them a big "Ta-da!"

He would tell you about the time, at the age of fourteen, he fell in with Dr. Dracula's Den of Living Nightmares, a broken-down spook show that toured the movie theaters of the Midwest, starring Card Mondor as the titular undead guy, and little Del as his sinister assistant. Near the end of their act, the theater would go completely black, the audience screamed, and Del would yell, "A plague of worms will descend upon you!" and toss handfuls of cold spaghetti onto the crowd. Then, for the finale, Dr. Dracula himself would appear at the footlights and lower a flaming torch down his throat. *Ta-da!*

The looks on their faces!

How Del wanted Mondor's secrets. But Mondor would not show his apprentice how it was done. So Del observed and stole.

"You call this entertainment?" came an angry voice from the back of the theater one night. "I just shit my pants!"

It took several failed attempts, but eventually Del discovered how to swallow fire, dousing a torch in gasoline and, as Whitey the Albino had showed him, taking it down without triggering the gag reflex. "It's a matter of the threshold of pain," he explained. "It's all over before I feel anything. You can die if you inhale the flames."

Yes, sir, Del thought. *I do call that entertainment. I want to squeeze you dry, whether it's of laughter or shit.*

Onward to Viola's son, Paul Sills, the future cofounder of the Second City, now a busboy at the University of Chicago coffee shop, where he let the nimble guy in the cheap toupee steal lunch off the paying customers' finished plates. ("I don't know why," Nichols said.) But that was Sills. He could see, in you, the truth you didn't know was there, and beneath Nichols's refinery — the grin, the ornate argots — he could feel the kind of emotional hunger, Sills, a rowdy street Jew, did not pretend away. Sills was early to self-acceptance. Growing up watching his mother transform mere humans into founts of inspiration, Sills had seen goodness burst forth from so many kinds of people so many times that — without devolving into a cheerful individual — he had started to cultivate something like faith. Not in God — though, unlike his mother, Sills hadn't ruled out the possibility — but in something God-like that manifested from the communal experience. Viola's games interested Paul, but less as an actor's tool, which is how she used them, than as a means of helping people throw their arms around each other and draw themselves together. "What I really want," he said, "is something that has the sense of the great periods of your youth when you're working with people — you know, some sort of activity, starting a magazine — Boy Scouts have it — this great sense of being part of a group doing something that's fun, only on an adult level." He sought community; small but socially oriented — "the way good theater should be." Sills, in 1944, had left his mother in California for the Francis W. Parker School in Chicago. He knew, had there been no community to buttress him, he never could have directed theater at Parker, played football, or had a place to live

— a hotel, with his girlfriend and her family. His parents sent money, but Sills owed his happiness to the people around him. It was only through community, he believed, that people could free one another. On their own, they were stuck inside.

When they finally did speak, Paul had a bite of food for Mike. "Right away," Nichols said, "we started bullshitting about the theater."

First off, they were in complete agreement about the state of the art in Chicago. There was virtually nothing of interest. If you were starving, you could head out to the Loop and see a road company on their way down from Broadway, but most of it was commercial bullshit and none of it Chicago's own; Chicago, Sills decreed, would remain a truly second-class city, at least theatrically, if it continued to accept New York's breadcrumbs for sustenance.

A. J. Liebling would later echo this stance in the pages of the *New Yorker*. In 1952, preceding its publication in book form, his thorough and weary valuation of contemporary Chicago — a place Liebling deemed America's "Second City" — unfolded over a series of three cheerily degrading installments needling every facet of the local character, which, he wrote, evoked "the personality of a man brought up in the expectation of a legacy who has learned in middle age that it will never be his." Chicago's theater scene, Liebling continued, "is outclassed by Oslo, which has a population of four hundred thousand": "Plays at Chicago theaters, for example, are always locally assumed to be inferior versions of the New York productions, or, if they *are* the New York productions, with original casts intact, the actors are presumed to be giving inferior performances. Taking an interest in the Chicago theater, therefore, is regarded as naïve . . ." Furthermore, Chicago theatergoing was prohibitively inconvenient. Potential audiences were stymied by "awful" after-hours public transportation to and from the suburbs. "And those great, silent, though densely populated, spaces, the outlying city wards, are peopled by frequenters of neighborhood movies who are now turning to television."

The on-campus options weren't much better. U of C had no actual theater department, and there was nothing in the University Theater, largely a well-behaved, meat-and-potatoes enterprise not worth reinventing. Had Mike heard of Tonight at 8:30, the only student-run theater group of U of C? It was still coming together, but for the theater people on campus it was the only thing going. Was Mike an actor or a director or a writer?

Actor, sort of.

Sills? Director, maybe. Sills had begun a series of open-invitation Spolin game workshops. Prior theatrical training was not required for admission. All Sills required of his amateurs was willingness. What would emerge from them would emerge. Sills intended only to create the environment for emergence.

Nichols, despite his curiosity about the workshops, couldn't quite digest the semimystical flavor of the experiment. His taste took him slightly to the right of Sills. A psychology student, devoted analysand, and Upper East Sider, Nichols was, at nineteen, predisposed to the Method technique and its acolytes. Beginning at eight o'clock, he remembered every shattering detail from December 3, 1947, the night his then girlfriend Lucy invited him to Broadway, to the Ethel Barrymore Theater, to see *A Streetcar Named Desire*. It was only the second performance. He remembered the great shock of Brando, how, at intermission, both he and Lucy found the other actually unable to stand, how they wouldn't dare hold hands the first act and held on all through the second, but mostly he remembered the substance of the production, the commingling of total reality the director, Elia Kazan, had merged with total poetry, neither negating the other.

Yes, that element there hit the bull's-eye in Paul Sills. Though the Method struck him (and his mother) as overly cerebral and dependent on the past — the theater, like play, happened here, now, in the present — the emergent director in Sills had already begun to dream of a best-of-both-worlds theater of his own hovering between real and ideal, community and spirit, rocks and sky. If he could just get the right actors together.

Over the course of many weeks, Sills and Nichols took their conversation from the campus coffee shop to Jimmy's, a local brick saloon with one rickety pinball machine and, to settle arguments, an *Encyclopaedia Britannica* on a shelf over the bar. The rest was tables. Whoever you were, as long as you could talk, you could find your table at Jimmy's: the Communist Table, the Aristotle Table, the Hegel Table, and of course the Theater Table. They were the informal symposia of the University of Chicago. And if you played them well enough, you got laid.

This was not Liebling's Chicago, but Saul Bellow's. "What we had [in Chicago] was a cultureless city pervaded nevertheless by Mind," he would write. "Mind without culture was the name of the game, wasn't it?" At U of C, it certainly was. If your half-baked idea seemed improbable, funny, or even ridiculous, all the better; it meant no one had ever thought of it before. "It was some sort of hotbed," Sills said. "You were where it was at. It must have had something to do with Hutchins." Robert Maynard Hutchins was elected president of the University of Chicago in 1931, at the age of twenty-nine. His revolutionary Hutchins Plan, aka Hutchins's "Chicago Experiment," emphasized thought for thought's sake; the idea was not to prepare students for the workforce per se, but to make good minds, and the earlier the better. One didn't even need a high school degree to get into U of C. Hutchins had done away with the university's age requirements. ("As a result of this generous stand," Liebling wrote, "the University of Chicago's undergraduate college acts as the greatest magnet for neurotic juveniles since the Children's Crusade.") To gain admittance, prospective students needed only to pass all of U of C's fourteen insanely difficult entrance exams. (Mike Nichols was a college freshman at fifteen.) Though they read everything — "five to six hours a night," U of C student Sheldon Patinkin recalled — what went into those minds mattered less to Hutchins than how his students played with them. Most classes were discussion-oriented, attendance was not mandatory, and there was only one examination per class, at the end of the year. "Your entire grade," Patinkin said, "was based on what you got on the final. Each was six to nine hours long, half multiple choice, half essay, and they covered the entire year. It was grueling. In the couple weeks before exams, there were occasional nervous breakdowns and suicides."

U of C students enjoyed a wealth of free time, mostly at places like Jimmy's, or Steinway's Drugstore, or the coffee shop where Nichols met Sills. Talk was the university sport, a twenty-four-hour game of ubiquitous critique played by the spectators. It didn't even matter if you were smart; you just had to be good. You had to provoke. Lie, guess, stumble, fail, but be interesting. Don't shrug. Take a side, whether you believe it or not, and squeeze it until something comes out of you. "There was so much hanging out," Nichols said. "That's where the education was, in talking to each other. That's when my life began. I suddenly came in contact with the other wonderful weirdos of the world, people like Sills and Susan Sontag. These people wanted to talk about the things I loved. The theater. Music. Eugene O'Neill, Yeats, Dostoyevsky. You can't imagine what a relief that was, to stay up all night and play with my people."

• • •

To cool off in the hot summer evenings, the folks of that part of Manhattan, Kansas, took to their porches, the orchestra seats of Pierre Street. The entertainment started as soon as the sun went down. Generally, the action was strictly small-town; a little gossip, some cards.

The night of July 8, 1951, certainly began that way. The Union Pacific arrived on schedule and the tired ambled home.

One of them, Del Close, was walking at a brisk pace, as if pursued. Wait, was that car following him? Porch audiences were rapt: Del started running, but he couldn't lose the black Packard on his tail. Suddenly its doors flung open and out flew two hoods with handguns. Two shots later Del hit the pavement; the hoods hauled his body into the car and sped out of view.

The police caught up with the Packard at a gas station not too far away. The bad guys — six high school kids — kept their eyes on the ground, away from the spinning red lights.

"Where's the body!" yelled Sheriff Goode.

Dozens of cops — from the Sheriff's Department, the Highway Patrol, and the City Police — held guard behind Goode, their guns pointing at the boys.

But there was no body. No one had shot Del. It was a prank, an act.

"Where's the body!"

Almost defiantly, Del raised his head, then his hand. "I'm right here," he declared. "I'm the body."

The looks on their faces! Yes — that's exactly what he wanted.

It was all very serious and important-sounding inside the third-floor theater of U of C's Ida Noyes Hall. The high arched ceiling, the echo, the Renaissance-y wraparound mural, *The Masque of Youth;* the play, *Miss Julie,* its author, August Strindberg; the growing reputation of the Tonight at 8:30 ensemble, hence the presence of critic Sydney J. Harris of the *Chicago Daily News;* and, more serious than the rest, Mike Nichols as Jean the valet, lecherous manservant to the Count, one in a bestiary of pricks his director, Paul Sills, had him play in any number of Tonight at 8:30 productions. There was Caesar, Shrike in *Miss Lonelyhearts* . . . "I knew all about those guys," Nichols said. "I was a ready-made prick."

Nichols did not suffer fools; in those days, they suffered him. The problem — part of it, anyway — was that he was so damn smart, even to the smarter-than-thou sets of U of C. "Mike was an absolute genius," Sheldon Patinkin said. "Everybody on campus knew that. So did Mike." An intimidator of intimidators, Nichols could defend his inner-Mikhail and twinkle his outer-Mike with a single stroke of wit paired to a Cheshire grin, kind and proud, at once a deathblow to your ego and an open hand to lift you off the floor. The effect made hating him or adoring him both impossible and inevitable, the bastard. How did he do it? Was it the supersonic hearing, the split-second advantage he had over the room, the class, the bar? Or was it his voice? You could practically hear him tasting those long consonants, rolling them around his tongue like a 1928 Château Lafite. *Hhhhmmmm-mmm, wellllll yessssssssssss* . . .

As Jean the valet, he plowed on with egregious hauteur, pointing fingers, raising fists, and declaiming into the spotlight, his attention breaking, line by line, from the play to the palpable rancor of the girl sneering at him from the front row. It was impossible to miss her. ("I could fucking hear her *breathing* hostilely," Nichols said.) She was four feet from the stage.

Every time Nichols edged out of the glare for a better look at her face, he was hit with a stream of contempt.

There was no denying it. "We loathed each other," Mike Nichols said, "on sight."

This person, he did not know, was Elaine May.

Distracted now from his stagework (which, ironically, might have helped his performance as Jean the valet), he managed to get a better look at her. She had bored black eyes and long black hair, chaotically bobby-pinned into a savage argument of strands, a basically beautiful face, and under that trench coat, probably great tits. In short, he decided, there was nothing pretty about her except her eyes, hair, face, and figure.

She did have one thing going for her, though. She could see he was terrible in the part. He had to respect her for that.

"That night," Nichols said, "I think she fucked Sills." Nichols pretended not to care.

The next morning, after a late stolen breakfast, Nichols was crossing the street outside Steinway's, rereading Sydney J. Harris's review in the *Daily News*. An amateur group reviewed in a national paper. That alone was extraordinary, but the review itself was a jawdropper. "This self-supporting all-student organization has maintained the highest possible level of repertory in world drama . . . Mr. Nichols exhibits an ease and intelligence in the ambivalent role of the valet, who is one of Strindberg's most perceptive creations. His technique is sometimes a bit ragged, but his emotional understanding of the role is more than adequate compensation." Nichols could not believe it, but there it was, still: a rave. It was about then that Nichols spotted Sills heading in his direction. With him was the evil girl from the night before. Now they were going to have to speak to each other.

"I want you to meet Mike Nichols," Sills said to the girl, "the only other person on campus who is as hostile as you are."

"Hello."

"Yes, hello."

"Mike," Sills continued, "this is Elaine May."

Of course he had heard of her. Everyone had. By 1951, Elaine May stories were already campus currency all across the University of Chicago. Drop her name and your coolness quotient doubled. Get her to talk to you, or better still, respect you, and you were hip for life. "Among the stories I had heard," Nichols said, "was about the time Elaine appeared in a philosophy class, and convinced everyone, including the professor, that everyone in Plato's *Symposium* was drunk. When she was sure she had gotten her point across, she got up and left the class." That she had never enrolled at U of C only added to her allure.

Even those who were not selected to spend the night with Elaine puzzled over the combination to her lock. "Elaine," Sheldon Patinkin said, "had everything." Uncommonly clever, impossibly informed, offhandedly dangerous, and biographically mysterious (was she Argentine? Philadelphian? Los Angeleno?), she didn't look like she knew her power. Elaine always seemed like she had just woken up someplace she didn't want to be and had gotten lost on her way back to bed. Lunch crumbs stuck to her blouse.

But Elaine was a scalpel. Though she was small and at times looked languid and vulnerable, she had no compunction about announcing you were completely wrong; she could make a good case for suicide; she had no interest in "niceness" or "being nice" and was called rude as often as she was called right, which she basically always was, about the fate of the world, and more terrifying than that, about you. That was Elaine's specialty. She was always right about you.

"Here," Nichols said, handing the *Daily News* over to Sills. Sills opened the paper and started reading the review. Elaine, too.

A rave? *That?* Elaine blurted "Ha!" and walked off.

And that's how Mike Nichols, who really did not like Elaine May, decided he had to have her.

David Shepherd, a tall, fiery patrician in the passenger seat of a truck, was hitchhiking, he decided, to Cleveland. He had with him about ten thousand dollars and a dream to found a people's theater in America, a neighborhood haven where any workingman or -woman could go after a long day and, for a few coins, have their world performed back to them. "My idea," he said, "was to have a theater close to where people lived so they could come without dressing up, without making a reservation; where there would be food and drink; where the circumstances would be informal; and where they could see plays that had to do with the life they led, and not with another class or another culture or another country." European voices had long since contaminated America's theater, especially in his hometown of New York. The whole East Coast, in a way, was like that; it seemed embarrassed to be American.

That's why David Shepherd (Harvard-educated, wire-frame glasses) was hitchhiking to Cleveland, to the Midwest, where the real America lived.

All this he told the guy beside him at the wheel, a truck driver on his way to Indianapolis. "Don't go to Cleveland," he said to Shepherd. "Stay with me."

"Why?"

"Because I'm going to crash on the road if you don't keep me awake telling me your stories."

He got off at Gary, Indiana, and started dreaming aloud his theater, but the locals were unresponsive. They had television.

Shepherd's theater, he argued unpersuasively, would steer clear of professional actors, conduits of the bourgeoisie. Shepherd's "actors" would be regular people just like you and me, getting up there after long working days to do scenes from our lives, about our problems, dreams, fears — anything. But us, not them.

A lovely notion, but how regular, everyday Americans could be made to act, David Shepherd wasn't sure.

From Indiana Shepherd continued on to Chicago — to Hyde Park, home of the University of Chicago — in the fall of 1952. He decided it might be wise to start first with educated bohemians, his tribe, and progress, hopefully, to the workers.

Word of Paul Sills's weekly workshops—whose meaning and effects mystified even its participants—pulsed the experimental strain in Shepherd, and spoke, somehow, to a means of getting regular people onstage. Sills, meanwhile, caught Shepherd in a Tonight at 8:30 production of *The Man of Destiny*, and although Shepherd was no actor, Sills sensed something pure that he respected. They agreed to meet at Steinway's.

Shepherd was the first to arrive. The motley assortment of students, professors, beats, day workers, and steelworkers swarming Steinway's told him of a genuinely diverse population at the threshold of great potential. "I wanted them in my theater," Shepherd said, "watching stories about Hyde Park." He took a seat at an open table and waited for Sills to appear.

Sitting at a table nearby, a leonine figure orating to a group of students with near-brutal conviction caught Shepherd's interest. It was hard to miss him. His charisma was tremendous.

Then Shepherd put it together. He was watching Paul Sills.

They picked a table, started talking, then seeing aloud. Then dreaming together. They agreed a new people's theater was necessary, and Brecht, whose writings had only just appeared in English, had something to offer them both—left-wing politics for Shepherd and community ideology for Sills. To move an audience to enlightened action, Brecht theorized, the theater had to favor didactic rather than emotional techniques. Involving stories and characters was empty escapism: it sedated audiences, failing to connect the stage drama to their own lives. To restore the connection, Brecht advocated, paradoxically, alienation. He decreed sets should be minimal; performers subdued; the action of the play vulnerable to interruption and bulging with allegory; the fourth wall broken. Distancing audiences from the illusory aspects of the drama, the full-fledged sets and costumes, would awaken them to their own objective minds.

Brecht's actors were talking to *you*.

But Shepherd didn't want to bring Brecht's plays to Hyde Park. Sills wanted to direct *The Caucasian Chalk Circle*, but Shepherd objected; they needed something closer to home. Bringing the people Berlin, even the people's Berlin, they would only be repeating the sins of Broadway. But Sills, inspired by Brecht's avant-garde techniques, was an entrancing speaker, and by the end of their coffee, Shepherd was convinced.

Sills decided to move toward a production of Cocteau's *The Typewriter*, and convened a handful of actors, including Mike Nichols, for one of his famous workshops. Using his mother's games, Sills urged his players to explore not their characters, but themselves. The play would come later. The two dozen students in attendance didn't quite understand what any of this had to do with Cocteau, but Sills's urgency was too compelling to question. "All Paul told us," Patinkin said, "was we were going to learn Viola's games. He didn't tell us why. I kept asking questions, but Paul did not want to discuss it. He wanted to keep us out of our heads and just *do it*." It was only later that Patinkin understood what was happening. "He was building an ensemble. That's what happens when you play the games."

Shepherd observed, amazed, as Sills watched his game players play. They were creating constantly, and without the help of lighting, costumes, sets, script, or even story. In or out of the theater, Shepherd had never seen such interconnection. These people were all working together, like a family, to alchemize empty space into art.

In the spring of 1953 Shepherd agreed to bankroll Sills's repertory theater, and Sills agreed to help Shepherd build his people's cabaret, the one he had dreamed about as he'd hitchhiked West.

Nichols could not afford music or girls with expensive taste (his), but realized, if he took a stack of LPs into the listening booths at the record store near campus, he could listen all day for free, and if he took a girl *and* a stack of LPs into that booth, expounded on a little music theory, and at the precise moment in the crescendo of that trio from *Der Rosenkavalier* ("You've done this before, haven't you?") casually name-dropped Saint-Saëns, he and the girl could be back in his dorm room in no time, listening to records all night. "I was good at that," Nichols said. "If you can believe it." Believe it: Big on nostril and short on jaw, Mike Nichols was hardly Chicago's most physically attractive resident, but he was probably its most seductive. Intelligence, sensitivity, charm, and all other courtly assets he had in natural abundance — that was the European in him. But what put Nichols over the top with girls — with anyone, really — was the gourmet quality of his attention. It was total. Total to the point of empathy. Glancing into that booth, you would not see him touching his concentration to hers, savoring her unrevealed self as Proust could intuit a full personality from a single scent, but if you were to listen, you could hear the cadence of a mind microscopically alert to the cues she didn't know she was giving him, like when to enter and when to exit conversation, when interjecting would help and when it would hurt. So Sherlock Holmesian was Nichols's sense of the other, and so powerful, it was construed as calculated by many who feared and admired it. But calculation you can hear in the pauses. They're empty, like white rooms. In seduction, Nichols's pauses, redolent with agreement, were full of the present moment — hers.

Sills and Shepherd invited Mike Nichols to join the Playwrights Theater Club, the repertory theater they set up in a converted Chinese restaurant (actors slept rent-free in booths downstairs), but mostly, he stayed faithful to his job as DJ at WFMT (which paid better), where his voice and musical tastes earned him some neighborhood fame. He appeared at Playwrights on a part-time basis, acting for Sills here and there in basically serious European classics like *La Ronde* and *Volpone* (on a break from summer stock, Del Close caught the show passing through Chicago and thought, *These strike me as the kind of people I'd like to work with* — which would turn out to be a prediction). Nichols soon came to imagine a professional life in the theater, but not in Chicago, where Playwrights was the only show going, but in New York, where Strasberg taught and Kazan directed. It was *The Fervent Years*. Reading Harold Clurman's personal history of the Group Theatre — as of then, the most impactful phenomenon in the history of the American theater — had given Nichols renewed purpose and direction. He would be an actor.

From WFMT's studios downtown Nichols walked to the nearby Randolph Street Station, where he picked up the train back to his apartment in Chicago's South Side. One evening, in the spring of 1954, he sailed through the station waiting room to his seat on a bench, and stopped cold — at a hostile thicket of black hair perched over a magazine.

It had been two years since Nichols had spoken to Elaine May. Two very good years.

He'd try to pick her up.

As benches go, it was a fairly long one, crowded with people Elaine hardly seemed to notice. Nichols, however, was fully aware of them, and the adverse effect they would have on his seduction scene. A rush of unwanted attention could make Elaine uncomfortable, or worse, awaken painful memories of Jean the valet. He would be wise to operate covertly.

So he sat down beside her.

He leaned toward her ear.

Out of the side of his mouth, in a German accent, he whispered, "May I seet down?"

Immediately, she replied, "If you veesh."

("I knew then," Nichols said later, "that she was the best girl I had ever met.")

Her eyes were on the magazine.

"Do you haffa light?"

"Yes, zertainly."

People turned to look.

"I het a lighter, but I lozt eet on Feefty-Seventh Street . . ."

"Oh, of course, you muzt be Agent X-9?"

"Shh."

They were still at it on the train home, gossiping in character.

May: "Who was it? Uh — Agent, uh — oh, we can say her name now, she's dead. Myrtle Henning."

Nichols: "*Mmm*yes."

"You know Myrtle?"

"*Mmmm.*"

"Ah. Well, I saw her two months ago, and she gained a lot of weight, and I find out that she's dead. Well, *can you . . .*"

"It's a terrible thing."

They weren't just parodying the spy genre; they were doing actual people. You could hear it in their delivery: praising Myrtle, but really, deeper down, congratulating themselves for praising her. Double agents have needs too.

They took the train back to her place, a basement apartment that looked like its inhabitant hadn't committed to moving in or moving out. Scribbled notes lay everywhere. "Elaine's shortcomings," Nichols observed, "were purely organizational." She made him her specialty, a hamburger with ketchup and cream cheese served on two pieces of toast, and they talked through what was left of the night.

She was born in a Jewish trunk, the daughter of Jack and Ida Berlin, showfolk of the Yiddish theater, and the trunk never stopped traveling. Philadelphia, she said, was where her parents "just happened to be . . . at the time" of her birth; from there, Elaine was bounced from Chicago to Mexico to California. It was her father's theatrical company. They toured. Ida printed tickets, worked the box office, and understudied when necessary; Jack handled the art. He starred in *Velvele Ganef*. He wrote, produced, directed, and starred in *The Dance of Death*, a play about drug addiction. Before she could walk, baby Elaine appeared with him onstage — "carry-on bits," she called them. When she got older, Jack sometimes gave her the boy roles, which lasted only so far as puberty, because "our people do not believe in breast binding." Not long after, Jack died of a heart attack.

Elaine and her mother (along with Elaine's cousin and aunt, widowed at almost the same time as her sister Ida) moved to Chicago, where Ida went into business with Uncle Louis. Uncle Louis was in deals. He bought surplus coffins from the army, opened a beauty parlor to straighten curly hair, and had an ulcer. An opportunity in lumber brought Uncle Louis and the gang out to Los Angeles, where Elaine made the rounds from Fairfax High to Hollywood High to John Burroughs Junior High until she turned fourteen and decided to quit formal education for good. She wrote advertising copy, studied the Method with Maria Ouspenskaya in Chicago, and the games with Viola Spolin in Los Angeles. At sixteen, she married toy and orthotics designer Marvin May and had a daughter, Jeannie. The marriage failed, Elaine decided then to become "extremely educated," left the baby with Grandma Ida in Los Angeles, and hitchhiked to the University of Chicago. Then it was back to L.A. and Jeannie and her mother, a tiny living working for small theaters, and eventually a letter from Paul Sills inviting her to return to Chicago and join the Playwrights Theater Club. She did.

She had come to Playwrights to lend a hand wherever she could, acting, directing, selling concessions, and leading the company through game workshops (after Sills, she was the most experienced Spolin game player), but "it was as a writer," Nichols remarked, "that Elaine decided she would achieve immortality." Her total concentration was evidenced in the forgotten *things* seemingly dropped around her basement apartment, left there, as if partway into trying them, she had reconsidered their usefulness and ran off to try something else, quickly, before she could forget what she thought she needed wherever she was going. "I always learn the same thing about Elaine, if it's then or now," Nichols said. "Physical reality does not interest her."

What interested Elaine, often to the exclusion of all else, was truth. Not poetic truth. Real truth.

Elaine, he understood, was addicted to the secret truths beneath the surface of people and events and conversations. The unsaid consumed her.

But this archaeological project came with a price — hostility toward apparent reality, the pervasive suspicion that people are not exactly who they claim to be, or even believe they are. A seasoned skeptic in his own right, Mike could appreciate Elaine's position — it was a variation of his own. "We analyzed voraciously," he said. Apart, each was perceptive, brilliant even; together, they were baroquely and gorgeously judgmental, Fred and Ginger on Freudian parquet. He had the gift of hearing, she the gift of paranoia. Distrust was her shovel. Jamming it into the soil between *what is* and *what really is,* she could dig up the world's entire catalogue of comedy problems. That's what so much of comedy is — problems. Take, for instance, the present seduction scene between Mike Nichols and Elaine May. In the wide shot, it is the story of a gleaming new romance. But move in closer, pursue the details to their crisis point, describe what's really, *really* happening, and you'll see the beauty and emotion give way to unavoidable facts. In that sense, yes, she believed comedy was more honest than drama. "In a comedy, as in life," Elaine said, "you meet a guy, you like him, you want to invite him up to your apartment. But you're thinking, 'My underwear doesn't match, my bra is on its last legs, there's a splotch of nail polish on the run on my pantyhose.'" Commit to the big beneath, to betrayal and personal hell. You'll find yourself miserable, but laughing a whole lot more than a happy person.

Oh boy, Nichols thought that night. *This is going to be fun.*

A few months later, David Shepherd was on his way to meet Roger Bowen, a writer, for coffee. They were going to talk about Shepherd's dream — what was left of it, anyway. For almost two years, the producer had watched the Playwrights Theater Club, under Sills, transform from a progressive young-people's theater with leftist tendencies, producing over twenty classic and original ensemble plays, about one every month, to a full-blown critical success, the highbrow puppet of Hyde Park's bourgeoisie. It was time, Shepherd decreed, to wipe clean the slate and open America's people's cabaret. Whatever that meant.

Any cabaret, he reasoned, that could survive the rambunctious atmosphere of a working-class crowd would have to be fast paced, direct, and inexpensive, something that could be packed up and transported from town to town. But in lieu of plays, Shepherd still didn't know what kind of dramatic material — "simpler forms than those of the contemporary theater," he once wrote — would work in that kind of environment. That's why he was meeting with Roger Bowen, a university law student and part-time theater critic for the campus newspaper. Bowen liked what he'd seen at Playwrights and was eager to hear what Shepherd had in mind.

Shepherd, meanwhile, was eager to hear what Bowen had in mind. Having placed ads in American and English publications calling for original plays — fables, satires, re-creations of important historical events — and subsequently rejecting all of them, he came to the U of C coffee shop directed only by an inclination away from the sort of theater he didn't want, and a single, confounding phrase, "scenario play" — borrowed from commedia dell'arte, the world's original people's cabaret — to point him toward the theater of his dreams. Shepherd asked Bowen to write one.

"What's a scenario play?" Bowen asked.

"We won't know until we've done it."

With only notions of simplicity to guide him, Bowen wrote an outline. Seven scenes. Four teenage boys. One used car for sale. Some complications along the way. Bowen called it *Enterprise*. Besides brief scene descriptions and briefer character sketches, the scenario provided the actors and their director only the most basic plot points and motivations — ingredients any nonactor could digest. The dialogue — none of it specified in the scenario — would be supplied by the performers every night. In that sense, Bowen and Shepherd's *Enterprise*, when it premiered at the University Theater in May 1955, would be improvised. And in that sense, it was the first improvised evening in theater history.

Mike Nichols, having left Chicago for New York to begin his career, was depressed. He lived in a miserable eight-dollar apartment on the Upper West Side and worked the smart-aleck shift at a Greenwich Village Howard Johnson's. The job, like the others, didn't last. Nichols said, "I was fired when somebody asked me the ice cream flavor of the week and I said chicken." He dreamed of chicken. He dreamed of cheese. "One night," he said, "I woke up so hungry that I ate the only thing I had in my room — a jar of mustard." He mooched off a couple of girls who lived across the street. They loaned him money when they could, and when they couldn't, he stole from their icebox. When they got wise to him, Nichols started going to the Automat. If he had enough for a cup of tea, he'd stir in some crushed crackers and ketchup and urge it toward tomato soup. Then, if he was still hungry, he would make more. Hot water was free.

As a student in Lee Strasberg's class, he cried his eyes out. Because that was the Method. You had to work very very hard at hurting yourself and then you had to cry it out in the scene. Strasberg's view of the director came easier to Nichols, and it hurt considerably less. The director's job, Strasberg explained, was to create the *events* of the play. The event is what the audience *sees*. And a good director creates an event for every moment in the play. "Every moment must be physically comprehensible," Nichols learned. "You must see people trying to do things that are not expressed in words. Very often they are the direct opposite of the words. And those are the events."

Alone in his apartment, Nichols switched his little television set from channel to channel, searching the employable faces of Philco Television Playhouse for some future sign of himself. He found none. According to the casting office in his brain, Mike Nichols did not exist. He was not a heavy, he was not a leading man; he was not urban enough for Paddy Chayefsky's work, or character enough for Rod Serling's. He wasn't ethnic. He wasn't even the Jew. Edward G. Robinson and Jerry Lewis — they were Jews. Or John Garfield. What was Nichols?

He missed Elaine.

Elaine would bring the typewriter into bed, prop it up on her knees, and lay there, sometimes very late, braining out a play from the puzzle-patchwork of papers she dumped out of coat pockets, handbags, the backs of drawers, onto the mattress around her. The unlucky ones never made it back to her bed. "I picked them up when I could," Patinkin said. "I, like everyone else, was in love with her." But she was living with someone else, an actor, Jerry Cunliffe.

Patinkin would put his own schoolwork aside to try to help Elaine hold the net over her ideas. His function was primarily organizational. "Not that it did much good," he said. "Elaine would write notes on anything." They were the middles, ends, and beginnings of plays, ideas for plays, like *Mikey and Nicky,* an idea she had about two small-time hoods, and the betrayal of one by the other. Her thoughts flew out too numerous to capture, and the few Patinkin managed to grasp left his hands the moment he opened his mouth. It was not a question of his intelligence but of speed. Elaine was simply gone. When she created, Elaine was possessed, removed from the writer's call to structure and story, to an infinite place where no one could find her. When she returned, it was with pages upon pages of new material that may or may not pertain to the play at hand. But relevance mattered less to her than possibilities. From those possibilities, buried troves of new relevance could surface. Hence the flood of papers Patinkin couldn't hold or hold back. "I helped her off and on for months, maybe years," he said. "The play she was working on, about a young warrior of some kind or another, reached two hundred and fifty pages and was nowhere near done."

Not too far from Elaine's apartment, David Shepherd played Sills his recording of a rowdy performance of *Enterprise,* watching his friend's stolid face for hints of enthusiasm. He still needed a director for his unborn cabaret theater, and Sills, Shepherd knew, needed a new theater. A few months earlier, the fire department had shut down the Playwrights Theater Club, citing its illegal second-floor space and lack of a fire curtain. ("I do think our politics played a part in that," Sheldon Patinkin said. "Most of us were just casual lefties, but it was McCarthy time.") Remembering the effect Sills's workshops had on inexperienced actors, Shepherd knew Sills was perfectly suited to lead his ensemble of real, working people. *Enterprise* was his bait.

"I don't know why they're laughing," Sills mused during playback. "But they're laughing, so it must be good."

Sills, a grumpy mystic, was conflicted. No one, least of all him, intended Spolin's games to get laughs. Until that moment, Sills never considered how unleashing one's spontaneous self—the intended result of his workshops —could be so funny. But that's what happens when your personal truth breaks out and blows up the socially acceptable one. Perhaps, he conceded, there was something mystical in comedy.

Shepherd had his director.

He also had his director's mother. Having just directed Playwrights' final production, Viola Spolin was an exile in Chicago. Back in Los Angeles, her marriage to Ed Spolin was crumbling, and the Young Actors Company, after ten years, had closed. Like her son, she also needed a new theater.

In the spring of 1955 Shepherd invited Spolin to lead a monthlong series of improvisational workshops, which he would open to anyone interested in learning the games. From this group of real people, he would build a company for his dream theater, the Compass, the first improvisational theater in the world.

2

1955–1956

To get to the Compass, a couple of doors down from Jimmy's, you had to walk the row of schlumpy storefronts that sat along Fifty-Fifth Street, into the semirenovated Hi-Hat Lounge, and continue through a hole they literally knocked in the wall that separated the bar area from the narrow next-door space they were calling a theater, though not officially. The dubious closing of Playwrights ("The same space was opened up three months later as a nightclub and got away with [the same violations]," Sills said) taught Sills and Shepherd the Chicago way of finagling a theater from a couple of back rooms: rub together a cabaret and liquor license, charge no admission fee, only for drinks, beer mostly. They split the proceeds with Hi-Hat's proprietor, Fred Wranovics, himself a U of C graduate and former bartender at Jimmy's, grossing the Compass team — at a capacity performance of ninety individuals — a grand total of fifty dollars six nights a week, before that sum was divided among the actors (at twenty-four dollars a week, more than the bartenders) and the various bill collectors, to about a twenty-five-dollar net, weekly.

In those days, Hyde Park was still "experimental," a transitional mix of working class and ivory tower, black and white. You could feel the friction, especially at night, during bar time, when young women were smart to check twice over their shoulders on their way into the street.

For a set, all Compass had was chairs and some colored louvers upstage that could be shuffled into place for entrances and exits.

One more thing: as opening night approached, no one was really sure who Shepherd and Sills had selected from Viola's workshop to join the permanent company. As ever, Shepherd knew what he wanted but not how to get it. "I was going on something you could not measure," he said, "which was a sense of their insight into what was happening in society and the ability to play a whole bunch of parts," an understanding of "the social world of our heads." To Shepherd, that meant Elaine May, certainly, and Roger Bowen, and the writer Robert Coughlan; there was the luscious and cautious and then quite suddenly insane Barbara Harris, and Shepherd too, if the need arose. But his attention, for the moment, was on the paucity of original material his dream cabaret had to offer. A forty-minute scenario, written by actors, Shepherd and Sills on a volunteer basis, could not sustain a full evening of theater, no matter how socially observant or civically engaged *Enterprise* demonstrated the form could be. He needed more.

Shepherd went to Bowen. "I want to have a 'Living Newspaper.'"

"What *is* a 'Living Newspaper'?"

"I don't know. I just know I want something called the 'Living Newspaper.'"

For the Living Newspaper segment — whatever that was — Bowen suggested he act as a kind of narrator, reading aloud bits of preselected clippings from news articles, film reviews, fashion pieces — whatever they deemed relevant to the common interests of their working-class, ivory tower, black and Caucasian audience — while a handful of other players stood beside him, supplying dialogue, playing Khrushchev, or anyone, or *anything*, when called upon, reinventing stage space, as they had been taught by Viola Spolin, throughout. This offering would come early in the show and last about twenty minutes, and they would make up a new one every day. It was, after all, the news.

Still, that wasn't enough entertainment. After a little curtain-raiser scene, the Living Newspaper segment, and the scenario, it was decided, for their second act, the Compass Players would improvise a scene based on a suggestion taken from the audience. "The idea," Bowen said, "was to keep them there a little longer and sell them another drink."

The Compass was scheduled to open on the hot summer night of July 4, 1955, but the air conditioner broke down and they rescheduled for the fifth. Rushing in and out of huddles, Sills, Shepherd, and the actors spent the day reading, clipping, and gluing together news items for the Living Newspaper, passing out flyers, and debating the scenario play ("The Game of Hurt," by Sills, starring May and Shepherd).

The young insurgents of the first improvisational theater lacked the time or energy to contemplate the cultural behemoth they were up against: the Man in the Gray Flannel Suit. In 1955, he was a bestseller, a national ideal, and the symbol of acquiescence and self-denial — the fictional antithesis of Spolin, Sills, and Shepherd — in short, *the* 1950s American. He was not a freethinker; he would have agreed with President Eisenhower's definition of an intellectual, "a man who takes more words than is necessary to say more than he knows." If he were to step out of his novel and tour American university life beginning in the late 1940s he would have found himself very much at home. "A vast hush had settled over the universities," historian William Manchester wrote of the late Truman years. "Liberalism had become tired and dull. There seemed to be no indignant young men on campuses, no burning causes, no militancy, except among a reactionary handful on the far right."

All over America, university students were as neat, unimaginative, and complacent as job applicants interviewing at Goldman Sachs, and in a sense that was what they were. They went to college to land jobs. Here and there, a baby beatnik like Elaine or Del kissed off Brooks Brothers with a show of brooding black jackets and denim, but the gray flannel epidemic — brought on by the postwar rush to free enterprise — leveled progressive youth culture with the McCarthy treatment. When the Compass opened, there was no *Animal House*. Because, in 1955, there were no Blutos. The developmental phase of experimentation known as adolescence, like improvisation, was only just being invented. "None of us had seen or heard anything on TV or the radio that dealt with what it was like for us to be young Americans then and there," Sheldon Patinkin said. "Compass was about its audience, and we knew it." Sills said, "We were the first people on stage to mention real names, real products, real streets. Everything was mentioned. Every time you said Coca-Cola in those days you got a laugh, or 55th Street where we happened to have the place."

None of them intended to be funny, least of all David Shepherd, but between Spolin and Hutchins, the Compass Players, at that moment in the summer of 1955, were the most liberated comedy ensemble in the country. The Marx Brothers had disbanded. Sid Caesar and *Your Show of Shows* had gone off the air a year earlier. *I Love Lucy* still played to large audiences, but no matter how brilliant the show, it was, like all network television and most movies, basically well behaved. The Compass Players did as they liked. With no script and no sponsors to obey, no Legion of Decency or family-friendly morality to uphold, they were saddled with no *nos*. The effect was instantly obvious to those ninety or so Hyde Parkers present on opening night. Even drunk, they felt it: as improvisers, these amateurs were like no one else on any stage or screen had ever been; they were like the rest of us offstage Americans actually ought to be: free to do and say as they felt. Free to criticize; free to guess; free to feel differently.

They were not comics, actors, or vaudevillians; they were not even professionals. They were their audience, Chicago people, Spolin-trained. They took suggestions.

"Just go to the people," Sills said, "they'll tell you what they want and you give it to them. That's what happened."

Mike Nichols was still in New York, still studying with Strasberg after two years and still depressed about his nowhere career, when Sills appeared at his apartment three months after Compass opened, in September 1955. With Sills was his twenty-year-old bride, Barbara Harris. She and Nichols first met in the early days of Playwrights, the afternoon Barbara, a local teenager with no theatrical experience, walked into their Chinese restaurant and asked, "What are you doing?" "We have a theater," someone answered her. "Do you want to be in it?" Barbara was handed something to clean with, and for the next four or five months, every time they looked up, she was mopping closer to the stage, and Sills. Eventually she made her way off the floor and into Brecht. Audiences loved her because she was adorable and real, a genuine innocent caught in the perpetual whirl of "wait, nevermind," with cherries for a face and a lovely voice that was sometimes nasal, like a librarian's. "When you watched her," Nichols would say, "you could actually see her brain working." She could retaliate apologetically.

Paul and Barbara told Nichols they were en route to the University of Bristol, where Sills, on a Fulbright Scholarship, would try Viola's games on the English before heading off through Europe to sample, among other theaters, Brecht's Berliner Ensemble. Their New York leg would be a short one — a disappointment to Nichols. He missed them, his old company. His friends.

They missed each other. In fact, that's why Paul and Barbara had come — part of it, anyway. They wanted Mike back in Chicago, in the Compass. A look around his tiny apartment — for furniture, there was only a Victrola on the floor, playing a Dietrich record — and they guessed Nichols probably wanted it, too. Though how to make the offer without implying he had failed as a Method actor in New York?

"Improvise?" he asked.

"You want to stay here stealing cheeses from the supermarket?"

Nichols, insulted, laughed. No matter how much they perplexed each other, he and Sills would always admire the other one's dream, Sills's to create theater communities and Nichols's to be taken into them.

"But, Paul — in front of an audience?"

Harris stepped in. "Please go," she quavered. "You'll see."

Nichols had improvised only in private, with Sills in workshops and Strasberg in rehearsals. The thought of actually getting up there in front of people, without a script, and, just . . . well — it sounded nuts.

Historically speaking, it was insane. David Shepherd, however, placed Compass very much in line with the commedia dell'arte, those bands of Renaissance actors that strolled European countrysides for nights of drinks and folk comedy. From that tradition, Shepherd borrowed his theater's scenarios, and with it, he believed, the improvisation required to animate them. Stretching the line of artistic parentage across four centuries, from Italy to Hyde Park, he was sincere; he was also attempting to legitimize an inchoate experimental free-for-all, as if, by giving the Compass an instant history, he could grant it cultural stability, like assigning a foundling to a family. But the Compass *was* a foundling — Shepherd sold his genius short — because improvisation, as they were practicing it in Hyde Park, had only just been found, and not in Italy, but in America, by Viola Spolin.

So Mike Nichols was correct. Before the Compass, no theater had ever charged audiences to watch actors — *players* — get up there and improvise. The sort of "improvisation" that Shepherd understood to take place in commedia performances was closer to ad-libbing. Commedia artisans modified performances to suit the language and temperament of a particular region, but most stuck to their roles for life. Repeating the mother, father, daughter, or count, patterns invariably developed. Speeches were set, and the longer the better: for in that age of slow-traveling news and limited entertainments, power went to those who retained most. Memory, not spontaneity, was the Renaissance player's tool.

Sills explained to Nichols how it worked at the Compass. After the first act, someone went out with a notepad and took suggestions from the audience. Movie styles, book styles, characters, settings — anything. Then, during intermission, the players sat around a table backstage, brainstormed scenes from those suggestions, and handed out parts. So, no, they weren't making it up *the moment* they got the suggestion, but still they were making it up that night . . . live . . .

But, to Nichols, the insanity of the undertaking was hardly a consolation. The avant-garde did not entice him. "What about Elaine?" he asked.

They all asked. In only three months at the Compass, May had already established herself as a master of the form — its first. "She only had to touch her shoe," Shepherd recalled, "and the focus went to her." And where many improvisers, in the rush to maintain a "funny" rhythm, blurted out some version of the expected response, Elaine would turn up singular, cliché-busting ideas, like the matronly (not embittered) whorehouse madam, who remembered the names of her client's mothers. May's preternatural ability was not simply a function of her complete focus, wit, intelligence, and imagination, though she had all that too, in spades. It was more like she had three brains, the actor's, the writer's, and the director's. With split-second efficacy, they thought as one, immersing her in character, whispering ideas into her ear, and showing her the stage picture without one diluting the other.

Thinking of her, Nichols felt a pull. "I wanted to explore more Elaine and me," he said. "It was her and that train station and those hamburgers she made me in her apartment, and what came with them that I was thinking about when I decided to go back."

The whole business of improvising in front of an audience, Nichols discovered, really *was* insane. It produced no evidence of art, none of the poetry of great or even merely good theater. Its gifts were intermittent and accidental. Its practitioners — amateurs all — were not penetrating psychological truths (imagine Strasberg's horror!) or achieving a deeper communion with the human predicament. They had no craft. In the fall of 1955 there were no rules, no methodologies, and no set of assumptions to pass for guidelines. The Compass, as Nichols first encountered it, was the Wild West, and with Sills in Europe, woefully lacking a sheriff. Not even Shepherd, his deputy, acting as director, could tame the outlaws, not with political ideology and not with workshops. What good were the teachings of Marx or Spolin to Mike Nichols, a trained Method actor, in the hot blaze of panic, drowning in the silence of ninety drunken intellectuals (some of them pretty girls) licking their metaphoric lips at his slow and delicious disintegration? They wanted him to fail! To feel better about *themselves*!

The first time Nichols improvised, sharing the stage with Compass Player Barbara Gordon and Elaine, he grimaced when one of them pulled a thumb-and-forefinger "gun," and asked, "Why are you pointing your finger at me?"

Some nights, the guilt and humiliation were so awful Nichols would have to run — out the back door of the theater, all the way to Lake Michigan, and jump in.

"Rehearsals" was a term Nichols found ridiculous in this context. How could anyone rehearse spontaneity?

Still, he went; it was his job (at twenty-eight miserable dollars a week). A late sleeper, Nichols ambled in to rehearsal approximately on time, early in the afternoon, a Kent Micronite cigarette held out in front of him with an air of *better than this* that was hard to miss. "And then," Nichols said, "we talked and debated and came up with ideas for scenes to do that night." More like a rabid book group than a theater, "rehearsals" were spent shouting around a table.

"The Kafka scene was weak last night —"

"I thought you were going to come in when I started —"

"Let's do something from *The Lonely Crowd*!"

"What about that Strindberg thing? Elaine, would you —?"

"That's great. What if —"

"What if Strindberg goes to Hollywood?"

(This was David Shepherd's people's theater?)

"Strindberg goes to psychoanalysis?"

"No more Strindberg, please —"

"They loved Strindberg two weeks ago —"

"No one loves Strindberg."

"*Ergo* he's in analysis. He's depressed!"

"Well, of course he's depressed."

"I could have told you that —"

"That's why it's funny . . ."

For all his wit and charisma, Nichols improvised from the brain, his conscious past of his proven jokes and highbrow deflections. He played by himself. He joked. He did voices. He put his voice in his nose, his throat, his stomach. No matter how convincing, it was technique, a trick, and the audience's silence told him so.

Nichols tried, but he could not learn from Elaine. She was too good to emulate. "The stuff never stopped coming out of her," Nichols said. "She threw it away with both hands." What came out of him? Variations on the Know-It-All, the Ego. But Elaine's range was voluminous. And where her fellow improvisers dutifully obeyed Spolin's space rules — a practice Nichols considered embarrassingly close to pantomime — Elaine ignored them. He delighted in these transgressions. They inspired him to do the same. On the occasion she blatantly ignored his "coffee table," Nichols announced, "Darling, you just walked through my Noguchi." As ever, Elaine justified her gaffe, instantly incorporating it into the scene. This was the improviser Nichols longed to be. "My impulse to learn from Elaine," he said, "came as an impulse to be near to her."

Improvisers connect for the same basic reason you and your friends connect.

Say you meet someone. You like something about them and they like something about you. Your mutual interest begets mutual play. Play begets cooperation and mutual understanding, which, trampolined by fun, becomes love. Love is the highest form of play.

It was as improvisers, backstage, in a loud little room packed with Compass Players and cigarette smoke that Mike and Elaine found that kind of love. They were an actual couple, Nichols said, "only sort of for a minute, but that clearly wasn't how it was going to be. It was more that we would go through all sorts of not terribly successful things with other people, and always tell each other everything." Taking down audience suggestions on a large pad of paper, and retreating from the noise of the cabaret to the shouts and sudden hushes of their debating table, Mike and Elaine discovered they shared, beyond rhythm, rapport, and intelligence, a predilection for certain themes and comedic ideas. Their first duet, a dramatic improvisation about a man deciding whether to rat on his friends, sprung easily from their comfort zones; his training in "serious," "truthful" acting, hers in the theme of betrayal, a lifelong obsession. The theme of pretension both knew and loved; and between his ear for sound and hers for language, and their deep and wide engagement in the canon, they were reference-ready to parody on command. Sitting at that table for those tense fifteen minutes between sets, as the five or six other improvisers deliberated over what to play and who would play it, Mike and Elaine, at the whiff of a girl and boy or mother and son, put their hands up at the same time.

"When you have to make things up on the spur of the moment," Nichols said, "you gravitate very quickly to the person who understands you most easily." But what, exactly, did they understand the most easily about each other? The secret in their special adhesive, as it is with any bond, would take Nichols and May all the way back to their beginnings, to the underground volcanoes of instinct Spolin deemed the place of improvisation. "Where Elaine and I really met most passionately," Nichols said, "was in being the offspring of classic Jewish mothers." Commonality drew them together; togetherness deepened their commonality.

In Germany, Nichols remembered his mother, Brigitte Landauer, to be a flower of music and intelligence, the object of many powerful attentions, a beauty and a muse. It was also how she remembered herself. "But when we got here," he said, "she just settled into being a Jewish mother." Though her marriage to Nichols's father had been deteriorating for years — young Mikhail absorbed innumerable fights and infidelities — losing her husband, her witness to her gloried past, precipitated a series of further heartbreaks for Mrs. Peschkowsky from which she never recovered. She became "a nightmare of accusation." "I raised you so you could say that to me? Thank you very much, I deserve that." There started the taking of pills. There were prolonged hospital stays. Why? Who could answer such a question! Everything hurt! Elaine's mother, Ida Berlin, also a young widow, was herself quite literally in the theater, the Yiddish theater; self-dramatization was her stock and trade. Both mothers, Nichols said, "were invaders."

From these volcanoes rose Mike and Elaine, Siamese twins. With no script to border their neuroses — their buried selves shot upwards with the force of a combined half-century of repressed hostility.

"Teenagers" was their first masterpiece. It began, like all the others, with a suggestion.

"Let's do a scene about two teenagers," she thought aloud.

"Oh, good, two teenagers in the backseat of a car."

That's it. No discussion. Just a premise: two kids, slightly younger than their actual ages, caught in the awkward tangle of premarital sex. The rest they improvised. "What we did," Nichols said, "came so easily to us that we were utterly confused by people making so much of it." With "Teenagers," first presented at the Compass late in 1955, Mike and Elaine defied a long-standing ideal of abstinence young Americans had been suffering in popular culture since the death of the flapper. But more than presenting the truth, Mike and Elaine presented the truth truthfully. This was not just sex; it was clumsy teenage sex in the backseat of a borrowed car. These teenagers were anxious, fraught with self-consciousness, cramped, stuttering, sweating, and palpably horny. She babbles on to distract herself from what they drove there, to the lake, to do. He stares at her body, pretending to listen. "Isn't the lake suicidally beautiful this evening?" she asks. *What?* He has to practically beg her to put out. "If I went any further," she warns him, "you wouldn't respect me." He stares right back. "Oh, you have no *idea* how I'd respect you. I'd respect you like *crazy*." His voice cracks, he swallows hard. He kisses her at precisely the wrong time, after she takes a drag from her cigarette, and she's so stunned she freezes in his stupid embrace. Both are frozen. A passionless moment later, she opens the side of her mouth to release a line of smoke.

"It wasn't that Elaine pulled me out of myself," Nichols said. "She pushed me into it."

With Elaine, Mike abandoned his previous go-to persona, Jean the valet, the prick-ego, in favor of the all-purpose nebbish. And by the law of emotional physics, Elaine inflated. Her repertoire of commanding personalities — shrink, actress, spy, queen, lover, intellectual, and pseudo-intellectual — blossomed in their work together. May's psychological acuity deepened. A juicy joke possibility often tempted Nichols, but May stayed ferociously committed to truth. "Elaine and I had a rule," he said, "never try for a laugh. Get the laugh on the way to something else. Trying for it directly is prideless and dangerous, and the audience loses respect. The audience should find the laugh itself." Relinquishing the need to be funny, he discovered, actually made him funnier. Because, in reality, people are, mostly, not trying to be funny. They're just reacting, being themselves — which, it turns out, is pretty funny on its own.

David Shepherd, suddenly the producer of a local hit, needed a bigger theater. Folks were driving in from all over to witness for themselves the uncanny spontaneous satirical conjurings of the twenty-five-year-old Mike Nichols and twenty-four-year-old Elaine May. How could it be that these kids were actually making this stuff up, live, every show? Was it a trick? Something they actually had memorized and rehearsed? On its own, the novelty of improvisation, in 1956, was news enough to fill the Compass, but as word spread and audiences grew, it could no longer be argued that this new theater turned on a gimmick. Now, on their way through the door, repeat viewers reassured the incredulous: "I went again last night, and it's true! They really *did* make it up!"

The irony was not lost on Shepherd. His socialist cabaret, its revolving team of nonprofessional actors and worker's sensibility, was ceding, rapidly, to the intellectual elite. Odd, then, that when it came time to grow, he moved his theater from the university milieu of Hyde Park to a larger venue called the Dock, on South Lake Park Avenue — farther from bohemia, yes, but closer to the bourgeoisie. "I forgot all about the audience," he would confess. "I should have been building audiences out there — training audiences how to improvise and direct and write and get into the act. But I wasn't." Paul Sills, if he were there, in Chicago instead of Europe, might have reminded him. But he wasn't.

Nichols went back to New York, on a short vacation from the Compass, to solve a little mystery. He knew something unusual was happening to Ruth Gordon at the Royale Theatre, where she was playing — rather, playing *with* — Dolly Levi in Tyrone Guthrie's production of Thornton Wilder's *The Matchmaker.* It was, in 1956, wholly inconceivable to Mike Nichols that these men, giants of the theater, would permit Ruth Gordon to interfere, even slightly, with a single piece of blocking, or phrasing; Gordon's every deviation, no matter how inventive, would topple the carefully assembled domino line of actors and stage people on the lookout for their own cues. Nichols was no director, but he knew Gordon was doing something unacceptable, something different technically, and considerably more real, more surprising and eccentrically human than he had ever seen in a comedy. Returning to the Royale a second time, he was determined to find out what.

Broadway comedy in the 1950s had no Elia Kazan. It did not engage in naturalism, poetic or otherwise. It had no, or negligible, psychology, and no matter how funny, bright, or whimsical, it portrayed human lives obliquely, through the pink filter of farce, or some equally confectionery form. Its master was George Abbott, the speed king. Where there were doors in need of slamming, or adulterers in need of escaping, there was the director of *Room Service, Where's Charley?,* and *The Pajama Game* to conduct actors through windows and out of closets. His comedies were immaculate laugh machines, but as much as Nichols admired them, he sometimes thought there wasn't much else there. Abbott, unlike he and Elaine, was famously uninterested in behavior or latent truth. Hence the famous exchange between a befuddled actor and George Abbott: "Mr. Abbott, what is my motivation here?" "Your paycheck."

The second time he saw *The Matchmaker,* Nichols believed his eyes. Here and there, Ruth Gordon was changing things, little things. Not the dialogue; she was changing her stage business, discovering new relationships to her physical world as if she weren't doing what she had been directed to do, but living, really living, as Dolly Levi, and not the way she lived the part the last time Nichols saw her, but as a person changed by the circumstances of tonight, alive once again for the very first time. "There were little moments that she just improvised every night," remembered Gordon's costar Robert Morse, "but there was this amazing eating scene between Dolly and Vandergelder. I watched it from the wings almost every night for about a year. It was brilliant. She would — not the dialogue, but the actions, the behavior — improvise that whole scene, that whole eating scene, and it was quite remarkable for that time. She was cutting and talking and chewing and doing different things. I was amazed at her peculiarity, pushing the plate toward him, offering him a bite."

"That was the best thing I ever saw," Nichols said. "I was obsessed with it."

It wasn't always a matter of inventing the whole thing from scratch. There were *kinds* of improvisation. There was the scenario kind, which came from an outline; there were his scenes with Elaine, which came from a suggestion they chewed over backstage; and there was what Ruth Gordon did, which erupted behaviorally from between the lines. He thought, "She respects the play too much to let habituation kill the work."

Unpredictably alive, Ruth Gordon, Nichols thought, was the Brando of comedy. This right here was how to act in a comedy.

Nichols saw the show again, for a third time.

A word now about Severn Darden, the improviser's improviser. This person — a description too limiting for Severn — did not distinguish stage and life. He lived as an improviser — you couldn't miss it — the cape, the walking stick, the buoyant stride. Fearlessly free and just as intuitive, he would always appear, somehow, at precisely the right moment, as if he had been waiting for it, his cue to launch the one-man parade. Don't look now, but he's standing in the door frame, stroking a stuffed parrot. "Good afternoon, fuckers!" The munificent entering or exiting of Severn Darden into or out of Compass rehearsals or anywhere else on earth was a Dadaist's Christmas to all who beheld its splendor.

There was the time, before the Compass, when Severn, still enrolled at U of C ("It was thought crass to graduate," he said), had snuck into the women's dorm and waited up all night in the bathroom, his hand on the shower rail, just so he could ask, as smoothly as a Dixie colonel, when a naked girl appeared the next morning: "Is this the way to Clark Street?" His name was on the dean's Ten Most Wanted list. "Severn was," Nichols said, "number one. He was the purest, the greatest, the best, the most gifted, the smartest, the finest, the best human being." The Tao of Darden, Nichols noted, was good religion; it espoused danger and spice. "Severn," Nichols said, "would leap first, fastest, and farthest. He was always inventing."

It was Severn — the first in a line of kamikaze improvisers who would take John Belushi and later Chris Farley for their archetypes — who suggested Del Close come up to Chicago and audition for the Compass. Del had no improvisational chops (it was 1956; who did?), but Severn recognized Del's crush on theatrical Russian roulette as approximately suited to Compass.

Del knew the players; he'd remembered them from a Playwrights production of *Volpone,* and liked what he remembered. They had brains as big as his own, but were much more sophisticated than he could pretend to be. Del's thick, chic glasses and skinny hipster tie would help, somewhat, to close the gap, and all that tech talk he appropriated from science fiction and comic books sounded good when he rattled it off at warp speed, but still Del was tentative. They, with their college educations, argumentative bent, and existential cult of Freud, looked a lot meatier than what he had grown up with in Kansas. He said, "I began to think of myself as Jewish or at least a Jewish fellow traveler because I thought the Jews were the hip people." Their whole psychological thing — on the titillating threshold of 1950s culture and counterculture — enchanted Del. If the Jews were on the outside of WASP America, as they claimed, then Del, who hailed from WASP America, was on the outside of the outside. He wanted in.

As if Freud himself were pulling the strings, Del, for his Compass audition, was paired with Elaine.

They were given characters and circumstances. Del was a businessman with a plane to catch; Elaine was the woman he wanted to go to bed with. Except for the businessman part, Del had a lot of real life to bring to the improvisation. He truly did have to be back at the Barter Theatre, in western Virginia, where he was under contract. He was a twin-engine plane ride away, which left him not much time to get to know more about Elaine, though he wanted to.

She spellbound him. It was her exotic Jewishness. And the way she tended to him onstage. "I really didn't know what to do up there," Del said, "but Elaine brought me through the scene and made me look good."

At the end of the audition, Del baffled them all by eating fire.

He was offered a place with the Compass, but couldn't accept. He owed the Barter more time. Improvisation, and Elaine May, would have to wait.

Imagine their shock, Sills and Barbara Harris, returning to Chicago and the Compass. What they saw bore only the slightest resemblance to the rough-and-tumble amateur theater they had cofounded a year earlier. Once again, Shepherd had moved his company — by now, all professional actors — into a bigger space. But the Argo Off-Beat Room, a slick, nightclubby venue on Chicago's North Side, was no cabaret; it had a balcony. It had a kitchen. Its audiences, martini people, came in gray flannel suits and ties. Scant were the black turtlenecks and professorial tweeds of Compass yore. Scant were the scenarios. Remember those? Though Shepherd and May had tried to keep the withering form alive, writing and rehearsing fresh forty-minute plays every two weeks was physically exhausting and clashed creatively and commercially with the ensemble's new unofficial mandate: be funny. Laughs sold. Critics came. Successful scenes, like "Teenagers," were repeated — "frozen," they called it. Jokes that worked last night would be punched up for tonight.

The first improvisational theater in the world had ceded to a polished revue-style entertainment.

Was improvisation, which Sills had intended to serve everyone, really just a theatrical bonbon for the skyscraper set? In Europe, he had begun to wonder. Returning to the Compass, in the summer of 1956, he knew for sure. "In the American culture," Sills said, "the working class has no understanding of itself as such, as you might find in Europe. So, it can have no theater. It doesn't have what Marx called 'class consciousness.' These people go directly to the popular culture on TV and movies without any sense of being wrenched out of their lives." Improvisation, for player and audience, was all about wrenching. One couldn't discover new lands without being cast out to sea.

His mother returned to Los Angeles, but perhaps it was for the better. Had she seen the Compass at its peak, I imagine Viola would have been heartbroken. None of these "improvisers" was connecting. They were merely talking, thinking fast, being brilliant, nearly dead to the mysterious moment in each other.

Not Elaine, though. The sea was her paradise. Once she hit land, she turned around and started out again.

Mike, a polisher of pearls, stood on the shore and watched her go.

Severn had pinwheels for eyes and a Ferris wheel brain.

Oh, the Compass Players were wonderful — Mike, Elaine, Severn, Andrew Duncan, Bobbi and Mark Gordon — but they were no longer a reactive ensemble. Not with each other and not with their audience. Kierkegaard jokes? Here outside the university? Those giant laughs: were they laughs of recognition, or laughs of outsider derision, the sound of suburbanites taking down the coeds? To Paul Sills, and to Viola, the distinction mattered. The Compass "was leaving the community from within," he said, "it was hardening into a professional form and so its ties with the community seemed to lessen."

Shelley Berman, the latest and most divisive addition to the schizophrenic unit, gave a face to the devolution. A trained actor, sometime sketch writer for Steve Allen, and combustible personality, Berman had "Compass" written all over him. But no one had told Berman that improvisation was not a one-man show. Instead they threw him out there, and to keep from drowning Berman did as any comic would: he went for laughs. Getting them, he tried for more. "Hey guys," Berman said one night. "Mike had three scenes in that set, and I only had two." (Nichols said, "It was a whole new idea in Eden to count.")

It was then that Berman's fellow players understood that no improvisational ensemble could sustain an atmosphere of competition. Good manners had nothing to do with it; creating spontaneous realities en masse demanded the sort of patience and consideration Berman's egotism could not tolerate. As a monologist — a form he was soon to reinvent — Berman alienated his team.

To stay in the game, the other players had to defend their laughs, or try to. It threw the Compass out of sync. "The next time you fuck me up on stage," Elaine said to Shelley one night, "I will pull down your zipper and pull out your dick."

Improvisation had gone funny. Paul Sills was outnumbered.

3

1956–1959

Theodore J. Flicker had a goatee. In 1956 that was interesting.

The learning impresario in him had begun to see most successful entertainment, low or high, as fascination, an almost erotic satisfaction of urgent interest. The job was to create that interest, like a magician. But in what theater? An erudite man in show business, Flicker's tastes ran too traditional for the avant-garde, too adventurous for Broadway. He had no home.

Months earlier in New York, before the Compass had begun to fray, Flicker's pal Severn Darden had introduced him to David Shepherd, and they'd discovered in each other flecks of the same dream, to create a popular theater in America. And neither was sure of his next steps. True, they were philosophically opposed — Shepherd was politics and Flicker was entertainment — but Flicker had money ($34,000), Shepherd had the theater, and together they would rescue improvisation from the university elite. Joining forces, Flicker and Shepherd decided they would bring Compass to New York City, where all the world could see it, and from there they would sow the seeds of improvisation across the country.

That's why Shepherd had invited Flicker to observe the Compass as it disintegrated — and most of what Flicker saw appalled him. In performance, the Argo players wore street clothes and smoked cigarettes. This was *theater;* where were the costumes? Where was the formality? And where, Flicker wondered, was their technique? Did they know *how* to do what they were doing?

A new low came the night Severn appeared onstage cupping his hands together around a little ball of air.

"Look at my rabbit . . ." he cooed to Shelley Berman.

Berman took a look at his partner's empty hands and glanced up at Severn as if he were crazy.

Flicker recalled, "He made the audience his ally in making a fool of Severn because there was no rabbit." It got Berman an easy laugh, but denying the existence of Severn's rabbit ruined the scene. Flicker immediately identified Berman's choice as "the cardinal sin of improvisation," and decided a better improviser would have instantly accepted any idea presented, no matter how outlandish, and run with it. He had to agree — to say yes. They needed rules, Flicker decreed. If improvisation were to catch on in New York, and spread on from there, it could not be *only* free — that would make it anarchy. If people were going to play together, Flicker reasoned, they needed some kind of bill of rights.

For the final performance of the Compass at the Argo, in January 1957, David Shepherd brought back the first-ever scenario, *Enterprise*, insisting the format was still, and should remain, the backbone of theatrical improvisation. Collecting the more successful scenarios, Shepherd believed, would provide Compass with the written material any theater needed to secure its position in American culture. The Group Theatre had Clifford Odets; Compass would have Shepherd, Bowen, and May. Right there, he had a massive problem solved, he thought; to disseminate this ephemeral form, as he and Flicker planned, they would disseminate these scenarios. "If I succeed," he wrote to Spolin, "the Compass may not make more money, or branch out more quickly, but it will be a better theater. The question is: how?" A year and a half after *Enterprise*'s premiere, he still didn't have an answer. Moreover, none of his fellow improvisers liked working from an outline. This essential dispute between freedom and form would become the driving tension of improvisational comedy for the next half century.

Del Close left New York in a virtually floorless Volkswagen that was so cold he had to burn a can of cooking fuel to keep from freezing. Ready or not, he was on his way — a trek of one thousand miles — down to St. Louis to join Ted Flicker. They were going to improvise. They were going to throw out everything and start over.

Shepherd had tasked Flicker with replicating his version of the Compass in St. Louis (their New York backers had withdrawn). Flicker nodded obediently, but the P. T. Barnum in him had other plans. Del at his side, he would transform the St. Louis Compass, *his* Compass — comprised of Close, Nancy Ponder, Jo Henderson, and himself, doubling as director — into a manic circus act of whimsical ingenuity and derring-do. "Ted's idea," Close said, "was to present improvisation as an intellectual feat, as an unusual human ability." "It was Del," Flicker said, "who brought the truly unknown into the improvisations of the St. Louis Compass." The rest they would figure out as they went along.

The scenarios, Del agreed, were total bullshit. This was improvisation! Del insisted on what he called spot-improv, improvising from a suggestion right there, *on the spot,* not from a concept agreed upon during intermission, and certainly not from a scenario, but the way he and Elaine had at Del's Compass audition — suddenly and without a plan. Flicker agreed wholeheartedly, but with a single caveat: an entire evening of spot-improv was too much of a commercial and artistic risk. Sure things were needed: good sketches and blackouts refined in rehearsal. Unlike the Chicago Compass, whose talky, cerebral explorations could drag on, sometimes for twenty minutes, Flicker impressed upon Close the need to play their scenes for speed. Speed and variety. They were improvisation's insurance against failure. Didn't like that one? Try this. Now this!

Removed from Spolin, Sills, and Shepherd, the St. Louis Compass banished its predecessor's utopianisms for an innocent ignorance, lightly and wittily trodden by just four players, improvisational virgins all, but each an artist and scientist both. The less ideology Flicker's Compass assumed, the more they would discover. Those discoveries they would call knowledge.

On opening night, April 2, 1957, they presented their earliest findings at St. Louis's Crystal Palace.

Under the aegis of impresario Flicker, the Crystal Palace traded Shepherd's Brechtian box for the antique cellar of a mad Victorian sorcerer, dressed up like a fairy tale in vintage old-world crystal chandeliers, crooked panes of stained glass, and black walls behind white marble busts glowing like real faces in the buttery light.

Lights up!

Del and Nancy Ponder — he in all black, she in black hose and scarlet blouse — appear through two revolving doors and perch on colored boxes downstage. They begin plucking things from space and eating them. It's pleasant. Nothing happens. They keep eating.

Then Flicker, from out of nowhere: "You've got to have conflict!"

In the corner of the stage, light falls on an imaginary apple tree. Del picks an apple for himself and takes a bite. He hands it off to Ponder.

She takes a bite, a change comes over her, and she looks him over. "You ought to be wearing a fig leaf."

Laughter! Blackout. Lights up!

Flicker reappears, as he will between scenes, as a sort of ringmaster, setting up characters and situations, all scripted, all short and fast. A Grand Guignol–style murder (of hyenas), a satire on the latest labor movement, and a gibberish play, "Mudpies in the Afternoon." In another scene, Flicker himself plays a farmer who wants to become a sycamore tree. He tells his wife. "Now you're twigging, George."

Blackout. Lights up! Intermission. (The men's room is soon out of commission.)

For the second act, Flicker tells his audience, they will improvise. Would a kind gentleman or gentlewoman of the audience please suggest four objects and an opening and closing line of dialogue?

"Iron maiden . . . beer bottle . . . cigarette butt . . . Roman candle . . ." These are the objects.

"'Our marriage is a failure.' 'You're so right.'" Opening and closing lines.

And now, announces Flicker, the Objects.

Lights up. Del, acting hard, does his best to inhabit the inner life of a Roman candle. The others pun around their objects. No dramatic situation develops.

Meager laughter and blackout. (Flicker running between light board and stage.)

Lights up on Nancy Ponder and Flicker, reading a pantomimed newspaper.

"Our marriage is a failure," he says.

"You're so right."

He turns an invisible page. "Our marriage is a failure," he repeats, a little slower.

"You're so right." Also slower.

As the married couple, Ponder and Flicker repeat these two lines, back and forth, over and over, getting sadder and older until they die. Blackout.

Lights up: Del and Jo Henderson. He grabs her by the throat. "Our marriage is a failure!"

"You're so right . . ." she gurgles, then dies.

Laughter, blackout, curtain.

How dumb. From these trifles, Del would "emerge burning with humiliation because we knew what we'd done in front of the audience was a con." He wanted more from improvisation. Something deeper. And farther.

Ted Flicker needed Mike and Elaine. He knew whoever had them had the future of improvisation. Writing constantly, he implored Chicago's local heroes to come to St. Louis, where they were rebirthing a new Compass every night, improvising how to improvise. "This is," Flicker wrote, "the most rewarding theatrical experience of my whole life." Mike and Elaine knew they had all the power, and no, they did not want to go to St. Louis, though Flicker begged them to reconsider. Mike had just married Pat Scott, a jazz singer ("Isn't this a beautiful first wedding?" Elaine remarked), and staying with her, in Chicago, where he and Elaine had pending job offers, including the chance to start a new, revamped Chicago Compass with Sills, kept Mike and Elaine closer to New York, their ultimate goal. (Plus, Missouri made Elaine queasy.) They could just go to New York now, and try their luck with agents, but without precedent for improvisation on or off Broadway, they foresaw many dreary months of no work. What if, Flicker suggested, they came to St. Louis in May or June of 1957, and in September headed east to open the New York Compass together? ("I shall take what I want from COMPASS," Flicker wrote to Severn Darden, "the COMPASS that I made, and I shall try and beat him [Shepherd] to the punch [in New York].") Flicker had saved ten grand for that very purpose, and he would keep looking for more, but in the meantime, he urged Mike and Elaine to be patient. Improvisation was still too raw for New York's imprimatur. Compass needed technique. And that's what they were doing in St. Louis, figuring this thing out, learning, mixing potions like mad scientists.

In the end, Flicker proved persuasive. They were coming. "Am very glad Elaine and Mike decided to go to St. Louis," Shepherd wrote Flicker. "Hope Elaine can start working soon on the weaknesses in the company: for instance fact that Del & Mike have many of the same weaknesses and same qualities . . . Del may fall into habit Andy [Duncan] did in Chi — competing with Mike in wit."

That summer, the power duo left Chicago and joined the other members of the St. Louis company at 4411 Westminster Place, an imposing brick mansion turned boardinghouse a half-hour walk from the Crystal Palace. Flicker had one of two bedrooms on the third floor, and perhaps out of deference to her position, gave Elaine the other. Mike, Del, and the rest took rooms below.

They became a team. Living and playing together congealed their appetites, and would become a modus operandi for their descendants for decades to come. Conversation was constant and focused; removed from the idealistic concerns of their Chicago counterparts, consistent improvisational theories sprang up and did not have to fight rocks to flourish. Troupe Flicker, united as entertainers, became the first ensemble devoted to cracking the "how" of improvisational comedy.

They worked out a plan. Mondays, designated workshop night, they would improvise an entire evening for paying customers. Flicker's Compass, beyond mere one- or two-word suggestions, would invite an audience member to the stage to monologue about themselves for as long as twenty minutes before converting their free-associative miasma of thoughts and experiences into entertainment. "This is not as exciting to rest of the audience as it is to the story teller and us," Flicker wrote to a friend, "but every once in a while we get some one who is obviously telling us something out of thir [sic] lives, and then the house gets very very still . . . sometimes uneasy . . . then we play it (adding that which we feel it needs) we usually get a very strong reaction from the story teller." On Tuesdays through Thursdays, experimentation was sidelined, somewhat, for scenes improvised off suggestions of a theme (love, art, war, and "almost every aspect of manufactured mass thinking"), and on Friday and Saturday, they presented the best of the week's findings. "We are testing new techniques and methods each night of the week," Flicker wrote, "and each week they work better. By the time we get to New York in the fall we will be able to take a word, any word, and creat [sic] a scene on the spot from it." By June of 1957 they had devised over two hundred scenes, and broken all financial records at the Crystal Palace. Most exciting of all, Flicker felt, "is that we are not appealing to just a special group, but it appears that people from almost all walks of life are taking up on us."

Flicker's successful experiments, and subsequent joy, he owed to "the most talented girl that I have ever known let alone worked with," Elaine

May. Every morning at 4411 Westminster Place, they met in the third-floor kitchen across from their bedrooms and discussed, over breakfast, what had been lost and what had been learned at the Crystal Palace the night before. They decided improvisations should be divided into two categories: public and private. In private, commensurate with the approach Spolin devised, one's only obligation was to one's intuition, one's inner life. In public, Flicker and May found that improvisers, to ensure scenes of dramatic integrity, had to establish a who, where, and what (as in, what are they doing?). To help players achieve and develop such scenes, they wrote, after weeks of breakfasts, what would be known as the Westminster Place Kitchen Rules. There were three:

1. Don't deny. If Severn says he has a bunny in his hands, he has a bunny in his hands.
2. Whenever possible, make a strong choice. The less obvious the better.
3. You are you. What you think of as your "character" is really just a magnified piece of you. Therefore, onstage, be you.

In time, the first rule, the rule of agreement, would be abbreviated to "Yes, and," signifying the composite virtues of agreement ("Yes") and embellishment ("and"), a player's duty to both accept his partner's reality and, in some form, enhance it. Established here, in St. Louis, the so-called rules of improvisation were made to be challenged, and indeed they would be, but Rule 1, the central tenet of agreement, would never be overturned. For the rule of "Yes, and" is the rule that makes cohabitation possible; it is improvisation's peace treaty, its bill of rights, evidence-based and favorable to amendment. Practicing "Yes, and" — in effect, agreeing to agree — gave Flicker's Compass the courage to forgo the open, hurried deliberations of "backstage" improvisation for the purity of spot-improv. What they discovered, almost immediately, was that they could do it; "don't deny" really worked. "You can't imagine the excitement," wrote Flicker, "of being able to plan it so that no matter what the audience gives us to play . . . we are able to play it instantly."

When Pat Scott visited her husband in St. Louis, Mike's late-night schedule made it hard for them to catch Sarah Vaughan — tops on their short list

—when she came to town. But they had her records. Some Saturday nights, after Mike's last set at the Crystal Palace, they would walk back to the skinny castle on Westminster Place, drop the needle on Vaughan's latest, and analyze her riffs till dawn. Riffs: that's what jazz was, how you played with the notes. Mike and Elaine, they made jazz of "Teenagers," by now a standard in their songbook. The dramatic beats of the scene were the melody they riffed around, always a little differently, every time they played it. "You can't plan jazz and you can't plan improv," Nichols said. "They must express you in the moment. You can have your central beats—those are the big laughs and the story points the scene needs—but your breaks have to be there in you and come out."

Livelier after dark than in the day, the Westminster Place think tank of improvisation doubled, at night, as an experiment in living. You could say —at least, Del would—that the two went together. Life is an improvisation, improvisation is life lived onstage. As his own audience, during the very late and lonely nights in St. Louis, Del began experimenting with a new form entirely, a two-person scene between his brain and his brain on drugs. Can I get a suggestion for a narcotic, please? Benzedrine? Morphine? Marijuana? Opium? Del got his from neighborhood antique stores. They sold dusty old bottles, some of them half-full, purchased, probably, from pharmacies that had been bought out or torn down. It was like having a chemistry set again, only with one beaker.

Proving Shepherd's prediction accurate, Del and Mike clashed. Only one vision of improvisation could rule when the company went off to New York: the Jew of the jazz riff or the hell-for-leather WASP. "It is so easy to go out and get laughs, it's ridiculous," Close argued. "To do something else, to drive them insane . . ." To enter unknown planes and capsize the audience's "perceptions of reality so that alternative possibilities enter." To Mike, Del's flamboyance was indulgent. Del saw Mike's variations as improvisation writ small. Each asserted the other was ego-driven, using his theory to rationalize a retreat from full spontaneity back to his creative comfort zone. Meanwhile, Ted Flicker, in awe of both minds, was weary of the single element they did share —highly literate hyperintelligence. Mike's and Del's styles he considered too rarefied for general consumption. How, then, were they to be free?

"The entire history of improvisational theater," Del concluded, "was balanced on a pinpoint there in St. Louis." They were a month away, Flicker promised, from New York.

Seeing the value in each — the witty, the visceral, the purely entertaining — Elaine sided with none. Rather, she played midwife to all. As she had with Mike in Chicago and Flicker in the third-floor kitchen, Elaine conjoined herself to Del, ripe with fresh ideas, on the promise of their mutual expansion. "Under Elaine's direction, my acting is improving," Del wrote to Flicker, then in New York, prospecting for their big opening. "I still can't play children, but I'm progressing apace with playing people." He may have meant *himself.*

While Del and Elaine let each other go and go, Mike often feared, and often rightly, that his tendency to (how to put it?) *direct* Elaine, whether by nudge or lasso, limited her. "She could explore any sort of character," Mike said, "and it sort of became my responsibility, or I *took* the responsibility — I don't know — of giving our scenes shape." Despite his young marriage and Elaine's long-distance relationship with Howard Alk, Paul Sills's friend in Chicago, the Del/Elaine experiments made Mike more jealous than he could have expected. Her subtle shifts of allegiance hit him like earthquakes, and what he didn't see onstage, he sensed.

At night, when Mike took to the town and Del enclosed himself in chemicals, Elaine and Flicker ceaselessly redressed their theories, he pacing her bedroom, she smoking and fingernail biting on the floor.

"Where does a girl get laid around here?"

Flicker looked up. "Del."

The next night's performance, Flicker recalled, "was the best improvisation would ever be." In place of frozen-Del was "Del Dionysus. He danced, he flew. He flung joyous madness into the sounds of all present. That night, stunned, and sated, the audience left in a post-coitus daze." Through Elaine, his only teacher, Del shot himself up with mythic forces of inspiration and destruction. She even looked like a needle.

He was in love with her. And he always would be.

Paul Sills tried, but he could not open his own Chicago Compass without Mike and Elaine. After losing them to Flicker, his deal for a space on Dearborn and Division, where Playwrights Theater Club had been, disintegrated. Soon thereafter, Flicker lost them to New York. They were tired of waiting and bigger things lay ahead.

Fall 1957.

You could not have picked a better moment to be Mike Nichols or Elaine

May, the first improvisers in New York City. Throughout the decade, notions of authenticity and intuition, from abstract expressionism to bebop to the beats, had been scratching at the shine on corporate American culture. Spontaneity was a counterattack, the artistic Left's minefield under the battleships of prepackaged mass communication, the cultural equivalent of the military industrial complex, which, since the end of World War II, had metastasized. Look at Archie and Veronica, Ozzie and Harriet: conformists anathema to improvisation. But we bought it because we needed it. Hollywood and Madison Avenue had been hard at work fabricating and selling an image of America the pristine and powerful to a country in serious need of a pick-me-up. In the days before the beats, who defined themselves by their spontaneous style, Allen Ginsberg said, "The air was filled with pompous personages orating and not saying anything spontaneous or real from their own minds, they were only talking stereotypes." By the end of the 1950s, you could no longer believe what you read, heard, or saw on TV. Was quiz-show prince Charles Van Doren *really* that good?

The avant-garde of the Depression had dealt in social reform; in the war-torn 1940s, with psychological disintegration; by midcentury, as the nation turned plastic, the revolution turned to the spirit. If God, Capital, Freud, and L. B. Mayer were the most popular enforcers of what Viola Spolin called approval/disapproval syndrome — the epidemic of the 1950s — then Spontaneity — or in its performance form, improvisation — was the cure.

Surely none of this crossed Jack Rollins's mind the afternoon he took Mike and Elaine to lunch at the Russian Tea Room.

Between bites of Stroganoff and borscht, Brooklyn-born Jack Rabinowitz listened, openmouthed, fork and cigar suspended in disbelief, as the boy and the girl comics, dressed in their showbiz best, did, according to Nichols, "a set of ad-libbed little skits we not only had never rehearsed but had never even thought of until that desperate minute."

The blood left Rollins's face. "I didn't laugh," he said. "In fact, I think I almost cried."

When the coffee came, Nichols breathed a sigh of relief as Rollins not only agreed to represent them but also picked up the check.

Rollins was still smarting from the loss of Harry Belafonte, his star client. His friend. Strolling Sheridan Square seven years earlier, Rollins had stopped at a restaurant window, and there was Belafonte, the singer, flipping hamburgers. "Why don't you become my manager?" he asked. "If you don't get personally involved," Rollins said, "there's no point in doing it." Rollins's personal involvement in Belafonte, his first client, was so complete, he turned down everyone else to focus exclusively on developing him. Hence Rollins's despair after Belafonte went calypso (Rollins's idea), got famous, and dumped him for another manager. Hence the scar tissue and subsequent gun-shyness and the tears he almost cried watching Nichols and May eat borscht at the Russian Tea Room. Rollins loved talent, and these kids — directed to his attention by Charles Pratt, a producer friend of Mike's — had talent to spare. But it wasn't simply a matter of quantity. Their talent had a special quality: it was their intimacy that captivated him.

Mike and Elaine weren't doing punch lines; they were doing scenes. It lent their work a behavioral honesty Rollins had never seen; in American comedy, no one had. Unlike Groucho, Sid Caesar, Lucille Ball, Jerry Lewis, Danny Kaye, Milton Berle, Phil Silvers, Burns and Allen, Jack Benny, and Francis the Talking Mule, the improvisers were too naturalistic for alter egos, shtick, gags, bits, acts, and one-liners. Mike and Elaine dealt in life, not jokes. They were real actors. With them, you could *feel* the humor. It was personal. That was new, too. Bob Hope and his generation of comics didn't write "their" stuff; they were showbiz, personalities. In terms of self-disclosure, Mort Sahl came closer. But he was a commentator, an American's editorialist. Nichols and May were . . . you and me. They spoke for us. Beginning at that table, Jack Rollins could sense the paradigm shift, he said, "from writers writing about 'take my mother-in-law please,' to human beings speaking."

And they *improvised* this? Which meant what, exactly? Pratt's advance description of their act — "They improvise, Jack" — had sounded like a fairy tale or bullshit to Rollins. But his idea changed that afternoon at the Russian Tea Room, and expanded later, after he incredulously asked Mr. Nichols and Mrs. May back to his office/cubicle, a former servants' quarters in the Plaza Hotel, for a closer look. Would they improvise something else for him, please? Per their request, Rollins suggested a first and last line and they improvised a scene right there just for him. "My god," he thought, "I'm finding two people that are writing hilarious comedy on their feet!"

Two days later, Rollins taxied them to the Blue Angel, New York's toniest nightclub. He wanted impresario Max Gordon, owner of the Blue Angel and Village Vanguard, to have a look at the kid geniuses. Short, round, and looking like he had never seen the sun, Gordon was their ticket. And not the friendliest. "We weren't frightened," Nichols said. "We had just decided to do the best we could and let it go at that." They, mere stars of the Compass, had only just arrived in New York. Neither expected a career in show business. "It was bizarre," Nichols said. "We never thought we would get that far, certainly not in one weekend." Mike's one suit was freshly pressed; Elaine's one dress wasn't. The Vermeer of displaced anxiety, she worried its subtle greenish tinge wouldn't show under the harsh lights. He was twenty-six; she was twenty-five.

When directed, they did "Teenagers" and their disc jockey piece — another Compass carryover — and waited out the uneven applause for the verdict. Gordon, they could see, had no reaction; but Jack Rollins was beyond speech. He explained, "They were totally adventurous and totally innocent in a certain sense." Max Gordon, meanwhile, had less interest in acts that didn't remind him of other acts. Saying nothing, he rotated himself, an inch at a time, toward Rollins. They had worked together since the Belafonte days. "What is it?" Gordon kvetched. "Is it a boy or is it a girl?" Rollins shooed Gordon and his cronies into the back office for what seemed to Nichols like a short eternity. Then Gordon reemerged, scotch-in-fist. "You can open in two weeks," he grumbled. "We have a new show coming in then."

But waiting two weeks in New York would not be easy for Mike and Elaine and the seventy dollars they had to share between them, some of which had been borrowed from friends. "Well," said someone near the boss. "You can fill in down at the Village Vanguard until then." That's what they did. For those two weeks, Nichols and May debuted their act — twenty minutes, "Teenagers" and First Line/Last Line — as an opener for Mort Sahl at the Vanguard. That is, when Sahl permitted it. "No, no," he would say, when he liked the crowd. "Skip them. I'm ready."

Uptown, the Blue Angel on East Fifty-Fifth Street looked to them like a movie star in gray quilted velvet. For Mike Nichols, who had waited his whole American life for a chance to commune with the inner circle of safety, assimilation, and, true to his European upbringing, class, the Blue Angel signified fulfillment. Almost. He was soon to learn Manhattan's cocktail crowd was distressingly unlike the Compass-goers whose attentions he and Elaine had captured instantly, every night. Even as an audience, presumably setting the day's cares aside, nightclub New Yorkers were hard at work, filling Nichols's distracted ear with the forced laughter and flirtatious chitchat of business transactions and foreplay. These New Yorkers were their own entertainment. Nichols felt like wallpaper, an outsider at his own show.

Under Strasberg, he had learned about the Event, the unspoken, bottommost, largely unconscious intentions of characters and real-life people. You have to look for them, Nichols said, "under and around and beside the words." They tell you the real truth, as New York audiences, in their unending ambition, showed Nichols theirs. Finding the Event, he suddenly understood, is the improviser's project. It makes him a psychoanalyst, answering the question, "What is this scene we're discovering *really* about?"

Quite often, and regularly in comedy, the Event is the complete opposite of the spoken dialogue. Like in "Teenagers": Nichols's character wants May's, but we receive in his voice and behavior signs of total terror. There's the Event. It grounds the joke. It adds complexity. It drives the scene.

It was sometime during Nichols and May's busy, popular, monthlong debut at the Blue Angel, in November 1957, that Mike Nichols's mother called him.

"Hello, Michael. This is your mother speaking. Do you remember me?"

Anger and laughter, an old duet. "Mom, can I call you right back?"

He called Elaine. "I have a great piece for us."

"What?"

He gave her the line and "she screamed with laughter." The rest happened that night at the Blue Angel. Mike and Elaine took their stools and improvised "Mother and Son," perfectly. "There it was!" Nichols recalled. "Our purest. It came out the way we improvised it and stayed there. The entirety of it onstage for the first time as we were searching."

New York understood that between and beneath the passive-aggressive (and aggressive-aggressive) "Mother and Son," a very Jewish, yet very relatable kind of Event — a story of repressed hatred and mutual codependence — told the rude truth about 1950s America's most inviolable folk hero: Mom. Jane Wyman? Donna Reed? Harriet Nelson? Ha! Elaine's "Mother" is a shape-shifting master manipulator, lethally swift with every weapon in her arsenal, beginning with guilt, which she detonates on her adult, aeronautical engineer son. "Arthur, I sat by that phone all day Friday, and all day Friday night, and all day Saturday, and all day Sunday, and your father finally said to me, 'Phyllis, eat something, you'll faint'" — he can't get a word in — "I said, 'No, Harry, no. I don't want my mouth to be full when my son calls me.'" Don't the other rocket scientists call their mothers? Is it so hard? To call his *sick* mother? Yes. Sick. It's her *nerves*. The doctor told her so. She's a very nervous woman. Didn't he, her son, know that? Just wait. Someday he'll find a girl, get married, have children ("Mom — Mother, please . . ."), and when he does, "I only pray that they make you suffer the way you're making me suffer. That's all I pray, Arthur. That's a mother's prayer."

Nichols said, "Each of our mothers thought it was the other one's mother we were talking about."

"Where's Del?"

Even without Mike and Elaine, the fledgling New York Compass — Larry and Rose Arrick, Severn Darden, Del Close, and improviser Paul Mazursky —had been developing nicely for a couple of weeks, playing to good reviews and small audiences in a restaurant near the Cherry Lane Theatre, when they got an exciting offer to appear on *The Steve Allen Show*. Two days before taping, Del didn't show up to rehearsal.

Telling no one, Del had given himself over to the psychoanalyst Theodor Reik and began a course of treatment that would prove unsuccessful. Terrified, secretly, that his unconscious mind might be smarter than he was, Del had always liked to show off, especially to Nichols, his contempt for analysis and analysands. His stubborn determination to prove himself right (and Nichols wrong) would have stood between Del and recovery, leaving the emotional basis for his stubbornness — so averse to improvisation — unexplored.

What had happened to Del? Mazursky and others asked. Who had hurt him? Did he remember? Laughing, Del liked to say that he had been there, in Del Close Jewelers, on December 15, 1954, the day his father killed himself. In some renditions of the story, Del senior, according to Del, kindly asked his son to pass him a glass of water Del didn't know was Drano. In others, Del watched his father gulp down battery acid and was instructed to stay put and watch what happened next. Sometimes Del didn't appear until the hospital scene: "He drank a quart of sulfuric acid and the fucking monotheists kept him alive for three days," was another version. "That's two days longer than Christ hung on the cross." It was, to Del's horror, a Catholic hospital. "They wouldn't kill him, the swine." The facts of the story always changed, but the feeling behind them never did; the suicide story, as Del told it, was a funny one. But when he told it, his audiences never laughed. And so, despite his work with Reik, Del's depression and addiction, compounded by the persistent public triumphs of Nichols and May and the personal blow, from which he was never to fully recover, of losing Elaine, body and soul, to Mike, persisted.

Two weeks after Del disappeared, the New York Compass folded.

No less than Arthur Schlesinger Jr. called the 1950s "the most humorless period in American history," and Adlai Stevenson, sounding like a Compass player, remarked, "You get your nose rubbed into this solemnity and this seriousness of our time and it begins to have its effect on you, it buries your own natural spontaneity of personality."

Satirists acknowledged the death of their industry. Groucho Marx was one of them. In 1958 he confessed, "There are no Marx Brothers movies because we did satire, and satire is verboten today." (*MAD* magazine? Anarchy, not satire.) It had been going on for years. In 1952 cartoonist Al Capp retired from *Life* because, he wrote, America had lost its "fifth freedom," the freedom to laugh. That same year, in the *New York Times Book Review,* cartoonist Walt Kelly published "A Crying Need for the Cleansing Lash of Laughter," a Hail Mary call to reenlist the intimidated. Then came cartoonist Robert Osborn, in the *Saturday Review,* protesting the "emasculation of American humor," and Kenneth Rexroth, in the *Nation,* with "The Decline of American Humor." The *Atlantic* ran "Vanishing Comedian"; the *Saturday Evening Post* asked, "Are You Afraid to Laugh?"

On the night of January 14, 1958, Mike Nichols and Elaine May did their sketch about two teenagers trying, and trying not, to make out, on the NBC program *Omnibus,* and America's fear of laughter began to subside. As the satirist Jules Feiffer recounted, "It was the first time I had ever seen a man or a woman, or a boy or a girl, talking about having sex, or not having sex, or trying to have sex on television."

Nichols awoke at 4:00 a.m. the morning after *Omnibus* aired and checked the papers. All raves. Raves beyond raves. After three months gigging New York nightclubs, they were nationally famous, stars.

He called Elaine. "What do we do now?"

Jack Rollins, the man who discovered Nichols and May, heard the office door open — he had upgraded to a bigger place at West Fifty-Seventh — and in peeked a small, shy, nervous person.

"My name is Woody Allen, may I come in?"

This nervous person had come, he said — actually, his friend, Len Maxwell, had dragged him there — because he wanted to write for Nichols and May, who he knew "were touching on some kind of truth — truth of character, social truth, truth of wit." But, Rollins explained, Nichols and May did all their own writing — though, technically, they never actually wrote, per se. They *improvised*. But yes, they generated their own material. Allen thanked him and left.

A month later, Allen returned and asked Rollins if he and his partner, Charles Joffe, would manage him, personally, as a writer. He then read, aloud, a sketch he had written. It was hilarious. He — doing it — was hilarious. But, again, Rollins had to decline. He and Joffe didn't manage writers. They managed performers. If the performers *also* wrote, like Nichols and May, then Rollins and Joffe handled their writing too. But Woody Allen didn't perform. He only wrote.

But Rollins had that feeling. He knew love when he felt it. They would take on Woody as a writer, just a writer, for a trial period of six months. In that time, Rollins said, "we suggested he should consider trying to perform."

Paul Sills got together with Howard Alk and Roger Bowen at the Greenwich Village Howard Johnson's — precisely where their famous friend Mike Nichols worked back when he couldn't afford to eat — to discuss jumpstarting another branch of Compass in Chicago. David Shepherd had declined their offer. Instead they found their backing in Bernie Sahlins, good to go on the six grand he'd earned from selling his share in a tape-recording factory. Since the earliest days of Playwrights, Sahlins had rallied behind Sills, and considered an investment in his latest venture a gamble safeguarded by the coffeehouse craze sweeping the beat scene. Espresso was big business and good people were available. Sills had interest from Bowen, Andrew Duncan, and Sills's ex-wife, Barbara Harris, then living on pennies she earned at her hospital job. And there was Severn Darden, out of place as a stand-up at the folk music venue the Gate of Horn. But the name "Compass" belonged to Shepherd, so with an ironic low bow to A. J. Liebling, who had famously trashed Chicago in his 1952 *New Yorker* series, they decided to call their place the Second City.

4

1959–1962

The two barely habitable storefronts at the corner of Wells Street and Lincoln Avenue, formerly occupied by Wong Cleaners and Dyers and a failed hat shop, did not exactly call out to Paul Sills as the ideal location for the Second City, his latest effort to bring improvisation to the people. Just off Lincoln Park, that block of Old Town Chicago—an industrial ragtag of warehouses and moving trucks—seemed never to have heard a laugh in its slow, silent life. But rent was cheap and you might say the neighborhood was ripe for discovery. Over there, across the street, the Lincoln Hotel sat atop the Lincoln Diner, open all night. Emma's Boarding House, where itinerant improvisers could find something like a bedroom, lurked a few steps away. New York City was to the east.

The Mob watched all through the summer of 1959 as Sills, Bernie Sahlins, and the multitalented who-knows-what Howard Alk stapled carpet to the floor (a dollar a yard) and filled the bar with martini and wine glasses Sahlins got, used, from a failed restaurant. To find the dressing room, upstairs, you had to leave the theater and take a separate flight of stairs. As for the box office—a card table—it would fold up and play the lobby during shows. Then, in daylight, they'd switch roles. Here and there, as Sills's team hammered and nailed, confused patrons of Wong's turned up at the table with claim tickets Sahlins could do nothing about. Wong left no forwarding address. Back to work: The creaky bentwood chairs—one hundred and fifty of them—Sahlins picked up at an auction (a dollar a piece), and the tables—Formica tops, cast-iron bottoms—looked like they had been conceived by schizophrenics and assembled by paraplegics. The décor originated as telephone booths painted black, artfully smashed and hung over a photo collage of Roman antiquities that had been cut out of coffee-table books. The lights Sahlins purchased secondhand, and under enough darkness the red dust around the clam-shaped stage could pass for a velvet curtain. Second City was black and red. "There was something very sexy about the look of the place," Andrew Duncan said. "A sin kind of thing." They had no money to advertise.

Meanwhile, Sills built the company. His recruitment strategy went something like this: "Severn, it's Paul. I'm doing this thing. Do you want to be a part of it?"

"Yeah, sure."

No need to audition.

They were Severn Darden, Barbara Harris, Andrew Duncan, Roger Bowen, Howard Alk, Bill Mathieu on the Wurlitzer spinet—Compass holdovers—Eugene Troobnick, and Mina Kolb, the funniest woman Sills had ever seen. Mina wasn't intellectual, physical, oddball, or an extremist. She wasn't like the others, hence her power. She had a way of blinking, of saying nothing, or just *one* thing—and after long bouts of silence—that would clarify everything around her. As she once put it: "I didn't know what was going on." You'd see her sitting one emotional inch outside of the scene, watching it unfold, seemingly vacantly, and then, out of Mina would come some approximation of what you didn't know you had been thinking; it hit the ensemble like a splash of cold water. She had never improvised before Second City.

So there they were. Now what?

"We weren't particularly definite in our plans," Sahlins said. He turned to Sills.

Thankfully, Sills had learned from Compass. For the first time, he had peopled his company—true improvisers all—with the knowledge that actors, like Mike Nichols, and stand-ups, like Shelley Berman, operated with too much personal need to cede themselves to chance. And though he cringed at the bald showmanship of Ted Flicker's team in St. Louis, Sills appreciated its variety and, when compared to the scenario-heaviness of Shepherd's Compass, its speed. It was apolitical. With Shepherd out of the picture (he was opening new Compass theaters along the East Coast), Sills could rid his theater of agenda and dogma—obstacles to communal discovery—and rush headlong into play.

Booze would help. There you have perhaps the most significant commercial innovation in improvisational history: this new experiment would have its own bar. One hundred percent of the proceeds would return to the proprietors, Sahlins, Sills, and Alk. Between a ceiling thrashed with exposed wires and a floor littered with broken bits of plaster, they workshopped. It was better not to know what. Common Sills directions were "No, no, no," "blah, blah, blah," and, in concise moods, "blah, no." Runners-up included "Do *something*," "Yes, fine," and "Goddamnit, stop!" When they were hot, Sills danced; when they stumbled, he would vault into such a rage, improvisers would duck preemptively. He threw chairs, stormed out, yelled—anything but discuss the work. "Severn," he might say, "do that after you do the other thing, then go back there and start over." Too much direction, he knew, would put the players in their heads. How do you talk about intuition? A false gesture from the improvisers and he would leap from his table and rush the stage, arms breaking the air, intoning passionately. "Most of the time," one said, "we had no fucking idea what he was trying to say. We didn't know if he knew." Sills wanted them to react. And if they reacted against him, fine: that was improvised.

A month before opening night, Sills could not have told you what he was going to present as his first offering. So unformed was his approach, he even told *Variety* he was opening Second City with an original play, "North Side Story," by Elaine May (it didn't happen). Sills started writing, of all things, a scenario, a picaresque about the Common Man, which didn't hold together. Time running out, he eventually broke it down into individual sketches, one of which, "The Dream of Richard Nixon," he asked David Shepherd to write. Bowen wrote, too, a scene called "Businessman," a parody of Nietzsche's Superman. (Facing a racist Woolworth's counter in Greensboro, North Carolina, Businessman declares, "Egads! That's not only unfair, that's contrary to the standard business practice of operating the Negro race at a profit.") Bowen's and Shepherd's sketches made it into the opening-night show, *Excelsior and Other Outcries*, along with an opera, a Freudian western, an Ingmar Bergman parody, "Seven Sealed Strawberries," and others.

A style emerged. The unimpeded marriage of Spolin and Satire, as observed by U of C graduate Philip Roth, joined "precise social observation with extravagant and dreamlike fantasy." Sills, Duncan said, "planned every second from the minute the light dimmed to the applause and bows" — a marked departure from Compass anarchy. Duncan himself — as cute as a Kennedy — would open the show with a simple, refined introduction that signaled Second City as a class outfit; it became, with few variations, a signature greeting. "Good evening, ladies and gentlemen. Welcome to the Second City. Tonight we're very pleased to bring you scenes originally improvised by actors both from their own ideas and suggestions from the audience, audiences such as you..." The whole of Sills's Second City presentation, from the cocktail attire of the improvisers to Bill Mathieu's Mozartian curlicues on the Wurlitzer, had an uptown elegance that would have been out of place at the Compass. This time, his commercial designs — situating Second City at the comfortably louche intersection of bourgeois and beat — were no secret. It was an older crowd; the improvisers themselves were older. But in keeping with the Compass format, Second City's second act would be improvised to the tune of "Ladies and gentlemen, we want you to give us ideas — from current events, your daily lives, the dark recesses of your minds — which we will dramatize for you. Just call out whatever comes to mind." Sahlins set admission at $1.50, intentionally cheaper than a movie.

Walking off the street the absolutely freezing night Second City premiered on December 16, 1959, you gave your money to the guy at the card table and your coat to Melinda Dillon, the girl someone told to take the coats. In the absence of an actual coatroom, Dillon hung them wherever she could in the ladies' room, but only when she was able to squeeze herself free of the sardine tin that was the lobby, from which a short flight of stairs took you into the theater, where a hostess led you to a table near where Kalujian, the rug dealer, on his hands and knees, was still nailing down the carpet. The waitress assigned to fade out the lights at the end of the show faced a challenge. On cue, she would have to cut a maze through the house to get backstage, to the light board, which, ordinarily manned by Howard Alk, who doubled as an improviser, would be abandoned at curtain if she didn't get there in time. The rest they had pretty well rehearsed. As Bill Mathieu started the opening song, "Everybody's in the Know," and Barbara Harris, in pearls and black shirtwaist dress, appeared to sing, Sills and Sahlins were still in the kitchen, in a frenzy of last-minute hamburger-flipping. One hundred and twenty Chicagoans filled the place that night and laughed for two straight hours. "The success of the early Second City company was an absolute shock to everyone," Bill Mathieu recalled. "It was astonishing. All of a sudden, we weren't just Chicago's darling, we were fucking successful!"

Months after they opened, *Time* declared the Second City the place where "the declining skill of satire is kept alive with brilliance and flourish," and *Playboy*, the company's neighbor in Chicago, raved "the best satire to be seen in the U.S.A. today." ("I practically lived at Second City" — Hugh Hefner.) Even if team Sills hadn't been wonderful, his theater might have won its praise by default. In 1959 Second City held the only comedy real estate in America. Outside of Jules Feiffer's syndicated corner of the *Voice*, you simply couldn't count on getting a regular fix of satirical storytelling anywhere else (certainly not on TV — yet). The *Chicago Tribune*'s chief theater critic, Richard Christiansen, spread the good word. "And it became, in those days, *the* thing to do," he said, "go to Second City." As the clock struck midnight on the 1950s, Sills, Sahlins, and Alk agreed they didn't have to advertise.

Ted Flicker and Elaine May were sitting in Central Park, discussing his next venture, a dream realized, opening the first permanent improvisational theater in New York. Years earlier, Compass had opened and closed in a restaurant off Cherry Lane — the result of bad management and a drugged-out nervous breakdown à la Del Close — but with the steaming success of Second City in Chicago, Flicker found the money, a basement saloon space at the corner of Bleecker and Thompson, and had a shot, he thought, at righting the wrongs of his predecessors. Star personalities and divergent philosophies shattered his St. Louis group (Flicker took partial responsibility; he had let them) — so he would build his new company, still unnamed, on a bedrock of unity and something like love. Whomever Flicker found, he vowed they would be individuals *together*. His conversation with Elaine diverged back to the Kitchen Rules. Did they still believe in what they wrote back in Westminster Place, these three years later? Basically, yes. You always start with a premise, a Who, What, Where —

"That's just what you ought to call it," she said. His new theater.
"Of course."
The Premise.

• • •

Paul Sills moved his mother to Chicago, installed her at the Lincoln Hotel, and hired her to run workshops at Second City, one for the professional improvisers and another for anyone in the community interested in learning and playing her games. Viola didn't go in for psychoanalysis — Freud was in the past, she in the present — but her public workshop sessions, true to Viola's original intentions as a social worker, were geared toward an undeniably therapeutic climax, personal liberation. Still, if anyone got metaphysical, she'd wag a finger. "Don't get misty-moisty!" But many in Viola's open group, children and adults, showed no professional interest in the theater. They had come to Second City just to play.

Taking a cue from Mike and Elaine and Shelley Berman, Del Close put on a Vegas tux and attempted to survive as a nightclub comic. He played the Gate of Horn in Chicago, the Hungry i in San Francisco, some holes in Jersey. It didn't work. Prematurely psychedelic, he went on about "Resistentialism," a little-known French school of philosophy, he joked, devoted to investigating "the inherent perversity of objects." Why are these coat hangers hell-bent on destroying humanity and where do they all come from? (From beer-can openers, their larval form.) You mustn't forget about the drugs: peyote procured from a cactus garden in Del Rio, Texas; LSD provided by the United States Air Force to determine, as Del put it to one journalist, "the best type personality for space travel"; and in basements and on fire escapes with friends in New York, mescaline, "a reality lubricant," sampled along with passages from Huxley's *The Doors of Perception*.

Del claimed he didn't need help, but Elaine looked out for him whenever she could. She gave him money; she doctored the script for his comedy album, *The Do-It-Yourself Psychoanalysis Kit*. He turned her on to grass.

Del was in Hollywood, barely making ends meet at the Club Renaissance, when he got the call from Howard Alk: Sills, their captain, had gone sullen and remote; success had once again "disturbed his muse," according to Sahlins. "Paul paled at the thought of endlessly doing shows in a single style. The telltale signs of his restlessness were evident." Sahlins overlooked Del's legacy of drinking and drug use, stubbornness, unreliability, lies, sadistic flashes, and his self-serving, often brilliant theories of improvisation, none of which paid heed to Sahlins's business, the making and selling of topical comedy to Chicago's bourgeoisie, and asked him to come to Second City. He suspected Del's presence would be a spur in Sills's side, and actually keep chaos away from Second City, which, considering what we already know about Del Close, was ironic to them both. It was the summer of 1960.

According to *Motion Picture Daily*, Mike and Elaine were the best comedy team in America. But they got stuck. TV notoriety, and the unyielding pressure to produce new and perfect family-friendly improvisations for network audiences, troubled the free flow that had come so easily to them in the Compass years, before the world started expecting genius a hundred times a night. Repeating and fine-tuning hit scenes was a worthy sacrifice to Nichols, a way to improve, sort of like rehearsing; but to May, for whom risk meant discovery, refinement was gilded barbed wire. "You cannot fail [in television], and because of that you can't try anything new." Nichols said, "Elaine May has a wonderful motto. The only safe thing is to take a chance. I think she means that if you stay safe, and don't take a chance — don't do something that's different from the last thing, something that makes you nervous and holds dangers — if you keep trying to do the thing that worked last time, the encrustations of mannerisms begin to take you over. And pretty soon you're no good at all — and therefore not safe at all."

It separated them. Nichols and Pat Scott bought grand furniture and moved into a spacious East Side apartment with air-conditioning in every room. May took a place across the park, on the Upper West Side, but didn't move in. Not right away. "If I ever get organized," she said, "I know I'll enjoy every minute of this dream too." Partying with the intellectual elite, she arrived in old slacks and sneakers. Mike came to the same parties shining like Gatsby. At Sardi's, an admirer approached Nichols with, "I understand you were born in Berlin." "Not anymore," he smiled.

By default Nichols became their spokesperson. He bloomed in conversation. Elaine, meanwhile, stayed quiet, forking her salad inquisitively, as though she didn't trust lettuce. "Because if I don't like the interviewer," she explained, "I become not so much hostile as sullen and childish. And if I *do* like the interviewer, I read the story and feel personally betrayed by what he's said." Moreover, once she said it in the press, she's said it permanently. She could never take it back, explain it better, start over. "It's like that terrible feeling you get after you drop the letter into the mailbox," she said. Television had the same effect.

Passionate and devoted analysands, Nichols and May still shared psychoanalysis, free associating, separately and expensively, five days a week, he with Dr. Rudolph Loewenstein, she with Dr. David Rubinfine.

To break the ice, Jack Rollins suggested Broadway, their natural habitat. As improvisers, Nichols and May could not be handled as actors; they needed to return to a live audience of their own species, the Manhattanites. Like Compass audiences, but with money, the upper Fifth Avenuers knew Brecht from Ben Hecht, Ingrid from Ingmar, and unlike nightclub crowds, they made ideal collaborators. "Everything we've done has happened with the three of us," Elaine said, "we two and the audience." Arthur Penn, whose productions of *The Miracle Worker* and *Toys in the Attic* were going strong on Broadway, would direct *An Evening with Mike Nichols and Elaine May*, a compendium of their best scenes, though he "was in this particular case more of a friend than a director," Nichols said, "an eye and an intelligence that we could trust absolutely."

Out-of-town tryouts, in Falmouth and Westport, Connecticut, were positive for Nichols, a chance to test and further clarify each scene's Event, a strategy of growing importance, he felt, especially as their Broadway debut approached. During one tryout performance of "Pirandello," about a play fight within a play fight within a (maybe) real fight, they actually did fight, drawing blood and real-life tears. Were the scenes improvisations anymore? If not, were they lying to their audience? If yes, shouldn't they rehearse once more? With opening night, October 8, 1960, rushing toward them, Nichols imagined his own humiliating reviews. Elaine, too.

Most nights, before they went out onstage, she would whisper, "I'm psychotic with fear," and he would come back, "I'm gibbering with fright."

Critics and audiences saw none of it. They loved *An Evening with Mike Nichols and Elaine May*, found it balm to the wounds of Broadway comedy. Feigning dumbness for a quick laugh, Broadway served up trivialities like *Critic's Choice, Send Me No Flowers,* and *Under the Yum-Yum Tree. An Evening with Mike Nichols and Elaine May* lacked the improvisational purity of their Compass days, but it was rich in character and plausibility and deep connection with its audience.

Every night, the show ended with a spot-improvisation, First Line/Last Line. They took suggestions for those first and last lines, and then for a style — literary, dramatic, or otherwise. Reviewing some of their suggestions, one marvels at the high reference level of their third partner, the audience. Theatergoers of late 1960 asked for Ibsen, Shakespeare, Chekhov, Tennessee Williams, Damon Runyon, Wilde, Gilbert and Sullivan, James Gould Cozzens (!), O'Neill, T. S. Eliot, Proust, Coward, Faulkner, Wordsworth, Shaw, Salinger, Brecht, Tolstoy, Kerouac, John O'Hara, Irwin Shaw, Joyce, J. M. Barrie, and Thorne Smith — and those were only their suggestions in previews, before they opened on Broadway. That night, October 8, 1960, Nichols and May treated the audience to not one but two rounds of First Line/Last Line. They were, Round 1: First Line: "Have you seen New Moods and Strange Fancies at that uptown art gallery?" Last Line: "No I haven't seen it." Style: Kabuki. Round 2: First Line: "I'd like to make my position perfectly clear." Last line: "And so to bed." Style: Elizabethan and *Open End* with David Susskind.

"When you do it every night," Nichols said, "your head gets weird and you could do things you could never again do," like improvise in styles you thought you never knew, or in Elaine's case, achieve the impossible, like the perfect verse she improvised one night, clear out of the blue, when Nichols, improvising as disc jockey Jack Ego, asked her, a movie starlet, about her new film, a musical adaptation of *The Brothers Karamazov.*

"Oh, could you possibly sing it for us?"

"Of course. *There was dashing Dmitri, elusive Ivan / and Alyosha with the laughing eyes / Then came the dawn, the brothers were gone, I just can't forget those wonderful guys.*"

It was, Nichols would reflect, the most beguiling of her many miracles.

Such was the cultural climate of Camelot, when improvisers and their audience could share Dostoyevsky and laugh. The dashing president's "best claim to greatness," Norman Mailer wrote, "was that he made an atmosphere possible in which one could be critical of him, biting, whimsical, disrespectful, imaginative, even out of line. It was the first time in America's history that one could mock the Presidency on so high a level, and we may have to live for a half a century before such a witty and promising atmosphere exists again." Sophistication was in.

Audiences reeled, and yet, to Mike and Elaine, all this was a bit like jumping through fancy hoops. Surrounded in champagne and accolades and the unexpected disappointments of success, the pair forged dutifully on. Tickets sold and they frayed. Laughter — when they got it and when they didn't — slowly eroded their innocence. She would say to him, one day late in their run, that she couldn't take it anymore. "Take what?" Nichols replied. "It's an hour and a half and all we do is talk!" Yes, but why? Why keep going? The improvisations hardened, the anger reversed course. Bitterness metastasized. What were they doing? "Satire is revenge," Elaine understood. But they had been avenged many times over.

Alan Arkin ambled into Second City a failure. He had lost, maybe, everything.

A year earlier, in New York, his wife, Jeremy, had taken their two children, Adam and Matthew, and left him.

A perfectionist since the age of five, when he first started imitating Chaplin and Danny Kaye, tearing apart his face in the bathroom mirror admonishing himself for being himself, Arkin was not a natural candidate for improvisation. Aside from Hugo's, the hot dog stand at the corner of Hollywood and La Brea, and his amazement at the prodigious gifts of Paul Sand, he barely remembered his six-month tenure at the Young Actors Company, and even if he had, Viola's games technique would not help him get where he needed to be — where he had been aiming his every grain of concentration for the last twenty years — onstage in New York, or on film in Los Angeles. But those parts were not forthcoming. He was a character actor, which is to say he didn't look like a leading man. He looked Jewish.

Depressed, he accepted a job at the St. Louis Compass (David Shepherd's wife, Honey, a friend of Arkin's, had recommended him). Arkin's summer at the St. Louis Compass — he joined Jerry Stiller, Anne Meara, and Nancy Ponder — was double-edged. Working a steady gig, finally, satiated the stage addict in him, but improvisation required an acquiescence of self he did not associate with art. Real acting was hard work. "I wasn't loose enough or facile enough," he reasoned.

Paul Sills, however, saw through the tension, deeper in to something strange and good. "If you ever want a job in Chicago," said the director to the actor, "come out."

At this, Arkin only nodded. *Yeah, right,* he thought. *I'm going to bury myself in the Midwest for a hundred bucks a week? I'd rather starve in New York.*

In New York a year later, Alan Arkin was a starving out-of-work actor, less a wife and two children. Only the offer from Sills remained. "Making that call," Arkin remembered, "was like phoning in my own obituary."

Arriving in Chicago in December 1960, he moved into Emma's Boarding House (a dollar a day, bathroom down the hall). The place reeked of failure, a smell Arkin knew well.

He did not like what he had to do at Second City. A trained actor, Arkin needed direction, dialogue, anything sure, "something solid out there that would fill the void," but improvising gave nothing solid; it was a hell of free will. To survive, an improviser had to fill that void with a piece of him, a tall order for most, but for Alan Arkin, who had spent his life pretending to be other people — Chaplin, Danny Kaye, Beethoven — it was paradoxical. "I had no interest in being myself onstage. In fact, there was no possibility of my playing myself on the stage because I didn't know who I was. I didn't have a clue." He read Dostoyevsky constantly. He didn't want to be funny.

When he wasn't alone at Emma's, felled by despair, he was with the group from morning until night, sometimes sixteen hours a day, rehearsing, performing, staying up late to beat the inevitable adrenaline rush that followed every show. Instead of sleep, Arkin and Sheldon Patinkin — hired, the day Arkin arrived, as Sills's assistant and the general company's "nervous Jewish mother" — would venture downtown, to the Clark Theater, for a bounty of foreign films, double features, a new pair every night, *La Dolce Vita, Through a Glass Darkly*. The Clark barely closed. Approaching sunrise, Arkin and Patinkin would debate Fellini versus Bergman back to the all-night diner under the Lincoln Hotel, nod at the friendly Mob guys in the next booth, and talk on through dawn, two nighthawks in a Hopper painting.

Arkin's first character — "a character that was serious" — was a working-class guy, not necessarily employed, and not from this country. Like Arkin at Second City, he was dislocated. Arkin's pain and isolation: you could see it in the way he played the character, the two or three feet Arkin put between himself and the others, the still, tense face not-erupting with repressed anger. And to his surprise, audiences laughed at this guy. "Then I found a body of characters that no matter what I did with them there was some humor in them," he said. Out burst a Dickensian assortment of fringe folk and foreigners, Arkin's autobiography in improvisation. "They were all unemployed or menials and yet they had an all-encompassing pride in their work," he said, "which was how I felt about the acting profession." A Jewish pretzel peddler, an Italian immigrant, a Puerto Rican kid who didn't want to go to school, and one night, six months after Arkin arrived at Second City . . .

"Beatnik." The suggestion.

After the intermission, Bill Mathieu at the piano played Arkin and Barbara Harris out onstage; Arkin, guitar in hand, wore a schlumpy jacket. Harris had on black glasses and a beret. Daintily, she scrutinizes something on the invisible wall, consults a guidebook, and scrutinizes again. Arkin watches her calmly, then breaks the silence with a sudden and crazy strum on his guitar. He stops.

"I don't mean to seem like a prude," she says, "but you're going to get kicked out of here if you don't watch out."

"I don't care. I gotta speak my mind."

"That's healthy! I mean, as far as I'm concerned, of course, it's all right with me. I mean, I know who you are."

"Who am I?"

"Well, I mean, I know who you are generically ... You see, I took a humanities course last year ... and I, uh, I —" She's scared and excited. He's her anthropological study. "I, uh, read quite a few of the generation's, the beat writers ..."

Harris smiles at her own hipness; Arkin doesn't smile.

She asks him about Allen Ginsberg, he asks her about the art on the wall (we're in a museum!), and from there, each unknowingly reveals to the other his tribal pretensions. Arkin and Harris's "Museum Piece," as it would come to be known, is a satire of ideology, and in the tradition of Second City under Paul Sills, a warm one. Long, too. At fifteen minutes, longer than most Compass scenes, "Museum Piece" exemplified Sills's taste for the so-called people scenes, bite-sized plays about relationships unfolding at the un-jokey pace of real life. We're serious, people scenes say; it's what we do and think that's absurd.

Arkin and Harris's collaboration "came out great," Patinkin said, "the first time they did it." "Museum Piece" would go into the repertoire, Sills decided. But turning the improvisation into a sketch, and putting it into the main portion of the evening, "took three weeks of screaming, cursing, and tearing hair out." It was Sills's fear — neurotic and also reasonable — of completion. When the scene "works," it's done, under glass, dead. When it's broken, the scene yields more surprises, more life. "I think Paul suffered," Patinkin said, "trying for perfection and then running away from it."

When Second City was approached to film a stage show for Canadian television, the first time most improvisers in Arkin's company would be on camera, "Museum Piece" got self-conscious. Striving for perfection, Barbara Harris clenched. She stopped responding to Arkin improvisationally. As if scripted, her reactions hardened and her attention shifted to herself and the audience's attention followed. "Museum Piece" became Harris's showcase. To stay alive in the scene, Arkin yanked as hard as he could in the opposite direction, going bigger, faster, louder . . . but it didn't work. The harder he tried to win back the audience, the uglier the scene got. All that once was wonderful in "Museum Piece" vanished. Arkin decided he hated Harris.

Out of ideas, he ventured into the only place left, the counterintuitive. One night, a day or so before the film crew arrived, instead of even improvising, he tried to love her. ("Where that idea came from," he said, "I will never know.") At first, Arkin felt like he was dying. Laughs were life preservers, and after casting them overboard, he felt himself drowning in blandness and humiliation. But on his way down he felt a quickening. Harris and Arkin connected. Real moments returned. Barbara Harris, and "Museum Piece," came back, and deeper than ever.

Arkin knew why. He had permitted himself to plunge, feet first, into certain failure. "The truth of the matter is," he said, "is if [improvisers] allow that to take place, and to be gone, and empty, it's gold." Egolessness; it was freedom, a state of grace Arkin would spend the rest of his creative life trying to recapture. "They are those rare moments when we are operating past our abilities," he wrote. "They are the most exhilarating moments in life. It is as if we are not responsible for our own actions but are witnessing them from some exalted vantage point."

He fell in love with Barbara Harris.

"When you do a show for a year," Nichols said, "especially on Broadway, you can't be best friends anymore. It's like when you've lived with somebody and fucked each other's brains out and you're so sick of them, you just have to get out of the house."

"Form is the thing that interests me," he now understood. "In the act with Elaine, we were doing little plays. She was the gifted one. She had the ideas. I gave them a beginning and end; I gave them form. I was the director and she was the author."

"I once saw a very rich man standing with his beautiful wife and maybe three or four other people," Nichols said. "He was leaving his apartment and giving instructions to the maid: and as he was doing this, he held the maid by her right breast. What interested me even more than the fact he held her by her right breast was that everyone, including his wife and the maid, acted as if he weren't. And I thought, the things that happen between people casually while they're just standing around are so extraordinary that if I can create that kind of behavior—I don't mean simply bizarre, but unique and revealing of character—if I can do that, I'm a director."

As an improviser entering a world he did not create, Del Close joined the Second City company—a completely revised edition—in the summer of 1961. Following the sold-out smash of *An Evening with Nichols and May,* Alan Arkin, Barbara Harris, Paul Sand, Severn Darden, and the other members of Second City's first generation had gone off with Sills to present their material on Broadway, a thrilling showcase for the organization and the improvisers both, but one that left the home front rather confused, improvisationally speaking. The campus/Compass foundation had gone. In came Avery Schreiber and Jack Burns, regular guys. Cabdrivers. Del's friend, John Brent, brought drugs into the scene. Few took to Spolin. Soon after their induction, the revolving cast, mostly virgins, were marched into Viola's workshops, but without Sills to ground their game work in actual scenes, a theatrical product that made professional sense to the actors, they resisted her. Del performed his disgust.

"This is fucking bullshit," he murmured, loudly, to improviser Larry Hankin. (Hankin agreed.)

"Concentrate on your 'Where,' people."

"Our *what*?"

Close fought everyone—and every theory of improvisation—at Second City. "Del had a problem with authority," Hankin said. "He didn't want anyone teaching him stuff. He was going to discover it himself, Goddamnit."

He fought Sahlins. Close argued for improvisation's inherent value as an art form in its own right, independent of the written sketches it emerged; his boss saw it as merely a tool, a means of arriving at the finished sketches he considered Second City's most significant contribution. He fought Sills (who reappeared erratically, tiring of the company in New York, to rehearse shows in Chicago). Their issue was satire, which defeated its own purpose, Del believed, "because assault in the sense of attacking is a tribute" to the thing being attacked.

We were just getting into Vietnam. "Why do you want us to do this political shit on stage, Paul?"

"To remind the audiences that we're living in the same world they are."

Del admitted Sills had something there. Politics *was* the Now, a moment uniting the community. But in the final analysis, comedy was about hurt and healing—end of story. "The issues are immaterial," Del said. "It is the response that is the only important thing and the rage that drives the comedian. In order to heal the audience, you have to heal the actors in the audience's presence and take the audience along, which is why I've been devoted to improvisation for such a long time because it does precisely that."

He fought one of his newest colleagues, a relentless, barrier-breaking, born stand-up, Joan Rivers. She denied, as Shelley Berman had denied in Compass. She didn't join anyone else's reality. She never said, "Yes, and . . ." But did Del? How often would his old stand-up material appear in sketches and improvisations? How often would Del choose to improvise as a professor, intellectual, or any other stringent, verbose character that justified a solo turn? He played generals, fathers, authority figures—fighters all—who took it out on Joan Rivers, a woman. "Del did not love women, no," Sheldon Patinkin said.

He fought Alan Myerson, his new director. "I have no idea why Paul hired me to direct," Myerson said. "I had no experience in improvisation except teaching acting in New York. But it was nothing like Second City." He and Sills first met in New York, through Myerson's ex-girlfriend, Roger Bowen's current girlfriend, a waitress at Second City. "It wasn't even an interview," Myerson said. "I think he was just interested in getting a sense of who I was." Del complained to Sahlins almost immediately. He called Myerson—a soft-spoken, analytical director, 180 degrees from the tempestuous Sills—a martinet, and worse. As the company's veteran improviser, to say nothing of his emeritus stature in the field ("Del was a mythological figure to us," Hankin said), he should have been next in line to direct Second City. Not Alan Myerson. "Del was also driven and determined," Myerson said, "whether it was taking over the show, getting a laugh, or scoring the speed." And Sahlins listened. For all the havoc Del wreaked, on himself and others, he had in frightening abundance the quality Sahlins admired above the rest, above humor even—Del had intelligence. It was Sahlins's motto. Spolin preached space, Sills community, Del risk and innovation, Mike and Elaine insight, and Bernie Sahlins would sacrifice all to keep his theater smart. "Always play at the top of your intelligence," he would advise the improvisers, almost singing, almost every day. Not IQ, mind you, but reason. Don't compromise truth or integrity for a laugh. Play characters as bright as you are. Let them know what you know. And don't goof. Wherever Del failed as an improviser, he forever stuck true to Sahlins's refrain — and Sahlins loved him for it. Five months after he'd been hired, Myerson was let go.

"Del was becoming a director," Hankin said. "You could feel it."

Ted Flicker had a methodology. It had taken him three meticulous months and over a thousand one-minute auditions and five hundred callbacks to find his Premise Players. Where Sills sought in his improvisers some ineffable, mysterious *x* quality, Flicker applied himself to building a functioning organism, people who, by following the rules — the Kitchen Rules — could play together. For each candidate, he briefly ran through the three points he had devised at Westminster Place with Elaine May, and then:

"Do you want to improvise?" he asked big-eyed Joan Darling. She was, like Elaine, dark, small, and smart.

"Now? Sure."

"Okay," Flicker said. "The place is a jungle."

"Okay."

Darling sat on the floor and started swatting at bugs. "They're early today."

He stopped her. "Is your thought the bugs come every day at a certain time?"

"Yes."

He hired her on the spot. Darling joined the group of George Segal, Tom Aldredge, and Flicker himself, perhaps the busiest man in "instant theater" (his term). At the Premise, a one-man auteur operation, Flicker emceed, directed, improvised, and produced everything. His mission — an antidote to the comic vacuity of televised entertainment and the insularity of Broadway theater — was "to find a form for improvisational theater that would not only train these actors in ensemble techniques, but would also explore methods of dealing with audiences in such a way as to genuinely affect their immediate thinking." Premise improvisation was not intended to be political or mystical; if it succeeded, Flicker's bite-sized off-Broadway basement would precipitate a total reinvention of the American theater, a revolution in show business. "The Premise," he wrote, "is a result of a conscious effort by serious theater people, dedicated to the theater, to find a means to save the theater from its slow death."

His ambition was huge; his budget was not. For lack of a liquor license

— the improvisation business's secret weapon — Flicker ushered the Premise into selling Danish and coffee. For lack of an aesthetic, he bought 160 colored doors and called them decorative. Instead of scenery, Flicker's improvisers had colored boxes. In lieu of an actual kitchen, an espresso machine hissed (during performances) just off stage right, and with no room for bistro tables, Flicker installed schoolhouse chairs with attached desks to hold cups and small plates.

For a dishwasher, Flicker hired an actor. "Dustin Hoffman tried out for the Premise," Darling said, "and we all wanted him desperately but he couldn't resist doing sexual or scatological material that was really too much for the time. Ted was concerned about his off-color material, which was really funny but at that time in the early sixties it wasn't really acceptable onstage. No one was really doing sex yet." (Flicker hired Hoffman's friend Gene Hackman instead.) But they all liked Hoffman and he needed a job, so Flicker brought him on to serve the hot chocolate and espresso during intermissions. When he could, Hoffman watched the show from the back. It was his first taste of theatrical improvisation, "the first time," he said, "I ever saw the audience creating the characters and the setup for the actors."

Above all else, Flicker advocated entertainment. Scenes had to be short and funny, an approach Flicker tested in St. Louis and perfected in New York. "We are going to do three kinds of scenes for you here this evening," he announced at the top of each show. "One type we will invent on the spot from suggestions made by you, another type is invented during the intermission from suggestions made by you having to do with events or on the political front that interest and amuse us all, and the third kind are scenes that we have created in the past either from audience suggestions or out of our own insanity that we repeat as often as we think we might get away with them." If a scene didn't find itself fast enough, Flicker would kill it, quickly, with a blackout (yes, he did lights too). And if he — running from stage to light board in the wings — didn't kill zombie scenes fast enough, improvisers were free to whip out their invisible "suicide devices" and do the deed themselves. Darling said, "If we were in the middle of an improvisation that didn't work — I had a long, deadly hat pin, Tom Aldredge had a poisoned ring — we would simply find a way to bring out our weapons and kill ourselves." Flicker, unlike Sills, had no patience for discovery, personal or otherwise. As emcee, he would regularly interrupt scenes to drive them in another direction — of the audience's choosing. "Freeze!"

Flicker leaps onstage midway through a parody of Paddy Chayefsky's *Marty*.

"All right!" he announces, laying a hand on Segal's shoulder. "How do you want this scene to end?"

The audience: "Happily!" "Homosexually!" "Heroically!"

"Heroically," Flicker repeats. "That rather intrigues me. Okay, fellows" — this to Segal and Aldredge — "take it from here to the end. Heroically!"

Segal glares at the audience, feigning anger to buy himself a second of thought. Then to Aldredge, "Well, Marty, why don't we duel?"

Though Flicker never aimed for political satire, he heeded New York's taste for news-related scenes. An improviser, he knew to agree. Village tastes forced the improvisers to keep up. "We had to read every newspaper and magazine," Darling said. "[Flicker] wanted us to cultivate a strong personal view." Back in Chicago, Bernie Sahlins, a businessman, preferred his politics in private, and Sills, a humanist, used it only as a tool of communal unification. It was because he improvised, responding to that third player, the audience, that Ted Flicker reintroduced political cabaret — long ago replaced by the jingoistic 1940s and somnambulant 1950s — to New York City. "Being political hadn't been popular for a long time," Darling said. "Not since the WPA and the Living Newspaper." Or as Flicker so succinctly put it: "They call out the names of people they hate and we improvise a scene."

As more and more journalists, tempted by dramatizations of the day's material, came to the Premise, Flicker began to think of his theater as much as a news source as an entertainment venue. He wrote, "They somehow liked seeing us say what they frequently [are] unable to say in the papers." Pining for Nichols and May, critics nailed Flicker for searching out gag lines and blackouts, and indeed they may have been right, but in his commitment to the political moment and concessions to popular tastes, he delivered improvisations his predecessors never would. Darling said, "Tom Aldredge did a composite of all the southern governors who were trying to stop the kids from going to school. He would string together all the names of all the governors, 'I'm Governor Orval Wilbur . . .'"

Reprioritizing in mid-1961, Flicker bowed out of improvising to focus full-time on directing, producing, and promoting. To replace him onstage, he hired — after a round of over seven hundred auditions — an ex-GI and Dartmouth graduate, Buck Henry. Outside of what he had seen of Nichols and May on Broadway, Henry had zero experience with the form. He loved it immediately because "it's a writer's device," he said. "[Improvisation] unlocked a way at getting at certain ideas." Like Nichols and May, Henry could speak in other voices, other styles. He came to the Premise with an Ivy Leaguer's knowledge of world literature and a native New Yorker's frisky cynicism. For the Premise, he invented an improvisational form, the ventriloquist and his dummy, often played by George Segal and Henry, respectively; Segal was better with accents, and Henry, smaller, fit nicely on his lap. The audience supplied political identities for both parts, and away they went, "and then, at the end," Henry said, "the dummy, who was getting politically fucked by the dialogue, stood up and folded up the ventriloquist." It became a Premise standard.

The Premise exploded. "Since Broadway got so square," wrote *New York Herald Tribune* critic John Crosby, and since "television's greatest satirist, Sid Caesar, has fled to Las Vegas, the last refuge of satire and the satiric sketch seems to be the supper club and the Greenwich Village basement." Harold Clurman, Tyrone Guthrie, A. J. Liebling, Sophia Loren, Arthur Miller, Paddy Chayefsky, Richard Rodgers, Jack Paar, Sarah Vaughan, Norman Mailer, Jules Feiffer, Kenneth Tynan, Nat Hentoff, Mel Brooks. They all came to the Premise. It was Greenwich Village in the early 1960s, the perihelion of cool, the Renaissance. Across the street from the Premise, you could catch Woody Allen at the Bitter End. "We saw Woody as often as we could, after our show got out," Darling said. At the Dugout, a bar a few steps away, "we would see Bobby Zimmerman, just sitting there." Around the corner, *The Fantasticks* had only just opened at the Sullivan Street Playhouse. Walking east from Tenth Street and Sixth Avenue was like trick-or-treating for comedy. You'd see masters gathered in doorways. Bill Cosby. Lenny Bruce.

Down the street from the Premise, on West Fourth Street, Sahlins and Sills opened a Second City outpost at Square East, and filled it with their original company — led by rising stars Alan Arkin and Barbara Harris — now that their Broadway run, a mixed bag, had ended. In came Flicker's team to spy and admire. Their more famous colleagues had the "wit" — often no more than a high reference level — "but we intended to be slicker," Henry said. Premise Players prided themselves on their six-minute scenes. Watching at Square East, Henry said, "I remember thinking, 'This sketch is going on for twenty minutes! What's the point of this?' We'd sit in the audience making faces and looking down the aisle at each other, thinking, *Is this ever going to end?"*

Premise and Second City improvisers were siblings, with all the attendant affection and competitive rivalry. But fundamentally they were one. Second City's Severn Darden, an old friend of Flicker's, was known to join the Premise Players onstage before his late show at Square East, and Del had an open invitation to teach Premise workshops whenever he was in town. "Del would tell us what we were doing right and wrong," Henry said. To Joan Darling, "We were a growing community, with Second City and among ourselves. Our show and their show had camaraderie to it. That was very important to Ted. We became so appreciative of each other. It is the only way to improvise. You must learn to trust the other person and you trust your own intuition." It was what Flicker had intended: a true ensemble.

"I can't believe what I'm seeing," Lenny Bruce said to him during one of his Premise visits. "You do it with love."

5

1962–1963

Mike Nichols found himself in Madison Square Garden, on May 19, 1962, standing inches behind Marilyn Monroe as she sang "Happy Birthday, Mr. President." The spotlight on Marilyn was so strong, he and Elaine could see right through her dress. "It was as though she were nude," Elaine said. "We were both riveted." And then, to their horror and delight, the dress split.

Except for that last part, it had all been rehearsed the day before. After Bobby Darin went off, Nichols and May would be announced. They would take the giant stage and read aloud from a list of imaginary birthday telegrams written to the president by important politicians (and one from Robert Frost). For example: "If things had been different, tonight would have been *my* birthday. Richard Nixon."

They did not improvise.

The American sense of humor, Elaine sensed, had changed, or needed to. Kennedy's election had so improved the country's mood, targets that once were evergreen had shriveled — a disappointing side effect of happiness. The nation's comics, most of them liberal, had less to protest now that their president, noted for his cinematic smile and grace with an ad-lib, proved to be something of a laugher himself. (Eisenhower never laughed.) The current gathering at Madison Square Garden, noted *Variety*, sealed the deal; it "dramatized, as no previous evidence has, that the present administration is enamored of, and in turn admired by, large segments of entertainment." How do you laugh at your own side, especially when your side is already laughing?

Elaine could not work this way. She needed the discomfort of parts unknown. Yet here they were, gripping their champagne at the after-party, nodding at the other VIPs, as far from artistic risk as they could possibly be, and incidentally, very, very close to Monroe and Bobby Kennedy as they danced by.

"I like you, Bobby," they heard.

"I like you too, Marilyn."

After three years at the top, Nichols and May were done as improvisers. "I would have gone on," Nichols said. "But she got sick of it."

With his base in Greenwich Village still going strong, Flicker opened successful Premise touring companies in Miami and Washington, D.C., where Vice President Johnson and Lady Bird really did laugh, and had begun to investigate opening Premises in Toronto and Puerto Rico, when the opportunity to play London came in the summer of 1962. It was a momentous offer for Flicker and the entire improvisational movement.

No one, American or otherwise, had ever improvised on an English stage. It was, quite literally, illegal to perform material previously unapproved by the Lord Chamberlain, Britain's censor, opponent of anything that might "deprave and corrupt those whose minds are open to such immoral influences and of a nature calculated to shock common feelings of decency in any well-regulated mind." Which posed two considerable problems for Ted Flicker and his players: one, their form, impossible to preapprove, and another, their content, which did not break for decency. So Flicker devised a plan. From some forty hours of New York–recorded improvisations a typed transcript over a thousand pages long was produced. "We thought they wouldn't possibly read all that," Joan Darling said. "If they ever came backstage and said you couldn't do that scene, we would say, you approved it. Look at page 724. Or if they had read it we would say, maybe it's on page 628." They sent the transcript overseas and it worked.

Until they got to London and slipped into their preview performances five sketches about the First Family and one incendiary sequence about a racist governor from the American South, who, upon dying, goes to heaven, and discovers God is black. That's where they were stopped. The satiric representation of heads of state, even American ones, violated the Theatre Regulation Act of 1843. The Lord Chamberlain's office demanded that Flicker send, posthaste, an accurate play text for its approval. Of course, he had no accurate play text to send. For backup, Flicker cabled his new friends, Premise fans, at the White House, "Do you have any objection to our continuing the Premise Kennedy scenes in London?" Within hours, Flicker got a response from Pamela Turnure, press secretary to the First Lady: "No objection Premise continue scenes." But the Lord Chamberlain was not going to take orders from Mrs. Kennedy, and without words on pages, threatened to send Her Majesty's troops to the Comedy Theatre, the scene of the crime, and forcibly shut down the Premise. So Flicker, a marvelous talker, began negotiations with the government. The Lord Chamberlain gave the improvisers a choice: either they could say they were improvising and secretly submit scripts for approval — a flagrant cheat, Flicker thought — or the reverse; they could improvise so long as they didn't advertise it. Fingers crossed behind his back, Flicker agreed to the latter. Three months later, the black God was back in the show, and just as he was about to cut into his steak dinner one evening, Flicker was handed a telegram from the Lord Chamberlain's office. "In view of the admission by certain actors that they improvise every night," he read, "I must ask you to forward immediately any explanation you may be able to offer. In the meantime, you will please take steps to insure that the play is performed in exact accordance with the licensed manuscript." Flicker laughed.

The Premise Affair, as it would be known, played out in the press for months, into the fall of 1962, stirring in the English a curious taste for Flicker's scandalous American technique. In came waves of sold-out audiences that included Peter O'Toole (drunk backstage, he presented Joan Darling a rose) and Stanley Kubrick, in London wrapping his film of *Lolita*. He and Flicker had known each other in New York; in fact, it was Flicker who had taught the director the Westminster Place Kitchen Rules. "I told him the best thing I could think of," Flicker said. "He had such great actors, he should explain some of the rules I had and then just let it go and have at least five cameras going from every angle." When it came time for Kubrick to film *Lolita*'s first scene, a long, dreamy whirl of James Mason and Peter Sellers, Flicker said, "That's what he did." But only with Sellers. "He was the only one allowed," wrote James Mason, "or rather encouraged, to improvise his entire performance." Kubrick told Flicker he was so pleased with the results, he planned to further explore the improviser in Sellers in his next film, soon to begin production, *Dr. Strangelove*.

Prime Minister Macmillan and Princess Margaret arrived together, and laughed, remarkably, at jokes directed against them. "They should have fled from the theater," mused Flicker during the show; so too did the anonymous angry young man that appeared backstage after the curtain call. "If you make fun of Prime Minister Macmillan," he berated the Premise Players, "and Prime Minister Macmillan comes to see you and enjoys it or does not leave the theater in a rage: or if you are able to get your president to wire you permission to make fun of him, you can't really be striking any telling blows, can you?" Flicker assured this person he was mistaken. The Premise was entertainment. It wasn't supposed to hurt.

"Can it be," wrote Kenneth Tynan, apropos of the Premise Affair, in September 1962, "that the European tradition, which regards improvisation as a means to a perfect, fixed and stylised end, is fundamentally inimical to the American tradition, which regards improvisation as an end itself — as the key, in fact, to a new kingdom of theatrical entertainment? If so, we had better reconsider; for our way of thinking excludes from the theater the kind of invigoration that jazz brought to music." Unimaginable where speech is not free, improvisation is both the prodigal son of the First Amendment, "an open forum" Barbara Harris called it, and, as the unmitigated expression of individuals joined in self-governed reinvention, a diorama of the American political ideal *e pluribus unum,* "out of many, one." It is the tree and fruit of the American mind.

Americans have always been improvisers. "In the language of the Declaration of Independence, for example, Americans accorded themselves the right to revolution, that is, the right to create new forms," writes Professor Kerry T. Burch. "The US Constitution's amendment process similarly codifies permanent revisability as a defining feature of our democratic-inspired political culture." Americans are a work in progress, an ensemble revolution, making it up as we go along. Changeability — the intended imperfection of our foundational documents — opens the way to a more perfect union. And individuals: "Because of the chemistry and the way people were playing off each other," Miles Davis wrote of jazz collaboration, "everybody started playing above what they knew almost from the beginning. Trane [John Coltrane] would play some weird, great shit, and Cannonball [Adderley] would take it in the other direction, and I would put my sound right down the middle or float over it, or whatever." Through improvisation, they made each other better. Giving themselves over to syncopation, playing, literally, off-beat — a term jazz shares with humor — they discover new beats. Surprise and variation, touchstones of improvisation, are requisites of both, amendments — to the melody, the scene, the "law" — permissible only when speech is free. "I think what we look for," explained jazz pianist Bill Evans, "is freedom with responsibility." Without that freedom, we would be perennially scripted, locked into quarter-note time, unable to evolve new rhythms out of those conflicts that arise from our melting pot morality or, as Del Close described it, the "democratic mess." We can clean it up with improvisation.

Normally, Del would appear at Second City just in time to witness the company at the height of panic, take a sip of the chaos he authored, and rejoin the group. But one night in 1962, an hour before showtime, the panic upgraded to fear. Where was he? Everyone knew about the drugs. "His idea was that his body was a wonderful toy and he could put any kind of chemical into it," Avery Schreiber said. "I once had to take him to the hospital when he accidentally shot up developing fluid." No one could ever be sure if Del's wife, Doris, would be home to intervene (or partake?) at the crucial moment. In fact, Doris was said to appear so erratically, some insisted she didn't exist at all. Or was she, as Del said, cooling out at the sanitarium? No one knew.

Unable to reach him by phone, Sheldon Patinkin raced to Del's apartment around the corner from the theater. Patinkin got no answer banging at the door, so he ran around the back, to a low window, where he saw Del inside, facedown on the floor. "Del!"

Patinkin collared the closest neighbor, got to a phone, and called Sahlins at the theater.

"Bernie —"

"What's going on?"

"Del's on the floor!"

In moments, Sahlins and an ambulance were outside Del's house.

"It was pills," Patinkin said. He was alive. From the hospital, where they pumped his stomach, Patinkin and Sahlins took Del to a small clinic on Chicago's South Side, "and got him committed." As Sahlins signed the papers and personally took care of the bill, Patinkin replayed the scene in his head. Del had picked an interesting time to try to kill himself, maybe the perfect time. Back at the theater, he knew they were an hour from showtime. He knew people would be there, waiting for him. He must have known someone would come and rescue him. In that sense, it looked staged. But the results of the stomach pump revealed traces of a lethal dose.

"Del wanted to direct," Patinkin said. Upon Alan Myerson's departure, the responsibility was split between Sills and Patinkin. Whenever Sahlins allowed Del to step in, he always found himself sorting out the mess.

A month later, the head doctor at the sanitarium where Del was being treated informed Sahlins that the patient could rejoin Second City on a supervised-release basis.

Patinkin acted as Del's chauffeur every evening for months. Mostly, their car rides were calm and quiet. But once onstage, Del would occasionally break scene to curse at the audience. Then he would join the scene again. Then Patinkin would take him back to the hospital.

Nichols and May — this time as Mike Nichols, actor, and Elaine May, playwright — stood on opposite ends of the Walnut Street Theatre in Philadelphia, seething. (She had written *A Matter of Position* specifically for him; he would play a young executive desperate to be liked.) It was "in every way a catastrophe," Nichols said, "first to last." She refused to implement the script changes he and Arthur Penn, the director, asked of her, cuts mostly. "Cuts and revisions were made up to the point where they would change the nature of the material and emasculate the play," she wrote in the *New York Times*, when their difficulty went public. "A play is more than a formula made up of words and jokes and scenes. Somewhere it must have something to do with the realities of human behavior. This has always been my premise for comedy." And Nichols could not bear to be alone up there. Not while she was down there, whispering to director Arthur Penn, probably, about everything he was doing wrong. It was *Miss Julie* all over again, with Elaine in the front row soundlessly eviscerating his Jean the valet. Nichols heard she was looking for other actors. Also whispering, but into May's ear, was her boyfriend, formerly her psychologist, Dr. David Rubinfine. What was he doing there? Finally, Arthur Penn quit, "because she wouldn't cut it," Nichols said. "Luckily my lawyer found a way out, which was I had director approval, and it was no longer Arthur, and I just closed it in Philadelphia."

Mike and Elaine, each feeling betrayed by the other, stopped speaking.

Now double divorced, from Elaine and from his wife, Pat Scott, Nichols buried his despair in New York's most epicurean circle — "the Blob" Stephen Sondheim called them — of Leonard and Felicia Bernstein, Richard and

Evie Avedon, Adolph and Phyllis Green, and Sondheim himself. Arm-in-arm with dear friends, and at the head of a luxurious table, Nichols had everything but one thing—her, which was him. "Elaine gave me myself," Nichols said. "I didn't exist as a performer or any kind of a theater person except because of her and through her. Which is why when we split up I didn't think I could do anything. I thought it was all over." He dated. He traveled. He joined the Blob in Jamaica.

"Oh, Mikey, you are so good," Bernstein consoled him one day. "I just don't know at what."

As he tired of Second City's format, and the constraints Sahlins placed on improvisation, Del rechanneled his risk addiction onto the real world, life outside the theater, where no one, and no theory, could curb his appetite for neurotheatrical inquiry. One day—or maybe night—Del came to in the Chicago sewers with an acetylene lamp taped to his head, a .32 automatic in his hand, and a circle of dead and wounded rats at his feet. He had a theory about LSD. It forces you to justify. Like an audience suggestion. That's how he had gotten to the sewer, probably. On LSD, your new brain, holding a gun to the temple of your old one, upchucks a rainbow of reality amendments and "you've got to make this kind of like a conceivable part of your normal behavior," Del said, "so you don't panic." You have to "Yes, and . . ." the LSD or else pull the trigger. Fear death, actual or metaphorical, and you're just replaying your old sketches. But court possibility, justify whatever materializes, no matter how strange or sinister the trip, and you'll be free.

For many months, since his return to the Premise in New York City, Ted Flicker had been brooding over the angry young man who had stormed backstage and accused him and his improvisers of satirical cowardice. His British success behind him, he began to see clearer now: the hypocrisy of his ostensibly left-leaning city, rife with racism, and the young president, a better actor than a politician. That angry young man, Flicker decided, had been right. "And I suddenly realized that we and The Second City were all giving a sort of intellectual stamp of approval to the very people we were satirizing by satirizing them gently; and suddenly we were the Establishment." He closed down the Premise immediately and began thinking seriously about revolution.

What was the most urgent, most sensitive issue in American life?

They did not have to look far. Their colleague Godfrey Cambridge told of hailing a taxi, which slowed as it approached, and then sped up once the driver saw he was black, "and Godfrey grabbed the handle of the door," Buck Henry said, "and ripped the door off the cab and threw it into the street." Joan Darling's best friend, Tony-winning black actress Diana Sands, "would come out of the theater," Darling said, "and a cab wouldn't stop for her." Applying for an apartment in the West Twenties, Sands gave Sidney Poitier as a reference. But "they turned me down," she said. The stories Flicker and Darling heard were grotesque; there was, however, something funny about how they, white folks, fumbled over what to call their friends — Negroes? Coloreds? Black people? It seemed a faux pas to even ask the question — "and they," Darling said, "had the same difficulty with us." Even for nonracists, the problems of race were mutually embarrassing.

"It was Ted's idea," she said, "to take three black actors and two white actors and do an improvisational theater from the point of view of the black person. Ted and I weren't just trying to do a show; we really wanted to learn the truth about the black experience from black people." They were Godfrey Cambridge, Al Freeman Jr., Diana Sands — black — and Jo Ann LeCompte and Calvin Ander — white. A year earlier, the integrated cast of *Purlie Victorious* survived several months on Broadway, but the Living Premise, codirected by Flicker and Darling, was the first integrated repertory theater in New York. And it would be improvised.

"I don't really know anything about Negroes," Flicker confessed at their first gathering in April 1963. "Do whatever you want to do."

They pulled up chairs and started talking. "Rehearsals," Cambridge said, "were a little like group analysis" — a new technique in improvisation. The conversation lasted over a month. Sands told of her first "nigger" experience; she was in an all-white school, and as she approached the others, they ran off, chanting, "Run, run! Here comes the nigger!" Sands only found out what it meant later that night, when, after telling her sister how fun school had been, she got slapped for using the word. "We all must learn to get along with each other," Al Freeman's teacher had said. "We must all learn to get along with the little Chinese boy and the little nigger boy." His father would have to tell Al what it meant. They had to carefully plan their evenings around *not* being able to get a taxi. Sands had a technique: she hid her face behind her coat until she got in. She remembered one promising date ruined after her suitor, trying to impress her, failed to catch a cab. Cambridge's wife pleaded for just one evening out with her husband where she didn't have to hear him call anyone a motherfucker. "It took a while for them to really tell us what they really felt about Kennedy," Darling said. "They had to find out that we really meant it, that it was absolutely okay for Godfrey to have a tantrum about Kennedy." Listening to Cambridge, Flicker radicalized. Do white barbers, he wondered, know how to cut Negro hair? "This morning, I was shaken by the fire hoses and the dogs in [Birmingham,] Alabama," he confessed to his notebook. "I'm beginning to side with the no compromise crowd — I resented Bobby Kennedy's suggestion that the demonstrations were ill-timed."

From the offenses, patterns of hate and ignorance, natural scenes emerged. An integrated married couple — he's Jewish, she's black — fight, and as the room heats with anger, he gets more Jewish and she gets more black. Then there was the scene about the sweet old couple trying to stage a lynching. Flicker had them switch roles; this time, black plays white. Play any race you want. Get angry. The results of the experiment astounded everyone involved. "The color line is slowly disappearing," Flicker noted, "with Negroes playing whites or Orientals and whites playing Negroes." And sometimes they went too far; unchecked caricature offended both sides. But the hurt was discussed. "If you do it right," Darling said, "you can't survive improvisation without really connecting."

The Living Premise opened on June 13, 1963, with a kiss — between a white man and a black woman. Unlike the Premise or Second City or Compass before them, Flicker's new team smashed audiences with flagrantly subversive sketches, intended, foremost, to disturb them to political action. Perhaps the most memorable, about a plot by two black men and a white woman to kidnap the First Lady ("He'll [the president] have to make a stand now"), featured imagery as graphic as, "When Mrs. Kennedy enters the ladies' room, I will open the can of chloroform, pour chloroform on the rag and place the rag over Mrs. Kennedy's nose and mouth." The sketch ends somewhere in the radical middle as the revolutionaries lose their nerve. Instead of waging war, they telephone Ralph Bunche, the first person of color to be awarded the Nobel Prize, and ask him to speak at a benefit dinner "to raise funds to finance a committee to study the possibility of making a survey on the question of the feasibility of a solution to the possibility of understanding segregation that might exist in some parts of the country."

The line "I want to see him [Kennedy] on TV, crying like I seen all them women down in Birm" was cut.

The night of the first performance, Flicker knew he had a success as soon as he heard the gasps. Some confronted him directly: "If you don't stop playing that scene I shall have to speak to the *right people.*"

But it was too late. The learning had already taken place. "Real dramatic integration is actually possible only in improvisation," Flicker said, "when all responses are quick, personal, and honest, and not the products of after-thought."

"And we all became *real* friends," Darling said, "because we suddenly could say anything to each other."

To save himself from summer stock, Nichols accepted, quite absurdly, an offer to direct *Barefoot in the Park* (originally titled *Nobody Loves Me*), the second play by Neil Simon. In 1963, Simon was already the nascent master of what Buck Henry called "the running character joke," an effective but sitcom-ish contrivance wholly out of sync with Mike Nichols's improvisational instincts. "[Simon] takes a character with a funny failing," Henry said, "and plays a joke off that failing, then refines that joke over and over, so that it becomes unbearably hilarious." In style and sensibility, Simon and Nichols could not have been more opposed; a bonbon, *Barefoot* was born old. You could say the same of practically all of Broadway comedy — before Nichols put his hands on it.

In rehearsal, if *Barefoot in the Park* started anticipating its laughs, Nichols would warn the ensemble, kindly, that they were not doing a comedy, "We're doing *King Lear* here." Quite consciously, he did not follow comedy "rules." Rather than blocking, as George Abbott would, the actors' every move with the precision endemic to Broadway comedies of the era, Nichols riffed. He wanted "to create an atmosphere of freedom for my actors." "The whole thing," by which he meant directing, can be seen as an "extension of improvisation. I don't like to go into rehearsal with a set plan — and even if I do know what I want in a particular scene, I would rather that it come from the cast." If the scene called for sadness, Nichols did not undermine the sadness in irony; staging a fight, he did not try for slapstick. "I wanted to do comedy as if it were just another play," he said of *Barefoot,* "as if the people were alive. I didn't want to keep tipping the comedy, having the actors running downstage, yelling, slamming doors, things like that."

Nichols permitted the entire ensemble the freedom to live between their lines, to perform the little actions of life that their characters would if they were actual people: light a cigarette, tie a shoe, stare off into space. It was an improvisational innovation utterly new to Broadway.

For the first time in years, Mike Nichols was happy. In his former life as an actor, Nichols felt like a petulant child, scared and insecure; as a director, he assumed the best qualities of a father. He saw what you needed and what you were doing, and as an improviser, saw the moves ahead.

He directed slightly and invisibly, as a careful teacher would. He allowed actors' questions, ideas, impulses, no matter how odd or off, the consideration to evolve. It was a form of kindness, an invitation ample with interest and permission. And yet it wasn't affirmation that gave the improvisation wings, but the gentle borders Nichols placed around possibilities, the way he said no without squashing what was good, or had potential, the way he said yes while adding a silver subtlety of his own.

After the smash opening of *Barefoot in the Park,* which would run for three and a half years, Nichols quickly became the hottest director in New York.

Producer Larry Turman did not share Hollywood's sense of humor. At Harold Pinter's plays, he laughed. The whole theater held its breath, but Larry Turman *tee-hee*d at those claustrophobic, menacing pauses, swarming with rage and jammed with betrayal. "Mordant," he called Pinter. Not black comedy — that had something of the grotesque — but uneasy, bitter comedy. That was Larry Turman's idea of a good time.

With a thousand dollars of his own money, he had taken an option on a 1963 novel, *The Graduate,* which he thought could make a Pinteresque movie, "a nervous comedy," he said, "with edge, and intelligence." In England, where Turman had just produced *I Could Go on Singing,* Pinter's sense of humor had taken root, but in Turman's native America, where the highest-grossing film of 1963 — the year *The Graduate* was published — was *It's a Mad, Mad, Mad, Mad World,* comic landsmen were harder to find. *The Pink Panther* came out the same year. "The reason I couldn't get any studio to finance the film," Turman said, "is because nobody thought it was funny." Because, really, *The Graduate* wasn't Hollywood-funny; it was *real* funny. Like Nichols and May.

Mike Nichols. Yes. Turman had seen *Barefoot in the Park.* "I thought it was oozing smart direction and style," Turman said. "Mike knew where all the laughs were." Could he direct *The Graduate*? He had never directed a movie before. "Yeah," the producer thought, recalling Nichols and May's comedy albums, "that *sounds* right." For the picture to work — to keep its seriousness and its humor — *The Graduate* had to be handled in the Nichols and May manner.

Turman would send the book to Mike Nichols.

John Brent called Alan Myerson. "Are you watching?"

"Watching what?"

"Turn on your television."

"What? Why?"

"This is the signal."

"What are you talking about? The signal for what?"

"The signal for all those lonely men who live in boardinghouses to pull out their weapons and become an army."

It was November 22, 1963. The president had been shot.

Sills thought: civilization is over. We are rushing into a time of madness and we may never recover. He had a wife, Carol, and children. His friends had children. Somewhere along the way they had lost touch with what was good. "We and everybody we knew were just amazed that such a thing could have happened," Carol Sills said, "and wondered what to do and started saying, 'We should get together with our community and make a life that's real.'" Sills called the owner of Square East, Second City's home in New York, and asked for his help. He needed to find a place, a bucolic setting outside the city, maybe upstate, where he could build, from scratch, a community of improvisers, and relearn how to live together.

The teacher waited until two forty-five to tell her class, eighth graders, that the president had been killed. Then she ended class early and told them to go home. But Billy Murray didn't do as she said. Instead of home, Billy ran to the drugstore across from school, where a crowd had gathered, men mostly, waiting for the afternoon paper to tell them exactly what had happened. They just stood there, strangers in silent riot, their distress mounting with every rumor. Billy's father was among them. He took his son's hand, and together they went home and turned on the TV to see — to actually watch, live — the country breaking. "That was when television really took over," Murray said. "That moment of waiting for the newspapers, it never happened again."

Elaine knew what would happen. Comedians would run from this. "But I don't think we should ignore it. I don't think we can ignore anything that is so much in people's minds all the time."

The night after, Del Close faced Second City's most apprehensive audience to date. "We do know what happened," he assured them. "Let's make a deal: we won't stand around wondering why you're here if you don't sit back wondering why we're here."

A connection was made, and the audience thawed. They had been understood. All through the sketches, they laughed, not wildly, but enough to assure Sahlins and Patinkin they had been right to open the theater. Many, they knew, didn't want to be home tonight. Television could only give so much; people had to be with people.

Del reappeared, before intermission, to take suggestions. He was a touch paler than normal, even for him, and zigzagging; it could have been the speed. "Ladies and gentlemen, I would like to ask you now —"

"The Kennedy Assassination!"

Del stormed downstage and scowled into the lights. "Just what the fuck was it you wanted to see, sir?"

Patinkin flinched when he heard it. Second City's first "fuck."

6

1963–1967

Second City was bleeding to death. Bernie Sahlins knew that.

Since his Square East improvisers had signed with big agents and scattered to Broadway — Arkin to *Enter Laughing* and Barbara Harris to *Oh Dad, Poor Dad, Mamma's Hung You in the Closet and I'm Feelin' So Sad* — Sahlins had woken up to a cruel irony of the little-theater business: as soon as his unknowns made a success with him, they left him. They would upgrade to more money, more power, just like Mike and Elaine had. How could they not? Second City was a wallflower at the show business ball. It needed to be. Improvisers needed to fail, and fail safely; and in the Midwest, far from Broadway and Hollywood, they really could. Second-class stature was the secret ingredient, a petri dish of comedic mitosis; Chicagoness set the stage for anonymity, risk, discovery, the mulch of intellectual progress. But when improvisers felt the entertainment business gazing on them, they turned Second City into their personal showcase, a full-time paid audition, and, suddenly fearing failure, they pulled back on their risky, responsive choices, got out of the moment, and froze their best scenes — *their* scenes. They were stars now. But improvisation, the art of the huddled masses, was constitutionally averse to kings. "Bernie," Patinkin said, "was borrowing all the time. Many times I thought we were going to close." It didn't make sense. Success led to failure, failure to success. What kind of business was this?

In five short years, Sahlins's theater had already achieved veteran standing in the improvisational world. Since none of its predecessors claimed runs longer than two or three years, and none of its contemporaries had stayed afloat — Flicker's Premises had closed, and Shepherd, somewhere in America, couldn't resuscitate a Compass — it was reasonable to conclude Second City's success had finally run out. In 1964 you could have pulled the plug in good conscience.

Camelot was over. "After the [JFK] assassination," Patinkin said, "we could not get audiences. People wanted to laugh, but I don't think anyone knew what to laugh at, or if they could." Audience suggestions turned to the nonsensical — "Waiter, there's an alien in my soup," "Ride red hyenas into the abyss!" — and in the miasma, Second City's brain trust evacuated. Howard Alk, cable to the cutting edge, sold his share of the company to Sheldon Patinkin; Del Close, the one Sahlins counted on for constant lunatic intelligence, lost his taste for Second City's success formula, became impossible to deal with, and was reluctantly fired; and Sills, though he still appeared at erratic intervals, no longer guarded the premises with his heart and soul. After the assassination, he suffered an identity crisis, too. The satire boom of the early 1960s had died that day in November.

It fell to Bernie Sahlins, the producer, to run the show. Smallish, Jewish, baldish, bookish, Sahlins looked like a producer; you'd want Bob Balaban or Wallace Shawn or someone good behind a desk to play him in the movie. A man of the arts, Sahlins could comfortably cross-reference his conversation with classical music and jazz, opera, movies, and literature; he took seriously the responsibility to serve good comedy to the people, and as a versed historian, he liked dreaming about Second City's place in world civilization. But his real strengths were kindness and good business sense. When his Chicago company disassembled and the time came to wonder, again, what could be funny now that the country's young hope had been murdered, Sahlins did not call on Compass reserves or Spolin's former students at the Young Actors Company to restock the Second City trenches. He did not pillage the small but growing world of unemployed improvisers Flicker and Shepherd had cultivated to fill the vacancy. Rather, to rebuild Second City, Sahlins and Patinkin enlisted the William Morris Agency, a heretofore untapped resource in the history of improvisational casting. Paul Sills and his mother had already proved anyone can improvise, but the Morris office did not deal in anyones. As far as Sahlins and Patinkin were concerned, they dealt in funny actors and comics. They dealt in money. And money, which Second City needed, was in the jokes.

"But I'm not political," Fred Willard insisted. "I can't do that stuff."

He was on the phone with his agent. "Fred, Fred, come on. They *like* you." Sahlins and Patinkin, he explained, had seen Willard and Vic Greco, his comedy partner, play the Gate of Horn in Chicago, and wanted him to audition for Second City.

"I'm not right for that," he persisted. "Have you seen those guys? I can't improvise about psychiatrists and philosophers. I can't improvise period!"

Willard, born in Cleveland, saw himself, accurately, as more of the silly type. Beholding his enormous, *Music Man* smile, you would think he was putting you on; no one could possibly be that genuinely happy, especially a funny person. But Fred Willard really was. Even in New York, where he had been trying to make it, he absolutely floated down the street, nodding cheery hellos like a small-town mayor in a Frank Capra movie. "I've always admired people who just didn't have a care in the world and said what they wanted to," he said. Onstage, his megaton innocence played like naïveté. "I like to play the guy that has no self-awareness," said Willard, "kind of the likable buffoon who will stick his foot in his mouth and say the wrong thing." He lived outside the world of Nichols and May. "Bernie [Sahlins] and I knew Fred was hilarious," Patinkin said. "We also knew he was different than what our audiences were used to."

Willard ended up auditioning (in a William Morris conference room in New York) with Robert Klein, a recent graduate of the Yale Drama School. Both got the job.

Sheldon Patinkin directed Willard, Klein, David Steinberg, and the others, Second City's latest wave of improvisers, with a blithe hand that could have been construed as no hand at all. He waited out rehearsals lotus-legged, a cigarette in his mouth, saving his energies for the show's running order — deciding which sketches should go where — a task Patinkin fulfilled with formulaic exactitude. He had learned from watching Sills. Start big, with a full company piece; let us get to know our improvisers. Once the audience is comfortable, give us smaller, two- or three-person sketches to deepen our relationship to the performers as individuals. By then we'll have had enough laughs to tolerate a more emotional piece, a people scene, the sort Sills once nurtured as director. Finally, we'll go back to funny again, but this time, because the players have grown on us, the sketches will be more intimate and sometimes stranger than before. Completing the circle, we'll feel as though we've actually gone someplace with these people and returned with something new. Black out on a big laugh.

Where Paul Sills, resolving the paradox at the heart of all good direction, gave individual company members rein to discover and express their uniqueness within the framework of his own, Patinkin was too technically minded, too mired in the business of stagecraft and running order, to manifest the ineffable glue of ensemble. But if Second City's mid-1960s shows lacked point of view, one could argue Patinkin was only taking the audience's suggestion. A cultural moment ago the targets were clear, but the transitional climate of the present era did not lend itself to satire. In the wake of President Kennedy's assassination, finding America's enemies was just as difficult as parsing the various conspiracy theories. What could really be understood? What were the facts? The only thing that seemed clear was that nothing made sense and every "truth" was in question. In December 1964, the Village Vanguard convened a panel of professionals under the banner "Is Satire Futile?" There among the turtlenecks, one satirist theorized, "Well, maybe everything today is so absurd you just can't make it any more absurd."

In this mad, mad, mad, mad world, certainty read like absurdity. It was smart to be dumb. Or play dumb. Consider *Dr. Strangelove*, and Peter Sellers's cartooning of the title villain (not to mention the effects of his tripling up on roles) — which, to Mike Nichols, comprised the best improvisational work he had ever seen — the antic senselessness of *A Hard Day's Night*, the giant pie fight that culminates *The Great Race*, the whole of Jerry Lewis, *Laugh-In*, *The Magic Christian*, the first gurgles of pop art and the burgeoning theater of the absurd. The culture of spontaneous impulse that gave birth to abstract expressionism and improvisation had slowed down and reversed course — toward the synthetic, a world of parody, not satire. Satire must take a stand. It must be violent. But America was too confused to be angry.

David Mamet, working then as one of Sahlins's busboys and ice-cream-soda makers, had a comparable association to the Second City style, likening it to Beckett and Pinter and Chekhov, the bleakest absurdists, whose plays he had discovered, over many afternoons, in the drama section of the Oak Street Book Shop not too far from Wells Street. "Pinter especially struck me," he said, "because it was so reminiscent of what I'd seen at Second City, 'cause the idea at Second City was the almost unquantifiable serial comedic sketch where it was funny and — I think it derived from the same place as Chekhov, the idea that life finally couldn't be quantified, that it was funny and sad and bizarre at the same time and yet it could be accomplished in a seven-minute blackout."

Hanging out backstage one night, Mamet watched Willard bound onstage to introduce an improvisation with "Let's take a sleigh ride through the snow-covered forests of entertainment!" At that precise moment, Mamet thought, he would not be following his father into law.

Fred Willard was the ideal vessel for put-on comedy. Forever switching channels between phony game-show hosts and deluded newscaster types, his brain was given to the sort of "people who you can listen to, and think that they're making sense," he said. "Then all of a sudden, you realize that what they're saying is complete nonsense." He loved nonsense, silly non sequiturs, and vacuity, comic notions that were funny precisely because they couldn't be fully understood. A satiric brain looks for truth, patterns, and logic; Willard went fast in the other direction. One of his wacky blackouts, still in the Second City repertoire today, begins with a man and a woman. "Miss Jones, take a letter," he says. As he dictates, she starts blinking uncomfortably. She tells him it's her contact lenses. "Here," he says, "let me help you"; he helps her remove her contact lenses and steps back in awe. "Miss Jones!" the man exclaims. "You're beautiful!" Apolitical, asocial, a-everything but funny, Willard introduced Second City to a weirdness that echoed the new enlightenment.

Sills didn't get it. Nor did he want to. When he appeared, mostly by surprise, the director threw out scenes and blackouts as hilariously oddball as Miss Jones, shoved Patinkin aside, and returned the show, block by block, to natural scale. It didn't matter how close to opening night they were. Sills would force Willard back to reality.

"Okay, Willard, get up there," he barked.

Willard did as he was told.

"You meet a friend on the street and by the end of it you're going into a hair salon. I don't care how long it takes. Go."

Willard and his partner began. Hello. Oh, hello, Joe. How are you, Jerry? Their conversation, as regular conversation tends to be, was chitchatty and bland. Willard got bored. "I think I need a haircut," he said.

"Stop!"

The actors turned to Sills. He was fuming. "You can't just *say* you need a haircut. You have to *get there together*." It sort of almost made sense.

Sills decided another scene needed an oblique reference to Brecht.

"Paul," Willard began. "I don't think the audience is going to get that."

"What do you mean?"

"That's pretty obscure."

Sills snickered at a passing waiter. "He never heard of Brecht!"

"No, Paul, I don't think the *audience* —"

Second City's most popular scenes were now pop culture parodies. Television, its viewers increasing in numbers and, one could argue, its content already decreasing in originality, both stole from Second City's audience and provided it a variety of clichés to offer as suggestions. "That was a big change," Patinkin said. "We became a little broad."

No matter how funny or fun, parody — or "friendly satire," to quote Elaine May — did not speak with subversive urgency. Neither were laughs a substitute for improvisational prison breaks of human intuition, but Second City, without Sills, was in the laughter business. Accordingly, Viola Spolin was let go. "I had to fire her," Patinkin said, "because she was saying a lot of not nice things about how we were running things." In her place, he promoted Spolin acolyte Jo Forsberg, a devoted presence since the earliest Second City workshops, and together, they founded Second City's — indeed the world's — first improvisational comedy training facility. Note the difference: Spolin-style improvisation had ceded to improvisational comedy or, as it would come to be known, improv comedy. Or just improv. "She began modifying many of Viola's games and adding her own exercises," wrote Forsberg's son, Eric. "She wanted to make the work as applicable as possible to developing sketch material and doing a show." Once trained, Forsberg's students might join her Second City Children's Theater, or a touring group, Second City's constellation of farm teams, and play colleges and business functions across the country. But there was no formal progression to the mainstage. To Sahlins, funny was funny; it didn't matter where it came from or if it had been properly schooled. Now, if he needed new improvisers in the resident company, all Sahlins had to do was pluck from either the Children's Theater or the road. It was an efficient innovation, providing the growing theater, and all its arms, a consistent stream of ready-made talent. But the joke was on Second City: in 1965, there were other, more convenient venues for the nightly intake of humor, some as close as the black box in the living room.

Elaine May was at a party on Riverside Drive with her former therapist, now husband, David Rubinfine. Normal people surrounded her. They were talking. That she could prove. She could see them talking. What she couldn't prove — what they were saying — she could intuit. There were tells. She knew them better than they did.

It had been years since Elaine had spoken with Mike Nichols, approximately the exact amount of time, to the day, since her last success, their final performance as Nichols and May. *Coincidence or correlation?* wondered the party, New York City, the comedy world, and every English-speaking man, woman, and precocious child who had ever stayed up late with *An Evening with Mike Nichols and Elaine May* on vinyl. What was she doing and what was going wrong? The one-act musical she had written for Bob Fosse, *Robbers and Cops,* she withdrew; the Third Ear, her own sketch-improv ensemble held at the onetime Premise Theater, was an early casualty of the new antisatire climate; *The Office,* directed by Jerome Robbins with Elaine as an incompetent secretary, played ten previews then closed.

One worried. Was she planning her long-awaited comeback? Or had she, the J. D. Salinger of comedy, disappeared for good? Had her ex-partner's winning streak demoralized her out of the game? Did she resent Mike Nichols? Or was she — quoting ancient publicity — too much a perfectionist to secure and sustain regular writing gigs in Hollywood? Or, actually, was it the other way around: was it Elaine who was through with *them,* through with rewriting other people's scripts (*The Loved One,* draft, June 1962)? In that case, why wasn't she writing her own stuff? Or *was* she writing?

It was not too early in the 1960s to regard May's career caesuras as the product of an insularly male industry. Betty Friedan and history could attest to that — a consistent deprivation of women directors on Broadway and in Hollywood. But women *writer*-directors! Women writer-director-*actors*? They were nonexistent. And of the zero percent, what percentage were mothers? May's household now consisted of four children: three from Rubinfine's previous marriage, and her teenage daughter, Jeannie Berlin (née May).

Domestic life galvanized Elaine's genius for procrastination. She designated a corner of her Manhattan brownstone's basement the office and started sharpening pencils and rearranging furniture. She accepted a part in the film of *Enter Laughing* — which director Carl Reiner let her improvise, partially — because "my typing finger needed a rest."

She still thought of *Mikey and Nicky,* the paranoid pas de deux she'd begun on napkins and legal pads over a decade earlier, in Chicago.

And trying to hide from her basement, Elaine went to parties, where she hid from people's questions, but they cornered her, and trying to evade them, she redressed herself in tailor-made aphorisms never intended to be funny, but they were, and people gathered, laughter built, crowds formed.

From the crowd that evening on Riverside Drive emerged her old partner, Mike Nichols, and his new girlfriend. He came toward her.

It had been years. First, pleasantries amid the discomfort, the jokey defensiveness, both fumbling for the impossible chord, social grace and raw honesty, the sound that said they were happy now despite the hurt, despite the past. They could not lie, not to each other. Because of old love, they laughed. He introduced the girlfriend. English. Porcelain. Lovely. Mike did everything well. He took hard weather better than she could, better than anybody. That had always been their secret, one of them, anyway; he was the sail, she was the storm. "But is he perfect?" she once asked. "He knows you can't really be liked or loved if you're perfect. You have to have just enough flaws. And he does. Just the right, perfect flaws to be absolutely endearing."

It was good to see her. "Everything felt different," Nichols said.

He said something funny to Elaine and Dr. Rubinfine, then kindly excused himself from their company to rejoin the party. "See?" May said to her husband, loud enough for Nichols to hear. "I told you Mike was wonderful."

He heard. "Life had renewed," is how Nichols described that moment. "It was back. It had begun again."

Fearing the worst, Sheldon Patinkin rushed to Del's apartment and, as he had before, banged on the door. He did not expect it to open, slowly.

"Will you come sit with me?" Del asked. "I'm being devoured inch by inch by the Spider King."

LSD.

Del's apartment, a hoarder's paradise of books and comic books, smelled of cats and cigarettes. Patinkin was told not to touch anything. "Everything was an experiment," he said. That pile of composition books represented a train of thought Del would resume as soon as he could plug — *watch out!* — that cable running through the living room into the camera he was building on the coffee table — so put your tea *there* — with technology he had adapted from ancient Mayan . . .

Though Del had been fired from Second City, he stayed in town, loitering, flailing. He had nowhere to go. From a distance, Sahlins, through Patinkin, kept semisympathetic watch on his well-being, trying not to get tangled in Del's web of promises and excuses. "I sat with him," Sheldon said, "until it passed."

Patinkin let him talk. "Del was so bipolar," Second City pianist Bill Mathieu said, "so up and down, so many glints of genius and so many arid stretches of nothing. He was completely unpredictable, a total mystery, and into drugs like Charlie Parker was into drugs or Miles was into drugs. You can't separate it from the work." Some of what Del explained to Patinkin he understood. When he couldn't evolve improvisationally, when he felt he couldn't grow the form, or test his experiments on real people, he decayed. Del was on a quest for improvisation's LSD. Could an ensemble improvise a play? Could improvisers sustain a narrative an hour or forty-five minutes long? He needed to know.

Bill Mathieu lived at 452 Webster — a big, wood-frame country house decked out in the Second City style with walls of crisscrossing old elevator grates and repurposed curiosities d'art — a mile from the theater. Severn Darden's ex-wife, Ann, had the second floor; Mathieu's acid hookup was stationed up on the third; Dennis Cunningham, Second City bartender and occasional improviser, could be found above the little studio inhabited by Fred Kaz, a skinny shipwrecked Ahab, and also a pianist, who could play Bach with his left hand as barroom jazz came out of his right. And at the nerve center of 452 Webster, Paul and Carol Sills, in love with each other, and increasingly with Martin Buber, humanist philosopher. It was on their first date, the year Second City opened, in 1959, that Paul and Carol discovered the other's passion for Buber. To achieve existence, Buber preached connection, the word "yes," a tunnel of yeses from one person into another. It was improvisation.

In the back of the house, they built a sound sculpture, "a jungle gym of junk," Mathieu explained, a heap of found objects they would add to over the years — four years, actually — and came together to play it, banging away at pipes and chairs and broken planks for hours after dinner. Music, Mathieu knew, had something to teach Second City improvisers. In a way, language was a barrier to full ensemble improvisations. "Because words don't mix, you can't have everyone improvising at once," he said. "But in music, sounds mix. You can close your eyes and listen." With Viola's encouragement, Mathieu developed musical games at Second City, "a discipline," he said, "from which freedom can arise." They were played in Spolin's (now defunct) workshops. She wanted to show the improvisers how every creative gesture, beyond a two- or three-person dialogue, could be the product of the entire ensemble, the collective mind. The question was, how would improvisers spontaneously create that mind and think with it together? To this end, Mathieu introduced a game he called Meat Stop. He said, "Everybody piles in sound like a pile of meat and then there's a sudden stop. You have to agree to stop at the same moment — without agreeing of course. No cue. Everybody stops on a dime. Or tries to." But the Second City actors, failing to see Meat Stop's application to comedy, weren't interested.

But Mathieu stayed the course. With the collective mind, he was on to something new, bigger, the next thing in improvisation. "Acid," he said, "was important to this." On one memorable trip, he hallucinated hearing language as a dog might, the sounds of the words clanging and humming together — a sound sculpture of human voices.

About ten improvisers — the Cunninghams, the Dardens, Mathieu, Paul Sand, and others — were all seated around the big oak table in the Sills's kitchen at 452 Webster when, after dinner, Sills started lecturing about Buber, and Mathieu — in boredom and accord — jiggled some silverware. Dennis Cunningham picked up on the sound and started tapping his wineglass. As Sills talked on, others joined in, tapping chicken bones, wobbling plates, "diplomatically," Mathieu said, "in the pauses Sills put in his speech," and after a moment, Paul reached for a pewter pitcher and accompanied himself. Getting up from the table, Carol Sills searched the kitchen cupboard and reappeared five bars later with a bag of rice, an ice tray, and, Mathieu said, "a gleam in her eye," as she dropped, slowly, tinkling rice into the metal tray, while the orchestra faded into place around her. Then, in the hush, she walked in a circle around the table, letting the rice from the tray fall over everyone's plates, cups, forks, "the finale," Mathieu said, "of a dinner symphony." Everyone cheered. This, Mathieu thought, was how church, or heaven, ought to be.

Paul Sills met Mike Nichols for lunch in New York.

It felt different now. The two friends used to eat dinner out of cans and argue about Brecht. Now, in New York, Nichols was living in a penthouse tower above Central Park and had four hits running (*Barefoot, The Knack, Luv, The Odd Couple*), and was, on his way to *Who's Afraid of Virginia Woolf?*, indisputably the most respected young director in America — and Sills, though he smiled across the table, hated all of it. "Paul didn't want to be successful," Nichols believed. "It was his own decision. But I think that his headlong rush away from success didn't deprive him of rage and envy." Sills was angry with his friend, and because of his anger, ashamed. His shame embarrassed Nichols, who could hear everything Sills wouldn't confess. Over lunch, they discussed their various projects, carefully.

"What are you working on?" Nichols began.

"Well, you know. We have this little group . . . You know, I'm just . . . I'm just doing what I always do. Trying to make a connection with the community."

After looking for new theater spaces upstate, Sills explained, he decided that if he were really going to press the reset button on civilization, which had grown so treacherous and deceitful since the Kennedy assassination, and build a new population of free people, he and Carol had to go back to Chicago, where their friends were, and improvise a theater. From play, he knew, a healthy community would come. Whatever "art" resulted was inconsequential, merely a by-product of the goal, harmonious, joyful cohabitation. The important thing was being.

At first, Paul and Carol met every Saturday in Lincoln Park, a space big enough to accommodate everyone who came. They played the old dance and folk games of Neva Boyd, Viola's mentor, and to their delight, friends came with friends and friends with children and the children brought more friends. Sills brought them all inside to play Viola's games — players were pulled from the audience — and soon everyone was playing and watching. There was no audience; the players *were* the audience. Sills called his community the Game Theater. Anyone was welcome. "Paul did it in order to explore the play that they'd been doing at Second City," Carol Sills said, "but to explore Viola's exercises as performance and to invite the community to not only offer suggestions but to get up and play." The Game Theater offered the only way to effect civic revolution. Government had no ear for the poor, the ethnic, the American unloved. Participatory art was their only refuge. The resultant stories didn't have to be "good." They were — from the people for the people — beyond art and comedy, as necessary as conversation. There were no sketches at the Game Theater. "With the games," said Sills, "you don't embalm the scenes so you can get the same laughs night after night." To sell a work, and therefore imply its completion, falsely implied a completion to human ingenuity. That was Nichols's thing, Sills thought. Perfecting, sealing, and selling.

Nichols's heart, soaring for Sills, broke a little for himself. "Paul," he replied, "you are still active and I am still passive."

Nichols was only making art; Sills could change the world.

But it was not that easy. The Game Theater was only a pistol fired on the starting line. To change the world, Sills had to grow beyond Chicago. He knew that eventually he had to spread his mother's games everywhere. He also knew, from the lessons of Compass and Second City, that by entering the world and spreading the games, improvisation would be embalmed. Just look at Mike Nichols.

Nichols felt the look and thought, *We are fucked.* Sills, who had started him in the theater, whom Nichols loved, didn't like him anymore. Having spent his entire life an outsider, desperate to belong, he had at last reached the inside, the penthouse, only to find himself, like Montgomery Clift in his favorite film, *A Place in the Sun,* as estranged from the people below as he once was from the giants above. He was different again.

It was one of those *before* moments. You could see, across the improvisational theater — and because improv is a mirror, you could see it in the streets too — the sense of dissatisfaction that portends decline and, hopefully, resurgence. Change had to happen. But it was not clear — at least to Second City — how improvisation had to evolve to mirror the new America.

With no intention of founding the Committee, improvisation's answer to the 1960s, Alan Myerson married Second City's Irene Riordan, left Square East in New York, where he had been directing, packed up his van, and together with his bride set off on a cross-country honeymoon to visit each other's parents in L.A. and Phoenix on their way to San Francisco, to meet a friend of Myerson's brother and a cousin of a cousin, "relative strangers," Myerson said, "but those were the times." Soon after greetings and chitchat, the inevitable question, "Where did you two meet?" and the answer, Second City, prompted an unforeseen follow-up. "Why don't you two do something in San Francisco?" *Why not?* The question stuck. Alan and Irene had no plans, and San Francisco, on the crest of revolution, was relishing a citywide improvisation of its own. *Our theater:* a place for the big-dreaming young of psychedelic San Francisco, a town hall unencumbered by literary "good taste," "good behavior," or any of the other Eisenhoweran refinery that along with wit, elegance, and polite satire was the stock and trade of Second City. At *this* our theater, personal authenticity and political urgency — not just discourse, but real *action* — would characterize the improvisations. Beyond the charge of entertainment or even satire, Myerson's company was committed to truth in all its dimensions. They called themselves the Committee, in ironic tribute to all that was awful about the House Un-American Activities Committee, or HUAC. In lettering evocative of the *New York Times* masthead, they hung their logo, like a coat of arms, above the entrance to their theater, a former Italian restaurant in North Beach. EAT MORE ART was scratched in the pavement out front.

Second City broke holes in the fourth wall and patched them up again; the Committee, by way of drugs and love, demolished the wall. "Most of our great moments," Myerson said, "had to do with including the audience, not just for suggestions, but in a really personal way." In one scene, improviser Howard Hesseman drops acid — not actually, although . . . maybe — and his scene partner, Chris Ross, walks in with a bag of apples.

"How's it going?" Ross asks, meaning the acid.

Hesseman ignores him.

"What do you see now?"

Tripping, Hesseman starts talking with the audience.

"You can't do that!" Ross protests.

"Why?"

"There's nobody there!"

"What are you talking about?"

To prove he isn't actually hallucinating, Hesseman drags people up onstage. *You see?*

"How did you *do* that?"

"I brought them through the heater grate."

Ross freaks out — like it's *his* trip — and Hesseman tries to calm him down.

On its own, far-out material did not suffice. It was not enough to simply improvise anymore; a Committee improviser had to improvise with improvisation. "Been there, done that," Myerson said of shortform sketches and blackouts. "I wanted a really sustained experience based on simultaneity and watching [separate] events [onstage] catalyze one another," a theatrical plaything that could approach the meandering randomness of actual life the way Lenny Bruce could extend a monologue by returning again and again to a particular theme or rhetorical device. One Bruce vehicle in particular had impressed itself on Myerson. "He started riffing on 'What if . . .'" Myerson explained. "'What if such and such was really such and such . . .'" If thoughts were tiny embryonic dramas, then every one of Bruce's what-ifs was like a link between scenes. What if Myerson improvised a series of what-ifs? Between workshops and performances, he developed a forty-five-minute sketch and improvisation sequence (interspersed with audio-visual excursions), the Fear, Guilt, and Impotence Collage. For example: What if . . . the mouth was a sex organ and we ate with our vaginas? (Would gynecologists give us fillings?) They did that scene, followed by another, followed by . . .

"I need a job." It was Del calling from California.

"Okay," Myerson said. "Come on out here."

Though Alan Arkin had scored, big-time, on Broadway, in productions of *Enter Laughing,* for which he won the Tony, and *Luv,* directed by Mike Nichols (for which *he* won the Tony), director Norman Jewison expected the studio wouldn't agree Arkin was perfect for *The Russians Are Coming, the Russians Are Coming.* Arkin had never been in a feature film before, let alone starred in one, and moreover, United Artists had originally intended the part of Yuri Rozanov, a Russian submariner dispatched to Cape Cod, for Peter Ustinov. But Jewison had loved Arkin in *Luv,* and through the grapevine heard he was a master of accents.

"Well, what do I have to do?" Arkin asked Jewison.

"You don't have to do anything. I just want to get a few feet of you on camera. We'll just talk."

They would shoot the test in New York on the set of Sidney Lumet's *The Group.* When Arkin arrived, Jewison explained that although he considered the *Russians* script nearly perfect, he had cast renowned improvisers Carl Reiner and Jonathan Winters in other parts. Should Arkin be given the role, Jewison added, he would surely be asked to respond improvisationally.

"Okay," Arkin said. "What should we —"

Jewison tossed him a heavy leather jacket. "Put this on," he said. "You're going to be a KGB Russian agent who is here with the ballet company and I'm going to do an interview with you, like a television interview."

Jewison rolled camera on Arkin for "a smart, funny, and lucid improv," Jewison said, "that proved to me that with a little work he could be wonderful." Arkin played a Russian actor in round one, drawing from his Second City catalogue of immigrant misfits.

"What is your name?" began Jewison, off camera.

"Constantin Gabrilich Stepanowsk."

"Is that your name?"

"Yes, is my name. Stepanowsk. It was longer, but I shortened it to go onstage."

"You play an instrument?"

"I am wiolinist."

Jewison tried to keep from laughing. "A wiolinist?"

"I denote a slice of humor on your part. We have our way of pronouncing. I don't make fun of the way you pronounce my name."

"Could I see you without your hat?"

Arkin took the suggestion. "This is my real hair and top-of-head. It was used very successfully in many films, in films of I. Pudovkin. In *Mother*, it was used in scene of infant's top-of-head. That was when I was very young."

Jewison, loving this, moved Arkin into his next character, a Russian officer claiming to be CIA, and then into:

"Constantin Mevedenko."

"How do you spell that?"

"M. E. V. A. U. W. Y. X. G. Evynik."

Jewison was losing it. Arkin was pressure in human form, a slow-burning nervous breakdown, but there was Zen in there. If stars are contradiction, the impossible person made real, then Arkin, anxious Buddha, had a real shot at making it in the movies. UA agreed. Based on his improvised screen test, they gave Arkin the part.

He said, "There's not a line in the film that I said as it was in the script."

Well in advance of shooting day one, *Who's Afraid of Virginia Woolf?* made people nervous on and off the Warner Brothers lot. The play, by Edward Albee, was notoriously difficult and unanimously admired, under glass and untouchable, like a painting in a museum; its adult themes and colorful language, direct assaults on Hollywood morality and the withering Production Code, recurrently aggravated studio head Jack Warner. The operatic volatility of Elizabeth Taylor and Richard Burton preoccupied Ernest

Lehman, *Virginia Woolf*'s screenwriter and first-time producer, who feared that first-time film director Mike Nichols, at thirty-four years old, would be powerless to corral his stars' drinking, egos, sex rows, and talent. Nichols's permissive attitude and playboy persona, his new Rolls-Royce and poolside weekends, panicked Lehman. "I have felt that Mike tends to leave the picture behind when he leaves the studio," he wrote, "and I think he goes off to a very happy social life in the evenings. Now perhaps it will all work out well, but I have worked with other directors, and it seems to me that if they were in Mike's position, directing their first picture — a picture as important and as difficult as this one — they would be burning the midnight oil trying to find all the answers to all the questions." Lehman had never worked with an improviser. On July 20, 1965, his first day as a film director, Nichols decided a little improvisation might open the production's emotional-release valve. Late in the afternoon, before rolling cameras, Nichols let Burton and Taylor play with scene one, shot one, the loopy, liquored moment when their characters, George and Martha, return home after a late-night party, and she surveys the premises and blurts out, "What a dump!" But just for laughs, Nichols had Taylor improvise as George and Burton improvise as Martha.

It was a wild idea and everyone laughed. Except Ernest Lehman.

Nichols called him at the end of the day, elated. "Did you hear me say Action?! I said it — the first time in my life. Wasn't I good?"

Nichols was already home, at his rented house, the Cole Porter estate in Brentwood; Lehman was still at the office.

"You certainly were," Lehman allowed. "Now you are a film director."

Lehman reserved his actual feelings for himself. Improvising in nightclubs was one thing, but in Hollywood, on film, where mere seconds cost thousands, free play smacked of immaturity and decadence; it showed artistic indulgence; disrespect for traditional studio hierarchy where producers and production heads controlled their directors and actors. Improvisation started with actors, not executives. It would be a fight between the Old Order and the New, but with Mike Nichols leading the charge, the New had a chance. Nichols had the star clout — and, as an improviser, the interpersonal finesse — to wrestle down guardians of the Old like Jack Warner and Joseph E. Levine, the independent financier of his next film, *The Graduate,* which Nichols had already begun to imagine. "My hope," he said, "is to make the picture free-wheeling, partly improvised. To make something happen that only happens once — and you've got it. The idea of doing it quite loosely interests me." He saw the character of Mrs. Robinson as a version of Elaine.

Buck Henry was in L.A., living at the Chateau Marmont, working on *Get Smart*, the show he created with Mel Brooks, and would, from time to time, drop by the *Virginia Woolf* set to check in on his friend, former fellow Premise Player George Segal, whom Nichols had cast in the movie. Since their Premise days, Henry had worked mostly as a writer, for Steve Allen's *Tonight Show*, briefly, and *That Was the Week That Was* (*TW3*), a satirical news show — the first of its kind — populated by Compass and Second City improvisers. On *TW3*, unlike other shows, they were actually allowed a regular platform to improvise. Nichols and May, Arkin, Andrew Duncan, Mina Kolb, and others made up a kind of revolving repertory company from episode to episode, taking suggestions from their studio audience. It was unprecedented.

"After *TW3* we all interrelated," Henry said. "Arkin and Nichols and everybody else. Everybody did everything with everyone. But there were always some people we couldn't fit into our new age of success. We couldn't get them out of Chicago and into the rest of the world. The most obvious two were Severn Darden — who was a god to all of us — and Del Close." They were always writing parts for scientists and inventors on *Get Smart*, an opportunity, Henry thought, to give Del the Hollywood break he needed. So Del came out to California, and met with casting director Pat Harris. Del arrived in a lab coat ("one doesn't ask," Henry said) carrying a little box that looked to Henry like something out of early Scientology. "It's really simple," Del explained to Harris, offering her the box. "You hold on to these two handles for about two minutes." She did, and he pumped her frail body with enough voltage to blast her off her chair. Del did not get the part.

Nichols and Buck Henry had instant shtick. New York Jews, expertly educated (Henry at Choate and Dartmouth), and acutely versed in show business custom and history (Henry's mother was silent film actress Ruth Taylor, his father, Paul Zuckerman, a stockbroker), they had the motor, means, and material to live up to each other's challenge. Nichols said, "I thought Buck was the funniest and most serious guy I'd ever met — simultaneously."

"You should read this book, *The Graduate*, and see what you think of it," Nichols told him.

Henry had written only one screenplay, *The Troublemaker*, a film Ted

Flicker made with the Premise Players. Nichols had never seen it (few had), but he didn't need to familiarize himself with Henry's writing to know he could write. Buck Henry could improvise. He knew that.

"I think you could do it," Nichols said. "I think you should do it."

Henry went back to the Chateau and read the book. He related. He could see how Mike related. They were Benjamin Braddock.

Del Close's Committee workshops, held in the empty theater during the late-afternoon hours, were inexpensive and open to the public. Putting his own spin on Spolin's "everyone can improvise" credo, Del said, "It's much more useful for me as a teacher to treat everyone as a poet and a genius because they're more likely to behave that way than if they're treated like they're an idiot." While most of professional San Francisco worked at their desks, about twenty or twenty-five twenty-year-olds, in beads and bell-bottoms, would trickle in to the Committee Theater, sober and stoned, and sit at Del's feet, which he flung over the edge of the stage.

His hair was long now, like a hippie's, but determined to stay, in some fashion, an apolitical beatnik, Del always pulled it back tight, in a ponytail, as if in old-man protest of time. Del's glasses were electric-taped at the bridge and held to his neck by a chain holding on to a rope. Up and down his arms, he'd like you to notice the constellation of broken veins and needle marks he called his track suit — a joke Del dropped with a Groucho double-bounce of eyebrows. The cigarette was his all-purpose costume. For Groucho, he would twinkle it out in front of him; for FDR, he flipped it up tall; he let it go limp for Parisian roué; for Barfly there was always the right corner; between the teeth for ventriloquist's dummy; and, ladies and gentlemen, the circus freak twirled a lit one up and under five dirty fingers and flicked it back into his mouth.

Because you got a different Del every day, you got a different lecturer, and differing lecture style — all improvised. Generally, the day's style and subject was influenced by whatever books Del's brain had eaten the night previous. What is the purpose of theater? he might ask them, crowded at his feet.

"To entertain . . ."

"To communicate?"

"To . . . connect."

"You want to know what Freud said was the purpose of psychoanalysis?"

he replied. "To discover the universal elements of our everyday lives. Those elements of our seemingly private and unique experience that are, in fact, archetypical . . ." Everybody is the same. With negligible variation, we face identical problems. Improvisation is finding and sharing solutions to those problems, a ritual we must repeat to discover the rituals we need. Think of the Minotaur and the maze. Tribes as geographically diverse as Africa, South America, and the Outback each had their version of the myth. In some tribes it's a dance, and you dance it your whole life so that when you die, and you cross the dark waters on your way to the beach, you're prepared. "Beyond the beach is a cave," Del said, "where your loved ones are waiting. On the beach is traced a complex path, which you must tread — on the beach is also a hideous monster in the shape of a vagina with teeth that erases half of the path, which you must reproduce by dancing it into the sand, and thus proving you are an initiate, and have the tribal right to paradise." And you can dance it because you've been dancing it your whole life. "Zowie," Del said. "Theater is in the same tradition as that peculiar, ancient maze dance." We, the improvisers, have to teach the steps. Workshops were for finding them.

Del led workshops for the professional company too, an ensemble made up of improvisers from all walks, from Compass to Premise to Second City, divided by ethic and training, but united in their weariness with shortform, two- or three-person scenes. Cut loose from the anchor of Second City and urged on by the radicalism he inhaled on both sides of the theater walls, Del urged Committee improvisers to *all* get up on the stage at once and let what happened happen — with a vengeance. Real art, powered by anger, ripped up brains; it should hurt both sides. Propelled by a similar urge, the Committee had been playing with group scenes of extended duration like Myerson's Fear, Guilt, and Impotence Collage since before Del's arrival, but Del, said Howard Hesseman, "was really urging you to try anything and . . . abandon all of the rules and notions of safety that you had." On the back wall, in block letters big enough for the improvisers to see from the stage, he had written FOLLOW THE FEAR.

Meanwhile, Alan Myerson, guest teaching improvisation at San Francisco State, was continuing his own experiments in longform, testing collages with the students. These collages arose by following an improvised scene with a Spolin game followed by an improvised scene . . . until one day, semimiraculously, the parts came together in a cohesive dramatic whole

—a short play instead of unrelated scenes. To all involved, this was a powerful awakening, nearly spiritual in the shared discovery of unconscious forces that had guided these improvisers toward a single organizing narrative. How had it happened? Without planning or discussion, Myerson's ensemble had unknowingly submitted to an awareness of impulses none of them had ever known as individuals. What?

Bill Mathieu, formerly of Second City, whom Myerson had hired as the Committee's musical director, had at that approximate moment, by coincidence, made an eerily similar discovery. Teaching musical improvisation at the San Francisco Conservatory to a class of actors, musicians, and singers, he alternated Spolin's games with his own musical games and reminded his ensemble, "Anything can happen at any time, commit to spontaneity, and listen." His musical collective, as if conducted by a ghost, would harmonize. "The ghost," Mathieu said, "was the musical narrative." What was happening? Close, Myerson, and Mathieu came together in the summer of 1967 to ask that very question. Comparing their notes over several months, they recognized in the simultaneity of their discoveries some verification of the zeitgeist. How else to explain these continuities? Just as the individuals in their three distinct workshop sessions had moved spontaneously toward a "group mind"—Del's phrase—so had Close, Myerson, and Mathieu, in activating their ensembles, been their own group mind. "We knew we had something here," Mathieu said, "but we didn't know how we were going to reproduce and sustain it time and again. Even if two or three were successful, the rest were abominable, but those two or three would be so brilliant I'd be happy to be alive." To lasso the free beast of longform improvisation, they needed guidelines like the Westminster Place Kitchen Rules, or the kind of preset structure Myerson had given his students at San Francisco State. But too much structure would be limiting. To truly develop and evolve, this form—whatever they called it—would have to have some built-in self-destructive outs, the flexibility to revise itself on a moment's notice; it had to be improvised alongside the improvisations themselves. But then again, too flexible and it would basically disappear.

Through the fall of 1967, the Committee played under the microscope, rotating the company through workshop directors Close, Myerson, and Mathieu, pitting three different personalities—the dangerous, the social-political, and the musical—against the longform beast to observe the results. Mathieu could tell the improvisers were none too thrilled with his abstraction, and neither was Del. Sitting at his stable, strung out in yesterday's clothes, and still as a stone, he watched the improvisers struggle and fail to implement Mathieu's musicality. At the experiment's end, in lieu of verbal feedback, Del dumped his can of apricot juice over his own head. "End of workshop," Mathieu concluded. "I was deeply offended by Del, but I learned I wasn't allowed to turn [the improvisers] into abstract motion and sound. What I did have was the freedom to change the scene with music, like adding the sound of a storm."

After one productive workshop, Committee members Ed Greenberg, Ruth Silveira, and Julie Payne were lounging around the theater, analyzing the day's efforts with Close, Myerson, and Mathieu. All buzzed on the high of new purpose.

"We gotta name this thing," announced Close. He was sitting apart from the others at one of the Committee's square bistro tables.

"How about Harold?" Mathieu joked. He thought of some guy named Harold, sitting in his undershirt with a dead cigar in the ashtray.

"That's a bad idea," Del said.

But the actors loved it. "Harold": as cheeky as George Harrison's *Hard Day's Night* answer to "What do you call that haircut?" ("Arthur.")

It stuck. "Harold."

But what was it?

For months, Mike Nichols and Buck Henry met in the house Nichols rented in Brentwood, settling every day in a sequestered back patio Henry called the Stone Room. They played records — Beethoven's String Quartet No. 15 in A-minor, Schubert's String Quartet in C-major, Duke Ellington — and improvised not so much scene ideas, but montage sequences, image by image, for *The Graduate*. Bouncing visual ideas off Henry, and having complementary visuals bounced back to him, Nichols gathered a complex, interconnected chain of free-associated images — switching from Ben's purposeless home life and his affair with Mrs. Robinson — linked by spacial symmetries, lighting accents, and color.

Hanging out was part of the job. Nichols needed to merge with his writers; he needed to play with them. When it came to putting words on the page, he would give Henry all the space he needed to earn his screenwriting credit, but the phase of exploratory prewriting, the ideation, Nichols extended all through the actual writing and rewriting of the script, for as long as time and money would allow, until he lost his writer to another project, until the actors needed their lines and the crew had to set up the shot. There the conversation ended. It had to. Until then, with Henry in the Stone Room, Nichols was forever asking, as he would in an improvisation, what is this film *really* about?

"I want this to be about not becoming a thing in a world of things," he told Henry.

Previous screenwriters had struggled to implement this concept. William Hanley, writer one, parted ways with *The Graduate* after declining Nichols's suggestions, and anyway, "Hanley had no humor," Larry Turman said. "He was capital-*D* dark. He didn't get this was a comedy." Calder Willingham's draft vulgarized the central love triangle and was summarily rejected; and Peter Nelson, recommitting the story to the source material, was perhaps too faithful to the novel. "And none of them," Nichols said, "were terribly funny. Buck improvised comedy." And unlike Charles Webb, the book's author, Buck Henry empathized with Benjamin. Simpatico with Nichols's description of Benjamin's alienation — the otherness that still beset Mikhail Igor Peschkowsky these thirty years after his arrival in America — Henry could play within Nichols's emotional parameters. "Working with Buck is very like what Elaine May and I used to do," Nichols said. "Both of them have spectacular inventiveness and hundreds of ideas and my role has always been to pull our certain threads and try to strengthen them."

Together, they turned *The Graduate* into a compassionate comedy, and the part of Benjamin Braddock, the WASP outsider, into a nervous nebbish. A Jew.

7

1967–1968

Mike Nichols and Robert Redford were playing snooker at Nichols's rented house in Brentwood. They'd just enjoyed a lovely dinner; Nichols decided the time was right to let Redford know he was wrong for *The Graduate*.

"You can't play it."

"Why?"

"Because you can't play a loser. Look at you."

"Yes I can! Of course I can play a loser!"

"Really? When was the last time you struck out with a girl?"

"What do you mean?"

Nichols had looked at countless actors for the part of Benjamin. Warren Beatty, Steve McQueen, George Peppard, Keir Dullea . . . "goy after goy," Nichols said. Crystal-eyed blonds fit the film's Beverly Hills, swimming-pool-and-palm-trees setting. WASPs were story-appropriate, and when it came to playing America's young men, represented a casting ideal as old as movies. "He [Benjamin] needed to be an outsider for this story to happen," Nichols said. "And we didn't even know that until we'd seen all these other actors not make it." It seemed obvious in retrospect, but considering Hollywood convention, equally improbable. Nichols had only to recall his own dark days as a starving actor in New York, when, alone and hungry in his mattress-sized apartment, he flipped depressingly from channel to channel in search of himself, and found nothing.

· · ·

Dustin Hoffman, on the phone with Nichols from his one-bedroom apartment on West Eleventh Street, was gratified to hear that a powerful and gifted film director had admired his work in the 1964 off-Broadway production of *Harry, Noon and Night,* but "I'm not right for this part, sir. This is a Gentile. This is a WASP. This is Robert Redford."

Hoffman was then appearing at the Circle in the Square, in *Eh?,* a British import on its third director. The first two, before they were fired, hadn't known what to do with Hoffman. One plainly instructed him to go to the movies and copy the mannerisms of actor David Warner, who'd starred in the original production. The third director, suggested by cast member MacIntyre Dixon, a former Second City player, was hired ten days before opening. Under the pseudonym Roger Short, director Alan Arkin took *Eh?* through to its successful run. Hoffman said, "Arkin was the first director that didn't want me fired and the first director that I connected with. We had the same sense of humor."

Eh? brought success to all involved, further proof that, after years of trying, Hoffman, at twenty-nine, had finally found a home in the theater. *I'm not supposed to be in movies,* he thought. *An ethnic actor is supposed to be in ethnic New York in an ethnic off-Broadway show. I know my place.* But Nichols pressed. He wanted Hoffman to come out to L.A. for a screen test.

Plus, Nichols had already seen everyone else. Hoffman was his only lead. But neither side was sure it was a good idea.

"Did you see this week's *Time* magazine?" Hoffman protested. It was lying there on his coffee table — "Man of the Year" in January 1967 was the collective "Now Generation," the under-twenty-five set, and the cover illustration featured a young guy, good-looking, screamingly master race. "That man, Mr. Nichols, that man on the magazine. That's the guy who should be playing it."

"You mean he's not *Jewish*?" Nichols joked.

"Yes, this guy is super-WASP. Boston Brahmin."

Nichols tried another tack. "Did you think the script was funny?"

"Yes."

"Well, maybe," Nichols improvised, "he's Jewish inside."

Hoffman, reluctantly, flew out to Los Angeles for a screen test. At Paramount, he was led into makeup, where they plucked and powdered him in preparation for the camera. The more they fussed with his face the more

Hoffman was convinced his original instinct had been correct; he was absolutely wrong for the part.

Nichols walked in and studied Hoffman's reflection in the mirror. He then turned to the makeup artist and, loud enough for Hoffman to hear, asked, "Do you think you could make him look a little less Jewish?"

If Hoffman was nervous before, he was exasperated now. Had he already lost the part? Was Nichols giving up on him already?

For the test, Hoffman was paired with Katharine Ross, who, auditioning for the part of Elaine Robinson, was just as uneasy as he was. It was a very long scene, a bedroom scene no less, and both Hoffman and Ross kept flubbing their lines. To casting director Lynn Stalmaster Hoffman mouthed, "What am I doing here?" When he glanced up at his director, he found him glaring back with an intense look that was not happiness.

Nichols called Hoffman aside. "Relax. Don't be nervous."

Hoffman extended his hand to shake Nichols's, and found the director's hand was so sweaty his own slipped out. *I guess I'm not the only one who's nervous,* Hoffman thought.

Hoffman returned to his place beside Ross, Nichols took some more film, and at last, released the actors ("I was so happy it was over," Hoffman remembered). Before he could flee, Hoffman approached the crew for a round of handshakes. Removing a fist from his pocket, he accidently scattered a cluster of New York subway tokens on the floor. The prop man bent over to pick them up. "Hey, kid," he said. "You're going to need these."

Hoffman returned to New York, to *Eh?* "Don't worry," he told a couple of actors in their shared dressing room. "I'm not going to get this one." Meaning, they wouldn't be closing.

A few days later, Hoffman was instructed to call Mike Nichols at nine o'clock on a Sunday morning.

"Hello?" It was Nichols. He didn't sound happy. He sounded like he had just woken up.

"Hi. Mr. Nichols, this is Dustin Hoffman. I was supposed to call? At nine o'clock?"

"No, nine o'clock *L.A.* time."

"I'm sorry —"

"No, no. It's all right."

For what seemed like an eternity, neither spoke. "Well," Nichols said, "you got it."

"Oh."

"You don't sound very excited."

"No, it's just — I just thought —"

What he thought was that Nichols had cast him because he had seen everyone else and was out of options.

Bernie Sahlins knew he'd made a mistake. From New York, he and Sheldon Patinkin had brought J. J. Barry and Martin Harvey Friedberg and Burt Heyman — stand-up comedians — to Second City. "We were losing big to television," Patinkin said, "and needed laughs." Burly, urban tough guys, the new crop earned their keep in prostate and gay jokes, and J. J. Barry made a convincing Mayor Daley, but their common denominatorism shifted Second City's center of gravity one notch farther from the intellectual domain Sahlins had once so zealously guarded. Still, these were desperate times. Many years of poor box office had backed Second City, clumsily, into vaudeville shtick.

"I want everyone to bring in some jokes," he ordered the company one evening. "We'll add the satire later."

The next day, when asked to deliver, Friedberg dropped his pants and made a fart sound. "You wanted a joke, Bernie? That's my joke."

The first time social worker Gary Austin saw an improvisation, in the spring of 1968, he was sitting a few seats down from Carl Reiner in the front row of the Tiffany, a converted movie theater off Sunset Boulevard. It was the Committee's opening night in Los Angeles, and Austin thought he'd like to see his pal, Committee member Christopher Ross, do his thing. Reiner's son Rob — a veteran of his own improv group, the Session, which he'd formed as a student at UCLA — was onstage, along with an ensemble that included Peter Bonerz, Nancy Fish, Jessica Myerson, Howard Hesseman, Carl Gottlieb, Chris Ross, Mel Stewart, Garry Goodrow, and Lewis Arquette. For Austin, their work, reverberant with that late 1960s sound of indignation and hope, and lifted high on the communal spirit of the Harold, shot an arrow through his heart. This wasn't ha-ha sketch comedy; this was oh-my, the theater of real life.

Backstage after the show, Austin approached John Brent. "How do I do this? Is there a workshop?"

"Yes. Every Saturday for one dollar."

Austin went habitually, joining as many as fifty other nonprofessional improvisers, "anyone off the street," Austin said, for workshops, each led by a different Committee member.

Del appeared to them a six-foot brick of black — black pants, black work boots, black turtleneck, glasses, and slicked black hair pulled to a ponytail — sucking down whole cigarettes, it seemed, in single draws.

"Hello, my name is Del Close," he boomed over them as he took the stage. "If any one of you thinks you can run this workshop better than me, then I want you to come up and lead it and I'll be your student. If I think I'm a better teacher than you, I'll get back up, and I'll continue to run the workshop. If you break one of my rules, and it works, I will applaud you. If you break one of my rules and it doesn't work, I'll castigate you. Let's begin."

Thus commenced Del's prescription of trust games, verbal abuse, chair throwing (inherited from Paul Sills), brilliant insight, and miscellaneous acts of violence, alternately engineered to prompt spontaneous responses and cause pain. Both, to Del, qualified as shows of truth, and therefore, art. There was talk of Del and improvisation's supple days in the St. Louis Compass. "You know that when Del and Elaine lived together," Austin was told, "she decided to become a dog for a number of days. She decided to do everything a dog does, so she crawled on all fours, she ate dog food, she drank out of water bowls, she shit on the floor and barked."

From those workshops, Close handpicked a company, which included Austin, to play the Tiffany on Monday nights, the Committee's night off. Soon Austin was inducted into the main company and shuttled up to San Francisco, where he learned, by the example of improvisers Howard Hesseman and David Ogden Stiers, to divest the ego of wants and simply "not give a fuck." "If [Johnny] Carson was in the audience," Austin said, "no one [in the Committee] cared. People would walk out of the audience on a Saturday night going, 'Fuck you! We paid money for this shit!' and no one onstage gave a shit." It was their composure onstage, their faces. In the storm of failure, Austin could see that they, by their own estimation, hadn't failed at all. "One time," Austin said, "I was with the Committee and we were flying somewhere and it got turbulent. It freaked me out. What I did to calm myself was I looked at the faces of the Committee sitting in their seats and saw they weren't scared and there went my fear. Gone." Austin was hooked.

• • •

Nichols originally conceived of *The Graduate* as partially improvised, and did in fact have the actors improvise on a Paramount sound stage for three weeks — an unusually long time for a Hollywood movie — inventing and playing with character backstories, including scenes from childhood, family get-togethers, and even an off-script affair between Benjamin's father and Mrs. Robinson. But by the end of the rehearsal period Nichols's company was so certain of their every move, Hoffman joked that they could take *The Graduate* on the road. Nichols had allowed them to play their way to there, to certainty.

"Benjamin's twenty-one years old," he said to Hoffman early in rehearsal. "Do you think he's a virgin?"

"If I had to guess, I'd say no. But I don't think he's had anything that was meaningful, like a girlfriend or anything."

"I agree. But I think with Mrs. Robinson he's as close to a virgin as you can get."

"Meaning?"

"Well, I don't think he ever fucked his mother before."

That became Hoffman's starting point. The tension around sleeping with his mother's friend, a woman he'd known since he was a kid. Hoffman could run with Benjamin from there.

Using Nichols's suggestion, Hoffman and Anne Bancroft ran the scene. Then Nichols called Hoffman over for a private conference. "Did you have any movie stars that you looked up to when you were a kid?"

"I don't think so. But I remember I saw *The Yearling* and I wanted Gregory Peck to be my father."

"Aside from that."

"Yeah. My brother was the only sibling I had. He was older, but he had little to do with me so any time he paid me any attention at all, I took it all in. At times, the phone would ring and some girl on the other end would say, 'Is this Ronny?' And I could imitate him. Yeah, he was my hero."

"Did you ever see him when he was uptight?"

"Yeah."

"What was he like?"

"I remember he would sort of stop breathing and exhale and . . ." Hoffman squeaked nervously. Nichols laughed at that; he loved it. Hoffman didn't know Nichols had made almost the same squeak playing terrified, put-upon young men in his improvisations with Elaine. ("I found out later," Hoffman would say, "that I was becoming a sort of alter ego for Mike. I don't think either of us knew it was happening.")

"Let's do the scene again," Nichols suggested. "Why don't you do it as if you're your older brother?"

They did. Then:

"Let's improvise the scene now. Don't be tied to the words. Just try to do the *essence* of your brother."

When they had played First Line/Last Line in the style of whatever literary figure the audience had suggested, Nichols and May used the author's essence as a shortcut to perceived notions, to improvise, seemingly, in their language and style. To them, Ibsen was as much a feeling as he was a writer.

"Remember the first time you touched a girl's breast?" Nichols asked.

"Yeah, I do."

"Tell me about it."

"I used to play 'Bumble Boogie' when we had assemblies in junior high school. I didn't know what else to play. And I was waiting in the basement for my turn to go on and this girl arrived and was sitting there and she was in blackface because she was going to do 'Mammy.' We were sitting there a long time and for some reason I had enough courage to put my arm around her and then put my hand on her breast, but I couldn't get too close because she was in blackface."

"Let's do the scene again, and this time, take Mrs. Robinson's sweater off. And I want you to hold her breast."

"When?"

"Whenever you want."

They tried it. As directed, Hoffman removed Anne Bancroft's sweater. Hardly turned on, her attention snapped to a stain in the sweater. She rubbed at it. Hoffman studied her a moment before landing a hand on her breast. Utterly invested in the cleaning, Bancroft proceeded as if he wasn't even touching her. "I thought this was so hilarious," Hoffman said, "that I started to laugh." To shield himself from Nichols, Hoffman simply turned and walked to the wall, certain that he was going to be fired for breaking up in the middle of the scene. But Nichols was laughing. He put the improvisation, as is, into the movie.

"That rehearsal was a magical time for me," Hoffman reflected. "It was the best rehearsal time of my life."

But once shooting began, the air of fun and discovery ended. Nichols, exuding worry, grew tense, and Hoffman, who still wasn't convinced he was right for the part, could sense why. "It's not that I felt the acting was so bad," he explained. "It's just that it was such a bold piece of casting. Benjamin Braddock, this little five-foot-six Jewboy? Nobody could understand it."

Halfway through production, the director Ulu Grosbard, a friend of Hoffman's, mentioned he had planned a lunch with Nichols.

"You gotta ask Mike if he thinks he made a mistake," Hoffman pleaded. "I just gotta know if I'm crazy. Please."

Grosbard agreed, and after lunch, returned to Dustin with the verdict. "You have to promise not to say a word to anybody."

"Of course not."

"He thinks he made a mistake."

"Now listen," Nichols barked at Hoffman and Katharine Ross at the end of an exhausting day, "you're going to get on that bus and you're going to laugh, because we've stopped traffic for twenty blocks and I can't do this over and over, so get on there and *laugh*."

It was to be the last shot of the film: Benjamin and Elaine, having fled the church, hail down a passing school bus and ride off, presumably, to the rest of their happy ending.

On the day, Hoffman and Ross did as they were told. Exhausted, they ran onto the bus, squeezed out a laugh, and waited for the director to yell cut. But for some reason, he didn't know why, Nichols didn't yell cut.

It wasn't until he reviewed the footage in dailies that he fell in love with it, with the air of distant preoccupation that had creeped into the actors' expressions. It was one hell of an ending. "That's usually the best work," Nichols said, "when you're not exactly sure neither what you're going to do nor why you did what you did."

He was working from his unconscious, like a Compass player. The scenes of Benjamin and Mrs. Robinson in particular borrow the rhythm and pathology of Nichols and May. (One actually lifts the cigarette gag from "Teenagers.") Indeed, the film is the very first direct descendant of Compass naturalism. *The Graduate* offers few "jokes," never panders to situational humor or embellishes for maximum impact. In keeping with Nichols's work on *Barefoot in the Park,* the film's humor emerges at its own pace, the pace of real life, and from character. "I got my feeling for people from working in comedy," Nichols said of his Compass years. "I approach comedy as if it were reality."

The Graduate was so good because it was so real. In the spring of 1968, in the middle of the student revolt at Columbia University, members of the Students for a Democratic Society arranged their protest so that every young revolutionary, by turns, had their chance to sneak out of the president's office, which they were occupying, to go see the movie. Benjamin, in slothful protest of his parents' plastic generation, embodied their dissatisfaction as none before him had, but it was his clumsily Jewish, normal-guy package that conveyed their alienation most powerfully.

In anger and solidarity, Alan Myerson listened to Howard Hesseman's tale of the night before, January 17, 1968. He and Committee members Garry Goodrow and Mimi Fariña were watching Johnson's State of the Union Address, surging with rage at the president's hypocritical profession of peace advocacy concomitant with sustained force in Vietnam, and his similar pledge to defend the home front with "more vigorous enforcement of all of our drug laws by increasing the number of federal drug and narcotics control officials by more than—" which so infuriated Hesseman, he leapt up and would have kicked in the television, if Goodrow and Fariña had not restrained him.

Hesseman, in that moment, was acting for millions, not only in San Francisco, but Chicago, Hollywood, New York, wherever impotent rage was breaking from the medium cool of nonviolence. He had improvised himself into a powerful metaphor, and it needed to be shared. "We're going to do what happened last night," Myerson told him. With the audience. Tonight. "Because this is why we are improvisers," he said. Activism—another word for audience participation—was the sole province of their theater. Action was up to them.

Myerson outlined a rough scenario—a longform cousin of the Harold—beginning with Hesseman, Goodrow, and Fariña watching TV as they had the night before. But Hesseman and the group resisted. No, they said, they would not perform it.

"If you don't do this scene," Myerson announced, "I'm out of here. I'm done."

Autocracy was not his style—giving decrees ran counter to their mission of personal authenticity — but he meant it. "We had to do this," Myerson said. "I knew it with every part of me."

The Committee agreed, "under duress," Myerson said, to improvise the scene that night. It would constitute the entire second act.

When the moment came, the improvisation began, per Myerson's suggestion, exactly as Hesseman had described the incident, with the trio watching Johnson, played by improviser Peter Bonerz in a cowboy hat. Immediately, the audience recognized the night before; they were, emotionally, on both sides of the stage now, through the looking glass, and looking back. In that fusion, the Committee became a community, and over the loudspeaker, improviser Jim Cranna read the salient parts of Johnson's speech, as Bonerz, gesticulating "on TV," grew adamant, and Hesseman, inflamed, ran over to kick his face in, and Goodrow and Fariña restrained him, as scripted. What followed, Myerson later said, "was the apex of improvisational theater in my experience."

Hesseman freed himself from his friends and mimed turning off the TV. But Bonerz did not turn off. He continued to gesticulate, and in response, Cranna, into the loudspeaker, said, and kept saying, like a mantra, "You can't turn me off; I'm you. You can't turn me off; I'm you. You can't turn me off; I'm you . . ."

Powerless, Hesseman turned his energy to the audience, and over the chanting, spoke. "This is actually what happened last night. I went to kick in the television and Garry and Mimi had to stop me. And standing here, part of me is deeply ashamed because I don't believe in violence. I grew up in a violent household. This isn't what I want to be. But do you know something? When I went to kick that thing in, I felt good. You get me? Anger felt good" — the room warmed — "I suspect you are all angry at Johnson for something." Throughout, the mantra persisted — *you can't turn me off; I'm you* — and in musical alignment with Hesseman's address, as Bill Mathieu, in workshops, had rehearsed them. Everyone synchronized. Every dissonance in rhythm.

"It's fun to hate," Hesseman continued. *You can't turn me off; I'm you . . .* "If you get really angry, I bet it will feel good." *You can't turn me off . . .* On piano, Mathieu joined in with ugly, atonal mud, and all grew louder together.

Myerson watched from the back of the house as Hesseman, letting loose, exhorted the audience to action. "It's fun to hate . . ." he repeated. Some gave it back. "It's fun to hate . . ." It spread. The full Committee took the stage to form a line behind Hesseman and picked up the refrain. "It's fun to hate," they chanted. *You can't turn me off; I'm you.* "It's fun to hate . . ." *You can't . . .* "It's fun . . ." As Hesseman got hotter, the audience became citizens, shouting the refrain back at him, with him, and momentum built. "It's fun to hate! It's fun to hate!" Then Hesseman released himself: "Let's kill this fucker!" he shouted, and the full audience leapt up from their tables, spewing filth and heartache out of their guts and onto the stage. Chairs were thrown.

Before it went too far, Myerson, offstage, caught Hesseman's attention and gave him the signal — a sign to change direction. "Okay," Hesseman said, and the room froze. "Okay, that didn't work." The hate chanting stopped, but *You can't turn me off* held. "We can't kill him," Hesseman continued. "Let's see if we can love him to death."

Mathieu first: the music turned joyous.

The improvisers embraced one another, in individuals and groups. *You can't turn me off; I'm you.* Real lovers kissed, friends held one another, "and because authenticity is contagious," Myerson said, the audience caught the feeling, and improvisers stepped off the stage and flooded the house and the Committee detonated in love — *You can't turn me off; I'm you. You can't turn me off; I'm you* — but the room did not listen; they had disappeared from Johnson into each other. Myerson and Hesseman too. Across the room, they caught eyes, Myerson gave the signal again, and on his cue, another change, this time: total blackout. "It was like cold water," Myerson remembered. Exact and sudden stillness. No sound. No movement.

Nothing. Just January 1968. Everyone in darkness.

And in the darkness, Mimi Fariña, in a clear, gorgeous voice spoke out: "Vietnam."

A king now, with a Best Director Oscar for *The Graduate,* Mike Nichols, at thirty-six, had nothing left to prove, another way of saying he had nothing left. No director in American history, not even Orson Welles at the top, had his combined record and youth. It was a problem.

Looking back, Nichols could argue he only knew normal for the give-or-take two years of Compass that preceded his overnight superstardom. He loved more people than he could bring with him. He had already lost Sills, he feared. He was losing all the time. He thought seriously about getting back together with Elaine and Sills and doing a play they all loved. He dreamed of their old theater. Of building a new one. The physical space didn't matter; in fact, Nichols didn't want one. "It seems to me that it is important to start with the people, not with a building," he said. Without real estate, his imagined repertory company would rove freely from stage to stage to screen, following each other everywhere, all the while deepening their shorthand and advancing their talent. Nichols got commitments from Elaine, Sills, Barbara Harris, Alan Arkin, former Compass Player Alan Alda, and others, all friends. In a sense, with *The Apple Tree*, a Broadway musical Nichols peopled with Harris, Alda, and Robert Klein, featuring a third act based on a Feiffer story, he had already begun the process of reunion. And he would build his next film, *Catch-22*, into a repertory dream. Beginning with a script by Buck Henry and with Alan Arkin in the leading role, Nichols said, "I plan to cast everyone I've ever worked with in the picture." But repertory meant more to Nichols than old friends. The ensemble of his mind's eye would stand as America's premier repertory company — a theatrical family that clung together over time, and grew. Nothing like it existed in America. "I am so sick of hearing how great the English actors are, and yet it is true," he said. "The reason they are so good is that they are able to go off into repertory and perform fifty plays in two years. There's no such opportunity for an American actor to do the same. That's why we need repertory."

A refuge from the world, Paul Sills's Game Theater gave two years of solace to Sills and his informal repertory of amateur improvisers, until Martin Luther King was killed, and then Bobby Kennedy, and Sills could no longer convince himself that his local theater of personal liberation meant a goddamned thing. He had to reach more people. Thinking, perhaps, that Second City had been right all along, that satire was the loudest megaphone, he considered opening "a bar where we could put the Democratic Party on trial for getting us into Vietnam in the first place," then reconsidered. Political satire was exclusive to grown-ups, the already-converted, and however popular its message, satire's appeal was esoteric. If the revolution was to spread, it had to come from primeval wisdom. If it was to be sustained, it had to begin early, with children. How to reach them?

Fairy tales. Ancient teachings that speak to intuition. Sills would use his mother's games — games anyone could play — to improvise with fairy tales — stories everyone knew. Perfectly matched, Spolin's 1963 text *Impro-*

visation for the Theater, and the Brothers Grimm. Both conveyed identical revelations about the power of personal transformation. "This 'invisible inner self,'" Sills explained, "is what fairy stories are about." It was what improvisation was all about. That alone was a revolution. "You can't reject outside authority until you realize you have a self," explained Sills's daughter, Aretha. "That's what the fairy tales were about for him, so they were political in a sense."

They moved into the original, abandoned Second City at 1846 North Wells, then set for demolition, renovated the space — Carol Sills designed a round stage surrounded by bleachers — and invited the community, anyone interested, in discovering with Sills the next outflow of his improvisational charge. "Paul," said improviser Cordis Heard, "was some sort of mystical, mythical figure at that point."

Heard was in the theater that first night, in the spring of 1968, as Sills marched into the empty space, a worn copy of *Grimm's Fairy Tales* tucked under his arm, and announced: "Let's just read. Let's just start."

Joining his evolving ensemble of experienced improvisers, Sills selected players from the audience of hippies young and old, matching first-timers to Grimm's descriptions of princes, princesses, and enchanted animals, handing them the texts — "The Blue Light," "The Fisherman and His Wife," "The Goose Girl" — and directing them to read *and* improvise, speaking from the pages and their hearts in both the third and first persons, pivoting their intuition between narrator and self. Heard explained, "You can use the text to tell you what happens, to take you into the magical woods, and then what happens there, in the woods, we improvised."

"I don't want your psychology," Sills told his players. "I just want you to tell me what you're doing and then do it." And: "Your political consciousness comes through the work, just being you, being free."

No props, no scenery — their absence would generate continual rediscovery of, as Sills said, "the free space and the whole person connected with other whole persons." The time was right. They spent the entire summer of 1968 discovering themselves in the fairy tales, discovering, moment by moment, the precepts of what Sills dubbed Story Theater.

"There are some guys calling themselves yippies coming to town for the convention," Dennis Cunningham, once an improviser, now a left-wing lawyer, explained to Sills. "They need a place to stay —"

"I'd like to, but —"

"Paul—"

"I just fixed it up."

"A *couple* of nights—"

He would not admit it, but Sills was scared. The yippies had made some provocative jokes—although they didn't sound like jokes—about their Chicago plans. "They can stay downstairs in the bar," Sills decided. "We have a mimeograph machine there. They'll want that."

In July 1968, as Chicago prepared to host the Democratic National Convention, Sills began to improvise a work about the Boston Massacre of 1770. Outside the theater, across the facade of the original Second City building, he draped a wide banner advertising the show—COMING SOON: THE AMERICAN REVOLUTION.

You didn't know how much the yippies were kidding. Even before they arrived in Chicago for the Democratic Convention, when they announced they were going to contaminate the city's water supply with LSD, you may have thought, *well, no, there's no way,* but still you wondered—and if you were Mayor Daley, worried—what outrageous incident they would provoke instead. "Essentially what we're going to do is throw a lot of banana peels around Chicago," their front man, Abbie Hoffman, warned the press. "It's all conceived as a total theater," he said, "with everyone becoming an actor." The idea was to put on a show, grab hold of the media's convention coverage, and direct America's attention where it belonged, to ending the war in Vietnam. Were it not for the uncomfortable amount of tension and the slight threat of crazy that accompanied the silliness, the yippie fanfare looked like a put-on. So did the preconvention calm. Anywhere you looked along the park, you could see cops eying pedestrians, and pedestrians disappearing around corners.

Just to be safe, Daley would err on the side of fascism. Insulted by their pseudo-seriousness and flamboyant disrespect for American manners— whatever that meant—Daley denied demonstration permits to the yippies and other antiwar organizations, a provocation that only inflamed the New Left and did not stop the yippies, hippies, Panthers, parents, undercover agents, Allen Ginsberg, and war protesters of every stripe from gathering ten thousand strong in Lincoln Park, the very hot afternoon of Sunday, August 25, a day before the convention, and two blocks from Second City's new home at 1616 Wells Street, wherein rehearsals for the next revue, *A*

Plague on Both Your Houses, showed the organization to be as divided as the Democratic Party. "We were all against Vietnam," Sheldon Patinkin said. "And *Plague* was [shaping up to be] what was for us a very political show, but we couldn't get our cast to work." Divided by age and sensibility, Second City's late-1968 troupe looked as vaudevillian, as philosophically divided, as its mid-1960s companies. Other than laughs, who were they? Topical satire had always been Bernie Sahlins's mantra, and for Second City's first years, when political satire still needed training wheels, his kindness served him exceptionally well. But in the Vietnam era, the mounting confluence of the political and personal spheres—better delineated in the Eisenhower and Kennedy years—changed the emotional tenor of politics. Sahlins was in the intelligent-laughter business, but now no one at Lincoln Park was laughing. As for intelligence, public discourse—the Committee understood this— was no longer a college seminar; it was a fight. A fight that had, outside the theater walls, permeated all aspects of Second City's domain, the comedy of everyday life. But inside, without Del Close or Paul Sills to push and prod, and a company dominated by stand-ups, their improvisation was ten years behind schedule.

That night, sometime after eleven, the Second City gang filtered out of the theater for goodnights and cigarettes and stopped short at the sharp smell of tear gas coming off the street. It preceded the noise, the yelling and honking and *pop pop* of firearms and the onrush of hundreds of feet smacking down North Avenue, toward them. Across from the theater, Sheldon Patinkin watched a couple of kids get thrown against a Walgreens and beaten by the cops. J. J. Barry, renowned for his Mayor Daley impression, ran for a barracks of sandbags the cops had constructed in an empty parking lot near the drugstore. Through the stampede, he saw policemen crouching behind the barricade, aiming automatic weapons into the melee. Out of the roar, screams and smashing windows, a distant chorus came from Lincoln Park, "We Shall Overcome."

The streets were blood. With allies in Paul and Carol Sills, certain protesters ran from Lincoln Park directly for Story Theater; others, with nowhere else to go, blindly followed, some actually pushed into the theater by the force of the mob. Acting fast, the Sills family transformed the theater's beer garden into a sanctuary. Abbie Hoffman, for a flash, took a safe spot at the fire pit. There was food. When the tear gas flew in over the walls, they moved the wounded into the theater, transformed now into an infirmary, letting in as many as they possibly could, piecing together details of the attack from story bits that poured in with the blood. The ten thousand demonstrators that had come to fill Lincoln Park were denied nighttime access, but with no place else to sleep, they held in together while the police, in helmets and gas masks and mounted on horses, lined the perimeter and moved inward, firing rounds of tear gas at citizens, beating their arms and heads with clubs and the backs of handguns. The protesters had no weapons. Some threw bags of shit. Some used their bodies and the backs of picket signs to protect themselves. Those that could ran west, for Old Town, while others, stumbling and out of breath, wheezing on the poison fumes and blind in the white fog, scrambled and fell on their way out. Not everyone made it to Story Theater.

Monday, the following day, as Democrats filled the amphitheater, Mayor Daley called in six thousand army troops, equipped with rifles, bazookas, and flamethrowers to join the six thousand Illinois National Guardsmen who had already been added to the twelve thousand Chicago policemen, and violence intensified. No one was spared. Pedestrians on their way home were chased after and thrown down, but the news media limited their coverage to the amphitheater, where Vice President Hubert Humphrey, tentatively committed to the war in Vietnam, was gaining the edge over antiwar candidate Eugene McCarthy. Outside, battle waged through the early-morning hours of Tuesday night, and settled to an angry hush by Wednesday afternoon, as protesters gathered, peacefully, for a rally outside the band shell in Grant Park. Again, the police pushed in. An unprovoked attack on peace advocate Rennie Davis catalyzed activist Tom Hayden, who took the microphone and, in outrage and disgust, rallied those who had come in love to steel themselves for war. He declared, "This city and the military machine it has aimed at us won't permit us to protest. Therefore, we must move out of this park in groups throughout the city and turn this excited, overheated military machine against itself! Let us make sure that if blood is going to flow, let it flow all over this city. If gas is going to be used, let that gas come down all over Chicago . . . If we are going to be disrupted and violated, let this whole stinking city be disrupted and violated."

John Belushi, a Chicago native, took in Davis's speech and the riot that followed. It was the summer after his freshman year. He had come to Grant Park with friends and his longtime girlfriend, Judy Jacklin, and at the close of the speech found himself standing about ten feet away from an enraged group of protesters who had taken control of a police paddy wagon, rocking it back and forth, and finally shoving it onto its side. "Democracy is no good unless it is dangerous," he had written to Judy from college. "We live in a country where we can speak out about what's wrong about the country *to make it a better place.*" Participating in political happenings and brushing up on his political literature, Belushi had radicalized. Deciding that the "so-called most radical student group," Students for a Democratic Society, was as useless as all those pot-smoking hippies with their childish dreams of brotherhood, Belushi, once among them, now aligned himself with action at all costs. That's why he had come to Grant Park.

The police swarmed the paddy wagon, and Belushi and his gang fled from the park, up Congress and down State Street, crowds roaring into the street behind them, and dove back into the protest on its march to the amphitheater. The National Guard launched another round of tear gas and Belushi, his eyes burning, doubled over, caught sight, up ahead, of a cop beating the shit out of a kid begging for mercy. Belushi ran over to help, the cop hit him in the ribs, and he bolted for cover.

Toward evening, the demonstrators were cornered at the foot of the Conrad Hilton Hotel where Humphrey, moments from winning the Democratic Party's official nomination, counted his votes twenty floors above the people. Down below, the yippies, having lost their candidate, were on their way to winning the media. "Theater — guerilla theater," Abbie Hoffman had explained, "can be used as defense and its offensive weapon," and now they were doing it. It was happening. News crews had turned their cameras from the convention floor — where shouts had turned to brawls — to the streets outside the hotel as police, supposedly sweeping the street clean of protesters, deceitfully blocked every escape route while civilians, between blows, chanted, "The whole world is watching! The whole world is watching! The whole world is watching!"

Inside the Hilton Hotel bar, McCarthy delegate Jules Feiffer heard the shouts coming from Michigan Avenue. Demoralized by McCarthy's loss, sickened by the violence, and despairing of the state of the union, he had been drinking with his pals Studs Terkel, William Styron, and Jim Cameron, a journalist from the *London Evening Standard*, nursing his wounds with martinis and dark laughs at the failure of the convention to acknowledge the massacre unfolding outside the amphitheater — "The horror," Feiffer said, "and the sense of shame that we're sitting here watching this roman coliseum" — when the picture window overlooking Michigan Avenue shattered and in crashed a dozen demonstrators. They fell onto the hotel floor, trying to gain their footing amid the broken glass. A wave of cops rushed in after them, clubs swinging, beating anyone they could grab, even those unmoving on the floor, while Feiffer, lifting the remains of his drink, thought, *Yes, well, this is the end of the country.*

Belushi recovered in Judy's brother's house that night. He was out of danger, for the moment, but still in pain, and swirling. After showering, he regained total consciousness and called Judy. "I can't believe how much tear gas hurts."

WE THE PUNKS

1969–1984

8

1969–1972

We take you now to a changing Second City, sometime in January 1969, where the savageries of the Democratic National Convention, already months in the past, still persisted in its improvisers, bartenders, waiters, and the venerable Bernie Sahlins. Sahlins pulled his hair out perseverating over Chicago's emotional collapse and what the senseless devastations in the park and on the streets had done to his funny little cabaret, where his mandate for ten years — play to the top of your intelligence — now had little to do with a country that, every day, seemed to have lost its ability to reason. Attendance was way down. Bernie's current batch of improvisers — the burlesque bunch that included J. J. Barry, Martin Harvey Friedberg, and Burt Heyman — lacked the original company's intellectual and satirical fervor. Come to think of it, so did Willard, Steinberg, Klein, et al., the wildcard company that had preceded them. But declining standards was the old complaint. Second City, they always said, was better — *then*.

Looking over his spreadsheets, Bernie could see that Second City's slow but sustained slip could be traced to a concomitant incline in laugh-oriented performers — those cattle calls at William Morris — a trend he, ironically, had perpetuated. He could see that losing Paul Sills, matchless in his power to turn those performers into improvisers, supported the thesis, and that in losing Del Close — firing him — Second City forfeited the laboratory environment it needed to flourish. All true, but for the immediate solution, Bernie had to leave his office, step onstage, and as an improviser would, assess his audience. Who was going to Second City today, now? What kind of suggestions did they give the improvisers? Where did they laugh? That would tell Bernie which improvisers were bringing it home. What did those audiences wear? (Suits and ties, mostly, the old uniform of the beatnik.) He had to look at their faces. (Glasses, glasses everywhere.) What did they smoke? (Not marijuana, but cigarettes.) They were his original audience — what was left of them, anyway — a decade later, the Jewish intellectuals, the Mike and Elaine set, the stalwarts thirty and forty years old, come in from the suburbs still hoping for a hit of the neurotic, Freudian old days, and not getting it. Satire had been their revolution. They got one Kennedy, lost two, and their revolution ended. Where were the successors?

Had Bernie looked out one particular night in January he would have seen one. Joe Flaherty, a six-foot mustachioed string bean with wild eyes and a *heh heh heh* laugh, watching the show, transfixed. At twenty-seven, he had never seen improvisation before. Flaherty, an actor, had come to Second City via the Pittsburgh Playhouse drama school, brimming with the catalogue of high theater, Arthur Miller to Shakespeare. In search of work, Flaherty wrote just about every prospective employer he could think of. A lone reply from Second City's current director, Mike Miller, came back with an offer. "I don't need an actor," Miller wrote, "but do you know anything about lights?" With zero experience and no alternatives, Flaherty became Second City's new stage manager. But instead of giving him a tutorial, the exiting stage manager — whose appetite for acid made him slow on the light board — directed his successor to a table in the house and told him to "take a look" at the show, and he did. Improvisational comedy, Flaherty saw, was the nexus of you and world. You could speak and be heard. "[This is] a chance to use all the comedic information that you've stored up in your head," Flaherty observed, "all the satiric takes on things, viewpoints that you had, things that irritated, bugged you, you could bring them out, you could do it right onstage. You could make it happen."

Flaherty raced into Jo Forsberg's improvisational workshops. After-noons, Forsberg's class took to the empty theater for a steady diet of Viola's games, and absorbed the secrets of collaboration. "Just play the game," Fors-berg advised her students, bead-wearing longhairs uncommonly open to communal give-and-take. Jim Fisher, one of Flaherty's classmates, learned to survey the stage for signs of ready improvisers, and then "pass to the open man," he said. "If Flaherty was on a run, then you fed him, and if you were on a run, you got fed."

Though Harold Ramis was new to improvisation, by virtue of his day job as *Playboy*'s jokes editor he was the most experienced comic in Forsberg's class. They looked to his reaction for an instant evaluation of a joke. Was Harold laughing? Or just smiling? "I would say in the first month [at *Playboy*], I already knew 95 percent of the jokes in current circulation in America," he said. "I could not hear a joke I didn't know." But — contrary to Bernie Sahlins's emphasis on learning and sophistication — intelligence is mostly at odds with spontaneous flow. To improvise, Ramis had to get out of his head; he could not write; he could not whisper suggestions to the others. But Ramis had trouble switching off his critical instinct. Why weren't they doing *x*? Didn't they see the problem with *y*? And yet Ramis proffered his insight only when asked, and with a self-deprecatory smile, and they loved him for it. "Everybody fought to be in a scene with Harold," Flaherty said, coming to admire, beyond Harold's skill with a line, his generosity in first polishing and then handing them out. They were handy in a pinch.

Flaherty and Ramis froze during one improv.

"Why don't you do that joke?" Ramis whispered.

Flaherty immediately knew what he meant: the doctor's office. "What are you here for?" he asked.

"Well, because my penis is red."

"That's 'cause someone's talking about it."

Flaherty got the laugh.

Others would guard their gold, their ticket to attention. Harold Ramis was the company's Giver.

Flaherty, the purest, oldest, most experienced of the group, became its Older Brother, responsible for elevating the level of play both on and off the stage — "adjusting egos," he said, to hold the scene, not its players, in the foreground and perpetuate a spirit of chaos that complemented Ramis's inclination to control. Where another improviser — a Mike Nichols, for instance — might favor his audience, Flaherty played to the other improvisers, provoking them, personally, with funny choices intended to flip them backward into the unknown. He might grab an invisible book off the shelf, toss it to Harold or Jim, and say, "I can't read this. It's in Latin." From out of left field came Flaherty's reminders that real life is not made of setups and payoffs, but accidents any improviser must arrange into a coherent pattern. "I guess I'm pretty much a structuralist," he conceded.

As a team, Flaherty's gang were promoted from Forsberg's class and her Children's Theater to the Second City touring company, playing engagements around and out of town that consisted mostly of classic Second City scenes like "Football Comes to the University of Chicago" and "Amateur Hour," and whenever they could, improvising in public, like at the Earl of Old Town, a saloon across from the theater, taking suggestions, adding improvised dialogue tracks to old industrial films, and developing a sensibility of their own. Jim Fisher — their stage manager and director and a part of the ensemble — filmed the improvisations for future study; until then, improvisations were recorded on audio only. Now they could actually *see* what they were doing. After a show at the Earl of Old Town, they would regroup at Fisher's apartment for a look and learn. What were their tricks, their bad habits? How could they break them? "We worked so well together as a group," Fisher said. No wonder they developed full company scenes so easily; they all wanted to improvise together. "Everybody would just fill in the background of a scene," he added. "It got to the point where all we had was group scenes." A look at the footage, and they understood the different responsibilities of a background versus a foreground improviser, and learned what choices paid off with their fans — drug-related and explicitly political material, and robust physicality. Beyond merely topical, "we were radical," Ramis said. "Our company was born out of the Chicago convention." Monday nights at the Earl of Old Town were selling out — to a college crowd distantly aware that what Abbie Hoffman brought to Lincoln Park, they were bringing to comedy.

From across the street, Bernie Sahlins took note. No, this was not his long-defended brand of intellectual satire plus exceptional acting, but unlike his current mainstage company — riddled with infighting, shtick, and culturally disconnected from its (aging) audience — the Old Town improvisers showed a refreshing optimism. It was in the way they felt about each other. "The previous bunch was always nipping at each other onstage," Fisher said. "They had no background in improvisation. We had a very different 'Yes, and' way of working." Never before had an unprofessional ensemble been so thoroughly trained and, inhaling the same political fumes, so thoroughly united by principle. Wiping his stage clean — Second City had never done this before—Bernie graciously escorted his current company to New York, installed them in an off-Broadway theater, and moved the Earl of Old Town punks back home. He called them the Next Generation. The youngest cast ever.

Alan Arkin was directing the 1969 revival of Jules Feiffer's lunatic postassassination satire *Little Murders,* which had had a short, unsuccessful Broadway run two years earlier, off-Broadway at the Circle in the Square. It was Feiffer's first full-length play; his first work for the stage, *The Explainers,* was a revue Paul Sills had commissioned in 1961 to inaugurate Second City's legit (and short-lived) theater, Playwrights at Second City, in a space adjacent to the mainstage. "In Jules's cartoons," Sheldon Patinkin said, "Paul saw the makings of a playwright with Second City values. We all thought he was one of us." *The Explainers* featured Del Close, Barbara Harris, and Paul Sand, and much like the Broadway run of *Little Murders,* didn't work.

"This is a great show," Arkin assured the cast of the new, off-Broadway *Little Murders,* "fuck the critics," but he was nevertheless struggling, in rehearsal, to get them through the first scene of Feiffer's play, which begins as Patsy Newquist (played by Compass Player Linda Lavin) brings her boyfriend, Alfred (Second City's Fred Willard), home to meet her parents. The Newquists go to ludicrous extremes trying to ingratiate themselves to Alfred, a depressive, whose persistent catatonia, rather than deter the family, elevates their gooey all-American kindness to a painful fever pitch. Where *Murders's* Broadway director smoothed the comedy's semiabsurdist mishmash of styles and tones—almost like a full evening at Second City—Arkin, in rehearsal, had his actors improvise their way to a deeper emotional understanding, a "paraphrase," he called it, in which Fred Willard, improvising as President Johnson, appeared as the Newquists' dinner guest. After five exhausting minutes of desperately trying, and failing, to entertain LBJ, the ensemble achieved the desired effect—hysteria. "They got the paraphrase completely," Arkin recalled, "and through the many months that they performed the play they never lost it." The rehearsal improv went out, but the manic intensity remained.

Arkin's handpicked company of trained improvisers built themselves, by virtue of their training, into a functioning stage family, "a real ensemble up there on stage," Feiffer said. "On Broadway, there was never a real family up there, even though the production was far more realistic, far less stylized. There was a lot of *talk* about having a family, but it never happened. This time, when I did look in at a rehearsal, I was amazed to see how much Alan had immediately solved by creating the feeling of a real family." And this time, under Arkin, the critics got *Little Murders*. Arkin had simultaneously tightened and loosened the production, and the play's harsh view of the new despair, in the years since its premiere, had expanded from prophetic to proven. The darkest, funniest, most clinically percipient comedy of mid-century America, *Little Murders* pulled all the cadavers from the morgue for a two-hour autopsy of the national character, born and killed in violence. Fired by improvisation and the erratic Second City–style gearshifts of cabaret comedy, the play fulfilled Paul Sills's expectation of Feiffer's dramatic abilities, and heralded Feiffer as the theater's leading satirist. "If you have ever experienced the unpleasant feeling that someone was watching you," wrote Clive Barnes in the *New York Times*, "I must tell you someone is. It is Feiffer."

Somewhere into the run, the cast changed, replacement auditions were held, and New York University graduate student Christopher Guest, while finishing his degree, won a part in the production. Guest's comedy, even then, showed the delicate, almost invisibly ironic sangfroid of Peter Sellers, a tightrope walker's control of any flamboyant personality, but it was Guest's meeting with Fred Willard, sui generis in any context, that marked his first flash of professional improvisation. Guest had improvised in college, forming "what we thought was an improv group" with Tom Leopold and fellow NYU classmate Jeannie Berlin, daughter of Elaine May ("We went up to see her, Elaine May," Guest said, "and did something in front of her that we thought was funny. So we did something — and I don't remember what it was — and she looked at us like this [blankly] and I don't know if there was any comment at all . . . and then we left"), and there was the everyday inventing he did automatically, riding the bus with his roommate, actor Michael McKean, doing characters, fooling around.

During that run of *Little Murders*, Guest, for the first time, was flipped head over heels into the improvisational deep, in front of a paying audience. "I knew something was off," Guest said, "when Fred [Willard] actually started doing lines that weren't in the play. To me." Guest was sitting onstage, following the script, during a performance, when "I heard these words that weren't familiar and I looked over and there was Fred of course . . . And I didn't really know what to make of it other than I just looked to him and nodded, and I said to myself, *You're different."*

"If I'm in the room and there's no one funnier than me," Harold Ramis would say, "I figure it's my job to lighten it up." He came by comedy and social consciousness — the humanitarian impulse channeled through laughter — as a boy in his mother's kitchen, playing whack-a-mole with her depression, using stolen jokes for a mallet, acting, absurdly, the role of grown-up to his own parent. "We tell kids that the world is a safe place," Ramis said, "that our leaders know what they're doing, that policemen are good, that your priest would never molest you. We know that the world is terrifying but we don't want them to be terrified, so we give them a false picture, which, as the kid gets older — it works when they're little — but when they get old enough to see what's really going on this cognitive dissonance develops." It's a sense of humor.

Even as a kid he had rescuer's dreams. TV and movies gave myths to the Robin Hood in him, burgeoning and converging Ramis's great goodwill and his political awareness. He had to "stand up for the little guy and save the village, save the woman, save the nation, whatever. It was always about saving somebody." At five, absorbing the newsreels, he decided he would be a fighter pilot, an American hero. At ten, watching civil rights disturbances on television, his mission grew more complicated. "Suddenly," he said, "television started introducing this nightmare into my life, and I began to see our culture for what it was, not all bad, certainly, but clearly not what was portrayed in the movies I had grown up on." As a teenager, he learned to play guitar, wore blue denim, and sang protest songs. He lived in middle-class Chicago but identified with the migrant farmworkers — and Groucho Marx. Ramis's father, a grocer, led him to *A Night at the Opera* and *Duck Soup,* which became "a great lesson in comedy and an actual political point of view," the triumph of the common lunatic over the pretensions and sterility of the ruling elite.

What does it mean to be crazy? The question interested him. To live outside the system, was that crazy? How different were the manic-depressives, the compulsives, the paranoids, the rebels, from the so-called sane? Or was it living within the system — you know, America, 1969 — that made you crazy? "I could see elements of it all in myself," Ramis concluded. "To some extent, it showed me how my own feelings and experiences were on a continuum with what it is to be alive."

After college, he took a job in a psych ward. At some point, most of us would have flipped out, probably, working the locked unit of the Jewish Hospital in St. Louis, where psychotics painted the walls in their own shit, and one patient, a June Cleaver type, told of spreading out on the lawn and masturbating in front of her family, but Ramis, a twenty-one-year-old English major just out of college (he had no medical training) was fine — better than fine, he was happy. Wherever he went, he showed a Buddha's talent for patience and empathetic flow. In a hurricane, Ramis could make himself comfortable; as the plane fell from the sky, he would set down his crossword puzzle, help himself to the oxygen mask, then turn to you and, in his Kermit the Frog voice, say, "This is going to be hard, but if you're open to it, it could also be really interesting. My name's Harold, by the way. How long will you be in Chicago?" Acceptance gave him serenity, the look of inner peace.

In coming to Second City, Harold Ramis had no plan, no urgent purpose. He liked to get high more than he liked to work. At $137.50 a week, Second City was a convenient way to conscientiously object — to "real" work, long hours, and, well, conscientious objection. (Flaherty said Ramis made Bob Dylan look like a GI.) So it was by default that Ramis became Second City's revolutionary-in-residence. Flaherty, grumbling or snickering, was born to play the Dad in the armchair; Brian Murray, the Neighborhood Bigmouth, you would find pouring himself another beer at the end of the bar; cute Judy Morgan was definitely the Girl; Jim Fisher, the Boy; Roberta Maguire, the Mom; and tough David Blum ideal for the Cop, or any variation thereof. That left the Hippie to Harold Ramis. Between his shaggy Jewfro, John Lennon glasses, and aw-shucks chuckle, he conveyed the sort of endearing antiestablishment good boy far too Mickey Rooney for the Committee, but perfect for Second City.

Accordingly, it was Ramis who opened *The Next Generation*, Second City's thirty-seventh revue, in October 1969 — and with a blackout, the most efficient way to deliver a message. As the lights went down, the piano played on the full company, shouting together in generic protest ("Rah! Rah!" "Power to the people!"). Harold pushed his way through and took the floor. "Brothers! Sisters! The fact that we are standing in the White House represents the people's triumph over the repressive forces of the imperialist power!" (Shouts of agreement.) "The streets now belong to the people!" Hooray! The people! "We must face the monumental task ahead!" Yeah! Yay! "The people's streets need to be *cleaned!*" Confused silence. Blackout.

"We bombed," Harold said. "It was terrible."

The conviction the Next Generation summoned for the alternative audiences of the Earl of Old Town seemed forced in their mainstage debut. Critics dismissed them. Certain nights, improvisers outnumbered their audiences two to one. Maybe it was the snow piling up outside the theater. Or the snark piling up inside: you could feel a little of that in the detached air of *We're only kidding here, folks;* it undercut the seriousness of the material. And there was a better show in town: the sustained, months-long improvisational innovations of the Chicago Seven. Their trial for conspiracy to cross state lines and incite a riot at the 1968 Democratic National Convention was drawing standing-room-only crowds to Judge Julius Hoffman's kangaroo courtroom. There, the "totally authoritarian, dictatorially oppressive atmosphere of wrongful persecution," to quote audience member Jules Feiffer, present on assignment for the *New York Review of Books,* played so absurd that Judge Hoffman's unabating perversions of First Amendment rights, which climaxed in the gagging of Black Panther Bobby Seale, provoked both cries of pain and sobs of laughter from the defendants, one of whom, Abbie Hoffman, had been known to spend his nights with Second City's Roberta Maguire.

The Next Generation set out to emulate the show playing out in real life and regain its authenticity. From the audience, they selected a jury and brought them onstage. "Ladies and gentlemen," began their introduction, "we take you now to Judge Julius Hoffman's courtroom. Please rise for the Honorable Judge . . ." Lights up. Sitting there, on the bench, in a choir robe snatched from wardrobe, was . . . Abbie Hoffman? At first the audience did not react. Abbie Hoffman and Harold Ramis had the same hair, so it was likely . . . *probable* . . . Out came the defendants, the seven members of the Next Generation, including Harold Ramis, to play the Chicago Seven. From there, Abbie Hoffman — it *was* him — presided over an improvised conspiracy trial, opening statements, cross-examinations, objections — the works. "Abbie," Fisher recalled, "was so into it, acting like a real asshole to get back at Judge [Julius] Hoffman." As insane as Abbie got (he brought a noose onstage and wasn't afraid to use it) their improvisation, being a counterpoint to judicial despotism, was closer to justice than the stuff Hoffman

and his guerilla ensemble were getting by daylight. The good feeling generated by the show amazed Ramis. The whole theater, 350 strong, converged
by means of a shared intensity of focus as liberation swallowed anger, and
for as long as Abbie Hoffman could — the Illinois Bureau of Investigation,
expecting trouble, was trailing him — he vindicated the house in buffoon-
ery. When someone out there heard the bad guys were on their way, the
Next Generation would smuggle their guest offstage, down the stairs, and
out the back door. The nights he got through the entire trial, to a verdict,
Judge Hoffman pronounced the Next Generation guilty, every time.

That spark charged through their next show, *Justice Is Done; or, Oh Cal
Coolidge,* which opened in March 1970, only weeks after the actual guilty
verdict, to the reviews they had been hoping for. Much of their material was
trial-related, but their attitude wasn't. "They are not as astringent as of yore,"
went the *Tribune.* "They're somewhat naive. In fact, they're almost charming. And, in a corny way, perhaps they're more fun." With July's *Cooler Near
the Lake,* which the *Tribune* ranked with the finest Second City revues ever,
the ensemble parlayed the fun into freedom.

In "PTA," a ten-minute sketch in which concerned parents and one har-
ried moderator discuss sex ed, Ramis rises out of the audience and, in an
uncharacteristically gruff voice, introduces himself. "I'm not speaking to
you tonight in my professional capacity as a teamster" — big, surprised
laugh — "only speaking as a concerned parent of the community. Now it
seems to me to introduce sex education into the schools is going to encour-
age, uh, a certain amount of *doin'* it among the kids. I got a young daughter.
She's sixteen years old. A lovely girl. She's a beautiful girl" — here a deep
breath — "and I cannot stand the thought of some young punk spreading
her creamy white thighs and violating her flowery pubescence. I'm *tortured*
by that vision night and day . . ." In the tradition of the best satirical acting, Ramis works his character into a disturbed frenzy as credible as it is
absurd, climaxing in an anguished hailstorm of pleas to save his daughter and himself, embarrassing everyone. Other impassioned parents jump
in, and the temperature rises. "I blame the parents," asserts the moderator, "certainly those children weren't *born* ignorant." Only gradually does
this well-intended discussion about the welfare of children devolve into a
sexual free-for-all fired by the parents' libidos. One mother confesses to
loving sex and hating her children, asking aloud "if Mr. Levin" — "*Levine!*"
— "Levine, has a way for me to have fun without having babies, then I'm

for Mr. *Levine.*" Flaherty as Levine: "Call me Russ" — blackout. A crack at town hall culture rich in suburban personality, full of polemical feeling but stripped of dogma, and a rather informed debate to boot, "PTA" is one of the Next Generation's finest ensemble pieces, their first of several permanent contributions to the Second City repertoire. Shows were selling out.

And yet, despite his development as an improviser, Harold Ramis could sooner see himself as a full-time tumbleweed than a professional funny person. "I loved writing and performing," he said, "but the idea of doing it for a living seemed so remote" — especially when the lodestars of his generation, rock musicians, conveyed limited, if any, satirical inclination. The children of Altamont did not share their parents' taste for dialogue and criticism. As the events of the Chicago convention had borne out, debate had failed them. Now, protest was lived. Instead of satirize, hippies dropped out. Instead of engage, they disengaged. You can see their point. What said *Fuck this* better than orgies, acid, Charles Manson, and a Hells Angel in a knife fight? Not the Smothers Brothers, not *Laugh-In,* and, despite their popularity, very little at Second City. There was more challenging, more pressing improvisation happening *out there* in real life, on the streets. In the fall of 1970, Ramis and his wife, Anne, took off for Europe.

"Why are you leaving, Harold?" Flaherty asked.

"Eh," he shrugged. "I ran out of jokes."

Well before the lights came up on the sneak-preview screening of *MASH,* which Mike Nichols and his producer, John Calley, had basically loved, Nichols knew they were fucked. Their carefully tweezered, labored-over production of *Catch-22,* only months away from its release, was many things — good, bad, funny, unfunny — yet, they conceded in that screening room, it stumbled far from the spirit of sustained, coherent anarchy Robert Altman spun out of his script and actors, many drawn from Second City and the Committee. He let them loose. "I almost passed out when I saw the movie," Nichols said, "because it was the first time Altman went nuts and improvised the hell out of the whole thing. It was brilliant and alive and it put us to shame. Certainly everybody else thought so and I secretly did, too. In terms of improvised comedy." Too holy a novel to play with and too intricate a script, by Buck Henry, to disobey, *Catch-22* would have disintegrated under Altman. But it froze under Nichols. Next to *MASH,* it looked old. In his satire, Altman captures the ant colony of self-absorbed

American strivers obsessed with their busy little projects, disconnected in pairs, but in the wide shot, seen as a social whole, the bugs add up to a little world of their own, a freak culture as good and dumb as any other. Indeed, the act of watching a film like *MASH* becomes an improvisational venture for the viewer. Where to look? What to hear? Altman's epic wide shots and multilayered audio tracks leave it up to you. "Everything that *Catch* couldn't have," Nichols said, "the freedom and the wildness and the half-assed improvised quality, made us seem even more stately."

What was happening? Had Robert Altman become the filmmaker Mike Nichols should have been? Nichols himself wondered.

Finishing *Catch-22* in Los Angeles, Buck Henry knew Nichols was grasping. Their film was "not about human behavior," he admitted. "That's one of the things that drove Mike crazy. He had no behavior to work with, just attitudes." Hence Nichols's relief when, midway into cutting the picture, he received a new play by Jules Feiffer, then called *True Confessions,* a darkly feminist and chauvinist work delivered to Nichols smack in the upswing of the women's movement, "about the fact that heterosexual men don't like women," Feiffer said. *Confessions* "startled me," Nichols said, "because it really was like an extended Nichols and May sketch in a lot of ways." Reading the play, Nichols kept thinking, to his shame and disgust, *Yes, this is true, this is true,* and passed the manuscript to Henry for a second opinion.

"Well, you've got to do this," was Henry's take.

"Yes, I think so."

The next day, Feiffer's phone rang.

"I want to do it," Nichols said. "But I don't think it's a play. It's a movie." *True Confessions* became *Carnal Knowledge.*

You could imagine why Paul Sills was distrustful of money — and Mike Nichols — and why, swayed by an alloy of survivor's guilt and admiration, and longing in his own right for the freedom and familiarity of a repertory company, Mike Nichols urged his pal Sills to come to New York and make a theater, again, with him and Elaine. Think of the old days, he said, and don't worry about the money; the names "Mike and Elaine" guaranteed the attention of all of New York, and if, ultimately, they wanted to return to independence, Nichols pledged to buy them away from their investors. "But Paul didn't think theater could happen in New York," said Carol Sills. "His experience was Chicago first, then New York." Sills spoke of his allegiance to Chicago, but Nichols heard the self-destructive — at best, regenerative — impulse Sills conflated with creativity. The commercial strictures of Broadway equaled paralysis; an improviser, Sills required transformation to live. Nichols saw Sills's point, somewhat, so he wrote Sills a check and wished him only the very best. With the money, Sills moved Story Theater into the Body Politic, an arts complex on Lincoln Avenue two blocks from the new Second City Theater, where, in October 1969, with Ovid's *Metamorphoses* added to his repertoire, Sills resumed his lasting excavation of human goodness.

He invited Del Close — rotting on the vine at the University of Texas at Austin, where, after shedding the Committee, he had attempted to form a theater company — to return to Chicago and join Story Theater. In the decade since their last collaboration, at Second City, much had changed for Del and Sills, but they still shared, and always would, a lust for experimentation. "So I took a leave of absence from guerrilla theater," Del said, "I was suffering from a broken shoulder anyway . . . broke it in a trust exercise." ("I knew the sixties were coming to an end when they dropped me," Del added.)

Joe Flaherty came by the Body Politic to check out Del Close at work. What he had heard of the master comedian bore no semblance to the Story Theater improviser before him, "jumping around like a chicken," Flaherty said. "I remember thinking, *Is this satisfying to him? Is it fulfilling?* I thought it was a waste of talent but I never said anything because it was Sills and Sills was a god." Word got back to Second City that Del, the genius manqué, had returned to Chicago, and, with Bernie Sahlins conveniently out of town, the improv comedians pulled him, after hours, into workshops, where he introduced students to advanced techniques, theories of mind expansion, Compass lore ("What a ball buster Elaine was," he'd growl wistfully), and whatever he was then calling the Harold. When Sahlins returned, he discovered in Close, in his popular workshops, a bridge between generations, and asked him to return to Second City. To direct.

The whole Hollywood equation runs counter to improvisation. If, say, the screenwriter hadn't decided on the exact details of his or her story, the studio, or any other entity responsible for financing and producing a film from the screenplay, would be unable to set a budget, sign a cast, secure locations — stay with me here — schedule the shoot, keep a crew, conceptualize a marketing and release strategy, or actually *shoot* the picture. How then could anyone responsible for any of the above do their job? Be accountable? Justify their professional existence? With many millions of dollars at stake, the reply "I don't know" is unthinkable; it hemorrhages liability. In the realm of independent filmmaking, however, where so many variables cannot be anticipated, "I don't know" or "Let's see what happens" are pronounced with courageous luster; they are a maverick's mottos, and in the case of their first king, John Cassavetes, said by men with modest crews and budgets.

But Elaine May was in Hollywood — where there are millions of dollars and thousands of personalities on the line, and the improviser's attachment to the undecided, so crucial to their success onstage, is widely taken for callousness, indulgence, ego, pathological ignorance, sadism, masochism, sadomasochism, and/or madness — and she was not a man. In 1968.

"I never wanted to be a director," she said. But she had written a script, *A New Leaf,* and Paramount wouldn't give her director approval, but they would, however oddly, buy the script and allow Elaine to direct, and star, for a relatively modest fifty thousand dollars — a good deal for them. "I pitched very hard," her manager, Hilly Elkins said, "on the fact that having a woman director would be of consequence." She had slipped into the contract a clause that would award her an additional two hundred thousand if she, a first-time filmmaker, were fired from the project. Which is about when producer Howard Koch got nervous. Why was she already digging her tunnel to safety? On their dime?

"Listen," Koch said to his boss, Gulf & Western chairman Charles Bluhdorn, "I don't know if I can handle her."

"Sure you can."

Happily, Paramount agreed to Elaine's terms. The price was good and so was the publicity: no one could remember the last time a woman wrote, directed, and starred in a studio film. And a woman, it was understood, would be easy to control.

When the script arrived at Walter Matthau's apartment, he thought, *Why not?*

After the first shot the very first day of filming *A New Leaf,* Elaine May called "Cut!" for the first time.

Producer Howard Koch rejoiced. *Yes,* he thought, *she is wonderful, a natural.* The scene had gone beautifully. They would be moving on.

"No," she said to Koch, "I want to do it again."

He didn't understand.

It was best, she'd decided, not to say too much too soon. Wait to see if the actor will get there himself. No director wants to say, "Do this," and no actor wants to hear it. Best to wait. So: "Do it again."

And then again.

Wow, Koch thought. *What the hell?*

A brave someone led May from the camera and warned, "You make the crew nervous."

She didn't want to scare them. In fact, she wanted them to like her, and for a time, she got them to. But, of course, docile Elaine May was not the only Elaine May. She was a shape-shifter, an improviser. "And when they found this out," she realized, "they hated me all the more. And I think that's what really happens." Being a woman, "they think [you] want to show that [you're] a nice person . . . And in the end, when it comes down to it, you're just as rotten as any guy. You'll fight just as hard to get your way. So I think the real trick for women is they should start out tough . . . In that way I think I did have trouble. But only because I seemed so pleasant."

"The first day," Koch recalled, "we did the scene five times. We thought, Tomorrow, we'll start again, but it went on and on and on."

Some thought she was lost. Others knew not knowing was May's way to the best laugh. It had to be discovered alive, like everything else. "Elaine does [all those takes] because she's looking for something other than that which is presented," said costume designer Anthea Sylbert. "She's not very fond of having an actor doing the scene exactly the same over and over again. I've seen her fire an actor because each of these takes was exactly the same as the one before."

Walter Matthau had countless opportunities to observe this person, Elaine May. He would see her out in front of the camera, guardedly looking about as if that very day was her first on a movie set, or earth. He dubbed her, lovingly, Mrs. Hitler. Sometimes as many as twenty takes wore him out — to fantastic results. "She's basically improvisational," Hilly Elkins assured the press, "but a genius, and she's *not* unconcerned about the economics." Maybe, but *A New Leaf* went forty days over — double the intended schedule and budget. Koch begged Paramount to remove May from the picture, but they didn't. They wouldn't. Per May's foresight, firing her would cost them two hundred grand.

After a year abroad, writing through Europe, Harold Ramis returned to Second City early in 1972, bounded into an improvisation, made straight for his power spot upstage, and stopped. A puff-haired two-legged brick, looking like an electrocuted plumber from a third world country, was already, and quite comfortably, there. So this was his replacement, the little Albanian Flaherty had written him about. Impressive. After only a couple of months, the brick had already found the power spot. Harold took an obliging step to the side and, along with the audience, waited to see what his replacement would do with his power. Incredibly, he did nothing. That also was impressive. Most beginners, afraid of the silence, would rush to fill it, firing blindly until they hit. The Albanian — summoning a poise such a runty-looking guy should not have had — sat in silence like it was his throne. Doing nothing, he seemed complete. And the audience, Ramis sensed, sensed it, too. And sensing them back, the Albanian turned his head slowly, unnaturally slowly, and wiggled his eyebrows at them. They flew out of their seats.

John Belushi.

Ramis said, "He made us all look good."

Not since Elaine May had an improviser so quickly accrued so much myth and speculation. There was no explaining his power, but as with that of any prodigy, Belushi's was too strange a force to accept on faith. Faced with the mystery, his fans and friends — he accumulated them wherever he went — traded theories like baseball cards. They said John's parents, Adam and Agnes, were remote, frustrated, depressed, "too lost in their own dramas," according to John's brother Jim, to convey much more than their own needs, making them more like an older brother and sister than the mother and father of two children. "Look, Mom and Dad are irresponsible parents," John said to his younger brother one night. "Just eat and sleep here. Go out for football, for track, for wrestling. Go out for chess club. I don't care what you go out for, but for your own good just stay out of here." Too young, John became, in his mother's words, her little man. For his independence and industry, she rewarded him. "By the time he was four," Agnes beamed, "he'd just wander up the street, walk into a neighbor's house, sit down and strike up a conversation." He needed company. Whenever dinnertime got tense — Adam carried home his repeated failures in the restaurant business

—John would go for a laugh, turning his eyelids inside out or doing an impression, anything to bring his family back. Harold Ramis had been there. Well versed in clown psychology, he could personally vouch for the formative, painful absurdity of being parent to one's parent. "When I was a little boy," Ramis explained, "I acted like a man." If Second City was the Juilliard of comedy, depressed mothers were Exeter.

Born in Chicago's Humboldt Park, and growing up funny in suburban Wheaton, it was inevitable that John Belushi would make the pilgrimage, sooner or later, to Second City. It finally came in 1967 in the form of a graduation present from Dan Payne, his high school drama teacher. John brought his girlfriend, Judy. Until then, John had seen himself as a traditional theater actor. Neither knew anything about their native art form, improvisational comedy. But that night they learned. In the hourlong car ride from Wheaton to Wells Street, Payne told them the story of Paul Sills, Mike Nichols and Elaine May, the Compass Players, Alan Arkin, and Barbara Harris, and inside the theater, John and Judy enjoyed the next chapter—Steinberg, Willard, and Klein—for themselves. Leaving Second City a little dazed, somewhat blindsided by the sudden contact with his certain future, John turned to Judy. "This," he said. "This is what I want to do."

At the College of DuPage, some twenty miles west of Chicago, he and his pals Tino Insana and Steve Beshekas started messing around, creating bits, and improvising comedy at the Student Center. They called themselves the West Compass Players. And they played original Compass games, like the Nichols and May classic First Line/Last Line. The night John's ensemble got the Last Line, "She came in through the bathroom window," he came out with a perfect Joe Cocker, honed to second nature by long drives with Judy in his busted Volvo, windows down, stereo up, crying out with Cocker on the radio. "As much as John loved being an actor and a comedian," Judy said, "at heart his fantasy was to be a rock and roll star." This was no caricature. Belushi *was* Cocker, all emotion, a wrecking ball. It was scary, his volatility, the constant threat that, lost in flow, gone from consciousness, he might impale himself on a mic stand or another human being. They more than laughed: the completeness of his immersion was so convincing that his audiences felt, through him, a communion with mysteries.

Joyce Sloane, Bernie Sahlins's right hand, caught the West Compass Players at DuPage and arranged for them to audition for Second City, and Sahlins, railroaded by John's magnetism, rushed him directly into the main company. Here Bernie felt his world begin to change. Against his heart, he was in awe of Belushi's obvious ability; to Bernie, Belushi was every day a bride, perennially commanding, because he knew he always was. The kid was as bold as Elaine May, Joe Cocker to her Miles Davis, but even then, Bernie could guess Belushi's blue-collar persona, his penchant for rough types and physical comedy, would not convey Bernie's own long-guarded investment in satire, intellectual or otherwise. "Television and rock 'n' roll," Belushi said. "The two greatest influences on my life." But Second City was not a sitcom. It was a theater. At least it always had been. "From our beginnings," Sahlins wrote, "we had tiptoed the boundary line where the classical spirit ends and the realm of commercial, popular entertainment begins." With Belushi's audition, a right turn appeared on the horizon. Second City, Bernie saw, would be saved from obsolescence, but at a cost.

At twenty-two, John Belushi, the only improviser of his generation to skip over workshops and the touring company, became the youngest Second City performer in history.

The current company let him right in. As experts in the rules of agreement, they accepted Belushi as swiftly as an audience suggestion. John loved being part of a family, especially this fun and happy one, but initially his inexperience with the "Yes, ands" of improvisation and his increasing awareness of his own stardom, the wedding-day shine Bernie so admired, kept him outside the synergy. Give or take an improviser, the Next Generation had been playing together for years now: Flaherty, Ramis, Fisher, Morgan, Brian Murray, Eugenie Ross-Leming — they could all toss the ball, but John didn't yet know how to throw it back. He stole focus. The coarse jokes and attention-grabbing tricks that got him big laughs with the college crowd — like upstaging a scene in progress with a pantomimed heroin injection and overdose — pulled the rug out from under them. After one too many steals, it fell to Flaherty to teach the new guy improv's golden rule. When the time came, he took him aside for a private lesson, and to Flaherty's surprise, John humbled. "I'm just having so much fun," he apologized. "I just get carried away. I'm sorry." More than anything, he wanted to join them. "Flaherty," Belushi would say, "taught me subtlety" — John's word for cooperation.

Thematic subtlety was another thing entirely. Unencumbered by Second City's roots in intellectual material, Belushi trampled through good taste like a pig at a garden party. Farts, burps, crotch grabs — you name it. One such character, the World's Most Obnoxious Houseguest, aka the World's Most Obnoxious Date, would saunter out with a self-satisfied grin, and to his host or the girl's parents — anyone ripe for offense — declare, "Wow, you won't *believe* this. I just took a shit a *foot* long!" John used his hands like a fisherman describing his catch. "I'm not kidding," he'd persist, awed at his own creation, "this thing really was a full foot. You ever seen that? And not in pieces! You know how hard that is to evacuate?" Cheap, you say? Easy? Do not mistake the content for the form. In Belushi's hands, the lowbrow laugh, elevated by his unqualified commitment to character and endless improvised elaborations, rose to something like shock art. "He made a fugue of the foot-long shit," said Ross-Leming. "If people didn't run for their lives, they died laughing." How Bernie squirmed! "We respected the rule that you say 'shit' maybe only once in a show," Jim Fisher said. He was backstage when he heard John, once again Mr. Obnoxious, tell another improviser to "eat a bowl of fuck." No one had any idea what he meant. But they laughed anyway.

Belushi's image alone gave him carte blanche. It was his flat nose. Those stump legs under his barrel torso. "John *looked* funny," explained Flaherty. "They laughed before he opened his mouth." And inside he burned. Making a six-course meal of his containment, slowly turning the crank of his own jack-in-the-box, he became a time bomb. They laughed at that too — the anticipation. Incredibly, he could set *himself* up. When they said Belushi was funny doing "nothing," this is what they meant; how, drawing out those silences, he tickled the air around him. This — despite the coarseness of his material — was all nuance and self-control. Flaherty called it Brando meets Lou Costello, inner heat and slapstick working as one. John would ram his body into walls if he had to, and when he did, he ran at them full force.

So Harold Ramis had to step back. Once the Crazy Hippie, he put up a white flag, ceded wacko duty to Belushi, and took up the role of Nerdy Sidekick, Kissinger, he said, to Belushi's Nixon. Thinking, getting stuck in his head, had always been Ramis's improvisational Achilles' heel. He could never fully observe the scene and experience it at the same time. But in his new incarnation as the smart guy, thinking became an essential part of Ramis's persona. From the class clown to the class clown's writer, he learned patience and relaxation. Where Ramis once twisted a scene, or an idea, to suit his incubating joke, he now watched and waited. Sharing the stage with Belushi, he had to. To Jim Fisher's astonishment, Ramis's jokes — seemingly prepared—"always fit. That was the rare talent. It didn't feel like when you were working with him, uh-oh, here comes a joke. Harold wasn't lying in wait for his setup; the setup would appear and the joke would well up in him." Others sweated out their jokes; Ramis merely shrugged and opened his mouth. His mastery was the company puppy dog they all wanted to play with.

During one rehearsal, Flaherty asked Ramis to do Rabbi Dithers, a favorite character. Typical of Flaherty, he decided to break an unwritten rule and, putting Ramis on the spot and in his head, interrogate his scene partner's character. The setting: deli.

"Are you Jewish?" Flaherty asked.

"Yes, yes, I am."

"What *is* Judaism exactly? Is it a religion?"

"Well," the rabbi considered, "it's more than that."

"Is it a way of life?"

"Well . . . it's less than that."

"What is it?"

Beat. "It's a way of eating."

Flaherty got such a kick out of Dithers, he convinced Harold to do the character, questions and all, in the improv set after the show. The audience loved it, and for several nights of sets, Ramis complied.

"You all set, Harold?" Flaherty asked before his entrance one night.

Standing in the wings, Ramis moaned a little, like Benjamin in *The Graduate*. That's when Flaherty realized, "The whole thing consisted of us just asking Harold to be brilliant! Say something brilliant! Say something brilliant!" But that was Ramis: they asked and, like a rabbi, he answered. He gave. Gaining strength, he found a home upstage, another power spot behind the other improvisers at the end of the audience's roaming eye line, where he could plant himself, glove ready, a catcher at the plate. Later, looking back, he would remember the psych ward as his first rehearsal, proof against luck that he really could keep his head—open an imaginary office, and think—while the crazies ran screaming around him. By their individual differences, balanced in antithetical accord like the counterarguments of a great debate, they matured into a protean marketplace of ideas, the perfect comedy democracy. In purely functional terms, variation encouraged cooperation—no one tried to be as silly as Joe Flaherty, for instance, because no one could be. As with Second City's first company, their diversity was an apt cross-section of types, a young mirror to the world outside. Sahlins had always peopled his teams with current sociology in mind, but here, with a group of "normal," everyday people, in some cases brought into Second City with a shrug and a *Why not?* (as opposed to the rarefied subsets of U of C or the William Morris office), the early 1970s set came closer than any ensemble to proving Viola Spolin's claim that anyone can improvise, to affirming Shepherd and Sills's efforts to create a nonexclusive community theater of the American Now. These improvisers were in some cases literally brought in off the streets. Look around; they were their audience as never before. Chicago — indeed, the changing world — was growing with angry young Belushis, wavering Ramises, working-woman Ross-Lemings, blue-collar Brian Murrays . . . Art? They just wanted to have fun.

9

1972

Anticipating contention with Elaine May, director of *The Heartbreak Kid,*
Neil Simon preemptively guarded his script, adapted from a short story by
Bruce Jay Friedman, against the likelihood of involuntary coauthorship.
He'd put a provision in his contract stipulating that she could change none
of the dialogue without his prior approval. If they agreed to a particular
modification, Simon asked that May shoot the scene in question both
ways, once his way and once hers. It is not customary in Hollywood for
the screenwriter to be setting terms for the production, to, in effect, direct
the director, but Neil Simon, the most successful playwright in Broadway
history — thanks in part to his collaborations with Mike Nichols — had the
clout to insist, and Elaine May wisely kept her mouth shut. She was still
on movie probation from the overages of *A New Leaf,* which she'd held
in editing for nearly ten months until Paramount's Bob Evans, anxious
for a finished picture, pried the film from her hands and recut it his way,
changing the story, thereby violating her contractual right (she argued) to
script approval, and incurring a lawsuit May filed against the studio and lost.
Her sights set on *Mikey and Nicky,* May had to first play nice on *Heartbreak,*
or at least pretend to. At least at first.

In rehearsals, which Simon attended, May asked her leads — Charles
Grodin and Jeannie Berlin, Elaine's daughter (who addressed the director as
"Miss Mother") — to sing songs their characters might sing together, happily newlywed, in the car ride down to their honeymoon hotel (where Grodin's character will fall, forgivably and unforgivably, for Cybill Shepherd's).

At this, Simon called halt. "Where does it say they sing?" (Ultimately, the songs appeared in the film.) Shepherd noted that rather than use the term "improvise" in rehearsals, May "spoke about the exploration of subtext, the meaning beneath the lines," which she allowed the actors to discover, first by rehearsing the scene as written, then throwing out the dialogue and playing the situation again with their own words.

Simon, meanwhile, was catching on. By the time the production began filming in Miami, May had her actors improvising in front of rolling cameras with and without Simon's approval. (Grodin was confused. "Didn't they have a conversation before they started, to let Neil Simon know Elaine May's intentions?" he said. "I found that odd.") In one scene, Grodin had to leap from a yacht onto a moving dock. To keep him improvising, May, take after take, kept increasing the distance between the two. Shooting on the yacht, she had those playing the yacht's owners call for a waiter, but secretly directed the waiter not to respond; then, on the retake, she instructed not one but four waiters to appear and turn their backs to the yachtsmen, capturing the improvised frustration of all. "She would hide [Grodin's] key prop on the set and his task would be *in the take* to find it," Nichols recalled. "She actually did do those things. And the fucking operator would have to find him." That operator, Enrique Bravo, had been well trained for this approach. He had cut his teeth in documentary before turning to features, shooting, before *Heartbreak,* loads of improvised material for director William Friedkin on *The French Connection,* a filmmaking style Friedkin designated "induced documentary."

In frustration, Simon took off for Barbados. "He wasn't around very much," Grodin remembered. "So there's a lot of improvisation in that movie." Elaine seized on her new freedom, and in time, producer Michael Hausman said, "that phone call [to ask Simon for approval] never got made," adding, "There was no yesterday and tomorrow for Elaine, it was all happening now, in the moment." So intense was her focus, abetted by the equally intense focus of her improvisers, and handfuls of NoDoz, that May, shooting in the freezing snow of Minnesota, didn't know her toes were frostbitten until Cybill Shepherd pointed out to her that she was limping. Improvisational opportunities proliferated — Grodin and Berlin in their hotel room bed (she's chomping on a candy bar, cooing, "We're going to be married forever . . ."); a conversation with Grodin, Shepherd, and her character's college boyfriend outside the University of Minnesota (where

Jeannie led improv workshops during the off-hours); scenes with Cybill Shepherd and her parents, played by Eddie Albert and Audra Lindley; and the ending of the film, Grodin's melancholy encounter with a carefree, innocent boy. These and others were largely or partially improvised. But like the best works of Samuel Beckett, *The Heartbreak Kid* was only funny in disguise. In Elaine May's hands, the security of genre conventions — the clichés taken for truth — are themselves a kind of betrayal she systematically disassembles until she finally arrives at bottommost reality where, surprise, there is nothing funny left.

"When I was little, and alone," said Brian Murray's kid brother Bill, "I used to sing songs to God."

There are two worlds. Even as a boy, he knew that. In one, you have to wake up early and go to school. You must do your homework. You must do what they tell you to do. It doesn't matter who you are or what you want; you have to follow the rules. In the other, you can be a cloud.

Boy Scouts and Little League kicked him out. In Catholic grade school — of course, he didn't tell the nuns he wrote poetry — Billy got bad marks and spoke out of turn. "It seemed as though everything we did broke one rule or another," Murray said. "So I figured I might as well be funny doing it. I thought if the person laughed, I might not get in trouble." Getting laughs was the unintended though pleasant result of standing up for himself, saying no. "Rather than the class clown," he said, "I was the kid who didn't buy the program." Grown-ups had ways of handling punk kids, but they couldn't figure out how, time and again, Murray could take the consequences without flinching, like it was part of the plan. Incredibly, he had courage — they never anticipated that in one so young. "I got plenty of punishment at home," he said, "and I got in enough fights with my brothers. So I wasn't afraid of anything or anybody . . ." The nuns of St. Joseph's called in his parents, Ed, a lumber salesman, and Lucille. They had six boys, three girls, never enough money, and in their middle son Bill, a mixed-up case of intelligence and idiocy, sensitivity and callousness — a problem the nuns could not solve.

He went to Loyola Academy, an all-boys Jesuit high school where they made fun of him for dressing in brightly paneled, ill-fitting golf shirts, not knowing, and in some cases knowing, that these clothes, passed down to Bill from his older brothers, were all he could afford. Wandering by the theater one afternoon, he heard music, peeked inside, and discovered all to himself a stage full of glittering dancing girls wearing next to nothing, auditioning for the school production of *The Music Man*. Murray, enchanted, took a seat out of view and watched them move. These were the fabled beings of Sacred Heart, the Rich Pretty Girls from downtown Chicago, as strange and exciting to a square-faced lumberman's son as a purple planet seen through a telescope.

"Now, who's going to audition to be a dancer?"

Billy jumped out of his seat. "I'm a dancer."

Later, when he told his friends he got the part — just by clowning around, he said — they furrowed their brows. A dancer?

"I'm a dancer now," he explained.

"What? *Why?*"

"I don't know. It's just an instinct."

Show business, he could see now, was the way to get in trouble without getting in trouble. Since rehearsal began at seven, Murray had the perfect excuse to leave home after dinner, "which was even better than leaving school," he said, and get next to these girls who turned out to be, like him, misfits, slightly nuts, and intellectually engaging in all kinds of surprising ways, and sipped gin they snuck into rehearsal in Coke bottles passed to Murray when their director left early. Flirting was the best kind of trouble-making, a way to let loose kindly, to play in the sandbox without doing damage. The opposition, those who told him to sit down and stay quiet, saw a goof-off and a jerk, but they were half-wrong; Murray had the courtly graces of a knight. Girls knew that. "We were inculcated with some sort of manners," he said, from his mother. "Her definition of a gentleman is someone who never makes anyone feel uncomfortable. I remember that sometimes. When I'm not making people uncomfortable."

Billy worked summers caddying at the Indian Hill Club in Winnetka, one of Chicago's tonier suburbs, studying the game he would come to love, and, at $3.50 a bag, absorbing the appalling class politics of country club culture. They weren't all snobs. Billy caddied for some very rich men who didn't appraise him by his father's income, treating him kindly and engaging him in meaningful conversation about golf and school, the hardships of growing up as he had. Others at Indian Hill barely deigned to look at him. In their company, Billy caddied for eighteen holes of hostile silence, speaking only when spoken to, then shutting up. In time, he layered his snap judgments, discerning at a distance the good from the mean, and adjusted his temperament, from warmth to ice-cold passive-aggression, accordingly, whatever the old power rules required. Over ten summers, he mastered them all. "It was an extraordinary chance to see how the world operates," he said. "You learn to spot bad apples real quick." As it had in school, private irony, the inside joke he had with himself, freed him from total subjugation. For every wrong glance loaded with insult, Billy cultivated the perfect country club antidote — a bullshit smile.

He went out West for college, dropped out after a year, came home to Chicago, and moved back in with his mother, a new widow after the death of Murray's father in 1969. In those days, both mother and son, both in need of the other, were unsure how to connect. "It was sort of a lonely thing," he said, "because I really wanted my mother's approval, but what she needed wasn't what I was delivering. I would wake up in the middle of the night and clean her kitchen." For money, he hauled concrete, mowed lawns, served pizza through a storefront window, anything. If it fell in his lap, he picked it up. Suffering over the loss of his father and the daily worry over his mother, working then in the mailroom of a hospital-supply company, Murray's thoughts of his own career, whatever that meant, hardly occurred to him. It was day to day. He was a jumper-aboard. You could say spontaneous. You could say lost.

He had this dream — he always would — of being at O'Hare with no luggage and no ticket, grinning for a moment at the giant board of departures . . . Bangladesh, St. Petersburg, New Delhi, Crete . . . *Just go.*

In the evenings, he would just go to Second City (for free) to watch his older brother, Brian Doyle-Murray (who added the "Doyle" to distinguish himself from another actor, Brian Murray), improvise comedy with Joe Flaherty and John Belushi. After the show, they'd hang out at Brian's apartment near the theater, or one of the bars on Wells Street. "They thought I was a riot — [a] weekend hippie," Murray said, "you know, going back to my straight life in the 'burbs every night." He didn't think about improvising himself, but his eyes opened wide at his brother's free and easy lifestyle, waking up late, laughing with his friends all day, and drinking on the house, after the show, all night. He couldn't control a scene like Belushi — *B'loosh*, to them — and he didn't have his big brother's eye for character, or Flaherty's versatility and flamboyance, but in his own way he knew he could connect to something funny. It was his stories. Sitting around the Earl of

Old Town with Brian or Joe, telling them about the time, only a year earlier, when, in the weird days after college, traveling the country selling weed out of a suitcase, he got arrested in Colorado, Murray could actually get them laughing. At first, it seemed like mere good luck, a ball pitched smack into the thick of his bat; then, repeating the story for different friends, trying out new ones, Murray got laughs again, proving that it was definitely the batter, not the ball. He didn't know what it was or how to control it, but Second City looked more fun than working the pizza counter, so on a lark he joined a workshop.

"I was so bad," Murray said, "I couldn't believe it." He walked offstage and decided never to go back.

Belushi's outfit took in Del Close like a favorite roughneck uncle, the one who always advocates for the kids against the parents (Bernie Sahlins and Joyce Sloane) for another hour of television, the good bad guy who, despite the Valium and morning cocktails, the filthy manners and the selfishness, comes through where it counts, not in ethics but — this being improvisation — risk. "Del," said Ross-Leming, "felt an obligation to be as provocative and subversive as possible, whether culturally, sexually, or politically. He pushed for that, always urging us to go darker. You might pull back from it, but there was a lot of, 'What if he sets fire to his wife's head?' He wanted you to be on the edge of good behavior — nastiness gave him new realities for us to play with. Even if you didn't always understand why you were doing what you were doing, you knew he represented intellectual liberation."

Prowling the lip of the stage, a highball and cigarette in one hand, a torn volume of mysticism in the other, Close directed, his leopard eyes searching the floor, in lectures seemingly intended for himself, as if Second City, instead of a barroom entertainment, was actually his secret laboratory that Bernie Sahlins had opened to the public. You could never be sure if Close was onto something or just on something, but the kids were so taken by his satanic glamour, his ties to Nichols and May and the green years of improvisation, and the incredible range of his spelunking mind, they "Yes, anded" his every fancy with a fervor and allegiance and openness that Close, up to that point, rarely had. "By the time Del came onboard," Flaherty said, "we started creatively exploding."

Close knew from the start that these kids, like him, saw improvisation as its own presentational art form. Recurrently breaking from a tradition as old as Second City, the Next Generation would improvise not just in the free set after the Saturday show, but often — to Sahlins's consternation — took audience suggestions *between* sketches, once in the first act and once in the second. Encouraged by Close, Fisher developed new improvisational formats — make that *spot*-improvisational formats — outside the comedy playbook. Fisher said, "Sometimes we'd hang three pads on the stage labeled Who, What, and Where — professions, activities, locations — and when we took our break the audience would come onstage with markers and write stuff down. Then we would come out after the break and read the pad and improvise off of that." The notepads did not amuse the boss. ("I was always getting in trouble with Bernie for dreaming stuff up.") But Sahlins — in his wisdom — only smiled and headed back to the office. Second City was his; the players were Del's.

Close told them to play with drugs.

One Saturday night, Harold and Eugenie ingested something that "made the improv and its requirements really challenging," she said, so she stayed very quiet and fled the crocodiles (serving cocktails) and hid behind Harold as the walls melted down around her.

"Eugenie," Harold whispered. "Are we standing?"

"Yes, I think we are."

He nodded, momentarily assured. "But on the ceiling, right?"

Acid, speed, angel dust, booze, weed, they tried them all, mostly to unfunny results. "Do I think Del influenced John's drug use?" mused Judy Belushi. "Certainly he was open about his drug use, and I think it did affect him — that it could somehow make you more creative." The show itself was a high, all that adrenaline, the heady buzz of raw laughter. "No one wanted to call it a night," Ross-Leming said. "Generally we were too wired. We all lived like a pack of wolves, going from one place to another till three, four in the morning. Let's get fucked up at John's place; let's go see who's playing at the Earl of Old Town. People just roamed. They slept wherever they ended up." The everlasting night was heaven for John Belushi; he thrived among friends, his family. When they left for bed, the show ended, so John lived to keep them awake, lunging for checks, passing out drugs, taking the stage at a crowded bar and releasing his most anguished Cocker into the microphone. Last call? Not tonight. For Belushi, they stayed open. He was so magnetic they almost had to. A collector of good times with good people, he was at home all over Chicago. Parting on a joke, Harold headed back to his wife, but John and Eugenie and Joe Flaherty's brother Paul, one of John's roommates, would sneak into a forgotten warehouse in a ragged part of town and jam — Eugenie on bass, Paul on guitar, and John on drums — until exhaustion knocked them off their feet. They would reconvene hours later, at about noon, at Lum's, a burger place near the theater, where a mix of Belushi, Flaherty, Ramis, and Doyle-Murray would spread their newspapers across the counter and circle in on the day's targets. Invariably TV talk would derail the news. Up late with the midnight movie, Belushi and Flaherty were in love with genre parody and celebrity impersonation — "Hey, Johnny, channel four! *On the Waterfront!*" — and with Del Close behind them, preaching full-body immersion, they didn't think twice about sidestepping critique and going broad. Why should the belly laugh be inferior? As Del had said, "Comedy's an art. Satire's propaganda. It's an attempt to have an intellectual effect on the audience instead of a cellular effect."

You could feel just that in Close's handling of *43rd Parallel; or, Macabre and Mrs. Miller,* their revue of March 1972, widely considered one of Second City's best. "Although there is a fair amount of satire in the program," wrote a *Variety* critic, "the strongest results come during items that approach slapstick and kindred yock techniques rather than the subtle, biting stuff." Close built "Funeral," *Macabre*'s immortal ensemble sketch, around the slow-rising rage Belushi, playing the son of the deceased, tries, and ultimately fails, to contain. The audience shares it. "How did it happen, Mrs. Smedley?" asks a concerned Flaherty at the top of the scene. The widow hangs her head. "He got his head stuck," she sighs, "in a gallon can of Van Camp's beans." (Del gave them that line.) At this, Belushi squirms in his seat; Flaherty, feigning grief for the widow, turns to hide his laughter. One by one, as characters enter, learn the cause of death, and stifle their giggling, Belushi's indignation becomes physically intolerable — until finally he explodes, banging his head against the wall, choking himself, ripping his clothes — and the audience, no longer in control, screams with laughter. They squeeze their guts and hit the floor. They hit each other. This — to see an improviser take over people's nervous systems, destroy their egos for a golden split second of freedom — was Close's Grail.

"During my days at Second City," Close said, "I was absolutely hung up on Belushi." Belushi named Close his biggest influence in comedy. "John worshipped him," Flaherty said.

Moved, deeply, by their commitment to full ensemble scenes, Close introduced them to the Harold, the still-gestating dream of group longform he believed to be the next inhabitable planet of improvisation. Via the Harold — Del's life's work in progress — improvisers could sustain thirty- or forty-minute improvisations far more complex than what could be achieved with mere two- or three-person sketches and games, forms too often limited by length and scant points of view. Feeding off the imaginations of seven, eight, or nine simultaneous brains, the Harold promised bigger, stranger results, pulsing with the gestalt truths of communal agreement, the Jungian reply to all that Freud Elaine May had given him so long ago.

He thought of her always, still. Especially when directing, making adventures for his players, as she once had for him. Elaine he loved twice, both as a woman and as a totem of investigation, whose dark current of daring he sparked from St. Louis memory and conducted into them, into the Harold.

Harolds began with a question to the audience, a real question. Maybe Close's improvisers would arrive at a serious solution. "Why am I so [fill in the blank]?" or "How do I get a date?" or "Why am I so concerned about [blank]?" would get an answer the team would use to trigger a round of monologues, "and out of that," Flaherty explained, "suddenly two people would freeze and start a scene." Concurrent with the first scene, on the other end of the stage, another scene — different, but related — would be taking shape. Say, for instance, separate conversations at the same restaurant. "That was something our group could do so well," Fisher said, "really listen to each other and have two scenes going at once. One would get a laugh and then the other would take over and then get a laugh and then the focus would go back. And you just intertwined all this stuff and build to something." Improvisers were free to freeze a scene, then flash it forward or back. "Thirty minutes later," Judy Morgan said, "we would come off and say, 'How did that happen?'" When the Harold's puzzle pieces clicked together sensibly, elegantly, supposedly on their own, they startled audiences and improvisers both. "Other times," Morgan said, "it would just sit there." And so what if it did? "They hate us," Joe Flaherty liked to cackle backstage. "Oh, they really *hate* us . . ."

In August 1972 Gary Austin, recently of the Committee, formerly a social worker, was now an out-of-work actor, accustomed to waiting on line at the California Department of Employment in Hollywood for his weekly seventy-five-dollar unemployment checks, which unceremoniously stopped one week, by way of a technicality he hadn't foreseen.

"I thought I had three more months . . ."

"No . . . sorry . . ."

Now what? He could teach.

The thought surprised him. Teach? He was an actor. He had never taught before.

On a Thursday, Austin called his friend, former Committee member Howard Storm — one of a tiny group of improvisation teachers in Los Angeles — in a panic. "I think I'm going to have to teach."

Austin procured the space Storm used at the Cellar Theater, then called Fred Roos, an ace casting director and Austin's manager, and asked him to notify all the actors he could think of, a list seventy-five names long that included Harrison Ford and Jeannie Berlin. "Call each of these people," Roos instructed Austin. "Tell them Fred Roos says to come to my workshop or else."

By Monday, Austin was facing a roomful of twenty-one actors, his students, "and no clue," he said, "what I was doing."

"You don't have to pay," Austin told them that first day. "I have no idea how to teach. If you come back, you can pay me then."

They came back — actors, improvisers, stand-ups, writers, songwriters, filmmakers — nineteen, to be exact, returned the following week to work on anything, everything, whatever they wanted, Molière, Pinter, Tennessee Williams, improvised scenes and monologues. Tracy Newman, whom Austin met while he was improvising with the Comedy Store Players, brought her sister, an actress, Laraine. She was not yet twenty, with a range of experience — Marcel Marceau in Paris, acting and improvising at CalArts — that suited the grab-bag variety of Austin's workshops. Before long, he was teaching at different venues all over town and almost every night, four hours at a stretch, growing more impressed with the work throughout, until, finally — a year after his last unemployment check — Austin decided the work was good enough to present. "Let's do a show," he announced to the faithful, though he didn't know what he meant, and neither did they. But catalyzed by their teacher's enthusiasm, they went ahead and presented the results of their workshops — miscellaneous scenes and improvisations, revue style — under the banner of the Gary Austin Workshop. When scenes faltered, in front of an audience, Austin would sometimes pause the scene, get up, and give notes. "I had never seen that done before," he said. Process was the product.

He wanted to formalize this thing. "Let's make a company," he proposed to his five closest students. "A company where we have workshops and do shows."

The name they settled on: the Groundlings.

Wandering through downtown Chicago one frosty afternoon toward the end of the year, Bill Murray came to the distinguished block of State Street dominated by Marshall Field's flagship store, then pulsing with a rush of holiday shoppers and the *bong bong bong* of its great clocks. Needing nothing in particular, he lingered a moment to absorb the spontaneous offering all around him, the *Why not?* spirit of the place, his hometown, the happy madness of the season, the curling wall of people, each one a secret door. Murray did not need a job or metaphysical purpose; he could make meaning just by doing this — leaving his mother's house with an ounce of curiosity in his pocket and riding the wind's suggestion. "There's a lot of goodwill out there," he said, if you can ready yourself to receive it, to practice willingness, you can walk through the mundane and live in Christmas every day.

Standing there under a chiming clock, he felt a tap on the shoulder and turned to face Jo Forsberg, Second City's workshop leader. "We'd like to offer you a scholarship," she said, "if you want to come back."

"Thanks, I will. Merry Christmas."

"Merry Christmas."

A miracle, he thought.

In exchange for classes, Murray painted Forsberg's kitchen (purple), a tedious job complicated by exposed piping difficult to brush around. "It was one of the biggest shit jobs I ever did," he said, about as fun as his first workshops under Forsberg. Murray knew he was bad; nobody wanted to work with him. Though he didn't blame them, he recoiled in consequence, grew tense, and got worse. For a while, he got up there, made faces, and no one laughed. "When you talk about paying dues," he said, "there are no dues like dying on stage." But after dying enough times, Murray realized that he was actually still alive, and that the feeling of so-called failure was just that, only a feeling, one of many, and came as soon as it went. The turnstile impermanence of improvisation meant no mood, good or bad, could be sustained, ergo, prolonged disappointment, he came to see, signified a problem with the improviser, not his potential for good work. To address the problem, Murray had to shift his inner magnet away from himself, toward chance, the other person, and wait for their invitation to transform again. "The fear will make you clench up," he said. "That's the fear of dying. When you start and the first few lines don't grab and people are going like, 'What's this? I'm not laughing and I'm not interested,' then you just put your arms out like this and open way up and that allows your stuff to go out. Otherwise it's just stuck inside you." With every thought and action, he had to choose fun, and the more fun he had improvising, the better he did. "Comedy is not effortless," he learned. "The key is to get in a good humor — to have fun. That's not as easy as you might think. Obviously, if you're going to work for eight to twelve hours, you're not going to be in a good mood all day. So it takes a lot of tricks." Through hard-won relaxation, Murray's hyper self-consciousness opened into awareness. "The reason so many Second City people have been successful is really fairly simple," he said. "At the heart of it is the idea that if you make the other actors look good, you'll look good." To improvise with Bill Murray was to be seen, held, carried by a swift and sensitive imagination ready to follow or lead you anywhere, even backward, through the gate, to the childhood playground you thought you had locked on your way out. "He had a very special talent," said Forsberg. "He could project the good part of himself, the part that is optimistic and charming, onto an audience. His darker side he'd show in private, but never onstage. But what I really loved about Billy was that he supported everybody so well."

Out of Forsberg's workshop and into the touring company, Murray came into regular contact with Del Close, its director. Unfortunately for Murray, his timing was off. Only a short time earlier, he would have caught Close at the peak of his enthusiasm, but as the high of returning to Second City wore off, Close's improv addiction got the better of him. He needed more — attention, innovation, risk — than just directing could offer. "It was clear Del didn't want to direct," said touring company member Douglas Steckler. "He wanted to be up there onstage, but his time had passed." His development of the Harold had stalled. He would leave workshops in medias res, coughing out excuses like "I gotta feed the cat" or "I gotta see a man about a horse," before heading home for a fix of Valium, speed, or whatever he could find between couch cushions. If he returned, it would be to the Second City bar, where he had an open tab, to fill one snifter after the next and bark at the students who had elected to sit there and wait out his drug run. "Get the fuck out of here now. Now!" "You, you're an idiot!" "You have nothing to give improvisation. Get out of my fucking class!" It took Bernie Sahlins longer than anyone to figure out why Second City's whipped cream bills were so high (nitrous oxide).

On the road with the touring company, some of Close seemed to have rubbed off on Murray. He was known to miss rehearsals and disappear in the evenings, returning to the performance space sometimes only moments before curtain, slipping in through the back door, into his first costume, and striding out on the stage with the authority of a man ahead of schedule. For Sloane, charged with corralling the touring company from her office at Second City, Murray conducted himself offstage pretty much the way he conducted himself in improvisations, as an irritant too charming to stay mad at. Those nights he went missing? Rumor placed him either at Saint Mary's women's college or a dive bar a short distance from the last place anyone had seen him, where it was said he treated the room to a round of drinks before jumping up on a table and crooning "Trouble in River City." "You had to give Bill space," Joe Flaherty said, speaking for many. "He could be volatile."

Workshopping a melodramatic parody of *Long Day's Journey into Night*, Murray, seemingly unprovoked, physically attacked the troupe's weakest improviser, a preppy button-down jokester reminiscent of the rich kids he knew, and hated, from his caddy days at Indian Hill. What's more, the improviser conveyed no personal convictions, and took direction like a lapdog, and always literally. "Billy did not think he was doing his job," Douglas Steckler said, "which in some invisible way provoked him." Murray picked up the innocent, pushed him against the back wall, and started yelling at him. Steckler ran over. "Guys, no," he said. "We can't do this . . ." Murray wouldn't drop him; the guy's feet were dangling off the floor. All attempts to reason with Murray's anger failed. If, on the other hand, he respected you, if you, unbeknownst to you, satisfied the requirements of his artistic and/or political code, Murray would be a dream to improvise with. His commitment and his willingness to support made him, at his best, pure fun to play with. To the others he could be violent. "Billy was quick to use his fists," Flaherty said. "He didn't know the value of a punch and got in fights a lot." Close enabled the punk in him; it didn't matter to whom he directed his volatility, or why. It seemed Murray sensed a calling higher than community, a moral superiority that lit him with arrogance. "Billy is angry, tough, bright," Close said. "He's got more rage beneath the surface than anyone I know."

But the recipient of Close's highest praise was Bernie Sahlins's mess to clean up, or have cleaned. Not one for confrontation, Sahlins enlisted Harold Ramis, a leader of the mainstage company, to speak to Bill about playing nice. "I think he respects you because you're Brian's friend," Bernie said. "Talk to him." They had met only once before, several summers earlier, just after Bill's high school graduation, when Brian Murray brought Harold to visit his little brother's ninth-hole snack bar, and then again that winter of 1968, outside the Treasure Island grocery store where Murray sold hot roasted chestnuts on the street. Since Ramis's return from Europe, their relationship had been collegial. From afar, Murray respected Ramis's intelligence and veteran standing, and Ramis ranked him with Belushi for fearlessness, and for interpersonal integrity, the care and patience he showed other improvisers in the scene — as opposed to the way he could treat them in real life — Ramis placed Billy Murray way up there in a league of his own. You would have to go back to Elaine May to find an improviser as whimsically inclusive. Why then Bill Murray seemed to turn around and punish people Ramis could only guess: "If he perceived someone as being too self-important or corrupt in some way that he couldn't stomach, it was his job to straighten them out," the satirical impulse improperly directed. He was the professor of a class no one knew they had enrolled in and every day was a pop quiz.

"You know," Ramis said, taking a seat beside Murray, "a lot of people in the cast are pissed off at you."

"Yeeee-eah."

"Do you care?"

"Nnnn-o."

"Okay." Ramis got up. "Good talk."

"Frank," said Howard Koch to Paramount's Frank Yablans, "I don't believe what I heard."

Elaine May was coming back to Paramount to make *Mikey and Nicky*, the idea she'd been polishing since her Compass days. To star, she'd cast improvisers Peter Falk and John Cassavetes.

"Howard, what happened to you happened to you; it's not going to happen to me. We've got an ironclad deal."

Koch replied, "I don't believe what I heard."

Disbelief would be the keynote of this production.

On the first day of filming, Elaine informed David Picker, Paramount's new head of motion picture production, that she wanted to move the white lines on a road.

The crew did not know what to make of her.

You would see her, on location in Philadelphia, in old shirt and blue jeans, ragged and talked-out after nights of no rest, hanging her head, and thin, like a Jules Feiffer cartoon. Then an idea would zap her back to life and she'd be off. Out sprayed a fireworks of creative possibilities, their coherence often obscured by May's concurrency of thought and cognitive speed; many were impractical, unrealistic even, but as they fell to earth, a wrong look, or the hint of perceived incredulity from an onlooker, and she would suck hungrily on a cigar or apple core and vanish in dismay, off to recover her equilibrium with a new idea on her own. Raising his voice in passionate agreement or frustration, Cassavetes could shake her down from indecision or urge her back into it. "John lost patience with her a lot," said cinematographer Victor Kemper. "'Come on, we're ready to go!' he'd say, then she'd contradict him and he'd raise his voice and she'd back off. When he spoke to Elaine she listened. More than listened; she shut down, like flipping a switch." So trusting were May and Cassavetes of each other's improvisational instincts, they appeared to the crew like codirectors, or lovers, forever disappearing to the darkened sidelines to discuss, while everyone waited, and waited, the direction for the scene or, as was sometimes the case, an idea for a new one. From these conferences, she would return with a new face, physically changed all the way through to her fingers, which, while cameras rolled, curled in synchrony with the improvisations. "It's because we respect [the script's] tightness that we can play with it," Cassavetes explained. "[May] would never ask that it always be done just the way she wrote it. Because something better might come out of it. A line, a quality, a mood. Like I say, filming the scene is like doing another draft." The more drafts she shot, the more improvisational latitude Elaine would grant her future self in the cutting room. They would not stop. She shot rehearsals. On a single night, according to one observer, she shot 16,000 feet with two cameramen (a two-hour film is 10,800 feet).

During one take, Falk and Cassavetes, absorbed in an improvisation, ambled out of the shot. The camera was now filming a dark and empty street.

"Cut!" called out camera operator Ricky Bravo.

Elaine went over to him, perplexed. "Why did you call 'Cut'?"

"There's no one in the scene."

"But they might come back."

For the improvisers, May always consented. She gave them everything they could think of to get them to go at it again, maybe deeper this time. Spolin had her games to get there; May worked, as Del Close did, from the muse of leap and free fall. Lunch, most days, was at 1:00 a.m.

Playing in the dark did in fact embolden the improvisers, like night swimming in the rain or trespassing, but their freedom, impossible to anticipate, and therefore impossible to light perfectly, was murder on May. Though they had rehearsed, Falk and Cassavetes were permitted to reinvent their blocking on film, but ignoring their marks, ducking in and out of the light — the little that existed — she couldn't always see them. It further destabilized her.

"Who's gonna see that?" she asked Kemper. "I can hardly see them with my naked eye!"

"Elaine, you have to trust me."

But she couldn't be absolutely certain, not until dailies, and she couldn't have faith. It was too risky. "Can we add more light?"

"Elaine, we'll have continuity problems —"

Cassavetes appeared. "What's your gripe, Elaine?"

"Well, I can't see anything!"

Cassavetes turned to Kemper. They had worked together, quite well, years earlier, on *Husbands,* a film that drew comparisons, fairly and unfairly, to *Mikey and Nicky.* ("The guys improvised on *Husbands,*" Kemper said, "but everyone understood John and he didn't shoot a lot.") "What's the scoop, Vic?"

Kemper explained the situation to Cassavetes; Cassavetes, squinting through his cigarette smoke, listened, understood, agreed, and went off with May to further convey Kemper's directive. The crew watched, waiting, again, for consensus, and the signal to proceed. It took time. It got later. "She never admitted that she didn't know what she was going to do next," Kemper said, "but at the same time she was always asking for help." Instead of unifying the company in collaboration, as they would have the Compass Players, these complicated frays of power and communication troubled the crew. "She had no concept of the waste that went on," Kemper said. "It was upsetting. It put everybody off." The production moved at a slow frenzy.

A focus-puller quit.

A script supervisor was rumored to have been locked in a closet. Some believed it had happened.

Once, an assistant tapped May on the shoulder and directed her attention to two women, citizens of Philadelphia, watching from the sidewalk. "These ladies want to know what's happening."

May paused. "What *is* happening?"

A gaffer who had worked with Nichols on his last film, *The Day of the Dolphin,* guarded his frustration. "[Nichols is] also improvisational," he said, "but it's more strict, more disciplined in the sense that there is a *way* he wanted it . . . He kept at it until the effect is achieved."

She was always running late. Working in a graveyard one long and heavy summer night, Elaine had two cameras rolling on Cassavetes and Falk. They were playing as usual, boldly shifting the fervor between them, sparking from the script and their own very real friendship multidimensional variations on the theme of *Mikey and Nicky,* standing there, at Nicky's mother's grave, laugh-crying like rundown wolves. "Elaine," Kemper said, "was in her heaven," in a sniper's tube of focus, when Kemper got the signal from both assistants, one on each camera, saying she had only one minute of film left.

Kemper tiptoed to her. "Elaine," he whispered, "there's only a minute left. If you can give them some kind of signal . . . to find a way to wrap it up . . . quickly—"

"Don't cut! Whatever you do, don't—"

"There isn't any film left—"

"If you cut, I'll fire you."

Kemper's assistants flashed him the thirty-second sign. He ran to the soundman. "Don't cut your recorder."

"Huh?"

He ran to the cameramen. "Keep rolling."

"Vic—"

"*Don't* cut!"

And on they went, Falk and Cassavetes, riding the moment for empty machines, for another five minutes. Maybe ten. Then, on their own, the actors came to a natural end and the big wave of feeling dribbled to shore. Cut.

"That was wonderful," Elaine said to Kemper. "Thank you."

What could he say? "You're welcome."

How could she, the director, get her collaborators to join her? If joined, how could she hold them there?

With scrupulous attention to creating an interactive environment that would permit spontaneous life to occur on film, as dense and boundless as actual life. Before rehearsal, while the crew waited and the budget escalated, Elaine filled the fridge, shelved the dishes, added pillows to sofas and removed them. Nuts? Listen to this: they weren't even *shooting* in the kitchen. For this scene, they were in the living room. Well, but what if — on that phrase the crew stopped breathing — what if they *did* move into the kitchen? The fridge couldn't be empty! So: the fictional owner of this fridge: What would she eat? Why would she eat it? And why hadn't she eaten it *yet*? Did she always buy too much? Did she just go shopping? — Could someone run downstairs and get a chicken? No, no — roast beef? Is *anything* open at 4:00 a.m.? Well, how *far* is the gas station?

And then, prepping a short scene, a page and a half, wherein Peter Falk's Mikey fights with the counterman at a coffee shop, her gaze latched on to a box of donuts sitting behind the counter. One at a time, Elaine examined the donuts. Those donuts she liked she kept in the box. Some she eliminated. Other donuts she separated into careful pieces, returned them to the box, arranged and rearranged them, and called over the prop man, Bob Visciglia, to inspect her work. Visciglia approved of some of it. Some he did not approve of. While the crew, failing to understand this, watched, Visciglia and May discussed the arrangement and decided to promote certain donuts from the pastry box to the donut display on the counter. They would be in the shot. Regarding the donuts in the display, they again analyzed their selections, reconsidered, and made the necessary adjustments. At last, they agreed. These were the right donuts. Quickly, May reordered them for maximum impact. Then, apparently satisfied, she excused herself from the counter display for other business, and a boy, someone's son up way past his bedtime, lifted the cover and took a donut for himself. Returning, May noticed the change immediately, fixed the pile, lowered a cover over the arrangement, and stepped back behind the camera to preview the composition. Not quite right. Again she removed the cover and rearranged, then decided, finally, to strike the donut display entirely, and moved it out of the shot. In its place, she put the box of rejected donuts, took another moment behind the camera, and smiled. There.

Tom Miller had observed this for about fifteen minutes. A publicist, he had been sent to the location and advised not to reveal his identity to May, who, he was told, hated publicists. "She'll think you're here to spy on her," Mike Hausman warned. So Miller, incognito, asked Pete Scoppa, May's assistant director, to explain the donut thing.

"For Falk to work with," Scoppa replied, "if he wants."

"How?"

"However he wants. If he wants."

They were ready to shoot. The target of a last-minute decision, Scoppa would improvise as the counterman. Having witnessed Falk, a die-hard Method actor, tear up previous scenes, and improvisers, he was more than scared, but —

May called action.

Rabid, crazed, dangerous, Falk went at Scoppa with everything he had to give. He saved nothing for the next take. "He could kill a man," Scoppa recalled, "and he wouldn't know what he was doing." Excess anger Falk directed to the innocent box of donuts, ripped open the pink lid, and tore every last one of them to bits. He threw plates. He burned the air. Screaming at Scoppa, terrifying him, he fired donuts against the wall, strangled them in his fists, spat them to the floor. Falk lunged over the counter, grabbed Scoppa by the throat, jammed donuts in his own mouth, then Scoppa's, lost his breath, collapsed in heaves, regained his strength, and went at Scoppa again — Miller resisted the impulse to leap into the shot and physically defend him — and by the end of the take, no donuts were left. Then a silent consensus: it worked. Falk was mesmerizing, more wildly alive for May than in life, a man in a state of truth. "Everyone was watching spellbound," Miller recalled, "Elaine visibly ecstatic." She shot that shot, a master shot, fourteen times before she went in for close-ups. "I couldn't imagine anyone else having invented improv comedy," Kemper concluded.

And then one day Bernie Sahlins walked into a rehearsal and asked, "Anyone here want to go up and start a theater in Toronto?"

The company scratched their heads. None of his cast knew much about Toronto, let alone Canada. Bernie himself knew only slightly more. Since the mid-1960s, he had seen moderate success bringing companies north to the Royal Alexandra Theatre, and at the urging of Nathan Cohen, *Toronto Star* critic and stalwart Second City fan, he guessed further investigation was in order.

"You'll love it," Sahlins insisted. "I saw *Medea* up there and they did the entire play *in Greek!*"

They didn't quite know what to say. Setting up in New York was one thing. Or Los Angeles. Or even playing Cleveland or Ann Arbor, as touring companies sometimes would. At least those cities shared their American sense of humor, topical references, and politics. But Canada? Comedy?

"Why don't I book you a show up there?" Sahlins suggested. "Look around. See what you think."

What the hell, Joe Flaherty thought. Old Town, the neighborhood around Second City, was starting to look a little dingy anyway. "Well, okay. Sure."

As the group's senior member and informal captain, Flaherty set the pace for the rest of the cast. In no time he was leading Harold Ramis, John Belushi, Jim Fisher, Eugenie Ross-Leming, and others to the University of Toronto to play a one-night-only show for college students, Bernie's ideal audience, and prospective backers.

To their astonishment, the whole experience came off: the show was a hit and the city itself, emerging from the conservative cold years of British cultural dominion, opening its arms to art and artists, basement coffeehouses and funky, folky sidewalk jam sessions, was ready for change. *How green,* Joe Flaherty thought, *how clean!* How much lovelier was young Toronto than old Old Town, which had only gotten rougher since Flaherty arrived in 1969. The trolleys, the red brick Victorian row houses, the nonstop sky; the streets around the university — it was a picture postcard of a booming pioneer town on the crest of a renaissance.

After the show Sahlins took Flaherty and company, along with some very happy backers, to a celebratory steak dinner near the University Theatre. In sadness and jubilation, Gilda Radner, who had been in the audience and loved the show, watched them leave without her. Ever since she was a girl, Gilda had known about these people, improvisational comedians. Her camp friends, Chicago kids, were the first to tell her about Second City. Years later, she saw them play Detroit, but it wasn't until Second City came to the University of Michigan, where Gilda, then a student, had started her own improv group, that the switch was flipped. "That's what you should do," someone said to her on their way from the auditorium. It was not Gilda, though, but a friend of hers who had been invited to join the improvisers for dinner that night in Toronto. Her nose pressed to the restaurant window, Gilda watched them throw their arms around each other and laugh. Their stage was their imaginations. "It's like getting to be a child again for a little while," Gilda thought, "to be naive, to have empty spaces that can be filled in. What's so sad about so many grown-ups is they lose those spaces."

Viola Spolin, mother of improvisation, 1946. She smelled sweetly of chicken broth, herbs, and cigarettes.

Courtesy of the Viola Spolin Estate

Viola rehearsing the children — children of all cultures — of Chicago's Hull House. "Everyone can improvise," she would write. (Note her son, Paul Sills, center, grimacing in short pants.) *Courtesy of the Viola Spolin Estate*

The Compass Players, circa 1955: Severn Darden, Larry Arrick, Elaine May, Shelley Berman, Mike Nichols, Rose Arrick, and Barbara Harris (napping?).

From the collection of David Shepherd, courtesy of Michael Golding

From her seat in the front row, Elaine May sizes up a Compass performance. She was universally feared and admired, rarely on time, artistically ambidextrous, never wrong, and would rise to prominence without resorting to the kind of burlesque, airheaded, or regressed personae of her predecessors, Fanny Brice, Gracie Allen, Phyllis Diller, and Lucille Ball. Every comedienne who eschews type and leads with her intellect follows suit, in May's footsteps. Thus there are two kinds of comediennes in America: Before Elaine and After.

From the collection of David Shepherd, courtesy of Michael Golding

Mike Nichols and Elaine May, before they were Nichols and May, in an early Compass version of "Teenagers."

From the collection of David Shepherd, courtesy of Michael Golding

Young Bernie Sahlins outside his theater, 1959.

Courtesy of the Second City Archive

Paul Sills, looking characteristically intense with an uncharacteristic mustache, inside the Second City, 1960.

Courtesy of the Viola Spolin Estate

The Second City company, December 1960: Eugene Troobnick, Barbara Harris, Alan Arkin, Paul Sand, Bill Mathieu (musical director), Mina Kolb, Severn Darden, and Andrew Duncan. *Courtesy of the Second City Archive*

Backstage at Second City with Barbara Harris (at the mirror), Andrew Duncan (in the center mirror), and Bill Mathieu. *Courtesy of the Second City Archive*

In January 1962, before the theater we call "improv" or "improvisational" was known to the public, the Premise, which Ted Flicker (pictured with Tom Aldredge) termed "Instant Drama," played Washington, D.C. — for a crowd that included Vice President and Lady Bird Johnson. *From the collection of Theodore Flicker, courtesy of Barbara Flicker*

The Committee, soon after director Alan Myerson established the group in San Francisco, May 1963. Top row: Garry Goodrow, Larry Hankin, Ellsworth Milburn. Middle: Irene Riordan, Scott Beach, Kathryn Ish. Bottom: Bob Camp.

Courtesy of Alan Myerson

Joe Flaherty was captain of Second City's Next Generation, keeper of John Belushi, curator/guiding force of Second City's first Toronto company, and the unofficial artistic director of *SCTV*.
Courtesy of the Second City Archive

For all of his friends, improvising at Second City was an accident. For John Belushi, in a Second City portrait from 1971, it was a calling. He was the first of his generation to arrive at Second City with previous improv experience. His West Compass Players incubated many of Belushi's best characters and impersonations, most memorably his Joe Cocker.
Courtesy of the Second City Archive

Circa 1972. "That river always makes me sad," Harold Ramis improvised. "Yeah? Why?" asked Joe Flaherty. "It's called the Crimea River."
Courtesy of the Second City Archive

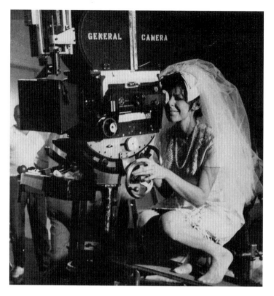

Elaine May, the director, takes over from Elaine May, the actor, on the set of *A New Leaf,* written by Elaine May, the writer. According to all who were lucky enough to see her play Chicago, St. Louis, and New York, May's tripartite skill fed her improvisational genius (and vice versa).

In April 1972, Martin Short, like his friends at 1063 Avenue Road (not to mention every other fledgling performer in Toronto), had no vision of himself as a comic actor.

Courtesy of Martin Short

Gilda Radner, Brian Doyle-Murray, Gerry Salsberg, Dan Aykroyd, Joe Flaherty, Jayne Eastwood, and Valri Bromfield in Second City's first Toronto company, June 1973.

Courtesy of the Second City Archive

Del Close in Toronto, 1976. When asked about this photo, improviser Steven Kampmann wrote, "My guess was Del was about to go insane or just was coming out of a breakdown or was actually still in it. Keyword is breakdown."

*Courtesy of
Steven Kampmann*

The original cast of *SCTV,* 1976: Andrea Martin, Catherine O'Hara, Joe Flaherty, John Candy, Dave Thomas, Eugene Levy, and Harold Ramis.

Courtesy of the Second City Archive

In the summer of 1978, with *Saturday Night Live* and its ancillary triumphs at their peak, Andrew Alexander rented the cast of *SCTV* a house in Bel-Air where writer Harold Ramis, then in L.A., would be close at hand. Most days they wrote in the morning, hung out together at night. The *SCTV* house party pictured on the opposite page marked their informal initiation into the Hollywood big time: (top) Eugene Levy and Chevy Chase; (middle) John Candy, Joe Flaherty, and Christopher Guest; (bottom) Steven Spielberg and Dave Thomas. (Not pictured but also in attendance were improvisers Fred Willard, Bill and Brian Doyle-Murray, and Laraine Newman.)

Courtesy of the Second City Archive

Chris Farley, Chicago improviser. "I'll never forget that first laugh," he said a year before his death. "The nun came over to my desk to yell at me for something and I said, 'Gee, your hair smells terrific,' like in that commercial. Well, all the kids laughed hysterically and it was like a revelation."

Courtesy of the Second City Archive

The Beatles, clockwise from top left, are Steve Carell (as Paul), Scott Allman (George), Dave Razowsky (Ringo), and Stephen Colbert (John), circa 1994. Gradually, they reveal repressed memories: Ed Sullivan, it seems, fondled each of them before the show. Except Ringo. *Courtesy of the Second City Archive*

Improviser Amy Poehler, pictured here around the time she met Tina Fey in Chicago, 1993. "I heard about Tina on the streets before I met her," Poehler said. "We were both new improvisers who had moved from where we were going to college to study improv, and we performed together on an ImprovOlympic team named after a bad porn movie called *Inside Vladimir*."

Courtesy of the Second City Archive

Tina Fey, Scott Allman, and Rachel Dratch in a scene from Mick Napier's 1996 *Citizen Gates,* which featured Second City Chicago's first original gender-equal cast, three men and three women. "What's made me laugh through the years," Napier said, "is stuff that doesn't make any fucking sense at all." *Courtesy of the Second City Archive*

The cast of *Piñata Full of Bees,* summer 1995: Scott Allman, Jon Glaser, Scott Adsit, Rachel Dratch, Jenna Jolovitz, and Adam McKay. *Courtesy of the Second City Archive*

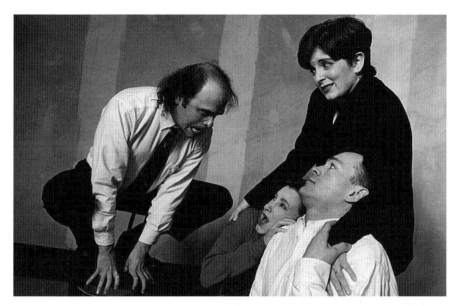

Scott Adsit, as a gargoyle on his first day of school, terrorizes Jenna Jolovitz, Tina Fey, and Kevin Dorff. Andrew Alexander called the sketch, from *Paradigm Lost* (2000), one of the funniest he had ever seen. *Courtesy of the Second City Archive*

2001. Second City's response to 9/11: *Holy War, Batman! or The Yellow Cab of Courage.* The cast from left to right: Keegan-Michael Key, Samantha Albert, Andy Cobb, Abby Sher, and Jack McBrayer. *Courtesy of the Second City Archive*

Amy Poehler, Matt Walsh, Ian Roberts, and Matt Besser. Here, the four founding members of the Upright Citizens Brigade perform at a live taping for *The UCB Show* at the UCB Theatre Sunset, August 2015.

Courtesy of Upright Citizens Brigade / Photo by Liezl Estipona

10

1973–1974

We go north now to Toronto through a mesh of maple leaves and up to a brick Victorian row house like all the others — at least from the outside — along the preposterously named Avenue Road. Inside number 1063, home of former McMaster college students Martin Short, Eugene Levy, and Dave Thomas, you would find anywhere from two to a dozen uncommonly free and funny people, many of them the McMaster boys' new actor friends from *Godspell,* then running downtown at the Royal Alexandra, gathered together for what they called Friday Night Services, their postshow all-night Big Chill of impromptu songs and comedy, wherein the likes of Danny Aykroyd and his partner, Valri Bromfield — Nichols and May, but insane — would take over the living room sofa and motormouth back and forth in characters they could sustain, to the wonderment of all, for literally hours, the pint-sized hurricane Andrea Martin, up for anything and already a thousand ideas ahead of you, crowded into the dining room with Dave and Eugene and Gilda Radner and Catherine O'Hara beside Paul Shaffer at the upright piano they had instead of a dining room table, playing the first big notes of Marty's entrance music, Short's cue to emerge from the proscenium archway to the kitchen, holding a spoon for a mic, and parodying out a signature tune they all recognized, courtesy of the Buffalo feed, from American television. "No one watched Canadian television," Short said. "It was no influence at all. Our influences were American television. We were kids who could never imagine being in show business because show business was on the planet Neptune. It was in the United States."

Though it was only just across the border, the paradise of American entertainment, what these twenty-two-year-olds had grown up watching on TV, was impossibly far away, likelier to appear in dreams than life. No, they would never make it; never *really* make it. This was Canada, after all, the Second Country, land of watch but don't touch. Short grew up in front of his parents' living room television, feasting on the dream people of Showland, Jack Paar and his guests, Nichols and May, Judy Garland, Oscar Levant, and the blindfolded uptowners of *What's My Line?* ("Are you opening a film this week?"; "Could I have seen you at Sardi's last night?") As a boy of ten, Marty wanted to be there, in tuxedo, howling with them at their inside jokes. "What sticks in my mind," he said, "is how hard these people were laughing. You felt like you were part of a party that there was no way you'd ever be invited to." Number 1063 was theirs.

They dreamed in ridiculous parody, aping the outsize careers they wanted but couldn't have, moving the coffee table out of the way and turning 1063 into an improv stage and laughing to life a living room carnival of their showbiz gods, their idols. "Everybody was really at their funniest," Shaffer said, "because the audience was each other."

They didn't have studio cameras, so they made cassette tapes. In one, they improvised as other *Godspell* cast members.

"This is so mean!" Shaffer laughed. "We can't be doing this!"

"Gilda, you play Avril!"

"The best roles! Always given the best roles!"

You had to be funny to get in, but to stay in, you had to stay funny, which was difficult when everyone around you, riff after spectacular riff, was actually getting *funnier;* when Andrea, who went farther than you could imagine, surprised everyone by actually going *farther,* dropping to the floor and improvising as a wolf getting eaten out. No one in North America was as funny as Andrea Martin. Except for Marty, Eugene, Dave, Gilda, Danny . . . huge-hearted maniacs and friends. The spirit of 1063 was fast and nurturing, a trellis of disparate blooms linking tendrils and curling upward, together. "Opportunity was inherent in Canadian culture," Bromfield said, "because nobody was looking at us; we were left alone in a hothouse to grow. Nobody said no to us. We pushed each other and we laughed at each other. And we made that the most important thing in our lives." There were no Eve Harringtons because, in the tiny world of Toronto entertainment, there were no Margo Channings; making a little money, working regularly, the denizens of 1063 were already living their dreams. Jealousy and competition, therefore, did not exist. "When we started in *Godspell*," Short said, "people just couldn't believe they didn't have to study for exams anymore. We had ambition, but it was 'I hope I can keep working so I don't have to go back to school.'"

Catherine O'Hara, at nineteen the youngest of the gang, was too shy to jump up and join Short and Shaffer at the piano. "Marty did so many characters," she said, "that he could improvise to infinity. He'll jump into anything. He just goes." O'Hara, however, felt a little like an interloper at 1063, which pounded with musical people; she had auditioned for *Godspell* and didn't get in. Though, as one of seven children, having grown up under funny parents and grandparents in a three-bedroom house where "freedom was encouraged from an early age," O'Hara was at home in a noisy room. After dinner at her parents' house in Toronto, she and her brother Marcus, and Gilda, would play improv games with Mrs. O'Hara, lifting her up in the air and bringing her down, "like one of those old workshop exercises."

"We were all family people," O'Hara said of her circle. "We came from big, loud families."

Those were days of surplus, of love and fleeting crushes, and resounding yeses to (d) all of the above. Marty Short marveled at Gilda, in overalls and pigtails, though, presently, she was spoken for and anyway Marty would come to love the bright and beautiful singer, Nancy Dolman; her brother Bob, dashing and erudite, would soon fall for Andrea and Andrea for Bob, though Andrea, for the moment, was with Eugene, who was soon to discover the adorable Deb Divine, whose roommate, Mary Ann, was seeing Paul Shaffer, and everyone, at some point, fell in love with Gilda. Let me revise that: everyone loved *period*. A huge laugh at 1063 induced in all a flutter of admiration, a ray of hot honey shot to the nerves. "In those days," Andrea Martin said, "sex was like an extension of laughter." "Or vice versa," O'Hara would add. "I find laughing sexy, so forget it. That's why everybody dated everybody. When you start laughing, you think, 'Oh, wait. Maybe . . .'"

You could say they had been perfectly cast. *Godspell*, a freewheeling Jesus musical by Stephen Schwartz and John-Michael Tebelak, wanted not traditional musical theater performers, but flavorful personalities, individuals. Technique they sidelined; Schwartz and his team were looking to cast the actor, not the role. Highly improvisational and ensemble-oriented, *Godspell* auditions were (and always have been) specifically geared to reveal the raw goods of young talent. "*Godspell* was basically the only comedy opportunity in Toronto," said Dave Thomas. "A lighthouse for like minds."

Most of the other theatrical opportunities for the hopefuls of Avenue Road were in small, stuffy dinner theaters, where you could drink and watch a deadly serious play — "my long, slow, snowy walk to death," the actress Jayne Eastwood dubbed the genre that was "incest and wolves" to improviser Robin Duke — but truthfully, you went for the booze. In those days, good Toronto bars were hard to come by. To win their liquor licenses, proprietors had to have restaurant licenses, ergo any theater that wanted to sell drinks had to be a restaurant too. That spelled dinner theater — not exactly a big draw to the world's foremost theatrical artists or Canada's untapped comedy fringe. And so, to a young funny actor in Toronto, *Godspell* was the sun coming up.

Eugene Levy dragged Marty Short out of final exams to audition the very day Andrea Martin blew through the theater like a gale wind, the same day he first saw Gilda, jacked up, Short recalled, "like a demented child at the peak of a sugar rush," blaring out to Schwartz and John-Michael Tebelak "Zip-a-Dee-Doo-Dah" with more charm than skill alongside piano accompaniment by Paul Shaffer, who had only come because a friend slipped him twenty bucks to play for her. (Spotting a good thing, Schwartz fired his musical director and hired Shaffer on the spot — a far better gig than playing the Hammond B-3 at the strip clubs of Yonge Street.) As for the others, they all got in. "This," Schwartz said, "was the funniest *Godspell* company we had ever seen." Those who didn't make the cut complained Schwartz & Co. didn't know what they were doing, just hiring kids off the street. In fact, though he didn't know it at the time — and neither, for that matter, did they — he hired born improvisers. "It's no accident that so many of the [Toronto] *Godspell* cast wound up doing Second City," Schwartz said, "because other than the musical component it's essentially the same skill set."

And so when Bernie Sahlins came to town with Del Close, Joe Flaherty, Brian Doyle-Murray, and Joyce Sloane to scope the talent for Toronto's first Second City company, he bought his recruiters seats to *Godspell*, the hottest ticket, probably, in the nation, and pretty much stopped the theatergoing leg of his search right there. "We didn't love the show," Flaherty said, "but we knew these guys were the real ticket." After the show, Joyce got in touch with the cast and invited them to audition. Del and Flaherty wanted Eugene; for a young actor in such a flamboyant show, he showed an impressive amount of self-control, Buster Keaton amid the Marx Brothers. When Bernie argued for the more attention-hungry Gerry Salsberg, Flaherty rolled his eyes. If they couldn't agree on the qualifications, why had Bernie invited them to come along? It seemed Bernie himself was improvising his way through the casting process, alternately looking for guidance from and giving direction to a panel of judges with tastes as disparate as their personalities. In the old days, casting would have been a job for Paul Sills, but without a strong, consistent artistic vision to lead the charge, the little band of improvisers, under Bernie, came to the plate like the Bad News Bears. Back at the Royal York hotel after the show, the discussion continued, and Flaherty confessed to Doyle-Murray he had his reservations about the whole business. "What are they" — meaning the Canadians — "going to know about improv?" he wondered aloud. Doyle-Murray agreed. How Canada's first improvisational theater would get off the ground was anybody's guess.

On the day of the auditions, Bernie's team took their seats in a church they rented in Yorkville, the Haight-Ashbury of Toronto, and crossed their fingers they were casting their net wide enough. ("Bernie," Flaherty said, "wasn't big on advertising.") Of those who trickled in, not one among them saw Second City as more than just another job opportunity. Among those who had heard or at least heard of Nichols and May, only a handful could trace their beginnings back to the Compass, and of that handful, only Danny Aykroyd and Valri Bromfield regarded their native medium as something like an art.

Aykroyd had been hip to Spolin for the better part of his adult life; at the age of twelve, his parents had enrolled him in improv classes at the Ottawa Little Theatre. "The instructor Brian Gordon was aware of commedia dell'arte, Pirandello, all the absurdist playwrights and also of the American improvisation movement that emerged in the late 1950s," Aykroyd said. "He was teaching us this stuff in the classes: sharing and giving; not to take too much; how to overcome fear and build self-confidence on stage; how to not be afraid of flying, dying and trying." Valri heard him before she met him. Aykroyd did characters in the tunnel connecting his Catholic boys' school to her Catholic girls' school. She thought: *That guy with one eyebrow is one funny guy.* "He reminded me of my brother," she said. "I loved him." Bromfield, who had lightning in her eyes and mouth and improvised unremittingly, did voices too, strong, pushy women, women on fire. They bubbled up in her in class when she should have been paying attention.

"Sitting there, bored," she said, "you just activate sporadically. It's a firing of one's brain. You get a fact in your brain and extrapolate on that fact." When Aykroyd walked between classes, the tunnels echoed with data, dates, facts, serial numbers. "He could have been a surgeon or a comic or anything," Bromfield said. "He knew everything in that wonderful obsessive way. I loved his brain. So we made friends."

At Carleton University in Ottawa, he went in for sociology and criminology and abnormal psych, anything that would bring him the full gamut of human deviance and diversity, "the hawks, the doves, the rights, the lefts," he said. "The radicals, the racists, bigots, humanitarians. The Feds, the criminals — I've got to know them all, because *those* are the stories." Those people lived in him. Aykroyd — whose friend Nancy Dolman recognized as ten people in one — was their warden, and the tunnel voices Bromfield heard, jailbreaks. From Toronto, she convinced him to drop out of college, join up with her, and develop their act. "I definitely led in the booking of things," she said, "in building our team." Of the two, Bromfield had the most professional experience. She had already worked with Lorne Michaels, whose secret combination of calm and ambition Bromfield found confidence-inspiring. "I had never met anyone so young," she said, "who had that."

For fifty bucks, they rented Saturday-night space at Toronto's Factory Theatre Lab, and paper-flyered the streets with news of a midnight show. People came. "We would dress up as parents," Bromfield said, "and improvise, sometimes for hours." From Nichols and May — "they were God," Bromfield said — Aykroyd and Bromfield learned the value of listening, of trusting the pauses, "the very thing," Bromfield explained, "that people are afraid of socially. That's where the laugh is." But they also understood speed. If Mike and Elaine waltzed the parquet, Danny and Valri dove onto it hands first, slid across the room, and flew out through the window. "Danny and Valri were wild," Dave Thomas said, "and so fast." Read this aloud at top speed: "Waiter, what's the soup de jour?" "What day is it today?" "Wednesday." "Wednesday soup."

They played wherever they could. In addition to late nights at Factory Theatre Lab and Global Village, they played coffeehouses and gay bars (following a transvestite named Pascal), 1063 Avenue Road, the backseat of Gilda's car, the front of Aykroyd's '63 Chevy, between stops on his mail run, during dinners of borrowed soup and beans, and out loud in public, up and down the busy streets of Toronto, spontaneously breaking into character for beguiling marathon arguments about absolutely nothing. "Everybody was improvising," Bromfield said. "I'd go to visit Marty and Gilda at Gilda's house and they'd put socks on their hands and do puppet shows. They just didn't capitalize on it the way Danny and I did."

Local comedy's homecoming king and queen, Danny and Valri were Second City shoo-ins, but they were nonetheless terrified of the "Five Through the Door" audition process. The form was clean and challenging. First, improvisers were broken into pairs. One to play a desk clerk; the other to enter through the stage door in character, engage the clerk, then exit and reenter as a completely different character — five times. Then the improvisers switch roles. Were each improviser's five characters distinct? Were they intelligent enough for Bernie? Fully inhabited enough for Doyle-Murray? Risky enough for Del? Funny enough for Flaherty? Did they have a point of view? Were they jokey or real? And most of all did the improvisers listen to each other?

In his anxiety — or so he claimed — Aykroyd begged his friend John Candy to please join him and Valri at the audition, if only to lend support. Candy, who could never deny a pal — his big body was mostly heart — showed up as requested and waited outside the church for Danny and Val to finish their audition. Second City was not for him. He lacked the musical ability and old-fashioned show business purview of Marty, Andrea, and the other *Godspell* players, and unacquainted with the writer's side of his brain, he disqualified himself from engaging in the sort of verbal antics Danny and Val improvised at Global Village. John Candy was an actor, plays mostly. To see that big Wallace Beery smile was to land in the center of a giant pillow fort, and though he was twice your size and strong as a castle, you still somehow felt Candy was the one who needed protecting. It was innocence, the ingenuous good manners of a Boy Scout. He gleamed with kindness. Candy was so instantly likable he made friends without trying, just by leaving the house. He didn't even have to open his mouth or look in their direction; that man-in-the-moon face pied-pipered the citizens of Toronto out from their daily routines to join him at whatever he was doing, and then on to whatever they wanted to do next. That's why Candy was so often late for his appointments. *Hey, who's hungry?* A second after meeting them, he would be buying another round for two dozen strangers before driving them back home for an all-night dinner of lobster and pizza and whatever else he had in the fridge. What he didn't have, he'd pick up on the way. For his local celebrity and peerless generosity, Aykroyd called Candy Johnny Toronto — and it stuck.

He only found out that Aykroyd had written "John Candy" on the audition sheet after they called his name and asked him to take the stage.

"What have you got to lose?" Aykroyd grinned as he bounded from the church.

"I'll kill you. I'll kill you for doing this to me."

Inside, Candy was given a partner and a crash course in "Five Through the Door." He made an immediate impression on Del. It was one of his characters — a gay boxer. For a guy with zero experience, going against type and against camp, Candy showed himself to be a risk taker of consequence. He did not need gimmicks or even laughs. He was real. As long as he stayed himself in an improvisation, that meant Candy couldn't fail.

"I want that guy," Del whispered to Bernie. "That guy's got it."

Then Candy and his scene partner switched roles. As directed, Candy took the stage behind his invisible desk and aimed his concentration at the other guy with the care and focus that had already made him a local hero. Listening to his partner monologue at him through one annoying character after the next, Candy did not angle for a way in, or interrupt his partner's speech. All support, he asked for no one's attention. Watching from his seat out front, Flaherty was amazed. Candy had intuited and applied the principle of give-and-take. "John was so good at listening," Flaherty said, "that he stole the scene almost by doing nothing." There was no question: this guy, in his own way, was as compelling as Aykroyd and Bromfield.

"I want that fat guy," repeated Del to Bernie. "I want that fat kid."

The skinny girl, Gilda Radner — also coerced by Aykroyd into auditioning that day — was a bundle of need in paper-doll form, a nervous toy person practiced, brilliant even, in failing herself before you could fail her. So she didn't want to audition. If she didn't get into Second City, Gilda knew she would hate herself forever. But if she just stayed home alone with her magazines and three-legged cat, she would never be loved like one of those beautiful skinny girls whose hair moved when they moved their heads. "I'd move my head," she said, "and my hair would just *stand* there." Her mother — her *perfect* mother — was forever telling Gilda to comb her hair, cover her blemishes, eat slower, eat *less*. Her father — who took her to the theater to see the beautiful dancing girls — Gilda lost at fourteen. A brain tumor.

"Show business is about families, series of families," she understood. "You get to be born in them, and to get all new parents and siblings." If this family — Bernie, Del, Flaherty, Brian Doyle-Murray — rejected her, she would die. So Gilda rushed through her audition, improvising as standard types — the Young Girl, the Old Woman — which she played as she perceived herself, with all the embarrassing, snot-nosed, donkey-laughing nerdiness of a six-year-old girl singing too loud in the shower. "I've just never let go of my child self," she said, "seeing things clean and clear like when I was just born. Being a child is being impulsive. Knowing hangs you up. You get inhibited. Keeping that part of me alive is very useful — in comedy, I can walk into a wall because I don't think ahead of time, 'Oh, there's a wall there, I might hurt myself.' I just go into that wall with abandon." Some comedians love their characters and hate the audience; some love the audience and hate their characters; some, like Gilda, loved both.

Bernie's team agreed, easily, on Aykroyd and Bromfield. "The Second City tradition was two women and a bunch of guys," Bromfield said, "but Jayne Eastwood, Gilda, and I would not leave each other's sides. So we made sure they couldn't get us apart. I think we forced Bernie into it." So three women this time, and instead of Eugene Levy, whom Del and Flaherty wanted, Bernie made a push for Gerry Salsberg. He had come on pretty strong in *Godspell*. Candy, Bernie thought, was too young, too shy, for the improvisational stage.

"Okay," Flaherty said. "We'll give you Gerry if you give us Candy."

Del piped up. "I want Candy in Chicago."

That settled it.

"Wow," Flaherty said at the end of their second day of auditions. "We have a cast."

Charged with leading the new company, Flaherty and Doyle-Murray gave the beginning improvisers basic Spolin technique and mixed in a little Del Close, but mostly they just hung out with them. It was the summer of 1973; Flaherty and Aykroyd tossed a football around an empty lot near the theater and stretched out in the park. "These guys had no artistic pretensions," Flaherty recalled. "They weren't that interested in politics and they weren't that interested in satire." To Flaherty's astonishment, some bungled the very word "improvisation" — "improvisions," they called it. In Toronto, Second City wasn't an art; it was a job. (Bernie appeared for one rehearsal, called out "Commedia dell'arte!," and Jayne Eastwood rolled her eyes.) Without

Sahlins's continual supervision, enforcing topical, intellectual material, or Del, demanding they bare their souls onstage, the first Toronto company, in their first workshops, had the freedom to redefine the criteria for successful improvisational comedy. When their captain, Joe Flaherty, asked them to "just play, just improvise," he really meant just have fun and be funny. "I just loved comedy," he said, though he could have been speaking for his ensemble. "It was always most important to make the audience laugh. After that you could make social comments, or make a point, anything, but first and most important make sure it's funny."

Oh, yeah: they needed somewhere to rehearse. Under the gun, Joyce Sloane reached out to the St. Lawrence Centre, a regional theater a short ways from Second City's future digs on Adelaide Street, to see what might be available, and the venue's man in public relations, Andrew Alexander, an easygoing twenty-nine-year-old show business entrepreneur (and after-hours speakeasy manager), directed Joyce to an open space. As for the theater on Adelaide — a cramped and sweaty black box evocative of the early Compass — it opened, without a liquor license, in June 1973 with a best-of-Second-City show, *Tippecanoe and Déjà Vu,* and was an instant hit. At least, the improvisations were. The old imported material fared all right, but when it came time for suggestion taking, Flaherty said, "half the city would show up." Danny and Valri were the draw. The insider following they had amassed playing the likes of Global Village and the gay bars of Toronto turned up in full force to watch them work, solidifying Second City's hipster reputation and virtually guaranteeing its immediate future. Gilda, as predicted, couldn't be matched for loopy vulnerability, the disarming mastery she had over her own inelegance — when she lost hold of an improvisation, they actually seemed to love her more — but for the late-night improv-hungry audiences of Adelaide Street, already versed in the verbal harmonies of Aykroyd and Bromfield, no one else compared. Desperate to win, Gilda got competitive; Jayne Eastwood recoiled from the pressure; and Gerry Salsberg struggled to keep up. "Danny and Valri raised everyone's level of work," Flaherty said. "That company was like horses chomping at the bit." In fact, the laugh-centric, me-me-me athleticism of the Adelaide improv sets — as opposed to the Chicago emphasis on scenes and team-work — was so compelling, audiences didn't seem to care how stifling it was in that beat-up theater beset with no ventilation during one of Toronto's hottest summers on record, or that they weren't drinking, because they, the young people of Toronto, were laughing, hard, at Canadians, for the first time in their lives. Before Second City came to Adelaide Street, the nascent generation merely chuckled at Canadian television with its geriatric Canadian Broadcasting Corporation programming and politely groovy variety shows, like Lorne Michaels and Hart Pomerantz's *Hart and Lorne Terrific Hour*— in which Pomerantz got huge laughs playing a beaver. Though it was apolitical and largely oblivious to the world outside, the frenzy they felt in Danny, Valri, and Gilda, the size and unnatural speed of their characters, conveyed the madness of the profoundly free. Had they been there, Spolin and Sills would have been horrified at all the showboating, but one could argue that Flaherty's ensemble, in throwing out Viola's rules and eschewing the high bars of Bernie Sahlins, achieved improvisation's most emancipated state yet. "Improv is human, but it's goofy," Bromfield said. "I think there's forgiveness in it. I think that's what an audience perceives. 'I'm seeing my weaknesses and everyone's laughing. It's okay.'"

Catherine O'Hara, waitressing at Adelaide with her sister, singer Mary Margaret, was "fascinated by Danny and Valri. They were freaky together," she said. "They were so good at knowing one or two facts about a subject and then sounding like experts." Serving up crepes, a Second City specialty, in that stifling hot room — Doyle-Murray would come out and do grumbling tirades against the heat, and Bernie — O'Hara came to see, for all the fun she was having watching the show, she could have more fun *in* it. *Please, oh please,* she thought, *please, let me be up there,* so she auditioned for Joe Flaherty, for the touring company — and didn't get in. "Keep up the good work," Flaherty told her. "Waitressing, I mean!"

Eugene Levy had never seen anything like it — the speed, the intelligence, the direct interface with the performers. He wanted to be up there, too; he wanted to invent and inhabit characters of his own creation, but improvising scared the hell out of him. And yet there was something in Brian Doyle-Murray's approach to the work that soothed the tension Levy, imagining himself improvising, had already begun to feel. In the whirl of language and scene stealing, Doyle-Murray, Levy recalled, "had a very economical way of performing. He mainly sat, always had a coffee, and didn't do a lot of moving around. He just waited for the right opportunity, then came out with a line."

Martin Short also came to Adelaide to watch his friends work. Practically all of *Godspell* had auditioned for Second City, except him. "I had zero agenda," he said, "of being a comedian." Of course, Short knew he was dependably funny, funny in college plays and *party* funny, the funniest guy in the room if that room were 1063 Avenue Road, he had Paul Shaffer on piano, and the audience members were his friends, but the future he had dreamed up for himself—born of Donald O'Connor, Sinatra, and all those American entertainers he had grown up watching on his parents' television —was absurdly far-fetched, comically obsolete. But it was also a fact. Martin Short, in his variety-show heart, was a song-and-dance man. The idea of improvising under pressure? "I couldn't imagine getting up there and trying to be funny without a script," he said. Until that show at Adelaide, the first time Short had ever seen Second City, his idea of comedy came mainly through the emotionally uninvolving "Take my wife, please" stripe of variety-show humor, but at Flaherty and Doyle-Murray's performance of the classic "Brest-Litovsk," a sketch about a college student bullshitting his way through an oral exam, Short was "gobsmacked. I was like, 'I get what this is now.' Because it was such a hilarious, true, sincere scenario, which we had all done. We had all gone to the professor with excuses. I was already laughing just from the expression on Joe's face because I knew he knew nothing."

"Greg," Doyle-Murray, as the professor, began. "I want you to explain and amplify the ramifications of the Treaty of Brest-Litovsk."

Flaherty goes blank. He says and does nothing for an incredibly long time. Then: "Is this multiple choice?"

It was Flaherty's pauses, the suppressed terror on his face. So much of the behavior, Short saw—the choices of when to smoke, when to sip coffee, subtle and hilarious displays of anxiety—deepened the scene beyond whatever laughs Flaherty and Doyle-Murray won with punch lines. The human realness of Second City comedy was to Short the revelation it had been to the audiences of the early Compass. He said, "To trust the power of sincerity and the power of knowing that if you get within in the way people think and operate and not try to be funny, you can do anything." The lesson he absorbed instantly and never forgot. "Laughter," Short said, "engulfed the whole audience."

For lack of a liquor license, the Adelaide theater closed six months later.

It was Bill Murray who, somewhere between Willy Wonka and the Artful Dodger, welcomed John Candy to improvisation, and his hometown,

Chicago, with a Cubs game and insider's tour of Wrigley Field, visits to the original McDonald's, the first International House of Pancakes, and some of Chicago's seediest corners, which Murray admired as if they were the great monuments of Europe. "This is my town," he was always saying to Candy, a little brother twice his size, "and this can be your town too!" Candy could feel in his guide the dark tingle of profanity, a sense of the unpredictable, of social exemption wholly unfamiliar to him. "He's the kind of guy," Candy reminisced in 1986, "who'd call me at 4 a.m. when the [Iran-Contra] hostages were freed and say, 'Thanks for being a Canadian.'" Candy, a bashful mountain, would never think of disturbing anyone, let alone at such a late hour. Not Bill Murray. He looked into placid eyes, into their ideas, with the calm clarity of a sniper. It was why he improvised, to quarrel with the rules. John Candy didn't know why he improvised. So, sharing the stage with Murray at Second City, he mostly hung back, as he had in his audition, and gave warmth. "He still had a ways to go," Flaherty said. "For a while there John would just disappear into the scene." If there is such a thing as too much of a team player, John Candy, in learning to be free in Chicago, might have been it.

Satirically upstaged by the ongoing soap opera that was Watergate, and generally bored of lampooning such easy targets as Richard Nixon and his gang of incompetents, Murray's group conscientiously put the whole enterprise of political commentary behind them. Washington, in effect, was turning out the best improv comedy in America; Second City had to do something different. "I think that what we try to do now is we don't go after the obvious targets," said improviser Jim Staahl. "You can sit at home and watch *Sonny and Cher,* and you can see the obvious targets get it." They subtitled their first show *Watergate Tomorrow, Comedy Tonight.*

Present in the audience one evening was Andrew Alexander, the bootlegger producer who had helped Flaherty's Toronto company find a rehearsal space only months earlier. "But this was my first time," he said, "seeing Second City." That Alexander, stifled by anxiety, had even made it out of his Canadian bed and bedroom was a miracle, but how he had managed to then leave his house and board a plane (thank you, Valium and vodka) for several hours of uninterrupted airborne claustrophobia only to get to his interview at Chicago's Ivanhoe Theater, and then actually put on a healthy face for the job of public relations director — which he got — even he couldn't tell you how. (Maybe, he reflected, it was his new white suit.) Most neurotics can at least attempt to stabilize their panic with practiced self-soothing or the sure knowledge that they have survived worse or comparable in the past. Not this guy; he was new to dread. He could remember a time, pre-anxiety, when he would call himself fancy-free, an adventurer, even, like that summer he and a friend, inspired by their favorite movie, *Lawrence of Arabia*, decided they had to see the sand, and from Canada thumbed it down to Ensenada, where, sitting on a beach drenched in a tie-dyed sunset, Alexander spotted a sailboat out there on the water — Omar Sharif flickering on the horizon — and years before he would ever hear of "Yes, and" — turned to his friend and mused, "I wonder where that sailboat is going?" One rowboat later, they had befriended the captain. "Do you have experience?" he asked. "Of course," they lied. Thus began their trip to France by way of the Panama Canal, which ended a week later with a mini-major storm that shipwrecked the sailors around Baja, marooning them for a week before they thumbed it back up north again. "My parents," Alexander said, "were kind of freaked out." *Freaked out.* Alexander didn't know the meaning of the phrase until later, in college, when he dropped acid for the first (and last) time and looked into the mirror, "which is probably the worst thing you could ever do," he said. "All of a sudden there were two or three of me and I was in a state of panic for about twenty hours. My life changed from that moment on in terms of anxiety, claustrophobia. I was a different person overnight. So the thought of ever getting on a plane or traveling anywhere within five miles of my bed . . ." And here on the Second City stage were Tino Insana and Jim Staahl, doing a scene about group therapy, wherein the therapist attempts to "enlighten" his patients with the satirical logic that "group therapy is not designed so much to solve your problems," as he explains, "as it is to convince you that you have them." Andrew Alexander loved the sketch; more even than that, he loved improvisation. It was like the lost version of himself: anarchic, ill-advised, impulsive, punk. Improvisation gave no time for nerves, no time for plans. It blessedly ruined every thought. He said, "The whole idea of the spirit of improvisation I had a visceral connection to."

In that improv set, Alexander saw Bill Murray and his joyfully nihilistic fusion of sincerity and sarcasm, the "blend of outrage and resignation, passion and black humor" historian Bruce J. Schulman identified as the distinctively skeptical style of the 1970s outlaw. One moment, Murray totally lost himself in character, as if improvising for Paul Sills; the next moment he seemed to be standing outside of not just his character but the entire scene, joking about joking, too blasé to even pretend to act. How did he switch so easily between them? Taking deep into heart the wisdom of Del Close, who advised Murray, as he did everyone, to wear his characters like a trench coat — knowledge that had been passed on to Del, years earlier, from Elaine May — Murray developed a relaxed pose of simple, subtle behaviors easy to slip into and out of. "Using small effects is from Second City," Murray reflected.

Crooning as a Las Vegas lounge singer, as he did in many improvisations offstage and on- throughout 1973, Murray, disco to Belushi's rock 'n' roll, would change his character name and shift from moronic dumb guy to dead-serious entertainer, exercising both muscles, intensity and irony, to incredible effect. Beside him at the piano, Second City's longtime musical director, Fred Kaz — a powerful presence at the theater for many years — had the stylistic fluency to follow Murray wherever his riffs bore him, and vice versa; a good musical idea from Kaz and his piano, like another improviser, could sway Murray in yet another direction. He really could play Bach with his right hand and Monk with his left. Squinting between beard and sailor's cap, Kaz was the paragon of nighthawk cool, Del's analogue in jazz, discoursing in mumbled cycles of images and epigrams aimed at the unconscious, the conductor, he thought, of a comedy orchestra. Some regarded Kaz as the longest-running member of the company. "He kept us all afloat," improviser Ann Ryerson said, talking to them with sounds, thinking music into their ideas. Kaz said, "Sure, you can say, 'If you play diminished chords, it's scary music. If you hold these notes down silently and strum the strings, it's like a harp.' But how do you say, 'This scene is really dragging and it's getting too serious and they don't know how to bust out of it, so what if you go "diddle dee, wang wang" on the piano, someone in the wings comes out in a funny hat and walks out like Charlie Chaplin.' Or what if you sense this is the real phrase of what is happening, where you can probably goose the response by taking the music out here, it makes a point and brings a response where there might not be a rise otherwise?" Kaz knew how. Out of the corner of his ear, Murray heard him.

"The whole lounge-singer thing," Tino Insana said, "was there so Bill could just play with the audience."

That character — making his mainstage debut as "Steve" — closed the first act of *Et Tu, Kohoutek,* Second City's forty-seventh revue, with "Las Vegas," a loosely structured outlet for Murray's sultry impertinence. Lending support, Insana introduces the sketch from offstage. "Ladies and gentlemen," he proclaims, "Caesar's Palace, right here in Las Vegas, is proud to present the comedy and song stylings of 'Read 'em and Weep!'" Into the spotlight comes Murray, singing, "Up, up and away in my beautiful, my beautiful balloon — balloon!" and makes straight for the audience. "Say, where're you from? Champaign? I love it out there . . ." Apropos of nothing, Insana runs on, pulled by an invisible dog on a leash — "Bow, wow, wow," Insana jokes — and runs off again. Murray awards him a false laugh. "Get out of here, you nut!," he says. "Ladies and gentlemen, Jackie Weep!" Then it's back to brownnosing the crowd ("Are there any grandmothers in the audience tonight?"), feigning sincerity, flaunting self-importance ("You know, a lot of people have been putting this country down . . ."), and finally getting down on one knee for the big bullshit finish, "Walk on, through the rain / Walk on, through the storm," which Murray full-throat belts, clutching onto Insana's leg until the lights black out. "Thank you very much! Goodnight!"

Andrew Alexander went to Bernie with a good guess. He had never done this before, so bear with him: What if Alexander got a small, seven-thousand-dollar investment from this guy he knew in the meatpacking business, a guy who had already invested in the Adelaide Street venture, and reopened Second City in the Old Fire Hall, the multistory former fire station that a lawyer and three doctors, one of them divorcing and in debt, had ineffectively converted into a dinner and dancing venue, and — here was the winning angle — serve dinner with the show? Bernie knew what that meant. With food, enough to satisfy the Liquor Control Board (crepes didn't cut it), Alexander could sell liquor, the absence of which had pretty much doomed the Adelaide enterprise. To keep the receipts looking fifty-fifty balanced between food and drink, Alexander would sell dinner-theater packages — food, booze, and entertainment rolled innocently into one. Of course, they'd have to get the improvisers back together, but it had only been six months, and —

"Sure," Bernie said, summarizing Second City's long-held business strategy. "Why not?"

Like that, Alexander — this quietly high-strung college dropout with few producing credits to his résumé — had the job. He called Joe Flaherty in Pittsburgh.

"Joe? I talked to the cast" — John Candy, Eugene Levy, Rosemary Radcliffe, and Gilda Radner — "and they said I had to get you back up here."

"Yeah," Flaherty said. "Sure!"

With its belfry and imposing brick archways, the Old Fire Hall looked like one of those cavernous orphanages out of Dickens, and after dark, when the drunk and homeless of Jarvis Street swarmed the liquor store opposite and that short block went *Oliver Twist,* you would have to second-guess your map if you were among those coming to Lombard Street dressed up for an evening of respectable Canadian dinner theater. "Nothing was bleaker," Flaherty said, "than Jarvis Street in the wintertime." But no, yes, you *were* at the right place. Inside, up the creaking, Miss Havisham staircase, you would begin with your prepaid dinner at the second-floor restaurant, a cranky "French" affair of gloved waiters and pretended elegance. "Most people with half a brain would never eat there," said waitress Sally Cochrane. "We had an hour and fifteen minutes to serve everyone before the show. Everyone in, everyone out." Soup or salad and pick your meat. "They'd be in a drunken bad mood after dinner," Flaherty said, "because of the food." The theater itself was its own bad mood. "You could barely see through the smoke," Cochrane said, "and it smelled bad. The chairs were uncomfortable. The tables were tiny."

Having replaced Flaherty three months into his Adelaide run, three months before the theater shut down, Eugene Levy entered the Fire Hall company an experienced beginner, a major asset to the sketch portion of the evening (memorably in his "Ricardo and the Trained Amoeba" skit, wherein, Levy said, "I do all the orchestral music while I'm working with this trained amoeba and then I crack the whip, he does a trick, and I take out my microscope to see if he's where he's supposed to be"), but when it came to taking suggestions, he clenched. Before the second set, while the others raced through improv suggestions backstage, Levy, uncomfortable with the go-go-go of Second City improvisation, held back. He could not lock in and commit to a scene element without reflecting on its consequences, and the consequence of those consequences, and the consequences of . . . time the intermission did not allow. "It's hard to just flip from 'Let's go with that' to 'All right, let's go with that,'" he said. "I'm not always *there* yet." Without a solid conceptual foundation for an improvisation, Levy couldn't launch. "Give Eugene a moment," was a common backstage refrain. "Hold on.

Wait for Eugene." He ate the same way . . . chewing, chewing, chewing . . . chewing . . .

Not that Levy was thinking slower, or less; if anything, he was thinking more, Bobby Fischer playing out chess moves, each one an idea, on several boards at once. Onstage, his steady deliberation, evocative of Jack Benny, one of Levy's heroes, paid dividends in segments like the fictional TV news anchors Earl Camembert and Floyd Robertson. The joke was that Flaherty, as Floyd, always delivered the important, big headline stories, where Levy, as Earl, got the scraps — cat stuck in tree, a forecast of light showers over the weekend. The opportunities for Earl's still and silent slow-burning self-doubt and humiliation, doubly hilarious next to Flaherty's cheery flamboy-ance, would be vintage Levy, and serve him beautifully for the rest of his career. No one at Second City could swallow a volcano like Eugene, then let the lava drip from the farthest corners of his expression, until, drip by agonizing drip, his eyes scream *I can't take it anymore* and, in a matter of milliseconds, explode.

Gilda was a different improviser entirely. She could not fail. "Her person-ality could bail her out of every situation," Levy said. "The audience loved her. If she got stuck, she'd look out at the audience, the audience knew, and they would just howl." Gilda didn't need "character"; Gilda, Martin Short observed, was more than enough. When, for instance, the ensemble needed to buy time between sketches — maybe, backstage, the right prop couldn't be located — an offstage voice would call out, "Stall!" and into the fray, a giggling Gilda, chewing a mouthful of sugarless gum, would appear on-stage, laughing in shared nervousness with the audience, and start talking. About her day, about her outfit, about her breakfast . . .

"Hi. I'm Gilda. I had toast today . . ."

Regressing to a childlike state, even when she played adults, Gilda spun out of pure sugar the character of Miss Eleanor Teably, based on her girl-hood nanny, Dibby. "I'm almost 32 years old," she said in 1978, "and some-times I look at my face and I don't see a grown woman. What I see is a child who has lived for many years." And so Miss Teably, shuffling along, squeak-ing about the inanimate objects she taught to speak on their own, came to life on the Second City stage, with the support of Eugene Levy. "She played a woman with a talking shoe," Levy recalled, "and I would be her interviewer." That shoe, Miss Teably beamed, was her prize pupil.

More than anyone else at Second City, the improviser in Gilda was *about* play, the poetic right to pretend, which the twenty-eight-year-old regarded, calmly and appreciatively, as permission to go comfortably insane. "If you think about it," she said, "the concept of creating a reality on stage, and then having to bend that reality to wait for the laugh . . . it's schizophrenic." That's just it. You could be crazy here. You could be everything that was you — and loved for it.

"What a gift," O'Hara said of Radner, "to have a place where you could go every night and express yourself. You have something to say? Get on the stage." O'Hara's time came at last, after her second tryout, when she won a slot as an understudy. Her first improvisation came midway into 1974.

The suggestion: Mosquitoes.

Backstage, racing through ideas, Eugene refused the rush to scene assignments. His deliberate consideration of each possibility, each choice and its ramifications, unnerved O'Hara, who, in the early days of their association — one that would span decades — was his precise opposite, ready to go with anything, fast. As preparation time ran out, she would nudge him into speech: "Eugene! Eugene! Eugene!" But he only cleared his throat, hedging to buy himself another thought. Between themselves, Flaherty, Candy, and the rest, they delivered each other to an idea: mosquitoes swarming the cottage country of Muskoka. Eugene agreed. They'd slap bugs the whole scene.

Then they were on. "Because I knew Candy the best," O'Hara said, "I stayed close to him, and because instinctively I knew he would be accepting, and because he had already hired me for the touring company, so I felt safe, I stayed next to him and slapped him for the whole scene, his whole body, just slapping him."

After the show, Candy taught O'Hara how to fake a slap. "Anyone else," she said, "would have killed me."

In the summer of 1974, O'Hara was inducted into the main company. "I was flying blind," she said. Until then, O'Hara's sketch and improvisational training consisted of watching Gilda and the others, the few workshops she took under Flaherty, and, going way back to high school, "a great theater arts teacher who wore lopsided wigs and let anyone who wanted to create material, get up and create it." When in doubt, O'Hara latched on to insane behaviors, unleashed her most argumentative self, and borrowed from real-life characters around her. "Getting the job at Second City gave me such a good excuse for watching people," she said, "but I did it anyway." At the encouragement of friends, who loved her imitations of a local woman she spied ambling around Aykroyd's place at 505 Queen Street East, O'Hara stuck out her jaw and cultivated Penny, a bossy, toothless, argumentative, arguably insane person. "When Catherine played a character," Levy said, "she *was* the character. She didn't just throw on a sweater and call herself an Old Woman. She became that character." It was a marked departure from the Del Close and Elaine May school of improvisational acting, which advocated a light touch, flexible in accord with a gestating scene. It was wholly in step, however, with the dawning school of legit theater-based, character-centric Toronto improvisation. "Maybe because everyone made me do it so I had so much experience doing it," O'Hara said, "I could improvise longer as Penny than I could as any other character." She — Penny — combined the cockiness and ignorance "at the core of every great comedy character," O'Hara said. "It's actually the core of life, going along as if we know what we're doing when really we don't." From that real-life core of false confidence can come the actual confidence — seemingly out of nowhere — to improvise comedy. "I swear," O'Hara said, "if life doesn't beat it out of you, everyone is born with the possibility of being funny."

Elaine moved *Mikey and Nicky* to Los Angeles, to the Sunset Marquis Hotel, a favorite of New Yorkers for its apartment-style suites and introverted, anti-Hollywood attitude, and spread her postproduction team and their equipment across several rooms, her own and theirs, where she could sleep and work a conscientious distance apart, and, in the spring of 1974, settled in to finish what she had been editing for many months already, beginning on location in Philadelphia and continuing in the Brill Building in New York. Since then — although, by some accounts, Elaine had already shot every scene at least once — she had come to Los Angeles to shoot even more. Finally, she really did have to stop; time, an accordion in Elaine's hands, could not be stretched any further. There were consequences now. According to her contract, a poem of legal concision and contingency, she had until June 1 — about a year since production began — to deliver a finished picture to Paramount. In exchange, they granted Elaine final cut. *In exchange.*

Did I mention she had a million feet of film? The equivalent of one hundred two-hour films? And that some scenes, shot with several cameras, she shot without a slate needed to sync sound to picture? And that at night, after her editor John Carter went to bed, she would tiptoe into the editing room and undo what he had cut together?

She decided that she and her team and their assistants required yet another set of eyes. In came Sheldon Kahn, assistant editor, to sync one of those slateless scenes, forty-eight hundred feet of film and six different cameras. Willing to work upwards of eighteen hours a day, six days a week, and, as a relative novice, too green to know the difference, Kahn took to Elaine's nocturnal schedule, 11:00 a.m. to 4:00 a.m., without objection. She promoted him to editor.

For months of nights, Kahn and Carter worked on separate KEM flatbed editing tables, each in his own office, converted bedrooms of their two-room suite. What would have been the living room became *Mikey and Nicky*'s film library, home base for assistants charged with dumping out ashtrays (empty film cans) and syncing and cataloguing the miles and miles and miles of film, racked and stacked in boxes floor to ceiling — you couldn't see wall — every frame of which Elaine had memorized. In editing, unlike production, no one ever had to wait for her. In fact, the opposite: Kahn and Carter had to race to keep up with Elaine's imagination. Those synapses were their only hope for making that June 1 deadline. "Elaine was so fast on her thinking," Kahn said, "that she would give me ideas of how to put a scene together and she would run over to John's [Carter's] room and work with him. She never had to wait for us to show her anything. She was always having ideas." Possibilities gushed out of her, two, three, four at a time. They crossed in the air, impossible to understand. "She thinks so fast," Kahn said, "that she would start a sentence and in the middle of a sentence go to the next sentence, and the thing is you learn when you're working with Elaine that you wait for her to come around the second time to get the complete idea because you may not get it the first time. Within three or four weeks, I was right on top of it."

For May, Kahn learned how to improvise with images. "I was willing to try anything Elaine wanted," he said. "I never said no."

Kahn, who had grown up listening to Mike and Elaine on LP, would begin every day with a joke he told May "purposely badly," Kahn said, "so she could turn to me and go, 'Oh, Shelly, *that's* not the way you tell that joke,'" which she did, and followed it with a pitch-perfect recitation as precise and seemingly practiced as if she were competing in a spelling bee. "And then," Kahn said, "she would tell me not only how far back the joke goes, but all the derivatives of that joke all the way from the beginning to where it is today." Abundant in variation, editing *Mikey and Nicky* worked in much the same way. Casually, improvisationally, Elaine would offer Kahn an editorial suggestion, a what-if or let's-try, and Kahn, not always knowing if she had shot and printed the material he needed to cut her thoughts together, had to dive into the living room of film, without thinking, the clock ticking, and swim around for places to drill drill drill. Story was oil, buried and liquid; but your ocean floor was Elaine's surface. So drill! Go! Like she had Falk and Cassavetes, Elaine freed Kahn to discover the best of him, and therefore, *them*, providing his fingers with enough film, enough variations in shot size and performance, for him to reply to her imagination, in pictures, almost any way he imagined. One scene they would try sixteen or seventeen different ways, and each way had to be assembled, finessed, discussed, compared, and viewed in context. Try explaining this to a studio: a scene that would have taken Mike Nichols four or five hours took Elaine May weeks. "When you've got a million feet of film," Kahn said, "you've got a lot of different ways to put a movie together." But how Kahn would justify logical impossibilities ("Wasn't Peter in the *kitchen* in the last shot?"), he had no idea. And yet he did. "I was learning so much from Elaine about how to put something together that shouldn't go together necessarily," he said. "I could get from one place to the next place because of Elaine, how to fake certain things in order to make it work. If she wanted me to cut something backwards and upside down — which she did — I would." And then, after he made it work, Elaine would return from John Carter's room to take a look at the results, nod at Kahn's little screen, and say, "Okay, well, now let's do that scene from John's point of view." And on through every point of view, and for each point of view there was a variation. "You know," she would say, returning to assess the results, "I like the third way we did it best."

The delivery date came and went.

Elaine never stopped. She couldn't. The sole indication of the world outside, the front door of the suite she kept open throughout. At two in the morning one night, she and Kahn were engaged in conversation at the KEM when she sensed, behind them, a disruption. A man was sitting in their cutting room, watching comfortably from a chair.

"Pardon us," Elaine said. "We're working."

"No, no. I'm sorry. Don't mind me."

"Well, this is sort of private. I know you're a guest of the hotel —"

"No, I'm very happy watching."

"Well," she said. "Then take off your pants."

He left immediately.

Precious few she allowed in, including hotel maids. She thought twice about the maids.

Exceptions she made for Falk and Cassavetes and of course, Mike Nichols. When in town, he would swing by the hotel and urge her to break for dinner, not in the lobby or at the KEM, but outside those physical extensions of her mind, at a restaurant, for a bite of real food instead of the candy and kefir she snacked on almost daily. She would accept Mike's invitation. Yes. For Mike she would take the time.

To buy herself more time, and more money, Elaine approached another ally, Paramount's Frank Yablans, with a highly plausible explanation. It was the sound. Falk and Cassavetes's dialogue she had recorded on two separate tracks — a strategy intended to provide her yet further variations in the editing room — but all these months later, she claimed, they still couldn't get the tracks to sync to picture. Yablans accepted Elaine's story, set a new delivery date, and allowed her to keep cutting, away from the studio, as was her preference, into the summer of 1974.

Of course there were rumors. Elaine, they said, was dive-bombing for disaster and taking the studio down with her. She was getting her revenge on Paramount, they said, for crib-stealing and mangling *A New Leaf;* they said that without the nonimprovisational checks of Walter Matthau on her first film and Neil Simon on her second, she had no one to rein her in, as Mike Nichols had in their act; they said she had lost control, that she had been working on this story too long, and the characters and actors, her friends, were too close to her for her to observe clinically. One rumor was certain fact: on *Mikey and Nicky* Elaine May had exposed more film than had been shot for *Gone with the Wind.*

Popping into the Sunset Marquis for a visit, cinematographer Victor Kemper had to see for himself. He was aghast at what he observed. Rather than narrow her focus, with more time to cut, she had amassed, incredibly, even more film in the editing suite. "She had printed the outtakes," Kemper said. It raised the question, had she scavenged tiny treasures from the scraps, or was she, returning to the drawing board, second-guessing her instincts? From Kemper's perspective, these outtakes had been abandoned for a reason. He said, "I thought her choices from a photographic point of view were off." But watching her work, he could see her intentions were earnest. If indeed she had lost control, as industry gossip stipulated, Elaine's eyes did not show it. "I think she worked," Kahn guessed, "twenty-four hours a day." Inspiration struck her physically; she would knock over an ashtray and keep talking.

"Vic," she asked Kemper, "do you remember that shot we were doing at the grave?"

"Of course I do." Who could forget it? They had run out of film.

"Well, I can't find some footage and it's critical to making this scene work."

"Elaine . . ."

"Have you any idea what could have happened to the film? I have no idea where to look . . ."

As she looked, Frank Yablans left Paramount, and when October 1, 1974, rolled around, Barry Diller had replaced him. Among his first orders of business: put an end to Elaine May's immunity once and for all.

11

1974–1975

Daniel Edward Aykroyd, purveyor of spirits and human miscellany, started bootlegging as a kid, back in his parents' basement. He kept a little bar for his friends and their friends, the cops, ex-cons, bikers, truck drivers, pole dancers, and undertakers of Canada's blue-collar underground. They knew, after the taverns closed for the night, the way to enhanced convivial deviance was down Mr. and Mrs. Aykroyd's coal scuttle to Danny's place. More even than booze, Aykroyd loved their company. As much as their company, he loved their expertise, their jargon, accents, accessories, firearms, uniforms, gadgets, the springs and gears of those gadgets, and the provenance of those gears.

If you didn't know Danny, you knew someone who did. Marcus O'Hara met him early in the decade at Toronto's Global Village Theatre, where, before the arrival of Second City, Andrew Alexander produced sketch revues and Marcus and his then-girlfriend, Gilda Radner, were ticket-tearers for the Aykroyd and Bromfield show. A college dropout nearing twenty, Aykroyd, O'Hara said, "had greasy hair, a chain wallet, the dirty fingernails of a guy who worked in a garage, and glasses with a bandage in the middle like a nerd." O'Hara — himself an actor, partygoer, and host to all — couldn't bottle the profusion. His new friend dressed like a punk, but he sounded off like a manic mechanic, like an instruction manual read at warp speed, and if you didn't know he was talking about carburetors and catalytic converters and discontinued locomotive technology, you could mistake his concatenations of industrial prose for the music of a bebop drummer. He had the verbal horsepower of a salesman, and the beneficence of a priest, but went with the Blacktop Vampire motorcycle gang — who, by the way, didn't ride motorcycles — and he believed in ghosts, but also in particle physics. Aykroyd's friends — i.e., all of Toronto — joked that his idea of perfect happiness was to commit a crime and then arrest himself.

The hangout à la Aykroyd was pitched at the awesomely nonviable and pathologically fast — always fast — like the time, soon after they met, when he raced Marcus through the moving subway, heaving open door after door to the very last car, then hurling his midsection over the guard chain to dangle inches above the tracks, his arms thrown back in flight. *Holy fuck,* O'Hara thought, *what a maniac. What a character!* "Jesus Christ!" Aykroyd yelled, pushing himself upright. "Marcus, get off at the next stop!" he instructed as he leapt off the subway and disappeared down the tunnel, only to reappear beside Marcus as planned, at the next station, thirty minutes later. "Why the fuck did you do that?" "I dropped my glasses," Danny said.

John Daveikis, Marcus, and Danny — "the Gentlemen Three," Aykroyd christened them — moved into 505 Queen Street East, a three-story storefront a quick trolley ride from Second City, back in the Adelaide days when there was nothing good to drink. Sobriety was tough on the patrons, but denying improvisers the sedative effects of alcohol — or fill in the blank — was like trying to put screaming children to sleep without a bedtime story. You couldn't just leave the theater and say goodnight to your friends, the funniest improvisers in Toronto and maybe the world. You needed to come down. But without access to an all-night bar — this being Toronto — the Second Citizens of Adelaide Street, at an inconvenient distance from 1063 Avenue Road, were in need. Knowing they had an ace bootlegger in Aykroyd, Adelaide's Jayne Eastwood approached the men of 505 Queen with five hundred dollars and a proposal. "I'll give you this money, if you guys open a bar," she said. "You don't have to pay me back, just make sure, when I come, I have waiting for me a glass of Canadian Club and a cigarette."

The Gentlemen Three obliged their beloved Jayne and opened the 505 Club on the first and basement floors of their storefront home, seven nights a week for dollar drinks served in glasses they stole, a little at a time, from Second City's kitchen, and if you didn't have that dollar, not to worry, as long as you were a friend of Danny's, and everyone was, and as long as the golden light inside the 505 gleamed onto the street between one in the morning and breakfast, which Danny, Marcus, and John took around lunchtime, the 505 would be open for you. "The 505 was unimpeded happiness," said 505er Bob Dolman, "encouraging everybody to do whatever calls you, and the place shook when the streetcar crawled by." On a great night, the 505 accommodated over a hundred illegal drinkers, improvisers, garbagemen, firemen, mailmen, and cops. "Hey, Marcus," the chief of police asked one night. "How do you get away with running this place? Isn't this a speakeasy?"

Yes, Officer, a speakeasy on one of the most trafficked streets in Cabbage-town, one of Toronto's most questionable neighborhoods, and flagrantly visible to passersby. Walled in glass from back to front, the 505 was designed to be a three-dimensional X-ray transparent from all sides, so that you could smoke out by the sixteen-foot marijuana plant in the backyard and see, across the party inside, to Queen Street out front. Signs of a bust, therefore, could be glimpsed from any vantage point, and just as quickly deterred. "Dan greeted the cops with such a friendly and welcoming confidence, they immediately softened and, if I recall, joined the party," said Dolman. "Such was his charm and his self-honed authority." Even the basement bathroom was glass, but Aykroyd shadowed the downstairs in dark lights suited to dancing and other clandestine sports. For Halloween, they trucked in hundreds of cubic feet of fallen maple leaves, and poured them in up to waist level, the perfect height, they agreed, for doing backflips. "We had tremendous evenings of fun there," Aykroyd said. "Cold, cold winter nights where we would sit and reminisce about the things we had just done onstage, and plan our futures." Regarding those futures, the 505 was home to a barber chair, regularly occupied by Lorne Michaels, a Second City fan, fellow comedian, and comedy writer.

Barreling through the 505 in driver's cap and bomber jacket, a baronial white scarf trailing behind him, John Belushi made for the proprietor, his friend of about three hours, Dan Aykroyd. They had only just met before the show that night, and though they enjoyed each other backstage in the Fire Hall's greenroom, it wasn't until they got up and improvised that John and Danny clicked into a single organism. "We took one look at each other," Aykroyd said. "It was love at first sight." Their fusion was instantaneous, complementary — John dangerous and loose, Danny loquacious and mannered — and, as with all natural duos, gave the impression of years of shared history. Of course, each knew basically nothing about the other, save for the lightning flash that had just struck them onstage, but that was enough for Belushi; he knew now that Aykroyd would be a great fit for *The National Lampoon Radio Hour*. The question was, was Aykroyd interested?

They took up stools at the bar and got down to it.

Radio Hour? What was that?

A comedy radio show produced by the magazine which Belushi was casting with improvisers of his taste, poaching from the best of Second City Chicago and Toronto. What's that music?

Curtis Mayfield. Who else was in?

Harold Ramis, definitely, there was no one better with a joke, and he actually *wrote things down;* Joe Flaherty, the ombudsman; Gilda, if Belushi could get her; and Brian Doyle-Murray, maybe the strongest actor of them all. And Christopher Guest and his friend from Bard, Chevy Chase, carryovers from National Lampoon's stage show, *Lemmings*. Crucial to Belushi, as he recruited his all-stars, was the prospective hegemony of Second City–style improvisation. Wait. Who's that now? (Muddy Waters.)

With *Lemmings*, a sinister Woodstock parody tangled in improvisatory sensibilities as oppositional as Guest's laconic hyperrealism and Belushi's theatricality, the producer in Belushi had learned a lesson. There were species of improvisers. If, interbreeding them, they couldn't find a common technique to bridge their disparities, then individual difference would damage the collaboration. Second City style — the aggregate of Viola Spolin, Del Close, and Bernie Sahlins — was one such technique. If the majority of the *Radio Hour*'s ensemble shared a language, Belushi could restore the camaraderie he enjoyed in Chicago and, so far, had lost in New York. It was, as ever, a family of friends Belushi was after. "That guy's voice. Who *is* that guy?" he asked Aykroyd.

"That's Hock Walsh, and Donnie Walsh, of Downchild, the preeminent blues band of this city and of Canada. That's the real stuff right there."

"Blues, huh? I don't listen to too much blues."

"You're from Chicago. You should know about the blues."

That the Chicago blues and the mind of Viola Spolin, wellsprings of improvisation, incubated only blocks apart — the former in the culturally diversified Maxwell Street Market, the latter in Hull House, where she mixed together the immigrants of Maxwell Street with her burgeoning theater games — lends credence to a prevailing theory of jazz as the American sound of spontaneous inclusion or, in the parlance of improv comedy, "Yes, and." "The real power and innovation of jazz," Wynton Marsalis explained, "is that a group of people can come together and create art — improvised art — and can negotiate their agendas with each other. And that negotiation *is* the art." For the first half of the twentieth century, at the Maxwell Street Market — at its height, the largest open-air market in the country — negotiation was essential to cohabitation. "Put quite simply," wrote folklorist Alan Lomax, "the Maxwell Street district is a living monument to American creativity, the site of some of the most profound social and cultural transformations of this century." Over fifty overlapping languages could be heard on a Sunday afternoon on Maxwell Street, where greenhorns became Americans, literally everything was for sale, and every indigenous music played — like the blues, brought up from the South with the Great Migration. With an estimated two cops per twenty thousand Chicagoans, vendors went unregulated, and as such flourished and multiplied as they never could in New York City, for instance, where the limitations of space and the efficacy of law enforcement seriously curbed the parameters of the cross-cultural hangout.

"Well, I'm not into blues," Belushi said. "I'm into grand funk and heavy metal —"

"That's all from the blues."

To prove his point, Aykroyd put on John Lee Hooker and Lightnin' Hopkins. Jazz musician Howard Shore, drawn by the sounds, joined Aykroyd and Belushi at the bar. Aykroyd and Shore watched Belushi physically absorb the rich, raw vocals and cool yearning of the electric guitar. He looked like he had just seen his first naked woman.

"You guys should start a band," Shore suggested when the song ended. "Call yourselves the Blues Brothers."

There was a time, before Belushi brought his friends to New York and the *National Lampoon*, when he felt terribly alone in Manhattan. It surprised him. Growing up in Chicago, he had always imagined New York to be a peppy achievement machine, the conveyor belt to destiny, but arriving in 1972, encountering in the *Lemmings* a comedy ethic of competitive one-upmanship, and a social scene fractured by constant distraction — in Chicago, they simply hung out all night in each other's apartments, crashed on couches, and went to Lum's for scrambled eggs the next morning — Belushi was not at home. "The contrast with Second City was striking," Judy Belushi said. "Second City provided a home for the cast. Here it was cold and impersonal." John got into cocaine and for a short time quaaludes. Though

Del advocated chemical enhancement, you couldn't get away with drugs as easily at Second City; for the most part, ensemble work, and improvisation's cabaret-sized audiences, wouldn't permit psychic alienation. But alienation was New York's mid-1970s chic, and the *Lampoon* sensibility — pitch-black, mercilessly offensive, slathered in sex and death — was the perfect excuse for damage. "We used humor as a weapon rather than a shield," said Lampooner P. J. O'Rourke. Crossing the line? At the *Lampoon,* there was no line. Second City, at its best, satirized, and mostly the right; the *Lampoon,* first in print and then onstage, gleefully massacred taboos with the indiscriminate "bad taste" of intelligent frat boys. If Second City was jazz, the *Lampoon* hit comedy with rock 'n' roll, the outraged dry hump of a country betrayed by Watergate, disabused of peace and love. To that end, they had the perfect front man in John Belushi, almost. He brought the unexpurgated *Fuck this,* but he needed like-minded improvisers to thrive.

Before Second City infiltrated the *Lampoon,* the maximalist in Belushi and the minimalist in Christopher Guest stuttered their theatrical collaboration. Remarkably, their systems coalesced in "The Perfect Master," an improvised *Radio Hour* interview Guest's Indian swami conducts with Belushi's American teenager. In their tone — a low-key ramble reminiscent of Nichols and May — they found common ground conducive to Guest's zero-joke threshold and a new Belushi, sounding like himself, talking with uncharacteristic ease. It was this conversational quality that appealed to Christopher Guest, who shared with one of his idols, Mike Nichols, an intelligence attuned to the slightest modulations of voice and sound. For Guest, a character began with the voice. It always had. "My first remembrance of being connected to what I thought was funny," he said, "was when I was quite young, 8 or 10, looking out the window and imagining the voices of the people I would see — this was New York City — on the street, and doing those voices." Finding a voice, he would cross the apartment to the bathroom, where the acoustics gave him a little echo, and discover more about his new person in front of the mirror. ("Christopher?" his mother worried behind the closed door. "Are you okay?") *Radio Hour* gave a stage to Guest's ear, namely his musical parodies, which he performed not as parodies but from the unironic point of view of seemingly real characters. The whiff of exaggeration or comment that was crucial to the Second City style had no purchase with him. "If you're playing a gay character," he said, "and there's some unconscious, subliminal message that . . . — 'This isn't really me, I'm straight, wink wink . . . but he's gay' — you're dead. You've got to be the guy."

The great Second City migration, courtesy of Belushi, began with one of Belushi's mentors, Brian Doyle-Murray. By the end of 1973, Murray was sleeping on the floor of John and Judy's Bleecker Street apartment. He'd be there for three months. "When Brian moved to town," Judy said, "it was the beginning of a new era." In no time they were back to the Second City rhythm of late breakfasts and open newspapers spread out like comedy maps. Soon after, Harold and Anne Ramis answered Belushi's call. Then Joe and Judith Flaherty sublet Christopher Guest's former apartment on Bank Street, not far from the Belushis; Gilda Radner moved nearby; Brian, falling in love with Gilda, got his own place a few blocks away. "John," Ramis said, "lifted us all and took us with him." Chez Belushi became Second City's makeshift New York outpost, the site of holiday gatherings, the improvisers' island on the island. When they moved uptown, into the *Lampoon* recording studio on Madison Avenue, to begin work on *Radio Hour*, a weekly broadcast Ramis described as "a fusion of the Second City working style with the *Lampoon* attitude," they were a rehearsed ensemble. Only the venue had changed.

Previously overseen by Michael O'Donoghue, the *Lampoon*'s mad priest of grisly laughs, the second iteration of *Radio Hour* flourished under the influence of its new creative director, John Belushi. Under O'Donoghue, one of the organization's star writers, the program was mostly scripted; Belushi turned *Radio Hour* into an improvisation. He didn't direct so much as lead by example, conveying the *Lampoon* edge "just by participating in those 'Yes, and . . .' discussions," Ramis said, and rolling tape on everything. Having their very own recording studio permitted a lot of improvisational experiment and discovery that Belushi's troupe never could have achieved on a rental basis. "Like Second City," Ramis said, "the *Lampoon* gave us an empty stage. They trusted our process and said, 'Here's the studio. Get in there.'" For the most part, the *Lampoon* writers stayed on their own floor, at their typewriters, whipping out manicured, pointed prose for the *Lampoon* magazine. With the notable exception of Doug Kenney, who made regular appearances in the eleventh-floor studio, the writers were as unsure of naturalistic comedy as the improvisers were of their "sophisticated" literary roots. As such, paper and pen were strange objects in the studio, equal parts organizational necessity and creative threat. They had to be handled responsibly, waiting nearby but at a distance, and by someone with one foot out of the ensemble, who knew structure but at the same time was friendly to freedom, a writer without ego, abounding with the Zen-like gift of letting go. That person was Harold Ramis. For some time he had been feeling outclassed as a performer, that he had been lucky to fall in with such talent. But it was not until *Radio Hour,* engulfed in personalities he had been assimilating almost every night for years, that Ramis realized he could think in their voices, just as Buck Henry, sitting down with Mike Nichols, realized he could "do" Benjamin Braddock. Radner, Belushi, Flaherty: their voices, even to Ramis, were stronger than his own. At a critical distance, he could join Belushi in thinking as Belushi, inciting him, like the kid sitting behind the class clown, to outrageous extremes. Seeing moves ahead, Ramis's imagination allowed the other *Radio Hour* improvisers to live in the moment; he held the straight line so they could zigzag. They trusted him to come up with ideas and write them down, with some narrative order, on actual paper.

The best of *Radio Hour* succeeded in bridging the contrary styles of Second City and the *Lampoon.* The intimacy of the radio format simultaneously restrained the Second Citizens' more theatrical instincts as it enhanced the level of cooperation among the Lampooners, forcing both sides to meet halfway out of their comfort zones. Downplaying *Lampoon* grotesquery to radio size, normalizing violence and political incorrectness, the hybrid style actually bolstered the effects of the satire, as in Chevy Chase's naturalistic reading of: "How can I really know if I'm a humorous person or an average, run-of-the-mill, I Don't Get It type? Quickly, slit your left wrist, taking care not to cut the tendons. Repeat with your right wrist. Okay? Now, if you thought I was serious about slitting your wrists, clearly you don't have a sense of humor at all."

By night, the Second City contingent was back at Belushi's place, or at Sandolino's, a twenty-four-hour Village café, assembling a set list that would become *The National Lampoon Show,* a touring sketch venture intended to duplicate the success of *Lemmings,* a show that, for all its misanthropy, had a clear target—hippie culture. The current targets were less tangible. "We're going to tell the audience they're assholes," Belushi told the group. "We're gonna shoot them the finger. No prisoners." A refreshing divergence, Flaherty thought, from Second City's tradition of liberal pandering, but wasn't indiscriminate satire, in its own way, just as easy as satirizing the right wing? "Harold and I would kinda look at each other," Flaherty said, "like 'John's running the show? What's this gonna be like?'" Amassing offensive material for the page or radio, Ramis understood and enjoyed, but antagonizing a live audience could embarrass everyone. Comedy had to have a point; otherwise it was just hostility. Flaherty agreed. "It wasn't like we were exploring black humor," Flaherty said. "A lot of the stuff we were working on was mean and crude." For openers, Belushi perverted "You're the Top" to "You're the Pits," to be sung with underwear on their heads. Gilda would do her Barbara Walters, a voice gag pretending to be a character. Then there was "The Rhoda Tyler Moore Show," in which she played a blind girl, with Belushi as her abusive boyfriend. (Belushi humps her leg. "What's that?" Gilda asks. "Just the dog, honey.") Sticking to Second City, Ramis improvised as the Swami, taking questions from the audience, and in "First Blow Job," a Second City–style people scene crossed with *Lampoon* humor, Flaherty and Gilda played father and daughter on the eve of her first date ("Do me one favor tonight, honey." "What's that, Dad?" "Don't give him a blow job. You know, that's how your mother died.").

There wasn't much of a point to this, Ramis lamented, but the *Lampoon Show*'s very pointlessness, the *We don't give a shit* attitude personified by Belushi, would be—not now, but soon—its secret weapon. In the meantime, as they set out in the fall of 1974, the conceptual division in the group rendered their set list an outrageous mishmash.

Partway into the tour, the elders were vindicated. "It had no real shape," Ramis said. "It was just a bad sketch show." Times two: most nights, they played an early and a late show, and never to interested audiences. On a budget, the *Lampoon* booked them into dive bars all the way to Canada. "We got dirty looks from motorcycle gangs," Flaherty said. "They came to hear rock 'n' roll and they got comedy." There were no tomatoes; the bikers threw beer bottles. Before one hostile audience, Ramis dropped a dollar bill and announced, "Partial refund." Some shows devolved into chug-a-lug contests between Belushi and the audience. "That's when I really started to miss Second City," Flaherty said. Radner, true to form, did all she could to keep the company buoyant backstage, but crowd control was out of her hands. Their show in London, Ontario, was miserable. Toronto was worse, a low point for the tour. Sales were dismal. An early close was likely. "I was getting tired of it," Flaherty said. "I wanted to go back to Second City."

Sitting with Eugene Levy at Toronto's El Mocambo was his college comrade, Ivan Reitman, a twenty-eight-year-old roll-with-the-punches Czech refugee, a director/producer and entrepreneur with basset hound eyes and the hustle of a fox. His inaugural short, *Orientation,* and second feature, 1973's *Cannibal Girls,* starring Levy and Andrea Martin, were pieced together, pragmatically, he said, with improvisation instead of a script. Made fast and on the fly, his first films rudely awakened him to the battles Elaine May — that very moment struggling through *Mikey and Nicky* — was only sometimes winning. "*Cannibal Girls* was a hundred percent improvised on a nine-page treatment and you can see it," Reitman reflected. "It taught me that you need a script if you want to go off script." From directing, Reitman had turned to producing — films, a children's television show with Dan Aykroyd, and *The Magic Show,* a successful Broadway musical — but he wanted to get back behind the camera. The Harvard-born *Lampoon,* he decided, was his ticket — "I thought these Harvard guys," he said, "really had a handle on where comedy was going" — and with characteristic self-sufficiency, he picked up the phone and cold-called Matty Simmons, the big name on the *Lampoon*'s masthead.

"Hey, I've got this hit show on Broadway," Reitman began. "Let's make a movie together."

"Everybody's calling me to do a movie, but I've got these really talented kids and I want to do some kind of a sketch comedy show off-Broadway. Do you want to produce it?"

"Yes."

"We're coming to El Mocambo with a version of the show," Simmons explained. "Why don't you go see it, then you can bring it to New York."

That night at El Mocambo, Reitman laughed at the jokes, but above and beyond the sketch work he was knocked out by the cast, Belushi's handpicked bouquet of Radner, Flaherty, Brian Doyle-Murray, and Harold Ramis. For all the show's cynicism, the fluidity of their give-and-take, their reciprocal amusement and support allowed a splinter of compassion to shine through the bitterness of the comedy. "The great skill of the people who come out of mostly Second City," Reitman understood, "was they're really trained to listen, which is the basis of all good acting. Not how you emote the line, [but] how you react to the line." They were connected.

Meeting them for the first time, "backstage" — really some dank closet behind the bar — after the show, Reitman sensed that that compassion did not extend to him, or to any outside authority figures. He was getting ready to explain he came in peace, that he was going to take them all to Broadway, when someone rushed in and announced: "No one's leaving."

Meaning everyone was staying for the second show. What? The company panicked. They couldn't just repeat the early show. Could they?

Reitman watched as the Lampooners, in the remaining moments before curtain, strategized next moves as if they were backstage at Second City, planning the improv set.

"Well," Harold Ramis, beacon of sober judgment, suggested, "let's do the same show over again and just change all the punch lines."

Back in the audience, Reitman, who could not believe the confidence he had witnessed backstage, watched the results in amazement; he would call it "the greatest example of comedic improvisational brilliance that I have yet to see." Each scene of the second set, beginning much as it had in the early show, the improvisers developed, sometimes, into completely new scenes, transforming, along with their material, the audience's mood. "Hey, what the fuck?! You just *did* that one!" became "Oh my god . . . What's going to happen?" Reitman was blown away. "If you weren't drunk," he said, "and a lot of the audience was, the show was funnier the second time around because you have the new joke and the spin on the old joke being retold. That's when I realized, 'Fuck, these are the most talented comedic minds I have ever seen.'" Reitman was overcome with their discipline, the right brain/left brain synthesis of cycling old material into new and back to old. "It just opened my eyes in terms of what the possibilities were in film, and I immediately knew I would have to make movies with them, that they would all be famous, that this was where comedy was going."

He would produce the *Lampoon Show* off-Broadway, and behind the scenes keep thinking Hollywood. "There didn't seem to be anyone making comedy movies for my generation," he said, "not antiestablishment movies." In an age of Woody Allen, Robert Altman, Peter Bogdanovich, Elaine May, Paul Mazursky, and Mike Nichols comedies — "serious" comedies for mature adults — there seemed no precedent for the filmed equivalent of the *Lampoon*'s "First Blow Job."

Whatever that antiestablishment *Lampoon* movie looked like, to get it going Reitman needed a story and a script. And the stage show needed an organizational overhaul. Assessing the possibilities, Reitman observed in Harold Ramis the "secret weapon," the seer of bigger pictures where other improvisers saw only scenes — theirs. Though Belushi acted as curator, se-

lecting scenes to suit his taste, it was Ramis who, in lieu of an actual director, impressed Reitman with his gentle leadership, and he enlisted him to
restructure the show for New York.

On their way, Flaherty dropped out, and in his place Belushi hired Bill
Murray, by then practiced in the *Radio Hour* and innately primed for what
lay ahead: grass, (free) beer, and the contentious barroom atmosphere he
never got at Second City. "That was the closest it ever got to the carnival life
for me," Murray said. "I was rooming with Belushi, because it was two to a
room. He was like my big brother." (Especially now that a romantic triangle
of both Murrays and one Radner spelled the end for Brian Doyle-Murray's
continued involvement in the *Lampoon Show*.) Offstage and on-, Belushi
and the younger Murray shared the *Lampoon*'s bias for provocation. "[Be-
lushi] wanted to see what they were like when they were uncomfortable,"
Murray said. They craved genuine intuition from the audience, even berat-
ing them, as Sills had his improvisers, out of their false selves. "Talk about
an explosion," Murray said. "We did a show that was like a brawl. It wasn't
theater; it was crowd control. Belushi would come out with a bullhorn and
do his stuff. We killed people." There — Del's influence. Get them, change
them, anyway you can.

Valri Bromfield was out in L.A., per producer Lorne Michaels's invitation,
to do some writing and performing on *The Lily Tomlin Special*.

He mentioned an upcoming variety program he'd be producing on NBC.
"It's the show I've always wanted," he said to her. "I've got it."

Gary Austin moved his new company, the Groundlings, into the minus-
cule thirty-seat Oxford Theater in East Hollywood, a part of Los Angeles
Laraine Newman described as "a good place to give up," and gradually, the
scripted segments of their repertoire faded away. With an ensemble evolved
from two years of workshops dozens of actors deep — even, at one time,
reaching a total of ninety performers, about thirty-five of whom became
a part of the shows — the Groundlings seemed predestined to improvise.
How else to include all those people (if you paid your tuition you were in)
creating their own material, scenes suited to their specific and unusual circumstances? "Everything we ever performed," Austin said, "came from improvising a scene over and over until we got it. We never said, 'What's the
story? What happens here?' We just did it. And if it worked, it worked; if

it didn't, it didn't." Unlike Second City and the Committee, the Ground-lings allowed for elaborate costumes and makeup and never worked with scripts. No one spoke of doing comedy. No one spoke of sketches. What did the *scene* need? "Nichols and May, Severn Darden, all those people, they weren't doing comedy," Austin said. "They were doing theater."

Days before their opening night, early in 1974, Austin realized Laraine needed more to do in the show, so he called a special meeting of the giant cast of fifty.

For four hours they improvised, to mediocre results. And none of it good for Laraine.

"All right, Laraine," Austin said as the group looked on, "there are times when we have to change the set in front of the audience — each one a minute or two each. Come back with three monologues, each a different character."

The next day, Laraine returned, as directed, with three delectable monologues for three different characters. They went right into the show between scene changes, and for being irregular solo pieces amid group scenes, stood out. Particularly memorable was Sheri, Newman's Valley Girl character, who caught the attention of audience members Lorne Michaels and Lily Tomlin, then casting, with Jane Wagner, Tomlin's upcoming TV special. Newman's Valley Girl, they could see, was practically made to order for the show's "Suzie Sorority" sketch, and from the theater off Oxford, she, Austin, and a handful of Groundlings were delivered to ABC, into the company of Valri Bromfield, Christopher Guest, and the other creators of *The Lily Tomlin Special.*

Michaels, meanwhile, kept returning to the Groundlings, his mind very much on finding the right kind of talent for his new venture, *Saturday Night,* a TV show tailor-made for his generation, the people who grew up watching TV. "I felt that American kids knew TV as well as French kids knew wine and that there *was* such a thing as good TV," Michaels said. "The problem was that no one in TV was accurately expressing what was going on. Carol Burnett sketches were dealing with the problems of another gen-eration — divorce, Valium, crabgrass, adultery." Michaels imagined a revue-style program of film parodies, specialty acts, stand-ups, rock music, and infused with the Monty Python, Beyond the Fringe, and Second City styl-ings he craved since his first taste of Nichols and May. ("They proved you could be smart *and* funny," Michaels said of improv's first stars, "that being smart and funny wasn't punished the way it was at school." The simplicity of Nichols and May's presentation also impressed Michaels. They didn't beg for laughs. Nichols and May were just two people sitting on stools, talking.) The idea to do the show live, and in New York, originated with NBC president Herbert Schlosser. "It should be young and bright," Schlosser wrote in February 1975. "It should have a distinctive look, a distinctive set and a distinctive sound. We should attempt to use the show to develop new television personalities."

"NBC doesn't expect it to work," Michaels explained to Austin at the Chateau Marmont. "I know everything's stacked against this. What's the worst night for television? Saturday. I know that. What's the worst time? Prime time. What's the worst cast? Unknowns."

Incredibly, this was how Michaels began his pitch. He had called Austin to his hotel to tell him he wanted Newman for his cast and Austin for a director, but not the sort that sat up in the booth cutting between cameras; Michaels wanted him to direct the *Saturday Night* ensemble as if he were directing the Groundlings. The show would be scripted, but unlike *Laugh-In, Smothers Brothers,* or any of the other variety shows of the recent past, this one would convey the anarchic, anything-can-happen spirit of improvisational comedy. Even if, on air, everything went according to plan, the mere fact of knowing that it might not lent the proceedings an air of danger, like watching a high-wire act. Such an anxious atmosphere would require a certain kind of dexterity in a performer, one that required a certain kind of director — a position for which Lorne Michaels, the producer, didn't have a title. But he wanted Austin for the job. Would he consider coming to New York?

No, thank you. Austin was going to stay in L.A. At the Groundlings.

"Look," Michaels continued, "they expect it to lose, but it's going to be a hit. Because it's going to be live."

The day Ivan Reitman showed up for the first *Lampoon* rehearsal in New York — in time to witness an argument between Belushi and Murray — he volunteered a resolution from the seat he had carefully selected in the back of the theater. "They're like soldiers together," he said, "who knew that each of them had their back and they were very mistrusting of anybody who was going to walk in." His presence was not appreciated. Bill Murray descended the stage, walked over to Reitman, and swung an arm around him like he was one of the family.

"Ivan, is this your coat?"

"Yes."

Deliberately, piece by savory piece, Murray re-dressed Reitman in his winter gear — coat, scarf, hat, gloves — and walked him to the door.

"Thanks for stopping by."

Reitman loved it. Undaunted, he came back to rehearsal the next day, and then the next, and by giving wide berth to their process, never questioning its apparent contradictions and mysteries, Reitman won their respect. "Finally, they realized I wasn't doing any harm. I had a great laugh and I'm very enthusiastic and they needed somebody in the audience to say, 'Well, how about . . . ?'" Basically, Belushi ran the show from the inside; Reitman, meanwhile, was warming to the paradox of improvisational directing. "Watching the process," he said, "I learned how these formidable comedians worked. I would never dare pitch a comedic line, but I think I had a better understanding of what makes a story and a character, and I sort of saw how we could do that together" — how it could work onscreen, how Reitman, if the off-Broadway show were a hit, could produce *and* direct them in the first *Lampoon* movie, especially now that, respecting their process, they respected him. As ever, Murray was the hardest get. "He lives his life to his standard," Reitman learned, "even though sometimes he's lazy and sometimes he's eccentric, and he's frustrating to other creative people and, frankly, unfair, because everything has to go on his clock. But he's worth it."

Rehearsal, for Murray, never ended; causing trouble was how he played, and play was for Murray, as early as Second City, indistinguishable from regular life. "He was always doing characters," improviser Dick Blasucci said. "We'd be driving around Chicago and suddenly . . . there he goes." Improvising offstage, in restaurants and on the street, Murray's characters interacted freely with unsuspecting civilians — just like real people. "He would play with anyone," Doug Steckler said, "but if people were confused by his launching into something, he would drop it. He didn't like confusing the innocent." Fellow improvisers didn't have to think twice; Murray was their movable playground. Jump on. "He had such an influence on all of us at Second City," said Aykroyd, who met Murray in Chicago months earlier, in the summer of 1974. "Just his boldness, his style. His character the Honker that he sort of does in *Caddyshack* — all of us at Second City were doing the Honker onstage and off."

Crossing the street with Reitman during *Lampoon* rehearsals in New

York, the Honker — a playful, seemingly brain-damaged oaf — emerged, out of nowhere, at full volume.

"Watch out! There's a lobster loose!"

People's reactions!

"Hey, get some hot butter, it's the only way to get 'em!"

The revised *National Lampoon Show* opened at the New Palladium in March 1975, and Harold Ramis left the show a month later, Reitman's cue to draw him into his big plan, a *Lampoon* movie. Was Harold interested? Could he write a treatment for a script somehow tying together these and other *Lampoon* sketches? Yes, but how to transform a revue into a single, feature-length narrative? Based on the most successful publication in the *Lampoon*'s history, the *1964 High School Yearbook,* Reitman suggested they go with a high school movie. A few false starts later, Ramis went to his wife, Anne. "Your college experience was so funny," she said, "and you've always wanted to write about it, so why not shape the material into a college movie?"

12

1975–1976

Their friends — Danny and Gilda — were leaving them for American television. None among them were certain that Danny and Gilda's decision to
take on a job as risky and perverse as Lorne Michaels's *Saturday Night* was a
sure thing, or even a good idea. Recalled one who was there, "they were saying, 'Oh, God. I hope we didn't make a mistake. We've got everything here,'"
a loving, creative kinship they might lose in the dispersive fray of New York.
To say goodbye, a band of 505ers lifted Gilda and a freight of bootleg liquor
onto a streetcar and rode her up and down College Street in sad celebration.

Elaine could tap-dance, and did, for an impressively long time considering,
but she knew, at some point, she would have to reckon with Barry Diller,
person to person. At this late stage — three trimesters into cutting *Mikey
and Nicky* — Paramount's new chief was entitled to a progress report, a
screening of a rough cut, no matter how rough, and a terminal, do-or-die
deadline she would stick to *or else*. So in May 1975 — two years after filming
began — Elaine came up with a plan. She consented to meet her boss, not
on the lot, where he was sure to make full use of his home-court advantage,
but somewhere in downtown L.A., not among the city's most comfortable
neighborhoods, but at one of those unsavory, broken-down diners tailor-
made to Diller's discomfort. She picked him up in a tiny rented Pinto. Diller
had to squeeze into the backseat.

   Elaine emerged from their détente with a new delivery date, September
15, 1975. *Or else.*

Then she returned to the editing room.

"I can't get this to work," she confessed to Kemper.

He surveyed the reels upon reels of cut and uncut film encircling her. "Elaine," he began, "are you trying to put everything we shot into the film?"

"Yes," she smiled. "That's why I shot it."

Fretful assistants looked up from their whirring spools to watch her, unbelieving. She was so happy. Too happy, some said, to ever finish it.

Upstairs, on the restaurant level of the Fire Hall, Sheldon Patinkin was directing "in the spirit" of the long-defunct Playwrights at Second City a production of Elaine May's one-act, *Not Enough Rope,* starring Andrea Martin as a suicidal girl without a noose, and Martin Short as her down-the-hall neighbor with twine only. Throughout, Patinkin marveled at their offstage chemistry. "Here were two of the funniest people ever, apart," he said, "but together . . . *together* . . ." Patinkin begged them to join the Second City company downstairs, but neither saw themselves in sketch or improv. Short, despite his prodigious ability, for all the support he won from his friends improvising in restaurants and living rooms, was "subconsciously afraid," he said, as anyone would be, facing the pressure to be funny on demand. "I should have been wanting it," he said, and though in a way he wanted it more than anything else—hence the terror—Short declined the offer and stayed the course as an actor. "I didn't see myself as a comedian," he said. Andrea Martin, who dreamed in musical comedy, was also unsure. Though Patinkin saw in her the potential to be "one of the funniest we had ever had, Chicago or Toronto," she was, like Short, only comfortable with a script. Granted, she knew she could be funny, sometimes really, really funny, but Martin owned none of it. At best, she attributed the good fortune everyone else called genius to some extrasensory groove that by the grace of God happened *to* her, and at worst, the recycled antics of a dancing chimp. Nevertheless, Martin assented—she loved the cast, her friends—and into the company she went, terrified to pieces.

It's easy to forget that despite the traffic jam of genius—Dan Aykroyd, John Candy, Eugene Levy, Andrea Martin, Catherine O'Hara, Dave Thomas, and others—appearing, throughout 1975, in some formation, most every night at the Fire Hall, Andrew Alexander struggled to keep the theater above water. "I was bouncing checks on them regularly, every week," he said. "Generally the first six who got to the bank would get paid." For the price of a sandwich and a drink, he brought in a posse of telemarketers from all walks of life — whomever he could find, he hired — to an office on the third floor of the Fire Hall. He charged them with selling dinner packages to CEOs — of McDonald's, condom factories, anyone — to fill the seats of the little theater. Bob Sprot, a silver-tongued salesman with a permanent hangover, came in every morning with a bottle of vodka, pulled the phone to his mouth and a trench coat over his head and, to Alexander's astonishment, sold hundreds and hundreds of dinner-theater packages — good for sales, but bad for improv. The Fire Hall went to corporate working stiffs given to general, barroom disrespect and uninspired suggestions ("Stripper!" "Toilet!"). Audiences talked throughout the show; others heckled; McDonald's employees threw money and crumpled Egg McMuffin coupons at the improvisers.

"Is there any point to this?" Thomas asked O'Hara amid the mayhem.

"Yeah," she said. "They paid their money."

Playing mostly to expressionless faces of their parents' generation — and sometimes only five or six of them a night — appreciators were scarce. Alexander tried pulling young people, the drunks and rock fans loitering on the street outside the Fire Hall, inside, bribing them with tickets and free beer if only to fill the seats. "We tried every plausible marketing strategy," Alexander said. "I even came up with something called the Oyster Moister, which was red wine and ground beef with an oyster in the center." But fifteen minutes after the show started, Alexander said, "there was, almost in unison, the sound of retching." Some guy threw up on Dave Thomas's shoe. He was only the first. Alexander said, "I'll never forget the sight of paramedics wheeling sick customers past the horrified patrons who were waiting for the second seating." Calamities such as these informed the work. "Second City Chicago grew out of academic roots and Second City Toronto grew out of bar roots," said Dave Thomas. "That defines the difference between the two theaters far more than the cultural sensibilities of the U.S. and Canada. Our audiences wanted a faster, coarser type of comedy."

Bernie Sahlins, when he appeared, could not compel them toward the topical, the prescient, the satirical *Right Now*. What about a political song, guys? The kind they did in Chicago? "He brought that tradition into Toronto," Thomas said, "and we hated it because we thought [those songs] were stupid and didn't give us a chance to play characters." Flaherty, their director — returned from his *Lampoon* stint in New York — stood with them. He reveled in characters, the Mitchums, Joan Crawfords, Barrymores, and B-movie types that rolled out of his movie-made unconscious. "I just wanted to get away from the politics stuff," he said. "I was tired of the politics. Eventually it was pandering." Respectfully nudging Sahlins aside, the improvisers, also weaned on television, slipped right into Flaherty's sweet spot. None among them had come to Second City with satirical, or even comedic, dreams; they were, like Flaherty, actors first. Performers. Fans of film and theater, their lifelong marinade, bubbling with the Canadian predilection for the gargantuan they inherited from the English. "Whenever we did a commercial parody or something involving television it would get the biggest response from the audience," Flaherty said, "because everybody knew that stuff, and there's nothing wrong with that." The emphasis on laughs — opposed to the Spolin method — edged them toward a broader, though equally nuanced style than their midwestern brethren. Even if their sketches and improvisations weren't always about show business — the sort of genre mashups Flaherty loved — their well-rehearsed gift for exaggeration, for exploding the already-exploded personalities of American entertainment, spilled over into their everyday civilian characters. Entertainment, for many in that group, was as much content as it was style.

For instance: Andrea Martin's Edith Prickley, improvised to life in the Fire Hall late in 1975.

In the tiny dressing room the cast shared backstage, and in the twenty minutes they had to cast the evening's every improvisation, the improvisers chewed over a flurry of audience suggestions, one of which, "Parent Teacher Conference," was quickly disseminated among them: O'Hara would be the teacher and the rest of the cast, including Martin, the parents. Frantically, the company grabbed for hats and props and glasses and wigs — whatever struck a chord — amassed secondhand over the years from vintage clothing stores and hand-me-downs, undressed and dressed with no attention paid to privacy, or why they were drawn to what was drawing them. O'Hara, reacting as the straight man, reached for a prim cardigan and pinned her hair in a twist, the men went for ties and glasses, and Andrea Martin, already laughing at a 1950s leopard-print jacket and matching hat once belonging to O'Hara's mother, snatched them off the rack, and riffing on the leopard theme of loud and garish, went for a pair of rhinestone glasses and the reddest shade of lipstick she could find. From the look, came the person. "The posture, the voice, the intonation, the laugh, the volume, the name Edith all came together the minute I entered the scene and Catherine christened me Mrs. Prickley," Martin wrote. What followed was automatic.

"It is very important that we all get involved with our children's schooling and help them with their homework," teacher O'Hara says. "What about you, Mrs. Prickley?"

"Oh sure, dear," Prickley blasted. "I help Sebastian all the time. I say the family who plays together, stays together. I do his homework. And he pours the drinks" — then that laugh — "*Pa-HA!!!*"

It wasn't until she discovered Prickley, who said everything she thought and feared nothing, that Martin discovered the indomitable feeling of freedom that comes to those who improvise out of their nervous selves and into their alter egos — the forgotten people they really are.

By September 25, ten days after Elaine's drop-dead deadline, *Mikey and Nicky's* original budget, estimated at $1.8 million, had more than doubled, to $4.3 million. The next day, September 26, Elaine asked Paramount for an additional $180,000 to finish cutting the picture. The studio refused. "We offered her all of the support possible to make the film she and we originally wanted," explained Arthur N. Ryan, Paramount's senior vice president. "But we were unable to get her to deliver the picture."

Paramount pulled the plug, but that didn't mean Elaine was going to pour her film down the drain. She remembered *A New Leaf.* Rather than stand by in impotent rage all over again, while the studio kicked down her door and recut her work, she turned around and, before anyone could steal her movie away from her, sold a $90,000 interest in *Mikey and Nicky* to Alyce Films, a company no one had heard of. With those completion finances in hand, she began to finish cutting *Mikey and Nicky* as fast as anyone possibly could, speeding through scenes, a film fugitive with the border in sight, hurdling executives on all sides, ignoring phone calls, locking her doors, drawing curtains against daylight and the moon to buy herself just one more moment's improvisation to set in stone a definitive record of the film, *her* version, that, after all the drafts, all the miles of exposed film, negotiations, refused compromises, samurai schemes, and mad evasions, the two decades it had taken her, from the University of Chicago to today, to get Mikey and Nicky, two living humans, on film, she would at last turn over to the studio for release, posthaste, before —

Paramount sued. It was their picture. Alyce Films?

Then — this is wonderful — Elaine countersued, contending that she was only within a few days of completing *Mikey and Nicky*. Hold on, she would have it in time for a Christmas release, she said. Isn't that what they wanted? Or were they now trying to sabotage *her*? "In total bad faith," argued May's lawyer, Bert Fields, "Paramount refused to put up more money. The studio apparently wants to take over the film, which we are looking forward to fighting."

In October 1975, a New York judge ruled that *Mikey and Nicky* did indeed belong to Paramount and issued a writ of seizure granting the studio immediate possession of all pertinent film materials. A phalanx of New York sheriffs set out for the film labs of Manhattan to claim Paramount's lawful property, which they recovered in short order — minus two crucial reels. They were missing.

"We had no idea how long ninety minutes was when we first started," Lorne Michaels said. By the afternoon of October 11, 1975, the day of the first show, there was no guarantee that they would be ready come eleven thirty, no guarantee that, loading up on last-minute alternatives in case of emergency, he hadn't *over* overbooked the show (in addition to the cast and host, George Carlin, he had the Muppets, two musical guests, solo performances by Andy Kaufman, Valri Bromfield, Billy Crystal . . .), his engineers were still referencing the instruction manuals for the new audio equipment Lorne had squeezed out of NBC for *Saturday Night,* the set was still a work in progress, and the Friday rehearsal had been awful. The lighting director had disappeared, there weren't enough people in the audience (warm bodies were being pulled in off the street), and the show ran two hours over. Writer Tom Schiller hid under the bleachers and tried to send out good vibes.

And Belushi still hadn't signed his contract.

"There was a spirit very much in the first few years," Michaels said, "that we were making it up as we went along."

Of course there was a script, but the spirit of the show, what would be communicated to the live and home audiences, came through the rebel immediacy of the under-rehearsed. The brick basement set, the audience positioned directly in front of and around the stage (and sometimes in the shot), even the music of *Saturday Night,* under the direction of Howard Shore, conveyed the living intimacy of a nightclub. "I think *Saturday Night* is about the closest thing you'll see on TV to Second City because it's live," Gilda Radner said, "and it's not being sweetened, and it's always under-rehearsed, and it's always opening night." Theoretically, home audiences would respond to that atmosphere. "Live" puts us in Studio 8H. "I think 'Saturday Night Live,'" Michaels said, "is about a contact with another group of humans coming through this tube." America is lost, *Saturday Night* said, but we have this: a show that is not a show, it's not pretending, like Washington, but it's really happening, and not in Hollywood, but a "real" place, New York, where things that shouldn't be going on could go on, and live on TV, so if something that shouldn't happen happened, nothing could be done about it.

About Gerald Ford, Jules Feiffer wrote that "he was the embodiment of the void left after the collapse of the American dream," but Feiffer could have been writing about television. When Belushi, in his first interview with Lorne Michaels, bragged that his television was covered in spit, he unknowingly spoke for an entire generation freshly out of love with the medium that raised them. *Saturday Night* rekindled their love affair. The show told them up front it knew what they knew: TV lies to us. The inverse of Gerald Ford, *Saturday Night* so reveled in its own inauthenticity, it came off as the only honest show on television. To a country still smarting from the smoke and mirrors of Watergate, that sense of *really happening* was payback, and at its cathartic peak, tantamount to a national cleanse.

Loading his ensemble of Not Ready for Prime Time Players with improvisers — Belushi, Radner, Aykroyd from Second City, Laraine Newman from the Groundlings, and the splendid glinting Jane Curtin, late of Boston's improv troupe, the Proposition — Michaels insured himself against catastrophe. Television executive Dick Ebersol said, "He had people who trusted in each other's instincts enough to play with it on the air." Chevy Chase and Garrett Morris, originally hired as writers, lacked their range. "I had much less of that Second City experience," Chase confessed, "and they were all better actors than me, but one thing I could do was look into a camera lens and mug with impunity to a certain degree." Chase's brilliant solo turns would alienate him from the improvisers. And Morris, a playwright, couldn't quite play with the majority. "Garrett didn't do improv,"

Curtin reflected. "Garrett, when he wrote things, he really concentrated on it and was methodical about it and so he did not come from that facile place that most of us came from."

Still, Belushi would tease Laraine Newman. "What's that group you're from? That group in L.A.?" Homesick and lonely and only twenty-three, Laraine at least had Gilda and Jane, big sisters in New York. Together, they shared a dressing room, innocence, bravery, and delicious panic. "Nobody really knew what was going on," Curtin recalled. "How could you? There was no template that we could follow." That night of their first show, Carlin swung by with a rose for each. It momentarily put them at ease. "I just wanted you to know," he told them, "I hope you have a lovely show. And good luck."

Bromfield's dressing room was already strewn with flowers — from lesbians. On her way past, Radner stopped at the door and stared at the pretty picture. "Wow!" she exclaimed. "I want to be a lesbian!"

Carlin coolly interrupted their conversation to ask Bromfield the question few would. "Are you a radical lesbian feminist?"

She looked to Gilda. "Yeah, honey, you are," Radner said.

"I am?" Bromfield grinned. "Yeah, I guess I am."

Carlin beamed back. Radical worked for him. "Have a great show."

Despite Radner's enthusiasm for *Saturday Night,* and Michaels's enthusiasm for Radner (she was the first player he cast), she missed the freedom Second City had granted her imagination. Improvising, she had the power of whim to make the Fire Hall stage, in Toronto, into the pretend worlds of her childhood. Regression was Gilda's asylum and furtive wellspring, the message of innocence she brought back to earth. But the invisible dolls and spontaneous playthings of Second City, the sudden tumbles, cartwheels, and spastic leaps Gilda so loved were not suited to the literal eye of the camera. "And you can't change lines because they base camera shots on them," she pointed out. On *Saturday Night,* then, she would recover her sandbox not in the transformation of studio space around her but in the changing worlds inside. Grabbing hold of an open moment, especially one between herself and Aykroyd or Curtin, Radner found she could push her concentration from the studio into the long tunnel of shared subjectivity, and be free. "When you look in their eyes onstage," she said, "and you're doing a live television show, there's somebody *home* there, you know?"

For the tense hour between dress and air, as Lorne recalculated time against laughs against a feasible running order, Bromfield huddled with Kaufman and Crystal on the hallway floor outside the studio, praying her bit wasn't going to get cut. "Everybody was pooing their pants," she said. "It was so scary. It was diarrhea time. It was so frightening. Ninety minutes live!" When the verdict came — they were going to have to slim their acts by a couple of minutes — Crystal fled the studio and was bumped from the show. *Fuck,* Bromfield thought, *I have to get ready,* and started cutting.

Around then, Michaels's manager, Bernie Brillstein, passed Bromfield on his way into Studio 8H. With only minutes left to air and the Crystal debacle quelled, Brillstein managed only seven or eight confident strides before he crashed into the middle of an escalating argument. Haggling with a producer, John Belushi, who had no agent, was already very much in costume for "Wolverines," SNL's first-ever sketch, still complaining about the contract he hadn't yet signed.

Belushi dangled the papers in front of Brillstein, his boss's manager. "He insists I sign this contract."

"So sign it. What's the big fucking deal?"

"What do *you* think? Would you sign it?"

Brillstein, who helped write the contract, urged Belushi that it was fair, and without twisting his arm, tried, politely, to get him to sign it immediately, before they counted him on . . .

"Tell you what," Belushi returned. "If you manage me, I'll sign . . ."

"You got a deal."

The Brillstein-Belushi association would deliver considerable power to both men and win Brillstein, among other clients, the finest improvisers in comedy. Aykroyd, Radner, Martin Short . . . "I was the dad to this group of loonies," Brillstein said proudly. His patrimony was sealed then, at that moment, with two minutes to air.

The next hour and a half of that Saturday night in October, Valri Bromfield described as "a ninety-minute race in your brain, in your body, and the audience was right there, racing with us. In Studio 8H they were so close, you could reach out and touch their hands. But you didn't need to. You could feel them from the stage. That's what people think of when they say electricity. I'm not religious, but I think that's what people feel when they go to church."

• • •

Joe Flaherty, in the strip mall in Pasadena where he had set up yet another Second City outpost, his second, was taking intermission at the bar when Belushi appeared on TV. The whole bar quieted and looked up to watch.

"Man," spoke a rocker on the stool next to Flaherty. "This show is really good."

On-screen, Belushi was hard at it, attacking *Saturday Night* with his trademark scores and the old personalities Flaherty knew like members of his own family.

Yeah, that's Second City, he thought. Belushi's doing Second City.

Flaherty couldn't watch the whole episode that night. Intermission ended and he went back onstage.

After the disappearance of the *Mikey and Nicky* reels, Barry Diller's telephone started ringing with personal requests from Elaine May's most influential friends, including Warren Beatty and Peter Bogdanovich, to please reconsider Paramount's cold-turkey policy and write the movie one more tiny check, an oily olive branch that smelled to Diller — who could easily picture Elaine in a postproduction cellar somewhere with the "missing" reels, holding a gun to their heads — more than a little like extortion. "She is a brilliant woman and a wonderful woman," Diller is reported to have said, "but she can go to jail or the madhouse for *ten years* before I will submit to blackmail!"

On grounds of criminal contempt, Paramount took Elaine back to court, in September 1976, whence some version of the truth emerged from Dr. David Rubinfine, Elaine May's psychologist husband. According to Rubinfine's deposition, on October 20, 1975, the very evening, a year earlier, that Paramount won its writ of seizure on all *Mikey and Nicky* film materials and the reels in question disappeared, Rubinfine hurried to the Carter studio in New York, where much of the film was being stored, removed about a dozen cartons, and hid them, overnight, in the trunk of his car. Who instructed him to do so? Paramount claimed Elaine May; she had been seen, an hour after the writ was issued, at Rubinfine's apartment. (They kept separate addresses.) Arguing on her behalf, Bert Fields denied May's involvement, describing instead a phone call placed to Dr. Rubinfine "from a person claiming to be speaking for May." In either case, Rubinfine drove the film over state lines, out of New York jurisdiction, to the Connecticut home of Dr. Andrew Canzonetti, unloaded the cartons, and called Peter Falk, who instructed Rubinfine to tell Canzonetti that someone would be by to collect the goods. In his deposition, Falk, also a Fields client, neither confessed to nor denied making this statement, only acknowledging that he "might have said it." It was Fields's contention that Falk himself drove to Canzonetti's the following morning, intending to transfer the film back to a safe storage facility, only to be told, upon his arrival, that an unidentified limousine driver claiming to be under Falk's employ had beaten him to the punch and made off with the film. It was gone — a kidnapping.

Alyce Films, by the way, had been traced to Falk.

"Can you help us with Elaine?" Diller asked Paramount's vice chairman, David Picker.

"Probably."

A friend to executives and filmmakers alike, Picker had the imprimatur of fair dealings and strong credits that characterized the very best of United Artists, his former home. With total cool, he simply picked up the phone and called Bert Fields. "We talked in 'what-ifs,'" Picker recalled. Like what if, no questions asked, the film were to materialize at Diller's door? Would the studio consent to preview Elaine's cut of *Mikey and Nicky* at picture-appropriate venues? From these and other hypotheticals, Picker and Fields found a comfortable middle ground and hung up satisfied. Several days later a package with Picker's name on it arrived at a Connecticut post office and was delivered to Diller's office in Los Angeles. *Voilà:* the missing reels.

And then, as agreed, *Mikey and Nicky* got its first preview at an appropriate venue. By the end of the screening, the audience reaction was loud and palpable.

"Are they cheering?"

"No," Elaine said. "They're booing."

They had expected a comedy by Elaine May. *Mikey and Nicky* was not a comedy.

It was, however, a very funny tragedy and, I think, flecked with forces of real, rabid danger, as only a nighttime experiment can be. You should see it.

Elaine May wouldn't direct another picture for ten years.

13

1977–1982

Joe Flaherty was directing a "best of" show at the Fire Hall when Bernie Sahlins and Andrew Alexander called him upstairs, to Alexander's office, and explained the situation. As long as Second City couldn't provide its improvisers with a larger platform for growth beyond its local theaters, *Saturday Night* would bleed them dry, poaching their stars from Chicago and Toronto. To keep them happy and at home, the bosses had struck a deal with Global Television, a local network, diminutive by any standards, a pebble to New York's 30 Rockefeller Plaza, for seven half-hour episodes of Second City comedy, though no one had yet decided what exactly that would be. In fact, no one had decided anything, hence the summoning and questioning of Joe Flaherty, their oracle. What if, Sahlins proposed, they simply broadcast the stage show as is, bentwood chairs and all? That's what they were good at, and anyway, at five thousand dollars an episode, they didn't have the budget to do much more. Flaherty laughed: "I was thinking, *What? We're going to go up against* Saturday Night Live? *With that? Yeah right.*" Lorne Michaels had known exactly what kind of television show he wanted; Sahlins and Alexander, theater producers, were making it up as they went along. So they passed the ball to Flaherty. Not like he had much experience with television either, but . . .

"Who do you want to work with?" they asked.

"Well," he said, "I like the cast I'm directing." It included Andrea Martin, Catherine O'Hara, and Dave Thomas. Eugene Levy wasn't in the current revue, but Flaherty, who gunned for Levy against Sahlins's inclination as early as the *Godspell* days, wanted him — and John Candy — back and in the show, whatever it was. "And me," Flaherty said, "I'd like to be in it too."

"What about writing? We're going to need some writers."

"Harold. Harold Ramis."

"I don't think he'll do it," Sahlins said, reluctantly, knowing the last time he offered Ramis a job in Canada, in the first Toronto company, he turned it down. Moreover, Harold was busy. He was in L.A. working piecemeal with Christopher Guest, and Billy and Brian Doyle-Murray, all recently sprung from ABC's failed *Saturday Night Live with Howard Cosell,* improvising comic journalism — documenting actual events, like the Oscars and the Super Bowl, tongue-in-cheek — for TVTV, a guerilla video collective heavy into broadcast satire; he was spotted in New York, writing with Doug Kenney and Chris Miller that *Lampoon* movie, *National Lampoon's Animal House,* which, under Ivan Reitman's supervision, would feature, they thought, a Second City ensemble of the Murray brothers, Aykroyd, John Candy, and Belushi as Bluto, the most animalistic of all the animals. Casting the first *Lampoon* movie with Second Citizens, they really could imagine *Animal House* would be the most successful comedy ever. "Our generation had broken into television with *SNL*," Ramis said, "and this was going to be the first 'new' Hollywood comedy."

"Okay, but let's try to get Harold," Flaherty urged Sahlins. "He's easy to work with and such a funny guy. And he should be in the show, too."

What Sahlins didn't know was that, despite all his work, Ramis had only about forty dollars left in his bank account.

"Has it occurred to you that you might not be successful?" Ramis's wife asked him moments before Sahlins called.

"Oh, man. It's occurring to me *right now.*"

Which is when the phone rang. Sahlins made the offer — writer/producer of this incipient, ill-defined show — and Ramis said yes.

A short time later, Sahlins and Alexander convened their brain trust — Flaherty, Ramis, Sheldon Patinkin, Eugene Levy, Dave Thomas, and, up from Chicago, the fabled Del Close — in Alexander's office to improvise a television idea to life.

Flaherty began. "I want to do television parodies," he announced. "They always work on stage because everyone can relate to them. Everybody watches television."

Everybody but Bernie Sahlins. "Are you sure you don't want to put the camera in the theater —"

"No, no, parodies work." Flaherty was thinking also of *Saturday Night Live*'s uncommonly reliable commercial parodies.

Del lit up. "What if we presented ourselves as the world's smallest television broadcasting company?"

Harold could see it: they would be what they really were, an actual low-budget production, charming in their makeshift desperation. They could aim for bad, for cheap. Why hide? It would be funnier to run toward the problem. That's what comedy was.

"We could play the people working at the studio," Flaherty added, "and we can play the people in the parodies."

"How about it's a programming day?" Patinkin suggested. "We start off with the morning news . . ."

"Then a soap opera . . ."

"Maybe a movie . . ."

"End the day with a sermonette . . ."

"We could call it," Flaherty said, "the Second City Television Network."

"Too long."

Flaherty tried again. "How about Second City Television?"

SCTV.

Typical of the laissez-faire policy he would master, Andrew Alexander did not deny the momentum, the spirit of consensus building in his office. He would not rule *SCTV* as Lorne Michaels did *SNL;* whatever aired would be, like a Second City improvisation, the collaborative outgrowth of the writer-performers. "How soon," he asked the room, "can you get working?"

Grabbing a free office at the Fire Hall, Flaherty, Ramis, and Sheldon Patinkin began by asking themselves who would run this fictional television network? And who would play him? "That was going to be Harold," Flaherty recalled. "Because that's who Harold was." And the network's star producer, the guy with big dreams too big for such a little network? "We were talking about an Orson Welles type of character," Flaherty said, "bigger than life. And that was obviously Candy because that's who John was. He did everything in this excessive way." Flaherty, who had been tracking Candy's improvisational development from his audition three years earlier to his current work at the Fire Hall, had earmarked, in addition to a remarkable improvement in Candy's self-confidence, his instant likability, a face

— "my five-hundred-dollar face," Candy liked to joke — that Flaherty knew would get its due on TV, in close-ups. "I could see Candy would be the guy," Flaherty said. "I had no doubts about that."

To find out more about this guy, the show's main character and, concomitantly, *SCTV,* Flaherty and Ramis went backstage before an improv set, and handed Candy his instructions.

"Johnny," Flaherty said, "you're gonna play a producer who's losing his job."

In a previous show, Andrea had improvised as a character she called Kitty LaRue. Flaherty never forgot the name.

"The guy's name," Flaherty told Candy, "is Johnny LaRue."

Seconds later, Candy, Flaherty, and Ramis were improvising for a Fire Hall audience.

"This is it, Johnny!" Flaherty announced in character. "Your career's over unless you come up with a hit!"

As suspected, Candy was perfectly cast. Paradoxically gargantuan and small-time, amplifying strains of a Canadian hang-up Dave Thomas described as "an inferiority complex covered by a very thin layer of braggadocio," in LaRue, a Quixote, their Canadian hearts tilted at the windmills of American entertainment. "Johnny LaRue really reflected that," Thomas said. "The guy with the big dreams but there was never the talent or the budget to pull them off. It was an artistic outgrowth of the actual reality of the show, which was we were always underfunded and underappreciated and always feared that we were second best to *Saturday Night Live.*" LaRue told their story.

They were too modest and too inexperienced to know that they — John Candy, Joe Flaherty, Eugene Levy, Andrea Martin, Catherine O'Hara, Dave Thomas, and Harold Ramis — were on the road to becoming the greatest television comedy ensemble in North America, probably ever.

None of them had any idea how to make this idea into a television show, not Andrew Alexander, producing his first series; not Sheldon Patinkin, a first-time editor cutting tape in an extempore corner of the Fire Hall; not Bernie Sahlins, uneasy with the idea of television parody that was the show's springboard premise; not the cast, doubling as writers, making $250 a week, and without any experience writing scenes on paper, and never exactly sure what their budget was, and therefore, never precisely clear on what they could afford to write. Working without a live studio audience, they had no idea whether their jokes were landing, or how they could produce seven half-hours of comedy against the clock at Global Studios, a third-rate production facility out in Don Mills, a neighborhood sagging with chintzy props and recycled sets, its own jury-rigged crew and an Egyptian director, Milad Bessada, unversed in American pop culture, who didn't always get the joke. Bernie tried to enforce literary parody, and the company begrudgingly obliged here and there. But Bernie was halfway MIA, in Chicago as much as he was in Toronto, which left Andrew Alexander the man on the ground. Alexander, wisely, made it his policy to disengage from the creative. "I set the table," Alexander said, "and let the people do what they'd been hired to do," so they looked to head writers Joe Flaherty and Harold Ramis for marching orders. But as trained improvisers, team players weaned on ensemble, neither considered himself at ease with the responsibility. "It was sort of a non-power structure," Flaherty said of *SCTV*. "The inmates ran the asylum. I would definitely have input, but I didn't want to make the final decisions." They had no Lorne Michaels. No thesis statement for their comedy. No clear production schedule. What they had, though, were characters, a vivid bench of outrageous but nuanced personalities refined by their tenures on the Second City stage — there was Candy's blustery, vulnerable Johnny LaRue, Eugene Levy's insincerely self-important comic, Bobby Bittman ("Now, in all seriousness, folks . . ."), Flaherty's obsequious talk show host, Sammy Maudlin, and Andrea Martin's tough-going (but inwardly depressed) Edith Prickley, all suited — in size and self-deception — to the world of show business that was *SCTV*'s métier, the fascination each had nurtured since birth, in front of their own televisions, and later, with each other. But for all their character work — among the best Second City would ever see — the stage did not prepare the ensemble for sketch writing. Their writing offices at 100 Lombard Street, a bland brick building next door to the Fire Hall, saw Dave Thomas, a former copywriter, comfortably producing on paper, but the other improvisers were constitutionally inclined to writing on their feet. Candy did whatever he could to avoid writing. He had to "run errands," meet friends, shop, buy a drink, strike up a conversation with someone on the street. Sometimes he scribbled out beginnings of things on cocktail napkins; Levy, meticulous in everything, took ages to press a single key of his IBM Selectric; Catherine O'Hara second-guessed herself to distraction; Andrea Martin struggled to write alone; and Flaherty simply didn't like to write.

Heading into the fall of 1976, it fell to Harold Ramis — "a man at peace in a storm," Alexander observed — to take stock of the offerings, collate the scraps, and, if possible, reconcile the goofy and the brainy. Ramis understood that parodying television, with its commercials, movies of the week, and five-second promos, accommodated ideas big or small, half-baked or overdone. "A lot of items that didn't make it as full-length parodies were fine as promos," Ramis said. "If someone had just the concept and nothing else, a premise, we could just do the premise." To every idea he was welcoming. Embracing the low-budget limitations of Global Studios, he urged the gang to embrace the comic mindset of the endearingly second-rate. They couldn't compete with *Saturday Night Live* for resources or broadcast muscle (Global played Ontario only), so why fight it? Why not make *that* the joke? It would be even funnier, Ramis reasoned, to pit this fictional network's limitations against its creative and intellectual grasp. He enforced a mix of low and high that appealed to his co-leader, Joe Flaherty, who laughed at the Three Stooges and Eugene O'Neill with equal passion. "We wanted to keep the Second City tradition going by doing things we found intellectually interesting," Flaherty said, "keeping the reference level high," combining, in effect, the unhinged comedy of Second City's Canadian improvisers with the smarty-pants strain that touched Ramis and Flaherty back in Chicago. "For somebody as smart as Harold was," Levy said, "he just loved the cheap joke." If they made Ramis laugh, they knew they were on solid ground.

But the measure of their intelligence, as Flaherty defined it, had less to do with the What than the How. Flaherty's recall was incredible. Remember that cheap movie, *South Sea Sinner*? Remember that hilarious sound effect from that Stooges movie? *Booioioioiiingggg!* Flaherty still laughed from "that sophomoric phase when you're young," he said, "and satirize everything cheap. Bad special effects, cheesy blue screen. 'You call that a *chariot*?!'" The cheaper the better.

Cheapness was both virtue and necessity. "When we wrote the parody of *Ben-Hur*," Ramis explained, "the production department said, if we build this set you will have spent your whole budget. You'll have to do one whole show out of that piece." So *Ben-Hur* became *SCTV*'s first extended film parody. Only then did Ramis realize just how bad the sketch was. "We had a twenty-five-minute *Ben-Hur* piece," he said, "and we rehearsed the piece and there wasn't a single laugh in it. And we were all dressed ready to go. We were on the set. Not one laugh and it was the whole show. So finally, I said [to Candy], 'John, do Ben-Hur as Curly'" from the Three Stooges — a page out of Flaherty's playbook.

Candy started improvising in Stooge and Harold doubled over. "Yes," he said, laughing, "that's the way to do it!"

Levy recalled, "It was like this big breakthrough. That's the show where we saw, yeah, it's okay to go cheap and still be clever."

In thirteen shows, they had come a long way from their pilot episode, "The Freud Show," which Ramis, Flaherty, and Patinkin built around a Sahlins-friendly *Masterpiece Theater* parody. Since then, Sahlins's affinity for the show, rocky from the start, began to strain. "The cast's idea of funny," observed Patinkin, "was clearly opposed to Bernie's."

"There's a better take than that," Dave Thomas said to Sahlins in the cutting room.

"No. I don't think so."

"There is, Bernie. Did you look at all the takes?"

"I did. I looked at them all."

Here the script supervisor spoke up. "No, Bernie," she said. "You didn't."

Thomas exploded and Sahlins stormed out.

Sahlins, and then Patinkin, left *SCTV.*

Think of the undersized office assigned to Bill Murray and writer Jim Downey — new recruits to *Saturday Night Live* on the seventeenth floor of 30 Rock, in January 1977, partway into the show's second season, crackling with silent tension. It wasn't working for Murray. Downey's Ivy League biases only fed his contempt for the writerly atmosphere of the seventeenth floor, the overall sense that, coming late to the show, he was invisible. "The writers made the show," he explained, "and the writers didn't know me, so they'd write for who they knew." Among Murray's Second City allies, only Aykroyd lobbied to write Murray into sketches, and when he did, they were mostly minor parts, CIA agents or law-enforcement officials without any lines. "People think that working on *Saturday Night Live* was fun," Murray said. "It was a *nightmare* — the most high-pressure job I ever had in my life." The laid-back, ensemble mentality of Second City was in constant jeopardy at *Saturday Night Live,* where the competitive pressures of writing under deadline for a broadcast audience of millions, fighting to protect one's personal piece of the show, and auditioning, constantly, for the writers' trust obliterated the freedom to fail that Bill Murray, and every improviser, had onstage. But here, Murray said, "If you blew a joke in somebody's sketch, you were history." Sensing their unease, he further distanced himself from the writers. Mutual discomfort drove a wedge through his chances. "If you say something to him he doesn't like," said head writer Michael O'Donoghue, "he does this thing called the Stare. When he just looks at you with, like, cold, flat, kinda icy hatred." Downey knew the look. "He would give me shit, abuse me," the writer said, "and I would just bow to him. It wasn't screaming matches — he was just pissed off at the writers in general. He was always angry."

In March, he and Michaels came up with the idea for "The New Guy." In the sketch, a respectful Bill Murray sits behind a desk, directly addressing the camera, and asks late-night America to just give him a chance. "Hello," he begins. "I'm Bill Murray. You can call me Billy, but around here everybody just calls me 'the new guy.' I want to thank the producer, Lorne Michaels, for urging me to speak with you directly. You see, I'm a little bit concerned. I don't think I'm making it on the show." The surprising transparency of the concept came off well, but Murray, a born insurgent, looked uneasy as a supplicant. With a pat on the back he was returned to the bench.

Though he rarely performed, he was still expected to put in long hours at 30 Rock. His Upper West Side apartment, seemingly unlived in, had no stereo or TV, a couple of wooden chairs for furniture, and a bare mattress tucked into a corner. The only hint of humor — soap in the shape of a microphone — hung on a rope in Murray's shower. It was a Christmas gift from Belushi's wife, Judy, an invitation to the latent lounge singer she knew waited inside him. When he was home, and showering, Murray took full advantage of Judy's present; it freed him to sing as he had at Second City, where the words were always his and always changeable. "I became attached to this soap on a rope," he said. "I would sing my guts out in the shower." Late in May, showering the morning before *Saturday Night Live*'s weekly Wednesday read-through, he found himself glaring at the soap, dreaming at it, then throwing on clothes and racing down to Rockefeller Center, grabbing Gilda Radner, and in twenty minutes, improvised a scene between husband and wife. He's in the shower, singing to an imaginary audience; she hears him and pokes her head in.

"Honey . . . ?" she asks.

"Ladies and gentlemen . . . *don't wanna leave her now* . . . a very special guest . . . *you know I believe and how . . .*"

"Honey . . ."

"My wife, Mrs. Richard Herkiman, Jane Nash! Come on in, Jane!"

"Honey, will you quit fooling around?"

Murray didn't have time to transcribe their improvisation before the read-through. He scribbled a few notes and ran into the conference room, late. They'd already read the week's sketches.

"Oh," he said, "I have one more," and Murray jumped into the character, a guy who keeps pulling people into the shower, first his wife, and then his neighbor, whom he introduces to the audience as "a surprise guest, the man she's been seeing behind my back for the last two years" — and to Murray's astonishment, he actually started getting big laughs from the writers at the table. Then he stopped cold. "I haven't finished the ending yet."

Writer Tom Davis volunteered to help Murray finish the sketch, and two days later, May 21, 1977, it went into the show. Radner played Mrs. Richard Herkiman; Buck Henry, making his sixth appearance on *Saturday Night Live,* played Cularsky, the surprise guest; and Murray, at last, found his center, reprising, live, a version of the lounge singer he'd discovered at Second City.

When confronted with pieces as hastily assembled and rehearsed as "Shower Mike," Murray's training came to his rescue. "[Improvisational actors] can solve it during the performance," he said, "and make a scene work. It's not like we were improvising when we made the shows, but you could feel ways to make things better. And when you get into the third dimension, as opposed to the printed page, you can see ways to solve things and write things live that other sorts of professionals don't necessarily have." At *Saturday Night Live,* the laughter of live, intimate audiences directed Murray's instinct — along with everyone else's — toward the solutions. "That's what that group could do," he said. "That was a really good group to watch."

After Murray caught on, he'd be recognized out on the street, walking with Jim Downey, who Murray's fans, fawning over *Saturday Night Live's* youngest star, had no reason to recognize.

"Well," Murray would say, pointing to his officemate, "he's the guy who writes the stuff."

Harold Ramis, having completed the *Animal House* script, left Toronto for L.A. early in 1977 to get his next movie — *Caddyshack,* cowritten with

Doug Kenney and Brian Doyle-Murray — off the ground. So, on the heels of *SCTV*'s second season, Andrew Alexander accepted Ramis's invitation and, that summer, brought Toronto to Bel-Air, renting for his cast a five-bedroom house (John Candy snagged the master), and charged them with writing sixteen half-hour shows in seven weeks. To Ramis, "this was the best group of people I had ever worked with, and the nicest group of people, and we just had so much fun creating this stuff sitting around the table." The day would begin around breakfast as Ramis arrived, lit a joint, and together with Flaherty, brokered an additive brainstorm directed at amusing not their bosses or sponsors — out of sight and out of mind — but themselves. Nearing lunchtime, the brainstorm naturally apportioned into pairs and trios. Those who laughed together went off to work together, seeing a good idea hatched earlier that morning through to a completed sketch. "We wrote *for* each other," Flaherty said, an ethic he attributed to Del Close's training.

By midafternoon, the improvisers would punch out, sort of. Because most were staying at the house, sleeping where they worked, the writing process never really stopped. Over billiards, or in the pool out back, the conversation continued. "It was one of the happiest times of my life," Ramis said, "because they were all so funny and generous and talented in their work." Flaherty, energizing them with chaos, spread a sense of happy panic to jump-start spontaneity; Ramis lassoed the ensuing good ideas and touched them up, grinning throughout.

Per Belushi's recommendation, Lorne Michaels had offered Ramis a writing position on the show, but the stories Ramis had heard — the cocaine, the late nights, the scrambling, the competition — put him off the idea of writing for *Saturday Night Live*. The improvisational atmosphere in Bel-Air was more to his liking, utterly noncompetitive. "The thing about Second City," he said, "is we all shared a technique, which was very important. So when we sat down at a table it wasn't a competition to see who could get their piece on the air. We would just sort of build on each other's ideas. If someone had a good idea there'd be six other people to take it one step further."

Back in Toronto, the spirit of idea building persisted. Ignited by the notion of a *Fantasy Island* parody, Flaherty and Thomas seized on the broadest-possible conception of fantasy, "opening it up to our imaginations," Flaherty said, and ran with it, using the TV show as a cheesy excuse to launch from fantasy to parodied fantasy — of Hope and Crosby, Fred and Ginger, *Casablanca,* and *The Wizard of Oz* — to build a surreal, maximalist movie-world free-for-all on the "Yes, and" logic of cross-breeding, to the edge of excess, iconic stars, and genres. The adventurous "multilayered" style of show business parody, born with the *Fantasy Island* episode — itself born from the additive improvisational writing techniques of *SCTV* — would come to characterize the show's strongest work, and some of the most complex TV sketch work ever, wherein laughs, as layered as the parodies themselves, get deeper and smarter as the best multilayered sketches unfold, building up from the ground level of accessible impersonation to imaginative clashes of entertainment icons (Orson Welles and Liberace?) bristling with esoteric show business savvy.

But despite terrific reviews and a devoted cult following, Global Television notified Andrew Alexander that *SCTV*'s second season would be its last; henceforth they wanted to go with American programming. In search of a new home, Alexander tried the CBC, whose executives told him they weren't looking for comedy. NBC's Fred Silverman took one look at what Alexander was selling and complained, "Far too intelligent." Alexander had no other leads.

Martin Short's childhood fantasies, played out in the attic of his parents' home in Hamilton, Ontario, were of celebrity entertainers like Jack Paar and Frank Sinatra. And yet, without knowing exactly why, in a farther-back part of his brain, where he stored his comedy albums, Short prized Nichols and May above all the others. "I used to feel," he said, "like when you're twelve or something, something happened. There's a dividing line. Either you wanted to be Mike Nichols and Elaine or you wanted to be Newhart. Why do people say 'I want to be a stand-up' and why do people say they want to do improv?" For years, Short repressed the impulse. He became an actor, moderately fulfilled, sometimes less so. In January 1977, in Los Angeles, Short and his wife, Nancy Dolman, were walking to meet their friend Paul Shaffer, and his friends Bill Murray and John Belushi, for dinner at the Sunset Marquis Hotel. Suddenly he stopped on Santa Monica Boulevard and told Nancy he had to sit down. There was a bench.

"What's going on?" Nancy asked.

"I can't go and hang at Paul's hotel. Not only do they all have success, but they have direction. I don't know what I want to do, and I'm so pathetically lost that I just want to sit on this curb. I feel fine as long as I stay right here."

Nancy took his hand. "How long are we going to sit here?"

About two hours, as it turned out.

The Shorts passed on dinner, and instead got tickets to see War Babies, the L.A.-based improv group playing the Cast Theater in nearby Hollywood. The show knocked Marty out. He knew what he had to do.

The next morning, Short called Andrew Alexander at the Fire Hall. "I want to join Second City."

Two months later, Short was back in Toronto, replacing John Candy in the Fire Hall's ninth revue, the Flaherty-directed *The Wizard of Ossington*.

Short threw himself into the work, fired by the open encouragement of the ensemble, his friends for five years, and the self-imposed pressure of making up for lost time. He ran directly to the cliff's edge. Taped improvisations Short brought home and diligently typed into sketches; characters he named and refined quickly — like the adorable nerd, Ed Grimley, who debuted in *Ossington* — giving nuance to their personality and physical life as an actor would, with uncommon and deliberate attention to detail. Grimley's voice he adapted from his brother-in-law's; his gray and orange shirt came from Short's teenage closet. But most significantly, for all his boldness, and oddness, and preposterous physical daring, Short committed to his characters' inner reality. In the case of Grimley, it was his panic and pervasive enthusiasm, "and I quickly understood . . . that it's not the action, it's the reaction, and that if you create a sincerity within a character, that sincerity has the power, not a joke." The lesson informed the rest of his career. "For me, it was very liberating because I was used to setups and punch lines." Henceforth, Short would not hold back: the greater his commitment to Grimley, inside and out, the greater the audience's commitment to him. As long as he came from *somewhere* emotionally, there was no such thing as going too far. "My work," he said, "completely shifted after Second City."

And then Del Close came up from Chicago to direct *East of Eatons* (a pun on the name of a Canadian department store chain).

In the name of art, Close offered up workshop ideas that raced past the edge. The Toronto improvisers, who, Flaherty said, "were more interested in show business and comedy and characters than baring their souls onstage," bridled at Close's exercises, especially the one Del called Autobiography. Meaning his own.

He assigned Dave Thomas the role of Doctor and Catherine O'Hara, Nurse. The scene: Del's father's suicide.

"Get the fuck out of here," Thomas returned. "I'm not doing that."

"Theater is not a democracy. I'm the director. You do what I say."

"I'm here to do comedy. I'm not bringing my own baggage into this and I'm sure as hell not bringing yours."

"Then you're fired."

"All right," Thomas said, "I'm outta here," and left.

Two hours later, Andrew Alexander got Thomas on the phone. "You're coming in tonight, right?"

"Only you can fire me. And unless you're firing me, I'm coming in."

After the show that night, Thomas offered Close an olive branch, a ride home.

"I would have done just what you did," Close conceded in the car. "Don't ever take shit from anybody."

There was a time when Close could improvise away the pain, but a quarter century of torrential brainstorms had exhausted his capacity for new ideas. Grasping, he hired an enormous bodyguard named Tiny to keep him from drinking. It didn't work.

When Close came in drunk, improviser Robin Duke asked, "Where's Tiny?"

"I gave him the night off."

Alexander had no choice but to divest Close of his directing responsibilities and send him back to Chicago. "Del could find the truth in the scene, asking what's real here," Alexander observed. "He was committed to it, but he wasn't so good at finding it in himself." Close responded to his dismissal by creating more havoc, clogging his hotel toilet with kitty litter and storming the theater that winter night — having drunkenly walked over a mile from his room on Bloor Street — in his socks, with no jacket, shivering and cursing Alexander with, "You demon! You Judas!" — and, finally, as if he had run out of ammo — "You cheeser!" John Candy intercepted Close's clumsy swing at Alexander, then, along with Dave Thomas and Sheldon Patinkin, rushed him out the back of the theater to his hotel lobby, where Close reached up, grabbed the bell clerk by his tie, and yanked his face against the desk. "Del wanted to kill Andrew," Patinkin said. "He was not kidding." They sat there in his hotel room amid the stink of kitty litter to be sure he didn't kill himself.

From Cook County Hospital in Chicago, Close would continue to send in ideas for new sketches and improvisation. They were mostly ignored.

In the summer of 1977 John Landis, the director of *Animal House,* flew to New York to meet John Belushi. The character of John "Bluto" Blutarsky, samurai-silent party animal, had been written specifically for John, and Landis was happy to bring him aboard.

Universal, however, was not so sure about any of it. The new crop of star filmmakers found zero political or artistic value in the script's tale of punks versus preps, and Hollywood's dwindling old guard saw nothing in its belligerent, tasteless, insolent, airheaded gags. The latter at least had the good sense to know it was out of touch with baby boomers, and as a sort of stopgap, allowed the *Animal House* script to linger in development for many drafts, not saying yes but not saying no either. Universal president Ned Tanen didn't get why the film's supposed heroes were such losers. "That was part of the trick of *Animal House*," Ramis explained. "Universal couldn't believe that those were the heroes of the movie — the slobs, the idiots. But that was a big thing when I was in college, the smartest people would act as stupidly as they possibly could." To Ramis, goofing off was a political act.

When Chevy Chase, *the* star of *Saturday Night Live*'s first season, turned down the lead in the film, Universal happily signed Tim Matheson, an actor on the rise. Coupled with a valuable yes from Donald Sutherland — "that's what got the movie green-lit," Landis said — the studio warmed to the idea of letting Belushi play Bluto. It was, after all, a small and ugly part. Someone had to take it.

Nearly as soon as Belushi bounded into Landis's room at the Drake Hotel, he was brandishing demands of a rewrite, pushing for additional Bluto scenes, calling up from room service an unbelievable order of beer, oysters, shrimp cocktails, margaritas — improvising in character, Landis realized, for a part he said wasn't big enough.

"Okay, I'll do it," Belushi finally conceded, asked if he could borrow twenty bucks from Landis — a trust test Landis passed — and flew out of the room.

Moments later, room service arrived with the food. Laughing, Landis picked up the phone and called Universal's Sean Daniel. "I think we got him."

On set in Oregon later that year, Landis found himself expanding Bluto, setting the stage for Belushi's run-amok by directing certain scenes like a silent film director, calling out to the actors during the take, yelling at them (cameras still rolling) with a smile on his face to do it again and again — "Stop! That's terrible! Do it again!!" — creating, between the takes, high-energy pauses for spontaneous action to occur and even spill into the scripted scenes themselves. Throughout, unscripted glimpses of Belushi's sweetness — the antidote to his savage side — kept presenting themselves, less in dialogue than behavior, insisting their way into Landis's attention. "John," Tim Matheson said, "was the only one Landis would let go off-script."

Though he was present at the creation, instrumental in taking *Animal House* from idea to screen, Ivan Reitman feared his creative contributions, upstaged by Belushi's bravura performance, Ramis & Co.'s sweetly tasteless script, and director John Landis's canny elevation of the ensemble, would be ignored by Hollywood and the press. With the *Lampoon* boat leaving the port and no time to conscientiously form his retaliatory movie, Reitman raced himself into production on his next feature, this time as director, "for my own confidence." There was no time to plan. Taking a cue from the innocent anarchy of *Animal House,* Reitman and writer Dan Goldberg decided on a summer-camp comedy. *Meatballs.* "Summer camp is so much fun," Reitman reasoned. "It's full of beautiful girls and guys having so much fun and falling off of ladders and stuff." They hammered out a draft in a month. Minimal revisions. Barely a second draft. And they started casting. Who did they like for the lead?

"It's got to be Bill Murray," Reitman told Goldberg. "Bill Murray's going to do it."

"Do we have him? Do we have a contract? Do we have a deal?"

Their casting director was unconcerned. "No, no, no, but don't worry. It's going to happen."

Without a commitment from Murray, or a plan B, Reitman began location scouting, hiring his crew, proceeding as if Murray's involvement was already secured. When Murray's name came up, generally within the context of, "Has anyone heard from him?" Reitman said, "I think he'll do it."

All summer long Reitman tried to get a yes from *Saturday Night Live*'s newest phenomenon, sending out script after script to wherever Murray had been sighted, whether in Washington, playing minor-league baseball with the Grays Harbor Loggers, or whatever address Murray's lawyer — who may even have been guessing — whispered to Reitman. Murray's replies, when they came back, were clear nos. He didn't like the script. (Who did?) Privately, Murray worried if, after a lifetime of shortform improvisation, he could sustain a feature-length scripted part — and the lead, to boot. "It's all artificial rhythms," Murray said of film acting, "that's the thing about movies, because they're manufactured. Stand-up comedy or live TV has its own rhythm because there's a natural oomph with the audience. But film is completely artificial, and that's why it's hard." But Reitman persisted; didn't Murray see that *Meatballs* could do for him what *Animal House* was doing for Belushi? "I'm only 30," Murray shrugged two years later. "From 20 years, I had no ambition to do anything, and then I got a job, sort of accidentally, and then another job, and another. But I don't think I want to be Charlton Heston. I don't want to be doing movies when I'm fifty years old." Better to spend his summer off from *Saturday Night Live* traveling around the country playing minor-league baseball and golf.

To lure Murray, Reitman hired Harold Ramis, *Meatballs*'s fourth writer, to punch up the jokes and focus the script, to write to Murray's strengths. Again, Murray declined.

"We're going to start shooting one way or the other," Reitman decreed.

Early in August 1978, a week after *Animal House* opened to life-changing box office — winning acclaim for everyone but Ivan Reitman — Reitman made good on his promise and, to the distress of many around him, began shooting *Meatballs,* a comedy with a weak script, no lead, a tiny budget, and a rigid schedule: when summer ended, the director would lose his background campers, the unpaid extras of Ontario's Camp White Pine.

On that very day, Murray's lawyer notified Reitman that "Mr. Murray was considering doing the movie." Unbeknownst to Reitman, Belushi had advised Murray that it didn't matter what or how bad the movie was as long as he was the star. In the meantime Murray was getting bored with minor-league baseball.

Two days later, Bill Murray arrived at Camp White Pine. He was wearing baggy pants and a Hawaiian shirt. "What are we going to shoot today?"

"Well, you know," Reitman said, "we're going to do this bus scene. It's not very good."

"It's *crap*." He threw the script pages away. "I got this."

So — for the first time in a feature film — Bill Murray improvised on camera. Instantly, Reitman understood what he had in front of him: a collaborator. "The thing about scripts is, they're two-dimensional," Murray said. "There's always something that's not accounted for. That's where I come in handy. I can make something happen there." More than merely hilarious, Murray's inventions, engendering spontaneous responses from the other actors, most of them untrained kids, facilitated honest reactions all around. Just by playing, he was spreading and receiving inspiration, making the movie better. "It's hard to call it a technique when it's something much bigger," Murray said. "When the cameras roll, I think: This is the most important thing I'm going to do. It's going to the biggest experience I'll ever share with other people. The biggest moment of contact with people right now. And if you're there, conscious of that . . . what you do doesn't look hard."

On day two of *Meatballs*, Reitman, quite consciously, really began to work with Murray.

"Bill," he said. "I want you to enter there —"

"Wait a second, Ivan. What about — how about this . . ."

Reitman had already set up the lighting to suit his original idea, but there was something special in Murray's idea, a kernel, that was better than what was written. "I knew I had a decision to make," Reitman said, "and I decided I just had to go with it. *You're going to have to be more nimble*, I said to myself. *You're going to have to be fast and smart enough, and learn when to control and when to let go.* That's how I got trained in improv directing. *Meatballs* was the training."

Those around Murray, Reitman directed not to initiate improvisations but simply react honestly to whatever Murray invented. "Actors can clash in improvisation," Reitman said. "The first way you gain control in those kinds of sequences is some characters should do it and some characters should not, or some characters should just react and not say lines." *Meatballs*, then, was built around Murray the improviser. "You see it in the wrestling scene," Reitman said. "Murray's just wrestling with her as part of the seduction and it turns out to be this sexually powerful thing choreographed in a real way." Before the scene, Reitman spent fifteen minutes with Murray working out his blocking in broad strokes, "and whatever else happened in the choreography of it was up to Bill." Reitman rolled two cameras on the improvisations, allowed three or four takes, each one different, and each one, Reitman said, "more delightful than the other."

With every improvisation, Reitman was witness to a new side of Murray, a big-brotherly sweetness at odds with his *Lampoon* and *SNL* personae. With women, he showed his playful innocence — it wasn't sex his characters wanted, but fun — and it lifted him, Murray, out of sarcasm. "On *Saturday Night Live*," Reitman said, "all you saw was this wacky sort of side, but [Murray] has a very warm, genuine quality. I think I brought out some glimpses of that . . ."

"And I don't think a director, as often as not, knows what is going to play funny anyway," Murray said. "As often as not, the right one is the one that they're *surprised by*, so I don't think that they have the right tone in their head. And I think that good actors always — or if you're being good, anyway — you're making it better than the script. That's your fucking job. It's like, Okay, the script says this? Well, watch *this*. Let's just roar a little bit. Let's see how high we can go." Far better than anything on the page, Murray's sensitivity to the younger actors sent the film in unanticipated directions, incurring in Reitman new ideas for scenes, as many as seven or eight story points — added later — to augment what was now the emotional centerpiece of the film, Murray's relationship to the character of Rudy, the lonely kid he charms out of his isolation. "We'd see a scene shot," Murray recalled, "and we'd say, 'This is garbage, let's look for another idea.'"

For *Meatballs* — his first starring role — Bill Murray got above the title credit. And Ivan Reitman had a hit.

"I saw *Meatballs* when it opened," said Columbia Pictures president Frank Price, "and though there were a lot of people in this business that didn't think Bill Murray was an incredible star, I thought he was going to be huge, and I knew that Ivan had great talent." Price would finance their next picture, *Stripes*. On Murray's insistence, Harold Ramis would cowrite and costar.

But a week before Reitman was scheduled to start shooting *Stripes*, no one could find Bill Murray.

Screams erupted when Dan Aykroyd, in black Ray-Ban 5022-G15s and skinny black tie, took to L.A.'s Universal Amphitheatre stage on September 9, 1978, as Elwood Blues, to the rousing accompaniment of Otis Redding's

"I Can't Turn You Loose." The audience, thousands deep, was split between *Animal House* togas, Blues Brothers T-shirts, and — in homage to Steve Martin, the top-billed act — foam arrows through their heads.

"Good evening, everyone, and welcome to the United States of America," Aykroyd spoke to the roar. "And indeed we have congregated here at this time to celebrate a most treasured wellspring of contemporary music . . . Tonight, assembled exclusively for your entertainment pleasure, from the music capitals of this continent, this is the hardworking all-star show from Jake and Elwood Blues. Ladies and gentlemen, these are the Blues Brothers."

Which is when John Belushi, with an agility incredible for someone with his physique, turned a triple-cartwheel to the microphone at center stage and started belting out "Hey Bartender."

Many in the audience had seen the Blues Brothers' debut months earlier on *Saturday Night Live*, but most had come to behold Bluto, the unexpected overnight star of *Animal House*, the biggest movie in America, soon to be the highest-grossing comedy of all time. In October, *Newsweek* would give Belushi the cover: "Eleven years ago, in *The Graduate*, Dustin Hoffman proved that a movie leading man need not be tall, chiseled, and dashing. Now John Belushi has demonstrated that he can even be a slob." Weary of the principled 1960s, and the failed principles of the 1970s, the nation needed a vacation from seriousness; instead of "Revolution" it needed an animal to bash in the folksinger's guitar and cry "Toga!" *Animal House*, through Belushi, gave them party politics, a demonstration in the form of a hall pass. "No one," Ramis said, "had represented that energy and that spirit on film before and we buried the politics, which meant it wasn't polarizing to anybody." America wanted more.

Hence the blank check show business wrote to Belushi and all he touched: nine sold-out nights at the Universal Amphitheatre; a Blues Brothers' live album, *A Briefcase Full of Blues;* continued appearances on *Saturday Night Live,* and a massive deal for a *Blues Brothers* movie. The cross-promotional potential — known as "synergy" to the new Wall Street accountants of Hollywood — heralded a major shift in the film industry. "The 1980s," wrote Stephen Prince in 2000, "thereby set in motion a dynamic that has yet to be arrested and a marketing logic that aimed to produce synergies between film entertainment content across a broad range of product formats and through a diverse set of distribution media." The Blues Brothers were among the new era's triple-cherry jackpots: on the heels of *Animal House,*

John Belushi, at thirty, would have the number one movie, the number one television show, and the number one best-selling album in the country.

Harold Ramis was in the audience that night. He thought: *John might not survive this.*

Bittersweetly, Bernie Sahlins understood what was happening. The Belushi phenomenon brought *Saturday Night Live,* entering its fourth season, its best ratings ever, reflecting glory back onto Second City as it entered its twentieth Chicago year. Garnering a financial security unprecedented in the short history of improvisational comedy, Bernie's theaters were, he sensed, fast becoming audition spaces, stepping-stones, shifting the improvisers' focus and affecting the work. You could almost hear the laugh track. "Once you start worrying about your career," Bernie would say, "you don't want to take risks. Once you avoid risks, you're hemmed in." You're not free.

Prospective improvisers came prepared, with agents and glossy headshots. Bernie had to wonder: Was it Second City they wanted or *Saturday Night Live?*

Improviser John Kapelos joined the Chicago touring company in 1978, at the crest of the phenomenon. "We were getting people, 'Toga, toga, toga!' all this stuff out in the audience," he said. "But I think in retrospect, what happened is that Second City and by extension *Saturday Night Live* and all its proxies flipped from being counterculture into popular culture, so there was a sea change and I think it made it more difficult as careers went on to do comedies and do other things."

"Lorne Michaels is coming in," Joyce warned Bernie Sahlins one afternoon.

"Don't let him in."

"How can I not let him in?"

Sahlins could remember a time when people read, when, at parties, the way to get a girl was to sit in the corner and brood. When owning one of Mike and Elaine's albums was an act of rebellion. "Neither the audiences nor the casts are as intellectually oriented anymore," he confessed in 1979. For the shift, he blamed America's "pernicious" misappropriation of Belushi's talent, and also television, perpetuator of contrived laughs. "In TV comedy," he said, "long after characters should know what's going on in a situation, they conspire not to. In real comedy, as in real life, a character sees something right away and acts on it. He doesn't lag behind his audience," principles in direct violation of Sahlins's motto number one: play to the top of your intelligence. Now they wanted, Bernie thought, "the comedy of insult and the zany." But that wasn't Second City. At least, it wasn't what Second City *had* been. It wasn't him.

Tired of directing and admittedly out of touch with audiences, Sahlins turned to Del Close. But Close, bored with Second City–style shortform improvisation, turned to drugs and alcohol. When he wasn't bored, he was sober, working with the cast on experimental Harolds. But Sahlins, ever weary of improv as a presentational art form, resisted. In the longform Harolds, he saw erratic results and limited sketch potential. Gone from Close were the Compass years of constant transformation and discovery, and back rushed the feedback loop of stifled creativity and Valium and alcohol that blurred him to the edge of oblivion. "I was likely to break down and cause serious trouble at any given moment," Close confessed, "but I was able to continue." Week after week, he'd come to Second City in the same clothes, smelling of cat piss and BO. "Nice work in the psychiatrist scene," he barked at improviser George Wendt. "Unfortunately, Mike and Elaine did it in 1958." Interrupting one of Steven Kampmann's scenes during an actual performance, Del rushed the stage, fuming, "Now we can do better than *that*, can't we?!" Out drinking with improviser Larry Coven, he switched gears into what Coven called "Devil mode." It was the alcohol. Coven said, "He would tell me things that he did, stories about things he did with Elaine May, and things he did to twelve-year-old girls . . ." Close would call Joyce Sloane, usually right before showtime. "Joyce . . ." he'd moan. "I've done it again." She'd send an ambulance. When Robin Williams came to Second City Chicago and asked to meet the Guru, he found Del Close collapsed in the greenroom. "There's your genius," the company told Williams.

Early in 1979 Andrew Alexander called a meeting at his office in the Fire Hall.

"Look," he said to the cast of *SCTV,* "we don't have any backing. We lost our distributor."

The conversation got heated. Among the cast, there was some sense, however misguided, that Alexander — the owner of a used Jaguar — had more money than he was letting on. He didn't. In fact, Alexander was still struggling to keep Toronto's Second City stage above water, trying to settle old debts — those of the Fire Hall's previous owners — that came with his purchase of the building years earlier.

"Would you guys consider taking fifty percent equity in the show? It would mean working for less." Considerably less.

The answer was no.

"Well," Alexander said. "It looks like we don't have a show."

Alone among the disbanded cast of *SCTV*, Joe Flaherty was willing to make any compromise necessary to get the band back together and on the air. "I must say, I was really upset," he said. "Everyone had bailed out. I didn't care if the budget was low. That didn't mean much to me. I thought we were doing good work and getting better." He met regularly with Alexander to check in on the financial end of things, and Alexander, though hopeful, always gave Flaherty some version of the same: "I'm still looking, Joe. I'm still looking." That the rest of the cast had gone on to other things Flaherty tried not to take for abandonment. They had to work; Joe Flaherty had to do the *right* kind of work.

To fill the time, he did some directing for Second City Toronto. "That was one funny show you had there," Martin Short would tell him.

"Hey, thanks, Marty. Thanks."

Fortunately for Flaherty, Alexander was a dogged producer, willing to cast his net ever wider to find investors, which is how, late in 1979, he got the peculiar invitation from his partner, Len Stuart, to meet Dr. Charles Allard, multimillionaire surgeon and part-time broadcaster, who offered to bring *SCTV* to his television studio in far-off Edmonton. Flaherty jumped at the offer, Dave Thomas, too, and Alexander made them head writers. But regrouping the rest of the cast was not as easy. Andrea Martin and Eugene Levy had gone to L.A. for pilot season; John Candy had his own show, *Big City Comedy*; Catherine O'Hara was looking to take a year off. Flaherty and Thomas got tentative commitments. The cast would do *some* new shows.

To fill in the vacancies, Flaherty corralled Second City improvisers Robin Duke and Tony Rosato, and Dave Thomas found a new guy — new to Second City and improvisation. Thomas met Rick Moranis, a local DJ, at an amateur rock concert — a band of former high school friends that included Bob Dolman, then engaged to Andrea Martin — that erupted into a huge party after the show. "At the end of the night," Dolman said, "Dave and Rick walked up onstage like they were their own band and started improvising imaginary musical instruments into the microphone. You could see these two had fallen in love."

Alexander hired additional writers to make up for the paucity of permanent cast members. Joining Flaherty and Thomas and the others, Martin Short's older brother Mike and (per Harold Ramis's recommendation) Second City alum Dick Blasucci, and Joe Flaherty's brother Paul were brought in to the smoke-filled writing offices off Lombard Street to come up with about three hundred sketches for twenty-six episodes of comedy, or barring that, as much as they possibly could the summer of 1980, before the schedule ordered them to the burning cold 3:00 p.m. sunsets and sterile expanses of far-off Edmonton, two thousand miles west of Toronto, where they would begin filming *SCTV*'s third season.

"Edmonton was flat and lonely," Thomas said. "There was nothing to do but hang out in each other's hotel rooms and work on the show." Work as many as eighteen hours a day, seven days a week, shooting six days and rehearsing on the seventh.

Banishing the *SCTV* ensemble to a snowy hell away from their families and locking the bunker door behind them forced the improvisers into deeper, odder reaches of their shared personality — the Bel-Air summer times a thousand. Coursing on a self-reliant, self-regulated group brain divorced from the outside real worlds of "Will they laugh?" and "Will this help our careers?," all they had was each other and an expanding catalogue of inside jokes and obsessions encouraged onto the page, and screen, by their own laughter. The topicality of *Saturday Night Live* — difficult to maintain when so much of *SCTV* had to be written in advance — was eschewed for an intricate, insular comedy universe of satirical programming and backstage dramas, reliant as much on the shared sensibility of its creators as it was on its stable of growing characters, called upon to reappear like figures in a soap opera. In a pinch, they could fall back on, and therefore refine, or shade, a familiar character or recurring sketch. "There was never enough material," Thomas said, "so we were relying on everyone." As Moranis put it at the time, "We sort of guard each other."

Everyone's opinion was solicited. Writers consulted set decorators; actors looked to the crew for laughs. With barely any time to rehearse new characters, improvisers had to discover their performances in the hair-and-makeup chair, moments before cameras rolled. It wasn't until makeup artist Beverly Schechtman painted Andrea Martin's teeth gleaming white, hairdresser Judi Cooper-Sealy fitted her with a mousy brown wig, and costume designer Juul Haalmeyer slipped her into a white blouse and plaid skirt that Martin knew who the character of Yolanda DeVilbiss was — and when Catherine O'Hara saw her in the chair, she took a look at those white teeth and suggested Martin give DeVilbiss a stutter. As in any true improvisational ensemble — even a scripted one, like *SCTV* — no one worked from ego. No one was that famous — yet. Ramis, watching on TV, observed, "It didn't allow any star trips since there was no feedback. The public did not make a star out of anyone in the show, which destroyed *Saturday Night* in the very first year."

That began to change when Andrew Alexander brought the news that the CBC had requested two additional minutes of Canadian content per episode. Thomas and Moranis, as protective as anyone of *SCTV*'s creative bubble, shot back, "What do you want us to do? Throw up a map of Canada and sit there wearing tuques and parkas?"

Alexander replied, "Yeah, and if you could have a Mountie in it that would be great too."

A map of the Great White North went up, Thomas and Moranis reached for tuques and parkas and, before a rolling camera, invented and began improvising as Bob and Doug McKenzie, ribbing just about every small-town Canadian cliché they could think of, and with the same casual, dream-easy flow they discovered in their first meeting onstage after that rock concert. In one hour of studio time, they improvised enough usable two-minute segments to satisfy the CBC. Pat Whitley was up in the control room, laughing along with the crew. "We all thought it was hilarious," he said. Each one of them knew that this was *SCTV*'s version of the Blues Brothers.

Thomas and Moranis were soon flooded with fan mail, media attention, personal appearance requests, and a record deal, and the show "no one" watched became the show with the McKenzie brothers. As it had at *Saturday Night Live,* the introduction of celebrity into the family cut both ways, compromising the ensemble environment that was *SCTV*'s secret weapon, but also raising the show's profile both in Canada and the States, where the loserish air of Bob and Doug McKenzie fed the nation's appetite for the anti-yuppie antics of John Belushi and Bill Murray, the humor of underachievement both grown-up capitalists and their children, the coming slackers, could relate to.

Joe Flaherty heard NBC president Brandon Tartikoff was connecting the dots from *Saturday Night Live* back to Second City and onto *SCTV*. With their numbers improving and Tartikoff, beloved by most in the business, at the network helm, it seemed to Flaherty his moment — *SCTV*'s moment — was finally upon them.

Formal recognition of Flaherty's contribution was overdue. Though as mentor to Belushi, Radner, and Aykroyd — to his entire generation of Second City improvisers — he could take partial credit for the success Lorne Michaels had made of them, the depth and breadth of his influence was still largely a trade secret. It naturally complicated his view of *Saturday Night Live*. "I didn't resent them, my friends on the show," he said. "It was all the media attention they got. We deserved it, too." Why was his company — by anyone's estimation, equal (if not superior) to Lorne Michaels's — relegated to Edmonton and an awkward, very-late time slot after *Saturday Night Live*?

At the end of the season — which, once again, marked the end to *SCTV* — Joe Flaherty, his brother Paul, and Dick Blasucci were at Universal working on a script that couldn't compare, at least to Flaherty, to what they had achieved, against all odds, in Edmonton.

He looked up to Paul and Dick. "You know what? I'm going to call Brandon Tartikoff. I'm going to call him right now."

"Get out of here," they said. "No way!"

"No, I'm going to do it. Why not?"

They watched as Flaherty picked up the phone, like it was no big deal, and dialed NBC. No one in the room, including Flaherty, knew that Tartikoff, before he had become a master of network television, had studied improvisation with Jo Forsberg back in Chicago. To him, the name Flaherty meant what it meant to Second City's other students: master.

"This is Joe Flaherty," the master said into the phone. "I want to speak with Brandon Tartikoff."

"One moment please."

Then Tartikoff's voice: "Hello?"

"Brandon? This is Joe Flaherty." Flaherty, chuckling at his hubris, never expected an answer. "We have a show, Brandon. A show we like a lot."

"I know. I know about your show."

"We'd really like to be on NBC."

"Well, we'll see what we can do about that."

A few days later, in March 1981, Andrew Alexander got his own phone call: *SCTV* was moving to NBC.

In the summer of 1979 Belushi was back in Chicago, shooting and running away from shooting *The Blues Brothers.* "In L.A. or New York," he said, "people look into the camera and forget to relate to the other performers. Here it's family. Ensemble acting, that's what Second City teaches you." To an overwhelming response, he and Aykroyd would make unannounced appearances on the Second City stage, performing with the likes of Tim Kazurinsky, and John's brother Jim. "[Belushi] was desperately searching for someone that saw his eyes, not his fame," Fred Kaz said. "I think to a large degree he found it at Second City." At the site of the former Sneak Joynt, Belushi's onetime hangout across the street from the theater, he and Aykroyd set up a Blues Bar, their second. Their first, a comedown refuge after *Saturday Night Live* tapings, was in downtown New York; this one, restored to their attention by John Candy, served a similar purpose, to keep the gang together. They bought a jukebox, a pinball machine, guitars, amps; Belushi hired his old colleague, former West Compass Player Steve Beshekas, to tend bar; and they opened the doors to Second City improvisers thirsty for a drink, or more, after the show. "That's one of the greatest summers of my life," Aykroyd reflected, "because it went back to the Second City roots." The bouncers, installed to keep the bar private, knew "Second City" was a password. Belushi wanted everyone close. He had already talked Steven Spielberg into letting Aykroyd, John Candy, and Joe Flaherty appear in his film *1941;* and although he and Aykroyd had only recently shot their last *Saturday Night Live,* he was already pining for a reunion. "I thought it was real," he said of one dream. "I thought everybody was together and everybody said, 'Let's do one more year; let's go back.'" He craved a spot with the current company of *SCTV.*

Del Close lived directly behind the Blues Bar. A year earlier, on the recommendation of his dear friend Severn Darden, he had checked into a Texas rehab facility and kicked his alcoholism with a form of aversion therapy Del compared to the "rehabilitation" scene in *A Clockwork Orange.* Off drink, he was indeed a changed man, but Del was still doing drugs, and Belushi, only thirty steps away at the Blues Bar, knew it. Crashing on cocaine ("We had a budget in the movie for cocaine for night shoots," Aykroyd said), Belushi knocked Del's door down for a speed injection. He was facing a dance sequence and fading fast and Del obliged him with a needle to his ass. "Junkies give the best shots," he said.

Before the first shot on the first day of filming *Caddyshack*, Harold Ramis's first feature as a director, someone asked him, "Where do you want to put the camera?"

"Well, let's, uh . . . I think I should shoot it this way."

"Uh-huh," replied the First AD. "So do you want us to move all those trucks that we've parked there, and the generator, and the lunch tables, and the tent, and the catering?"

"Let's not do that."

When the soundman called "Speed!," production assistant Trevor Albert looked over to Ramis.

"Harold," someone fed him his line sotto voce. *"Action."*

He was in Davie, Florida, sent there by Orion to reproduce, from a script by Ramis, Doug Kenney, and Brian Doyle-Murray, the magical moneymaking elixir of *Animal House*. Ramis had originally pitched Orion an explicitly political dark comedy — a true story — about the proposed Nazi march in Skokie, Illinois, but Orion's Mike Medavoy asked Ramis to dial it down. "If you have something urban and contemporary," he offered, "I'd be happy to consider it." The writers came back with *Caddyshack*, an unruly-kids-against-the-dour-grown-ups story rife with Doyle-Murray's memories of country club social strata and Ramis's gentle leftism. It wasn't exactly what Medavoy asked for, but it was just what he wanted: another invisibly political anti-institutional comedy, *Animal House* on the green.

"And I want to direct it," Ramis told producer Jon Peters.

"Yeah," Peters replied. "You *look* like a director."

Months later, Ramis was on set, squinting over the Rolling Hills golf course, thinking, *This directing thing, it really doesn't seem so hard. They ask you questions; you answer them.* The task was to make everyone comfortable, to sacrifice, if he had to, admiration for affection. "I want everyone to feel good on a movie set," he said. "So I spend maybe too much of my day making sure everyone's happy." To enhance the collaboration, he would, like a socialist leader or improvisational director, willingly defer artistic authority, shocking cast and crew with an honest confession of "I don't have a fucking clue what to do at this point."

His theory was he was in good hands: theirs. "We knew we were funny," Chevy Chase said. "They were a tight group coming in," explained editor William Carruth. "They trusted each other and backed each other. Everybody stood behind Harold and tried to help him as much as they could."

"I never saw reason not to improvise," Ramis said.

As Carl, Billy Murray played a version of the Honker, a character Ramis knew from Second City. For one of Carl's scenes, sparsely designated in the shooting script, sans dialogue ("Carl, the greenskeeper, is absently lopping the heads off bedded tulips as he practices his golf swing with a grass whip"), Ramis used his understanding of Murray's muscle to produce a most memorable improvisation.

"Bill," he said, "when you're playing sports, do you ever just talk to yourself like you're the announcer, and you're actually —"

"I know exactly what you mean. Say no more."

In one take, two cameras rolling, Murray improvised the film's famous commentator monologue: "What an incredible Cinderella story . . . This unknown, comes out of nowhere, to lead the pack . . . at Augusta. He's on his final hole. He's about 455 yards away, he's gonna hit about a 2-iron I think. [Swings, decapitates a flower] Oh, he got all of that. The crowd is standing on its feet here at Augusta. The normally reserved Augusta crowd . . . going wild . . . for this young Cinderella who's come out of nowhere. He's got about 350 yards left; he's going to hit about a 5-iron it looks like, don't you think? He's got a beautiful backswing . . . [Swings, decapitates flower] That's — Oh, he got all of that one! He's gotta be pleased with that! The crowd is just on its feet here. He's a Cinderella boy. Tears in his eyes, I guess, as he lines up this last shot. He's got about 195 yards left, and he's got a . . . looks like he's got about an 8-iron. This crowd has gone deadly silent . . . Cinderella story, out of nowhere, former greenskeeper, now, about to become the Masters Champion. [Swings, another flower] It looks like a mirac — It's in the hole! It's in the hole!"

Following an improvisation, Ramis would turn to the production crew: if they laughed, Harold moved on; if they didn't, he asked the improvisers to try again.

Ramis started shooting with a script hundreds of pages long, and his try-again attitude made the material pile up even more, confusing the storyline, and him. Amid the jokes, Murray's inspired embellishments around the hostile gopher subplot, came the whispers: "What is this movie about?" Looking back, Ramis said, "We were afraid of communicating anything real in the *Caddyshack* days. Romance embarrassed us, along with real emotion of any kind, admitting any kind of vulnerability." They were — in violation of Second City ideals — going for laughs *über alles.* "I see where the movie's going," Ramis said, "but then, *Oh boy,* there's a great joke over *here.*"

"The atmosphere was chaotic and creative and infused with the scent of confidence and marijuana," said Trevor Albert. The pot was Harold's; the coke was theirs, mostly. Rodney Dangerfield carried a quarter gram with him every day. "The significant part of Harold's job," Albert added, "was going to be creatively focusing this immensely talented cast with an all-you-can-snort paid vacation to Florida." It was fall 1979: they were young, celebrated, and knew they could get away with a little anti-institutionalism of their own. After-hours parties, hangovers, and jam sessions raged through a motel they had colonized right off the golf course. ("If you say you remember *Caddyshack,*" said actor Michael O'Keefe, "you probably weren't there.") Hijacking golf carts, cast and crew were spotted on the fairway spinning donuts at two in the morning. One night, Ramis and Kenney decided to re-create the Patton/Rommel tank battle and destroyed a dozen golf carts in the process. "I developed a mantra on *Caddyshack,*" Ramis said, "which was, 'It's not my money.'"

"You know there's a hurricane coming," Ramis warned Carruth in the motel's ad hoc pot-encumbered cutting room. "You got your supplies?"

"What do you mean?"

Ramis dropped two grams on the table.

"You got your *supplies.*"

Still unclear about his story, which had fractured into funny set pieces like a Second City revue, Ramis got lost under all that footage. There was always an "on the other hand . . ." Inviting outside opinions, Ramis's collaborative approach only intensified his indecisiveness. "Editing," Ramis said, "was a disaster."

Caddyshack's first cut was four and a half hours long. In Hollywood, veteran editor Ralph Winters did what he could before abdicating the film to editor David Bretherton. He came up with an eleventh-hour solution, a flimsy through-line on which to hang all of *Caddyshack*'s disparate material: add more gopher.

•   •   •

There was a banging on the door. "Chrissie, wake up and get dressed."

It was her roommate, her best friend, Donna.

"Bill Murray is downstairs and we have to take him to Long Beach . . . I'll explain in the car."

Out on the street, Bill Murray was indeed sitting there in Donna's Honda Civic. With him was his friend John Byrum. In bumper-to-bumper traffic on their way out to Long Island, the guys had gestured for the girl in the Civic to pull over. "Can you tell us how to get to Long Beach?" Byrum asked. "Hey," Donna replied, "your friend looks like Bill Murray." Then Byrum told her; it *was* Bill Murray. "Let me stop and get my roommate," Donna returned, "and we'll take you to Long Beach."

Upstairs in the apartment, Byrum and Murray offered Chrissie a large bottle of Pabst Blue Ribbon and off they went.

Murray and Byrum were traveling the country, road-writing a feature film adaptation of *The Razor's Edge,* Somerset Maugham's novel of spiritual seeking and rebirth. Denver, Iowa City, L.A., and now, with Donna and Chrissie as their guides, onward to Long Island, New York, Murray and Byrum were seeking out loud bars and restaurants where they could write their movie in the chaotic middle of life. "We weren't trying to make a funny movie," Murray said, "but the intention was to show that this search doesn't mean you lose your sense of humor." Byrum would direct and Murray would star.

In the spring of 1981 Murray was a movie star, the famous face of the high-grossing *Meatballs,* and his next hit — *Stripes* — was only months away from release. He had signed with Michael Ovitz, the most powerful agent of Creative Artists Agency, the most powerful agency in Hollywood. "Bill was always difficult to find," Ovitz said. "A call would come in from India, and it would be Bill saying, 'Here I am at the Taj Mahal.' I wouldn't believe him, and he would put his Indian taxi driver on the line to prove he was out there. Or he'd show up at my house in L.A., out of the blue, ring my doorbell and say he was a pizza delivery-man. We'd let him in, he'd actually have a pizza, we'd eat it and then he'd disappear again." Years later Murray would explain, "I live a little bit on the seat of my pants, I try to be alert and available. I try to be available for life to happen to me. We're in this life, and if you're not available, the sort of ordinary time goes past and you didn't live it. But if you're available, life gets huge. You're really living it."

Arriving at the beaches of Long Island, the writers checked into an unsatisfactory motel and took their recruits to dinner. Chrissie had her first martini and Bill Murray sang her "Happy Birthday." It was not her birthday.

After dinner, the writers decided to forgo the motel, forgo Long Island altogether, and return to Chrissie and Donna's apartment, back in Queens, and watch *Judgment at Nuremberg*. They had a print and a projector with them. The girls slept through the movie.

The next morning, Murray sat with Chrissie as she put on her makeup and readied herself for work. Just shut the door, she told him on her way out, and it would lock. Okay, he said. She uttered a transfixed goodbye to Bill Murray, and left.

When she returned home that night, she found the projector cover and a bottle of Pabst Blue Ribbon sitting in her refrigerator.

SCTV's original deal with NBC, settled in the spring of 1981, was for nine ninety-minute shows, a major increase in running time. To speed up the flow of material, Dave Thomas, head writer of this new *SCTV*, suggested the "three-minute-and-under rule," which allowed cast members to circumvent the customary table read and get any sketch they wrote immediately into preproduction. "We needed to get things moving fast," Thomas explained. "And we had to trust each other enough to move these shorter sketches to the front of the line." Shorter material meant more material, about twenty to thirty pieces a show, and more material meant more writers, so Andrew Alexander hired Bob Dolman, John McAndrew, and Doug Steckler, a former Second City improviser, born and raised in the small town of Vermillion, South Dakota, who showed, early on, a knack for writing the best "local" humor pieces about Melonville, *SCTV*'s fictional home base. ("You really want to know where Melonville is?" said Dolman. "Vermillion, South Dakota.") In no time the rookies learned that the best way to get a piece on the big board was to first pitch it to a cast member and, with joint enthusiasm, refine it together in advance of the table read. Collaborative writing was especially useful to improvisers like Andrea Martin and John Candy, who, insecure on their own, ignited in the presence of others. "Actors would 'Yes, and' us writers until it didn't go anywhere or it caught fire," Steckler said. "They would give you all the fish line you needed to get the idea out there."

"*SCTV* wasn't a show that was heavily improvised on tape," Moranis said. "It was improvised in the writing room."

Improvisers and writers would meet in their individual offices off the conference room to play out the beginnings of a promising idea. "Improv is very much the first draft," Dolman said, "the creation of something by saying 'Yes, keep going.' At *SCTV* we had the freedom to use that tool to generate a lot of material." From office to office, word of funny scenes spread with the sound of laughter, and stealing away from their desks, their own pieces, writer-improvisers followed the scent through half-opened doors, pulled up chairs without asking to come in, and, in effect, touched their paintbrushes to the idea incumbent, layering in a character or idea of their own, and watched the colors change together in the swirl. "You welcomed the input," Steckler said. "No one got possessive of an idea."

By week's end, all convened in the conference room to present their work.

"It was like taking a test," Dolman said. "But that was the extent of our creative censorship. Our only judges were our peers at that table, but they were all funny people we admired." With ninety minutes to fill, table reads worked more democratically than ever. Rarely was a scene argued out of the room; a laughing or quiet consensus made obvious the distinction between good and less good, and anyway, Flaherty said, "when we did those shows we needed so much material we didn't have time to second-guess our instincts, and by that time, our instincts were so good." So good, in fact, Flaherty encouraged a certain amount of flop sweat at the table. After all, one never knew if the initial discomfort around a rickety sketch would lead to the threshold of uncharted comic territory. On the rare occasion a scene was rejected, Dolman said, "we never felt ostracized from the family. We knew it was safe to fail, so we allowed ourselves to risk. Our fear was 'I hope this is good,' not 'I hope I don't lose my job.'" As Del Close would, Flaherty directed the table toward the unknown, the potential bomb, but where the demon in Del relished the sadistic, Flaherty watched in grateful amusement, and as "an American observing Canadians observing Americans," in Steckler's words, he was their tuning fork — "the anchor" Dolman and Andrea Martin called him — not always making sense, but never wrong. Still, as in every family, feelings got hurt. "As a writer," Flaherty said, "you take offense to someone who doesn't like your thing. There was some of that, I think. More than we wanted to admit. It's one thing when someone else is taking the heat — like Lorne Michaels. It doesn't affect the group. But when it's coming from inside the group, there can be some resentment there that builds up."

To release hostility, the ensemble had an ideal outlet. Resisting, as one, the rotation of dutiful executives NBC dispatched to control them encouraged the sense of underdog purpose at *SCTV* and further focused their oppositional tastes. When one unsuspecting batch of executives called Dave Thomas into their office to present him with their list of demands, he shot back, "The cast wants to do it their way. If you don't like it, you have the right to cancel the show," and into the writing room would come another network disciplinarian, "because NBC had to have some guy in there," Dolman said, like Barry Sand, Al Rucker, or Don Novello (aka Father Guido Sarducci), who all found themselves offering unsolicited suggestions, getting a round of blank nods from the conference table, and ultimately retreating to a back office. NBC didn't understand that *SCTV* didn't work like *Saturday Night Live*. "They weren't used to the fact that the cast and the writers were running the show," said *SCTV*'s own producer, Pat Whitley. "They never understood that there was no Lorne Michaels."

Relocating to Edmonton to shoot season four further suppressed the threat of network interference. "NBC," Doug Steckler recognized, "was afraid of the cold," and finally left them to themselves. Their director, John Blanchard, "knew that the cast was going to tell him what they wanted and he could either contribute or back off," Whitley said. "He was really politically conscious and he also had a great eye." In an era when VHS copies were difficult to come by, Blanchard, in preparation of a parody, always managed to find his source material — as he did with *SCTV*'s ambitious send-up of *The Godfather* — bringing to set detailed visual notes that would be essential to the show's brilliant, and even beautiful, cinematic jokes, adding his own layer of visual satire to the segment. And after a take, Flaherty said, "we would sit at the monitor and all of us would have to okay it." In between, Flaherty might offer notes on an impression, or another cast member would contribute an idea. In an *SCTV* sketch, even the utility players are rich in detail; one gets the sense that any supporting character could be the center of his own sketch, and sometimes would. Hence Moranis's introduction of Skip Bittman, Bobby Bittman's brother, or Candy's William B., Sammy Maudlin's Ed McMahon, who, in a misguided effort to host his own talk show, fails. The web of interconnected characters — show biz failures, phonies and dreamers fighting their own delusions, the fearful shadow side of 1063 Avenue Road — further indemnified *SCTV*'s evolving creation of a world apart, like one of those magnificent volumes of nineteenth-century literature where you get not only the stories of individuals but an entire society, *Middlemarch* cum Melonville. "In terms of television sketch comedy," Del concluded, "I don't think it's ever been equaled."

That season, *SCTV* earned its first Emmy nominations — four of the five in a single category, Outstanding Writing for a Variety or Music Program — ultimately winning for their "Moral Majority Show," an ornate and eloquent exposé of the sort of network hypocrisies they nearly suffered under NBC. When presenter Milton Berle announced the winner, the episode's eighteen writers and performers — all credited writers on *SCTV* — took the stage to accept the award, and Berle, baffled by the size of the company, turned back and asked, "Who's gonna make the speech?"

"Me."

"Which one?"

"Me," said Flaherty, trying to get to the podium.

"Oh?" Berle scoffed. *"You?"*

"Yes."

Berle, milking his last moments before an audience, gave a hurry-it-up sign to Flaherty and won a round of strong laughter from the room. "No, I'm kidding," Berle said, and repeated the hurry-up signal to even more laughter.

Flaherty had to push past Berle to begin his acceptance speech. "I can't believe that we've got something up here bigger than the cast of *Hill Street Blues,* which —"

"That's funny," inserted Berle with considerable sarcasm.

"Sorry, Uncle Miltie," Flaherty improvised. "Go to sleep" — a rag on Berle's famous *Texaco Star Theatre* sendoff, and a typically Flahertian reference to boot, as knowingly inside as *SCTV*'s best stuff.

With that, Joe Flaherty, on behalf of his writers, won back the audience. Berle scrambled to riposte, but came out stammering.

This time *SCTV*'s cast and crew knew they'd be back for another season.

Dustin Hoffman had been developing *Tootsie* for years. The script had gone through several writers, most recently Larry Gelbart, who, heeding a brilliant assist from Hoffman's partner, the writer Murray Schisgal, elevated what could have been a routine cross-dressing comedy into a story for the modern feminist man, about an actor, Michael Dorsey, who becomes a better man by being a woman. Running with Schisgal's insight, Gelbart and Hoffman holed up in Malibu for hours and hours of improvisations, some of which, like Dorsey's "Nobody does vegetables like me!" rant would make their way to the film. But drafts later, the director, Sydney Pollack, was still unsatisfied, and Gelbart was released. They needed a new writer.

"You haven't tried a woman," Hoffman's lawyer, Bert Fields, pointed out. "Why don't you try Elaine May?"

May reviewed the script, and in short order, Hoffman, Pollack, and Schisgal met her in her apartment for the verdict. She was, Hoffman noted, an avid reader of mysteries. "You have the complete works of Agatha Christie?"

"She's a great structuralist."

With mathematic elegance, May proceeded to tell them exactly what the script needed.

"Your character needs a roommate."

"I'm forty years old. I don't want a roommate. They're going to think he's gay."

"Michael needs a shadow, someone he can tell his feelings to. For the audience. And he has to have a girlfriend. And I'm telling you right now, I'm writing the part for Teri Garr. But the girl he's in love with should be having a relationship with a guy who's a real asshole. And she should drink. And she should have a kid, so you see she needs somebody like Michael. And she should have a father and he should fall in love with Michael."

Early in 1982 she was hired. "It's a tilt," May said of her *Tootsie* revision. "The movie, when it started, the hero didn't like being a woman, and he couldn't stand his clothes, and he just wanted to see women naked, but Dustin himself just loved his part. He would come in during a script conference and say, 'I hate my dress! This is a horrible wig and my makeup is . . .' and I thought: He loves this part! He's a true Method actor!" She re-dressed *Tootsie*'s soap opera scenes, wrote Hoffman's climactic confessional monologue, deepened the female parts, and built up the farcical avalanche of lies and cover-ups to collapse just on schedule, when Michael's professional success is at its apex. ("Some of these changes may be useful, some may not," May scribbled on Pollack's script. "At this point I only care if they're legible.") She gave Jessica Lange, Michael's love interest, a tender monologue — the wallpaper speech, whispered to Michael-as-Dorothy, in bed beside her — "so she'll get nominated" (she didn't), and, as was her policy on rewrites, she refused screen credit. "Elaine is the one who made the movie work," Hoffman concluded. Mike Nichols deemed the work "Elaine's most spectacular save." She completed her revision in three weeks.

On a hunch, Columbia president Frank Price, the first studio head to bet on Bill Murray, sat Murray next to Pollack. "I didn't know what would come of it," Price said. They were two of the eighteen Price had invited to Christ Cella, the renowned New York steakhouse, to celebrate his wife, Katherine's, birthday. Dustin Hoffman and his wife, Lisa, two of the others, were seated on Murray's other side, inadvertently drawing Murray into their conversation about *Tootsie*. Price watched them from across the table. "At the party," he said, "Dustin really got onto Bill and was recruiting him." He was thinking of Murray for the character of Jeff, his roommate.

That night, throughout the dinner, as Hoffman thought of Murray for his roommate, Murray thought of being asked. Even a small part playing second banana to Dustin Hoffman, Murray knew, would showcase a different side of his talent, the "real" actor side he hoped would come through in *The Razor's Edge*—if he ever got it made. "Playing number two makes you more free," Murray explained. "You don't have as much responsibility and you're free to look different." At the end of the meal, he presented Katherine with her gift—earrings—and the party said their goodnights.

Outside the restaurant, Hoffman pulled Pollack aside. "Gee," he said, "I think he'd be a great roommate for my character."

Pollack had enjoyed Murray's company that evening, and admired him as a sketch comedian, but did he have an actor's range? He wasn't sure.

But Hoffman was. "Whoever we get has to feel like my best friend," he argued, "the sort of guy I can just have dinner with and not feel like I have to talk to. Billy's that guy."

Murray led the Hoffmans to his Volkswagen and drove them back to their apartment. He and Dustin stayed up that night until two in the morning, just talking, hanging out. Like roommates. "We fit, Billy and I," Hoffman said. Yes, he decided the next day, I would live with Bill Murray.

Hoffman called his new friend, and over the next few days, over the phone, started to tell Murray the story of *Tootsie*, and "like *that*," Hoffman said, Murray agreed.

Pollack, however, was still unconvinced. "He was in *Meatballs*!"

Hoffman stood firm. "Sydney, Sydney. There's an *actor* under there."

Soon after, the director came around. "It wasn't until I screened [Murray's] films at Dustin's urging," he said, "that I saw what a satisfying actor he could be." Still, he'd have to read him with Hoffman.

At the audition, Bill Murray exercised Second City technique, "where you can make the other person look good," he said, "which is my training. We did it and we did it again, then a third time, and each time I made it more his scene." The fourth time, Hoffman locked eyes with Murray. "Okay," he began, "let's do it one more time," and this round, Hoffman, recalibrating, found moments to give back to Murray. Neither trying to upstage the other, star and support found themselves playing together, taking and giving. "When it was over," Murray recalled, "both of us looked at each other like *that's right*. And from that moment on, anything was okay."

Murray got the part, his first opposite a major actor.

Somewhere between a Tab and vodka and a jolt of cocaine, nearing four in the morning on February 17, 1982, Belushi moseyed through someone's mansion a short distance from the Chateau Marmont, leading his new friend, UCLA student Jeffrey Jolson-Colburn, away from the after-party crowd, from the bar into the kitchen, where they could begin the impromptu interview that would be Belushi's last.

Why had so many original *Saturday Night Live* players become stars? "You couldn't help it," Belushi explained. "We learned to play off each other. I don't give a bleep how many tickets *Stripes, Modern Problems,* or even *Neighbors* sold. We were best together. We worked better as a whole than as individuals." What did Belushi make of the new *Saturday Night Live*? "It sucks," he replied. "A group has to develop a good rapport, and it takes at least six months to do that." Six seasons in, the departure of Lorne Michaels, an expert in team building, left the show to a cast of talented individuals unversed in ensemble, a far way from the original Not Ready for Prime Time Players. Jean Doumanian, Michaels's replacement, summoned Del Close to Studio 8H, Del said, "to come in and try to give a semblance of a feeling of a company." Christening himself "house metaphysician," Close led the company through workshops and had them improvise for the writers to results that earned him the respect of Dick Ebersol, Doumanian's replacement. Entering season seven, Ebersol, with Close and Belushi's guidance, swept through Chicago and Toronto and hired a slew of Second Citizens —Robin Duke, Mary Gross, Tim Kazurinsky, and Tony Rosato—in an effort to restore *SNL* to its improvisational roots. And yet, as Belushi observed to Jolson-Colburn that night in the kitchen, the company still lacked "emotional affinity."

Throughout their conversation, Belushi waved away girls and joints, saving what remained of his attention for punk rockers, expressing his admiration for Dan Aykroyd, and excusing himself, erratically, to re-up on coke.

"Do you always take drugs?"

"Whenever I can," he joked.

If *Saturday Night* sucked, and *Fridays* — ABC's answer to *Saturday Night* — sucked for the same reason, Belushi said, because the ensemble showed "a typical L.A. comedy style — everybody out for themselves," then what show, Jolson-Colburn wanted to know, didn't?

"*SCTV* is a great show," Belushi answered. "But in the wrong time slot."

He was scheduled to appear, as himself, on the first episode of *SCTV*'s 1982 season, in a series of sketches called "Box Office Poison" — Belushi's last pictures, *Continental Divide* and *Neighbors* had bombed — begging Guy Caballero, played by his mentor, Joe Flaherty, to save him from further humiliation in Hollywood and give him another shot, this time back in the ensemble, as a regular player on the show. "We all loved that guy," John Candy would say. "He was so loyal."

Dan Aykroyd was in New York, at his desk in Phantom-Black Rhino, the company he shared with Belushi, working on *Ghostbusters,* the script he was writing for the two of them. Midway into typing a line of dialogue for Belushi's character, Peter Venkman, the phone rang. It was Bernie Brillstein in L.A.

"Danny," he said, "sit down . . ."

Bob Dolman heard the wailing coming from another room at *SCTV*'s writing offices and someone said Belushi was dead. He went toward the wailing and found John Candy, still wearing his massive winter coat, bent forward over his desk, staring down at a hung-up telephone. "His whole giant body," Dolman said, "was seething with sobs."

Doug Steckler appeared as Candy, emerging from his office, was repeating, over and over, "It's starting! It's starting! It's starting!"

"What's starting, Johnny?"

"The deaths. The deaths. It's all starting."

Steckler put his arms around as much of Candy as anyone could, but Candy was "beyond human consolation," Steckler recalled. "I never felt so helpless, nor ever again saw him in such wretched, mournful despair."

The avalanche of Candy's grief was compounded by the sudden picture he saw of his own demise, a death also driven by unappeasable appetites, the addictions of so many in the business of — whether one was aware of it or not — turning rage into laughs, mistaking those laughs for love, and gorging oneself on the placebo relief they gave the hunger. "I found it an incredible high," Robin Williams said. "Performing is a drug, and you've O.D.'d. It's like body surfing on big waves. If you catch a big wave and get through it alive, you get the same rush."

There are kinds of laughter. One is an exorcism; it frees the mind of injustice, and if one laughs hard enough, the body too. The other, shoving down the demons, kills so slowly it can be mistaken for happiness.

What's starting, Johnny? As he held his friend, Steckler interpreted Candy's refrain to mean that "the harvesting of keen talents, driven by an excess of earthly temptations, had begun."

The afternoon of Belushi's memorial, Del Close threw his hypodermic needle into the street. He would keep the cigarettes, the pot, and sundry psychedelics, but from that day forward, Close swore off injectables and cocaine.

To aid in his recovery, he joined, in Toronto, a coven of witches. At his banishment ceremony, Close, donning the pentacle, took in each fist a rock and a candle, and backed by the ensemble concentration of an all-female Wiccan collective, transferred to those objects the anima of all he wanted to banish — invoking "the images of the universe of the pagans," he said — hurled the totems into a great fire, and danced in and out of the flames until he collapsed.

It — or something in it — worked. Sampling a gram or two a few weeks later, Del got horrifically ill.

Amazed at the effectiveness of the ritual, he called the collective's high priestess in Canada. "Is this the way it's supposed to work?"

"Well, yeah, it takes about three weeks for it to work its way through your unconscious. It took me that long to get off heroin."

Back at Second City Chicago, where rumors of devil worship swirled through his workshops, Del experimented with an improvisational exercise he called the Invocation.

Around midnight, some days after John died, Judy Belushi was startled by a knock at her apartment door.

It was Bill Murray. He should have been at home with Homer, his new baby boy.

Inviting him in, Judy could see he was restless. Over tea in the living room, she waited for Murray's self-assurance to return, but he remained oddly distracted, surely searching himself for a certain way to talk to her about John. As he thought, his eyes interrogated the living room, the shelves, the ceiling, the furniture, then he stood up and began wandering silently, like a detective in a museum.

Murray turned to face her. "Have you felt John around here?"

"No. I haven't felt him at all."

"Yeah," he conceded. "I don't feel him at all."

14

1982–1984

In his senior year, 1982, Chris Farley was unexpelled from Edgewood High School. That was Farley: you couldn't stay angry with him. Even his basest, most disruptive pranks, like mooning the whole of Colonel McGovern's geometry class (to incredible laughter), won him the embarrassed affection of deans and principals and his parents, who couldn't help but see, beneath the attention-starved troublemaker, a pure-hearted Catholic boy sincerely terrified of offending anyone, even the girl in typing class, who looked down at her workspace to find a message typed out by Farley's penis, which is how he got expelled from Edgewood midway into his junior year. "When he got in trouble, even as a kid," Farley's brother Kevin explained, "it was like something would take control of him that he couldn't help but cut up and make people laugh, even though he knew he'd get in trouble for it." Regaining some kind of consciousness after the laugh, he'd be the first to whip himself with a "Fuck! *Idiot!* Can't believe I did that." But his expulsion from Edgewood changed nothing; wherever he went, he kept pranking. He had to. When Chris Farley made you laugh, no matter how much the laugh debased him ("Dance, fatty, dance!"), his eyes said, *Thank you, thank you, friend, for laughing.*

His best nights — family nights — two parents, three brothers, and a sister — Farley spent in front of the television, swallowing into his memory *Animal House, Meatballs, Caddyshack, Stripes,* and *The Blues Brothers,* drawing inspiration he didn't need from Murray, Ramis, and especially John Belushi — his idol, his north star. Here the paradigm shifted. The children of improvisation's third decade — the stars Farley fell in love with — came of age in an entertainment culture diversified by all manner of comedy; their influences ranged from the Marx Brothers to Nichols and May to Lenny Bruce and beyond, and rarely esteemed above them the improvisers of Second City. Murray and Ramis had come to improvisation accidentally. Many, like Joe Flaherty, arrived with no knowledge of their predecessors. In the 1970s, when they started out, Second City was still only a job, not a calling.

But *Saturday Night Live* coupled with the box-office triumphs of *Animal House* and its progeny focused the generation that would follow them on the work of this talented handful. They were something like the Beatles, and by the power vested in the new blockbuster Hollywood, they were cross-platformed, franchised, and merchandized directly to kids like Farley.

This was teenage comedy, boys mostly. Heavy on the underdog, heavy on the physical, Farley's favorite movies had the populist (some would say gross-out) appeal absent from the work of older Second Citizens. "I'm a zit!" Bluto announces in *Animal House*, before expelling the mashed potatoes in his mouth with his fists. "Get it?" You could grow up on *Meatballs*, on Bill Murray; how many American adolescents knew Nichols and May's "Adultery"? Time and technology were not on Mike and Elaine's side. In their brief reign, they produced only a handful of albums, and their films, before the VCR, could be adored but would be gradually unremembered. Unless you had seen *The Graduate* fifteen times in the theater, in 1967, you couldn't memorize — as Farley's generation did *Caddyshack* — your favorite bits. You couldn't do them with your friends. You couldn't easily fetishize and deify your comedians. Moreover, in 1967, you wouldn't want to: young Americans, hippies, dreamed in revolutions. Entering the 1970s, the disillusioned young began to dream in *Easy Rider*, in the movies, in show business. After *Animal House*, some dreamed — for the first time — in improv comedy.

"Chris," asked Farley's college dean on learning the sophomore hadn't preregistered for the next semester, "what do you want to do?"

"I want to be at Second City. It's a comedy company in Chicago."

Sydney Pollack, anticipating improvisation, saved Bill Murray's scenes for the last three weeks of production. "He knew we would be trouble," Hoffman confessed. His first day of shooting, Murray arrived late, having stayed up the night before, drinking with his brothers. According to Pollack, Murray did "an enormous amount of improvising" in *Tootsie*. He had very few scripted lines. "In that sense," he concurred, "it was like *Caddyshack*. The only difference was that this time I was working with Dustin Hoffman, a really incredible actor." And Hoffman, true to Murray's audition, worked right back. "Every take he does is amazing," Murray observed, "and they're all different."

It was Elaine May who insisted Pollack improvise the film's birthday-party sequence on the grounds that party scenes, when written, never come across as parties. The director took the director's note. "Bill," Pollack said before one such take, "can you say something that sounds almost profoundly true but is really nonsense?" Pollack didn't warn the extras — a group of admiring women hanging on Murray's character's every word — that an improvisation was imminent, so when Murray, as Jeff, a playwright, started in on how he imagined his ideal audience, not a full house at the Winter Garden but a group of people who had just come out of the worst rainstorm in history ("These are people who are alive on the planet"), and from there, wishing for a theater that was *only* open when it rained, Pollack captured — along with this perplexing sprint of dialogue that Murray balanced, perfectly, on the pinpoint of seriousness — the incredulous reactions of the extras. And in one take.

Fred Willard's agent called and said Rob Reiner wanted him in his first feature, *This Is Spinal Tap*. The part — a colonel on a military base — struck Willard as another one of those square types he'd grown tired of playing, but he knew and liked Reiner and Harry Shearer, one of *Tap*'s band members, and had vague memories of working with Christopher Guest on Broadway, in *Little Murders,* so, with some nudging from his agent, Willard agreed to at least take the meeting.

On the day, while Reiner was at lunch, Willard watched the twenty-minute demo reel of improvised scenes, interviews, and heavy metal numbers Reiner had cut together. "What I was looking at was extraordinary," Willard said. He had never seen anything like it — indeed, no one had — a rock documentary about a "fake" band so serious and considered in its presentation — shot on 16mm by Peter Smokler, who had handled rock documentaries like *Jimi Plays Berkeley* — it was easy to mistake Reiner's demo for an *actual* documentary, which in a way it was. The only detail distinguishing these twenty minutes from *The Last Waltz* or *Don't Look Back,* classics of the form, was that these musicians — and Guest, Shearer, and Michael McKean *were* actual musicians — were improvising as fictional characters, but with such stunning commitment to natural, low-key reality, they passed for the real thing.

"They're improvising?" Willard said at the TV screen. "You mean they're not real people?"

By the time Reiner came back from lunch Willard had made his decision. "I want to be in this movie."

"We don't have a lot of money —"

"I don't care. I want to be in it."

Reiner was himself no stranger to improvisation. In 1961, his father — actor, writer, director Carl Reiner — and Mel Brooks improvised *The 2000 Year Old Man* on vinyl and television from characters they had been fooling around with for years, and as a nineteen-year-old student at UCLA, Reiner junior had founded his own improvisational troupe, the Session, with his friends Larry Bishop, Bobbi Shaw, Richard Dreyfuss, and another second-generation improviser, David Arkin. The Session — primarily social satirists — found their own theater on Sunset, disbanded after a year, and Reiner joined the Committee, first in San Francisco, and then, in the late 1960s, appeared with them in Los Angeles. He said, "It seemed like there was a tremendous cross-pollination between the rock & roll world and the improvisational-satire world. These rock & roll people were all fascinated by what we did — we improvised onstage — and they were always hanging around: Mama Cass, guys from Blood, Sweat and Tears, David Crosby, Stephen Stills, Neil Young, Steve Miller, Janis Joplin."

A decade later, in 1978, Reiner, Shearer, Guest, and McKean came together to work on *The TV Show,* an hour-long sketch spoof of television genres — including the rock 'n' roll variety show. "We were shooting a take-off on *Midnight Special,*" said Shearer, "just lying on the ground waiting for the machine that was supposed to make the fog effect to stop dripping hot oil on us — and to relieve the tension of that moment, we started adlibbing these characters that had nothing to do with the show." Reiner joined in, and playing Wolfman Jack, introduced the others, members, as it turned out, of a British metal band. "Michael and Chris pretended to be childhood chums from Squatney," Reiner recalled. "Harry said he came from Nilfordon-Null, a small village in the British midlands not far from Wolverhampton." They worked a version of their improvisation into *The TV Show* and made their first appearance as Spinal Tap.

The characters stuck with them. "At that stage," Reiner said, "there was no cohesive plan, just a sense of 'let's take this further and see where it goes . . .'" Discussions of doing some kind of roadie movie were abandoned after the release of *Roadie* in 1980, but whenever the improvisers reconvened, the conversation resumed. The idea to do *Tap* as a feature-length documentary seemed a triple boon, first because documentary was a natural habitat for rock bands in the movies; second, "we wanted to improvise as much as possible," Guest said, "and the documentary form allows you to do that"; and third, the form, said Shearer, "lent itself to the exposure of the self-important." Filming *Spinal Tap* as a documentary — the province of mostly high-minded, socially conscious filmmaking — delivered its own irony: a solemn, deadpanned look at a bunch of idiots.

Features had been improvised before, and the faux-documentary approach had already been used to successful effect — on radio, in *War of the Worlds,* and on film, in *Take the Money and Run* and *All You Need Is Cash* — but a fusion of the two, a fully improvised film in the documentary style, a genre that would come to be known as mockumentary, came to the fore with Reiner & Co.'s concept for *This Is Spinal Tap.*

Development money customary for a script, Reiner spent on a scene-by-scene outline — which began as a two-metalheads-and-a-girl, Yoko Ono, story — a detailed history of the band and its members, and a demo reel intended to lure further investors (and, as it turned out, Fred Willard). "We were literally walking from one lot to the next," Reiner said, "with a can of film under our arms. Columbia, MGM, Twentieth, Orion. We went everywhere." The yes finally came from Avco-Embassy in the form of just over two million dollars: five weeks to shoot an outline of all Whats and no Hows. McKean said, "Going into each scene, improvising, we knew what information had to be conveyed, but the dialogue was totally flexible. The questions you see Rob Reiner asking us in the film were the first time we'd heard them." Rarely did Reiner need more than three or four takes of each scene. "The first time," he said, "I'd just turn on the cameras and see what happened. The second time, we added things or changed focus. The third time was to get variations and the fourth time was for cutaway shots." Throughout, Reiner kept his attention on the characters' attitudes, maintaining their parameters. He looked out for the story. Was each improvisation consistent with what had already been established and where *Tap* needed to go? Was a tangent compelling enough to reevaluate the outline, or was it what Reiner called a comic "wild card," hilarious, but liable to lead them astray? "It's the discipline," Shearer said, "of what is otherwise a free form of expression."

When Fred Willard improvised his scene, Christopher Guest, to keep from laughing and ruining the take — a priceless moment impossible to recreate, even on a second take — had to physically hide behind McKean to keep his reaction from the camera. Willard, Guest decided on *Spinal Tap*, was one of the funniest guys in the world, an enormous asset to any improvised scene, but to the other improvisers in that scene, an equally enormous liability. When Willard was on, some would literally have to walk — or run — out of the shot to keep from breaking up.

"That day shooting *Spinal Tap* led to me being in the movies Christopher Guest would make years later," Willard reflected. "So it was an afternoon well spent."

In the summer of 1983 Billy Murray was shooting *The Razor's Edge* through remotest Europe and India, where Columbia executives, impatient about his approaching start date on *Ghostbusters,* couldn't reach him. Their messages, increasingly desperate, didn't find the production until they hit Ladakh, a scarcely populated region of mostly monks in the north of India. "Is Bill finished?" came one such missive, three days late. "He's supposed to be doing *Ghostbusters* on the 25th."

Rushing from Delhi to London, Murray returned via Concorde to New York, exhausted and underweight, and shifting metaphysical gears from a movie about the search for freedom and meaning to a Hollywood comedy about ghost hunting, thinking, *What am I doing here? Slime?* "I mean," he said, "you'd look around on the set in Ladakh, and there were thirty-five monks looking at you, just looking at you. And you realized that they were looking for a reason. It was a reminder all the time. A reminder that you're a man and you're going to die, so you'd better not waste this time here." Where to go and how to be there: this was the quandary in Murray that Ramis saw as "always checking situations out for the moral quotient. What do I really feel? What do I really want? Is this good, is it moral, is it with it? Is it the right thing to do?" To fully feel the moment, to allow his liquid self to flow through its secret message toward a new becoming, was Murray's life's improvisation, often unfriendly to understanding. Even by his friends. Aykroyd said, "He's off on another kind of journey that people, including me, don't always understand."

It was not slime, but his ensemble allegiance to Aykroyd, Ramis, and Reitman, and theirs to him, that brought Murray there, to *Ghostbusters,* to a part Aykroyd had written for Belushi. "I think after John died," he said, "we all realized we had been getting away from each other and we should stick closer together and help one another out." He was returning the favor Aykroyd paid him some time earlier, when, putting his own film, *Ghostbusters,* on the line, he advised Murray, "Tell whoever wants *Ghostbusters* that they have to take *The Razor's Edge* too," a gamble Columbia's Frank Price — a longtime supporter of Murray's — was willing to risk. "The word in Hollywood," Price explained, "was I was making a stupid decision. *Ghostbusters* was expensive, special-effects comedy, and it was generally conceded that comedies had a ceiling on how much money they could bring in."

By any standard, *Animal House, Meatballs, Stripes,* and *Caddyshack* were low-budget investments; *The Blues Brothers,* approved at $17 million and coming in at around $27 million, approached *Ghostbusters'* $30 million budget, but where the former had the security of Belushi's bankability, and arrived in theaters at the tail end of *Saturday Night Live's* first great wave of popularity, *Ghostbusters'* elaborate special-effects plan was a sink-or-swim proposition liable to bury the whole production — and *Saturday Night Live's* star, having slipped from the firmament, didn't mean what it once had. Timing the film's release to the summer of 1984 — primetime for high school audiences — Price made Reitman guarantee a finished film almost exactly one year from the day he gave the go-ahead, in June of 1983, giving Reitman and company a mere twelve months to write Aykroyd's deliriously impractical outline into a script, and shoot, edit, and add the two hundred or so special-effect shots no one was certain they could pull off. "I wasn't asking for the impossible," Price said. He thought, worse case, *Ghostbusters* would break even.

Columbia's president and CEO, however, did not. Fay Vincent was so nervous about the budget, he sent his lawyer to Los Angeles to talk Price out of his decision.

Price's explanation was, simply, "I've got Bill Murray."

The ticking clock was loud in Ivan Reitman's mind when he and Harold Ramis drove out to collect Murray, that day in October 1983, from La-Guardia Airport, where they found him sauntering through the terminal, brandishing a stadium horn and chatting up the locals. ("If I see someone who's out cold on their feet," he reflected, "I'm going to try to wake that person up. It's what I'd want someone to do for me. Wake me the hell up and come back to the planet.") Rushing Murray into wardrobe, Reitman still had no idea if he'd actually read the script. In truth, Bill Murray had barely even thought about his character; but supported by Aykroyd and Ramis, doing double duty as improvisers and screenwriters, he knew *Ghostbusters,* though closely scripted, would be treated as a work in progress. "Having your writers as actors means you have them on the set all the time," Reitman said. "We basically did our final draft while we filmed." Wherever there wasn't a line — if the script allowed it — "We just made stuff up," Murray said.

"We trusted each other so implicitly," said Ramis, "because of our mutual training at Second City." A similar dynamic united Reitman and Murray. "Because we've worked together," Reitman said, "Bill trusts me. He's willing to be lousy because he knows I'll cut it out. That allows him to be spontaneous."

Trust curbed the impulse to deliberate every detail, allowing Reitman to work fast — "four writers, three directors, no waiting," Aykroyd said — shooting sometimes as many as fifteen setups a day, which he moved along with a shorthand — potentially off-putting to an untrusting ensemble — his improvisers understood.

"Be smarter . . ."

"Be cheaper . . ."

"Do it different . . ."

"Shooting was precious," Reitman said, "so you don't want to waste it on bullshit." To keep the pace, Reitman would restart scenes while the camera was rolling, and in twenty seconds the prop department would reset the props, the assistant director would get the background players back to first positions, and Reitman would call out to the principal actor, generally Murray, "the energy source," he called him, a shorthand direction, the improvisation would begin, and Reitman, "in some unsaid musical way," would feel, in his gut, the scene drawing to its natural ending point. Rhythm — he had it. When "Cut" finally came, Reitman would pull Murray to the camera. "You know where you said *this* instead of *that*?" he would say. "Let's do it again, and this time, let's try it with that." Reitman would try to hold on to the strongest discoveries — not just improvised jokes, but improvised story or character turns. Before rolling film on one library scene, Reitman said, "Let's just put a stack of books over here . . ."

"I'm just going to knock this shelf over," he warned before another library take, "so get ready . . ."

Laughing — Reitman was an ace laugher — kept the improvisers hot. "There's this Second City theory," said costar Sigourney Weaver, new to ensemble improv, "that says if you'll help the people around you to be good, you'll also bring out the best in yourself. That philosophy was so powerful I think it had a lot to do with why the film was such a breeze — it was just so much fun to make." Half the job, Murray knew, was maintaining that sense of fun; without it, that other half, spontaneity, wouldn't occur, and moments like the one between Murray and Weaver, playing at hunting ghosts in her character's apartment — Murray tinkling the living room piano and deadpanning, "They hate that" — would have never happened. Murray found the key to fun in looseness and relaxation, the blank, Zen mind from which his instinct could spring. On *Ghostbusters*, it was palpable. "Being on the set was one of the great experiences of all time," said Michael Ovitz, then Murray's and Aykroyd's agent. "The looseness was crazily fantastic."

Looseness grounded in story, Reitman said, "was the key to *Ghostbusters*. There's improv all over the place, but at the same time, we had a really great script." So successful was Reitman's give-and-take, watching *Ghostbusters*, you can't tell where the improvised scenes end and the closely scripted scenes begin. The net result, a structural integrity uncommon to the improvised film work of the 1980s, stamped *Ghostbusters* as the smoothest, most professional film of the post–*Saturday Night* comedies. "*Ghostbusters*," Aykroyd said, "was really ten years in the making if you think of the formation of my career and Billy's and Harold's and Ivan's. What we did was interlock and interweave the training we got from the three main comedy institutions in America — Second City, *Saturday Night Live,* and National Lampoon" — taming, in the process, the gross-out defiance of mid-'70s *Lampoon* humor with friendly goodwill. In *Ghostbusters*, it is the improvisational mood of pure fun enjoyed at City Hall's expense that shows the punk spirit Ramis wrote into *Animal House* and *Caddyshack* — indeed, all his films of the late '70s and early '80s.

"I feel that even as slight as films that I have worked on may seem to critics," Ramis said, "each one has a buried message to the audience — and I consider that audience a very impressionable one." *Animal House* delivered its message through tits and togas; *Caddyshack,* shit in the pool; but in *Ghostbusters* there is nothing to offend, no puerile attacks on power, no Belushi. Here Ramis and his cowriters, softened by years of success, channeled their 1960s radicalism into kinder terms, more palatable to mass audiences. Ivan Reitman, reaching his crest as an improvisational director, resolved the stylistic irregularities of their previous collaborations, *Meatballs* and *Stripes* — works beset by awkward shifts from scripted to improvised scenes — into polished, blockbuster form.

When *Ghostbusters* hit screens in the summer of 1984, "the money," Frank Price said, "was coming in in such huge amounts. It was like the movie *Boomtown*. The geyser kept pouring out. It kept gushing and gushing and . . ." This gusher was quickly followed by a sea change in Hollywood. Suddenly, Ovitz said, "everyone was clamoring for *SNL* people. Within a 12-month period, the entire attitude of people in the business regarding television personalities changed."

Judd Apatow could remember back to his teenage years on Long Island, how he went to see *Ghostbusters* opening day with his mother, and how the theater was completely packed, and the audience's laughter, during the library scene, was the biggest his sixteen-year-old ears had ever heard.

"In the beginning," Tina Fey said, "I was probably more motivated by *SCTV* and *Saturday Night Live* than anything else." She couldn't put her finger on it, but even then, as a girl, getting to stay up late, after *SNL,* and watch *SCTV,* Fey felt something different — different than *Saturday Night Live*. She didn't get all of it ("My brother was eight years older and *he* was into it"), but it made her laugh ("I knew Edith Prickley was funny"), and its complexity, what she didn't fully get, the way *SCTV* interwove its backstage stories with the "on air" shows within the show, made her aware of *SCTV*'s writers. Comedy writers. She followed them back. To Toronto, to Chicago. "I knew that most of the actors on those shows had come from Second City," she said, "and that at least inspired me to get to Chicago."

WE THE NERDS

1984–

15

1984–1987

On Halloween of 1982, Del Close had appeared, wand in hand and co-cooned in a floor-length robe, at a candle-lit art gallery in downtown Chicago. This getup was no costume; in pagan solemnity, Del was to lead a cast of ten improvisers through an Invocation, first by calling forth gods, good and evil, from the four corners of the earth, then by asking the audience to suggest a common object and summoning its essence, a four-phase process wherein the players address the object first as object, then as people, gods, and finally, as themselves, newly imbued with the object's spirit, scenes are improvised.

Around one thirty in the morning Del began his conjuring of spirits. Among his players that night was Charna Halpern, a fiery improviser proficient in Spolin and ImprovOlympic, David Shepherd's latest effort to return improvisation to the nonprofessionals. Halpern came that night in search of deeper, bigger modes of improvisation, but recoiled at what she saw as Close's recklessness. Her own training in Transcendental Meditation mandated a ritual "white-lighting" against danger, which Close had brazenly omitted.

She approached him after the performance. "You had a lot of nerve invoking demons," she admonished him. "People weren't protected."

"I protected the building."

"You can't do that."

"Yes, I can."

Early the next year, Halpern spotted Close outside Crosscurrents' cabaret, temporary home to Halpern's own branch of ImprovOlympic, apart from Shepherd. In the months since she and Close had last met, and clashed, Close had cut ties with Second City yet again. This time, the feeling was mutual: Del's suicide attempts had finally gotten the better of Sahlins, and Sahlins's retrograde views of improvisation had become intolerable to Del. "In reality," Close concluded, "if it were not such a sound business proposition, Second City probably should have closed . . . because we've done nothing but repeat ourselves for the last six or seven years. So long as the shows are not so much worse than television, [audiences] won't be disappointed." A victim of its own success, the former temple of satire had at last ceded to the tastes of tourists, who came en masse, looking for live versions of their favorite TV shows and movies. This, Halpern knew, left an artistic and perhaps even commercial opening in the improvisational marketplace.

"Hey," she said to Close outside Crosscurrents. "How'd you like to make two hundred bucks and some pot?"

"What do I gotta do?"

"Just teach one three-hour class."

"Can I do anything I want?"

"Yeah."

"Can I invoke demons?"

"Yeah," she conceded. "What the hell."

At that workshop, Halpern said, Close opened up for the students the secrets of the universe. He taught Invocation, a version of which Halpern had seen at the art gallery the Halloween before. The results were staggering. "He just embarrassed all of us," Halpern recalled.

Afterward, Halpern confessed to Close that ImprovOlympic, with its reliance on shortform games, had stopped satisfying her long ago. "I know there has to be something for improvisation beyond what I'm doing," she told Del.

"Well," he returned, "then you're not a twit after all."

Close suggested Halpern put aside her "little game theater" and, with her students as test cases, help him remake the Harold into a sustainable, teachable means of producing longform improvisations.

"If we made a structure . . ." Del said to Charna, "if we plugged some of your games into the Harold, maybe we could come up with something . . ."

They joined forces. At Crosscurrents, a black box theater squeezed into a skeevy row of pawnshops and liquor stores, Halpern took over the beginners classes, freeing Close to run wild with his experimental cadre of advanced students. "You never knew what he was going to do in class," Halpern said. Freshly fascinated with *Drawing on the Right Side of the Brain,* Betty Edwards's 1979 text on enhancing creativity, Del played with reversing the book's paradigm: he had his students hum aloud to dampen their right lobes to see what effects the ersatz lobotomy had on their left. "You gave me your money," he would say to the hesitant. "You've paid me to fuck with you, so I'm doing my job." Whereas an ambitious Second City student would, and often did, resist such techniques, his acolytes came to Crosscurrents open, for the most part, to following him, and the Harold, wherever it took them.

That Del Close had cleaned up his act gave his muse a new credibility. He no longer came to workshops high on anything weirder than weed or Valium, he had stopped drinking entirely, and he had virtually no veins left for needles. You could say Close didn't need the hard stuff anymore: a steady supply of his favorite drug — artistic freedom — he got at Crosscurrents. Aiding in his recovery, Halpern remade Del's derelict apartment — a Grey Gardens of comic books, unread mail, cockroaches, and cat shit — into an inhabitable living space. She convinced him to abandon his cashbox for an actual bank account, use tea bags only once before throwing them away, and get a telephone. Until then, Close was convinced merely owning a phone would lead to his arrest.

"Why would you be arrested?" Charna asked.

"When the president would come on TV to give his state of the union speech, I'd get mad, and I'd call and threaten his life and they'd come and arrest me, so no phone."

It was Close who turned down sex, because "(a) I might gross you out," he told Halpern, "and (b) I might end up killing you, and I want us to stay together for a long time."

"Then we'll be like family," Charna said.

Still, he was jealous. Del asked Charna to keep her romances away from him, and she complied, but as Charna got serious with one man, Del picked up the scent and tried to revise their arrangement. No, Del would not share her. There were only two women he ever loved, he pleaded: Elaine and her. But Halpern, if she imagined it, could see how that would end. The best thing for both of them, and for improvisation, would be to keep their relationship familial.

Where they came together, heart and mind, was in the Harold. Experimenting with the Time Dash, one of the shortform ImprovOlympic games Halpern taught in her beginners workshops, Close foresaw a structure. If Charna's Time Dash — a scene sequence that followed a suggestion through three jumps in time — formed the basis for three separate storylines (that's nine scenes total) and was set in motion, at the beginning of the improvisation, by an audience suggestion, the Harold could build, scene by scene, to a satisfying ending to all storylines. Ideally, in the final scene of the final Time Dash — the point of the story pyramid — character and narrative elements of previous scenes, the foundation of the pyramid, would coalesce. For Close, that interconnectedness was the artistic by-product of his great metaphysical adventure — not to make comedy per se, but to join together human beings, as Paul Sills tried to, in an act of communal creation. Hence "slow comedy," a strategy Close introduced to discourage the manic, laugh-oriented atmosphere of Second City improvisation, and attune the Harold's six or eight improvisers to what was really happening now. Act on your third thought. Your fourth thought. And rather than react, he would say, *Think. Feel.* It will fasten you to yourself and the thinking, feeling selves of others.

And so it was that, at Crosscurrents' cabaret, Baron's Barracudas, the first-ever Harold team, figured out how to Harold. They thought of themselves as Close's guinea pigs. Halpern dubbed them the pioneers.

They would tell Bill Murray, star of *Ghostbusters,* the highest-grossing comedy up to that time, that he could now do anything he wanted. Now even Clint Eastwood pitched him a movie idea. But what, Murray asked himself, did *he* want to do? He wasn't sure. "I didn't have a plan," he said.

Having taken possession of the blockbuster audience, Murray realized that if he wasn't careful, they would take possession of him. If he were to play into their expectations, reteaming with his Second City ensemble for a sequel to *Ghostbusters,* Murray would become the comedian they, the audience, wanted him to be. It would curb his freedom. And yet, if he were to turn his back on the heat, he could lose the power — and with it, a certain kind of freedom — that came with superstardom.

In 1984 he chose, instead of Hollywood, Paris. Without much of a plan, Murray, his wife, Mickey, and their son, Homer, left for half a year.

In Paris, Murray enrolled at the Sorbonne. He studied French grammar in a classroom with a view of the Eiffel Tower; his phonetics class (the professor called him William) took him across the Seine. He studied history, and the writings of the Armenian mystic George Gurdjieff, who believed humanity had lost touch with ancient teachings that could reverse ingrained patterns of mind and wake us from our psychic sleepwalks. For lunch, Murray would stop at his favorite chocolatier, pick up 150 grams, and offer handfuls to people as he walked down the street. It was a good way, he knew, to start a conversation.

The afternoon he found himself at the Cinémathèque Française, Murray happened on a screening of *A Romance of Happy Valley*, a D. W. Griffith silent that hit him, he said, "like a thunderbolt." Could he convey with his face alone all that the actors in the film could? "What would a guy like me do at that time?" he wondered. "Without a tongue, who am I?" He went to the Cinémathèque as much as he could, sometimes taking in two movies a day, after class. Most movie stars, he would see, didn't share the focus, but Cary Grant "really made other people look good. That's really what they taught us at Second City . . . you never think of a movie where he was just, you know . . . dominating someone in a scene or being much bigger than they or something. He was always very aware of them, you know, gave them focus." He loved Margaret Sullavan in *The Moon's Our Home* — a movie, Murray said, about "two famous people who are running away from their fame and they bump into each other and fall in love" — because of how free she was in the physical comedy, seeming to take blows from Henry Fonda without the careful or stylized physicality he noticed in too many other stars of her era. Above all, Murray kept thinking, "How could you see all these movies and make some of the movies that are made today?"

He resolved, upon returning to work, to choose carefully. His first choice was to costar with Dustin Hoffman in an art versus commerce comedy to be directed by Ivan Reitman, about two lawyers fighting over the estate of the artist Mark Rothko. But when Hoffman answered the call — from Elaine May — to star in her next film, *Ishtar*, Hoffman withdrew from the project, Robert Redford replaced him (and the Rothko idea), and Murray lost interest.

He would stay in Paris a little longer.

After Second City's Twenty-Fifth Anniversary, in the spring of 1985, Bernie Sahlins met Andrew Alexander at Chicago's Ambassador Hotel to finalize their agreement, the sale of Second City. Sahlins hadn't really explained why he was selling — not to the buyers, Alexander and his partner, Len Stuart, and not to his home team — but Alexander, reading between the lines, sur-mised "a combination of things. Bernie had a lot of legacy employees he didn't know what to do with and he couldn't fire anyone, so I think that laid on him." And of course Bernie, then in his sixties, was only getting older than his improvisers, too old for their aging brand of boomer comedy, a derivative form of *SNL,* which bored and baffled him. "I was getting to the point," he said, "where nothing was new enough." His onetime avant-garde theater had degenerated into a sketch revue, just as its cultural stock — as evidenced by the windfall of *Ghostbusters* — had reached a new apex. ("If you're not interested," Sahlins had said, perhaps bluffing, to Alexander, "I have a studio interested.") It was the time to sell, and Alexander — who had ushered the Fire Hall into the black and brought Second City into big media with *SCTV* — was the perfect buyer.

After dinner, the paperwork signed, Bernie announced, "I'm going to go talk to Joyce."

Alexander was shocked. Joyce didn't know what was taking place? Sah-lins's right hand since 1961, Joyce Sloane had long ago transcended the role of touring-company manager, den mother (buyer of birthday cakes, hostess of Thanksgivings), and all-purpose handler of emotions; she had virtually become Bernie's coproducer. She was family. The news would level her.

There was nothing Alexander could do. Onward from the Ambassador, he followed Sahlins to Second City and to the threshold of Joyce's office.

Behind a closed door, he heard Bernie's voice: "I'd like to talk to you . . ."

A few minutes later, Sahlins reemerged. "Okay," he said to Alexander. "I told her," and walked off.

Alexander rushed in to assure Sloane that everything was going to be okay, "but she was in a state of shock," Alexander said. "I did give her fifteen percent of the business right off the bat, but she and I had quite an unpleas-ant relationship for many years after that."

By the time Andrew Alexander left Sloane's office, Bernie Sahlins was gone.

By the age of ten, Stephen Colbert had already discovered, horribly, the truth about everything on earth: what matters now will not matter a thou-sand years from now, or one hundred years from now, or tomorrow. "In the line of eternity," his mother explained, "what does this matter?"

In 1974 her husband, Stephen's father, had been killed in the crash of a commercial airliner in North Carolina, along with Stephen's brothers Peter, age eighteen, and Paul, fifteen.

His mother's wisdom was offered in consolation. Giving her nine surviving children a God's-eye view of their place and time, Mrs. Colbert was taking them to the water's edge and pointing out the horizon. Look how small you are. Everything passes. Nothing important really matters. That's the good news and the bad. "The world didn't make any sense," Stephen, ten years old at the time, reflected, "and so it was easy to remove yourself from the world." When it all can be undone, instantly and for no reason, why go to school, invest in friends, do homework? Why do or, for that matter, feel anything?

He detached.

"I think that really helps if you're doing comedy," he would say, "or maybe even specifically doing satire, is that what seems normal no longer has status." Cynicism was also a numbing agent; it pushed out suffering. "Belated grieving is what it was," said Colbert, "and it lasted till I got out of college."

College, at first, was Hampden-Sydney in Virginia. Colbert's uniform was "poet-jerk," black pants and turtleneck, and his major was one of his lost father's loves, philosophy, which he found suitably hopeless. "I was just incredibly depressed," he said, "and then I thought, well, if I'm going to pick my liver this hard I might as well get something from it." As a serious actor (with the beard to prove it), Colbert reasoned he could share his misery with an audience. He would be Hamlet or Bob Fosse, performing his anguish. "There was something viscerally attractive to me," he said, "about living this sort of life that might kill you young."

In year 1984, he transferred to Northwestern, in Chicago, to study theater, and was asked, for the first time, to reveal himself onstage. His acting professor found Colbert's rage unnervingly powerful. It was too much.

"I think you could probably use a little therapy," she said.

"Oh, really?"

"Yeah, because I was physically afraid that you were going to punch me today in class."

Over lunch, professor and student discussed the origin of his offstage default position, clowning, and how it defended him from emotion.

"Well," Colbert explained matter-of-factly, "it might have something to do with the fact that my father and two brothers were killed in a plane crash when I was 10, and I was left home with a grieving mother. And my main mission became to make her laugh."

"We didn't have a TV," recalled Mary Scruggs, one of Colbert's roommates at Northwestern, "so you'd just hang out in someone's living room, and he'd adopt a character, someone else would adopt a character, and we'd have conversations that way for an hour." What emerged from these improvisations were not so much characters as heightened versions of Colbert's natural intelligence, all of them fancifully articulate and insanely erudite. "Stephen was fascinated with language and semiotics," roommate Anne Libera said, "with the way people tell their stories." Words were his way in.

Colbert's friend Chris Pfaff took him to Crosscurrents to watch Improv-Olympic's Harold teams grapple toward longform. Del Close's lifelong ambition, the crossbreeding of "low" improvisation with "high" theater, drummed both sides of Colbert's heart, and where most, if not all, beginning improvisers cowered from their fear of the free fall, Colbert, who had been in free fall for a decade, recognized its secret right away. Laugh or no laugh, time was like Kleenex, easy come, easy go. "And I think some of that comes from my mother," Colbert said. "I don't actually believe that the present social norm is some sort of eternal truth." Life had already proven, tragically, that there were no laws. He could be an asshole, he could be a saint. This thing, the Harold, said nothing *is*.

"I have to do this," Colbert said to himself at Crosscurrents. "I have to improvise."

Always in process, incessantly and restlessly sprouting new theaters and theatrical forms, only to halt them before they bore fruit, Paul Sills — co-creator of the Compass Theater, the Game Theater, and Story Theater — relocated his magic to the cozy Heliotrope Theatre in Hollywood, where his jangling band of old-timers — you remember Severn Darden, Mina Kolb, and their friends? — could draw back from their film and TV work, draw back almost to the 1960s, into Sills's dream of togetherness. They reunited to work on a scripted play, but no one could remember the lines, so Sills, with his mother, Viola Spolin, at his side, took up a copy of Spolin's 1963 book, *Improvisation for the Theater,* and they started from the very beginning, playing her games again, but this time as grown adults. "I've done musicals and plays and Story Theater," Sills said, "but I always keep coming back to the games. If you wanted to analyze it, you could say it's a neurotic thing about my mother, and maybe it is, but I don't think about my mother when I'm doing the games. We're just working on something that seems to be interesting." Second City improviser Tony Holland christened the group Sills and Company, "and we started playing on Fridays and Saturdays," Sills said, "going out for a beer afterward, just like in the old days."

They opened in 1985. For only seven dollars a ticket, I heard, anyone could see them play the hundred-seat converted-garage theater, transformed by Carol Sills into a readily adaptable imagination space of white sheet curtains and risers, which her husband, tearing at his hair like an angry sorcerer, would trample on his way to the stage, to shove one of his company, the world's most professional children, an inch deeper into their freedom.

"I'm going to crack you!" he would shout. "Crack you like a lobster!"

They played full evenings of Viola's games; there were no sketches to freeze, no mythic forms to ensure spiritual pertinence. Just improvisation. "Nobody," Sills said, concurrent with Close's experiments in longform, "has ever done that before."

From Los Angeles, Sills took them to Chicago, and then to Broadway.

Del Close thought he'd be dead before the IRS caught up with him. But he was, unfortunately, still alive when he got notice that he owed twenty thousand dollars in back taxes. In a panic, he confessed all to Charna Halpern, who responded swiftly with a plan of action.

"You remind me of Elaine," he told her.

"I do?"

"You're strong. No one takes advantage of you."

One night at dinner, Close and Halpern explained the tax details to Bill Murray, who devised, on the spot, a mutually beneficial rescue plan. Murray would cover Del's debt; in return, he asked that Del help him supervise an improvised feature film, something Murray had in mind for Sydney Pollack to direct. Bringing together some of his favorite actors, mostly untrained in improvisation, Murray envisioned a workshop process, from which a script would emerge. Of course Del said yes.

In January 1986 Murray assembled his ensemble — a team that included his brother, Brian Doyle-Murray, Dana Delany, C. Thomas Howell, Jami Gertz, Bill Irwin, O-Lan Jones, and Bud Cort — at Crosscurrents' cabaret.

Pollack would observe the workshops, noting tantalizing story and character discoveries, as he himself discovered improv à la Close. ("It was new to him too," Delany said, "though he would never admit it.")

Day one, Close started them off, two at a time, with a simple game of Freeze. In two days, he was giving them Where suggestions, beginning with: circus. Taking the stage, Delany became a tightrope walker.

"Continue the tightrope analogy," Close instructed the next players.

The subsequent scene — asking your boss for a raise — he explained was inspired by the previous one. They would go on like this, Close said, birthing, by association, one scene from the last. "We were learning the Harold," Delany reflected. "We would do it over and over again."

"Breathe in the events of the world," Del called out, "and exhale comedy." That was, he said, the metabolism of improvisational performers.

When the energy flagged, Close led them in a game of Machine, which he based on Newtonian pool table physics. Each player, their own part of a human Rube Goldberg, is not activated until they are "dinged" by another. Once activated, they ding someone else, and onward, until all parts of the machine ding together as a unit. An ensemble.

Then: "Has anyone had a nightmare recently?" Close asked.

Yes, of course.

Up jumped a volunteer to tell his story and the company leapt up behind him to fill in the details and add nightmares of their own. ("When you're in somebody's dream," Murray observed, "you have a responsibility.")

Leaving Close in Chicago, they moved onward to New York. Gaining comfort in the process, Pollack started a discussion about the quality of emotion in these, Close's exercises, namely, how to combine spontaneity with deeper truths and experiences, or as Pollack termed it, "a more Method improv."

Bill Murray took the floor to remind everyone what they were really doing here. He shared with his company his growing ambivalence about being a movie star and how improvisation was the cure. In a quiet voice, he imagined aloud the film they might improvise together — his admiration for Kurosawa's *Red Beard,* how the film begins in apparent simplicity and expands, planting narrative seeds, he said, some of which grow, some of which don't . . .

"Is there a way," he asked the group, "to start with a small town and *braid* the film around it?"

They began to discuss a sort of *Our Town*. Without scenery, they could move through time; the living would speak to the dead; the Stage Manager would transform himself, like a Spolin player, playing as if Thornton Wilder had written a game instead of a play. Off they went: Bud Cort improvised as the town's blustery big fish and Bill Irwin a café owner with big dreams. O-Lan became a hairdresser having an affair with Brian, the fire chief, married to Dana, society matron, whose bad-boy son, Tommy Howell, didn't want to go away to college. Bill Murray played the town's mayor.

By the time they arrived in Los Angeles, in February 1986, the screenwriter Steve Kloves had joined them. From their improvs, he would write a script.

Close flew in to check on their progress. He had them reimprovise the same scenes over and over, "an automatic editing process" he implemented to eliminate all the unnecessary material; only what they remembered, he taught them, would be truly essential. After each run, he asked, "What did you discover? Is there anything you want to add?" Then they ran it again. Then more discussion.

"You go from improv to improv to improv to dramaturge," he reiterated, "and then back, and we pull up the richness of our unconscious." And also:

"Have faith that the scene is going to eventually make sense."

"Always look for the solution to the problem, not the conflict."

"Hold until you see the other person react to what you said."

Wherever possible, Close said, choose the poetic interpretation. Slow down. Choose the second thought.

Watching them improve, Pollack thought: *We're almost as good as children.*

They were performing full Harolds now, debating the formal characteristics of their story (linear or with flashbacks?), testing monologues, each one a townsperson's memory, or dream. From those monologues, scenes, bits of dialogue:

"I got beat up once before," Murray improvised. "I sure learned my lesson!"

"It doesn't sound like it," O-Lan replied. "You just got beat up again."

"Well, shit, Jackie, there's more than *one* lesson in life."

And when improvisers left the moment in progress in pursuit of a joke, or a jab at wit, Close interrupted them for a lesson in what he called comedy-aversion therapy. "You don't have to be funny," he taught them. "We *are* hilarious — to be a human being is to be funny."

The film was never made. But I'm told videos exist. Steve Kloves, do you have them?

Caught between boss and interloper, Andrew Alexander didn't want his first acts in office to be construed as disruptive, so he maintained a "business as usual" policy at Second City as hands-off as his producership of *SCTV*. With genuine goodwill, he invited Bernie Sahlins to come back and direct (three consecutive) shows and asked Joyce Sloane to run the theater as she always had. But he was scared. "I really felt like an outsider," he reflected, "and I was flying by the seat of my pants. I really didn't know what to do with this." Spending most of his time in Los Angeles, where he went to work, as Sahlins never had, setting up Second City television pilots and developing movies, Alexander protected himself from the backlash (he feared) awaited him back at Wells Street. "For years," he said, "I flew over Chicago"; it was a decision he would come to regret. Alexander said, "I wasn't paying the kind of attention I should have." While Del Close and Charna Halpern were invigorating improvisation with a freshness and fervor it hadn't seen since its inception, Second City, left, ironically, with Sahlins and Sloane once again, fell farther behind the times.

There was, however, one area where his attention gravitated. A non-required step to the touring company or mainstage, Josephine Forsberg's Players Workshop and Children's Theater comprised, for decades, Chicago's only improvisational training facility and its sturdiest link to the Spolin principles that, depending on who you asked, were or were not the foundation of improv comedy. Alexander, glimpsing something of the future in improvisational education, opened Second City's own Conservatory, an on-site school, yearlong, for advanced students. Now, Forsberg's beginners would earn their advanced diplomas at the Conservatory.

"You know what intimacy is?" master teacher Martin de Maat would say to his advanced Conservatory students, "It's into-me-you-see . . . it's allowing someone to know who you are when you have all these defenses to keep them from knowing."

And: "I think many of us go through our life not fully having permission to be who we are and what we're going to become."

And: "I'm way out in theory here; it's the study of what the power is, the power in improvisation and why it changes lives . . . The power is love, if you want to know the truth. It's love and unconditional acceptance."

Love was de Maat's workshop. Love for self, for the other, for the work, a love that settled the ego and freed the intuition. Wholly opposed to the Del Close model of teaching by stick, not carrot, de Maat's sermons had the urgency of a man talking to himself. He believed in what he called "pure potential." Comedy was merely an outgrowth of the transformation. "Humor is simply the lubricant that makes our points of view palatable," he wrote. "It is necessary and honorable but not the entire entertainment." That — for de Maat, as it was for Spolin — was you.

On probation from Marquette University, Chris Farley would squeeze out the rest of his academic burden at the University of Wisconsin, performing, wherever the opportunity arose, stand-up comedy and his own fall-down brand of gregarious bar theater, but it wasn't until the summer of 1986, after he launched himself, one night, into a sprint of audience participation at Madison's Ark Improvisational Theater, that he discovered his destiny was improvisation. Farley stumbled back into the theater a night or two later, and stammered to Dennis Kern, the Ark's director, a dribble of pleas and garbles so unintelligible, Kern took the twenty-two-year-old Farley for brain-damaged.

"Wanna do . . . comedy . . . improv, I wanna — gotta do this . . ."

"Look," Kern said. "We're having a rehearsal tomorrow. Why don't you come by and join us then?"

Kern didn't think he would actually show up to audition, but Farley did. With a case of beer.

Farley's audition was so powerfully, dangerously physical, those present had good reason to question his and their own safety. When Farley fell, and he fell hard, like someone with a grudge against the floor, he didn't throw out his hands to brace himself or twist shoulder-down at the last split second to protect his face from impact. There was no sleight of hand to a Farley fall. He just dove. "The total commitment Farley had," explained Ark improviser Brian Stack, "was amazing. Taking those falls, anyone else would be in the hospital. But Farley wasn't anyone else. I remember thinking, seriously thinking, *Is it just me, or is this the funniest guy who ever lived?*"

Farley's go-to fat shtick was his fail-safe. It could bail him out of any jam, in life or onstage, but where even the best improviser's bag o' tricks gets old with use, Farley infused his physical life with the emotional urgency of a great actor, elevating the lowest-brow maneuver with the highest in personal stakes. If he was on his way to becoming the most powerful slapstick improviser of all time, it was because, like his idol Belushi, Farley conveyed a vulnerability as real as those falls. "Some of the funniest stuff Farley would do would have nothing to do with his size," Stack said. "Like I remember he did this hilarious and heartbreaking character who was a local weatherman who had gotten a letter from a little girl because he had predicted sun and her picnic had been ruined by a rainstorm. You could see how much it hurt him to have messed up her picnic."

Improvising, Farley seemed to say, Hurting me is fine, even good, the way to a laugh and maybe even love; but he couldn't abide hurting others. "I want to be a good Catholic," he confessed late in his life, "but I'm a hedonist, my friend."

He did fly. At the Ark, Farley — who had studied ballet to improve his football — could be seen literally pirouetting, with zero irony, his hundreds of pounds into the shape of an airborne swan. Beast into beauty, the transformation suffused Chris Farley with the poignancy and grace of the greatest clowns. But if you told him so, he would look to the ground and laugh, "Naaahhhh," he would tell you, and mean it, "not me."

As she underwent chemotherapy, Gilda Radner would improvise with herself. She would poll her brain's audience for suggestions, pick one, and assign the Cytoxan a character, like a dancer, no, a line of Russian dancers, arms crossed, in big leather boots, dance-kicking the cancer cells out of her body.

At the end of their first shooting day in Morocco, Elaine May, writer and director of *Ishtar*, assembled her allies to review the day's rushes, which consisted entirely of shots of the film's stars, Dustin Hoffman and Warren Beatty, mounting camels. One shot after the next: camels in the sand. Mounting them. "Five minutes, ten minutes, fifty minutes," Hoffman recalled. "Camels. You knew what you were in for right then and there." He turned to gauge Elaine's reaction. But she was, to his amazement, sitting calmly, chewing gum, scribbling notes on every take.

She wanted choices.

"Elaine, what if—"

"Try it."

More than her previous films, *Ishtar* was full of crafted jokes. Improvising, she knew, was unlikely to improve them, but she encouraged the actors to improvise on their way there.

"Wait, wait," Beatty said to Hoffman before a take. "What are we going to say?"

"No, we're going to improvise."

"I know, but what are we going to talk about?"

Hoffman paused. "Warren, you don't —"

"Come on. Just tell me the first sentence."

This was *Ishtar,* an Elaine May production. It was made, unmade, and made again in the cutting room. Refusing to slow down for exercise or meals, May sat beside editor Stephen Rotter (and a weight bench, brought in just for her) in their postproduction suite at New York's Sound One, trying not to smoke. Chomping gum, guzzling Tic Tacs, pecking at bagels she'd spear with a pen and hold up like lollipops, she interrogated the footage — "an enormous amount of film," Rotter said — well over a million feet of *Ishtar.* She had to be reminded to change clothes. "Elaine had this whole network of people that would check in on her, that wanted to make sure she was taken care of," Rotter added. "It frees her mind to these flights of fancy or whatever you want to call them where she creates this incredible stuff." She started smoking again.

May was, as usual, agonizingly behind schedule and overbudget, the turbulent epicenter of Sound One's *Ishtar* floor (yes, a whole floor), and the subject of an unfunny industry-wide joke created and maintained by the Hollywood press. Everything nasty one could write, they wrote about *Ishtar,* and before seeing a single frame, as if the way the film was made, or even bungled, should have some bearing on how audiences received it. "It was about creation for Elaine," Hoffman said. "She loved process. Those are dirty words when you're shooting." *Ishtar,* the *Heaven's Gate* of Hollywood comedy, they wrote, had already run up quite a bill. Now they waited for catastrophe, or "the Reckoning," as *Ishtar*'s hoped-for downfall was known in executive circles. To say public opinion had turned against Elaine May, her stars Dustin Hoffman and Warren Beatty, and their new buddy movie — Elaine's first film in nearly a decade — was also to say the yuppie obsession with box office, the infiltration of Hollywood by Wall Street, had reached a level of absurdity equal to the national bias against *Ishtar,* though Elaine was only still cutting it, and would be, for nearly a year, through 1986. "The thing that makes Elaine stop is running out of time," Rotter said, "so until you're running out of time, you're always trying something. What can we do with the building blocks we have? She's always writing, whether it's improvising in shooting, or improvising in editing. It's always approached as a 'What if?,' or 'Let's try this.'"

Side by side in Sound One, May and Rotter were looking at the first thing she filmed, a purely improvisational scene of Hoffman and Beatty on location in Morocco, trying to mount a camel. It took her two full days to shoot the scene.

"You know," she confessed to Rotter, "I never meant for this to be in the picture."

With careful attention to language and sound, May mixed her jokes like they were a musical score. So attuned was her ear, May would sweat the syllables to get her dialogue to pitch. "Could you take the *S* from that line," she asked Rotter, "and put it into this one?" But there were important exceptions. *Ishtar*'s memorable opening, in which Hoffman and Beatty ad-lib with preexisting (and perfectly bad) song lyrics, would be the film's funniest scene — "We never shot it the same way twice," Hoffman said — and, with its ridiculously earnest high highs and low lows, its desperate and awkward lunges at inspiration, one of the movies' truest pictures of artistic collaboration.

As ever, May prospected her streams of improv for sparks of life, fearing throughout that her postproduction stay, reextended many times over, would one day run to zero, and the studio would turn up at Sound One and take her gold away. Paranoid? It had happened before. May said, "Every movie I made except for *The Heartbreak Kid,* the studio changed regimes in the middle of the movie."

"This was her sandbox," Hoffman said. "She would never leave if it was up to Elaine."

There were big wooden desks at Sound One, as thick and nicked as old prison furniture. Well into *Ishtar,* sound editor Michael Kirchberger opened a desk drawer and found a strip of film taped to a back corner. It was eight frames of *Mikey and Nicky.*

Stephen Colbert graduated Northwestern in 1986, choosing to forgo drama school in New York, though he had been accepted, and linger instead in

Chicago and search for theater work, or any work, waiting tables, serving scrambled eggs at the Blind Faith Café in Evanston, and nights, making futons for money. Reconsidering his plan one fruitless year later, Colbert reapplied to that drama school in New York, and this time was rejected. He fell hard into despair. "Stephen was very, very depressed," his friend Anne Libera said. "His friends were worried." For hours on end, he would lose himself in his carpentry, hammering away in the basement of their duplex, surfacing for the odd class with Del Close.

"Stephen," Libera said to him, "come work at Second City. I can get you a job at the box office."

Colbert accepted reluctantly. He had already cultivated the snobbish attitude toward Second City that was de rigueur in the early years of ImprovOlympic, but he was in no position to turn down money, especially when working for Second City came with free improv classes. Moving from box office to merch table to bar to waiter, advancing through Second City's training program, Colbert began to enjoy himself despite himself, and over the course of a year revised his prejudice against sketch and improv comedy's old-fashioned way. "Once I was there for a while," he said, "I realized that this sort of was a place for me. I liked the atmosphere of it, I liked the fact that a lot of people who worked there were sort of damaged — I enjoyed that." Damage, he found, was talent, the precursor of personality. "Damaged people are very interesting," he said. "The way they behave to cover up their damage is usually very entertaining."

A short time later, Colbert was hired into a touring company that included, among others, Paul Dinello, Amy Sedaris, and Chris Farley. ("He was actually a great guy to improvise with," Colbert said of Farley. "He wasn't a hog.") But the other Colbert, the young actor, was still convinced his destiny was Hamlet. Throughout his tenure with the touring company, he kept leaving Second City to pursue local opportunities in legit theater. Dinello took Colbert's ambivalence (and preppy wardrobe) for high-mindedness, and along with his girlfriend, Amy Sedaris, relished every opportunity to corrupt Colbert's pretensions in flagrante delicto. Colbert was trying his hardest to squeeze his improvisations, as best he could, into controllable entities. He clung to his formidable intellect and preset ideas of theatrical rights and wrongs, but he was no match for the taunting and unchecked silliness of Dinello and Sedaris. Before long, they broke him down, cracked him open, and set him free. He abandoned ideology entirely. "Those three were inseparable," Libera said. "Like siblings," a family within a family.

Intentionally apolitical, the trio sidestepped references to real places, people, and things to foreground the weird, insular realities of their freak show characters. Colbert said, "We wanted the joke to stay the same five years from now, hopefully." If the Toronto improvisers of the early '70s loved to invent phonies and buffoons, Dinello, Sedaris, and Colbert worshipped at the altar of the grotesque, the damaged, the gleefully offensive. "Paul and Amy allowed [Colbert] to be who he was," Libera said, "allowed him to have all that darkness and be playful at the same time, so he can actually live with the dark parts of himself as well as the playful parts of himself, which characterized the best of his work at Second City."

"And I made a conscious effort then not to do political stuff when I first started out," he said, "because I found so much political humor false — stuff that just told the audience what they thought already about a political situation. I mean, the example is people making Ted Kennedy drinking jokes, which didn't seem to be informative or satirical. They just seemed mean-spirited and just told the audience what they thought already." He was just as gracious by day as a waiter at Scoozi, an Italian restaurant where Colbert, in gold waiter's jacket, worked the lunch shift, learning Spanish and Italian from the other employees. "What was interesting about my day shifts spent working along Stephen Colbert," wrote one of his coworkers, "is that the guy seemed to avoid the trappings of the waiter gabbing about his ship about to come in routine. Instead, Colbert helped the backwaiter/busboys with all sorts of tasks that weren't his responsibility. He loaded giant sized aluminum oval shaped trays placed on bus stands with dirty dishes. He was essentially busing tables which he didn't have to do."

There was that one time when Steve Carell, a Second City mainstage player, needed a last-minute understudy.

"You're on for Carell in six days," the director warned Colbert. "Can you play the baritone horn?"

"What is a baritone horn?"

"Ah, we'll have Scott Adsit do it."

"I'll do it!"

Colbert had never played a brass instrument, and the production wouldn't rent him a practice horn, so he rented his own miniature tuba, and in under a week, with lips puffed up "just like a baboon's ass," he learned the bass line to "Anchors Aweigh."

Whenever Carell had to leave town, Colbert would go on for him, but such opportunities were rare. After two years of intermittent touring, living off a puny income, and wondering if he ever would be elevated to his own position on the mainstage, Colbert began to think seriously, again, of leaving Second City for the dramatic stage. He went out, meanwhile, with Second City's Northwest ensemble, a gang that included Nia Vardalos and Paul Dinello, and toured "Ku Klux Klambake," directed by Mick Napier, one of Colbert's first improv teachers at Second City, who watched Colbert come to recognize his own strengths. "You try so many different scenes in the improv sets," Napier said, "that you learn everything you need to know about yourself. So Stephen Colbert would be able to learn that it works really well when he has this high-status character that's a little bit quirky and a little bit weird. He learns time after time that it hits." And yet comedy was only a stopgap on Colbert's career path.

Some months later, waiting in the wings during "Where's Your God Now, Charlie Brown?" at Second City's adjoining stage, the e.t.c. theater, Colbert and Dave Razowsky watched Jenna Jolovitz take on "Whales," a surefire blackout, which begins as Jolovitz, playing a folksinger, proudly tells the audience that she'd like to do a little song for the whales. Jolovitz then tunes up her guitar, deadly earnest, as the expectation builds, until finally, she clears her throat and barks like a whale. "It's not a great joke," Colbert would say, "but it never fails." But one night it did: Jenna bleated out the whale noises and got back not a single laugh.

Colbert whispered to Razowsky. "What?"

"This always kills."

Then Jenna, onstage: "Oh, I forgot to tell you! It's a song for whales!"

Colbert and Razowsky threw their arms up, Colbert recalled, "and hugged each other in the joy of her agonizing failure! But it wasn't schadenfreude! It was just like, 'Oh, we know what she's going through and it's agonizing and how hilarious, what a perfect fuckup to make,' and her trying to save it and now what can she do? And they're not taking the lights out on her and she's burning in silence out on stage." Howling with laughter in each other's arms, Colbert and Razowsky fell to the floor ("like a deflating teepee," Colbert said), their legs poking onto the stage, failing to kick themselves back up they were laughing so hard. And then Jolovitz started laughing.

This is healthier than straight theater, Colbert thought between gasps. "Because in straight theater, when someone fails, you come backstage, and people are very quietly sort of touching up their makeup, going, 'How's it going out there? It seems pretty quiet.'" In straight theater, there are mistakes. There is terror. But in improvisation, where, as the saying goes, the only mistakes you can make are sex and casting, Colbert understood there can be no real unhappiness, "because if there can be this much joy at a moment of this much agony and failure, there's something very healthy about that." In that moment, covered in Razowsky's tears, Colbert said to himself: "I will do comedy and not drama."

Chris Farley took a job with his dad at the Scotch Oil Company selling asphalt and waited a year for Pat Finn, his best friend from Marquette, to graduate, before making the pilgrimage to Chicago, together, in June of 1987. Farley and Finn thought, half-joking with each other, if they just showed up outside Second City and looked funny, someone would notice them. "Hey, you two!" "Who, us?" "Yeah, you! We need two more people for the show tonight! Why don't you come in and join Second City?" But they knew better. Upon their arrival in Chicago, Farley and Finn stopped by Second City to see how they might get into classes, when Farley spotted a familiar face walking in their direction, toward the theater.

"Hey, wait, look . . ." he loud-whispered to Finn. "Over there! There's Joel Murray, Bill and Brian's brother!"

Finn, a native Chicagoan, knew Joel, a little, from elementary school.

"Go say something!"

"Farls . . . I don't know . . ."

"Come on, do it! C'mon! That's why we're here! You've got to!"

By then, Murray was too close to ignore. Someone had to say something.

"Joel . . ." Finn began. "I'm Pat Finn . . . From St. Joe's?"

Yeah, sure, Murray remembered Finn, and in the course of their catch-up gave him and Farley the line on Second City: you couldn't just *walk in* anymore and get a part in the company, the way you did in the old days. Now you started at the Training Center. Along with hundreds of other hopefuls, you studied five levels of improvisation on your way, maybe, into one of the touring companies, a chance that only sometimes led to a part at the e.t.c. theater or the mainstage. Throughout his explanation, Murray couldn't help but take note of the big guy quietly bursting next to Finn. ("Being with Chris was like walking around with a panda," Finn said. "He was so wide-eyed you couldn't help but be ingratiated to him.")

"What do we do?" Farley asked.

"Take classes here," Murray instructed, "and go study with Charna and Del."

Farley already knew all about Del Close, the master teacher Belushi cited as his biggest influence in comedy. Now, it seemed, he was about to meet him.

As directed, Farley and Finn signed up for Second City's level-one class and Charna Halpern's beginning workshop at ImprovOlympic (iO). Working where they could, they earned only just enough to cover rent, food, and improv instruction (Farley, at one low point, barely covered his Second City class fee with an exchange of forty dollars for his guitar — "a major sacrifice for Chris," Finn said), but they didn't care; they had arrived. "We liked the style of both," Finn said, "the satirical mode of Second City and the Wild West feeling of iO." They shared their Second City classes with doctors, lawyers, and businesspeople curious about improv; but the atmosphere at ImprovOlympic, Finn said, "was more blood-and-guts improv. There was this kind of energy because no one knew where we were going but everyone felt confident in the people that were there. We felt like the pirates of the theater community."

Although Farley was eager to learn, he played, at first, with an idiocy verging on desperation, flashing his ass crack, screaming when just speaking would do, and more than once injuring other players. "I really didn't like him at first," Halpern said; it worsened when he started begging her, nagging her, to prematurely release him from the safety of the workshop environment to improvise for an audience at Orphans, their current venue, a bar on Lincoln Avenue.

"I want to be onstage," Farley told her, sometime into his third week of classes. "I want to be onstage now, I'm going nuts."

"You're not ready."

"Come on!" Farley bellowed, slamming his fists on the wall above her head. "Let me play tonight! I want to play!"

"I'll tell you when you're ready —"

"Come on!"

He badgered Charna until she lost her patience.

"I'm not going to put you onstage. I'm going to put your friend Pat onstage."

Finn, standing by, thought he could see Halpern beginning to warm to Farley. Or had he just worn her down?

"You could get on my stage tonight," she said finally, "and if you screw up, you'll never get on my stage again. And," she added, "take Pat with you."

That night, with Finn as support, Farley pummeled the stage, "and," Halpern said, "he was hilarious." ("Charna was mesmerized," Finn said. "You could see there was this 'wow' in her eyes.")

When he returned to Halpern's beginners workshop, Farley was changed somehow, still a tornado, but now, having proven himself, Charna noticed how well he could listen — to her instruction, the other improvisers, and his own ideas. Instead of reacting, onstage, with his first and neediest thought, or defaulting to "Fatty Fall Down" mode, Farley would take a short moment's consideration — a version of the slow comedy Del taught to his advanced students — to reveal his complete self, a sweet little boy in a big shouting man. This was something Charna had never seen: an improviser who was smarter onstage than he was off-. "I don't know how that could possibly be," Halpern would say. "But onstage he could do a movie review, he could do a joke, he could talk about anything, he could be the physicist. Then offstage you'd go 'Farley, why are you drinking and smoking? It's dangerous.' 'Really?' He'd be like an idiot."

At first, Farley didn't understand what Halpern meant by making truthful choices.

"Chris," she explained, "you have brothers, right?"

"Yeah."

"Pick one of your brothers and do them. Go ahead."

Finn watched as Farley grew a seed of truth into something more. "He learned," Finn said, "that it's better to emulate someone than making someone up out of the blue. That became a big part of it for him."

Late in Farley's beginners training, Charna invited Close to watch him perform. It was immediately obvious to Close what he was seeing.

"Oh," he said to Charna, as though it were fact, "that's the next John Belushi."

And then, at last, Farley arrived in Del's class, and the Guru was indeed the comedy wizard Farley had been hoping for. ("Try to kill the audience,"

Del instructed Farley. "Fucking kill them. I want you to make them laugh so hard that they vomit and choke on their own vomit.") Del said, "[Farley] didn't have to learn how to be honest and intelligent onstage because he didn't know any other way to be. He didn't put on a different persona to walk onstage and improvise. Improvising was just a seamless continuity with his regular life." That was a quality Gilda Radner had better than anyone, Del explained to Farley's class: that and her ability to make everyone else in the scene look good. She may not have been the funniest all the time, he said, but she was the best to play with because she was always herself, or versions of it.

"Chris was an athlete," Finn said, "and he knew the importance of a coach because a coach can see what you can't see. And that's what Del did. Del guided him." Del's challenge to Farley was to swirl his thoughtful and his violent selves — instructions Farley accepted gratefully. Why, for instance, is today different for this character? What does he bring onstage with him? It was a question Farley brought into Second City. Finn said, "When Chris took a suggestion of Waiter and made it that waiter's first day on the job, and he kept forgetting menus, and chastising himself for it, he was being the intelligent improviser Del wanted him to be."

"It truly was a family," said Farley's fellow ImprovOlympic player Jimmy Carrane. "You'd do a show, you drink till two in the morning, you'd end up at Farley's apartment, he'd do something crazy, like you'd be in the hall getting drunk and all of a sudden you'd see Farley drop his pants." And throughout, they were always discussing the work, what they had seen, what they had done, what succeeded, what needed improving. Finn said, "Sharing that camaraderie we became better because the better you know someone, the better you can work with them onstage, the better your chemistry."

The chemistry only improved as the prejudicial line between Improv-Olympians and Second Citizens — put in place by Close's campaign to push improvisation out of Sahlins-style entertainment into an art form — began to fade with ImprovOlympic's growing success. Monday nights, Second City's dark night, Close invited students past and present to informal Open Harolds. It was like a class reunion. "Wow," Farley and Finn said to each other, "this place must be pretty great if [Second City's] Joel Murray and [Dave] Pasquesi are coming here on their night off." Word spread. As Del and Charna continued to look for a permanent home base, the venue for Open Harold Night kept changing, and growing. "Hey," a friend would tell you, or you would pick up secondhand, "Del's at the Red Lion Tavern Monday . . ." It was improvisation's all-star night, when the cognoscenti played for the cognoscenti. Improviser Dave Razowsky said, "We would all get together afterwards and talk about what we saw, like 'That was weird? What happened there? Did that work? Why didn't that work?' We thrived on that interaction. When you thrive on that interaction with like-minded people, it doesn't matter where you are, whether you're Second City, or ImprovOlympic, shortform or longform. You have this new toy called improvisation that somebody suddenly rejiggered into a newer toy and what you thought you could do with it, you could do more."

There was no longer just one way to improvise in Chicago. There were many ways, maybe infinite ways.

And when a directorial vacancy opened at Second City, Joel Murray and David Pasquesi requested that Del Close — mostly sober and the father of the rising new wave of improvisation — return to direct one more show. Their timing was apt: Second City's previous show, its seventieth, *Kuwait Until Dark; or, Bright Lights, Night Baseball,* was yet another serving of soft satire, and Joyce Sloane, always ready to embrace Second City's extended family, conceded the time was right to give Close another try. Close accepted Sloane's offer on the condition that he be allowed to handpick his own cast — trained in his very own style. Sloane agreed, and onto the Second City mainstage went Del's brainchildren, Tim Meadows, Joel Murray, Dave Pasquesi, and — after only a short time in a touring company — Chris Farley.

16

1988–1994

If you approached Harold Ramis at this moment, as he stood atop the Everest of his career, and asked him to reflect on how he got this far, to *Ghostbusters II,* he would not have had to think long — for he was always asking himself the same question — before he answered, chuckling, that he didn't really do much at all except be at the right place at the right time, take some chances, wear glasses, and live at the top of his intelligence. It was his talent, he once said, "to float with it," to improvise. To live easy.

As his college roommate, David Cohn, had before her, Harold's wife, Erica Mann Ramis, deepened his engagement in Buddhism, whose precepts he could summarize in a single word: kindness. Ramis, who had kindness to spare, funneled the surplus into the writing of *Ghostbusters II.* "My idea," he said, "was that negative human energy collects under big cities and has explosive potential on a psychic level. So people would have to be nice to each other." The river of ectoplasmic slime that runs beneath New York City was the suffering the Ghostbusters, like civic therapists or spiritual gurus, had to exterminate. From that premise (which, Ramis conceded, did not lend itself to satire), the writers struggled to find a villain both in keeping with the theme and as surprising as the original's Stay Puft Marshmallow Man. So they enlisted Elaine May for a consultation.

Initially, there was some concern that May, for all her experience doctoring scripts, wasn't the Ghostbusters' ideal consigliere. "What was really great," Reitman said, "was I thought she was going to come in and crap all over what we'd done, but she liked the script; she thought it was really funny and understood how it worked." Rather than ply them with suggestions, May offered specific, often mundane, story questions ("If the guy can do this, why can't he do that?" or "What does the photograph have to do with the painting?") that she and Ghost Corps debated over a coffee table, like a Second City ensemble at intermission. Reitman called it "throwing script around." A week later, Ramis found himself on surer ground. "It made it all clear," he said, "at least in our own minds."

In 1988 Mike Nichols reached another mountaintop. He released two films, *Biloxi Blues* and *Working Girl;* directed *Waiting for Godot,* starring Steve Martin and Robin Williams, at Lincoln Center; and married television journalist Diane Sawyer.

"Do you think I'm passive?" he once asked her.

"No more than a set of wind chimes."

When news of their engagement broke, Sawyer heard one of her relatives was calling everyone she knew, bragging, "Did you hear Diane is marrying Mike Nichols and Elaine May?" (To which Sawyer thought, "I should be so lucky.")

Nichols's incredible success, at work and at home, embarrassed him. "I am, and have been, terrifyingly lucky," he said. "I never thought I was hot shit. I thought I kept getting away with it." His self-reproach, his fugitive's nose for troubles ahead, crept into his relationships with two of his best friends, pals from the University of Chicago days, acting teacher George Morrison, and Paul Sills. Thinking of them, the wind chimes in Nichols tinkled their resentment. He feared they loved him with an asterisk. "I did everything I did with them because of guilt," Nichols said. "And I couldn't make it up, I couldn't get it out. And they hated me more and more. It was a terrible thing we were all trapped into. And I helped with the school because of the obvious guilt and so forth."

The school, the New Actors Workshop, was an intimate, two-year training program founded by Nichols, Sills, and Morrison to blend the contradicting powers of the Method with improvisation, as Nichols and May once did, to build a more flexible actor, facile with depth and spontaneity. "As actor training," said student Diane Paulus, "it was a profound combination to be exposed to both." Along with classes in technique (voice, speech, etc.), workshop students were given four hours of Spolin games a week, taught by Sills; a unique version of the Method by Morrison; and a weekly master class in scene study from Nichols. Viola Spolin's sister, renowned improvisational dancer Beatrice Lees, taught movement. Friday nights were devoted to improvisational shows, and every year culminated in a production of Story Theater.

In 1988 they opened on an upstairs floor of a Greek Orthodox church on the Upper West Side. Carol Sills painted a large blue circle in the center of the floor and designated it the playing area.

"You played the game," Sills would commend his students. "Well played."

Nichols conducted his weekly, four-hour master class like a University of Chicago symposium. There were no "lessons," no skills to master. Rather, every week, three pairs of students would present a scene of their choosing, which Nichols would watch, grinning from front row center, "completely present in the moment," Paulus said. Then he would talk. He would remember. "He would tell stories," Kathy Hendrickson, student, and later vice president, said, "on the way to answering questions pertinent to the scene." Though he posed it to the actors, Nichols's foundational question — "This is like when you . . . what?" — prompted his own answers, asides, epiphanies, anything, really, that came to his mind. "I think those master classes allowed Mike a place where he could just hang out," Hendrickson said. "Sills, in the end, really didn't like me," Nichols reflected. "I think that his headlong rush away from success didn't deprive him of rage and envy. And I realized to my great sadness, after all the years of the school, he out and out hated me because [he and Morrison] couldn't take me being successful. So we were fucked. We were stuck. There was no way I could undo it." Still, Nichols held on. For the next twenty years, every week, schedule permitting and without pay, he would open his master class to first- and second-year students and New Actors alumni, establishing, not by accident, an informal legacy of like-minded rookies and veterans, "sort of like a rep company," Hendrickson said, an extended theatrical family. The one he used to dream of. "Mike's hope," wrote his student Johnny Zito, "was that we would all form a company together outside of school."

Del Close was at Crosscurrents, not drinking at the bar, when he heard the news. Gilda had died.

Ovarian cancer. May 20, 1989.

"Look at this," he said to improviser Rick Thomas, on the stool beside him. "It's on all the wire services."

Thomas took the paper.

"We're bigger than John Lennon," Del added. "We're bigger than Christ."

If his intonation were any less sincere, Close's callousness would have offended Thomas. But Close wasn't angling for a reaction, and he wasn't celebrating in bad taste. "I don't think he was being ironic," Thomas reflected. "I think he was making a point about improvisation as a movement."

The country was catching on.

After shows, when the bars closed and everyone went home, Chris Farley would haul himself up the stairs to the little apartment above the Mexican place on Wells Street, a block from Second City, and dial his old friend Father Matt Foley. "He was really struggling," Foley said, "he was so damn lonely." Farley's phone voice buckled with drugs and booze and the shame of a Catholic morning after; he hated himself for sinning against the talent he considered a gift God gave him to give to the audience. But at the same time, as a disciple of John Belushi's, he knew intoxication was his Faustian comedy juice, a self-sacrifice made in the name of harder laughs. Did that redeem the sinner in Farley? Killing himself for their enjoyment? Foley listened as Farley's addicted brain tried to explain itself, swinging from altar boy to funny fatso, neither forgiving the other, then rationalizing himself out of blame, then confessing. Was he going to hell?

"There was heavy betting," Del Close said, "that he wouldn't make it a week on the mainstage because of drugs and alcohol. But he could always cut the gig."

Farley went to Mass every Sunday. "Then, fourteen hours later," explained Second City's Jill Talley, "I'd be carrying him home from a bar and putting him into bed."

The night Second City's Bob Odenkirk brought Farley home, he watched helplessly as the drunken bull threw heavy furniture across the room — until suddenly, Farley slowed and turned, his face shining with sweat.

"Odie," he said, "do you think Belushi's in heaven?"

Onstage, Farley gravitated toward role-model characters — dads, coaches, older brothers. Their efforts to rehabilitate youngsters invariably ended in touchingly impotent outbursts, which Farley cribbed from his own father, in a voice that began in kind admonishment ("Aw, Billy, what you've got to understand is . . .") before exploding ("I AM GOING TO KILL YOU!") without shifting gears in between.

At first, these characters didn't have a sketch; but they were so popular, director Tom Gianas asked Odenkirk — who had, strangely enough, come to Second City backwards, from the *SNL* writer's room — to write one. "I went home," Odenkirk said, "and I thought the simple thought of what about a guy who uses himself — a motivational speaker who uses himself as an example of what not to be." Odenkirk played directly into the improviser's sweet spot, welding Farley's two masks and creating a catchphrase — "I live in a van down by the river" — that teed up the character for an emotional swan dive. Odenkirk wrote the sketch quickly, perfectly, in one shot, handed it to Farley the next day, and watched as it became one of the funniest in Second City's history.

The night "Motivation" debuted, on July 26, 1990, Farley's mentors, Del Close ("Coach," Farley called him) and Father Matt Foley were in the audience. When Farley's character stormed on, hiking his pants under his gut, he introduced himself as Matt Foley — and the actual Foley welcomed the tribute. And the name stuck.

The sketch was so popular that come 9:15, Second City waitstaff would routinely leave their posts to watch Farley go. "Doing this sketch with Chris Farley at Second City eight times a week was the best thing I ever had in show business," Odenkirk would say. "It was like doing ecstasy for seven minutes or however long it lasted because Chris would keep improvising it and pushing it further."

Casting Chris Farley, *SNL* coproducer Robert Smigel said, may have been the easiest decision Lorne Michaels ever made.

Before Farley left for New York, Close and Halpern took him to dinner. They wanted to teach him to act like a professional ("He was such a slob, a child, an innocent," Halpern recalled), and drum into him, one last time, the gospel of Belushi's bad examples — as Del once explained, "There is, in effect, this whole industry dedicated to turning you into your public image." Farley was too happy fulfilling his destiny to hear them, and for all his happiness, too sad and too afraid to leave his improv families, the Jewish-motherly duet of Joyce Sloane and Charna Halpern, and venture out of Chicago's Old Town onto the world stage of American comedy. On NBC, in New York, the pressure, self-generated or otherwise, to push Fatty farther would be so hard to withstand, broken coffee table after broken coffee table, Saturday night after Saturday night. "Although I love this kind of comedy," Farley said, "sometimes I feel trapped by always having to be the most outrageous guy in the room. In particular, I'm working on trying not to be that guy in my private life. Lorne told me that that's what killed Belushi more than anything else."

Improvisers Matt Besser and Matt Walsh felt there was something new waiting for them, for everyone, on the other side of unspeakable idiocy.

They found a venue in Chicago and started doing sketches.

"I'm Matt."

"And I'm Matt."

"And *I'm* Matt."

"And *I'm* Matt."

It was so stunningly dumb it may have been actually smart.

Stephen Colbert's first night as a professional improviser began with a note from veteran Second City director Jeff Michalski:

"You've got to learn to love the bomb."

It took time for Colbert to understand the deeper implications of the remark, that Michalski wasn't speaking of the thick skin an improviser has to grow over his own, but the rodeo ride Slim Pickens takes, crashing down to earth in *Dr. Strangelove*. "You gotta learn to love when you're failing," Colbert explained. "The embracing of that, the discomfort of failing in front of an audience, leads you to penetrate through the fear that blinds you." To train himself, Colbert began, consciously, to court humiliation. He took the stage in his underwear. In real life, he got into a crowded elevator singing too loudly. He paid for a bus ride in pennies. "I like to do things that are publicly embarrassing," he said, "to feel the embarrassment touch me and sink into me and then be gone."

Colbert's ensemble — indeed his entire generation — had a particular fascination with the excruciatingly uncomfortable. Into the 1990s, as "indie" and alternative sensibilities fought their way free of '80s corporate culture, frolicking in perversely "bad taste" became as much a political gesture as a cultural one. While comedy innovation always turns on violation — Mike Nichols, Elaine May, and others were "sick"; the *Lampoon* descendants rejoiced in blow jobs, acid, and Belushi — Second City's third great generation took theirs as an antidote to political correctness. Evil was good. Good was evil. Marginalized subcultures would now marginalize the mainstream. Improviser Amy Sedaris said, "We laugh at what you cry about."

"I like characters that can't be easily defined," Carell explained. "You don't know whether you should like them or hate them." Carell and Amy Sedaris wrote a scene about a woman (Sedaris) who runs into Chuck, a friendly serial killer (Carell), at a Laundromat. She teases him because he won't tell her exactly how he murders people. "Aw, come on," she pleads. "I'm not going to steal your idea." In "Clowns," Jackie Hoffman plays a deaf clown, and Colbert, Razowsky said, "was literally trying to rape Jackie" (Razowsky, wheeled on, plays a child from the Make-A-Wish Foundation). Scott Allman, Carell, Colbert, and Razowsky played the Beatles. One by one, as suppressed memories reveal themselves, they all remember Ed Sullivan touching them inappropriately. (Well, almost all of them. Ringo: "Mr. Sullivan didn't touch me.") Offstage Dinello proudly referred to himself, Colbert, and Sedaris as misfits. The same could be said for their onstage creations.

Of all the marginalized subcultures, none was more prevalent on the current Second City stage than the nerds. But these were not the lovable frog-prince nerds of the John Hughes era; the '90s nerds were pathetically and irrevocably uncool (which, worn proudly, as a badge of transgression, made them cool). Amy Sedaris loved to ugly herself up with sad wigs and buckteeth; Colbert, a former Dungeons and Dragons devotee, liked to remind Dinello that he had only three characters, the Geek, the Kid, and the Geeky Kid; and Carell would go on to play a virgin his own age. They tried that one in the improv set: Colbert, Dinello, and Scott Allman played the sexually experienced friends uncomfortably surrounding Carell at a guys-night poker table. "We tried it a few times during an improv set," Carell said, "but it never made it into a show. We never figured out how to tell that story. It was basically just a bunch of guys sitting around, regaling each other with these tales of sexual conquest, and there's one guy who clearly can't keep up." Carell's character tries to keep the lid on his nerdy secret, but it gradually becomes clear this guy has never been with a woman:

"You know how breasts are so powdery?" ventures the virgin.

"What do you mean?"

"You know, how they feel like a bunch of grapes?"

"What are you talking about?"

". . . they're like these big bags of sand."

As Carell, master of repressed embarrassment, tries to hedge exposure, laughing too loud, his eyes shining with pain, he evokes the best of Alan Arkin, master of repressed rage. Emotional layering grounded both in the stuff of legit stage acting. Others, like Colbert and Sedaris, favored energy; but for Carell, it was about psychological clarity and control. "I look at improvising as a prolonged game of chess," he said. "There's an opening gambit with your pawn in a complex game I have with one character, and lots of side games with other characters, and another game with myself—and in each game you make all these tiny, tiny moves that get you to the endgame." The Forty-Year-Old Virgin was classic Carell, an absurdity rendered with ferocious sincerity.

You could say improv's ascent from its early days as Chicago's local, cabaret divertissement to America's most influential theatrical phenomenon happened gradually, through the decades, as the form itself improvised to the suggestions of the eras, from Mike and Elaine's brainy shortform to the Committee's peace-and-love communal longforms, all the way through the corporate complacency of early-'80s Second City, the failure of which paved the way for iO's Harold Revolution. Peopled by a generation of young improvisers driven by their exposure to *SNL*, *SCTV*, and other epochal works of their predecessors, the new revolutionaries sought out Del Close en masse. His sermon of risk, discomfort, destruction, and reinvention—of innovation at all costs—because that's what improvisation is, innovation in real time, before your very eyes—had them awake at all hours, drinking up new ideas in their month-to-month semifurnished apartments, talking of, one day, filling a theater with the savviest improvisational audience ever assembled and figuring out, together, what it meant to improvise their own way. They would do for Close's longform what Mike and Elaine did for shortform. They would elevate their nerd's obsession with improv—"we understood the history," iO's Jimmy Carrane said—to the high level of theater art, Del Close's dream.

Treat your audience like artists and poets, Del had told his students, so they might have a chance to become them.

Earlier generations were comprised of accidental improvisers pit-stopping at Second City en route to careers as dramatic actors; these kids, born into Second City America, were Sills throwbacks, improvisers committed to improvisation. "It was a religion," iO's Dave Koechner said. "There was no one that spoke about being famous. There was a passion about being better, and better, and be the best, and be the best, and be the best." Most of their parents had never heard of improv. Those who had confused it with stand-up comedy. "One of the cool things about those days was that groups would come out and see each other," Brian Stack said. "We would support each other the way musicians sometimes influence each other and admire each other. It was a magically fun time in Chicago."

You could say it was happening gradually, but quicker now than ever before. Chicago in the 1990s was the Florence of the improv renaissance. The philosophical advances of ImprovOlympic, which had challenged Second City's forty-year monologue on improvisational theory, turned the future of the art form into a dialogue. Many dialogues. Now that Del and Charna had broken ice on the Harold, in came *Ed,* in 1990, the first longform show to be performed not in a storefront cabaret or black box, but a legitimate theater. "Just placing improv in a different environment, a theater," *Ed*'s Pete Gardner said, "made people take it more seriously." Second City's e.t.c. theater picked up the scent and, in June 1991, offered *We Made a Mesopotamia, Now You Clean It Up,* which made the critic Jack Helbig, who had all but given up on Second City, into a fan again. He wrote, "I'm willing to forgive all of *Mesopotamia*'s minor lapses in light of its two great strengths: the tight, playful ensemble work — not once did anyone in this cast of six talented actors try to steal focus from anyone else — and the performers' and director Barbara Wallace's experiments, however tentative, with the Second City format. Several sketches are performed not on the stage but in the aisles or the light booth or at the back of the theater." In March 1992, the e.t.c. opened *The Heliotrope Players' Production of Thornton Wilder's American Classic, Our Town, as Directed by d'Eric Blakemore; or, Cash Stations of the Cross,* which asked for audience suggestions in the middle of George and Emily's famous love story.

You could also say that it happened suddenly in the summer of 1992, as a handful of *Ed* veterans, mingled with choice iO alumni, "started to workshop," Pat Finn explained, "to see if we could push ourselves in new directions and venture into directions that seemed a little unfamiliar to us." Caught in an artistic limbo — post-ImprovOlympic, but pre-professional — the ensemble rehearsed with a frequency uncommon to improvisation, as much as three hours a night, five nights a week. "We approached it like it's a theater show," said Carrane. "Can you commit to six weeks of rehearsal? Can you commit to us and not the [Second City] touring company, if you get it? We want you to put all your eggs in one basket." Working in Chicago's Live Bait Theater, an actual legit stage, compelled the improvisers to approach scenes with as much "real" emotion as possible, as if they were playing in classical drama, not sketch comedy. Most Harold teams were constantly on the lookout for the next scene, moving the story forward; the Live Bait group was not afraid to slow down, stay with a character, let a situation breathe. "The scene work," Brian Stack said, "was richer than most Harolds. We were giving scenes a lot more time to play out." If they weren't funny, they weren't funny; most important was to play together and go deep. "If you had an interesting character," Carrane said, "you could follow the life of that character. What was that guy like at home? At work? At the gym? In the Harold, you couldn't follow that guy."

A new form emerged: two-person scenes interrupted by tag-outs, whereby an offstage improviser would retire an onstage improviser and introduce himself into the scene, taking the remaining character backward or forward in time. That offstage players were literally offstage, as opposed to onstage, waiting and watching from the traditional upstage line, enhanced the sense of proper theater, as did the deliberate, smooth cohesion of the ensemble — a stellar bunch that included Kevin Dorff, Brian Stack, Rachel Dratch, Dave Koechner, Noah Gregoropoulos, Pete Gardner, Miriam Tolan, Carlos Jacott, Chris Reed, Pat Finn, and Jimmy Carrane — longtime friends and collaborators from all corners of the Chicago improv world, who played the way they felt about one another, with patience, kind curiosity, and love. They called themselves Jazz Freddy.

A class act, a reunification of a slowly diversifying community, a hot ticket, a triumph of improvisation's DIY ideal, Jazz Freddy at the Live Bait Theater was the most influential, organizing improv experience of its generation. Among its fans was Del Close. He could take credit for instilling in Jazz Freddy their paradoxical appreciation of his teachings and their willingness to throw all of it out the window and improvise. "Del really liked the stuff, that we were messing with the form, taking the Harold in a new direction, that we were being patient, and doing serious scene work," Finn said. "That was so gratifying for all of us because we all owed him such a tremendous debt."

"We're in the midst of a real, you know, a real *something*," Close said in 1993. "I generally get everything backwards. Like I don't drive in L.A. and I had a car in New York. I didn't go to Woodstock, I went to Altamont. But I've also been in a lot of the right places at the right time, and I think that this improvisational ferment that's going on in Chicago at the moment is another one of those."

Tina Fey got to Chicago and enrolled in Second City's introductory classes with "people who worked office jobs and would brave the cold just to learn improv and then go out and have a drink after." *How beautiful,* Fey thought; *their curiosity to try this thing, just to see where it took them, how it felt.* She was only slightly more prepared than they were, having earned a theater degree from the University of Virginia, sampled some improv in drama class ("but we weren't really doing it"), and watched some *Whose Line Is It Anyway?*, which, if you weren't in Los Angeles or Chicago — Fey grew up in Upper Darby, Pennsylvania — really was the only way to see improv. Martin de Maat, who "was all about trust and loving your partner," would be her soft landing into Second City's Training Center. A rougher guide, like Del Close, might even have scared her away. "[De Maat] wasn't as much about finding comedy as [he] was about finding this magic that would happen, making something together that could not be made alone, finding that unexpected thing that will be ephemeral now and inexplicable later."

Kevin Reome, her friend at Second City, told her about ImprovOlympic. "Some buddies of mine are going to see this place tonight," he offered. "Wanna come?"

Adam McKay, coming to terms with his limitations as a stand-up, heard about Del Close from his friend Rick Roman.

"There's this old hipster," Roman told him, "teaching this form where you get onstage and you can do whatever you want, like you improvise plays and anything you say happens. Oh, we're on the moon —"

"I'm coming out there. Hold on."

McKay had never heard of Second City. He had never heard of improv comedy. Like most of his generation, he had worn out his VHS copies of Bill Murray movies, but he had never put two and two together — it started there, in Chicago.

Two days later, he dropped out of college (in the middle of his senior year), sold his comic book collection, bought a used Chrysler New Yorker ($800), drove out to Chicago and into an iO show at Papa Milano's restaurant. The place was packed. The Harold team was Blue Velveeta. McKay was knocked out. "I can't believe this exists," he thought, and signed up for classes.

Close was, for this brief period, teaching iO's beginners in Papa Milano's basement. Treacherous even for many advanced improvisers, his candor and intensity were invigorating to McKay. "Your job is to lead the audience, to push them," Del preached. "There is no failure in result; there is only failure in process." McKay came prepared, fortified by his stand-up experience and Close's respect for McKay's intellectual urgency. Charna Halpern said, "Adam's belief is you have to have something to say otherwise don't get onstage." Where few in his circle engaged with topical issues, preferring instead to play with the cultural marginalia of nerdom, McKay, something of a throwback, showed the insurgence of a radical. At the same time, he had no aversion for the absurdly apolitical, like a Committee improviser crossed with a Python, born into Generation X.

In the Victim's Family—a Harold team built by Halpern, with improvisers McKay, Roman, Miles Stroth, Neil Flynn, and, in time, Matt Besser and Ian Roberts—Close found the best possible coconspirators. "They were real smart and real fast, as fast as Jazz Freddy was slow," Halpern recalled. "Del used to describe them as watching six men fall down the stairs and land on their feet." They played with an unprecedented level of risk and emotional freedom, and almost always their Harolds came together—when they did, Close would call it "seeing Harold"—proving, at last, the viability of Del's once-unplayable form, and solidifying the team's position as the most exciting improv ensemble in the city, the country, the world. Their most challenging invention, "Horror," a favorite of Close's (and reviled by Halpern), began with a gruesome or distasteful newspaper headline. One Horror, about a valedictorian killed by her stalker boyfriend an hour after she delivered her commencement speech, had some in the audience crying, pleading for the improv to end. Del reveled in it; you could hear him, under especially grim improvs, cackling in the back, near the bar.

In fact, the Victim's Family, later condensed to the Family, worked so well together, it seemed almost inevitable that they would keep growing. "We wanted to write sketches," McKay explained, "do street stuff, do some assaultive comedy" — the antithesis of the lucrative sitcomy "observational" humor that crested with *Seinfeld*. Oversaturated in media clichés, they recoiled from laugh tracks and tidy setup/punch line jokes, anything that smacked of corporate aesthetics. "Money," McKay would say, "has swamped our culture too much." If it wouldn't sell, if it alienated, or violated, good taste, it called to McKay and his iO compatriots Rick Roman, Matt Walsh, Matt Besser, and Horatio Sanz.

"We just started hanging out," Walsh said, "causing trouble, and putting up shows." They started performing "really insane shit," McKay said, as Cerebral Strip Mine, a group name they hated. They'd play the Roxy, a variety-show venue, celebrating rude, volatile improvs to the tune of: "For a suggestion, we need a reason to eject a homeless person," or "I need a tuber. Please give me a tuber." For "Machine Gun Blackout," they took a suggestion and rushed into conflict to see how fast the scene could degenerate into a screaming argument. Roman, joking, had an idea to improv as an imaginary social-action organization, the Upright Citizens Brigade. McKay loved the name so much he suggested they take it for their own. And so, "Thank you, we've been Cerebral Strip Mine" became "Thank you, we've been the Upright Citizens Brigade."

They had no money. To eat, they would haunt happy hours, order one orange juice apiece, and fill up on bar snacks. "Adam was so poor," Halpern said, "I used to have to send him pizzas." At one time, she put him up in her living room.

The aim of their first show, *Virtual Reality*, was to push the fourth wall to the precipice. Before each show, audience members were assigned a number, and if their number was called, they'd be pulled into the improv. The improvisers could be forceful. But they lived for violation, within reason. If anyone resisted them, Sanz had stationed a friend in the back with a lab coat and stun gun. "If people leave or get out of control," they warned, "they will be dealt with by one of our assistants."

"We were maniacs," McKay said.

"We had no respect for any other comedy enterprise in Chicago," Sanz said. "I'm sure we weren't liked for that."

Once they brought the audience back to McKay's apartment and staged a murder scene.

Once they intentionally incited a riot. ("They put [Sanz] in cuffs and put him in the back of the car and drove off," Besser said, "and it happened so quickly that the audience felt we had put the cops in the show. We were like, 'Nope, that wasn't part of the plan.'")

Once they put up flyers with McKay's headshot: "Attention. On February 28, 1992 Adam McKay age 23 will kill himself during the performance of VIRTUAL REALITY NO JOKE Friday at Midnight." At the designated time, a tremendous audience (which included Stephen Colbert and Del Close) gathered at the foot of a five-story building, and looked up.

"You want this?" McKay yelled down to the mob. "You think this is a joke? Man, this is fucking hell, and you came here for entertainment."

("Jump! Jump!" Del screamed up at him.)

On cue, a CPR dummy, dressed exactly like McKay, flew off the roof. The Grim Reaper hauled the dead dummy away and McKay, stationed on the ground, reappeared "back to life." "There was just this freedom," McKay recalled. "There was just a freedom to try to get away with whatever you felt you could get away with. Del Close encouraged that."

The Upright Citizens Brigade — UCB — won praise from theater critic Helbig, and even a financial investment from Mike Nichols, who wanted to add his name as producer and bring them to New York. But the death of Rick Roman, by car crash, in 1992, halted UCB's ascension.

The Victim's Family became the Family. And they kept going.

The confrontational, form-breaking spirit of UCB directly influenced Del's next comedy experiment. Appropriating the tag-out from Jazz Freddy, the Family, under Del, developed the Movie, a speedy longform structure intensified by screenplay-like stage directions — "We zoom in on the mouse's face"; "We cut to a Ferris wheel spinning in the distance"; "The house bursts into flames" — called out, during a scene, by observing improvisers. They invented the Deconstruction, a cubist longform that, as its name suggests, continually revisited, revised, and expanded upon its initial two-person scene. The Family presented the results in "Three Mad Rituals," an iO triptych consisting of a classic Harold, a Movie, and a Deconstruction, all set into motion by a single suggestion — a line of poetry. And where most Harolds clock in around thirty or forty minutes, "Three Mad Rituals" stretched to an hour and forty-five, taxing its improvisers' imaginations to the brink, leaving them breathless and electrified. "My God," McKay sighed after one show, "my mind feels like a hot machine gun. Somebody better piss on my head."

Tina Fey would go see the Family any chance she got. "They were the ultimate aspirational Harold team, Murderers' Row," she said. "Going to see them do the Movie was, like, our weekend." How articulate they were. How deft they were with story, especially when, Fey knew, "improv was usually the enemy of story." And the Family's media savvy, in its hyper self-consciousness, seemed to predict the near future of storytelling. The Movie, Fey said, was "ahead of its time in the way young people now process everything as a reality show or a movie because [the improvisers were] calling out the devices that manipulate us."

Amy Poehler, a beginning iO improviser, would sneak through standing-room-only crowds and up to her friends in the light booth just to get a chance to lay eyes on them. It was, for Poehler, the beginning of a transformation. The risks she wasn't taking, they took. Their trust and fierce commitment, she wished she had. And they were all very tall. "I want to be like them," Poehler thought.

This time, Harold Ramis was waiting for just the right script. It had been years. He hadn't directed since 1986's *Club Paradise,* a comedy marred by the "Yes, and" ethic that had alchemized *Caddyshack.* Those days, and that spirit, were behind him now. Mellowing on his way to fifty, Ramis's improviser had passed the torch to his storyteller, and the question How do I make this funnier? became How do I make this meaningful? or, in Ramis's words, "so silly and so broad and yet so serious?"

Danny Rubin's original screenplay, *Groundhog Day,* which Ramis's partner Trevor Albert discovered in 1991, offered Ramis, with some rewriting, the beginnings of his long-sought Grail, a truly spiritual comedy. Albert said, "I think we both felt like we had something with great commercial, and more importantly, with great artistic potential and I'd never seen Harold more serious about the writing." Script development had become, suddenly, Ramis's high priority. "Humanizing the film was of course in Harold's wheelhouse," Albert added, "but taking apart the script was a very delicate and difficult endeavor . . . Needless to say, it took endless revisions to get it to a point where we felt satisfied."

Groundhog Day's central premise, about a man forced to relive a single day, over and over, until he gets it right, demanded from Ramis a new level of premeditation. "You could improvise on *Caddyshack,*" said Albert, who had been Ramis's assistant on the film, "but because of the continuity issue [matching days], improvising on *Groundhog Day* was much trickier." But Bill Murray, their star, was an improviser. It was the actor's job, he believed, to make improvements, and any director that refused him that freedom was acting the tyrant. "I can't make Bill do the script," Ramis said. "I can't make him do anything. There's a great sigh of relief when he actually comes to the set." Unpredictability was the price Ramis would have to pay for, well, Murray's unpredictability. Ramis knew as much going into *Groundhog Day*, Ramis and Murray's sixth film together, but this time out, Murray's volatility shocked him. And right away.

Eight weeks before filming began, with the locations secured, the schedules set, and the script one development year stronger, Murray decided he wanted to change the tenor of the comedy. He wanted *Groundhog Day* darker, meaner. "There were big changes in his personal life happening at that time," Ramis said. "His marriage ended and a new one began during that film, and I think he felt kind of isolated from the production. He was never happy. He seemed to be suffering a lot. I think he was convinced it wasn't going to be good and that he wasn't going to be good in it." Murray said, "Harold, you see, felt that it would work best if we centered on the romantic aspect between Andie [MacDowell]'s character and myself. Harold thought that is what could make it successful, the idea that true love can save you from a life of monotony. But I disagreed. I wanted to center on the wild comedy."

When Ramis and Albert heard — not through Bill Murray — that he wanted Danny Rubin in New York to make his changes, they were apoplectic. Albert said, "This was the first we had heard that Bill had any issues with the script and we knew only too well how insanely difficult it had been to disassemble the script and put it back together over the course of a year." What's more, Rubin hadn't worked on *Groundhog Day* in months. The script had advanced considerably since then; unraveling it at this state could be catastrophic.

The stink of sabotage was in the air.

"Gee whiz, you know this is *perfect* for Bill Murray," said the film's legendary production manager, C. O. Erickson, to Ramis.

"I wish *he* thought so."

Murray forced himself into the casting and hiring process normally reserved for the director and producer. His kindess tested, Ramis tried to let him in, but no matter his concessions, Murray was dissatisfied. Finally, it seemed to Ramis there was nothing he could do to sway him. The actor was petulant, unreasonable, enraged. "What I'd want to say to him is just what we tell our children," Ramis said. "'You don't have to throw tantrums to get what you want. Just say what you want.'" But Ramis was a diplomat, not an autocrat. He kept quiet and gently maintained his air of business-as-usual. But those close to him knew he was miserable. Most were; Murray's mean streak, beyond mere hostility, carried intimations of actual violence. "Going to the set every day," Trevor Albert said, "you think there is the possibility you're going to get slugged by the star. It was like working with a wild animal where you have no idea how they're going to behave."

Three weeks into production, Murray, inexplicably, stopped speaking to Erickson. "He will get it in his head that he doesn't like *somebody* on the crew," Erickson recalled, "and that fellow, you know, better stay out of sight somehow, if he wants to continue on. You've got to hide him in the office or send him to the department or something. You *can't* have him on the set. And it has no rhyme or reason."

"If I had been on my first movie," recalled actor Stephen Tobolowsky, "he'd have brought me to tears more than once."

Ramis had introduced them on Tobolowsky's first day of shooting. It was dawn, all were exhausted and freezing; the weather in Woodstock, Illinois, was as it had been and would be for the rest of the shoot, viciously cold. Still, Ramis managed to be personable as he brokered hellos between Murray and Tobolowsky, who was to play the part of exasperating insurance agent Ned Ryerson.

"Bill, this is Steve —"

Murray cut him off. "So," he spoke at Tobolowsky. "What are you going to do? Is it funny?"

Tobolowsky, auditioning, it seemed, all over again, had no choice but to offer Murray a taste of what was to come.

"Okay, okay." Murray held up his hand. "You can stop. That's funny."

Five hundred townspeople, come to see Bill Murray make a movie, had gathered all around them. To Murray, these were the good guys, the "real" people, the proverbial caddies of the world. Now Murray was rich and powerful, but he was determined not to act the part. At least not in front of them.

"Do you know what these people need?" Murray glinted at Tobolowsky. "Danishes!"

Murray raced Tobolowsky into a local bakery and declared, "I need every

Danish in this place," piled Tobolowsky's arms high with boxes of donuts and bear claws, and together they ran back to the set and Murray tossed the pastries into the crowd.

The crew snickered at this lavish show of humanity. They knew another story.

Murray, meanwhile, held Ramis and Albert responsible for the uncomfortable working conditions, the miserable weather actors and crew had to endure while he, the director, got to sit out the freezing cold in his expensive parka. "When we did *Groundhog Day*," Murray said, "I felt like Harold had become sort of like a mogul." Yet by all accounts it was Murray's behavior that fit the description. Albert said, "Bill knew Harold as his fellow improv guy who based on that philosophy was open to anything. It was all about collaboration. The fact that *Groundhog Day* was a script that was more than a template and needed to be respected put them into a different power structure. Now Harold was indeed in charge and Bill needed to serve the script and ultimately Harold."

Their feud continued through the end of filming.

It continued through postproduction.

They stopped speaking. "I don't call him, he doesn't call me," Ramis would say. "But it's not like he's — I have no idea. It'll be one of the great mysteries in my life, and I'm sure that's how he wants it — to be a mystery."

Before they met at iO, Tina Fey and Amy Poehler heard good things about the other. "Oh, she's really good, she's so great," someone told Fey, then Adam McKay's beginning student. ("I was all about you gotta crush the individual ego to create the group mind," McKay said. "I don't think I had Tina do an improv scene the entire time she was with me.") In addition to her classes at the Second City Training Center, Fey was taking a playwriting class at Chicago Dramatists Workshop. A few choice details from those classes made their way to Poehler, in a separate beginner's class at iO: "I remember Tina Fey wrote a play about Catherine the Great fucking a horse and I thought, 'That lady is hot stuff, I wanna know her.'"

For their predecessors, improvisation had been a layover, a gig; for Fey and Poehler, it was a calling. "The first time I went to see a Second City show," Fey said, "I was in awe of everything. I just wanted to touch the same stage that Gilda Radner had walked on. It was sacred ground." The light went on for Poehler at Boston College. Her first week of freshman orientation, she saw BC's improv group My Mother's Fleabag perform; Poehler roomed with one of the players and through her learned about iO. *Yeah, she thought, I can do this.* Poehler would follow her roommate to Chicago after she graduated.

Poehler and Fey came together in Del Close's advanced class; Tina, in overalls and old sweaters, Amy in T-shirts and bleached hair. Their rapport developed in the back of the class as they snickered to one another about Del, who terrified them.

"He's a fucking old man."

"What the *fuck* is he talking about?"

Nichols and May had bonded in much the same way. "[Tina] was very judgmental," noted iO improviser Kevin Reome, "but at the time it was good to be on that side of the fence with her, making fun of all the other 'terrible' people. She was a little catty that way. That's maybe what made her fun."

Close was not an instant friend to young women, had pretty much heard every idea in improv history, and was typically downright grumpy. His new false teeth hurt like hell and he looked to Tina Fey like a monster.

"What do you think that scene's about?" he croaked in her direction, after yet another boring patient-doctor scene, his millionth.

"The conflict," she stammered, "the conflict between —"

Close let her squirm before correcting her. "That scene was about bad improv."

Matt Besser, one of Fey's first iO teachers, advised her, "You have really good characters, but I think you came here with those characters." He was right. She had a tendency, as Harold Ramis did, to write first, improvise second, and yet she didn't suffer from the beginner's need for audience approval — Close would have nailed her for it. "The main thing you learned from Del," she said, "was not to be cute or precious because he would just call you out and eat you alive." Later, she realized that Close's note applied to many women improvisers. They were often slower to risk. "It was a funny sort of pattern in the improv world," she reflected. "The girls were all these well-educated, nice, obedient girls, and improv is some sort of outlet. Then there were a lot of guys who did two years of college or one year of college" — like Adam McKay — "they never finished and they liked to buck authority. So the reasons they're drawn to improv and sketch are the opposite." Not that Fey and Poehler were timid. "They were not the typical women who get steamrolled by men," Charna Halpern saw right away. "[They] were no shrinking violets. They were bold and ballsy and fearless." But as with any beginner, Fey tended toward her perceived strengths, in her case favoring harmless (but raunchy) lower-middle-class mothers and daughters, types that didn't completely free her, as Del endeavored to, into brave new regions of self. "Some people are more fully in it," she confessed.

There was often a remove between Fey and her improvised people, as if she wasn't really, truly inhabiting their bodies and feelings, but regarding them as a writer would her characters. But she was fast and grounded, always grounded, and played without tricks. Her choices — marked by an ideal fusion of the credible and the unforeseen — were staggeringly productive; that she looked, in those days, just like any other girl only heightened her impact. "The thing that interested me about Tina was that she was so non-descript and quiet," said fellow improviser Joe Bill, "but onstage she was so fucking smart and quick."

Del was now in the habit of saying, "Play at the top of your intelligence — or higher." Tina Fey did.

Lost in a scene? Turn to Fey. She easily gave herself to others' ideas, good or bad; she could take what you gave her and improve it. "You enter a scene and decide that your character is in a bar," she said, "but your partner thinks you're performing dental surgery. The combination of those two disparate ideas melds into something that could never have been created on its own." Her taste for crossbreeding ideas was less the actor's "What can I do?" than the writer's "Where can this scene go?" "If it wasn't daunting," Bill added, "if you had any measure of confidence in being able to play a strong character, you'd love to play with her, because she'd never let a scene go bad." If Fey was not exactly in her character's shoes, you could find her up in the lighthouse, watching the horizon.

She was five years old, at home playing in the yard, when someone she had never seen before slashed her cheek and disappeared. It was one of those inexplicable, godless tragedies, like Colbert's, that either takes a person down or inures her against the future. "It's the attack out of nowhere," Fey would explain. "Something comes out of nowhere, it's horrifying." In improvising, it must be said, she could synthesize conceptual attacks like none other.

Meanwhile, Poehler took a class led by the Family's Matt Besser. She fell in love with him and his ambitions for the Upright Citizens Brigade. They needed a girl, he said after McKay left for e.t.c., and Poehler accepted. "Once they got Amy," McKay said, "they went into turbo drive."

It was Charna Halpern who first matched Fey and Poehler, placing them in Inside Vladimir, a six-person team named after a gay porn movie. They were Vladimir's only women. Playing together regularly, their affection turned professional; they found how completely they had to rely on each other. "Once you [improvise] with someone," Fey said, "and you don't fail miserably you love them because anytime someone doesn't bail on you in front of an audience you love them." They grew closer, and rabid for improv, went to see whatever they could. Each show, it seemed, changed their lives. "It was all-encompassing work at the time," Fey said. "When you're in Chicago and you're an improviser, it is everything to you. It is a complete cult, and a church, and everything to you." Together, they haunted Second City, idolizing the senior class of Carell, Colbert, and Sedaris. Poehler stayed up and went out, but improv hours were tougher on Fey. Unendingly tired, she had to leave her apartment every morning before dawn to get to her day job at the front desk of the Evanston YMCA, by 5:30 a.m. "I made, like, $7 an hour," she said, "and it was freezing in Chicago — but I was so happy. I was doing comedy with the best people in the world."

She fell in love with Jeff Richmond, pianist in residence at iO. "She was quite round," Richmond said, "in a lovely, turn-of-the-century kind of round — that beautiful, Rubenesque kind of beauty." But they told no one, she said, "because I didn't want it to affect the dynamic of our team. That's how important improv was to us."

On Paul and Carol Sills's suggestion, David Shepherd went to visit Viola Spolin at her cabin in the Hollywood Hills, still very much her home since the sandbox days of the Young Actors Company. Now eighty-seven, Spolin was no longer driving. She was confined to a wheelchair after suffering a stroke. Speaking was difficult for her.

Viola's husband, Kolmus Greene, greeted Shepherd at the door and led him inside, to a glow in the center of a big room. It was Viola's hair. It was Viola, sitting in her wheelchair, radiating warmth.

Shepherd sat down beside her, and with Kolmus acting as interpreter, was guided into a kind of communication with Viola, who smiled throughout. Still, Shepherd could not be sure she knew who he was.

Then Spolin reached out and took his hands.

It surprised him. "Do you know who I am?"

"Yes."

"I must tell you it was a very moving experience," Shepherd would write to Paul and Carol Sills. "I felt there was real communication going on between Viola and me, in spite of her silence. She really seemed to be relating to me, in some mysterious way, and the vibes were all positive, benign, warm, and glowing."

Viola Spolin died a year later, November 22, 1994.

Paul Dinello and Amy Sedaris left Second City early in 1994, and Colbert's depression returned. Losing his truest friends was too much for one who had already lost too much, and what's more, losing his partners left Colbert unsure about his professional future. Colbert, newly married, wanted a family of his own, but how could he earn a living without his team, Dinello and Sedaris? He said, "I realized, 'I want kids and I don't want to be traveling all over the world to go to this gig and that gig.' And I had a complete nervous breakdown." Anne Libera gave Colbert the name of her therapist. "He would lie down backstage before the show," Libera said, "and try to figure out how he was going to get through it."

Colbert said to himself, "I want to do a scene where I play Maya Angelou."

It was after Bill Clinton's inauguration and Angelou's subsequent launch, after serving as Clinton's inaugural poet, and they were working on a new show, Colbert's first without Dinello and Sedaris. It would include "Doug," a therapist scene featuring Colbert and Razowsky, which Colbert named for his and Libera's doctor, and something, still gestating, about going home. Going home, Colbert knew, always changed him into the southern person he used to be, a version of himself his Chicago friends had never met and wouldn't understand.

In rehearsal, director Tom Gianas suggested Colbert somehow combine his Angelou idea with his concept for a homecoming scene. Colbert asked Carell to improvise it with him.

"I'm going to do this as small as I can," Carell warned him.

Without further discussion, they improvised—live on a Tuesday night —as complete a scene as Second City had ever seen. Lights up:

Carell: This is great.

Colbert: Yeah, I love my hometown.

Carell: It is just beautiful.

Colbert: Yeah. I don't know if this happens to you, but when I come home I act differently, people treat me different — it's a great feeling.

A few lines later, Ruth Rudnick enters with a southern accent. "Shirley! Shirley Wentworth! It's me, Missy!"

Colbert glides toward her. "Missy Kensington! Oh, Lord, how you've grown! Missy!"

He twirls her. Carell looks on, confused.

"Shirley! I have two kids of my own now and I named my girl Shirley and my boy Wentworth."

"Well," Colbert smiles, "I'm twice blessed."

When she exits, Carell finally gets to ask the question we've been waiting for. "What was that all about?"

"We're old friends."

"Shirley Wentworth?"

"Oh, I forgot to tell you. When I'm home, I'm an old black woman. Let's get something to eat. C'mon."

The high point of the scene — which they would call "Maya" — comes as Dave Razowsky steps on stage and humbly greets Shirley, hat in hand. We soon see how much they loved, and still love, each other, though in this southern town there is no future for a white man in love with an old black woman. The tragedy hangs over them:

"May I call on you later?" Razowsky pleads so tenderly.

They stare at one another, obviously yearning. (Carell, watching upstage, is speechless.) Too scared to breathe, Colbert and Razowsky try to fight what we know is coming, but their love knows no color. It is too strong. Slowly, sweetly, their faces draw together, and they kiss. It is not a sloppy comedy kiss, but a beautiful kiss, held well past the point of discomfort and not played for laughs. "When that scene debuted," Razowsky recalled, "we had people in the audience just shouting the worst names at us. I could not believe it and Stephen could not believe it, but that's the guts we had and that's the chutzpah that Stephen had in that moment, in 1994, to go, 'I am going to kiss that man, *that way.*'"

"Acceptance [of suffering] is not defeat," Colbert would say. "Acceptance is just awareness." He loved what J.R.R. Tolkien had written, "What punishments of God are not gifts?" It required gratitude.

It required discomfort — what Jeff Michalski meant when he told Colbert he had to love the bomb — but living through it, that was freedom.

"Boy," Colbert said, "did I have a bomb when I was 10. That was quite an explosion. And I learned to love it. So that's why. Maybe, I don't know. That might be why you don't see me as someone angry and working out my demons onstage. It's that I love the thing that I most wish had not happened."

The high-profile success of Jazz Freddy was a mixed blessing for Del Close, on the one hand drawing attention to his dynastic influence, while on the other, setting off an artistic chain reaction that cribbed iO's monopoly on innovation. Duly wowed by Jazz Freddy, Second City's fervent youngblood producer, Kelly Leonard, hired many of its rising stars, along with some iO veterans, into Second City's touring company. "Del knew what that meant," Pat Finn said. It was now only a matter of time before Close's original, long-form thinking seeped into Second City's mainstage, and from there, perhaps even America's mainstream. He wanted glory. And he deserved it.

As appetite for longform grew, Halpern's phone started ringing with improv questions from all over the world. What was iO, this training ground for *SNL*'s Chris Farley? Who was Del Close? What, or who, was Harold?

The time had come, she reasoned, to answer everything in a book, to write a comedy manual for students. It could do for improv comedy what Spolin's *Improvisation for the Theater* did for pure improvisation.

"I want nothing to do with it," Close snapped.

"Come on," Halpern returned, "you have to write it with me."

"It would be like writing a religion. As soon as you've got it down on paper, it's going to be out of date."

"But the basic tenets about how to care for each other onstage, that's how you start. That isn't going to change."

So Halpern began writing on her own, and enlisted Kim Howard Johnson, formerly of Baron's Barracudas, to help edit and furnish the manuscript with interviews.

"Who's going to buy a book on improvisation?" Close asked Johnson partway into writing. "Maybe some people in Chicago. Maybe."

But after reading the finished draft, Close changed his tune. He contributed here and there and came to endorse the project wholeheartedly. When the book, *Truth in Comedy,* came out in 1994, it brought a new flood of interest to the iO theater. All across the country, improv groups of amateurs and professionals alike took it as their bible, quoting its "rules" (made to be broken) like psalms. Thus did Del's longform begin to supplant shortform as the artistic superlative of improv comedy. "By 1994," Kelly Leonard wrote, "there were enough of these longform improvisers in [Second City's] system and they were itching to do longform work — so we decided we needed to give them an outlet as we didn't want to lose them — so we created 'Lois Kaz' as a new kind of alternative show that we would do on normally dark nights in the e.t.c." Directed by Noah Gregoropoulos and featuring the likes of Scott Adsit, Kevin Dorff, Adam McKay, Nancy Walls, Dave Koechner, and Brian Stack, *Lois Kaz* was Second City's first fully improvised longform show, much like Jazz Freddy in form and structure, but with an added touch of Spolin-style space work (like the time Kevin Dorff played a wave). The show was a huge hit, earning Leonard "the cultural buy-in to do more adventurous casting" and signaling, to Del Close, the bittersweet end of an era. The Harold had grown up and left home.

He dedicated *Truth in Comedy* to Severn Darden, Ted Flicker, and Elaine May.

Mike and Elaine were out to dinner.

She looked up. "You know what bothers me about God?"

"That he hates arrogance so much, but doesn't seem to mind cruelty?"

"Exactly."

Adam McKay never thought he'd find himself at Second City, tourist trap and, of late, bastion of family-friendly comedy, but on a lark, he auditioned (he was broke; they paid), and to his amazement, got in. Like a spy stationed across enemy lines, he would incite a touch of UCB-style havoc wherever his touring company went. There was that time in Dallas when upperclassman Steve Carell paid a visit to his future wife, Nancy Walls, then touring with McKay, when McKay invited Carell to join him onstage for a bit of audience participation. (It had all been rehearsed.) As planned, Carell's "improv" was so embarrassingly inept, McKay lambasted him onstage (Carell cried), and the audience left horrified. ("We weren't invited back," Kelly Leonard said.)

As McKay climbed the old hierarchy from TourCo to e.t.c., he began to miss his antic UCB days of staged suicides and public malfeasance. He was thinking of quitting when Second City director Tom Gianas, bored with the thirty-five-year-old sketch and blackout conventions of the mainstage show, approached McKay in 1995 and began what would be a monthlong conversation, one that would permanently mutate the chromosomes of Second City.

"I'm doing a mainstage show," Gianas told him. "I want to break every rule and I want you to do it."

"For real? Like we can really do whatever we want to do?"

"Yes. I mean it."

It was long overdue. A string of bad press, the incessant innovations of iO graduates, and — the last straw — Second City's horrible best of show, 1994's *Old Wine in New Bottles*, directed by Sheldon Patinkin, practically demanded a total reconfiguration. Easily the coolest improv in Chicago was taking place on Monday nights at iO. *The Armando Diaz Experience*, named (by McKay) for its first guest monologist was, to Tina Fey, "the big thing in improv culture," a loosely structured longform suggested by a day in the life of the guest monologist. Favoring the everyday as reported by anybody, the Armando recalled Sills and Shepherd's intentions for the early Compass. Fey said, "I always thought that was the appeal of it. 'I'm going to have my random friend who is not an improviser just tell about his day.'" But where Sills and Shepherd endeavored to create playable forms not just *about* the people but *for* the people, the Armando was strictly experts-only. "It was so far from Spolin," Fey said. "No one would start a scene by polishing apples or doing the dishes [while waiting for an idea to develop]. If you were in an Armando, you didn't find your way to the scene; you entered with an idea right away in a way [Spolin] would have discouraged." The most satisfying Armandos wanted both kinds of player, UCB and Spolin, to "enter strong [with an idea]," Fey said, "and *then* improvise. There's regular jump rope and then there's double Dutch," Fey added. "That's what this was." She knew she had earned the respect of her predecessors, the most skillful improvisers in Chicago, when she was asked, one night, to be the guest monologist.

Gianas and McKay, meanwhile, started having lunches at Second City.

"If you could open a show any way you wanted, what would you do?"

"Well," McKay said, formulating the first of many UCB-esque answers, "I'd put the cast in gas masks and I'd accuse the audience of crimes against humanity."

"All right. Great. What else would you do?"

Improvise.

Ironically, improv, at America's foremost improvisational theater, had become an endangered species. Most of Second City's after-hours "improvisations" were really unscripted rehearsals; the audience suggestion was often little more than a conduit to sketches in progress. "We wanted to change all that," Kelly Leonard explained, "and do an all-improvised mainstage show."

The idea evolved. "We know we can make them laugh," improviser Scott Adsit reflected. "Can we do anything else on the way to the laugh?" Gianas and McKay would break all rules, and eliminate jokey blackouts, reuse characters from scene to scene, and replay old scenes with variations (like one of Del's Deconstructions) — creating a scripted show that looked like a Harold, but with all the effrontery of the Upright Citizens Brigade. The rumor that Blockbuster video was covertly editing their cassettes for content led to a "What if they asked the audience to throw their Blockbuster cards at the stage and the improvisers ran around with scissors, picking them up and cutting them up?"

They called the show *Piñata Full of Bees*, which is what it was.

Piñata played against a wall of exposed brick, not the friendly old colored doors, the lights stayed low, and instead of the regular piano accompaniment, they played prerecorded tracks, some harsh. "But these packaging differences are nothing compared to the material itself," raved the *Chicago Reader*'s Jack Helbig, "easily the funniest and most intelligent, surprising, and creative stuff Second City has done in a long time . . . The show contains some wonderfully dark, taboo-breaking humor: skits about a killer ferret, a sweet meet in an elevator that ends in murder, and a harrowing journey worthy of R. Crumb through the dark side of the '50s. Second City proved a long time ago that a comedy troupe can survive and even thrive (thanks to tourists, conventioneers, and suburbanites) long after its artistic death. Now they're showing that there's artistic life after death."

Sheldon Patinkin appeared back stage after one performance to chastise the ensemble for their overt polemicism, but Andrew Alexander and Kelly Leonard, good to their word, their commitment to Second City's legacy of self-regulation, stuck by them.

Close's view of the show was more conflicted. As McKay would admit, *Piñata*, something of a written Harold, owed Del a portion of its existence.

"You took my work," Close complained to McKay.

"Yeah, but you taught it to me!"

McKay knew they had something with *Piñata* when, during the show, as flurries of Blockbuster cards rained down around them, he caught himself thinking, *People can be awesome.* In the course of the run, McKay estimated they collected thousands of shredded Blockbuster cards, an inviolable affirmation of their stated intention — despite some of their most alienating gambits — to really connect with the audience.

And then, one night, McKay had a horribly adventurous what-if: What if they told the audience that President Clinton had been assassinated? Scott Adsit, the strongest stage actor in the ensemble, volunteered to break the news.

"Adsit," McKay asked, "do you think you can seriously and sincerely tell the audience the president was shot?"

He did. Here's how it went:

"I'm sorry," Adsit began, crying. "We have to stop the show. The president has been shot. We don't know the details, but there are monitors out in the lobby, and we can watch the coverage. You're welcome to stay."

Before a gasping audience, McKay rolled out a TV monitor and flipped it on, not to coverage of the assassination, but sports bloopers.

Adsit interrupted. "I want to change the channel."

"No, wait. Wait."

Adsit made for the TV, but McKay, laughing at a referee getting kicked in the nuts, fought him back.

"Everyone loves sports bloopers!" McKay cried out.

Adsit, not disagreeing, sat himself next to McKay and watched.

The two of them just sat there, laughing and laughing at the bloopers on TV, until the audience realized the assassination never took place, they had been lied to, and filed out of the theater, weeping and enraged. End of show.

Improviser Rachel Dratch hated the idea from the start.

Jon Glaser thought the prank too wild to truly disrespect.

After they tried it, Jenna Jolovitz said, "It was like we raped a whole audience emotionally."

But the show itself was a milestone. "That breaking of form [in *Piñata*]," Fey said, "in hindsight it seemed so simple, but changing the [scene] transitions from just light changes with piano to extreme light changes with music broke that form open. Those things just weren't allowed at Second City shows. That's all McKay. It's just crazy that it took Second City so long. He had the audacity to question things and we all knew that he was the leader, for sure, and the future there." Scouting for talent, Lorne Michaels recognized it too, and in 1995 hired McKay off *Piñata* to write for *Saturday Night Live.*

Mike and Elaine loved *La Cage aux Folles,* a farce of incomparable elegance and warmth, and for twenty years, since the release of Édouard Molinaro's film, regularly discussed the possibility of one day remaking it. Nichols said, "It would always come up between us, how we loved this plot, but we could never get to it." The moment the rights finally became available, Nichols attached himself to direct, and when producer John Calley asked whom he wanted to write the script, Nichols spoke the name of Calley's old flame, Elaine May. "The next day," Calley said, "she said yes." It would be their first collaboration as film writer and director, marking a kind of Nichols and May reunion, though, technically, since their film careers began, they hadn't ever been apart. "I never once made a movie," Nichols said, "without first showing Elaine the script and listening to her ideas or bringing her in to talk to the writers." She had more than once rescued Nichols; on *Silkwood,* on *Wolf,* turning in new script pages throughout filming, as close to the finish line as the very last day of shooting, all the while refusing screen credit; it was Elaine's custom to keep her name off projects she didn't control. But collaborating with Nichols on *La Cage,* she could be assured they'd work side by side throughout and free of divisive creative differences. "Any small differences between us have burned away," Nichols had explained. "We have only pleasure. What I don't think, she thinks of; what she doesn't think of, I think of." Forty years after their first meeting, their shared sensibility had been preserved, still glistening, an old masterpiece under glass. "The old sketches are still as funny for us," May said. "I still find Mike so funny — what he says, even his expression when he's not speaking. That hasn't changed one whit, tittle or iota." They fortified their ensemble with first-class improvisers; Robin Williams, of course; the boundless Hank Azaria; Gene Hackman, once of the Premise Players; and Nathan Lane.

Where the majority of writers, even in the happiest arrangements, are held from production at an arm's length — close enough to the director to lend assistance, far enough not to interfere — Nichols, from the start, drew in May as his de facto codirector, encouraging her to come to rehearsals and speak openly to actors. He knew, putting her name on a script she wasn't directing, she was making an exception. "Mike was very protective of Elaine's script," Lane said, "and Elaine herself." In the midst of conversation, he would reach out to brush the crumbs off her blouse.

"We're going to rehearse it like a play," Nichols told his company at the outset of *The Birdcage*, "so that by the time we're ready to shoot, you could almost perform this as a play yourselves. Elaine and I are going to be sitting there, so pitch all your ad-libs and try everything you want to try in rehearsal, and we're going to write down what we think is the best of all the ad-libbing, and we're going to put it in the script. But then I want you to *stick to what we have,* because I don't want to have to cut a lot. I want everything to play as continuous actions, so I don't want to stop and try nineteen different alternate lines or different versions."

In rehearsal, Williams asked Nichols if he could play with an existing dance sequence. "Can I just make it into a history of dance?"

Already Nichols was laughing. "Let's try it."

Williams took the stage and, from the suggestions Nichols called out to him — Fosse, Martha Graham, Michael Kidd — they produced a manic medley of dance steps . . .

"Stop!" Nichols pleaded, out of breath from laughter. "I don't want to see this again until we're doing it!"

They still needed something, a line maybe, to cap the improvisation, a point to build to.

"How does it end?" Nichols asked aloud. "How do we get out of it?"

A half second later, Lane delivered Williams the perfect topper — "But you keep it all inside" — and Elaine slipped it into the script.

The idea was to get all the improvisations out up front, but that wouldn't be easy: there was no bottom to Robin Williams. "[Robin] was always joking around and being really silly and improvising, not just within the script, but at anything that came along in life," Azaria said. "If he asked you what you did that weekend and you said I went bowling, he would do a ten-minute routine on bowling."

Between setups, there was a lot of downtime, waiting, mostly, for the director of photography, Emmanuel Lubezki, aka Chivo, to light a scene. On *The Birdcage*, he favored the glow of lantern-like orbs that put Robin Williams in an Asian frame of mind. "Mr. Chivo!" — this in his most offensive accent — "We need more balls! More balls, Mr. Chivo! More balls!" These breaks in filming were no breaks for Williams. One incredible riff, performed just for Nathan Lane, Williams based on a toy store owner he had met in Paris. "Robin became this pretentious and arrogant French toy store owner," Lane recalled, "annoyed by Robin looking for presents for his children." At one point he handed Robin what he called an existential toy — an empty box. "Robin kept going and going, and I laughed harder and harder until I was crying and begging him to stop. It made him very happy." "One day," Nichols remembered, "Robin improvised a gay football player for about three hours. The whole approach was that he couldn't grasp what he was. He would say, 'You suck a cock or two, but come on! What's the big deal?' We were all in very serious danger of death by laughing. It was so painful. He wouldn't stop it. You thought you might die. It was infinitely beautiful. It was simply unbelievable. It was a masterpiece."

"How much of that do you remember?" Mike asked Robin the next day. "How much of that could you do again?"

"None of it."

Particularly moving to Nichols were Williams's deferrals to Nathan Lane. To watch the great soloist so graciously cede the spotlight filled him with a respect beyond even the admiration he had for Williams's talent. "Nathan and Robin were as brilliant as a practiced comedy team," Nichols said, "but in the *way* they worked they were like brothers." They sustained that circle of respect throughout the production. "That was one of the one or two happiest times of my life," Nichols said, "making *The Birdcage*." Making a family. Which is what *The Birdcage* was about.

The film was an instant smash, and quickly identified as a landmark American film. Where its antecedents took the "problem" of gayness for their dramatic conflict, *The Birdcage* takes its sexuality for granted, presenting instead of anguish and isolation an array of shame-free characters more interested in their everyday lives and families than the whys and wherefores of who they love. The great joke here isn't that the characters are out of the closet; it's that for the sake of family unity, they're pretending, and failing, to get back in it. For a "gay" comedy of its time, that alone was a revolution.

Tina Fey brought her notebook to a performance at the e.t.c. theater and wrote to herself, "Is there a difference between guy funny and girl funny?" After absorbing Jenna Jolovitz's work in the show, she had her answer "No."

Fey dove deeper into improvisation. It was the lure of the mainstage and the ontological implications of Marty de Maat's teachings, the coming awareness that the rules of improvisation, turned to life, opened your eyes wider to every mote of experience. "I was so sure that I was doing exactly what I'd been put on this earth to do," she said, "and I would have done anything to make it onto that [Second City] stage. Not because of *SNL,* but because I wanted to devote my life to improv." If this right here was it for her, that would be fine. Fey could see a perfect life for herself in Chicago just teaching improvisation, growing into the next de Maat or Close, the Mrs. Chips of Second City. "For many of us," she said, "improv was close to religion."

Moving up, Fey secured an understudy position with a touring company at seventy-five dollars per show (plus twenty-five dollars per diem if it was an all-day gig—they would often drive around all day to qualify), Fey's promotion to the tiny circle of paid improvisers allowed her, at last, to leave her awful YMCA job and brought her closer to BlueCo improvisers Rachel Hamilton, Ali Farahnakian (also of UCB) and her former iO teammate Amy Poehler. With every stop on the tour, from Waco to Kansas, high schools and business conventions, Tina and Amy fell a little less in love with the classic Second City scenes on their program. "If you found anything [in the Second City archive] that was with Alan Arkin and Barbara Harris, you found a treasure," she said, but mostly old scenes were out of date and no fun for a woman improviser raring to break out of the bland rotation of Girlfriend, Mother, Wife parts. Poehler had her own outlet with the UCB; Fey found her own in the role of writer, building new scenes for the touring company. "With Ali's encouragement," she said, "we would take things out, then we would put a couple of our own blackouts in. We got in trouble because by the time we got to Texas the stage report went back and showed we were doing 80 percent original material." It became their custom, every night, to replace a classic scene with a new one. She began, for the first time, to write sketch in earnest.

Eight months later, Jon Glaser left *Piñata Full of Bees,* and Kelly Leonard put Fey into the cast. The addition was a milestone for Second City, the first time a mainstage company, traditionally (and unofficially) comprised of four men and two women, featured a gender-equal cast, three men, and three women.

Fey almost couldn't believe it. Second City's brick walls, mantled floor to ceiling in the black and white faces of improvisation's first fifty years, triggered in Fey her most honorable burden, to live up to them. She felt so good. The life she had dreamed of was turning out to be the life she was living, and more so every day. "When the show was open in the summer," she said, "[boyfriend Jeff Richmond] and I would ride our bikes to the lake in the morning, go for a swim, get back on our bikes, go rehearse at Second City. The greatest life." Walking into the theater, passing under those famous faces every evening, she thought, overcome, "I work here."

"It was the best job I ever had," she said. "The most fun job I ever had."

As a professional, Fey was reverently committed to the Second City process; she was a hard worker and a fair teammate, prepared to concede to a better idea, but never willing to lie down for the wrong one. "She was never like crazy confrontational," said Scott Adsit, "she was just right." And she could make her case clearly, unemotionally, like a comedy lawyer.

Yet for all her resourcefulness, she worried about how she would come off as a performer. She rarely booked the commercials everyone else seemed to, and at Second City curtain calls, she never got anywhere near the best applause and would come home to Richmond, crying. "Oh, I'm not making it . . ."

Adsit, she thought, had it all: real acting chops, tremendous physicality, a true Spolinite's feel for space work, and the patience to wait out a meandering, laughless improvisation until it really found itself. Fey would catch herself falling back on bad habits: finger waving, crossing her arms when angry, and, when playing the Mother, resorting to the old hands on hips.

At first, Fey was reluctant to share her ideas with director Mick Napier. In private conferences, he would implore her to bring her ideas to the group, and in time, she could.

Years earlier, in 1989, the improviser Mick Napier was teaching at Second City when he saw two images — a prison and a circus clown fighting a drag queen — collide nonsensically in his imagination. Without knowing why, he wrote down the phrase "coed prison sluts," and read it aloud to his students.

"Do you think," he asked them, "this is a funny title for a musical?"

Yes. They said it was.

It was ideas like these that made Mick Napier a strange but welcome presence at Second City, teaching at the Training Center and directing Colbert, Sedaris, and Dinello at Second City's Northwest resident company. But for all that he loved about Second City in practice and tradition, he dreamed in improvisational forms bigger than sketch, and far more theatrical. A lifelong devotee of nonsense, and its evil twins, madness and defiance, Napier "developed," he said, "an anti-comedy sensibility very early." There was a little Severn Darden in him; in high school, Napier kept a journal of Dadaesque non sequiturs. He loved to walk down the street speaking sentences that made no sense, "just to jumble my brain up." To Napier, straight comedy was a salesman faking a grin; he laughed at the dark, the rude, the stupid, the unfunny. His favorite play, Artaud's *Jet of Blood,* opens with a nun and a whore eating each other's eyes out. Napier was as much the son of the director John Waters as early *Saturday Night Live,* and as tired of the so-called rules of real life as he was of the rules of rehearsed plays. He came to improvisation in college, a constricted theater major looking for freedom, and without a clue of how to do this thing he had only read about. But that was the beauty part. To improvise, you don't have to know anything. In fact, the less you knew, the freer you were, right?

So, conceptually naked, Napier started his own improv group and made up his own rules as he went along, all the way to Chicago, where, in 1987, he met Del Close at iO, and for the first time encountered the Kitchen Rules, all but unchallenged since they were first implemented by the St. Louis Compass thirty years earlier. The irony of this was not lost on Napier: Del Close, the original madman, followed the rules? Rules for improvisation? "Yes, and"? Support your partner? (What about support yourself?) "I noticed," Napier said, "that when people made a strong choice for *themselves,* that supported the scene, and *that* supported their partner." When your plane goes down — and in improvisation it always does — you put your own oxygen mask on first.

Hence Mick Napier's first show as director, *Splatter Theater,* a bloody comedy he opened upstairs at Crosscurrents, a floor above iO's big stage, in October 1987.

Then, in April of 1989, came *Coed Prison Sluts,* created from improvisation, which would become the longest-running musical in the history of Chicago.

"I had no intention to start a theater or have a theater company," Napier reflected, "but after *Coed Prison Sluts* that's what happened. We got kind of tight as a company and a group of friends and we started a conversation about getting a building. That's when we decided to become a company." They called themselves the Annoyance Theatre, and became, in Napier's words, a magnet for fun freaks. "I think," he said, "in reaction to theaters like Second City and iO, that we kind of wanted to be an annoyance in a way."

Second City, basically, was a sketch theater; iO, with a few excursions, was a Harold theater; the Annoyance, running, at its height, as many as thirteen different shows a week — Del Close could be heard in the lobby, bellowing, "Where are you, Mick Napier, you prolific motherfucker?!" — really was whatever you wanted it to be, and also precisely what you didn't. Such was the nature of freedom. And an Annoyance improviser, enriched by Napier's homegrown school of break-the-rules Rules, was built especially to violate, and as only an improviser can. "Because this," Napier would say, "really is the freest art form in the world."

At the back of one of Napier's theaters, he hung a sign, in glorious cursive: *THEATER SUCKS.*

The Annoyance attitude really was an attitude. You could feel it onstage (*Manson: The Musical*) and at their after-parties, where Annoyance players, like most beginning revolutionaries, made no effort to hide their superiority, turning up their noses at improvisers who didn't share their sense of anarchy. It was a different version of the same territorialism you saw in iO or Second City improvisers; *we* are the real thing, you're not. "The Annoyance," Napier conceded, "was mean and contentious when it started out. I took full accountability for that." He woke up. He saw, clearly, absurd contention across the entire improv community, and realized, true to the spirit of improvisation, the more iO, Second City, and the Annoyance played together, the stronger the whole of Chicago improv — and every improviser in it — would become. So he called a meeting. "It was very important to me to get Charna and Andrew and Kelly [Leonard] and myself together," he said, "and we did and we agreed to stop being contentious with each other and promote healthier, more collaborative relationships between the theaters." In the wake of their détente, it was not uncommon to see the same improviser, in the space of a single evening, appear onstage, say, in Second City's first show, iO's second, and a midnight show at the Annoyance.

As the theaters, and their improvisers, cross-pollinated, Kelly Leonard invited Napier back to Second City to direct his first show on the mainstage; it would be Second City's follow-up to Adam McKay's magnum opus. "Don't worry, Mick," they kept telling him. "It doesn't have to be as good as *Piñata.*"

Napier, casting his show, took Second City improviser Scott Allman out for a drink. "Who's good?"

"This girl Tina. She's great. She's . . ." and on he went.

Napier, who had never seen Tina Fey before, caught up with her in a five-minute clip and was sold. He got Alexander and Leonard's approval, and Fey went into Napier's company — with Rachel Dratch and Jenna Jolovitz, they made it Second City's first gender-equal opening night cast.

Napier was Fey's only director on the Second City mainstage, "a more palatable Del," she called him, intent on breaking improvisers out of their emotional comfort zones. "Second City," Fey said, "was a place where you could easily settle into a role unlike you were in real life, like, 'Honey, we've got to get to the mall!' [Napier] could loosen you out of that. He would do a thing called Taboo Day where you had to come in and present the most upsetting, inappropriate idea for a sketch you can think of." For one scene, he asked Rachel Dratch to fly into an angry rage ("She wasn't comment-ing on it," Fey said. "She was actually doing it") and, for another, allowed Jenna Jolovitz the time to disintegrate, slowly, silently; it was as raw and intricate a nervous breakdown as anyone had ever seen in a sketch show. But Napier and his company weren't out to provoke; their version of Sec-ond City showed Napier's dedication to three-dimensional characters. "I like a kind of disconcerted feeling for a scene," Napier said. A chance to ex-plore personality, to push psychologies beyond the limitations of sketch, the longform, for Napier, was a telescope he expanded, scene by scene, to peer deeper into uncomfortable truths. "We knew that he was bringing the long-form sensibility," Fey said, "continuing what McKay had started, to what was feeling like a too-venerable institution."

Offstage, in rehearsal, he worked much the same way, bringing improvis-ers out of themselves the way he would characters out of the improvisers. Having never written a Second City show, Fey, for all her experience, was not quick to share her ideas. Only after Mick called lunch, and everyone left, would she approach him.

"I *think* I have a good idea for a scene."

"Bring it up in rehearsal."

"Oh. Okay."

She did.

Fey would say, "It's easy to lose [your courage] when you're trying to write a show and trying to be topical, to dive in with abandon. But Mick encouraged that." At the Golden Apple Diner, where her company, a favorite of the waitstaff, would gather after hours for cheap eats and prolonged deliberations on the nature of comedy, she gained a leader's confidence. "She expects as much professionalism from others that she expects from herself," Adsit said, "which is a very tall order because she is one of the hardest-working people in show business. And so she knows enough to also give people the benefit of the doubt, or give them a little wiggle room, or cut them some slack. But in her perfect world everyone would be working as hard as she is." Mad courage showed in *Citizen Gates*, the show they evolved, Second City's eighty-first, and one of its best ever. It was every bit as good as *Piñata*, polished where McKay's was raw, uncomfortably human where it was political. Napier's vision of sketch comedy pulsed with the visual rhythms of a musical. Painting his stage with coordinated colors, moody (not comic) lighting effects, elegant transitions, and dance-like choreography, he leavened *Citizen Gates* into a fluid dramatic creation, and a new benchmark for sketch comedy. It was as if Second City, the theater, was dreaming. "I want a Second City show to be very very funny," Napier said, "and very very beautiful."

17

1995–2001

"Hello?"

"Eugene?"

"Yes . . ."

"This is Christopher Guest."

The call was unexpected. Strange even. Eugene Levy had met Guest a couple of times, but they had no professional or even personal relationship. Now, out of the blue, Guest was calling Levy — at home.

"I'm putting together a movie," Guest explained. "I'm wondering if you want to work on it with me."

Levy didn't know this was how Guest worked, by intuition. His hunch about Levy — that they shared a sensibility — Guest based exclusively on Levy's work on *SCTV*, one sketch in particular, "Perry Como: Still Alive," in which Levy, as the titular king of relaxation, crooned the disco anthem "I Love the Nightlife" from bed, tucked cozily under a blanket, half-asleep, as a lively gaggle of dancers and backup singers rocked the stage around him. The sketch was unforgettable based on the premise alone — Guest was calling Levy some fifteen years after it first aired — but it was Levy's performance, far more sophisticated than a mere impersonation, that made it a classic. The effect was the product of "real" acting, seasoned with minutely observed behavioral touches, like a single finger, which Levy, seemingly not asking for laughs, tapped laconically, in time to the beat. Guest's sensibility dwelled in this kind of naturalism, on the scarcely satirical hairline separating editorial and reportage. *SCTV*, he thought, was the funniest show of all time.

Levy, meanwhile, was just as big a fan of Guest's *Radio Hour* pieces, and like everyone else in comedy, worshipped *Spinal Tap*.

But all this admiration went unspoken. Guest, never one for effusion, kept conversation tidy, and Levy was too flummoxed to ask Guest what Levy was really thinking, which was, *How many people had to turn you down before you decided to call me? A hundred?*

Guest's movie idea didn't have a story yet, but he told Levy he was interested in setting it around a community theater. There was an *SCTV* flavor in that: show business small-timers, a provincial setting. "I suppose I've always been interested in behavior that's obsessive and unaware of the outside world," Guest said. "Everyone has their own version of that in their lives." And like *Tap*, Guest's film would be improvised. But Guest didn't want it to feel improv-y. The manic quality of bad improv didn't carry the awkward rhythms of real life, a pause held too long, the sadly absurd things people think but don't say. "Uncomfortable to the point of poetry," Guest would explain. "That's what I was going for."

"You want to come to my cabin in Idaho for a few days?" he asked Levy. "We can talk more."

Levy hesitated. Did he want to hang out with this guy? "Chris was very reserved," Levy would say. "You never got a gauge of what he thinks of you. You got some strange reactions if you said good morning. He's made people cry and he won't know or understand why."

Why not give it a shot? If it wasn't working out, Levy could always leave.

Guest picked him up at the airport. Almost as soon as they drove away, they had each other laughing, "and that's the way it stayed," Levy said.

Back at the cabin, Guest manned the legal pad, taking note of the good ideas they laughed out of one another. Guest hadn't fully cast the movie — about an ensemble of untalented amateurs putting on a musical — but knowing he and Eugene would have parts, and hoping to get Catherine O'Hara and Fred Willard, they had enough familiar faces and personalities to focus their conversation.

"What if the guy" — Levy's character, Dr. Pearl — "takes off his glasses and his eyes are crossed?"

Guest laughed. "Good."

Good? Levy was joking. "You really want me to do that? I'm not going to do that."

"Why?"

"I'm not going to cross my eyes on the big screen."

"Why? It's funny."

"A lot of things are funny."

"Is it because you don't *want* to get a laugh?"

"I do, but I just think it's like, you know, cheap . . ."

They kept a fairly regular working schedule, a few hours in the morning, a long break — fly-fishing for Guest; some golf for Levy — a few more hours in the afternoon, then dinner. In two weeks' time, they had their characters.

Leaving Idaho for L.A., Guest and Levy arranged their brainstorm into an outline, a few descriptive paragraphs for each scene, and scouted the Second City and the Groundlings present and past for their cast. "We weren't looking for the Robin Williams type," Levy said. "You had to know when to speak and when not to speak." The camera, Guest knew, craved the pace of real life, the looks that did for empty silence what Robin Williams could do with language. Guest said, "There's always been something more interesting to me about normal conversation, as opposed to something that's supposed to be enlightened or clever." He wanted listeners.

"We're doing this movie," Guest told Fred Willard. They went back thirty years, to Arkin's revival of Feiffer's *Little Murders*. "I think it's going to be called *Waiting for Guffman*."

"That's a strange title!"

"Other than Eugene, you're the first person I've asked to be in it. There's no script."

"I'm in!"

"I ran the idea by Marty Short," Guest continued, "and he loved it. Marty said, 'Let's do,' but I had to tell Marty, 'No. We want people who aren't well known.'"

That Parker Posey was not an improviser didn't trouble Guest. All instinct, he cast her after one meeting. Most of the others — Brian Doyle-Murray, Paul Dooley, Linda Kash, Dawn Lake, Deborah Theaker — came from Second City. Michael Hitchcock was Groundlings. Lewis Arquette came via the Committee and Sills and Company.

Once assembled, the improvisers were left alone to work out the specifics of their characters. Wardrobe, personality, mannerisms, props — everything except the story they were provided in the outline — were not preap-proved by Guest; he would see their choices at the same time as the rest of the company, on set. Catherine O'Hara's preparation consisted largely of interior work, questions she asked herself, notes she made about her character's relationships and goals, all of which, she knew, could change in an instant; Fred Willard, playing the part of her husband, used a real-life model to frame his character; Levy developed Dr. Pearl from the outside in, the way he worked at Second City, beginning with those big glasses. "You kind of need one thing," he said, "and the rest falls into place. For me, it usu-ally happens pretty quickly. But that was the toughest part, locking in your character, because that's the guy you're going to be improvising with for four or five weeks." This degree of freedom was most unusual, even for an improvised film. On *Caddyshack,* on *Mikey and Nicky,* dialogue had been written, characters agreed upon; on *Spinal Tap,* Reiner's ensemble was al-ready familiar with each other's characters; but on *Waiting for Guffman,* the director actually knew less about his movie than his improvisers.

Levy's first day of filming:

"I think we're pretty much ready to go," Guest said to his cowriter. They were in Lockhart, Texas.

"Where do you want to go over it?" Levy asked.

"What do you mean?"

"I mean the scene. You want to talk it through?"

"We're ready to go."

"What do you mean?"

"We're ready to shoot."

"So we're not going to even — oh, okay. Interesting."

There would be no rehearsal on *Waiting for Guffman.* Save for the film's musical numbers, what happened in front of the camera would be happen-ing for everyone for the first time. Even the dialogue of the film's "inter-view" scenes, in which the characters, as if in a documentary, appear to be speaking to an unseen filmmaker, were a surprise to Guest. There were no questions from off-camera; he called action and they just started talking, or rather, thinking. "I want a lot of this to be unspoken," he told the cast. "I don't want you to articulate everything." Otherwise, Guest kept his influ-ence to a minimum, directing gently. From take to take — rarely more than three of a given scene — he might ask an improviser to develop a certain strain he liked in a previous take ("Let's do that part again where you talk about the foot"), but it was more common for him to stay quiet. He laughed infrequently, and smiled less. In fact, it was not always clear if his opacity was a real personality trait or a directing technique intended to further reduce his influence. At times, his remove could be disconcerting to an improviser hungry to know how he was coming off. Then again, perhaps that was their own anxiety projected onto Guest's blank stares. "You're directed by the outline," O'Hara said, "and everyone else around you."

In O'Hara's case, she got certain cues from Fred Willard, her screen husband. Before takes, he was given to enthusiastically telling O'Hara how to react on camera.

"I'm going to go on about this," he told her on one occasion, "and you're going to get *really* mad —"

"Do I have to get mad? Can I just react the way it feels right to react?"

"Sure! Yes, of course!"

"Yes, anding" the whole of Fred Willard, O'Hara decided his penchant for directing them off-camera would form the basis of their characters' marriage, his strength and her suppression. "I am grateful for Fred being so strong," she reflected, "because I love playing argumentative women and I probably would have gone that way." ("He taught me to ignore my instincts," she improvised in one "interview" scene.) Simply, he would be the talker; she would be the listener. What her character could never say aloud, O'Hara conveyed through those awkward, silent moments Guest sought out at every turn.

Fittingly, O'Hara imagined her character's lifetime of suppression would one day erupt, probably inappropriately. The opportunity would come in a late-addition scene at a Chinese restaurant. It started as Willard's idea. "Fred thought it would be a good idea if we went on a double date [with Dr. and Mrs. Pearl]," she said, "and Chris agreed, so I thought, okay, on this date, if I'm drunk, I can be someone who lets the truth come out." In the scene, O'Hara achieved the sort of poetic discomfort that would make her Christopher Guest's ideal conduit and one of the most fluid improvisers of her generation. Others may be crazier; none were as elegantly at ease. O'Hara fit anywhere she landed because she always created to meet the needs of the scene, and when she created, she did so in full, with characters whose most vulnerable secrets reached all the way to the present moment. It was never sketch-comedy acting for O'Hara. "To me," she said, "the most rewarding improvising is having agreed on an idea beforehand, where the scene might go, who your character is, or what might be possibly funny about your character, and at the same time be completely open to the other people because you're not alone."

After twenty-six days of improvising, Guest returned to L.A. to watch his footage. The daunting task of reducing fifty-eight hours of raw material to a ninety-minute feature would have stymied a less disciplined editor, but Guest, unlike Elaine May on *Mikey and Nicky*, was not out to explore his bounty; his task, he knew, was to cut abstemiously, to the original outline. Certain lessons he had learned from *Spinal Tap*. Shooting *Guffman* in a documentary style allowed Guest to cut the movie like a documentary; it was an enormous advantage he had over the likes of a Harold Ramis or Ivan Reitman, who had to keep their Hollywood product looking smooth, free of jump cuts, jerky camera movements, and haphazard compositions. Working in "documentary," by contrast, allowed Guest to preserve choice footage that would have been unusable to others, and legitimize the slipshod style of the final cut. It was, he understood, the ideal venue for an improvised feature film.

Cutting took a year and a half.

When Guest finally called in Eugene Levy to look at his rough cut, virtually all of Guest's greatest scenes, as the wildly closeted Corky St. Clair, were missing.

"What happened?" Levy asked. "Where did all your stuff go?"

"I don't know if it stands up."

This was preposterous. Guest's improvisations were easily the funniest in the movie.

"Chris, can I just tell you how far off the mark you are?"

"There's a lot of me already in it."

"Can you do me a favor? Give me a couple of days with this, okay?"

Guest excused himself from the cutting room, and with the editor at his side, Levy went back through the footage, found all of Guest's best stuff, mainly from *Guffman*'s rehearsal scenes — "scenes," Levy said, "that would pay off when you saw them later in the show" — and put them back in the movie.

Released in 1996, *Waiting for Guffman* was immediately recognized, in comedy circles, as a benchmark film, if not one of the funniest movies ever made, then the most impactful comedy of the 1990s. If the equally beloved *Spinal Tap* didn't inform, as *Guffman* would, the future of film and television comedy, it was because *Tap*'s use of the improvised "mockumentary" — a term Guest despises — came before its time. In the 1980s, before the entire culture became camera-conscious, the formal epiphanies of *Spinal Tap* or *The Larry Sanders Show* or Albert Brooks's ingenious *Real Life* were celebrated, mainly, as inside jokes. Unpracticed in metafictional storytelling, many of *Spinal Tap*'s first audiences had been confused out of their laughter, but by the time *Guffman* hit, "the Real World" and the unscripted ordeals of O. J. Simpson (not to mention *Piñata Full of Bees*) had already made "reality" a question, and the cultural fascination with "Is this really happening?" — i.e., is *Guffman* a "real" documentary? — primed general reaction for the Guest ensemble. Wellspring of all other mock-documentary creations to come, *Waiting for Guffman* did to film and television comedy what *The Graduate* and then *Animal House* had done before. It created the next template.

In March of 1996, the latest incarnation of the Upright Citizens Brigade decided to leave Chicago for New York. Their purpose was clear: to get their own TV show.

Never an improv town, New York, UCB decided, was open for impact and presumably offered a safer landing than L.A., where Hollywood made it impossible for improvisers to fail the way they had to. And the UCB had allies formerly of iO and Second City, already stationed at *Late Night with Conan O'Brien* and *SNL,* like McKay, Dave Koechner, and Tina Fey, whom Adam McKay had brought to Lorne Michaels's attention. New York could be like coming home again.

Charna Halpern hosted a send-off fundraiser, and with only a dream for a plan, UCB filled two cars with every prop they had, and headed out. Matt Besser and Amy Poehler, turning down her shot at Second City's mainstage, clunked along in their rented U-Haul; Matt Walsh and Horatio Sanz barely managed in their old van. They agreed that if after six months in New York they hadn't made significant steps toward that TV deal, they would reevaluate.

It didn't take long to find their audience. Despite the prevalence of stand-up venues, New York's punk attitude had no comedy correlate until UCB appeared on the scene, passing out flyers and yelling at passersby through megaphones. Pop-up shows on busy street corners and open-mic nights at KGB Bar, Rebar, or Luna Lounge (where they got the audience high) won

UCB a following they led, eventually, to their own space, Solo Arts, a forty-seat hole in Chelsea.

To pay the rent, the UCB began teaching classes. They quoted Del Close and Charna Halpern, focused students on the "game" of the scene, discovering its comedic premise, how to heighten it, and then heighten it again. "It just developed unintentionally," Walsh said. Soon their students were putting on their own shows three or four nights a week. Sunday nights the UCB four — Besser, Walsh, Roberts, Poehler — reserved for their own concoction, a derivation of the Armando they called ASSSSCAT 3000; it was New York's first exposure to the mind of Del Close and longform Chicago-style improv. ASSSSCAT was free. "We kept it free because we wanted that vibe," Poehler said. "We wanted it to be an event rather than something we could make money off of."

It worked. Conan O'Brien put the UCB four on his talk show and more opportunities followed. In 1998 Comedy Central gave them their television show, which featured an opening title voice-over from Del Close and showcased sketches adapted from ASSSSCAT improvs. Walsh said, "In essence, in improv terminology, the theme of the show was our suggestion, and we would take existing scenes or write scenes that related to that topic or explored that idea, then we would start to weave it together, like the Harold does." They upgraded to a new theater, a five-floor walkup in a former strip club/secret brothel in Chelsea. Said one improviser, "The ladies would bring dudes up from the back and take the fire escape to the apartment directly above the theater, which had mattresses on the floor." They could handle it. The UCB's comfort with the ad hoc ethic of guerilla comedy inured them to squalor, almost. The UCB came together to clean the place up, chopping down the strippers' runway, breaking mirrors off the walls, and in Poehler's case, dropping to the bathroom floor to fish used condoms out of the toilet. "The women's locker room was all Prince mixtapes and bikinis," she said. "It was as if there'd been a nuclear disaster and everyone had just turned into dust and left all their shit behind." Even after they opened, sailors in town for Fleet Week would turn up looking for hookers. Some Hasidic Jews, too.

The publicity garnered from ASSSSCAT's famous and up-and-coming guest monologists, comedy celebrities and friends of friends, drew significant audiences. "I was like a cousin of the [UCB] family," Tina Fey said. "When I moved to New York to write for SNL that would be my whole Sunday. I would sleep till two and then go down there and do those

ASSCATTTs [*sic*] then eat a whole pizza solo." Jeff Richmond, Fey's other half, was directing Second City back in Chicago.

"One night they asked me to do the monologue," Conan O'Brien recalled, "and I said, 'What happens?' Because I'm a guy who likes to prepare. And they said, 'Don't prepare — just take a word from the audience, start talking, and see what happens.' So someone shouted out 'Dog!' and I started telling this story about a night that I pissed my dad off because I refused to take the dog out, and how he blew up — how I could hear him running down the stairs to get me. I told it in this comedic way, and people were really laughing, but I realized that I had, like, a sense memory of this big conflict I'd had with my dad in 1979. It was actually therapeutic." ASSSSCAT Sundays were old home week, a Chicago reunion, meeting place for initiates Ed Helms, Jack McBrayer, Jenny Slate, Ellie Kemper, Aziz Ansari, Julie Klausner . . . and a way for *SNL* employees to burn off steam on Sunday nights away from the pressures of the writer's room.

"The Dirtiest Sketch Show Ever" was exactly what it sounds like. "Me and my boyfriend at the time," said one improviser, "did this disgusting, disturbing sketch of a brother and a sister that can't find anyone on Valentine's Day, and they decided to fuck each other. And while they're having sex, they're talking about putting their grandma in a nursing home." The show's host, Adam Pally, remembered, "I saw someone have sex with a chicken. I saw two people vomit into a bucket and then drink each other's vomit." (Yes, it's true.) The UCB never said no.

To go to an ASSSSCAT show in those early years was to join a sick family of fun-loving derelicts undivided by the standard show business pecking orders. Everyone, no matter their experience level, could improvise. The same was not true of iO or Second City, where an improviser had to prove himself to earn stage time. To accommodate everyone, the UCB had shows of nearly every kind at nearly every hour. Walsh, who lived upstairs, felt like Peter Pan to the Lost Boys when he emerged from his bedroom at two in the morning to the smell of marijuana and beheld the strange picture of a couple of kids giving each other haircuts. Yes, and there was nerd sex under the stage and in the bathroom; for some, it was their first time.

Chris Farley, late of *Saturday Night Live* and his hit movie, *Tommy Boy,* had left Chicago a prodigal son and returned a comedy king, liable to drop in at Second City or iO, swoop up the players and pied piper them around the corner for a steak breakfast and a beer, as Belushi had, as John Candy had. Or Farley could pile into a cab with them and head downtown, back to his apartment at the Hancock Center, for pizza and heroin as the sun came up.

Farley knew heroin was bad; he said he felt the devil in it. Each time, he said, it took a piece of his soul away.

None of his stints in rehab had worked, and with each failure Farley lost a little more faith, not so much in God but in himself. He could temporarily recover a rush of good feeling getting laughs turning cartwheels upon request, or letting the kids ice-cream his fat face. But those humiliations cost him too. Reflecting on his *SNL* work, he said, "I've still got sores on my back and aches in my body from going out a window or falling down steps or landing on a coffee table. I dislocated my shoulder. I broke my leg." But he could not stop. If comedy was its own devotion, as he had confided in Father Joe Kelly, of St. Malachy's in New York, then getting laughs was his penance, and any club or restaurant, his church.

Early in 1997 Farley was spotted having dinner on the North Side. "Unable to sit still," one witness wrote, "he worked the room as if his life depended on it, going from table to table in an effort to elicit laughs from strangers — some of whom were more amused than others. Finally someone from the restaurant's management told Farley he'd have to stay at his table and behave himself — but as soon as the manager exited the room, Farley bounced back up and was back at it."

In December, Charna Halpern was visiting Farley when a couple of filthy guys walked into his apartment clutching a strange object she almost didn't recognize.

"Is that a crack pipe?"

"Yeah."

Charna threw the lowlifes out.

"You should be hanging out with people who love you!" she railed. "Not guys who are going to say 'I got high with Farley before he died'!"

They fought and she left.

He overdosed in his apartment two weeks later, the morning of December 18, 1997. Farley was thirty-three years old, the same age as John Belushi.

Del was hallucinating. Colors.

"It might be best," he told Charna by phone, "if you drove me to class."

There was no way she was letting him come to class. The previous summer, over half a year earlier, they had been warned: it was emphysema. Del had a year, the doctor said, at the very best.

In the months that followed, Close continued teaching at iO, undaunted, even driven to develop new improvisational structures like the Wake, a longform set at a funeral home. But the physical signs of Close's deterioration were undeniable, at least to everyone other than Close. They saw he no longer breathed freely. He struggled walking to the theater. He had difficulty standing. Students came to class prepared for coughing attacks, waiting at the ready with cups of water. Del knocked them to the floor. "Why the hell does everyone bring me water every time I start coughing?" he roared. "I don't breathe water. Just for once, I'd like for someone to get me a fucking tracheotomy tube."

Now the hallucination, February 27, 1999. Charna, on the phone with Del, put an end to the game playing. These hallucinations weren't drug-related; they told her, as the doctor predicted, his brain was asphyxiating. He was going to the hospital.

"No, no," he commanded. "I don't mind the colors. It's fine. I have a class to teach."

Soon after arriving at Illinois Masonic Hospital, Del was restored, with the aid of inhalation therapy, basically, to his normal abnormal self, but in a matter of hours, the Reaper tagged in and he had to be resuscitated. Charna found him with a tube down his throat. "He was crying," Halpern remembered. He wanted the tube out.

If they took him off the ventilator, the doctors warned Close, he would die. Did he understand that?

Yes, he nodded. He understood.

Unable to talk, Close reached for a pen, and as they switched off the machines, he wrote to Charna, joking mostly ("Get me a big stack of our books unsigned — price goes up!"), and also semiserious. He wrote that Charna was now allowed to have a boyfriend ("like me but younger"), and Charna encouraged him to hang in there, at least to March 9, his sixty-fifth birthday, so they could throw him a party.

Then again, why wait? This was it.

Charna called Bill Murray and told him all; they wanted to have the birthday, possibly his last, the very next day. Murray insisted he foot the bill.

Phone call invites went out around the country, nurses scoured Del's arms for usable veins ("Sorry! I got there first!") and local friends and colleagues appeared to say goodbye, entertain, and receive Del's freshest wisdoms on death and comedy. Barbara Harris came. It was too much for her, so she busied herself cleaning and reordering the hospital room and frantically tending to Del's requests. When she finished Del's hospital room, Barbara took off for his apartment, and with Charna's help, began scrubbing, washing, tidying up. ("I told Barbara," Close explained to Mina Kolb by phone, "that if the choice was whether to stay with her or die, I'd rather die.") Halpern drove Harris home, and by the time she returned to Del's bedside, she found Harris, too nervous to be on her own, sitting there as if she had never left. David Shepherd was sitting beside her.

Alan Myerson called. They spoke for quite a while before Myerson got around to it: "How do you feel about dying?"

"There's nothing to be done really. I just want to be as conscious as I can possibly be."

For a guy who had spent his life getting loaded, Myerson thought, that sounded like a leap into the last unknown.

On the day of the party, Del's current and former students — forty years' worth of fear-loving high divers — gathered in the hospital dining room for a living wake of balloons, flowers, cake, two saxophone players, a coven of nurses, two pagan priests, and a camera crew dispatched by the Upright Citizens Brigade. They were filming in New York and couldn't make it.

"You know," he told UCB, through an oxygen mask, by phone, "as I leave it, I begin to realize that we really haven't done such a bad job." It was not immediately clear if Close was speaking about the human race, or his effort — their effort — to legitimize improvisation. "And I think that we need, oh my fellow Conspiratorians, to recognize this, and, yeah, we're not doing such a bad job for the world. And if maybe a few more conspirators out there would realize that we're — what is this conspiracy? It's a conspiracy of geniality, of hope."

Close, in his wheelchair, wore a high-collared robe of red, yellow, and black stripes.

Bill Murray asked Del if there was anything he could get him. Close asked for a drink — his first in ages — a white chocolate martini.

Harold Ramis was there.

Joyce Sloane and Bernie Sahlins were there.

"It's an art form!" Del called out to Bernie.

"Del," Bernie replied, kissing him, "for tonight, it is an art form."

At the designated hour, they all drew together in the center of the dining room and fell silent, waiting for a word from Del.

"But as I said before," he said, after a sip of his martini, "there's no reason to burn it out tonight. We might get lucky . . ."

There followed a short pagan ritual, beginning with a blessing, an invocation of the deity. "We invoke you, goddess, the goddess we call by many names, Astarte, Hecate, Diana, Penelope, Earth Mother. Please come with us tonight. Send your blessing over all these people, and most of all, our guest of honor here, celebrating his birthday and celebrating his journey through life."

Del hung his head, his hands clasped.

Friends read poetry and prose.

"Blessed be," Del said.

"Blessed be."

Another blessing was read.

"Blessed be."

The room grew quiet again.

Gravely serious, Close said, "In the words of a wise woman from a foreign land who is often misunderstood, 'Death is not important. Life is important. And life is eternal, and life is now.' Leni Riefenstahl."

Early the next morning, around 3:00 a.m., the pain had become unbearable. Charna took his hand.

"No matter what," he told her, "you'll give the skull to the theater." He had already asked her to leave his skull to Robert Falls, director of Chicago's Goodman Theatre, so Del could play Yorick for eternity.

"Yes . . ."

"You'll put my ashes in the theater" — their theater, iO — "where I can affect the work."

"I will."

"You'll tell them" — the students — "we succeeded. We created the Theater of the Heart, where everyone takes care of each other, where everyone treats each other like a genius."

Then, Del Close's final experiment: morphine.

March 4, 1999.

Gary Austin, returning to the Groundlings some years after his resignation in 1979, stepped into the greenroom and noted, with disappointment, actors typing up their sketches as if they were in the writer's room of a television show. "That's completely backward from what we did [originally]," he said. "We were doing theater. It was alive; it came out of living, living on our feet on the stage." Though many of sketch and improv's funniest performers —Jennifer Coolidge, Will Ferrell, Phil Hartman, Jan Hooks, Lisa Kudrow, Melissa McCarthy, Maya Rudolph, Kristen Wiig— developed here, at Los Angeles's premier comedy theater, the Groundlings, they had all but abandoned their roots in improvisation. "We were actors who wrote," original Groundling Victoria Carroll would remind Austin. "These are writers who act." Many at Second City were guilty of the same, but under the artistic direction of Kelly Leonard, the temerity of new-blood directors like Mick Napier, and the everlasting aegis of Del Close, Second City was rethinking the so-called rules of improvisational form. The Groundlings were like sitcom sidekicks, regarded for the outrageousness of their kooky characters. "They still produce a lot of good work," Austin reflected. "But I hate the process." One is sketch, he thought, the other theater. One improv comedy, the other improvisation. "Even if it's exaggerated," he said, "comedy has to represent truthful human behavior. We have to see *you*. We have to see ourselves."

When ABC canceled *The Dana Carvey Show* in 1996, leaving Stephen Colbert and Steve Carell (along with a legendary assemblage of comedy talent including Robert Smigel, Charlie Kaufman, and Louis C.K.) out of work, Colbert was hired by ABC's *Good Morning America,* he said, "because I kind of looked straight but they wanted somebody to be funny—but like a weatherman is funny." At the time, Colbert's wife was also unemployed, and they had a baby girl, so Colbert, with no journalism experience, took the job. He said, "I did exactly two reports." They were barely amusing. One, in which Colbert ("Steve Colbert") interviewed contestants from the Ninth Annual National Rube Goldberg Machine Contest, showed him a mere shadow of his future self. Colbert, playing straight man to the kooks, looked out of place, like some rich network uncle got him the job. Apparently, ABC felt the same; after Colbert's piece aired, they rejected all thirty of his next story ideas.

Looking for work, Colbert took an interview with Madeleine Smithberg, cocreator, with Lizz Winstead, of *The Daily Show,* Comedy Central's late-night replacement for *Politically Incorrect with Bill Maher.* Smithberg already knew Colbert's work. She had loved him (and Carell) in the stupidly hilarious "Waiters Who Are Nauseated by Food" sketch from *The Dana Carvey Show*. More than funny, it showed that Colbert's direct gaze — "Waiters" was shot head-on, Colbert looking straight into the camera — suggested a kind of compatibility with the network news format. He could make a convincing mock-anchor. ("If you have an opportunity to give it right to the audience," Colbert would say, "there's a special connection that you make by looking at the camera.") *The Daily Show* was only in its first season.

"What are you doing now?" they asked Colbert at his interview.

"I'm a correspondent at *GMA*."

"You're kidding."

Colbert pitched them the nearly thirty story ideas *Good Morning America* rejected. *The Daily Show* loved them, and Colbert. In those early days, *The Daily Show* creators were most interested in lampooning the news media (as opposed to lampooning the news itself, like *SNL*'s Weekend Update), and Colbert came perfectly cast. "My joke is always that Stone Phillips really deserves a 'created by' credit on *The Daily Show*," Smithberg said. "We studied that guy. It became, Okay, we pretend we're him and mix it with stories that are much more absurd."

In 1997 Colbert was hired for season two. "I did not believe in the show," he would confess. "I did not watch the show, and they paid dirt."

One of a handful of *Daily Show* field reporters, Colbert played a Stone Phillips type assigned to the inane human-interest stories on the local news. His most ambitious work on *The Daily Show* came in the field, as his subjects began to reveal themselves. Real people, they had no script, which forced Colbert to throw out all his preparation, all his jokes, and improvise. Take, for instance, "Come Out, Come Out Wherever You Are," the *Daily Show* piece about Gaydar, the product — invented by a heterosexual boy — that helped gay people find each other (and inadvertently attracted squirrels). "But then we got there," Colbert said, "and it turns out the guy was a hairdresser, a professional dancer, and a makeup artist, and a wedding photographer, and liked to dress up as the Village People, and *was not* gay." Colbert spends the interview trying to get him to come out.

"Are you . . . *gay*?"

"No. Not at all."

"Let's say you're — I don't know — gay. You've got Gaydar. What happens?"

"What I would do is look around. Hopefully someone else would be looking around as well."

"And if you made contact, then you could go get all gay someplace . . ."

"That's right, yeah."

". . . you could gay it up . . ."

"Yeah."

". . . go someplace and gay off . . ."

"Yeah."

"But you're not gay."

"No, no."

It was Colbert who suggested his old Second City scene partner to *The Daily Show* executives.

"You guys should hire this guy named Steve Carell," he said, "there's nothing he can't make funny."

Already a fan of Carell's from "Waiters Who Are Nauseated by Food," Smithberg watched his audition tape ("The top half of his body was dead straight but the bottom half of his body was going nuts") and only loved him more. She offered him the job. But in 1999, *The Daily Show* was only just another cable show; Carell's agents urged him not to accept.

Carell ended up taking the job, though it disturbed him trying to win laughs at his subjects' expense; it was the ugly opposite of his Second City training, to make the other person look good. And it was shooting fish in a barrel. Colbert felt the same. "In the olden days [of *The Daily Show*]," he said, "you wanted to take your soul off, put it on a wire hanger, and leave it in the closet before you got on the plane to do one of these pieces. We had deep, soul-searching discussions on flights out to do stories, going, 'We don't want to club any baby seals.'"

Carell went to Colbert for advice. "You can't be yourself," Colbert advised him. "You have to go out there in the armor of a correspondent and play a role. Play it as a journalist taking it very seriously; it just happens to be a ridiculous story." Playing himself as a character, a buffoon, "a failed national news anchor who was demoted, and was now doing this cable show, and had a real attitude about it," Carell could share in the humiliation. "And that was also a way to protect yourself," he said, "because it was very scary to be in front of these people, essentially improvising with someone who doesn't know they're doing a scene with you."

Carell approached the interviews as if he were improvising with the best scene partner imaginable, someone so good they don't even seem like they're playing a part. "Short of having both a comedic background and journalistic experience," he said, "I would say having any sort of improvisational experience is probably the biggest help [to working on *The Daily Show*] because essentially you're doing these pieces and you're improvising with someone who doesn't know that they are your improv partner."

Still, in those first years of *The Daily Show*, mean-spiritedness trumped its creators' original intentions, to satirize the glut of twenty-four-hour news channels and attendant influx of time-filling "news." Excepting the show's self-mocking field reporters, most memorably Colbert and Carell, a certain snarky nihilism, the comic position of choice for the internet's adolescent years, undermined the satirical integrity of *The Daily Show*.

Harold and Erica Ramis were on their way to LaGuardia when the first plane hit. They watched the second plane hit on an airport lounge TV, and simultaneously, through the airport window.

Second City improviser Keegan-Michael Key went to Joyce Sloane. "You've been here for forty-four years. Is this the worst thing?"

"It's the worst thing, Keegan. It's the worst thing that has ever happened."

"Vietnam."

"Worse."

"Kennedy . . ."

"Worse."

18

2001–2008

After a half century as a professional satirist, decoding American "logic" and behavior from Eisenhower to George W. Bush, Jules Feiffer hung up his outrage and retired from cartooning. He said, "It seems to me what made me a serious political artist was that I always believed that what I did, along with other cartoonists, could effect change in some way. I no longer have that illusion. Nothing I could do is going to change the mind of Paul Wolfowitz, Donald Rumsfeld or Dick Cheney." He would illustrate children's books. He would teach. "This is an essentially conservative country," he concluded, "that had a left-wing fling in the '30s, during the New Deal, because everyone was broke." The conspiratorial dissent of the '50s was gone. "We were members of a comic underground," Feiffer wrote, "meeting in cabarets and cellar clubs, making startlingly grave and innovative jokes about virginity, Jewish mothers, HUAC and J. Edgar Hoover."

Thank God, he thought, for *The Daily Show*. He watched every night before bed.

The 2000 Bush vs. Gore presidential election was a Kafkaesque sitcom of hanging chads and Floridian quagmires. Remember? We were all wondering who was winning and who was *actually* winning? "By day fourteen," *Daily Show* creator Madeleine Smithberg explained, "the 'real media' did not know what to do, and they would use our clips [because] we dealt in absurdity and were the only ones who could make sense of it." If insane was the new sane, then *The Daily Show* was the sanest show on the air. "All of a sudden," Smithberg said, "the pets were running the pet store."

But it was their 9/11 coverage, and the leadership of host Jon Stewart, that elevated *The Daily Show* even higher, from the country's sanest news source to its most honored.

Following the 2001 attacks, *The Daily Show* went off the air for nine days. When it returned, on September 20, Stewart recouped his viewers with a deeply personal, highly vulnerable opening, more confessional than journalistic. "I wanted to tell you why I grieve, but why I don't despair . . ." The nine minutes to follow were piercingly humane and in levelheaded contrast to America's other, bigger TV news sources, then drowning in sensationalism. At that moment *The Daily Show* finally became its intended self: the pinprick to the bloviated balloon of TV news.

To Jules Feiffer, it was — as he had been fifty years before in the *Village Voice* — a long-silenced cri de coeur, the only meaningful political satire available.

Paul Sills loved *The Daily Show.*

Alan Arkin's improvisation workshops were open, as Viola Spolin's once were, to people of all kinds, from Bennington College students to the Native Americans of New Mexico. The players, naturally, began in fear, but with time and trust, their playing sparked spectacular fireworks of personal revelation. A communal state of grace; Arkin had been there before. He explained, "In every spirit tradition that I know . . . that's the whole problem of human existence. Just letting go and seeing what occurs. Letting go of your agenda. Seeing who you are without any external impulse and [discovering that] the whole promise that's deep inside is more exciting and glorious than anything you can invent." So, to free them from second-guessing themselves out of their instincts, Arkin prohibited all attempts at humor or imagination. Instead he had his students throw around the old invisible ball, then transformed it into a piece of rope, a suitcase, a squirrel, and in a matter of minutes, the whole room, without trying to, transformed into a creative entity.

"You failed!" Arkin would laugh. "The instruction was not to be creative, not to be interesting. Why were you creative?"

Almost always the answer would come back: "It's our nature to be creative."

They had — to use Arkin's phrase — become like idiots of God.

Invariably, at the end of every workshop, a student would ask Arkin, "How do we bring this back to the real world?"

The question always made him laugh. "This *is* the real world!"

The improvisers T. J. Jagodowski and Dave Pasquesi did not begin with a suggestion from the audience. When the lights came up onstage, at the start of one of their hourlong improvised two-person plays, T. J. and Dave would be watching each other's eyes, waiting for subliminal cues. An unconscious gesture, a mood, a look in one stirs something in the other, which stirs something back—a suggestion—and a scene begins. Call it a process of elimination. "Before those lights come up," Jagodowski explained, "literally the possibilities are infinite. But as soon as the lights come up, a bunch of possibilities are removed. And someone moves or someone looks at something—other possibilities are removed. What we end up trying to get to is this sense that we are now doing the one and only thing that this was absolutely from the beginning." Each meaning gleaned from the other's gleaning spun off a character from the hurricane of possible characters, as variable as the world's population, swirling invisibly around them. In T. J. and Dave's mind these characters were real people, merely waiting to be discovered. They had full lives, children, jobs, histories, pets. T. J. and Dave's job was to step into the swirl and bring them down to the stage. The stare was their séance, their "discovery of what is already there," Pasquesi said, "not what I can make it into."

Former students of Del Close's, T. J. and Dave were Chicago's foremost practitioners of slow comedy. Other improvisers, citing Bernie Sahlins's golden rule, talked of playing at the top of their intelligence, but in truth, only paid lip service to the lessons of honesty and not going for the joke. T. J. and Dave really did respect the pace and people of real life. Patience gave them the time to feel each other out for what they called "heat" and "weight." Heat was the energy of their relationship. Do we *feel* like an old married couple? Do we feel like teammates? Enemies? Weight was their predicament.

T. J. and Dave, the steadiest improvisers since Nichols and May, played without a net. They never "stepped outside" the scene to "take you to" another time or location. Unlike improv comedians, they did not work to heighten a funny idea. It's the wind of the relationship that moves them. If no wind comes, they just wait. "Improvisation is itself an exercise in faith,"

Pasquesi said. "In faith of Improvisation. That if I do the next tiny thing, all will be fine."

Career improvisers, T. J. and Dave were not auditioning for Lorne Michaels or developing material for their comedy pilot. Their show — Wednesday nights at 10:30 p.m. at iO — was their intended and final destination. The first time Bernie Sahlins saw them, he turned to his wife, Jane, and conceded that, yes, after fifty years, improvisation was something more than a tool. In the right hands, it was an art form.

In Los Angeles, Elaine ran into Victor Kemper, *Mikey and Nicky*'s fired and then rehired cinematographer.

"By the way," she said. "Remember that scene we shot? At the graveyard?"

"Yes. I remember."

"Wasn't there something else? Didn't I shoot a scene to cover that?"

They hadn't seen each other in thirty years.

"Elaine," Kemper said. "I don't store that stuff."

On September 20, 2004, the day after Mike Nichols's *Angels in America* became the most-awarded show in Emmy history and *The Daily Show* added two more Emmys to its CV, Stephen Colbert met with Doug Herzog, head of Comedy Central, to discuss the idea for a *Daily Show* spin-off. It was the surge of fan mail and phone calls imploring Comedy Central to air episodes of "The Colbert Report," which at the time was no more than fake promos these *Daily Show* viewers had taken for real. ("I'm Stephen Colbert and this is the Colbert Report. It's French, bitch.") "With Stephen," said executive producer Ben Karlin, "we said, 'Let's not just let him go off and become a huge star and not be working with the guy.'" And so *The Colbert Report* got its green light in much the same way Colbert and his team of writers — most of them trained improvisers and regular guests at UCB in New York — would come to green-light their own segments: through an improvisational feedback loop of on-air initiations and audience responses.

In fact, Colbert thought of *The Colbert Report* as a living exchange between his character, self-satisfied archconservative pundit "Stephen Colbert," and his audience. It was a drama of ideas, an ongoing twenty-two-minute, two-character scene. Night after night, his character's intention was to further indoctrinate his acolytes and recruit their total sympathy and devotion.

Its success would come from Colbert's gutsy balance of script and improvisation. Colbert knew that hewing to the jokes — carefully preassembled by him and his writing staff — was vital to sustaining his argument, but also that the emotional life of "Stephen Colbert," what elevated his show from commentary to art, he drew from real-time listening and reacting. "The trouble with the jokes," he explained, "is that once they're written, I know how they're supposed to work, and all I can do is not hit them. I'm more comfortable improvising. If I have just two or three ideas and I know how the character feels, what the character wants, everything in between is like trapeze work."

Before every taping, Colbert — the real Colbert — would appear before his live audience for a question-and-answer session, a conversation geared to warming them up but also, and perhaps more importantly, creating a connection between them, host and acolytes. After he took the last question, he would explicitly state as much. "This show has two characters," he would say. "I'm one and you're the other. Have a good show."

What followed was the trapeze act, a half-hour swing from the teleprompter to the dog whistle of room tone. "If a particular moment goes well," Colbert said, "if there's a roll from the audience, if I manage to catch the wave of their enjoyment, I might vamp a little bit on the back end, do a little filigree on the back end of each of those laugh moments," back and forth until the guest interview, Colbert's somersault in midair. "I'm prepared for the idea of [each interview]," he explained, "but the moment is improvised." Preparation consisted of visiting each guest before the interview and assigning them their "character." Rather than react to "Stephen Colbert" as their exact selves, he asked that they perform themselves with a degree of patience. "I do the show in character," he would explain. "He's an idiot. He's willfully ignorant of what you know and care about. Please honestly disabuse me of my ignorance and we'll have a great time" — or, as producer Emily Lazar put it, talk to Colbert as if he were a harmless drunk on the next barstool.

Colbert's mock-antagonistic interviews took the form of real debates. Throwing his guests off their intellectual balance and, in turn, reacting to their reactions, Colbert engineered one of the only extended improvisational segments on television, the rare broadcast interview that was actually an interview. Thus did *The Colbert Report,* a parody, become more real and more credible than most real news programs. To say nothing of Colbert's celestial wit, speed of association, and cogency, this fact alone — the simple decision to really improvise with his guests — electrified his interview segments with the slight charge of media criticism. Why is this guy, an improviser, who by his own admission knows very little about politics, showing up the pros?

A miraculous triple axel of political satire, television parody, and legitimate journalism, *The Colbert Report* had only been on the air a couple of months when, early in 2006, the little Algerian woman who sold Colbert his morning coffee noticed a change in him.

"Stephen," she said, "you look so tired, why do you look so tired?"

"Well, Anna, I've been working late after the show. I'm writing a script to get ready for the Correspondents' Dinner. I'm going to perform for the president."

"You perform in front of the president?"

"Yeah, I'll be like five feet from him."

"But you're a satirist. You're a critic. You're going to do your jokes right next to him?"

"Yeah."

She took his chin in her hand. "This is a good country."

Mike Nichols climbed into bed with Diane Sawyer and *The Colbert Report* as often as he could, with awe and gratitude, and for what Colbert had accomplished, a surge of grandfatherly pride. "Every time I watch Colbert," he said, "I am reminded that we really live in a free country." Despite all he had, watching Colbert or Stewart, Nichols would always yearn a little for his old improvisational platforms, the Compass and Elaine May, the satirist's prerogative to win revenge instantly, and that thing that happens in living theaters, when ten or a thousand evolving people, formerly strangers, are thrown off their scripts and joined together in laughter and self-discovery.

A monumentally clever, breathtakingly treacherous, backhanded compliment to the Bush administration and the press, Colbert's White House Correspondents' Dinner roast was received about as well as could have been expected by those present. But as for the rest of America — a zealous portion of which "Stephen Colbert" addressed as "Nation" — the performance was the era's defining satirical expression. While the *New York Times* did not cover Colbert's speech, the C-SPAN video went viral overnight, prompting

C-SPAN to order YouTube to remove the video (they would make it available for download at $24.95) a short time before it was uploaded again. The discrepancy between big media and the tastes of the internet generation was never more pronounced, signifying more strongly than ever the death of one by the birth of the other. Colbert's "Nation," after the Correspondents' Dinner roast, really was Colbert's.

He ran into Martin Short at a party a few days later.

"Were you scared?" Short asked.

"No. That day when I was a kid. When the plane crashed. That day I was scared."

Colbert's monster, which had begun as a joke, had gained, literally overnight, the support and power of an actual autocrat, and with his own television show to command his subjects to action, he upgraded the object of his satire from extremist punditry to the entire mechanism of unchecked authority. The joke was not a joke: the producer in Colbert found himself, in his own words, "Yes, anding" opportunities to take "Stephen Colbert" out of the studio and, with an air of is-this-or-isn't-this? reminiscent of an Andy Kaufman happening, place his alter ego, or his influence, in real-world situations, "as a pebble that I can throw into the news and then report on my own ripples." For instance:

After Bing West, assistant secretary of defense in the Reagan administration, appeared on *The Colbert Report,* West extended a big hand to Colbert and noticed, on Colbert's wrist, a silicone WristStrong bracelet, a running *Report* joke on Lance Armstrong's LIVESTRONG bracelet, in support of the Yellow Ribbon Fund, a program to help veterans returning from the wars in Iraq and Afghanistan. General David Petraeus, Colbert told West, had noticed the bracelet — it had prompted him to invite Colbert to Iraq.

"If General Petraeus invites you to do your show in Iraq," West returned, "you should do it."

"Gosh," Colbert thought to himself, "an improviser would say, 'Yes.'"

And then they were in Iraq. "The people in Iraq were so grateful that we came," Colbert said, "but the feeling of gratitude we had in return was enormous. It was a physical thing in the air during the shows. It was almost as if I didn't see the audience — I only saw the grateful space between us. It was as beautiful and awesome as a night sky."

The audience. They were playing with "Stephen Colbert." And Stephen Colbert, and his writers, played back. He said, "These initiations and these responses are where we make our discoveries and they give us games." On air, Colbert joked about wanting to name a new bridge over the Danube the Stephen Colbert Bridge. Suddenly, fourteen million people, voting in an online naming competition, cast their ballots for Colbert "and that," Colbert said, "led to a continuing game." He did a "Better Know a District" segment with Congresswoman Lynn Woolsey from Marin County, and joked about George Lucas, a Marin resident, contributing, in some form, with his own green screen special effects. The next morning, the Colbert staff discovered a YouTuber had already begun the process. That turned into a three-month game, the "Green Screen Challenge," in which viewers were invited to place Colbert in a digital environment, a concept the band the Decemberists then used for one of their own music videos, which brought on Colbert's retaliatory segment "Stephen Colbert's Rock and Awe: Countdown to Guitarmageddon." (One such game, The Colbert versus Willie Nelson feud, was resolved with a treaty Colbert signed as Compass and Second City improviser Eugene Troobnick.) "All those things," Colbert said, "were extended improvisational games with my audience."

The lines blurred and the breadth of Colbert's games grew with his courage, one feeding the other, until Colbert's long-latent activism began to show.

In 2010 he appeared, in character, to testify before a subcommittee on illegal immigration. (They invited him; he replied, "You know this is going to be a terrible idea?")

"Good morning," Colbert began, sitting before the subcommittee. "My name is Stephen Colbert and I'm an American citizen. It is an honor and a privilege to be here today. Congresswoman Lofgren asked me to share my vast experience spending one day as a migrant farmworker. I am happy to use my celebrity to draw attention to this important, complicated issue, and I certainly hope that my star power can bump this hearing all the way up to C-SPAN1."

He responded, under fire, to questions in character.

Q. "How many of those individuals were illegal and how many were legal?"

A. "I didn't ask them for their papers, though I had a strong urge to."

And:

"Does one day in the field make you an expert witness?"

"I'm sorry I can't hear you."

"Does one day working in the field make you an expert witness, do you think?"

"I believe one day of me studying anything makes me an expert in something."

"Is that to say it's more work than you've ever done before, right?"

"Excuse me?"

"It's more work than you've ever done before in that —"

"It's certainly harder than this."

And:

"I actually was a corn packer. And I know that term is offensive to some people because 'corn packer' is a derogatory term for a gay Iowan and I hope I didn't offend anybody."

Colbert's astonishing leap from comedy personality to national spokesperson was without precedent. You would have to go back to Bob Hope to find someone approaching an analog, but even still, Hope's commentary never surpassed or even reached that of his contemporaries in the news media. Colbert's had.

As TV news's emphasis on entertainment reached new highs (lows?), and the internet, with each passing year, broke another hole in old journalism's monopoly, a space opened for a commentator with a new kind of integrity, one that openly acknowledged the lack of integrity sweeping the profession. Playing both sides at once — thank you, irony — Colbert not only solved the problem, he managed to convince both the left and the right he was on their side. The internet made it so; it let him improvise for the world. Mere hours after it aired on Comedy Central, everyone with Facebook or Twitter (and increasingly the online outlets of Fox News, MSNBC, and the *New York Times*) would be sharing Colbert's latest achievement. You can't imagine the same ever happening to a Wolf Blitzer — unless something went hilariously wrong on the air.

Still, something even bigger was happening. By way of first Jon Stewart, and now Stephen Colbert — in 2009, the written-in addition to *Foreign Policy*'s list of the world's top twenty public intellectuals — comedy, surpassing entertainment, became the country's rhetoric of choice for serious discourse. In an age of partisan politics ad absurdum, it was far less ridiculous than reporting seriously on the world.

• • •

Years later, Harold Ramis would still have Bill Murray dreams. In dreams, they were friends again, the way they were for the first comedies. In those days, no matter the state of the script, Murray was always next to Ramis. He could be counted on to improvise an ailing scene back to health. "That was our alliance, kind of, our big bond," Ramis said. "I could help him be the best funny Bill Murray he could be, and I think he appreciated that then. And I don't know where that went, but it's there on film."

Finally, after a complete round of rejections from every studio in Hollywood, Adam McKay and Will Ferrell got *Anchorman* its green light. *Old School* had made a movie star of Ferrell, and the windfall raised his comedy circle — a company that included McKay, Judd Apatow, and a host of other improvisers — to a new premium. Many had been friends for years. That most were represented by the United Talent Agency made them easier to package, that they had grown up on the same comedies made them a coherent ensemble. "We are all the spawn of [Harold] Ramis," Apatow said. "We all grew up on *Stripes* and *Caddyshack* and *Animal House*."

Among all the improvisers on *Anchorman*, McKay's first film as director, Steve Carell was probably the most attuned to the financial implications of improvising on a movie. As they played, he could actually hear the film, the money, running through the camera, a reminder that Hollywood was not Second City, his improvisational choices, or "alts," should be modified accordingly, and that despite the freedom the executives had conferred on McKay's ensemble, they should not roam from story. The 2000s were not the '70s. *Anchorman* was not an Elaine May movie, where all was subject to rediscovery; it was not a low-budget Christopher Guest movie, where improvisers could know where they were going but not how they were going to get there; *Anchorman,* emblematic of the new Hollywood comedy, was a big-budget home movie, caught between convention and invention.

It was three or four takes as written, then McKay, his camera still rolling, would call out ideas, loudly, for the actors' immediate implementation. "I know the rules of improv," he would explain, "I know I've got to make the actors feel safe enough to fail, so I start throwing out ideas, and some of them suck, and so they get it. They know that it's cool." Often, he would get so involved in the scene yelling out ideas he would go home hoarse.

Judd Apatow, an *Anchorman* producer, approached Carell between takes. "You have any ideas for a movie?"

Carell told Apatow about a scene he used to do at Second City, the one they improvised a bunch but never put into a show, about a middle-aged virgin pretending he was sexually experienced. Carell still remembered the line about breasts: the virgin claimed they felt like big bags of sand.

Apatow loved it. "I could walk into a studio right now and sell this based on that line alone."

Which is what he did.

Carell and Apatow completed a draft of *The 40-Year-Old Virgin* early in 2005. It would be Carell's first starring role and Apatow's first film as director.

Apatow worked like McKay, and as Ramis and Reitman before them, making comedy by committee. "It's almost a think-tank approach," Will Ferrell explained, "and it gives you about thirty percent more options." The collaboration extended from the improvisations on set — which, in Apatow's films, could run out entire magazines of film, and leave hours of unused footage — to postproduction, a process Apatow centered on test-screenings. Seeking audience feedback on his film's every aspect, from jokes to song selections and even, in one case, a five-second-long music cue, Apatow continued to rediscover his film up to its very release. "Judd is like a feedback machine," said director Paul Feig. "He wants feedback of the person he doesn't even like or trust."

Owing largely to the strength of Carell's performance, *The 40-Year-Old Virgin* exceeded test audience's expectations. "What became clear very early is that people wanted the story," Apatow said. "They didn't want a joke fest. All the notes were: You can cut the jokes." It is an ancient custom of working writer-directors to envision a dream film too personal, too challenging to match reigning commercial tastes; Apatow embraced his executives as part of the creative team. He said, "They didn't tell me anything I disagreed with." Either the director had his finger on the pulse, or the pulse had its grip on *40-Year-Old-Virgin;* the movie was a breakthrough for the star, the director, and the slacker style and substance of the Apatow signature, inconceivable without improvisation. "I look at the people I meet," Apatow said. "No one's dying to have a lot of responsibility in their lives." His selective use of improvisation, not dialogue, conveys it. Apatow said, "It's very hard to capture the energy of men joking around with each other if it's completely scripted. You just feel its stiffness. It's very hard to fake laughter, the way you laugh when a friend says something crazy." He might, over the course of an improvisation, write down funny lines on Post-its, as reminders to hand back to the actors after a take. "Say that again!" He might shoot the same scene with different costumes, in different locations just in case, in editing, he discovered the scene was better *here* than *there*.

At the Deauville Film Festival with *Virgin*, Apatow and Seth Rogen discovered they were staying at the same hotel as Harold Ramis, a hero to both in two different ways. "As a Jewish actor with a very deep voice who was kind of large," Rogen said, "he was kind of the only precedent there was for success." Abounding with lovable underachievers, Ramis's comedies spoke to the eternal boy in Apatow; they made him want to make Ramis's kinds of movies in Ramis's kind of way. "If I was 20 years old," he reflected, "I would sign up for classes at Second City or iO — that's, like, the ultimate life I wish I lived." So it was with humility and disbelief that Apatow called up to Ramis's hotel room and introduced himself, or rather, reintroduced himself. They had met before, Apatow explained, twenty-three years earlier, back in Long Island, when he interviewed Ramis for his high school's radio show. Ramis didn't need an explanation. He remembered the article in the *New York Times;* Apatow had said they were all the spawn of Harold Ramis.

In short order, Apatow and Rogen went to see Ramis's new film, *The Ice Harvest,* and all three went out to dinner. The connection was instant. "We're in the same business," Ramis said, "and we all speak the same comedy language. There was a familiarity and a family feeling." The next night, they switched. Ramis went to see *The 40-Year-Old-Virgin,* all went out to dinner again, and Apatow told Ramis about his next movie, *Knocked Up*. It would be Rogen's first starring role, he explained, but of course, they were still writing it.

"I never finish a script," Apatow would say. "I just start."

He would cast a spiritual father, Harold Ramis, to play Seth Rogen's screen father. Their scenes, improvised from script, were, for Rogen, "a thrill that I constantly remind my real father that he can never ever actually live up to."

"Do you have any weed on you?" Ramis asked Rogen after the shoot.

"I don't have any *on* me, but I do have some at my apartment . . . It's around 45 minutes away."

"Okay."

And off they went.

Elaine May, Mike Nichols, David Shepherd, and other original Compass members gathered at the New Actors Workshop in New York for Paul Sills's memorial. He died on June 2, 2008.

Elaine turned to her old cohorts, sitting all in a row beside her, and with little-girl enthusiasm Shepherd thought so unlike her, chirped, "Isn't this great? Don't you think? To be all back together?"

Sills, Shepherd mused, would certainly think so. He died knowing nothing is ever finished.

Oftentimes, days after the fact, Bill Murray would look back and realize, no, he hadn't been connected to himself, he hadn't always felt the feelings, his actual *actual* feelings, and the succulent sense of calm that comes to all who feast on the present. What had stopped him? Fame, mostly; his persona, and the stale and automatic reactions it incurred in him. Who got to decide what Bill Murray was? "Fuck loss of privacy," he said. "That's not the least of it. That you can handle. You can buy privacy, to an extent. What you really lose is yourself, your real self. Every time you're reminded that you are the guy from TV, you sort of gravitate to being that guy. You leave yourself to answer that need for someone else." Fame was a script, but Murray was an improviser.

So he left the script that fame imposed upon him; he got lost.

There was the time in the Australian jungle when he moved in with a posse of surfers and lived on rice and night swims. ("I ended up staying seven weeks. It was more than a vacation. It was right on the edge of expatriation.")

There was the time he was watching TV, saw something about the Strait of Malacca, flew to Indonesia to see it, checked into an expensive hotel, reconsidered, rented a motorcycle, and ended up at the edge of a volcanic lake, took a room for sixty cents a night, where he watched the live crater through his open window.

"Would you sign this for my sister?" a fan once asked. "She's a real die-hard."

"Try hitting her when she's sleeping," he said, putting pen to paper. "Wait till she dozes off, and . . ."

There was the time, in New York, when he dropped a bill in a panhandler's bag of coins, then ferreted around in the bag for change.

"Sorry, I don't do autographs," he told one girl. "Gave 'em up for Lent. I do impressions."

"Impressions?"

"Yeah, impressions," he said, taking the paper from her hand and biting it. "*Dental* impressions."

There was the time, bored at a fancy benefit dinner, when he entertained himself by throwing silverware, one piece at a time, through an open window.

There was the time, at the Friars Club, when a kid came up to him and asked for an autograph. "Sidney," the kid instructed. Murray took Sidney's outstretched pencil and pad, and wrote, "Sidney, run away from home tonight — Bill Murray."

Bill Murray had been running away from home, moment by moment, long before he became famous. It's what brought him to Second City. But why should that first fateful "Yes, and" be his last? "Why," he asked, "should I devote my whole life to this career which happened so accidentally?" Better to devote his life to accident. He would stay light on his feet, always alert to audience suggestion. Kickball? Roosevelt Island? "We just figured he was someone's dad on the other team and kept playing, NBD," wrote a kickballer on a website devoted to Bill Murray sightings. "The man kicked the ball and ran pretty well to first base, trying to round to second, but one of my teammates chased him back to first, deciding not to attempt to peg the man. That was when everyone on my team realized who he was . . . BILL MURRAY DECIDED TO PLAY KICKBALL WITH US!"

The internet gave Murray a stage for the greatest improvisational run of his career, a venue for those Bill Murray stories formerly confined to rumor and word of mouth. Seen goofing on Pebble Beach, Wrigley Field, or a pub in Scotland, Murray, as the internet's Zelig, man of a thousand men and Robin Hood of free play, liberated himself from the prison of typecasting. Google Search contained his multitudes, the spiritual and social splendors of a life lived improvisationally.

In 2013 he was spotted in his hometown of Chicago, first in the house and then onstage, standing near the back of the ensemble, as they sang Second City's "Good Night Song" at the memorial for Bernie Sahlins.

• • •

Mike said to Elaine:

"You've changed more than anybody I've known in my entire life. You changed from a dangerous person to someone who is *only* benign. I have not —"

"What a vicious thing to say."

"But it's true! All the things about, say, certain heroines have come true of you. If you can't say anything nice, you don't say anything. You never ever attack people to their face or behind their back. You're the most discreet person about other people that I have ever met in my life. I haven't heard you unkind for fifty years. You have done a complete 180 degree turn."

"This is such a horrible thing of you to say."

"I'm really sorry."

"I feel exactly the same way about you too."

"You bitch."

"Blackout."

Laughter.

"That was great, Mike."

GOODNIGHT, EVERYONE

I have no idea what improv does next — no one does — but if it's anything like *The OkStupid Show*, the form I chanced on in early 2016, at UCB's Franklin Avenue outpost in Hollywood, a mile and a half from the original site of Viola Spolin's Young Actors Company, Spolin's vow, "Anyone can improvise," may finally be proven irrefutably true. One of the sincerest, funniest, most painfully raw and exuberant nights I've ever had in an improv theater began as two civilians — amateurs, in accord with David Shepherd's original intentions for a people's Compass — took their chairs on opposite sides of a bistro table that had been waiting for them in the dead center of the stage. Before the show, these two individuals, in this case a man and a woman, had been matched online, via a dating website. Now they had come to UCB Franklin to have their first date live, in front of us, a tiny, one-hundred-person audience. Scary? Terrifying. Two "cupids," trained improvisers, were stationed at the table's edge to goose slips into small talk, keep the scene moving forward (to a clear rejection or possible next date), and refill the prospective couple's red plastic cups — with alcohol, of course — like waiters in an actual café. Other than that, the figuring-it-out couple — with no concept of the "rules" of improv — are left to themselves. And the date begins.

One might think that under such contrived circumstances, neither participant could really feel, or act, "themselves," but whatever self-consciousness blights these untrained performers as they grapple toward each other, awkwardly, under the hot lights, is canceled out by the self-consciousness and awkwardness accompanying any first date. Remember Mike and Elaine in "Teenagers"? In this "game," the unnaturalness *is* natural. Soon we forget — as these newborn improvisers have — that this is a show. Emotionally, we leave the theater. Now I'm a voyeur, at that imagined café, listening from the next table, rooting for him to break down her wall, for her to see he's not worth her time, for phoniness to be exposed or romance to fly. I — we — saw it all (for seven dollars a seat), a complete abridgement of the human adventure as good as any performance of anything, Shakespeare to Jules Feiffer. For if there is no better drama (or comedy) in the world than the comedy (or drama) of actual life, the inventors of *OKStupid,* in returning, as Paul Sills did, improvisation to the "real" people of the audience, have erased the dividing line between art and being, and through spontaneity, united all.

As it is a truth universally acknowledged that the tenets of improvisation, founded on playful cooperation and mutual self-discovery, contain so many, if not all, of the ingredients of love, it follows that the sustained and meaningful practice of one regularly leads to the other. The inclinations of each ensemble change with the times, but climb all the way down to the bottom of the family tree, to Mike and Elaine, sitting there in the waiting room of Illinois Central's Randolph Street Station, and note the slight dilation of their pupils. Those are the eyes of Spolin and Sills, 1063 Avenue Road, the 505, Amy Poehler and Tina Fey . . .

Joy, improvisers understand, is a custom of the form, and providing you play by the rules — "the rules of improvisation," Eugenie Ross-Leming told me, "are just good manners" — you will never be in short supply, even when you get lost, because all the fun is in getting lost, and so the more lost you are, the more fun there is, and *therefore,* for the best results, get lost as often as you can, pursue the strange, the "impossible," the horrific, the very far away.

Failure, improv teaches, is actually freedom's friend; it may score less, but it lives a whole lot more. And the more it lives, the stronger it gets. Despite what you might think about age stealing genius the way it erodes the body, improvisers prove that when dauntless instincts agree to play, the exact opposite is true. With exercise, those tendons strengthen. With practice they renew. In any context, Elaine still leapt; Mike still caught her. Years and years later, their perfect convergence held.

There are people you've known for years — actual friends and loved ones — who remain remote no matter how many times you see them, or how hard you try to connect; a good improviser, no matter how new your acquaintance, incubates you in warmth. He makes you better. In his company, you are safe to be free and confident, because this person, in his understanding, sees *you*.

Wherever there is improvisation, anyone can speak her mind, and that mind, folded in with others', will form a totally original, harmonious entity — thesis, synthesis, antithesis — the democratic spirit channeled through art. Improvisation, then, is inherently egalitarian; it is about how we can be free *together*. Improvisation, then, is also inherently social; as Spolin and Sills knew, its singular power to fire rooms full of strangers into instant families burgeons real trust. And where there is trust, there is, as Nichols and May recognized, the fearlessness to plunge into the unmapped oceans of one's psyche, one's many personae, and surface onstage with the treasures of infinite selves. Improvisation, then, is inherently metaphysical; as Del Close, seeking for himself altered realms of consciousness and higher peaks of experience, intuited early on, it teaches you that there is more, that you don't know *you*. Not all of you. You only ever know the you you know. The rest of you, the complete and boundless you, is a prism of infinite refraction, waiting for a shock of light — a spontaneous impulse from another — to surprise a beam of unknown you to life.

ACKNOWLEDGMENTS

This book began thirty years ago in the Pacific Palisades with Jack and Joe Dolman, Andrea Martin, and Bob Dolman, and the taste of waffles and carpet, the flavor of laughing so hard at *SCTV* I fell over, mouth first, and regurgitated breakfast at the floor. Over the years — the Bestor Years, as we call them — my lips spent more time on that carpet than on any person, food, or drink. It was there, many detergents later, that I first asked myself, Who *are* these people, the people of *SCTV*? What miracle brought them — the funniest ensemble, I still believe, ever assembled — together? And while most bands end, and end acrimoniously, what keeps this one, even to this day, so close? That last question was the one I wanted answered most of all; it was the one that could pertain to me, to my friends and me, and answering it, I knew, would make life better. The how of comedy was incidental; what mattered then, as now, was how artists, in life and in work, collaborate, fall in love, and stay together. I had a hunch paradise was on the other side of that one.

Hundreds of conversations and three decades later, I found myself on February 24, 2014, catalyzed by the loss of Harold Ramis, following the breadcrumbs back to Second City, Toronto, Chicago, Nichols, May, and Viola Spolin, then forward to *The Graduate*, to *Saturday Night Live* and on. That's when I started writing. How fortunate, then, that I happened to have Marshall McLuhan right there, and could turn to Andrea and Bob. But more than offering information, they energized me. They joined in. They opened every door, materialized doors where I saw walls, and where there seemed no way through helped me carve out caves and gladly walked me in. When it was too dark to see, Jeffrey Wasson, Cindy Wasson, Sophie Wasson, and Maria Diaz lit candles. When I was hopeless, they waited, with patience and imaginative understanding.

Every step of the way, Andrew Alexander, Kelly Leonard, Erica Ramis, and Martin Short gave me more than everything I asked for. I am so grateful to you.

What I always hope for in an interview is someone who, in addition to having a gigantic memory for emotion and detail, is willing to entertain my theories and ideas no matter how farfetched, to let us play with the whys and wherefores of their own experience, to improvise with me. This is where I was lucky. I got to improvise with improvisers about improvisation. They were Annie Abrams, Trevor Albert, Andrew Alexander, Alan Arkin, René Auberjonois, Gary Austin, Ronnie Austin, Dick Blasucci, Valri Bromfield, Jimmy Carrane, William Carruth, John Carter, Sally Cochrane, Larry Coven, Nell Cox, Dennis Cunningham, Joan Darling, Dana Delany, Deb Devine, Lena Dolman, Leslie Dolman, Robert Dolman, Robin Duke, Murphy Dunne, Jayne Eastwood, Phyllis Epstein, Robert Falls, Jules Feiffer, Tina Fey, Pat Finn, Jim Fisher, Joe Flaherty, Barbara Flicker, Bruce J. Friedman, Nancy Geller, Kathy Greenwood, Charna Halpern, Larry Hankin, Barbara Harris, Michael Hausman, Cordis Heard, Kathy Hendrickson, Beth Henley, Buck Henry, Dustin Hoffman, Tino Insana, Norman Jewison, Kim "Howard" Johnson, Jackie Joseph, Elaine Kagan, Sheldon Kahn, Judith Kampmann, Steven Kampmann, Victor Kemper, Michael Kirchberger, Joe Klein, William Joseph Kruzykowski, Nathan Lane, Martha Lauzen, Kelly Leonard, Eugene Levy, Anne Libera, Joe Liss, Andrea Martin, Allaudin Mathieu, Paul Mazursky, Adam McKay, Lorne Michaels, Michael Miller, Judy Morgan, Robert Morse, Gregory Mosher, Alan Myerson, Mick Napier, Mike Nichols, Catherine O'Hara, Marcus O'Hara, Sheldon Patinkin, Diane Paulus, David Picker, Judy Belushi Pisano, Frank Price, Erica Mann Ramis, Harold Ramis, David Rasche, Dave Razowsky, Ivan Reitman, Eugenie Ross-Leming, Stephen Rotter, Gena Rowlands, Harvey Sabinson, Jane Sahlins, Paul Sand, Stephen Schwartz, Michael Segel, Cybill Shepherd, David Shepherd, Katherine Short, Martin Short, Nancy Short, Aretha Sills, Carol Sills, Brian Stack, Lynn Stalmaster, Douglas Steckler, David Steinberg, Violet Stiel, Dave Thomas, Rick Thomas, Stephen Tobolowsky, Larry Turman, Pat Whitley, Fred Willard, and Bill Wrubel.

Thank you to the librarians and archivists: foremost, Sondra Archer,

Jenny Romero, and everyone at the Motion Picture Academy's Margaret Herrick Library in Beverly Hills; the great Ned Comstock at USC's Cinema Arts Library, who was still thinking about my book even after I left; Michael Golding, who allowed me to look through David Shepherd's most valuable papers; Barbara Flicker, who trusted me with treasures; Sam Shaw, who took a break from his work on a forthcoming Committee documentary and helped, always promptly, with queries and photos; those at Northwestern University who saw me through Viola Spolin's archive; Chris Pagnozzi, who let me run wild through the Second City Archive, and who never let on that I was bothering him, if I was bothering him, which I hope I wasn't; and as ever, Patrick Hoffman, et al., at the New York Public Library's Theatre on Film and Tape Archive, which is even better than Willy Wonka's Chocolate Factory, I promise. You all put me at ease, stretched the rules, lent me your expertise. Thank you.

Thank you to Caroline Aaron and Jamie Foreman, Janet Cross, Colleen Dodson-Baker, Nicolette Donen, Nancye Ferguson, Jenni McCormick, Hendriik Riik, Lisa and Dustin Hoffman, Deborah Solomon, George Stelzner, and Alicia Van Couvering, who facilitated interviews, and in the case of one particular interview, tried very hard.

There aren't many things in this life I love without qualification. The Robbins Office is one of them. As the grace and dignity of my friend and agent, David Halpern, is not native to our era, his presence is as rare as good luck. And his counsel refined as diamonds. This is not hyperbole. Thank you, David and Kathy Robbins, once again, for giving me a life as a writer and a home on Park Avenue. Thank you, Rick Pappas, for recommending me to Mike Nichols; I was overcome by your endorsement. I still am. Thank you to Arielle Asher, Rachelle Bergstein, and Lisa Kessler for being so warm when I was in a cold panic, and Lucinda Blumenfeld, for every restaurant you brightened, thank you.

At Houghton Mifflin Harcourt, my editor, Eamon Dolan, made everything smarter; like a good parent, the director of a years-long improvisation, he was there when I needed him and obligingly absent when I didn't; he yanked the weeds from my mind and where I thought nothing could grow burgeoned the most exotic flowers, many of which he was wise to cut back entirely. Thank you, Eamon. If you're proud, I'm proud. To Rosemary McGuinness, whose voice is a lullaby, and Melissa Dobson, whose copyedits were a dream, thank you for your soft handling of this tired writer.

The complete story of improvisational comedy—which is changing and becoming even as you read this—can be written only after the whole thing ends, when its last theater closes and its last player dies. But until then, which I hope is never, its history will be a work in progress, and any telling of it, like this one, only a draft. For this and too many other reasons, I don't recommend anyone write a history of improv comedy—or, for that matter, a history of anything still with us—but if you must, and I hope you do, you should surround yourself with (in addition to the names listed above) the likes of Jeanine Basinger, Amy Blessing, Peter Bogdanovich, Maria Chilewicz, Gary Copeland, Marla Frazee, David Freeman, Judy Gingold, Liz Hanks, Beth Henley, Alex Horwitz, Allyn Johnston, David Jones, India Jones, Suzanne Joskow, Nathan Lane, Natalie Lehmann, Zander Lehmann, Lynne Littman, Veronica Lombardo, Jill Mazursky, Jocelyn Medawar, Brandon Millan, Graham Moore, Jackie Nalpant, Amanda Parker, Jane Parkes, Lynn Povich, Nic Ratner, Sarah Shepard, Steve Shepard, Katherine Short, Holland Sutton, Ted Walch, and Simone White. The only way I could get myself to write this book was to dangle at the end of every working day the carrot of your company so that I might peek over the anxiety to the coming night of laughter.

Sam Wasson
December 2017

NOTES

This book is especially indebted to Jeffrey Sweet's *Something Wonderful Right Away*, Janet Coleman's *The Compass*, and Kim Howard Johnson's *The Funniest One in the Room: The Lives and Legends of Del Close*. They were with me throughout, and if you're interested in the subject, they should be with you too.

EPIGRAPH

page

vii *"Ours is the only modern country"*: Harold Clurman, foreword to the 1957 edition, in his *The Fervent Years: The Group Theatre and the Thirties* (1945; New York: Da Capo, 1983), viii.

HI, HOW ARE YOU?

xii *"It's kind of like fireworks"*: Del Close, in *The Second City 15th Anniversary Special*, directed by Eugene Levy (SCTV, 1988), DVD.

1. 1940-1955

3 *tag, jacks, marbles, hopscotch*: Carol Sills to author.
"Play means happiness": Neva Boyd, "The Theory of Play," Intuitive Learning Systems Foundation website, www.spolin.com, accessed June 5, 2017, http://spolin.com/?page_id=1068.

4 *"When we find ourselves"*: Ibid.
"qualities which cannot be talked about": Clayton D. Drinko, *Theatrical Improvisation, Consciousness, and Cognition* (New York: Palgrave Macmillan, 2013), 18.
"a non-authoritarian climate": Richard Christiansen, "Second City's Founding Father Comes Home," *Chicago Tribune*, September 21, 1980.
"The unfolding of the scene": Viola Spolin, *Improvisation for the Theater: A Hand-*

book of Teaching and Directing Techniques, 3rd ed. (Evanston, Ill.: Northwestern University Press, 1972), 257.

"the first intelligent question": Lenny Kleinfeld, "Del Close," *Chicago,* March 1987, p. 146.

5   *"My grandfather":* Ibid.

"Every few months, the cast": Viola Spolin Papers, Northwestern University, Box 1, Folder 4, Early Work, "Creative Recreational Theater."

In 1940, in Chicago: Howard Vincent O'Brien, "All Things Considered," *Chicago Daily News,* May 26, 1939.

On a trip out West: Carol Sills to author.

6   *"It was like stepping":* Paul Sand to author.

roast chicken, herbs, and cigarettes: Ibid.

"Viola was a powerful woman": Ronnie Austin to author.

"The games were really": Jackie Joseph to author.

"We were guinea pigs": Paul Sand to author.

"some surprise little thing": Jackie Joseph to author.

"Viola gave me, by her laughter": Ibid.

7   *"The games really are":* Ronnie Austin to author.

"We had to get a lot of safety pins": Paul Sand to author.

"See each other with your toes!": Carol Sills to author.

"I remember Sand": Alan Arkin to author.

"We didn't have a lot of money": Ibid.

"I grew up with a lot of these games": Leslie Bennetts, "If It Works, It's Theater. If It Doesn't . . . ," *New York Times,* June 8, 1986.

Mother and son: Carol Sills to author.

8   *"the diamonds":* Paul Sand to author.

"As a kid": Robert Wahls, "Del Close Is Way Out — But Just for His Part," *New York Daily News,* May 24, 1959.

The glass bottles, beakers, burners, droppers: Kim Howard Johnson, *The Funniest One in the Room: The Lives and Legends of Del Close* (Chicago: Chicago Review Press, 2008), 8.

"Every kid assumes": Kleinfeld, "Del Close," 147.

9   *"pre-Nazis, really":* Mike Nichols to author.

"Basically, they beat my grandfather": Ibid.

"I'm incredibly lucky": Mike Nichols, interview with Stephen Galloway, "Director Mike Nichols on His 60-Year Career: 'Trouble Always Seemed Glamorous,'" *Hollywood Reporter,* May 10, 2012, http://www.hollywoodreporter.com/news/mike-nichols-death -salesman-career-322677.

"I don't speak English": Mike Nichols to author.

10   *"Is that allowed?":* Henry Louis Gates Jr., *Faces of America: How 12 Extraordinary People Discovered Their Pasts* (New York: NYU Press, 2010), 18.

"I don't know what happened": Lillian Hellman, "And Now — An Evening with Nichols and Hellman," *New York Times,* August 4, 1970.

"I think there is an immigrant's ear": Peter Applebome, "Always Asking, What Is This Really About?," *New York Times,* April 25, 1999.

"They fucked me on baseball": Sam Kashner, "Who's Afraid of Nichols & May?,"

Vanity Fair, December 20, 2012, audio recording accompanying article, VanityFair .com.

"The kid was as far outside": John Lahr, "Making It Real: How Mike Nichols Re-created Comedy and Himself," *New Yorker,* February 21, 2000, http://www.newyorker.com /magazine/2000/02/21/making-it-real-2.

"He's the one": Ibid.

"That was cast in bronze": Ibid.

"It makes for being socially adept": Kashner, "Who's Afraid of Nichols & May?," audio recording accompanying article, VanityFair.com.

11 *"I was motivated then":* Gavin Smith, "Without Cutaways," *Film Comment* 27, no. 3 (May/June 1991), 29.

attempt the leftovers method: Mike Nichols to author.

Del would tell you about the time: Del Close bio in Theodore J. Flicker Collection, University of Southern California Cinematic Arts Library.

and Whitey the Albino: Johnson, *The Funniest One in the Room,* 24.

Dr. Dracula's Den of Living Nightmares: Noted in source as "Dr. Dracula and His Tomb of Terror"; over the years, Close gave the show several different names. Kleinfeld, "Del Close," 146.

"A plague of worms will descend upon you!": Ibid.

12 *"You call this entertainment?":* Ibid.

"It's a matter of the threshold of pain": Wahls, "Del Close Is Way Out."

I want to squeeze you dry: Kleinfeld, "Del Close," 146.

("I don't know why"): Mike Nichols to author.

"What I really want": Paul Sills and Charles L. Mee Jr., "The Celebratory Occasion," *Tulane Drama Review* 9, no. 2 (Winter 1964), 167–81.

"the way good theater should be": Robert Koehler, "Sills Always Trying to Improve on Improv," *Los Angeles Times,* April 24, 1985.

13 *"bullshitting about the theater":* Mike Nichols to author.

in the pages of the New Yorker: A. J. Liebling, "Profiles: Second City: I — So Proud to Be Jimmy-Jammy," *New Yorker,* January 12, 1952; "Profiles: Second City: II — At Her Feet the Slain Deer," *New Yorker,* January 19, 1952; "Profiles: Second City: III — The Massacree," *New Yorker,* January 26, 1952.

Had Mike heard of Tonight at 8:30: Mike Nichols to author.

14 Encyclopaedia Britannica: Stephen Metcalf, "A Heady Brew," *New York Times,* Septermber 21, 2008.

your table at Jimmy's: Ibid.

"a cultureless city pervaded nevertheless by Mind": Saul Bellow, *Humboldt's Gift* (New York: Penguin, 1996), 69.

15 *"It was some sort of hotbed":* Beverly Solochek, "Daily Closeup," *New York Post,* November 10, 1970.

"As a result of this generous": Liebling, "Profiles: Second City: III — The Massacree."

"five to six hours a night": Sheldon Patinkin to author.

"Your entire grade": Ibid.

"There was so much hanging out": Mike Nichols to author.

16 *To cool off:* Johnson, *The Funniest One in the Room,* 14.

"I knew all about those guys": Mike Nichols to author.

17   *"Mike was an absolute genius"*: Sheldon Patinkin to author.
"I could fucking hear her breathing *hostilely"*: Mike Nichols to author.
"We loathed each other": Helen Markel, "Mike Nichols & Elaine May," *Redbook* (February 1961), 99.
"I think she fucked Sills": Mike Nichols to author.
"This self-supporting all-student": Sydney J. Harris, "Praise for U. of C. Players," *Chicago Daily News.*

18   *"I want you to meet Mike Nichols"*: Mike Nichols to author.
"Among the stories I had heard": Ibid.
"had everything": Sheldon Patinkin to author.
"Here," Nichols said: Mike Nichols to author.

19   *"was to have a theater"*: Lee Gallup Feldman, "A Critical Analysis of Improvisational Theater in the United States from 1955–1968," PhD diss., University of Denver, 1969.
"Don't go to Cleveland": David Shepherd to author.

20   *"I wanted them in my theater"*: Jeffrey Sweet, *Something Wonderful Right Away: An Oral History of the Second City and the Compass Players* (New York: Limelight, 1978), 5.
They agreed a new people's theater was necessary: David Shepherd to author.
but Shepherd objected: Ibid.

21   *"All Paul told us"*: Sheldon Patinkin to author.
"He was building": Ibid.
Shepherd observed, amazed: David Shepherd to author.
"I was good at that": Mike Nichols to author.

22   people I'd like to work with: Sweet, *Something Wonderful Right Away*, 138.
It was The Fervent Years: Mike Nichols, *Inside the Actors Studio*, season 3, episode 7, hosted by James Lipton, aired May 18, 1997.
it was a fairly long one: Mike Nichols to author.

23   *"Elaine's shortcomings"*: Ibid.
a hamburger with ketchup and cream cheese: Robert Rice, "A Tilted Insight," *New Yorker*, April 15, 1961, p. 47.
"just happened to be": Michael Braun, "Mike and Elaine: Veracity-Cum-Boffs," *Esquire*, October 1960.

24   Velvele Ganef: "Jack Berlin in Four Mason Appearances," *Hollywood Filmograph* 9, no. 22 (June 1, 1929), 15.
The Dance of Death: Ibid.
"carry-on bits": John Keating, "From Bistros to Broadway," *New York Times*, December 18, 1960.
"our people do not believe in breast binding": Thomas Thompson, "Whatever Happened to Elaine May?," *Life*, July 28, 1967, p. 54B.
surplus coffins: Sidney Fields, "In Mama's Footsteps," *New York Daily News*, December 19, 1972.
"extremely educated": Gordon Cotler, "For the Love of Mike — and Elaine," *New York Times*, May 24, 1959.
"it was as a writer": Mike Nichols to author.
"I always learn the same thing": Ibid.

25 *"We analyzed voraciously"*: Ibid.

"In a comedy, as in life": Robin Updike, "Elaine May on Comedy: That's a Laugh and a Half," *Seattle Times*, September 24, 1997.

Oh boy: Mike Nichols to author.

A few months later: David Shepherd to author.

"simpler forms than those of the contemporary theater": Janet Coleman, *The Compass: The Improvisational Theatre That Revolutionized American Comedy* (Chicago: University of Chicago Press, 1991), 47.

26 *"What's a scenario play?"*: Ibid., 86.

Bowen called it Enterprise: Ibid., 87.

Greenwich Village Howard Johnson's: Ibid., 255.

"I was fired when somebody": Guy Flatley, "A Day in the Country with Mike Nichols," *People*, 1976, available at *Movie Crazed* (blog), http://www.moviecrazed.com/outpast/mikenichols.html.

"One night": Mike Nichols, "A Show Soliloquy: Mike Nichols and the Midas Touch," *Show: The Magazine of the Arts* 5 (March 1965), 32.

crushed crackers and ketchup: Rice, "A Tilted Insight," 60.

27 *"Every moment must be physically comprehensible"*: Nichols, "A Show Soliloquy," 33.

Philco Television Playhouse: Ibid.

Elaine would bring the typewriter into bed: Sheldon Patinkin to author.

28 *David Shepherd played Sills:* David Shepherd to author.

("I do think our politics"): Sheldon Patinkin to author.

"I don't know why they're laughing": David Shepherd to author.

No one, least of all him: Carol Sills to author.

Shepherd invited Spolin: David Shepherd to author.

2. 1955–1956

29 *a hole they literally knocked in the wall:* Coleman, *The Compass*, 98.

Hyde Park was still "experimental": Sheldon Patinkin to author.

30 *"I was going on something"*: Sweet, *Something Wonderful Right Away*, 6.

"I want to have a 'Living Newspaper'": Ibid., 28.

"The idea": Ibid., 31.

air conditioner broke down: Coleman, *The Compass*, 101.

31 *"a man who takes more words"*: William Manchester, *The Glory and the Dream: A Narrative History of America 1932–1972*, vol. 2 (New York: Little, Brown, 1974), 580.

"A vast hush had settled": Ibid., 576.

"None of us had seen or heard anything on TV": Sheldon Patinkin to author.

"We were the first people on stage": Paul Sills and R. G. Davis, "A Dialogue," *Yale/Theatre* 5, no. 2 (1973), 26.

32 *"Just go to the people"*: Ibid.

Barbara, a local teenager: Barbara Harris to author.

she was mopping closer to the stage: Coleman, *The Compass*, 60.

"When you watched her": Mike Nichols to author.

33 *He missed them, his old company:* Ibid.

a Victrola on the floor: Barbara Harris to author.

"Improvise?" he asked: Mike Nichols to author.

"But, Paul": Ibid.

artisans modified performances: Natalie Crohn Schmitt, "Improvisation in the Commedia dell'Arte in Its Golden Age: Why, What, How," *Renaissance Drama*, n.s., 38 (2010), 225–49.

34   *"What about Elaine?"*: Mike Nichols to author.

"She only had to touch": David Shepherd to author.

"I wanted to explore more Elaine and me": Mike Nichols to author.

35   *"Why are you pointing your finger at me?"*: Mike Nichols, in *Becoming Mike Nichols*, directed by Douglas McGrath (HBO Documentary Films, 2016), DVD.

Lake Michigan: Sweet, *Something Wonderful Right Away*, 68.

How could anyone rehearse spontaneity?: Mike Nichols to author.

Kent Micronite: Sweet, *Something Wonderful Right Away*, 51.

"we talked and debated": Mike Nichols to author.

shouting around a table: David Shepherd to author.

"The Kafka scene": Mike Nichols to author.

36   *He put his voice in his nose*: Ibid.

"The stuff never stopped coming out of her": Ibid.

"Darling, you just walked through my Noguchi": Nichols, *Becoming Mike Nichols*.

"My impulse to learn from Elaine": Mike Nichols to author.

"only sort of for a minute": Joan Juliet Buck, "Live Mike," *Vanity Fair* (June 1994).

37   *a dramatic improvisation*: Nichols, *Becoming Mike Nichols*.

"When you have to make things up": John Keating, "From Bistros to Broadway," *New York Times*, December 18, 1960.

"Where Elaine and I really met most passionately": Mike Nichols to Alice Arlen, "Mr. Success," *Interview*, December 1988, p. 121.

"But when we got here": Ibid.

innumerable fights and infidelities: Galloway, "Director Mike Nichols."

"a nightmare of accusation": Lahr, "Making It Real."

started the taking of pills: Ibid.

"were invaders": Mike Nichols to author.

38   *"Let's do a scene about two teenagers"*: Ibid.

"What we did": Mike Nichols to Alice Arlen, "Mr. Success," 121.

"It wasn't that Elaine pulled me out of myself": Mike Nichols to author.

"Elaine and I had a rule": Clifford Terry, "Who's Afraid of Virginia Woolf, Richard Burton, Liz Taylor, or Even Hollywood, California? Not Director Mike Nichols," *Chicago Tribune*, July 3, 1966.

39   *David Shepherd, suddenly*: David Shepherd to author.

"I forgot all about the audience": Sweet, *Something Wonderful Right Away*, 9.

Thornton Wilder's The Matchmaker: Mike Nichols to author.

40   *"There were little moments"*: Robert Morse to author.

"That was the best thing": Mike Nichols to author.

41   *"She respects the play"*: Ibid.

"It was thought crass to graduate": Sweet, *Something Wonderful Right Away*, 90.

snuck into the women's dorm: Coleman, *The Compass*, 9.

"number one": Mike Nichols to author.

"would leap first": Ibid.

come up to Chicago and audition: Sweet, *Something Wonderful Right Away*, 138.

42 *"I began to think of myself as Jewish"*: Stephen E. Kercher, *Revel with a Cause: Liberal Satire in Postwar America* (Chicago: University of Chicago Press, 2006), 474.

"I really didn't know what to do up there": Ibid.

What they saw: Barbara Harris to author.

43 *polished revue-style entertainment*: David Shepherd to author.

"In the American culture": Paul Sills and Charles L. Mee Jr., "The Celebratory Occasion," *Tulane Drama Review* 9, no. 2 (Winter 1964), 167–81.

"was leaving the community": Ibid.

44 *"Hey guys"*: Shelley Berman to author.

"It was a whole new idea": Lahr, "Making It Real," 268.

"The next time you fuck me up on stage": Coleman, *The Compass*, 164.

3. 1956–1959

45 *as fascination*: Dickson Terry, "Let's Face It: Beards," *St. Louis Post-Dispatch*, November 23, 1958.

($34,000): Kliph Nesteroff, "An Interview with Theodore J. Flicker," *Classic Television Showbiz* (blog), December 3, 2014, http://classicshowbiz.blogspot.com/2014/12/an-interview-with-theodore-j-flicker.html.

Joining forces: David Shepherd to Ted Flicker, July 11, 1957, Flicker Collection, USC, Box 2.

And where, Flicker wondered: Barbara Flicker to author.

46 *"Look at my rabbit"*: Nesteroff, "An Interview with Theodore J. Flicker."

"He made the audience his ally": Ibid.

"the cardinal sin of improvisation": Ibid.

They needed rules: Ibid.

Collecting the more successful scenarios: David Shepherd to author.

"If I succeed": Shepherd to Spolin, December 8, 1955, Spolin Papers, Northwestern University, Box 6, Folder 20.

floorless Volkswagen: Johnson, *The Funniest One in the Room*, 65.

47 *"Ted's idea"*: Coleman, *The Compass*, 215.

"It was Del": Ted Flicker, "Some Fragments of Memory," *Performink* 11, no. 31 (March 12, 1999).

The scenarios, Del agreed, were total bullshit: Coleman, *The Compass*, 214.

Flicker impressed upon Close: Ibid., 215.

Lights up!: Myles Standish, "Compass Players Act in a Rococo Barroom," *St. Louis Post-Dispatch*, April 7, 1957.

49 *"emerge burning with humiliation"*: Sweet, *Something Wonderful Right Away*, 141.

"most rewarding theatrical experience": Ted Flicker to "Harold," June 27, 1957, Flicker Collection, USC, Box 2, Folder 5.

"Isn't this a beautiful first wedding?": Coleman, *The Compass*, 219.

Missouri made Elaine queasy: Elaine May to Ted Flicker, undated letter, Flicker Collection, USC, Box 2, Folder 5.

What if, Flicker suggested, they came to St. Louis: Flicker to Elaine May, Del Close, Nancy Ponder, and Severn Darden, October 7, 1957, Flicker Collection, USC, Box 2, Folder 5.

"I shall take what I want from COMPASS": Ted Flicker to Severn Darden, October 16, 1957, Flicker Collection, USC, Box 2.

he urged Mike and Elaine to be patient: Flicker to Mike Nichols, August 25, 1957, Flicker Collection, USC, Box 2, Folder 5.

"Am very glad Elaine and Mike": David Shepherd to Ted Flicker, undated letter, Flicker Collection, USC, Box 2.

50 Flicker had one of two bedrooms: Classic Television Showbiz (blog), "An Interview with Theodore J. Flicker," December 3, 2014.

They worked out a plan: Ted Flicker to "Harold," June 27, 1957, Flicker Collection, USC, Box 2, Folder 5.

"This is not as exciting": Ibid.

"almost every aspect of manufactured mass thinking": Ibid.

"We are testing new techniques": Ibid.

"is that we are not appealing": Ibid.

"the most talented girl": Ibid.

51 Every morning at 4411 Westminster Place: Sweet, Something Wonderful Right Away, 160–61, and Coleman, The Compass, 225.

"You can't imagine the excitement": Ted Flicker to "Harold," June 27, 1957, Flicker Collection, USC, Box 2, Folder 5.

Sarah Vaughan: Mike Nichols to author.

52 "You can't plan jazz": Ibid.

Del began experimenting: Johnson, The Funniest One in the Room, 54.

Del and Mike clashed: Mike Nichols to author.

"It is so easy to go out": Kleinfeld, "Del Close," 146.

"perceptions of reality": Ibid.

"The entire history of improvisational theater": Coleman, The Compass, 231.

53 "Under Elaine's direction": Del Close to Ted Flicker, undated letter, Flicker Collection, USC, Box 2.

"She could explore": Mike Nichols to author.

made Mike more jealous: Ibid.

"Where does a girl get laid": Nesteroff, "An Interview with Theodore J. Flicker."

And he always would be: Charna Halpern to author.

Paul Sills tried: Shepherd to Flicker, July 18, 1957, Flicker Collection, Box 2, Folder 5.

54 "The air was filled with pompous personages": Daniel Belgrad, The Culture of Spontaneity: Improvisation and the Arts in Postwar America (Chicago: University of Chicago Press, 1998), 198, n.10.

Between bites of Stroganoff and borscht: Rice, "A Tilted Insight," 70.

"a set of ad-libbed little skits": Nichols, Becoming Mike Nichols.

"I didn't laugh": Robert Wool, "Mike and Elaine: Mirrors to Our Madness," Look (June 21, 1960), 46–52.

When the coffee came: Nichols, Becoming Mike Nichols.

"Why don't you become my manager?": Jack Rollins to Betsy Borns, "Jack Rollins," Interview (September 1985).

55 "They improvise, Jack": Mike Nichols to author.

"My god," he thought: Mike Nichols, in "Mike Nichols and Elaine May — Take Two,"

American Masters, season 10, episode 5, directed by Phillip Schopper, aired May 22, 1996 (Eagle Rock Entertainment).

56 *"We weren't frightened":* Betty Etter, "Nichols & May, Unlimited," *Radio TV Mirror,* July 1958.

"It was bizarre": Mike Nichols to author.

Mike's one suit: Etter, "Nichols & May, Unlimited."

"They were totally adventurous": Jack Rollins, in "Mike Nichols and Elaine May — Take Two," *American Masters.*

"What is it?": Kashner, "Who's Afraid of Nichols & May?," audio recording accompanying article, VanityFair.com.

"You can open in two weeks": Etter, "Nichols & May, Unlimited."

seventy dollars: Ibid.

"You can fill in down at the Village Vanguard": Ibid.

"Skip them. I'm ready": Kashner, "Who's Afraid of Nichols & May?"

57 *"under and around":* Mike Nichols, *Inside the Actors Studio,* season 3, episode 7, hosted by James Lipton, aired May 18, 1997.

"What is this scene we're discovering really about?": Peter Applebome, "Always Asking, What Is This Really About?," *New York Times,* April 25, 1999.

"Hello, Michael. This is your mother speaking": Mike Nichols to author.

"she screamed with laughter": Ibid.

"There it was!": Ibid.

58 *"Each of our mothers thought":* Susan King, "Graduate Degree," *Los Angeles Times,* June 9, 2010.

"Where's Del?": Paul Mazursky to author.

the psychoanalyst Theodor Reik: Johnson, *The Funniest One in the Room,* 61.

59 *"the most humorless period in American history":* Kercher, *Revel with a Cause,* 4.

"You get your nose rubbed into this solemnity": Ibid., 95.

"There are no Marx Brothers movies": Ibid., 348.

its "fifth freedom," the freedom to laugh: Ibid., 26.

"emasculation of American humor": Ibid., 52.

"It was the first time I had ever": Jules Feiffer to author.

"What do we do now?": Gavin Smith, "Of Metaphors and Purpose," *Film Comment,* May/June 1999.

"My name is Woody Allen": Betsy Borns, "Jack Rollins," *Interview,* September 1985.

60 *"were touching on some kind of truth":* Lahr, "Making It Real."

A month later, Allen returned: Borns, "Jack Rollins."

"we suggested he should consider trying to perform": Ibid.

six grand he'd earned: Johnson, *Something Wonderful Right Away,* 179.

4. 1959–1962

61 *Wong Cleaners and Dyers:* Bernie Sahlins, *Days and Nights at the Second City: A Memoir with Notes on Staging Review Theatre* (Chicago: Ivan R. Dee, 2001), 24.

The Mob watched: Ibid., 38.

stapled carpet to the floor: Sweet, *Something Wonderful Right Away,* 180.

To find the dressing room: Sheldon Patinkin to author.

bentwood chairs: Sahlins, *Days and Nights at the Second City,* 37.

62 *"sexy about the look of the place"*: Sweet, *Something Wonderful Right Away*, 54.
"Severn, it's Paul. I'm doing this thing": Carol Sills to author.
funniest woman Sills had ever seen: Ibid.
"I didn't know what was going on": Sheldon Patinkin, *The Second City: Backstage at the World's Greatest Comedy Theater* (Naperville, Ill.: Sourcebooks, 2000), 33.
"We weren't particularly definite in our plans": Sweet, *Something Wonderful Right Away*, 159.

63 *"Most of the time," one said*: Bill (Allaudin) Mathieu to author.
"North Side Story," by Elaine May: Les Brown, "Stung by Off-B'way Try Last Year, Chi Going in for Cabaret-Legit," *Variety*, November 18, 1959.
the Common Man: Sheldon Patinkin to author.

64 *"precise social observation"*: Philip Roth, *Conversations with Philip Roth*, edited by George J. Searles (Jackson: University Press of Mississippi, 1992), xi.
"planned every second": Coleman, *The Compass*, 259.
your coat to Melinda Dillon: Mike Thomas, *The Second City Unscripted: Revolution and Revelation at the World-Famous Comedy Theatre* (New York: Villard, 2009), 7.

65 *"The success of the early Second City company"*: Bill Mathieu to author.
"the declining skill of satire is kept alive": Thomas, *The Second City Unscripted*, 5.
"the best satire to be seen in the U.S.A. today": "Playboy After Hours — Theater," *Playboy* (December 1961), 16–18.
"I practically lived at Second City": Thomas, *The Second City Unscripted*, 9.
"And it became, in those days, the thing to do": Ibid., 8.
Ted Flicker and Elaine May were sitting: Feldman, "A Critical Analysis of Improvisational Theater in the United States."
be individuals together: Joan Darling to author.

66 *Paul Sills moved his mother to Chicago*: Carol Sills to author.
He played the Gate of Horn: "Gate of Horn, Chicago," *Weekly Variety*, August 12, 1959.
"the inherent perversity of objects": Kleinfeld, "Del Close," 1987.
about the drugs: peyote: Johnson, *The Funniest One in the Room*, 63.
"the best type personality for space travel": Wahls, "Del Close Is Way Out."
"a reality lubricant": Kleinfeld, "Del Close," 1987.
She gave him money: Johnson, *The Funniest One in the Room*, 143.
The Do-It-Yourself Psychoanalysis Kit: Johnson, *The Funniest One in the Room*, 73.
He turned her on to grass: Sweet, *Something Wonderful Right Away*, 144.
"disturbed his muse": Johnson, *The Funniest One in the Room*, 47.
Sahlins overlooked Del's legacy: Jane Sahlins to author.

67 *Motion Picture Daily*: *Motion Picture Daily*, January 13, 1960, 14.
"You cannot fail": "Mike & Elaine: 2 Kids with Some Grown Up Thoughts About TV," *Variety*, June 25, 1958.
"Elaine May has a wonderful motto": Barbara Gelb, "Mike Nichols: The Special Risks and Rewards of the Director's Art," *New York Times Magazine*, May 27, 1984.
"If I ever get organized": Margaret McManus, "TV's New Ad-Libbing Comedy Team," *Baltimore Sun*, August 10, 1958.
old slacks and sneakers: Edmund Wilson, "Bunny in Winter," *GQ*, February 1993.
"I understand you were born": Mel Gussow, "Mike Nichols: Director as Star," *Newsweek*, November 14, 1966.

"Because if I don't like the interviewer": Joyce Haber, "Elaine May Has a Thing on Not Talking to Press," *Los Angeles Times*, July 7, 1968.

"It's like that terrible feeling": Kevin M. Johnson, "Elaine May: 'Do You Mind Interviewing Me in the Kitchen?,'" *New York Times*, January 8, 1967.

Passionate and devoted analysands: Stephen Farber and Marc Green, *Hollywood on the Couch: A Candid Look at the Overheated Love Affair Between Psychiatrists and Moviemakers* (New York: William Morrow, 1993), 202.

68 *"Everything we've done"*: Gordon Cotler, "For the Love of Mike—and Elaine," *New York Times*, May 24, 1959.

"was in this particular case": Gavin Smith, "Of Metaphors and Purpose," *Film Comment*, May/June 1999.

drawing blood and real-life tears: Mike Nichols to author.

"I'm psychotic with fear": Mike Nichols, in *Becoming Mike Nichols*.

Theatergoers of late 1960: Alexander H. Cohen Papers, New York Public Library for the Performing Arts, Box 61, Folders 17 and 18.

69 *That night, October 8, 1960*: Ibid.

"When you do it every night": Mike Nichols, in *Becoming Mike Nichols*.

"Oh, could you possibly sing it": Ibid.

"best claim to greatness": Kercher, *Revel with a Cause*, 238.

"Take what?": "This Is 40: Judd Apatow & Mike Nichols Q&A," video capture date December 13, 2012, https://www.amazon.com/This-40-Judd-Apatow-Nichols/dp/BooL4ST68Y.

70 *"Satire is revenge"*: Kashner, "Who's Afraid of Nichols & May?"

the bathroom mirror: Alan Arkin, on *Kevin Pollak's Chat Show*, no. 158, October 14, 2012, https://www.youtube.com/watch?v=LTbezHCVdBo.

Hugo's, the hot dog stand: Alan Arkin to author.

"I wasn't loose enough": Alan Arkin, *An Improvised Life: A Memoir* (Cambridge, MA: Da Capo Press, 2011), 38.

"If you ever want a job": Alan Arkin to author.

"Making that call": Arkin, *An Improvised Life*, 39.

71 *"something solid out there"*: Ibid., xii.

"I had no interest in being myself": Ibid., 41.

"nervous Jewish mother": Sheldon Patinkin to author.

"a character that was serious": David Galligan, "Carol Burnett on Alan Arkin: 'I Love Him,'" *Hollywood Drama-Logue*, June 4, 1981.

"Then I found a body of characters": Alan Arkin to author.

"They were all unemployed": "Alan Arkin is Coming," *Life*, July 22, 1966, p. 33.

72 *"I don't mean to seem like a prude"*: Second City Archives, The Second City, Chicago.

"came out great": Sheldon Patinkin to author.

"took three weeks of screaming": Sweet, *Something Wonderful Right Away*, 234.

"I think Paul suffered": Sheldon Patinkin to author.

73 *"Where that idea came from"*: Arkin, *An Improvised Life*, 47.

"The truth of the matter is": Alan Arkin, on *Kevin Pollak's Chat Show*, no. 158, October 14, 2012, https://www.youtube.com/watch?v=CncBFKdL7oQ.

"They are those rare moments": Alan Arkin, *Halfway Through the Door: An Actor's Journey Towards the Self* (New York: Harper & Row, 1979), 5.

"When you do a show for a year": Mike Nichols to author.

"Form is the thing that interests me": Cecil Smith, "Mike Nichols' Midas Touch with Broadway Comedies," *Los Angeles Times,* December 26, 1965.

"I once saw a very rich man": "Interview with Mike Nichols," *Playboy,* June 1966.

74   *"This is fucking bullshit"*: Larry Hankin to author.

"Del had a problem": Ibid.

He fought Sahlins: Jane Sahlins to author.

"because assault in the sense": John Guare, "Comedy and Rage," *New Theater Review,* Spring 1988.

"Why do you want us to do": Ibid.

75   *"The issues are immaterial"*: Ibid.

born stand-up, Joan Rivers: Sheldon Patinkin to author.

"Del did not love women": Ibid.

"I have no idea why": Alan Myerson to author.

"It wasn't even an interview": Ibid.

"Del was a mythological figure": Larry Hankin to author.

"Del was also driven": Alan Myerson to author.

76   *"Del was becoming a director"*: Larry Hankin to author.

a thousand one-minute auditions: Nesteroff, "An Interview with Theodore J. Flicker."

"Do you want to improvise?": Joan Darling to author.

"instant theater": Nat Hentoff, "Instant Theater," *Reporter,* March 30, 1961.

"to find a form for improvisational theater": Ted Flicker to Howard Taubman, April 27, 1963, Flicker Collection, USC, Box 3, New York Premise Publicity.

"The Premise," he wrote: Ibid.

77   *"Dustin Hoffman tried out"*: Joan Darling to author.

"setup for the actors": Dustin Hoffman to author.

Scenes had to be short: Joan Darling to author.

"We are going to do three kinds": Ted Flicker to David M. Dorsen, June 1962, Flicker Collection, USC, Box 3, Folder 13.

"If we were in the middle": Joan Darling to author.

78   *parody of Paddy Chayefsky's* Marty: Jerry Talmer, "Theater: The Premise," *Village Voice,* January 1, 1960.

"We had to read every newspaper": Joan Darling to author.

"Being political": Ibid.

"They call out the names of people": William Wolf, "Off-Beat and Off-Broadway, Flicker's New Show Clicks," *Asbury Park Sunday Press,* December 18, 1960.

"They somehow liked seeing": Ted Flicker to Bernard Bralov, December 28, 1961, Flicker Collection, USC, Washington, DC, Premise Publicity, Box 3.

"Tom Aldredge did a composite": Joan Darling to author.

79   *"it's a writer's device"*: Buck Henry to author.

"and then, at the end": Ibid.

"Since Broadway got so square": John Crosby, "Celebrations and Coffee," *New York Herald Tribune,* January 30, 1961.

Harold Clurman, Tyrone Guthrie: Flicker Collection, USC, Washington, DC, Premise Publicity, Box 3.

"We saw Woody": Joan Darling to author.

"but we intended to be slicker": Buck Henry to author.

"I remember thinking": Ibid.

80 *"Del would tell us"*: Ibid.

"We were a growing community": Joan Darling to author.

"I can't believe what I'm seeing": Nesteroff, "An Interview with Theodore J. Flicker."

5. 1962–1963

81 *"It was as though"*: Kashner, "Who's Afraid of Nichols & May?," audio recording accompanying article, VanityFair.com.

"If things had been different": Mike Nichols to author.

The American sense of humor, Elaine sensed: Thomas Thompson, "Whatever Happened to Elaine May?," *Life*, July 28, 1967.

"dramatized, as no previous evidence has": Robert J. Landry, "JFK — Show Biz in Love," *Variety*, May 23, 1962.

82 *"I like you, Bobby"*: Kashner, "Who's Afraid of Nichols & May?," audio recording accompanying article, VanityFair.com.

"I would have gone on": Mike Nichols to author.

"We thought they wouldn't possibly": Joan Darling to author.

83 *"Do you have any objection"*: James Feron, "Quips on Kennedy Barred in London," *New York Times*, July 21, 1962.

threatened to send Her Majesty's troops: Leonard Harris, "Americans Defy British Censors," *New York World-Telegram and Sun*, April 6, 1963.

secretly submit scripts: Ibid.

"In view of the admission": James Feron, "Britain Curbing American Revue," *New York Times*, October 20, 1962.

Peter O'Toole: Joan Darling to author.

"I told him the best thing": Matt Fotis, *Longform Improvisation and American Comedy: The Harold* (New York: Palgrave Macmillan, 2014), 37.

"He was the only one allowed": Ed Sikov, *Mr. Strangelove: A Biography of Peter Sellers* (New York: Hyperion, 2002), 160.

84 *"They should have fled"*: Kevin Thomas, "Improvisation Advocate Tries to Turn On Actors," *Los Angeles Times*, June 22, 1967.

"If you make fun of Prime Minister Macmillan": Theodore J. Flicker, "Safe and Unsafe Satire at the Living Premise," *Daily Times*, July 27, 1963.

"Can it be": Kenneth Tynan, "Theater," *London Observer*, September 23, 1962.

"an open forum": Coleman, *The Compass*, 303.

"In the language of the Declaration": Kerry T. Burch, *Democratic Transformations: Eight Conflicts in the Negotiation of American Identity* (New York: Bloomsbury, 2002), 168.

"Because of the chemistry": Miles Davis, *Miles* (New York: Simon & Schuster, 2011), 221–22.

85 *"democratic mess"*: Kercher, *Revel with a Cause*, 486.

"His idea was that his body": Jack Helbig, "Friends and Coconspirators Recall the Crazed Career of an Improv Olympian," *Chicago Reader*, March 11, 1999.

Del's wife, Doris: Sheldon Patinkin to author.

Sheldon Patinkin raced: Ibid.

"It was pills": Ibid.

86 *"Del wanted to direct"*: Ibid.

"in every way a catastrophe": Mike Nichols to author.

"Cuts and revisions were": Sam Zolotow, "Role in Musical to Carol Burnett," *New York Times*, October 10, 1962.

Also whispering: Mike Nichols to author.

"Luckily my lawyer": Ibid.

"the Blob": Buck, "Live Mike."

87 *"Elaine gave me myself"*: Joseph Gelmis, "A Dolphin Among Directors," *Los Angeles Times*, December 16, 1973.

Blob in Jamaica: Buck, "Live Mike."

"Oh, Mikey, you are so good": Mike Nichols, interview with Stephen Galloway, "Director Mike Nichols on His 60-Year Career."

acetylene lamp: Kleinfeld, "Del Close."

"you've got to make this": Ibid.

"And I suddenly realized that we": Feldman, "A Critical Analysis of Improvisational Theater in the United States."

88 *most sensitive issue in American life?*: Flicker, "Safe and Unsafe Satire at the Living Premise."

"and Godfrey grabbed the handle": Buck Henry to author.

"would come out of the theater": Joan Darling to author.

"they turned me down": Leonard Harris, "Success Not Enough, Negro Actress Finds," *New York World-Telegram and Sun*, September 2, 1963.

"same difficulty with us": Joan Darling to author.

"It was Ted's idea": Ibid.

"I don't really know anything about Negroes": Jay Carr, "Geoffrey Cambridge Makes a Sentimental Journey," *New York Post*, September 4, 1963.

"like group analysis": Ibid.

89 *"It took a while"*: Joan Darling to author.

"This morning, I was shaken": Ted Flicker, Rehearsal Notes: May 4, 1963, Flicker Collection, USC, Box 2.

Flicker had them switch: Joan Darling to author.

"The color line": Ted Flicker, Rehearsal Notes: May 7, 1963, Flicker Collection, USC, Box 2.

"If you do it right": Joan Darling to author.

with a kiss: Scripts, The Living Premise, Flicker Collection, USC, Box 1.

"When Mrs. Kennedy": Ibid.

90 *"If you don't stop playing"*: Flicker, "Safe and Unsafe Satire at the Living Premise."

"Real dramatic integration": Ibid.

"And we all became": Joan Darling to author.

"the running character joke": Marcia Seligson, "Hollywood's Hottest Writer — Buck Henry," *New York Times*, July 19, 1970.

"We're doing King Lear *here"*: Nichols.

"to create an atmosphere": Paul Gardner, "News of the Rialto," *New York Times*, September 8, 1963.

"The whole thing": William Glover, "Mike Nichols: Performer Turned Stage Director," *Bridgeport Post*, September 20, 1964.

"I wanted to do comedy": Mike Nichols to Elaine May, "Elaine May in Conversation with Mike Nichols," Walter Reade Theater, New York City, July 2006.

91 *For the first time in years*: Mike Nichols to author.

He directed slightly and invisibly: Jules Feiffer to author.

"Mordant": Larry Turman to author.

"a nervous comedy": Ibid.

"The reason I couldn't get": Ibid.

"I thought it was oozing": Ibid.

92 *the Nichols and May manner*: Ibid.

John Brent called Alan Myerson: Alan Myerson to author.

civilization is over: Carol Sills to author.

"We and everybody": Ibid.

Billy ran to the drugstore: Rich Cohen, "What's So Funny?" *Rolling Stone*, October 2, 2003.

93 *"That was when television"*: Ibid.

"But I don't think we": Stuart W. Little, "Elaine May, An Improviser," *New York Herald Tribune*, April 27, 1964.

Second City's most apprehensive audience: Sheldon Patinkin to author.

6. 1963–1967

94 *"Bernie," Patinkin said*: Ibid.

95 *"After the [JFK] assassination"*: Ibid.

"But I'm not political": Fred Willard to author.

96 *"I've always admired people"*: Jenelle Riley, "Fair-Weather Fred," *Backstage West*, July 24, 2003.

"I like to play the guy that": Joe Rhodes, "Second Wind for a Professional Oaf," *New York Times*, February 24, 2008.

"Bernie [Sahlins] and I": Sheldon Patinkin to author.

Robert Klein: Fred Willard to author.

Start big: Sheldon Patinkin to author.

97 *"Is Satire Futile?"*: Talk of the Town, "Over and Out," *New Yorker*, December 19, 1964.

the best improvisational work: Mike Nichols in Conversation at MoMA, April 18, 2009.

"Pinter especially struck me": David Mamet, interview with Rick Kogan, Chicago Public Library, October 13, 2006.

98 *"Let's take a sleigh ride"*: Ira Nadel, *David Mamet: A Life in the Theater* (New York: Palgrave Macmillan, 2008), 29.

"people who you can listen to": Daniel Schweiger, "Fred Willard Makes a Comedic Touchdown in 'Back to You,'" *Venice*, September 2007.

"Miss Jones, take a letter": Second City Archives, the Second City, Chicago.

"Okay, Willard, get up there": Fred Willard to author.

99 *"Paul," Willard began*: Ibid.

"That was a big change": Sheldon Patinkin to author.

"friendly satire": Kashner, "Who's Afraid of Nichols & May?," audio recording accompanying article, VanityFair.com.

"I had to fire her": Sheldon Patinkin to author.

"She began modifying many": Eric Forsberg, "Josephine Raciti Forsberg: An Important Part of Chicago Theater History," paper presented at Columbia College Theater Symposium, Chicago, May 20, 2011.

To Sahlins, funny was funny: Jane Sahlins to author.

Elaine May was at a party: Mike Nichols to author.

100 *Carl Reiner let her improvise:* Thompson, "Whatever Happened to Elaine May?"

"my typing finger needed a rest": Marjory Adams, "Film Star Elaine May Is Different," *Boston Globe,* August 15, 1967.

101 *Mike Nichols, and his new girlfriend:* Mike Nichols to author.

"But is he perfect?": Bruce Weber, "Mike Nichols, Urbane Director Loved by Crowds and Critics, Dies at 83," *New York Times,* November 20, 2014.

"Everything felt different": Mike Nichols to author.

"See?" May said: Ibid.

"Life had renewed": Ibid.

"Will you come sit with me?": Sheldon Patinkin to author.

102 *"I sat with him":* Ibid.

"Del was so bipolar": Bill Mathieu to author.

lived at 452 Webster: Ibid.

their first date: Carol Sills to author.

"a jungle gym of junk": Bill Mathieu to author.

104 *"Paul didn't want to be successful":* Mike Nichols to author.

every Saturday in Lincoln Park: Carol Sills to author.

"With the games": Leslie Bennetts, "If It Works, It's Theater. If It Doesn't . . . ," *New York Times,* September 8, 1986.

105 *"Paul," he replied:* Mike Nichols to author.

Alan Myerson married Second City's: Alan Myerson to author.

107 *"Well, what do I have to do?":* Norman Jewison to author.

"Put this on," he said: Ibid.

108 *"a smart, funny, and lucid improv":* Ibid.

"Constantin Mevedenko": Mel Gussow, "Alan Arkin: The Matchless Maskmaker," *Holiday,* October 1966.

"There's not a line in the film": Ibid.

109 *"I have felt that Mike tends":* "Fun and Games with George and Martha — Journal 1965–1966," Ernest Lehman Collection, Academy of Motion Picture Arts and Sciences Margaret Herrick Library, Box 2, Folder 8, p. 9.

On July 20, 1965: Ibid., 125.

"Did you hear me say Action?!": Ibid., 126.

"My hope," he said: Philip K. Scheuer, "Nichols: The Whiz Kid Whizzes Onward," *Los Angeles Times,* February 5, 1967.

110 *a version of Elaine:* Mike Nichols to author.

"After TW3 we all interrelated": Buck Henry to Steve Lafreniere, "Buck Henry," *Vice,* October 1, 2010.

"one doesn't ask": Buck Henry to author.

"I thought Buck": Seligson, "Hollywood's Hottest Writer."

"You should read this book": Buck Henry to author.

111 *"It's much more useful for me":* Kleinfeld, "Del Close."

"the purpose of psychoanalysis?": Del Close Improv Workshop Notes, assembled by Joey Novick, Workshop of October 11, 1968, http://c3467x.com/wp-content/uploads/2014/03/Applied-Improv-Network-Del-Close-Notes.pdf.

112   *"was really urging you to try"*: Helbig, "Friends and Coconspirators."

     his own experiments in longform: Alan Myerson to author.

113   *"Anything can happen at any time"*: Bill Mathieu to author.

     "The ghost": Ibid.

     "We knew we had something": Ibid.

114   *can of apricot juice:* Ibid.

     "I was deeply offended": Ibid.

     "How about Harold?": Ibid.

115   *"I want this to be about not becoming"*: Mike Nichols, in conversation with the *New York Times, TimesTalks,* live stream, May 7, 2012, http://original.livestream.com/nytimes/video?clipId=pla_b3bbca7b-a0ff-48fc-aa6d-2619b51a7a64.

     "Hanley had no humor": Larry Turman to author.

     "And none of them": Mike Nichols to author.

     Buck Henry empathized with Benjamin: Buck Henry to author.

     "Working with Buck is very like": Betty Rollin, "Mike Nichols: Wizard of Wit," *Look,* April 2, 1968.

7. 1967–1968

116   *"You can't play it"*: Mike Nichols, in conversation with Chip McGrath, *TimesTalks,* live stream, May 7, 2012, http://original.livestream.com/nytimes/video?clipId=pla_b3bbca7b-a0ff-48fc-aa6d-2619b51a7a64.

     "goy after goy": "This Is 40: Judd Apatow and Mike Nichols Q&A."

     "He [Benjamin] needed": Mike Nichols in Conversation at MoMA.

117   *"I'm not right for this part"*: Sam Kashner, "Here's to You, Mr. Nichols: The Making of The Graduate," *Vanity Fair,* March 2008.

     actor David Warner: Dustin Hoffman to author.

     "Arkin was the first director": Ibid.

     I'm not supposed to be in movies: Ibid.

     "Did you see this week's Time magazine?": Kashner, "Here's to You, Mr. Nichols."

     "he's Jewish inside": Dustin Hoffman to author.

118   *"Do you think you could make him"*: Ibid.

     "What am I doing here?": Lynn Stalmaster to author.

     "Don't be nervous": Dustin Hoffman to author.

119   *"We were losing big to television"*: Sheldon Patinkin to author.

     "I want everyone to bring": Murphy Dunne to author.

     The first time social worker Gary Austin: Gary Austin to author.

121   *"Benjamin's twenty-one years old"*: Dustin Hoffman to author.

123   *"Now listen," Nichols barked:* Gold Standard screening of *The Graduate.*

     "That's usually the best work": Ibid.

     "I got my feeling for people": Leonard J. Berry, "Mike: He Applies 'The Nichols Touch' to What May Be the Most Eagerly Awaited Film of This Generation," *Boston Globe,* December 7, 1969.

124   *tale of the night before:* Alan Myerson to author.

"*more vigorous enforcement of all of our drug laws*": Deborah Kalb, Gerhard Peters, and John T. Wolley, *State of the Union: Presidential Rhetoric from Woodrow Wilson to George W. Bush* (Washington, D.C.: CQ Press, 2007), 648.

"*We're going to do what happened last night*": Alan Myerson to author.

127 "*It seems to me that it is important*": Bob Thomas, "By Mike Nichols: Repertory Company Eyed," *Austin Statesman*, February 10, 1967.

"*I plan to cast everyone*": Ibid.

"*I am so sick of hearing*": Ibid.

"*a bar where we could put*": Laurie Ann Gruhn, "Interview: Paul Sills Reflects on Story Theatre," *Drama Theater Teacher* 5, no. 2 (Winter 1993).

128 "*This 'invisible inner self'*": Ibid.

"*You can't reject outside authority*": Aretha Sills to author.

improviser Cordis Heard: Cordis Heard to author.

"*You can use the text*": Ibid.

"*I don't want your psychology*": Ibid.

"*Your political consciousness*": Ibid.

"*There are some guys*": Dennis Cunningham to author.

129 "*Essentially what we're going*": Abbie Hoffman on Yippie Tactics — 1968, video, https://www.youtube.com/watch?v=2oujcg_Tifw.

"*It's all conceived as a total theater*": Abbie Hoffman on the 1968 Democratic Convention, video, https://www.youtube.com/watch?v=gcXKeuOW3lQ.

130 "*We were all against Vietnam*": Sheldon Patinkin to author.

a barracks of sandbags: Sweet, *Something Wonderful Right Away*, 359.

transformed the theater's beer garden: Carol Sills to author.

Abbie Hoffman, for a flash: Eugenie Ross-Leming to author.

131 "*This city and the military machine*": David Farber, *Chicago '68* (Chicago: University of Chicago Press, 1988), 196.

132 "*Democracy is no good*": Judy Jacklin Belushi, *Samurai Widow* (New York: Carroll & Graf, 1990), 24.

Belushi had radicalized: Judy Jacklin Belushi to author.

"*so-called most radical*": Ibid.

hit him in the ribs: Bob Woodward, *Wired: The Short Life and Fast Times of John Belushi* (New York: Simon & Schuster, 1984), 41.

"*Theater — guerilla theater*": Jerry Rubin, Address to the Yippie Convention, Great Speeches of the 20th Century, video, https://www.youtube.com/watch?v=-TphuwosYrQ.

Inside the Hilton Hotel bar: Jules Feiffer to author.

133 "*I can't believe how much tear gas hurts*": Woodward, *Wired*, 41.

8. 1969–1972

138 "*I don't need an actor*": Joe Flaherty to author.

"*[This is] a chance*": Joe Flaherty, interview hosted by Mark Warzecha, Second City and Beyond, Los Angeles, July 30, 2008, video, https://www.youtube.com/watch?v=UJd_ear6Dak.

"*pass to the open man*": Jim Fisher to author.

139 "*I would say in the first month*": Mike Sacks, *And Here's the Kicker: Conversations with 21 Top Humor Writers on Their Craft* (Cincinnati: Writers Digest, 2009), 40.

"*Everybody fought to be*": Joe Flaherty to author.

Flaherty and Remis froze: Ibid.

"*adjusting egos*": "A Bit of a Chat with Ken Plume and Joe Flaherty," *A Bit of a Chat* (podcast), January 27, 2013, A Site Called Fred, http://asitecalledfred.com/2013/01/27/joe-flaherty-ken-plume-chat/.

140 "*I guess I'm pretty much*": Ibid.

"*We worked so well*": Jim Fisher to author.

"*we were radical*": Donna McCrohan, *The Second City: A Backstage History of Comedy's Hottest Troupe* (New York: Perigee, 1987), 169.

Bernie Sahlins took note: Jane Sahlins to author.

"*The previous bunch*": Jim Fisher to author.

141 "*In Jules's cartoons*": Sheldon Patinkin to author.

"*They got the paraphrase completely*": Arkin, *An Improvised Life*, 99.

"*a real ensemble*": Tom Burke, "Feiffer: If at First You . . . ," *New York Times*, January 26, 1969.

142 "*If you have ever experienced*": Clive Barnes, "Reappraisal: The Comic Horror of Little Murders," *New York Times*, October 2, 1969.

"*what we thought was an improv*": Christopher Guest on *Kevin Pollack's Chat Show*, no. 113, October 13, 2012, https://www.youtube.com/watch?v=CncBFKdL7oQ.

"*We went up to see her*": Ibid.

"*I knew something was off*": Christopher Guest to Charlie Rose, *Charlie Rose*, aired May 12, 2003, PBS.

143 "*If I'm in the room*": Harold Ramis to Jake Jarvi, *Sheridan Road Magazine*, February 26, 2014, audio recording, https://www.youtube.com/watch?v=tMG7om-GVgU.

her depression: Ibid.

"*We tell kids*": Ibid.

"*stand up for the little guy*": Harold Ramis, interviewed by Eric Spitznagel, *Believer*, March 2006.

fighter pilot: Harold Ramis, Jack Oakie Lecture on Comedy in Film, audio recording, AMPAS Margaret Herrick Library, Beverly Hills, CA.

"*Suddenly*," he said: Ibid.

"*a great lesson in comedy*": Harold Ramis lecture, Chicago Humanities Festival, November 4, 2009, http://chicagohumanities.org/events/2009/laughter/2009-ramis-history-film-comedy.

144 "*I could see elements*": Ramis interview, *Believer*.

their own shit: Brett Martin, "Harold Ramis Gets the Last Laugh," *GQ*, July 2009.

masturbating in front of her family: YouTube video, Harold Ramis shared insights on Jewish Creativity *Rosh 5770 @ Aitz Hayim, https://www.youtube.com/watch?v=xSloTBCx424.

Second City's thirty-seventh revue: Second City Archives, the Second City, Chicago.

145 "*We bombed*": Thomas, *The Second City Unscripted*, 42.

"*totally authoritarian, dictatorially oppressive*": Jules Feiffer, Tom Hayden, and Jon Wiener, *Conspiracy in the Streets: The Extraordinary Trial of the Chicago Eight* (New York: New Press, 2006).

"*Abbie*," Fisher recalled: Jim Fisher to author.

146 "*They are not as astringent*": William Leonard, "Sweet Simplicity at Second City," *Chicago Tribune*, March 5, 1970.

147　*"PTA"*: Second City Archives, Second City, Chicago.

"I loved writing and performing": Ramis interview, *Believer.*

"Why are you leaving, Harold?": Joe Flaherty to author.

sneak-preview screening of MASH: Peter Biskind, "Who's Afraid of the Big Bad Wolf?," *Premiere*, March 1994.

"I almost passed out": Mike Nichols on Charlie Rose, October 19, 2011, https://charlie rose.com/videos/13356.

148　*"Everything that* Catch *couldn't have"*: Mike Nichols, on "Commentary," *Catch-22*, directed by Mike Nichols (Paramount Pictures, 1970), DVD.

Nichols himself wondered: Sweet, *Something Wonderful Right Away*, 86.

"not about human behavior": Carol Kramer, "Catch-22: 'It's Really About Dying,' Says Writer Buck Henry," *Chicago Tribune*, June 28, 1970.

"about the fact that heterosexual": Jules Feiffer to author.

Confessions *"startled me"*: David Fear, "Mike Nichols on *The Graduate*: The Director of This 1967 Classic Reflects on Its Making," *Time Out New York*, April 10, 2012.

"Well, you've got to do this": Mike Nichols, "Mike Nichols & Jason Reitman Talk Carnal Knowledge," Film Society of Lincoln Center, Walter Reade Theater, 2011.

"But Paul didn't think theater": Carol Sills to author.

149　*Nichols saw Sills's point:* Mike Nichols to author.

"So I took a leave of absence": Kleinfeld, "Del Close."

"I knew the sixties": Ibid.

"jumping around like a chicken": Joe Flaherty to author.

"What a ball buster": Ibid.

150　*"I never wanted to be a director"*: Michael Rivlin, "Elaine May: Too Tough for Hollywood?," *Millimeter*, October 1975.

"I pitched very hard": Rachel Abramowitz, *Is That a Gun in Your Pocket?: Women's Experience of Power in Hollywood* (New York: Random House, 2000), 61.

"Listen," Koch said: Andrew Tobias, "Elaine May: A New Film, But Not a New Leaf," *New York*, December 6, 1976.

Matthau's apartment: Wayne Warga, "'California Suite,' an Exercise in Spontaneity," *Los Angeles Times*, May 21, 1978.

151　*"I want to do it again"*: Abramowitz, *Is That a Gun in Your Pocket?*, 61.

"You make the crew nervous": Rivlin, "Elaine May: Too Tough," 17.

"And when they found this out": Elaine May, "Elaine May in Conversation with Mike Nichols," Film Society of Lincoln Center, Walter Reade Theater, 2006. Published in *Film Comment*, July/August 2006, https://www.filmcomment.com/article/elaine-may -in-conversation-with-mike-nichols/.

"The first day," Koch recalled: Abramowitz, *Is That a Gun in Your Pocket?*, 61.

"Elaine does [all those takes]": Ibid., 62.

Mrs. Hitler: Elaine May, "Elaine May in Conversation with Mike Nichols," 2006.

twenty takes: Betty Baer, "If Mike Can, Elaine May," *Look.*

"She's basically improvisational": Army Archerd, "Just for Variety," *Variety*, August 22, 1969.

152　*the power spot:* Ramis, Jack Oakie Lecture on Comedy in Film.

"He made us all look good": Martin, "Harold Ramis Gets the Last Laugh."

"too lost in their own dramas": Judith Belushi and Tanner Colby, *Belushi: A Biography* (New York: Rugged Land, 2005), 31.

"*Look, Mom and Dad*": Ibid.

"*By the time he was four*": Ibid., 17.

153 "*When I was a little boy*": Debba Kunk, interview with Harold Ramis, *On TV*, June 1982.

"*This*," he said: Judy Jacklin Belushi to author.

"*She came in through the bathroom window*": Belushi and Colby, *Belushi: A Biography*, 32.

"*As much as John loved being*": Ibid., 8.

154 "*Television and rock 'n' roll*": Michael Segell, "John Belushi: Every Night Live," *Cosmopolitan*, December 1981.

"*From our beginnings*": Sahlins, *Days and Nights*, 92.

"*I'm just having so much*": Joe Flaherty to author.

"*Flaherty*," *Belushi would say*: Marshall Rosenthal, "Stamped with His Own Brando," *Chicago Daily News*, April 18, 1972.

155 "*He made a fugue*": Eugenie Ross-Leming to author.

"*We respected the rule*": Jim Fisher to author.

"*John* looked *funny*": Joe Flaherty to author.

Kissinger, he said: Ramis, Jack Oakie Lecture on Comedy in Film.

156 "*always fit*": Jim Fisher to author.

Rabbi Dithers: Joe Flaherty to author.

"*You all set, Harold?*": Ibid.

he really could keep his head: Erica Ramis to author.

9. 1972

158 *provision in his contract*: "Dialogue on Film: Neil Simon," *American Film*, March 1978, p. 38.

("Miss Mother"): David Sterritt, "She Acts, Writes, Teaches, Observes Human Reactions," *Christian Science Monitor*, March 9, 1973.

to sing songs: Cybill Shepherd to author.

159 "*Where does it say they sing?*": Nathan Rabin, interview with Charles Grodin, A.V. Club, May 20, 2009, http://www.avclub.com/article/charles-grodin-28125.

"*spoke about the exploration*": Cybill Shepherd to author.

"*Didn't they have a conversation*": Rabin, interview with Grodin, 2009.

leap from a yacht: Sidney Fields, "The Face Is Familiar, but . . . ," *New York Daily News*, April 26, 1972.

"*She would hide*": Mike Nichols to author.

"*induced documentary*": Visual History with William Friedkin, Interviewed by Jeremy Kagan, Director's Guild of America, conducted over three days in 2007, 2009, and 2014.

Barbados: Army Archerd, "Just for Variety," *Variety*, February 16, 1972.

"*He wasn't around very much*": Rabin, interview with Grodin, 2009.

"*that phone call*": Michael Hausman to author.

NoDoz: Cybill Shepherd to author.

160 *improv workshops during the off-hours*: Sterritt, "She Acts, Writes, Teaches."

"*When I was little*": Chris Chase, "At the Movies," *New York Times*, July 3, 1981.

"*It seemed as though everything we did*": Stephen Farber, *Moviegoer*, June 1984.

"*Rather than the class clown*": Gene Siskel, "Bill Murray Earns His Stripes," *New York Daily News*, June 17, 1984.

"*I got plenty of punishment*": Ibid.

161 *school production of* The Music Man: Lynn Hirschberg, "Bill Murray, in All Seriousness," *New York Times*, January 31, 1999.

"*Now, who's going to audition*": Timothy Crouse, "The Rolling Stone Interview: Bill Murray," *Rolling Stone*, August 16, 1984, p. 23.

"*I'm a dancer now*": Ibid.

"*which was even better than leaving*": Ibid.

sipped gin: Chris Chase, "Bill Murray: More Than Just a Funnyman," *Cosmopolitan*, December 1984.

"*We were inculcated*": Fred Schruers, "Isn't He Romantic?," *Premiere*, October 2003.

162 "*It was an extraordinary chance*": Josh Tyrangiel, "The Many Faces of Bill," *Time*, January 10, 2005.

"*It was sort of a lonely thing*": Dotson Rader, "'Life Is Easier If You Can Share the Burdens,'" *Parade*, February 21, 1999.

"*They thought I was a riot*": Crouse, "The Rolling Stone Interview: Bill Murray."

163 *selling weed out of a suitcase*: David Felton, "Bill Murray: Maniac for All Seasons," *Rolling Stone*, April 20, 1978.

"*I was so bad*": Chase, "Bill Murray."

"*Del," said Ross-Leming*: Eugenie Ross-Leming to author.

"*By the time Del came*": Joe Flaherty to author.

164 "*Sometimes we'd hang three pads*": Jim Fisher to author.

"*made the improv and its requirements*": Eugenie Ross-Leming to author.

"*Do I think Del influenced*": Helbig, "Friends and Coconspirators."

"*No one wanted to call it a night*": Eugenie Ross-Leming to author.

165 *sneak into a forgotten warehouse*: Ibid.

spread their newspapers: Joe Flaherty to author.

"*Comedy's an art*": Del Close, "Comedy and Rage: A Conversation with Del Close and John Guare," *New Theater Review* 3 (Spring 1998): 9–12.

"*Although there is a fair amount*": "Second City, Chi," *Variety*, April 12, 1972.

(Del gave them that line.): Jim Fisher to author.

"*During my days at Second City*": Mitchell Glazer and Timothy White, eds., "John Belushi: Made in America," *Rolling Stone*, April 29, 1982.

"*John worshipped him*": Joe Flaherty to author.

166 "*and out of that*": Ibid.

"*That was something our group*": Jim Fisher, in *The Second City: The First Family of Comedy*, directed by Sharon Bartlett (Very Scary Productions, 2006), DVD.

"*Thirty minutes later*": Ibid.

"*Other times," Morgan said*: Ibid.

"*Oh, they really hate us*": Joe Flaherty to author.

In August 1972 Gary Austin: Gary Austin to author.

168 *Marshall Field's flagship store*: Chase, "Bill Murray."

"*There's a lot of goodwill*": Josh Tyrangiel, "The Many Faces of Bill," *Time*, January 10, 2005.

"*We'd like to offer you a scholarship*": Chase, "Bill Murray."

"It was one of the biggest": Roy Blount Jr., "Have You Heard the One About Bill Murray and the Himalayan Women?," *GQ,* November 1984.

"When you talk about paying": Stephen Farber, *Moviegoer,* June 1984.

169 *"The fear will make you clench"*: Scott Raab, "Bill Murray: The ESQ+A," *Esquire,* May 23, 2012.

"Comedy is not effortless": Pat H. Broeske, "Murray the Mouth," *Stills,* December 1984.

"The reason so many Second City": Roger Ebert, "Bill Murray: 'Quick Change' Artist," *New York Daily News,* July 13, 1990, available at http://www.rogerebert.com/interviews /bill-murray-quick-change-artist.

"He had a very special talent": Josephine Forsberg quote, "Bill Murray on Acting," Lost in Translation Fan Forum, http://www.weareawake.org/litforum/viewtopic.php?t =927&sid=f587906829083d1ce54dfd9bb3ba9651.

"It was clear Del didn't want to direct": Douglas Steckler to author.

"I gotta feed the cat": Ibid.

170 *"Get the fuck out"*: Ibid.

Saint Mary's women's college: Thomas, *The Second City Unscripted,* 63.

"You had to give Bill space": Joe Flaherty to author.

"Billy did not think he was doing his job": Douglas Steckler to author.

"Billy was quick to use his fists": Joe Flaherty to author.

171 *"Billy is angry, tough, bright"*: "Second City's Bill Murray to Play Hunter Thompson," *Chicago,* August 1979.

"I think he respects you": Thomas, *The Second City Unscripted,* 62.

Treasure Island grocery: Christopher Connelly, "The Man You Are Looking for Is Not Here," *Premiere,* August 1990.

"If he perceived": Martin, "Harold Ramis Gets the Last Laugh," 2009.

"You know," Ramis said: Jeff Labrecque, "Bill Murray: The Curious Case of Hollywood's White Whale," *Entertainment Weekly,* August 27, 2013.

"I don't believe what I heard": Tobias, "Elaine May: A New Film."

172 *white lines*: David Picker to author.

"John lost patience with her": Victor Kemper to author.

"It's because we respect": Tom Miller, writing as Tom Cranford, *A Fever of the Mad: A Movie Publicist Works with Francis Coppola, Elaine May, John Cassavetes, Peter Falk, and Richard Gere and Survives to Tell the Tale!* (Hollow Square Press, 2013), 75.

16,000 feet with two cameramen: Tom Miller's Notes, Folder 108, Mikey and Nicky Publicity, Tom Miller Papers, AMPAS Special Collections, Margaret Herrick Library.

173 *"But they might come back"*: Victor Kemper to author.

"Who's gonna see that?": Ibid.

174 *A focus-puller quit*: Tom Miller's Notes, Folder 108, Mikey and Nicky Publicity, Tom Miller Papers, AMPAS Special Collections, Margaret Herrick Library.

locked in a closet: Ibid.

"These ladies want to know": Ibid.

"also improvisational": Ibid.

"Elaine," Kemper said: Victor Kemper to author.

175 *Elaine filled the fridge*: Dan Rottenberg, "Elaine May . . . or She May Not," *Chicago Tribune,* October 21, 1973.

a box of donuts: Miller, *A Fever of the Mad,* 75.

176 *"I couldn't imagine anyone else having invented":* Victor Kemper to author.

"Anyone here want to go up": Joe Flaherty to author.

177 *"You'll love it":* Ibid.

Her camp friends, Chicago kids: Sweet, *Something Wonderful Right Away,* 363.

University of Michigan: Ibid., 363.

178 *"It's like getting to be a child":* Ibid., 67.

10. 1973–1974

179 *We go north now:* Martin Short to author.

"No one watched Canadian television": Ibid.

180 *"What sticks in my mind":* Ibid.

"Everybody was really at their funniest": Paul Shaffer, in *The Second City: The First Family of Comedy,* directed by Sharon Bartlett (Very Scary Productions, 2006), DVD.

"Opportunity was inherent": Valri Bromfield to author.

181 *"When we started in* Godspell*":* Martin Short to author.

"Marty did so many characters": Catherine O'Hara to author.

"freedom was encouraged": Ibid.

"like one of those old workshop exercises": Ibid.

"We were all family people": Ibid.

"In those days," Andrea Martin said: Andrea Martin to author.

"Or vice versa": Catherine O'Hara to author.

the actor, not the role: Stephen Schwartz to author.

182 *"Godspell was basically":* Dave Thomas to author.

"my long, slow, snowy": Jayne Eastwood to author.

"incest and wolves": Robin Duke to author.

Short recalled, "like a demented child": Martin Short, *I Must Say: My Life as a Humble Comedy Legend* (New York: Harper, 2014), 75.

"This," Schwartz said: Stephen Schwartz to author.

"It's no accident": Ibid.

"We didn't love the show": Joe Flaherty to author.

Del and Flaherty wanted Eugene: Ibid.

183 *Flaherty confessed to Doyle-Murray:* Ibid.

"Bernie," Flaherty said, "wasn't big": Ibid.

"The instructor Brian Gordon": Peter Robb, "Dan Aykroyd: It's All About McNamara's Band and the Ottawa Little Theatre," *Ottawa Citizen,* May 23, 2014.

"He reminded me of my brother": Valri Bromfield to author.

184 *"Sitting there, bored":* Ibid.

"He could have been": Ibid.

"the hawks, the doves, the rights": Carol Caldwell, "The Aykroyd Chronicle," *Playboy,* June 1982.

"I definitely led in the booking": Valri Bromfield to author.

"I had never met anyone so young": Ibid.

"We would dress up": Ibid.

"the very thing": Ibid.

"Danny and Valri were wild": Dave Thomas to author.

185 *"Everybody was improvising"*: Valri Bromfield to author.

That's why Candy was so often late: Bob Dolman to author.

lobster and pizza: Sheldon Patinkin to author.

186 *a gay boxer*: Dave Thomas, *SCTV: Behind the Scenes* (Toronto: McClelland & Stewart, 1996), 221.

"I want that guy": Ibid.

"John was so good at listening": Joe Flaherty to author.

hate herself forever: Sweet, *Something Wonderful Right Away*, 364.

"I'd move my head": Elizabeth Stone, "Gilda Radner: Goodbye, Roseanne, Hello, Broadway," *New York Times*, November 9, 1980.

187 *"Show business is about families"*: Stone, "Gilda Radner: Goodbye, Roseanne, Hello, Broadway."

the Young Girl, the Old Woman: Sweet, *Something Wonderful Right Away*, 364.

"I've just never let go": Edwin Miller, "Gilda Update," *Seventeen*, January 1981.

"The Second City tradition": Valri Bromfield to author.

"Okay," Flaherty said: Joe Flaherty to author.

"These guys had no artistic pretensions": Ibid.

188 *"I just loved comedy"*: Ibid.

"Danny and Valri raised": Ibid.

189 *"Improv is human"*: Valri Bromfield to author.

"fascinated by Danny and Valri": Catherine O'Hara to author.

Please, oh please: Ibid.

"Keep up the good work": Ibid.

scared the hell out of him: Eugene Levy to author.

Doyle-Murray, Levy recalled: Ibid.

"I had zero agenda": Martin Short to author.

190 *"I couldn't imagine getting up there"*: Ibid.

Short was "gobsmacked": Ibid.

"Greg," Doyle-Murray, as the professor: Second City Archive, The Second City, Chicago.

He said, "To trust the power of sincerity": Martin Short to author.

191 *tour of Wrigley Field*: Patrick Goldstein, "Candy Tells Tales on Some of His Favorite Comics," *Los Angeles Times*, August 28, 1986.

"This is my town": Ibid.

"He's the kind of guy": Ibid.

"He still had a ways to go": Joe Flaherty to author.

"I think that what we try to do now": "'Et Tu, Kohoutek; or Take 47' Cast Interview," January 15, 1974, Second City Archives, Second City, Chicago.

"But this was my first time": Andrew Alexander to author.

192 *"All of a sudden"*: Ibid.

"blend of outrage and resignation": Bruce J. Schulman, *The Seventies: The Great Shift in American Culture, Society, and Politics* (New York: Da Capo, 2001).

193 *wear his characters like a trench coat*: Dave Itzkoff, "With Bill Murray, Just Take the Trip," *New York Times*, November 28, 2012.

"Using small effects": Mark Leviton, "Dan Aykroyd and Bill Murray Believe in Ghosts," *BAM Magazine,* June 15, 1984.

"He kept us all afloat": Ann Ryerson, Fred Kaz Memorial, Second City, September 30, 2014.

"Sure, you can say": Hugh Boulware, "It's Fred Kaz and All That Jazz: 'Last Hipster' Is the Musical Glue That Held Second City Together," *Chicago Tribune,* December 18, 1988, http://articles.chicagotribune.com/1988-12-18/entertainment/8802250816_1_musical -director-piano-player-second-city/2.

"The whole lounge-singer thing": Tino Insana to author.

194   *"Ladies and gentlemen," he proclaims*: Second City Archive, Second City, Chicago.

Andrew Alexander went to Bernie: Andrew Alexander to author.

195   *"Nothing was bleaker"*: Joe Flaherty to author.

"Most people with half a brain": Sally Cochrane to author.

"They'd be in a drunken bad mood": Joe Flaherty to author.

"You could barely see through": Sally Cochrane to author.

"I do all the orchestral music": Eugene Levy to author.

"It's hard to just flip": Ibid.

196   *"Her personality could bail her"*: Ibid.

"Stall!": Martin Short to author.

"I'm almost 32 years old": Diane Rosen, "Gilda!," *TV Guide,* July 29, 1978.

"She played a woman with a talking shoe": Eugene Levy to author.

197   *"If you think about it"*: Sweet, *Something Wonderful Right Away,* 370.

"What a gift," O'Hara said: Catherine O'Hara to author.

"Because I knew Candy the best": Ibid.

"I was flying blind": Ibid.

"a great theater arts teacher": Ibid.

"Getting the job at Second City": Ibid.

198   *"When Catherine played a character"*: Eugene Levy to author.

"Maybe because everyone": Catherine O'Hara to author.

"at the core of every great comedy character": "Catherine O'Hara on the Art of Playing Stupid and Cocky," *GQ,* June 1999.

"I swear," O'Hara said: Catherine O'Hara to author.

199   *In came Sheldon Kahn*: Sheldon Kahn to author.

Elaine had memorized: Ibid.

"Elaine was so fast": Ibid.

"She thinks so fast": Ibid.

"I was willing to try anything": Ibid.

"purposely badly": Ibid.

200   *"When you've got a million feet"*: Ibid.

"I was learning so much": Ibid.

"Pardon us," Elaine said: Ibid.

201   *"She had printed the outtakes"*: Victor Kemper to author.

"I thought her choices": Ibid.

202   *"I think she worked"*: Sheldon Kahn to author.

"Vic," she asked Kemper: Victor Kemper to author.

11. 1974–1975

203 *"had greasy hair"*: Marcus O'Hara to author.

204 *raced Marcus through the moving subway*: Ibid.

"I'll give you this money": Ibid.

205 *"Dan greeted the cops"*: Bob Dolman to author.

"We had tremendous evenings": Aykroyd, from Bob Dolman's notes.

"We took one look at each other": Ned Zeman, "Soul Men: The Making of *The Blues Brothers*," *Vanity Fair*, January 2013.

206 *"That guy's voice. Who is that guy?"*: Brad Wheeler, "Dan Aykroyd's Got the Blues," *Globe and Mail*, November 9, 2009, https://www.theglobeandmail.com/arts/dan-aykroyds-got-the-blues/.

"The real power and innovation": Ken Burns and Geoffrey C. Ward, *Jazz: A History of America's Music* (New York: Knopf, 2000), 16.

207 *"Put quite simply"*: Steve Balkin, "The Roar of Irony Is Deafening: Statement on Preservation Conference on UIC Campus," *Roosevelt University Blogs*, February 9, 2012, http://blogs.roosevelt.edu/sbalkin/uic-preservation/.

"Well, I'm not into blues": Judith Belushi to author.

"You guys should start a band": Ibid.

"The contrast with Second City": Belushi and Colby, *Belushi*, 62.

208 *"We used humor as a weapon"*: Ellin Stein, *That's Not Funny, That's Sick: The National Lampoon and the Comedy Insurgents Who Captured the Mainstream* (New York: Norton, 2013), 161.

character began with the voice: F. X. Feeney, "Christopher Guest's Tender Follies," *Los Angeles Weekly*, February 14, 1997.

"My first remembrance": Ian Daly, "Wiseguy: Christopher Guest," *Details*, October 2009.

"If you're playing a gay character": Feeney, "Christopher Guest's Tender Follies."

209 *"When Brian moved to town"*: Belushi and Colby, *Belushi*, 80.

"John," Ramis said, "lifted us all": Martin, "Harold Ramis Gets the Last Laugh."

"a fusion of the Second City working style": Stein, *That's Not Funny, That's Sick*, 194.

"just by participating": Belushi and Colby, *Belushi*, 85.

"Like Second City": Stein, *That's Not Funny, That's Sick*, 194.

210 *"We're going to tell the audience"*: Joe Flaherty to author.

211 *"Harold and I would kinda look"*: Ibid.

"It wasn't like we were exploring": Ibid.

"It had no real shape": Sacks, *And Here's the Kicker*.

"We got dirty looks": Joe Flaherty to author.

"That's when I really started": Ibid.

"I was getting tired of it": Ibid.

212 *"Cannibal Girls was a hundred percent improvised"*: Ivan Reitman to author.

"I thought these Harvard guys": Ibid.

"Hey, I've got this hit": Ibid.

"The great skill of the people": Ibid.

213 *"let's do the same show over again"*: Ibid.

"the greatest example of comedic": Ibid.

"If you weren't drunk": Ibid.

"It just opened my eyes": Ibid.

"There didn't seem to be anyone": Ibid.

"secret weapon": Ibid.

214   *"That was the closest it ever got"*: Gene Siskel, "Bill Murray Earns His Stripes," *New York Daily News*, June 17, 1984.

"[Belushi] wanted to see": Judy Stone, "A Serious Bill Murray's Quest for Meaning of Existence," *Datebook*, October 14, 1984.

"Talk about an explosion": Siskel, "Bill Murray Earns His Stripes."

"It's the show I've always wanted": Valri Bromfield to author.

"a good place to give up": Julie Miller, "40 Years of Improv Comedy: An Oral History of the Groundlings," *Vanity Fair*, June 5, 2014, http://www.vanityfair.com/hollywood/2014/06/groundlings-oral-history.

"Everything we ever performed": Gary Austin to author.

215   *"Nichols and May, Severn Darden"*: Ibid.

"All right, Laraine," Austin said: Ibid.

"I felt that American kids": William K. Knoedelseder Jr., "The No Longer Interested in Prime Time Players," *Los Angeles Times*, November 18, 1979.

"They proved you could be smart and funny": Evelyn Reynold, "Nichols and May — Together Again at Last," *New York Daily News*, May 19, 1985.

216   *"It should be young and bright"*: Woodward, *Wired*, 69.

"NBC doesn't expect it to work": Gary Austin to author.

"Look," Michaels continued: Ibid.

"They're like soldiers": Ivan Reitman to author.

217   *"Ivan, is this your coat?"*: Ibid.

"Finally, they realized I wasn't doing any harm": Ibid.

"Watching the process": Ibid.

"He lives his life to his standard": Ibid.

"He was always doing characters": Dick Blasucci to author.

"He would play with anyone": Douglas Steckler to author.

"He had such an influence": Dan Aykroyd to "J.J.," interview, April 2015, *As Little As Possible* (blog), http://aslittleaspossible.blogspot.com/2008/10/ghostbusters-25-and-lost-dan-aykroyd.html.

218   *"There's a lobster loose!"*: Gavin Edwards, "Being Bill Murray," *Rolling Stone*, October 28, 2014, http://www.rollingstone.com/movies/features/being-bill-murray-20141028.

"Your college experience was so funny": Frank Lovece, "Ramis' Realm: Comedy Creator Surveys Career from Second City to 'Year One,'" *Film Journal International*, February 25, 2014.

12. 1975–1976

219   *Recalled one who*: Anonymous to author.

tiny rented Pinto: Abramowitz, *Is That a Gun in Your Pocket?*, 67.

220   *"I can't get this to work"*: Victor Kemper to author.

"in the spirit": Sheldon Patinkin to author.

"Here were two of the funniest": Ibid.

"subconsciously afraid": Martin Short to author.

"I should have been wanting it": Ibid.

"I didn't see myself": Ibid.

"one of the funniest we had ever had": Sheldon Patinkin to author.

Martin owned none of it: Andrea Martin to author.

"I was bouncing checks": Andrew Alexander to author.

221 *Bob Sprot*: Bob Dolman to author.

"Is there any point": Dave Thomas to author.

"We tried every plausible": Andrew Alexander to author.

"there was, almost in unison": Ibid.

"I'll never forget the sight of paramedics": Ibid.

"Second City Chicago grew": Dave Thomas to author.

"He brought that tradition": Ibid.

222 *"I just wanted to get away"*: Joe Flaherty to author.

"Whenever we did a commercial": Ibid.

Andrea Martin's Edith Prickley: Andrea Martin to author.

"The posture, the voice": Andrea Martin, *Andrea Martin's Lady Parts* (Toronto: HarperCollins, 2014), 305.

223 *indomitable feeling of freedom*: Andrea Martin to author.

"We offered her all of the support": "Par, Elaine May Sue Each Other; Film Over-Budget and Incomplete," *Variety*, October 29, 1975.

$90,000 interest in Mikey and Nicky: Abramowitz, *Is That a Gun in Your Pocket?*, 67.

224 *"In total bad faith"*: Jim Harwood, "Suits Fly as Par, Elaine May Bicker Over 'Mikey' Pic," *Variety*, October 22, 1975.

"We had no idea how long": Lorne Michaels on *Charlie Rose*, 1992.

Friday rehearsal had been awful: Doug Hill and Jeff Weingrad, *Saturday Night: A Backstage History of Saturday Night Live* (New York: Beech Tree, 1986), 86.

"There was a spirit very much": Lorne Michaels on *Charlie Rose*, 1992.

225 *"I think* Saturday Night *is about the closest"*: Sweet, *Something Wonderful Right Away*, 371.

"I think 'Saturday Night Live'": Morgan Gendel, "Lorne Michaels: Live From New York — Again," *Los Angeles Times*, September 7, 1985.

"he was the embodiment": Jules Feiffer, *Jules Feiffer's America: From Eisenhower to Reagan*, edited by Steven Heller (New York: Knopf, 1982), 169.

covered in spit: Charles M. Young, "John Belushi: Son of Samurai," *Rolling Stone*, August 10, 1978, http://www.rollingstone.com/music/news/john-belushi-son-of-samurai-19780810.

"He had people who trusted": William K. Knoedelseder Jr., "Trying to Resurrect 'Saturday Night Live,'" *Los Angeles Times*, March 29, 1981.

"I had much less of that Second City experience": Stein, *That's Not Funny, That's Sick*, 239.

"Garrett didn't do improv": Archive of American Television Interview with Jane Curtin, conducted by Jenni Matz, New York City, May 28, 2015.

226 *"What's that group you're from?"*: Laraine Newman, *Kevin Pollack's Chat Show*, no. 105, March 20, 2011.

"Nobody really knew": Archive of American Television Interview with Jane Curtin.

a rose for each: Valri Bromfield to author.

"Wow!" she exclaimed: Ibid.

Carlin coolly interrupted: Ibid.

she missed the freedom Second City had granted: Sweet, *Something Wonderful Right Away,* 371.

"And you can't change lines": Ibid., 369.

"When you look in their eyes onstage": Ibid.

227 *"Everybody was pooing":* Valri Bromfield to author.

"He insists I sign this contract": Bernie Brillstein, *Where Did I Go Right?* (Beverly Hills, Calif.: Phoenix, 1999), 139.

"I was the dad to this group of loonies": Archive of American Television Interview with Bernie Brillstein, conducted by Dan Pasternack, Beverly Hills, CA, November 14, 2001.

"a ninety-minute race in your brain": Valri Bromfield to author.

228 *Joe Flaherty, in the strip mall:* Joe Flaherty to author.

Warren Beatty and Peter Bogdanovich: Peter Bogdanovich to author.

"She is a brilliant woman": Tobias, "Elaine May: A New Film."

criminal contempt: "Par Charges Criminal Conduct in 'Mikey' Suit Vs. Elaine May," *Variety,* September 15, 1976.

Carter studio in New York: Ibid.

"from a person claiming to be speaking": Cameron Stauth, "Hollywood Law," *California Magazine,* November 1987.

Dr. Andrew Canzonetti: "Par Charges Criminal Conduct in 'Mikey' Suit," *Variety.*

229 *he "might have said it":* Ibid.

Alyce Films, by the way, had been traced to Falk: Abramowitz, *Is That a Gun in Your Pocket?,* 67.

"Can you help us with Elaine?": David Picker to author.

"We talked in 'what-ifs'": Ibid.

"Are they cheering?": Elaine May, "Elaine May in Conversation with Mike Nichols," Film Society of Lincoln Center, Walter Reade Theater, 2006, published in *Film Comment* July/August 2006, https://www.filmcomment.com/article/elaine-may-in-conversation-with-mike-nichols/.

13. 1977–1982

230 *"I was thinking, What?":* Joe Flaherty to author.

"We're going to go up against Saturday Night Live?": NBC officially changed the name to *Saturday Night Live* in March 1977.

"Who do you want to work with?": Ibid.

231 *"Our generation had broken into television":* Martin, "Harold Ramis Gets the Last Laugh."

"Okay, but let's try to get Harold": Joe Flaherty to author.

"Has it occurred to you": Martin, "Harold Ramis Gets the Last Laugh."

"I want to do television parodies": Joe Flaherty to author.

232 *"How soon," he asked the room:* Andrew Alexander to author.

"That was going to be Harold": Joe Flaherty to author.

"We were talking about an Orson Welles type": Ibid.

233 *"my five-hundred-dollar face":* Ibid.

"I could see Candy": Ibid.

"Johnny," Flaherty said: Ibid.

"an inferiority complex": Dave Thomas to author.

"Johnny LaRue really reflected that": Ibid.

234 *"I set the table"*: Andrew Alexander, interview, *ADD Comedy with Dave Razowsky*, January 9, 2013, audio recording, http://podbay.fm/show/572391530/e/1357707600?auto start=1.

"It was sort of a non-power structure": Joe Flaherty to author.

235 *"a man at peace in a storm"*: Andrew Alexander to author.

"A lot of items that didn't make it": Thomas, *SCTV: Behind the Scenes*, 35.

"We wanted to keep the Second City tradition going": Joe Flaherty to author.

"For somebody as smart as Harold": Eugene Levy to author.

"that sophomoric phase when you're young": Joe Flaherty to author.

"When we wrote the parody of Ben-Hur": Thomas, *SCTV: Behind the Scenes,* 59.

"We had a twenty-five-minute Ben-Hur*"*: 1999 Aspen Comedy Festival, SCTV Tribute, *SCTV,* Vol. 1: Network 90 (Los Angeles: Shout Factory), DVD.

236 *"It was like this big breakthrough"*: Eugene Levy to author.

"The cast's idea of funny": Sheldon Patinkin to author.

"There's a better take than that": Dave Thomas to author.

undersized office assigned to Bill Murray: Saturday Night: A Backstage History of Saturday Night Live, 49.

"The writers made the show": Timothy Crouse, "The Rolling Stone Interview: Bill Murray," *Rolling Stone*, August 16, 1984.

only Aykroyd lobbied: Lewis Grossberger, "Bill Murray: Making It Up as He Goes," *Rolling Stone,* August 20, 1981.

"People think that working": Stephen Farber, *Moviegoer,* June 1984.

237 *"If you blew a joke in somebody's sketch"*: Crouse, "The Rolling Stone Interview."

"If you say something to him he doesn't like": Christopher Connelly, "The Man You Are Looking for Is Not Here," *Premiere,* August 1990.

"He would give me shit": Jim Downey, *Saturday Night: A Backstage History of Saturday Night Live,* 252.

"I became attached to this soap on a rope": Rich Cohen, "What's So Funny," *Rolling Stone,* October 2, 2003.

238 *"Oh," he said, "I have one more"*: James Andrew Miller and Tom Shales, *Live From New York: The Complete, Uncensored History of Saturday Night Live as Told by Its Stars, Writers, and Guests* (New York: Little, Brown, 2014), 143.

"[Improvisational actors] can solve it": "Bill Murray Here: OK, I'll Talk! I'll Talk!" Reddit, archived post, https://www.reddit.com/r/IAmA/comments/1vhjag/bill_murray _here_ok_ill_talk_ill_talk/.

"That's what that group could do": Edward Douglas, "Interview: Bill Murray Checks into the Grand Budapest Hotel," ComingSoon.net, February 14, 2014, http://www .comingsoon.net/news/movienews.php?id=114604.

"he's the guy who writes the stuff": Miller and Shales, *Live From New York,* 304.

239 *"this was the best group of people"*: Harold Ramis, in *SCTV Remembers*, Volume 1, Network 90 (Los Angeles: Shout Factory), DVD.

around breakfast: Eugene Levy to author.

"We wrote for each other": Joe Flaherty to author.

"It was one of the happiest times of my life": Richard Christiansen, "All Herald Ramis," *Chicago Tribune,* January 31, 1993.

"The thing about Second City": 1999 Aspen Comedy Festival, SCTV Tribute, *SCTV*.

"opening it up to our imaginations": *Tomorrow*, Tom Snyder with *SCTV* cast Joe Flaherty, Eugene Levy, Catherine O'Hara, https://www.youtube.com/watch?v=TrnVIr635bU.

240 *"Far too intelligent"*: Andrew Alexander to author.

"I used to feel": Martin Short to author.

"What's going on?" Nancy asked: Martin Short, *I Must Say*, 13.

241 *Short threw himself into the work*: Martin Short to author.

"and I quickly understood": Ibid.

"For me, it was very liberating": Ibid.

"My work," he said: Ibid.

"were more interested in show business": Joe Flaherty to author.

242 *"Get the fuck out of here"*: Dave Thomas to author.

bodyguard named Tiny: Robin Duke to author.

"Del could find the truth": Andrew Alexander to author.

"Del wanted to kill Andrew": Sheldon Patinkin to author.

243 *Universal president Ned Tanen*: *The Yearbook: An 'Animal House' Reunion*, directed by J. M. Kenny (Los Angeles: Universal Studios Home Video, 1998), DVD.

"That was part of the trick": Manohla Dargis, "'Don't Go into Retail': Ten Years of Days in the Life of Harold Ramis," *Los Angeles Weekly*, August 9, 1996.

"that's what got the movie green-lit": John Landis, in *The Yearbook: An 'Animal House' Reunion*.

"Okay, I'll do it": Woodward, *Wired*, 118.

244 *"Stop! That's terrible! Do it again!!"*: *The Yearbook: An 'Animal House' Reunion*.

"John," Tim Matheson said: Belushi and Colby, *Belushi*, 140.

"for my own confidence": Ivan Reitman to author.

"Summer camp is so much fun": Reitman, in "Commentary," *Meatballs*, directed by Ivan Reitman (1979; Sony Pictures Home Entertainment, 2007), special edition DVD.

"It's got to be Bill Murray": Ivan Reitman to author.

"Has anyone heard from him?": Ibid.

245 *Grays Harbor Loggers*: Grossberger, "Bill Murray: Making It Up."

"It's all artificial rhythms": Ibid.

"I'm only 30": Chris Chase, "At the Movies," *New York Times*, July 3, 1981.

"We're going to start shooting": Reitman, in "Commentary," *Meatballs*, special edition DVD.

"Mr. Murray was considering doing the movie": Ibid.

"What are we going to shoot today?": Ibid.

246 *"The thing about scripts is"*: Joshua Rothkopf, "What's So Funny?," *Time Out New York*, April 8, 2004.

"It's hard to call it a technique": Blount, "Have You Heard the One About Bill Murray."

"I want you to enter": Ivan Reitman to author.

"I knew I had a decision": Ibid.

"Actors can clash in improvisation": Ibid.

"You see it in the wrestling scene": Ibid.

"and whatever else happened": Ibid.

247 *"more delightful"*: Ibid.

"*On Saturday Night Live*": Chase, "Bill Murray: More Than Just a Funnyman."

"*And I don't think a director*": Dan Fierman, "Bill Murray Is Ready to See You Now," *GQ*, August 2010.

"*We'd see a scene shot*": Clarke Taylor, "The Serious Side of Bill Murray," *Los Angeles* magazine, July 3, 1981.

"*I saw Meatballs when it opened*": Frank Price to author.

248 "*Eleven years ago, in* The Graduate": Tony Schwartz, "College Humor Comes Back," *Newsweek*, October 23, 1978.

"*No one,*" Ramis said, "*had represented*": Harold Ramis, Pinewood Dialogues, Museum of the Moving Image, June 12, 2009.

"*The 1980s,*" wrote Stephen Prince: Stephen Prince, *A New Pot of Gold: Hollywood Under the Electronic Rainbow, 1980–1989* (Berkeley: University of California Press, 2000), xiv.

249 John might not survive this: Belushi and Colby, *Belushi*, 201.

Bittersweetly, Bernie Sahlins understood: Jane Sahlins to author.

"*Once you start worrying*": Lawrence Christon, "Why the Longevity of Second City Troupe?," *Los Angeles Times*, March 26, 1983.

"*We were getting people*": John Kapelos, interview, *ADD Comedy with Dave Razowsky*, audio recording, http://www.stitcher.com/podcast/add-comedy-tour/add-comedy-with-dave-razowsky-and-ian-foley/e/john-kapelos-36388319.

"*Lorne Michaels is coming in*": Thomas, *The Second City Unscripted*, 166.

"*Neither the audiences nor the casts*": Linda Winer, "Second City Is Still First in Comedy," *New York Times*, August 19, 1979.

"*pernicious*" misappropriation: Bruce Weber, "Industrial-Strength Comedy," *New York Times*, December 21, 1999.

"*In TV comedy*": Christon, "Why the Longevity of Second City Troupe?"

250 "*the comedy of insult and the zany*": Winer, "Second City Is Still First in Comedy."

"*I was likely to break down*": Kleinfeld, "Del Close."

"*Nice work in the psychiatrist scene*": Wendt, quoted in Johnson, *The Funniest One in the Room*, 198.

"*Now we can do better*": Steven Kampmann to author.

"*Devil mode*": Coven, quoted in Johnson, *The Funniest One in the Room*, 203.

"*There's your genius*": Thomas, *The Second City Unscripted*, 142.

"*Look,*" he said to the cast: Andrew Alexander to author.

251 "*I must say, I was really upset*": Joe Flaherty to author.

"*That was one funny show*": Ibid.

"*At the end of the night*": Bob Dolman to author.

252 "*Edmonton was flat and lonely*": Dave Thomas to author.

"*There was never enough material*": Thomas, *The Second City Unscripted*, 142.

"*We sort of guard each other*": Gerald Levitch, "Second City Fever," *TV Guide*, May 23, 1981.

253 "*It didn't allow any star trips*": 1999 Aspen Comedy Festival SCTV Tribute, *SCTV*.

"*What do you want us to do?*": Dave Thomas to author.

"*We all thought it was hilarious*": Pat Whitley to author.

254 "*I didn't resent them, my friends on the show*": Joe Flaherty to author.

"*I'm going to call Brandon Tartikoff*": Ibid.

255 *"In L.A. or New York"*: Lewis Grossberger, "Belushi: Has Changed, Never Changes
—Check One," *Rolling Stone*, January 21, 1982, p. 21.
"[Belushi] was desperately searching": Belushi and Colby, *Belushi*, 186.
"That's one of the greatest summers": Thomas, *The Second City Unscripted*, 128.
"I thought it was real": Grossberger, "Belushi: Has Changed, Never Changes," 21.
He craved a spot: Dick Blasucci to author.
Texas rehab facility: Johnson, *The Funniest One in the Room*, 269.
"We had a budget in the movie for cocaine": Ned Zeman, "Soul Men: The Making
of *The Blues Brothers*," *Vanity Fair*, December 10, 2012, http://www.vanityfair.com/holly
wood/2012/12/drugs-john-belushi-making-blues-brothers.
256 *"Junkies give the best shots"*: Woodward, *Wired*, 172.
"Where do you want to put the camera?": Ramis, Jack Oakie Lecture on Comedy in Film.
"Action": Trevor Albert to author.
"If you have something urban": Ramis, Jack Oakie Lecture on Comedy in Film.
"And I want to direct it": Ibid.
"I want everyone to feel good": Harold Ramis, interviewed by Resolutions Productions Group, 2009, https://vimeo.com/87816359.
"I don't have a fucking clue": David Rensin, "Dr. Jokes," *Playboy*, September 2000.
257 *"We knew we were funny"*: "Caddyshack: The 19th Hole," *Caddyshack* (Blu-ray,
Warner Home Video, 2010).
"They were a tight group": William Carruth to author.
"I never saw reason not to improvise": Tom Legro, "Conversation: Harold Ramis
and Bernard Sahlins on Second City's 50th Anniversary," Art Beat, *PBS Newshour*,
December 17, 2009, http://www.pbs.org/newshour/art/conversation-harold-ramis-and
-bernard-sahlins-on-second-citys-50th-anniversary/.
"Carl, the greenskeeper": "Caddyshack: The 19th Hole," *Caddyshack* Blu-ray.
"Bill," he said, "when you're playing": Ibid.
if they laughed: William Carruth to author.
258 *"We were afraid of communicating anything real"*: David Eimer, "Multiple Choice,"
Time Out London, September 18, 1996.
"I see where the movie's going": Dargis, "'Don't Go into Retail.'"
"The atmosphere was chaotic": Trevor Albert, Ramis Memorial, Montalban Theater, Los Angeles, June 17, 2014.
"If you say you remember Caddyshack": Michael O'Keefe, in *Caddyshack: The Inside Story*, directed by Amelia Hanibelsz (New York: Pangolin Pictures, 2009), DVD.
"I developed a mantra on Caddyshack": Ibid.
"You know there's a hurricane": William Carruth to author.
"Editing," Ramis said, "was a disaster": Ramis, in *Caddyshack: The Inside Story*.
add more gopher: Ibid.
259 *"Chrissie, wake up"*: Story submitted by Christine, "A Trip to Long Beach with Bill
Murray, A Long Time Ago," June 12, 2013, http://www.billmurraystory.com/2013/trip-to
-long-beach-with-bill-murray/.
"We weren't trying to make a funny movie": Dale Pollock, "Murray Walks the Razor's Edge in Hollywood," *Los Angeles Times*, October 21, 1984.
"Bill was always difficult to find": Lynn Hirschberg, "Bill Murray, in All Seriousness," *New York Times*, January 31, 1999.

"I live a little bit on the seat of my pants": Bill Murray on *Charlie Rose*, 2014, http://www.hulu.com/watch/595859.

Arriving at the beaches of Long Island: Story submitted by Christine, "A Trip to Long Beach with Bill Murray."

260 *"We needed to get"*: Dave Thomas to author.

"where Melonville is?": SCTV, Vol. 2, "The SCTV Writers" (Los Angeles: Shout Factory), DVD.

"Actors would 'Yes, and' us writers": Douglas Steckler to author.

"SCTV wasn't a show that was heavily improvised": Thomas, *SCTV: Behind the Scenes*, 93.

261 *"the first draft"*: Bob Dolman to author.

"You welcomed the input": Douglas Steckler to author.

"It was like taking a test": SCTV, Vol. 2, "The SCTV Writers" (Los Angeles: Shout Factory), DVD.

"when we did those shows we needed": Joe Flaherty to author.

"we never felt ostracized": Bob Dolman to author.

"Canadians observing Americans": Douglas Steckler to author.

"the anchor": Bob Dolman to author.

"As a writer": Joe Flaherty to author.

262 *"The cast wants to do it their way"*: Dave Thomas to author.

"because NBC had to have some guy in there": Bob Dolman to author.

"They weren't used to the fact": Pat Whitley to author.

"NBC," Doug Steckler recognized: Douglas Steckler to author.

John Blanchard, "knew that the cast": Pat Whitley to author.

"we would sit at the monitor": Joe Flaherty to author.

263 *"In terms of television sketch comedy"*: Del Close, quoted in Thomas, *SCTV*, 214.

"Who's gonna make the speech?": YouTube Video, SCTV Wins 1982 Emmy for Outstanding Writing in a Variety or Music Program, https://www.youtube.com/watch?v=H4HXCyfcD6M.

264 *"You haven't tried a woman"*: Dustin Hoffman to author.

"You have the complete works": Ibid.

"It's a tilt": Mike Nichols in Conversation at MoMA, April 18, 2009.

"Some of these changes may be useful": Sydney Pollack Papers, Folder 576, AMPAS Margaret Herrick Library.

"so she'll get nominated": Mike Nichols in Conversation at MoMA, April 18, 2009.

264 *"Elaine is the one"*: Dustin Hoffman to author.

"I didn't know what would come of it": Frank Price to author.

"At the party": Ibid.

"Playing number two": Sara Nelson, "Bill Murray," *LA Herald Examiner*, October 14, 1984.

"Gee," he said: Dustin Hoffman to author.

"Whoever we get has to feel": Ibid.

stayed up that night until two in the morning: Ibid.

"We fit, Billy and I": Ibid.

"He was in Meatballs!": Ibid.

265 *"It wasn't until I screened"*: Timothy White, "The Rumpled Anarchy of Bill Murray," *New York Times*, November 20, 1988.

"where you can make the other person look good": Fred Schruers, "Isn't He Romantic?," *Premiere*, October 2003.

Tab and vodka: Jeffrey Jolson-Colburn, "Belushi's Last Party," *US*, May 11, 1982.

"You couldn't help it": Ibid.

"to come in and try": Johnson, *The Funniest One in the Room*, 222.

"house metaphysician": Thomas, *SCTV: Behind the Scenes*, 207.

267   *"We all loved that guy"*: Mitchell Glazer and Timothy White, eds., "John Belushi: Made in America," *Rolling Stone*, April 29, 1982.

Dan Aykroyd was in New York: Woodward, *Wired*, 404.

"His whole giant body": Bob Dolman to author.

"It's starting!": Douglas Steckler to author.

268   *"beyond human consolation"*: Ibid.

"I found it an incredible high": Aljean Harmetz, "Robin Williams: Comedy for a Narcissistic Time," *New York Times*, December 28, 1978.

"the harvesting of keen talents": Douglas Steckler to author.

threw his hypodermic needle: Kleinfeld, "Del Close."

"the images of the universe": Ibid.

"Is this the way it's supposed to work?": Ibid.

269   *Around midnight, some days after John died*: Judy Jacklin Belushi, *Samurai Widow*, 93.

14. 1982–1984

270   *typed out by Farley's penis*: *I Am Chris Farley*, directed by Brent Hodge and Derik Murray (Network Entertainment, 2015), DVD.

"When he got in trouble": Tom Farley Jr. and Tanner Colby, *The Chris Farley Show: A Biography in Three Acts* (New York: Viking, 2008), 29.

271   *"Chris," asked Farley's college dean*: Ibid., 41.

last three weeks of production: *A Better Man: The Making of Tootsie*, directed by Charles Kiselyak (Sony Pictures Home Entertainment, 2007), DVD.

"He knew we would be trouble": Dustin Hoffman to author.

272   *"an enormous amount of improvising"*: Sydney Pollack Commentary, *Tootsie* (Blu-ray, Criterion Collection, 2014).

"In that sense," he concurred: Stephen Farber, *Moviegoer*, June 1984.

"Every take he does is amazing": Ibid.

improvise the film's birthday-party sequence: Sydney Pollack Commentary, *Tootsie*.

"Bill," Pollack said: Ibid.

Fred Willard's agent called: Fred Willard to author.

"What I was looking at was extraordinary": Ibid.

273   *"They're improvising?"*: Fred Willard, Archive of American Television Interview, conducted by Amy Harrington, Encino, CA, September 28, 2012.

"I want to be in this movie": Ibid.

"It seemed like there was a tremendous": Michael Goldberg, "'This Is Spinal Tap': The Comics Behind the Funniest Rock Movie Ever," *Rolling Stone*, May 24, 1984.

"We were shooting a takeoff on Midnight Special*"*: Peter Occhiogrosso, "Shearer on Tap," *Village Voice*, March 6, 1984.

"Michael and Chris pretended to be": Spinal Tap Production Notes, AMPAS Margaret Herrick Library.

274 *"At that stage"*: Ibid.

"we wanted to improvise as much as possible": Terry Ilott, "Reiner's 'This Is Spinal Tap' Set for Cult Status in US, Now Opening in UK," *Screen International*, September 9, 1984.

"lent itself to the exposure of the self-important": Goldberg, "'This Is Spinal Tap': The Comics."

Yoko Ono, story: Rob Reiner, *Kevin Pollack's Chat Show*, no. 108, https://www.youtube .com/watch?v=ODVfTltkoRc.

"We were literally walking from one lot": Goldberg, "'This Is Spinal Tap': The Comics."

"Going into each scene, improvising": Mark Leviton, "Spinal Tap's Metal Memories," *BAM*, March 23, 1984.

"The first time," he said, "I'd just turn": Aljean Harmetz, "Reiner Has Last Laugh with His Rock Spoof," *New York Times*, April 25, 1984.

275 *a comic "wild card"*: Spinal Tap Production Notes, AMPAS Margaret Herrick Library.

"It's the discipline": Leslie Wolf, "The Splendors of Stupidity: *This Is Spinal Tap*," *LA Weekly*, May 3, 1994.

physically hide behind McKean: Christopher Guest, *Kevin Pollack's Chat Show*, no. 113, https://www.youtube.com/watch?v=CncBFKdL7oQ.

"That day shooting Spinal Tap": Fred Willard to author.

"Is Bill finished?": Crouse, "The Rolling Stone Interview: Bill Murray."

"I mean," he said, "you'd look": Ibid.

"always checking situations": Christopher Connelly, "The Man You Are Looking for Is Not Here," *Premiere*, August 1990.

276 *"He's off on another kind of journey"*: Tyrangiel, "The Many Faces of Bill."

"I think after John died": Siskel, "Bill Murray Earns His Stripes."

"Tell whoever wants Ghostbusters": Stephen Farber, *Moviegoer*, June 1984.

"The word in Hollywood": Frank Price to author.

"I wasn't asking for the impossible": Ibid.

"I've got Bill Murray": Ibid.

277 *"If I see someone who's out cold"*: Edwards, "Being Bill Murray," http://www.rollingstone .com/movies/features/being-bill-murray-20141028.

"Having your writers as actors": Michael London, "A Movie Maker Who Tamed High-Tech in 'Ghostbusters,'" *Los Angeles Times*, July 13, 1984.

"We just made stuff up": Crouse, "The Rolling Stone Interview: Bill Murray."

"We trusted each other so implicitly": *Ghostbusters* Blu-ray, "Cast and Crew Featurette" (Sony Pictures, 2009).

"Because we've worked together": Ivan Reitman to author.

"four writers, three directors": Austin Film Festival Ghostbusters Q&A with Harold Ramis and Ernie Hudson.

"Shooting was precious": Ivan Reitman to author.

"the energy source": Ibid.

"in some unsaid musical way": Ibid.

"You know where you said this": Ibid.

278 *"put a stack of books"*: Ibid.

"There's this Second City theory": Pat H. Broeske, "A Group of 'Ghostbusters,'" *Drama-Logue,* June 21–27, 1984.

"Being on the set": Lesley M. M. Blume, "The Making of Ghostbusters: How Dan Aykroyd, Harold Ramis, and 'the Murricane' Built 'the Perfect Comedy,'" *Vanity Fair,* June 4, 2014.

"was the key to Ghostbusters*"*: Ivan Reitman to author.

"Ghostbusters," Aykroyd said: Mike Bygrave, "The Exorcist," *Time Out,* December 6, 1984.

"I feel that even as slight": Margy Rochlin, "Behind the Scenes," *Los Angeles Reader,* September 28, 1984.

279 *"the money,"* Frank Price said: Frank Price to author.

"everyone was clamoring for SNL *people"*: Blume, "The Making of *Ghostbusters.*"

Judd Apatow could remember: Ibid.

"In the beginning," Tina Fey said: Tina Fey to Eric Spitznagel, *Believer,* November 2003, http://www.believermag.com/issues/200311/?read=interview_fey.

"My brother was eight years older": Tina Fey to author.

"I knew Edith Prickley was funny": Ibid.

"I knew that most of the actors": Fey to Spitznagel, *Believer.*

15. 1984–1987

283 On Halloween of 1982: Charna Halpern to author.

"white-lighting" against danger: Charna Halpern and Jason Chin, "Episode 64: The Life and Legend of Del Close," *Poor Choices Show* (podcast), hosted by Mark Colomb, Nerdologues, March 7, 2011, https://www.nerdologues.com/podcasts/poor-choices -archive/episodes/episode-64-life-and-legend-del-close.

"You had a lot of nerve": Ibid.

284 *"In reality,"* Close concluded: Johnson, *The Funniest One in the Room,* 240.

"Hey," she said to Close: Charna Halpern to author.

the secrets of the universe: Halpern and Chin, "Episode 64: The Life and Legend of Del Close."

"He just embarrassed": Ibid.

"I know there has to be": Ibid.

"little game theater": Ibid.

"If we made a structure": Charna Halpern to author.

285 *"You never knew what he was going to do"*: Ibid.

"You gave me your money": Ibid.

"Why would you be arrested?": Halpern and Chin, "Episode 64: The Life and Legend of Del Close."

"(a) I might gross you out": Ibid.

286 *"I didn't have a plan"*: Scott Raab, "The Master: Bill Murray," *Esquire,* December 1, 2004.

French grammar: Catherine Belmont, "Paris 1985," February 26, 2014, Bill Murray Stories, http://www.billmurraystory.com/2014/paris-1985/.

287 George Gurdjieff: Lynn Hirschberg, "Bill Murray, in All Seriousness," *New York Times,* January 31, 1999.

favorite chocolatier: Gavin Edwards, *The Tao of Bill Murray: Real-Life Stories of Joy, Enlightenment, and Party Crashing* (New York: Random House, 2016), 22.

"like a thunderbolt": "Under the Influence: Elvis Mitchell Interviews Bill Murray," Turner Classic Movies, https://www.youtube.com/watch?v=Q14JhdJ7QHI.

288 *"a combination of things":* Andrew Alexander to author.

"I was getting to the point": Thomas, *The Second City Unscripted,* 152.

"If you're not interested": Andrew Alexander to author.

"I'm going to go talk to Joyce": Ibid.

"In the line of eternity": Neil Strauss, "The Subversive Joy of Stephen Colbert," *Rolling Stone,* September 17, 2009. http://www.rollingstone.com/movies/news/the-subversive-joy-of-stephen-colbert-20090917.

289 *"The world didn't make any sense":* Stephen Colbert to Howard Stern, interview, August 18, 2015, audio recording, https://soundcloud.com/user-959658576-310443415/colbert-on-stern.

"I think that really helps if you're": YouTube Video, Stephen Colbert on getting to play himself, https://www.youtube.com/watch?v=Z2QLoGc6pjc.

"Belated grieving is what it was": Charles McGrath, "How Many Stephen Colberts Are There?," *New York Times Magazine,* January 4, 2012, http://www.nytimes.com/2012/01/08/magazine/stephen-colbert.html?ref=magazine.

"poet-jerk": Cate Plys, "The Real Stephen Colbert," *Northwestern Magazine,* Winter 2010.

"I was just incredibly depressed": Stephen Colbert in conversation with Tim Goodman, Herbst Theater, San Francisco, January 16, 2006.

"There was something viscerally attractive": Seth Mnookin, "The Man in the Irony Mask," *Vanity Fair,* September 24, 2007, http://www.vanityfair.com/news/2007/10/colbert200710.

"I think you could probably use": "An Interview with Stephen Colbert," August 11, 2003, IGN, http://www.ign.com/articles/2003/08/11/an-interview-with-stephen-colbert.

"Well," Colbert explained matter-of-factly: Plys, "The Real Stephen Colbert."

290 *"We didn't have a TV":* Ibid.

"Stephen was fascinated": Anne Libera to author.

"And I think some of that comes from my mother": Strauss, "The Subversive Joy of Stephen Colbert."

"I have to do this": Plys, "The Real Stephen Colbert."

"I've done musicals and plays": Richard Christiansen, "Sills & Co. Games Still Work Fine," *Chicago Tribune,* June 9, 1986, http://articles.chicagotribune.com/1986-06-09/features/8602110214_1_paul-sills-second-city-99-seat-theater.

291 *"and we started playing":* Ibid.

"I'm going to crack you!": Carol Sills to author.

"Nobody," Sills said: Christiansen, "Sills & Co. Games."

"You remind me of Elaine," he told her: Charna Halpern to author.

292 *"It was new to him too":* Dana Delany to author.

Day one, Del started them off: Sydney Pollack, "January 7, 1986," Sydney Pollack Collection, "Bill Murry [sic] Improv Group Undated," AMPAS Margaret Herrick Library.

"We were learning the Harold": Dana Delany to author.

"Breathe in the events of the world": Sydney Pollack, "January 9, 1986," Sydney Pollack Collection, "Bill Murry [sic] Improv Group Undated," AMPAS Margaret Herrick Library.

Newtonian pool table physics: Ibid.

"Has anyone had a nightmare recently?": Ibid.

"When you're in somebody's dream": Sydney Pollack, "February 10th Eve LA Odyssey," Sydney Pollack Collection, "Bill Murry [sic] Improv Group Undated," AMPAS Margaret Herrick Library.

Kurosawa's Red Beard: Sydney Pollack, "January 16th Sheridan Square," Sydney Pollack Collection, "Bill Murry [sic] Improv Group Undated," AMPAS Margaret Herrick Library.

"Is there a way," he asked: Ibid.

293 *"an automatic editing process"*: Sydney Pollack, "Los Angeles 2–10," Sydney Pollack Collection, "Bill Murry [sic] Improv Group Undated," AMPAS Margaret Herrick Library.

"You go from improv to improv": Ibid.

"I got beat up once before": Sydney Pollack, "February 12th — Odyssey," Sydney Pollack Collection, "Bill Murry [sic] Improv Group Undated," AMPAS Margaret Herrick Library.

294 *"I really felt like an outsider"*: Andrew Alexander to author.

"You know what intimacy is?": Martin de Maat, interview, *Monthly Aspectarian*, August 2008.

"I think many of us go through our life": Ibid.

"I'm way out in theory here": Ibid.

295 *"Humor is simply the lubricant"*: Martin de Maat, "Notes from Martin," May 15– July 30, *Boiling Point Improv Blog*, July 24, 2014, https://boilingpointimprov.wordpress .com/2014/07/24/the-last-days-of-martin-de-maat/.

"Look," Kern said: Tom Farley Jr. and Tanner Colby, *The Chris Farley Show*, 55.

"The total commitment Farley": Brian Stack to author.

296 *"Some of the funniest stuff Farley"*: Ibid.

"I want to be a good Catholic": Erik Hedegaard, "Chris Farley: On the Edge of Disaster," *US Report*, September 1997.

As she underwent chemotherapy: Gilda Radner, *It's Always Something* (New York: Avon, 1990), 164.

"Five minutes, ten minutes": Dustin Hoffman to author.

297 *"Wait, wait," Beatty said:* Ibid.

"an enormous amount of film": Stephen Rotter to author.

"Elaine had this whole network": Ibid.

"It was about creation for Elaine": Dustin Hoffman to author.

298 *"The thing that makes Elaine stop"*: Stephen Rotter to author.

"You know," she confessed: Ibid.

"Could you take the S from": Ibid.

"We never shot it the same way": Dustin Hoffman to author.

"Every movie I made except": Elaine May, "Elaine May in Conversation with Mike

Nichols," Film Society of Lincoln Center, Walter Reade Theater, 2006, published in *Film Comment,* July/August 2006, https://www.filmcomment.com/article/elaine-may-in -conversation-with-mike-nichols/.

"This was her sandbox": Dustin Hoffman to author.

big wooden desks: Michael Kirchberger to author.

299 *Blind Faith Café:* "For Stephen Colbert, Chicago Roots Run Deep," CBS Chicago, http://chicago.cbslocal.com/2015/09/09/for-stephen-colbert-chicago-roots-run-deep/.

"Stephen was very, very depressed": Anne Libera to author.

"Stephen," Libera said: Ibid.

"Once I was there for a while": "An Interview with Stephen Colbert," IGN.

"Damaged people are very interesting": Ibid.

"He was actually a great": Stephen Colbert to Howard Stern, interview, August 18, 2015, audio recording.

300 *"Those three were inseparable":* Anne Libera to author.

"We wanted the joke to stay the same": Colbert to Stern, interview, August 18, 2015.

"Paul and Amy allowed": Anne Libera to author.

"And I made a conscious effort": Stephen Colbert to Terry Gross, "A Tribute to Stephen Colbert, A Self-Proclaimed 'Junkie for Exhaustion,'" *Fresh Air,* NPR, December 18, 2014, http://www.npr.org/2014/12/18/371659078/a-tribute-to-stephen-colbert-a-self -proclaimed-junkie-for-exhaustion#.

Scoozi: Mike Thomas, "How Chicago Shaped Stephen Colbert," *Chicago Reader,* http:// www.chicagoreader.com/chicago/stephen-colbert-second-city-late-show/Content?oid =18958403.

"What was interesting about my day shifts": Behan, "A Man of Character," Daily Kos, September 24, 2010, http://www.dailykos.com/story/2010/9/24/904944/-.

301 *"You try so many different scenes in the improv sets":* Thomas, *The Second City Unscripted,* 202.

"It's not a great joke": Stephen Colbert, interview, *ADD Comedy with Dave Razowsky,* November 21, 2012, audio recording, http://addcomedy.sideshownetwork.libsyn pro.com/stephen-colbert.

Colbert whispered to Razowsky: Ibid.

"and hugged each other": Ibid.

"like a deflating teepee": Ibid.

302 *"Because in straight theater":* Plyś, "The Real Stephen Colbert."

"because if there can be this much joy at a moment": Colbert interview, *ADD Comedy with Dave Razowsky.*

"I will do comedy and not drama": Plys, "The Real Stephen Colbert."

"Hey, wait, look": Pat Finn to author.

303 *"Being with Chris was like walking":* Ibid.

"What do we do?" Farley asked: Ibid.

"a major sacrifice for Chris": Ibid.

"We liked the style of both": Ibid.

"was more blood-and-guts improv": Ibid.

"I really didn't like him at first": Charna Halpern to author.

"I want to be on stage": Ibid.

304 *"Charna was mesmerized":* Pat Finn to author.

"*I don't know how that could possibly be*": Charna Halpern to author.

"*He learned,*" *Finn said, "that it's better*": Pat Finn to author.

"*Oh,*" *he said to Charna*: Charna Halpern to author.

"*Try to kill the audience*": Erik Hedegaard, "Chris Farley: The Wild Ride and Sad End," *Rolling Stone*, February 5, 1998, http://www.rollingstone.com/tv/features/chris-farley-the-wild-ride-and-sad-end-19980205?page=2.

305 "*[Farley] didn't have to learn*": Mark Caro and Allan Johnson, "For Farley, Comedy Was His Life," *Chicago Tribune*, December 21, 1997, http://articles.chicagotribune.com/1997-12-21/news/9712210153_1_chris-farley-lorne-michaels-cook-county-medical-examiner/2.

"*Chris was an athlete*": Pat Finn to author.

"*When Chris took a suggestion*": Ibid.

"*It truly was a family*": Jimmy Carrane to author.

"*Sharing that camaraderie*": Pat Finn to author.

306 "*talk about what we saw*": David Razowsky to author.

16. 1988–1994

307 "*to float with it*": The Full Harold Ramis Audio Interview, *Sheridan Road Magazine*.

a single word: Erica Ramis to author.

"*negative human energy*": Martin, "Harold Ramis Gets the Last Laugh."

"*What was really great*": Ivan Reitman to author.

308 "*If the guy can do this*": David Ehrenstein, "Ramis on the Serious Side of Silliness," *Los Angeles Herald Examiner*, June 16, 1989.

"*It made it all clear*": Ibid.

"*Do you think I'm passive?*": Buck, "Live Mike."

"*Did you hear Diane is marrying*": Diane Sawyer, "Mike Nichols," *60 Minutes*, hosted by Lesley Stahl, aired March 10, 1996, http://www.cbsnews.com/news/mike-nichols-remembered/.

"*I am, and have been, terrifyingly lucky*": Mike Nichols to author.

"*I did everything I did with them because of guilt*": Ibid.

"*As actor training,*" *said student Diane Paulus*: Diane Paulus to author.

309 "*completely present in the moment*": Ibid.

"*He would tell stories*": Kathy Hendrickson to author.

"*I think those master classes allowed Mike*": Ibid.

"*Sills, in the end, really didn't like me*": Mike Nichols to author.

"*Mike's hope,*" *wrote his student*: Johnny Zito, "Remembering Mike Nichols," *BIRTE* (blog), January 9, 2015, http://irteinfo.blogspot.com/2015/01/remembering-mike-nichols-by-johnny-zito.html.

"*Look at this*": Rick Thomas to author.

310 "*I don't think he was being ironic*": Ibid.

"*He was really struggling*": Tom Farley Jr. and Tanner Colby, *The Chris Farley Show*, 82.

"*There was heavy betting*": Alex Tresniowski, "Requiem for a Heavyweight," *People*, January 12, 1998.

"Then, fourteen hours later": Tom Farley Jr. and Tanner Colby, *The Chris Farley Show*, 90.

"Belushi's in heaven?": Ibid., 92.

311 *"I went home"*: Bob Odenkirk, *Improv Nerd with Jimmy Carrane*, no. 114, http://www.feralaudio.com/114-bob-odenkirk/.

"Coach," Farley called him: Ibid.

"Doing this sketch with Chris Farley": Ibid.

the easiest decision Lorne Michaels: Tom Farley Jr. and Tanner Colby, *The Chris Farley Show*, 101.

"He was such a slob, a child": Reed Tucker, "That Was Awesome," *New York Post*, December 16, 2007, http://nypost.com/2007/12/16/that-was-awesome/.

"There is, in effect": Caro and Johnson, "For Farley, Comedy Was His Life."

"Although I love this kind of comedy": "What a Wiseacre," *People*, February 4, 1996.

312 *"I'm Matt"*: Brian Raftery, *High-Status Characters: How the Upright Citizens Brigade Stormed a City, Started a Scene, and Changed Comedy Forever* (Orange, Conn.: Megawatt Press, 2013).

"learn to love the bomb": Rebecca Ascher-Walch, "The Right Stuff," *Los Angeles Times*, June 1, 2009.

"You gotta learn to love when you're failing": Antoinette Bueno, "Stephen Colbert Reveals the One Thing He Won't Make Jokes About on the 'Late Show,'" ET Online, August 17, 2015, http://www.etonline.com/news/170104_stephen_colbert_covers_gq/.

"I like to do things that are publicly embarrassing": Joel Lovell, "The Late, Great Stephen Colbert," *GQ*, August 17, 2015, http://www.gq.com/story/stephen-colbert-gq-cover-story.

"We laugh at what you cry about": Dan Via, "Amy, Paul and Stephen Get Wiggy," *Washington Post*, June 6, 2003.

313 *"I like characters that can't be easily defined"*: Steve Carell to Eric Spitznagel, "Steve Carell: The Playboy Interview," June 2008, published on *Eric Spitznagel* (blog), June 1, 2008, http://www.ericspitznagel.com/playboy/steve-carell/.

"was literally trying to rape Jackie": David Razowsky to author.

"We tried it a few times": Steve Carell to Eric Spitznagel, "Steve Carell: The Playboy Interview," June 2008.

314 *"I look at improvising"*: Tad Friend, "First Banana: Steve Carell and the Meticulous Art of Spontaneity," *New Yorker*, July 5, 2010.

"we understood the history": Jimmy Carrane to author.

Treat your audience like artists and poets: Charna Halpern to author.

"It was a religion": David Koechner, *Improv Nerd with Jimmy Carrane*, no. 21, http://www.feralaudio.com/21-david-koechner/.

315 *"One of the cool things"*: Brian Stack to author.

"Just placing improv": Pam Victor, "Geeking Out with Jazz Freddy," *My Nephew Is a Poodle* (blog), May 22, 2013, http://pamvictor.blogspot.com/2013/05/geeking-out-withjazz-freddy.html.

"forgive all of Mesopotamia's*"*: Jack Helbig, "We Made a Mesopotamia, Now You Clean It Up," *Chicago Reader*, June 6, 1991. http://www.chicagoreader.com/chicago/we-made-a-mesopotamia-now-you-clean-it-up/Content?oid=877741.

"started to workshop": Pat Finn to author.

"We approached it like it's a theater show": Jimmy Carrane to author.

316 *"The scene work"*: Brian Stack to author.
"If you had an interesting character": Jimmy Carrane to author.
"Del really liked the stuff": Pat Finn to author.
"We're in the midst of a real": Tony Adler, "The 'How' of Funny: Chicago's New Wave of Improvisation Aspires to More than a Punchline," *American Theatre*, December 1993.
317 *"people who worked office jobs"*: Tina Fey to author.
"There's this old hipster": Adam McKay, *WTF with Marc Maron*, no. 119, November 1, 2010, http://www.wtfpod.com/podcast/episodes/episode_119_-_adam_mckay.
318 *"Your job is to lead the audience"*: Adam McKay to author.
"Adam's belief is you have to": Charna Halpern to author.
"They were real smart and real fast": Ibid.
"We wanted to write sketches": Adam McKay to author.
"Money": Alex McLevy, "*Big Short* director Adam McKay on Political Comedy in 'Fucked-Up Times,'" A.V. Club, December 18, 2015, http://www.avclub.com/article/big-short-director-adam-mckay-political-comedy-fuc-229832.
319 *"We just started hanging out"*: Improv Resource Center Forums, https://improvresourcecenter.com/forums/index.php?threads/improv-interviews.43043/page-3.
"really insane shit": Adam McKay to author.
"Adam was so poor": Charna Halpern to author.
"We were maniacs": Adam McKay to author.
"We had no respect for any other comedy": Brian Raftery, "And . . . Scene," *New York*, September 26, 2011, http://nymag.com/arts/comics/features/upright-citizens-brigade-2011-10/.
"They put [Sanz] in cuffs": Brianna Wellen, "Matt Besser Discusses the Good Old Days of Chicago Comedy," *Chicago Reader*, January 7, 2016, http://www.chicago-reader.com/Bleader/archives/2016/01/07/matt-besser-discusses-the-good-old-days-of-chicago-comedy.
320 *"There was just this freedom"*: Mike Sacks, *Poking a Dead Frog: Conversations with Today's Top Comedy Writers* (New York: Penguin, 2014), 121.
financial investment from Mike Nichols: Adam McKay to author.
"My God," McKay sighed: Ibid.
"They were the ultimate aspirational": Tina Fey to author.
321 *"I want to be like them"*: Amy Poehler, *WTF with Marc Maron*, no. 183, June 13, 2011, http://www.wtfpod.com/podcast/episodes/episode_183_-_amy_poehler.
"so silly and so broad and yet so serious?": Richard Christiansen, "Harold Ramis at the Forefront of Comedy," *Chicago Tribune*, March 9, 1993, http://www.deseretnews.com/article/279786/HAROLD-RAMIS-AT-THE-FOREFRONT-OF-COMEDY.html.
"I think we both felt like we had something": Trevor Albert to author.
"You could improvise on Caddyshack": Ibid.
322 *"I can't make Bill do the script"*: Steve Weinstein, "Happily Living on the Cranky Comic Edge," *Los Angeles Times*, February 12, 1993.
"There were big changes in his personal life happening at that time": David Rensin, "Dr. Jokes," *Playboy*, September 9, 2000.
"Harold, you see, felt that it would work best": Clark DeLeon, "Punxsutawney Paparazzi: Hollywood Comes to Dubois," *Philadelphia Inquirer*, February 3, 1993.
"This was the first we had heard that Bill": Trevor Albert to author.

323 *"He will get it in his head"*: Oral History of C. O. "Doc" Erickson, AMPAS Margaret Herrick Library.

"If I had been on my first movie": Stephen Tobolowsky to author.

324 *"When we did Groundhog Day"*: Bill Murray to John Walsh, interview, *Grantland Podcasts*, November 13, 2014, http://www.espn.com/espnradio/grantland/player?id=11869899.

"Bill knew Harold as his fellow improv": Trevor Albert to author.

"I don't call him, he doesn't call": Bill Murray to John Walsh, interview, *Grantland Podcasts*.

"Oh, she's really good": Brad Balfour, "Tina Fey and Amy Poehler Team Up to Make a Baby Mama," PopEntertainment.com, April 23, 2008, http://www.popentertainment.com/feypoehler.htm.

"I was all about you gotta": Adam McKay to author.

"I remember Tina Fey wrote a play": Nina Metz, "Welcome to the Renaissance of Chicago Comedy," Newcity Stage, August 8, 2005, http://www.newcitystage.com/2005/08/25/welcome-to-the-renaissance-of-chicago-comedy/.

"The first time I went": Fey to Spitznagel, *Believer*, November 2003.

325 *My Mother's Fleabag*: Amy Poehler, *WTF with Marc Maron*, no. 183.

"He's a fucking old man": Ibid.

"[Tina] was very judgmental": Kevin Reome, *Improv Nerd with Jimmy Carrane*, no. 119.

"What do you think that scene's about?": Ed Zareh, "Godfather of Improv," Studio 360, August 14, 2009, http://www.wnyc.org/story/108204-godfather-of-improv/.

"You have really good characters": Tina Fey to author.

"The main thing you learned from Del": Ibid.

"It was a funny sort of pattern in the improv world": Maureen Ryan, "Tina Fey's Climb to the Top of the Comedy Heap," *Chicago Tribune*, September 30, 2007, http://articles.chicagotribune.com/2007-09-30/news/0709290408_1_comedy-show-tina-fey-lorne-michaels/3.

"They were not the typical women": Reed Tucker, "The Girlie Show!," *New York Post*, October 17, 2012, http://nypost.com/2012/10/17/the-girlie-show/.

326 *"Some people are more fully in it"*: Tina Fey to Howard Stern, interview, March 1, 2016, audio recording.

"The thing that interested": Joe Bill, Improv Resource Center Forums, https://improvresourcecenter.com/forums/index.php?threads/improv-interviews.43043/page-2.

"You enter a scene and decide": Fey to Spitznagel, *Believer*, November 2003.

"It's the attack out of nowhere": Maureen Dowd, "What Tina Fey Wants," *Vanity Fair*, December 1, 2008, http://www.vanityfair.com/culture/2009/01/tina-fey200901.

327 *"Once they got Amy"*: Adam McKay to author.

"Once you [improvise] with someone": Amy Poehler to Howard Stern, interview, October 27, 2014, audio recording.

"It was all-encompassing work at the time": Tina Fey, full interview from *The Second City: First Family of Comedy* (Acorn Media, 2007), DVD.

"I made, like, $7 an hour": Kelly Tracy, "Funny Girl," *Seventeen*, January 24, 2008, http://www.seventeen.com/celebrity/advice/a9037/tina-fey-feb08/.

"She was quite round": Ibid.

"because I didn't want it to affect": Tina Fey to author.

On Paul and Carol Sills's suggestion: Viola Spolin Papers, Northwestern University, Box 24, Correspondence — Shepherd, David to Paul Sills, 1965, 1993, 2003.

328 *"I must tell you it was a very moving experience":* Ibid.

"'I want kids'": Stephen Colbert to Howard Stern, interview, August 18, 2015, audio recording, https://soundcloud.com/user-959658576-310443415/colbert-on-stern.

"He would lie down backstage": Anne Libera to author.

"I want to do a scene where I play Maya Angelou": Maureen Dowd, "Jon Stewart and Stephen Colbert: America's Anchors," *Rolling Stone,* November 16, 2006, http://www.rollingstone.com/tv/news/americas-anchors-20061116.

"I'm going to do this as small as I can": Friend, "First Banana."

329 *"When that scene debuted":* "He Brought . . . a Sense of Class and a Sense of Intelligence: A Look at Stephen Colbert's Time at Second City," WGN Radio, September 6, 2015, http://wgnradio.com/2015/09/06/he-brought-a-sense-of-class-and-a-sense-of-intelligence-a-look-at-stephen-colberts-time-at-second-city/.

"Acceptance [of suffering] is not defeat": Lovell, "The Late, Great Stephen Colbert."

330 *"Boy," Colbert said, "did I have a bomb":* Ibid.

"Del knew what that meant": Pat Finn to author.

"I want nothing to do with it": Charna Halpern to author.

"Who's going to buy": Howard Johnson to author.

331 *"By 1994," Kelly Leonard:* Kelly Leonard email to author.

"You know what bothers me about God?": Peter Applebome, "Always Asking, What Is This Really About?," *New York Times,* April 25, 1999.

"We weren't invited back": Marc Caro, "'Anchorman 2': The Chicago Roots of Adam McKay," *Sun-Sentinel,* December 6, 2013, http://www.sun-sentinel.com/news/chi-adam-mckay-anchorman-2-interview-20131206-column.html.

332 *"I'm doing a mainstage show":* Adam McKay to author.

"the big thing in improv culture": Tina Fey to author.

"If you could open a show": Adam McKay, *WTF with Marc Maron.*

333 *"We wanted to change all that":* Kelly Leonard to author.

"We know we can make them laugh": Scott Adsit, *ADD Comedy with Dave Razowsky,* February 17, 2014, https://soundcloud.com/addcomedy-1/scott-adsit-11.

"But these packaging differences": Jack Helbig, "Pinata Full of Bees," *Chicago Reader,* July 6, 1995.

"You took my work": Adam McKay to author.

334 People can be awesome: Ibid.

"That breaking of form": Tina Fey to author.

335 *"It would always come up":* Mike Nichols to author.

"The next day": Bernard Weinraub, "'Birdcage' Shows Growth in Older Audience's Power," *New York Times,* March 12, 1996.

"I never once made a movie": Mike Nichols to author.

"Any small differences between": Newsweek Staff, "Why Mike Nichols Is Working Without a Net," *Newsweek,* May 5, 1996, http://www.newsweek.com/why-mike-nichols-working-without-net-178372.

"The old sketches are still as funny for us": Glenn Collins, "A Double Reunion, 2 Decades Later," *New York Times,* May 2, 1992.

"Mike was very protective": Nathan Lane to author.

336 *"We're going to rehearse it like a play"*: Will Harris, "Hank Azaria," A.V. Club, September 14, 2011, http://www.avclub.com/article/hank-azaria-61696.

"Can I just make it into a history of dance?": Nathan Lane to author.

"[Robin] was always joking around": Scott Chiusano, "Hank Azaria on Working with Robin Williams and the Impact 'The Birdcage' Has Had on LGBT Progress as the Film Turns 20," *Daily News*, March 29, 2016, http://www.nydailynews.com/entertainment/movies/hank-azaria-working-robin-williams-birdcage-article-1.2581394.

337 *"Robin became this pretentious"*: Nathan Lane to author.

"One day," Nichols remembered: Mike Nichols to author.

"Nathan and Robin were": Ibid.

"Is there a difference": Tina Fey, *Second to None*, directed by Matt Hoffman (HMS Media, 2001), DVD.

338 *"I was so sure that I was doing"*: Fey to Spitznagel, *Believer*, November 2003.

"For many of us": Tina Fey to author.

"If you found anything": Ibid.

"With Ali's encouragement": Ibid.

339 *"When the show was open"*: Tina Fey to Dean Richards, *Dean Richards' Sunday Morning*, WGN Radio, aired March 23, 2014, http://wgnradio.com/2014/03/23/tina-fey/.

"It was the best job I ever had": Tina Fey, *Second to None*.

"She was never like crazy confrontational": Scott Adsit, *ADD Comedy with Dave Razowsky*.

"Oh, I'm not making it": Jason Gay, "Meet Four-Eyed New Sex Symbol, 'Weekend Update' Anchor Tina Fey," *Observer*, March 5, 2001, http://observer.com/2001/03/meet-foureyed-new-sex-symbol-weekend-update-anchor-tina-fey/.

343 *"She expects as much professionalism"*: Scott Adsit, *ADD Comedy with Dave Razowsky*.

17. 1995–2001

344 *"This is Christopher Guest"*: Eugene Levy to author.

345 *"I suppose I've always been interested"*: David Eimer, "Pedigree Chums," *Sunday Times*, March 4, 2001.

"Uncomfortable to the point of poetry": Feeney, "Christopher Guest's Tender Follies."

"Chris was very reserved": Eugene Levy to author.

346 *"There's always been something more interesting"*: David Eimer, "Pedigree Chums."

"I think it's going to be called Waiting for Guffman": Fred Willard, Archive of American Television Interview, conducted by Amy Harrington.

347 *Catherine O'Hara's preparation*: Catherine O'Hara to author.

"You kind of need one thing": Eugene Levy to author.

"I think we're pretty much ready to go": Eugene Levy to author.

"I want a lot of this to be unspoken": Feeney, "Christopher Guest's Tender Follies."

348 *"You're directed by the outline"*: Catherine O'Hara to author.

"I'm going to go on about": Ibid.

"Fred thought it would be a good": Ibid.

"the most rewarding improvising": Ibid.

349 *"What happened?"*: Eugene Levy to author.

351 *"It just developed unintentionally"*: Improv Resource Center Forums, https://improvresourcecenter.com/forums/index.php?threads/improv-interviews.43043/page-3.

"We kept it free because": Amy Poehler, interview for the *Onion,* A.V. Club, September 2, 1998, http://www.avclub.com/article/upright-citizens-brigade-13550.

"In essence, in improv terminology": Improv Resource Center Forums, https://improv resourcecenter.com/forums/index.php?threads/improv-interviews.43043/page-3.

"The ladies would bring dudes": Raftery, "And . . . Scene."

"The women's locker room": Ibid.

"I was like a cousin": Tina Fey to author.

352   *"One night they asked me to do the monologue"*: Raftery, "And . . . Scene."

"Me and my boyfriend at the time": Raftery, *High-Status Characters.*

"I saw someone have sex with a chicken": Ibid.

Peter Pan to the Lost Boys: Matt Walsh and Chris Gethard Share Stories on the Beginnings of the UCB Theater, 92nd Street Y, June 24, 2016, https://www.youtube.com/watch?v=gzDxu__xj2o.

353   *"I've still got sores on my back"*: David Rensin, "20 Questions: Chris Farley," *Playboy,* September 1997.

"Unable to sit still," one witness: Richard Roeper, "Chris Farley: He Was a Story of Excess," *Chicago Sun-Times,* December 23, 1997.

"Is that a crack pipe?": Charna Halpern to author.

Del was hallucinating: Johnson, *The Funniest One in the Room,* 350.

354   *"Why the hell does everyone bring"*: Jeff Griggs, *Guru: My Days with Del Close* (Chicago: Ivan R. Dee, 2005), 42.

"He was crying": Charna Halpern to author.

"Get me a big stack of our books": Ibid.

"like me but younger": Ibid.

"Sorry! I got there first!": Ibid.

355   *"I told Barbara"*: Johnson, *The Funniest One in the Room,* 354.

"How do you feel about dying?": Helbig, "Friends and Coconspirators."

"You know," he told UCB: Del Close's Last Birthday Party (Part 1 of 2), https://www.youtube.com/watch?v=7N2GHwPNiVU.

356   *"But as I said before"*: Ibid.

"We invoke you, goddess": Ibid.

"In the words of a wise woman": Ibid.

"No matter what": Charna Halpern to author.

357   *"That's completely backward"*: Gary Austin to author.

"We were actors who wrote": Ibid.

"They still produce a lot of good work": Ibid.

"Even if it's exaggerated": Ibid.

"because I kind of looked straight": Stephen Colbert to the *Onion,* interview, A.V. Club, January 22, 2003, http://www.avclub.com/article/the-daily-shows-stephen-colbert-rob-corddry-ed-hel-13795.

"I did exactly two reports": Stephen Colbert to *MediaBistro,* interview, 2003. Published in Pamela Engel, "Here's the Only Clip of Stephen Colbert from His Days as a 'Good Morning America' Correspondent," *Business Insider,* April 10, 2014, http://www.businessinsider.com/stephen-colbert-on-good-morning-america-2014-4.

358   *"If you have an opportunity to give it right to the audience"*: Dave Itzkoff, "Comedy Ahead of Its Time (If That Time Ever Comes)," *New York Times,* May 7, 2009.

"What are you doing now?": Stephen Colbert to the *Onion,* interview, A.V. Club.

"My joke is always that Stone Phillips": Jennifer Keishin Armstrong, "Meet the Woman Who Invented 'The Daily Show,'" *DAME*, January 27, 2015, http://www.dame magazine.com/2015/01/27/daily-show-creator-i-cant-believe-cbs-put-another-white -man-late-night.

"I did not believe in the show": "An Interview with Stephen Colbert," IGN, http://www .ign.com/articles/2003/08/11/an-interview-with-stephen-colbert?page=6.

"But then we got there": YouTube Video, The Daily Show — Carell and Colbert on improv: Paley Center.

359 *"You guys should hire this guy named Steve Carell"*: Stephen Colbert to Nathan Rabin, interview, The A.V. Club (website), January 25, 2006, http://www.avclub.com /article/stephen-colbert-13970.

"The top half of his body was dead straight": Armstrong, "Meet the Woman Who Invented 'The Daily Show.'"

"In the olden days": Stephen Colbert to *The Onion*, January 22, 2003.

"You can't be yourself": Jenelle Riley, "No More Mr. Nice Guy," *Variety*, November 11, 2014.

"a failed national news anchor": Ibid.

"And that was also a way to protect yourself": Steve Carell to Nathan Rabin, interview, The A.V. Club (website), August 23, 2005, http://www.avclub.com/article/steve -carell-13949.

360 *"Short of having both a comedic background"*: YouTube Video, *The Daily Show* — Carell and Colbert on improv: Paley Center.

when the first plane hit: YouTube Video, Harold Ramis @ Aitz Hayim after Dinner "A," https://www.youtube.com/watch?v=5mMeDhHn86I.

"You've been here for forty-four years": Thomas, *The Second City Unscripted*, 232.

18. 2001–2008

361 *"It seems to me what made me a serious"*: Mel Gussow, "A Cartoonist's Chance to Soar," *New York Times*, March 4, 2003.

"This is an essentially conservative country": Deborah Solomon, "Playing with History," *New York Times*, June 15, 2003.

"We were members of a comic underground": Jules Feiffer to author.

"By day fourteen": Kurt Orzeck, "Stumbling Into Brilliance: An Oral History of 'The Daily Show's' Early Years," *Flood Magazine*, June 22, 2016, http://floodmagazine .com/37319/stumbling-into-brilliance-an-oral-history-of-the-daily-shows-early-years/.

"All of a sudden," Smithberg said: Armstrong, "Meet the Woman Who Invented 'The Daily Show.'"

362 *only meaningful political satire available*: Jules Feiffer to author.

Paul Sills loved The Daily Show: Aretha Sills to author.

"In every spirit tradition that I know": Alan Arkin to Gerald Bartell, Kirkus Q&A, March 1, 2011, https://www.kirkusreviews.com/features/kirkus-q-alan-arkin-an -improvised-life/.

piece of rope, a suitcase, a squirrel: http://theslenderthread.org/broadening-the-arc -of-devotion/.

"You failed!" Arkin would laugh: Ibid.

idiots of God: Alan Arkin to author.

363 *"How do we bring this back to the real world?"*: Alan Arkin, *An Improvised Life*, 181.

"Before those lights come up": Pam Victor, "Geeking Out with TJ Jagodowski (Part Two)," My Nephew Is A Poodle (blog), October 2012. http://pamvictor.blogspot .com/2012/10/geeking-out-withtj-jagodowski-part-two.html.

"discovery of what is already there": Pam Victor, "Geeking Out with Dave Pasquesi (Part Two)," My Nephew Is a Poodle (blog), June 14, 2012, http://pamvictor.blogspot .com/search/label/Geeking%20Out%20with . . .Dave%20Pasquesi%20%28Part% 20Two%29.

"heat" and *"weight"*: Victor, "Geeking Out with TJ Jagodowski (Part Two)," My Nephew Is A Poodle (blog), October 2012.

"Improvisation is itself an exercise in faith": Victor, "Geeking Out with Dave Pasquesi (Part Two)," My Nephew Is a Poodle (blog), June 14, 2012.

364 *turned to his wife, Jane:* Jane Sahlins to author.

In Los Angeles, Elaine ran into Victor Kemper: Victor Kemper to author.

"With Stephen," said executive: Adam Sternbergh, "Stephen Colbert Has America by the Ballots," *New York Magazine*, October 8, 2006, http://nymag.com/news/politics/22322/.

365 *"The trouble with the jokes"*: Charles McGrath, "How Many Stephen Colberts Are There?," *New York Times Magazine*, January 4, 2012, http://www.nytimes.com/2012/01/ 08/magazine/stephen-colbert.html?ref=magazine.

"This show has two characters": Colbert, *ADD Comedy with Dave Razowsky*.

"If a particular moment goes well": Stephen Colbert to David Plotz, "Working with David Plotz" (podcast), *Slate*, October 16, 2014, audio recording, http://www.slate.com /articles/podcasts/working/2014/10/stephen_colbert_on_his_improv_background _and_how_he_gets_in_character_for.html.

"I'm prepared for the idea": YouTube Video, Stephen Colbert New Late Show Host, Interview Process, https://www.youtube.com/watch?v=LS85-jH59KQ.

"I do the show in character": Stephen Colbert to David Plotz, "Working with David Plotz" (podcast), *Slate*, October 16, 2014.

366 *"Stephen," she said, "you look so tired"*: Judd Apatow, *Sick in the Head: Conversations About Life and Comedy*, 458.

"Every time I watch Colbert": Mike Nichols to author.

367 *"Were you scared?"*: David Kamp, "The Cat's Meow," *Vanity Fair*, December 13, 2012, http://www.vanityfair.com/hollywood/2013/01/martin-short-hollywoods-most-be loved.

"as a pebble that I can throw": Colbert, YouTube Video, Stephen Colbert: "America Again: Re-Becoming the Greatness We Never Weren't," Talks at Google, https://www .youtube.com/watch?v=-HpBHWUPa8Q.

"If General Petraeus invites you to do your show": Neil Strauss, "The Subversive Joy of Stephen Colbert," *Rolling Stone*, September 17, 2009, http://www.rollingstone.com /movies/news/the-subversive-joy-of-stephen-colbert-20090917.

"The people in Iraq were so grateful": Ibid.

"These initiations and these responses": Stephen Colbert, "Panel Discussion: The Colbert Report, Second City 50th Anniversary Celebration," December 11, 2009.

368 *"led to a continuing game"*: Ibid.

"All those things": Neil Strauss, "The Subversive Joy of Stephen Colbert."

"You know this is going to be a terrible idea?": Colbert, YouTube Video, "America Again: Re-Becoming the Greatness We Never Weren't."

370 *"That was our alliance, kind of, our big bond"*: Steve Heisler, "Harold Ramis," A.V. Club, June 19, 2009, http://www.avclub.com/article/harold-ramis-29410.

"We are all the spawn": Harold Ramis to Robert Loerzel, "11 Questions for Harold Ramis: An Unpublished Interview," *Chicago*, February 24, 2014.

he could actually hear the film: Tad Friend, "First Banana."

"know the rules of improv": Adam McKay to author.

"You have any ideas for a movie?": Steve Carell to Eric Spitznagel, "Steve Carell: The Playboy Interview," June 2008.

371 *"I could walk into a studio right now"*: Ibid.

"It's almost a think-tank approach": Tad Friend, "First Banana."

"Judd is like a feedback machine": Joel Stein, "Judd Apatow, Seriously," *Time*, August 10, 2009.

"What became clear very early": John Horn, "Keeping 'Virgin' funny, but with its pants on," *Los Angeles Times*, August 14, 2005, http://articles.latimes.com/2005/aug/14/entertainment/ca-virgin14.

"They didn't tell me anything I disagreed with": Ibid.

"I look at the people I meet": Sharon Waxman, "Giving the Last Laugh to Life's Losers," *New York Times*, May 6, 2007.

"It's very hard to capture the energy of men": Jay A. Fernandez, "'Knocked Up' cast was quick on the uptake," *Los Angeles Times*, June 1, 2007, http://articles.latimes.com/2007/jun/01/entertainment/et-knockedset1.

372 *"As a Jewish actor with a very deep voice"*: Seth Rogen, Harold Ramis Memorial, Montalban Theater, Los Angeles, CA, June 17, 2014.

"If I was 20 years old": Gwynedd Stewart, "Judd Apatow answers questions about asking questions," *Chicago Reader*, June 12, 2015, http://www.chicagoreader.com/chicago/judd-apatow-sick-in-the-head-amy-schumer-trainwreck/Content?oid=17980311.

"We're in the same business": Harold Ramis to Steve Heisler, interview, A.V. Club (website), June 19, 2009.

"I never finish a script": Stephen Galloway, "The Angsty Existence of Judd Apatow," *The Hollywood Reporter*, December 12, 2012, http://www.hollywoodreporter.com/news/judd-apatow-this-is-40-400607.

"a thrill that I constantly remind my real father": Seth Rogen, Harold Ramis Memorial, Montalban Theater, Los Angeles, CA, June 17, 2014.

373 *"Isn't this great? Don't you think?"*: David Shepherd to author.

"Fuck loss of privacy": Lewis Grossberger, "Bill Murray: Making It Up as He Goes," *Rolling Stone*, August 20, 1981.

("I ended up staying seven weeks"): Richard Price, "Bill Murray's Wild Ride," *New York Daily News*, May 24, 1991.

Strait of Malacca: Ibid.

"Would you sign this for my sister?": Blount, "Have You Heard the One About Bill Murray."

panhandler's bag of coins: Judith Harney, "Bill Murray, in All Seriousness," *New York Times Magazine*, February 21, 1999.

374 *"Sorry, I don't do autographs"*: David Friedman, "Juiced but Loose," *New York Newsday*, March 4, 1993.

bored at a fancy benefit dinner: Benjamin Svetkey with Ray Bennett, "Quick Change Artist," *Entertainment Weekly*, July 20, 1990.

the Friars Club: Harold Conrad, "At Large with Bill Murray," *Smart,* July–August 1989.

"Why," he asked, "should I devote": Chase, "Bill Murray: More Than Just a Funnyman."

"We just figured he was someone's dad": Brett Martin, "This Guy Could Be President," *GQ,* January 2013.

Bill Murray sightings: "A classic 'Bill Murray Story,'" according to the explanation on the website billmurraystory.com, "is a tale, told in the first person," featuring "Bill Murray doing something ridiculous. Typically these stories end with Murray saying 'No one will ever believe you,' or something to that effect."

"You've changed more than anybody": Kashner, "Who's Afraid of Nichols & May?"

GOODNIGHT, EVERYONE

378 *"the rules of improvisation":* Eugenie Ross-Leming to author.

INDEX

Abbott, George, 40, 90
ABC (American Broadcasting Company),
    215, 231, 267, 357
absurdity, 97–98
Adderley, Cannonball, 84
Adelaide Street theater, 188–90, 194, 204
Adsit, Scott, 300, 331, 333, 334, 339
Albert, Eddie, 160
Albert, Trevor, 256, 258, 321–24
Aldredge, Tom, 76, 78
Alexander, Andrew
    SCTV, 230–31, 234, 235, 250–51
    Second City Chicago and, 191–92, 287–88
    Second City Toronto and, 188, 194–95,
        220–21
Alk, Howard, 60, 62, 95
Allen, Woody, 59–60, 79
Allman, Scott, 313, 345
Altman, Robert, 147–48
Alyce Films, 223–24, 229
"Amateur Hour," 140
American culture
    of the 1950s, 31–32, 54, 59
    of the 1960s, 88–89, 97
    of 1970s–1980s, 270–71
    founding principles of, 84
    during wartime, 124–26, 129–33
Anchorman, 370–71
Ander, Calvin, 88

Angels in America, 364
Animal House, 218, 231, 238, 243–44, 248
Annoyance Theatre, 339–41
Ansari, Aziz, 352
Apatow, Judd, 279, 370–72
Argo Off-Beat Room, 42
Ark Improvisational Theater, 295
Arkin, Alan
    Broadway acting and directing of, 107,
        117, 141–42
    film acting by, 107–8
    "Museum Piece," 71–73
    on Sand, 7
    work at Second City, 70–71, 79
    workshops by, 362–63
Arkin, David, 273
The Armando Diaz Experience, 332, 351
Arquette, Lewis, 119, 347
Arrick, Larry and Rose, 58
ASSSSCAT 3000, 350–52
Atlantic, 59
Austin, Gary, 119–20, 166–68, 214–16, 356–57
Austin, Ronnie, 6, 7
Aykroyd, Dan
    Belushi and, 205–6, 267
    Blues Brothers, 247–49, 255, 276
    Bromfield and, 179, 183–85, 187, 188, 189
    description of, 183–84, 203–4
    505 Club of, 197, 204–5, 219

Ghostbusters, 276–79
    on Murray, 236, 276
    Saturday Night Live, 219, 225
    work at Second City Toronto, 183
Azaria, Hank, 335, 336

Bancroft, Anne, 121
Barefoot in the Park, 90–91
Barnes, Clive, 142
Baron's Barracudas, 286, 330
Barry, J. J., 119, 130, 137
Beatty, Warren, 116, 228, 296–97, 298
Belafonte, Harry, 54–55
Belushi, John
    Animal House, 243–44
    Aykroyd and, 205–6, 267
    Blues Brothers, 247–49, 255, 276
    in Chicago DNC riots, 131–32, 133
    Close and, 165, 303
    contract and management of, 227
    drugs and death of, 164, 207, 267–69, 354
    early life and humor of, 152–53
    Ghostbusters and, 276
    as influence, 41, 296, 310, 312, 353
    The National Lampoon Radio Hour, 206,
        207–9
    The National Lampoon Show, 213–14
    Ramis on, 152, 155, 249
    Saturday Night Live, 226, 227, 228
    at Second City, 152, 153–54
Belushi, Judy, 131–32, 133, 153, 164, 269
Berle, Milton, 55, 263
Berlin, Ida, 23–24, 37
Berlin, Jack, 23–24
Berlin, Jeannie, 100, 142, 158, 160, 167
Berman, Shelley, 43–44, 46, 62, 66, 75
Bernstein, Leonard, 86, 87
Beshekas, Steve, 153, 255
Bessada, Milad, 234
Besser, Matt, 312, 318, 326–27
Bill, Joe, 326
Biloxi Blues, 308
The Birdcage, 335–37
Bishop, Larry, 273
Blanchard, John, 262
Blasucci, Dick, 217, 252, 254

Blue Angel, 55–57
BlueCo, 338
Blues Bars, 255
Blues Brothers, 207, 247–49
The Blues Brothers (movie), 248, 255, 276
blues music, 206, 207
Blue Velveeta, 317
Body Politic, 149
Bonerz, Peter, 119, 125
Bowen, Roger, 25–26, 30, 60, 62
"Box Office Poison," 267
Boyd, Neva, 3–4
Brecht, Bertolt, 20, 32, 98–99
Brent, John, 74, 92, 119
"Brest-Litovsk," 190
Bretherton, David, 258
A Briefcase Full of Blues (Blues Brothers),
    248
Brillstein, Bernie, 227, 267
British censorship, 82–84
Broadway comedy, 39–40, 68–69, 74
    See also specific shows
Bromfield, Valri
    Aykroyd and, 179, 183–85, 187, 188, 189
    Saturday Night Live, 214, 226, 227
Brooks, Mel, 110, 273
Brothers Grimm, 127–28
Bruce, Lenny, 79, 80, 107, 271
Buber, Martin, 102, 103
Burch, Kerry T., 84
Burnett, Carol, 215
Burns, Jack, 55, 74
Burton, Richard, 108
Byrum, John, 259

Caddyshack, 217, 238–39, 256–60, 271–72
Calley, John, 147, 335
Cambridge, Godfrey, 88, 89
Canadian culture, 179–81
    See also Toronto
Candy, John
    on Belushi's death, 267–68
    Big City Comedy, 251
    description of, 185–86, 187, 191
    SCTV, 231, 232–33, 234, 239, 251
    Second City audition of, 186, 187

Cannibal Girls, 212

Canzonetti, Andrew, 228–29

Capp, Al, 59

Carell, Steve, 300, 313–14, 331, 359–60, 370–72

Carlin, George, 224, 226

Carnal Knowledge, 148

carnival entertainment, 11–12

Carrane, Jimmy, 305, 314, 316

Carroll, Victoria, 357

Carter, John, 198, 199

Cassavetes, John, 150, 171–76

Catch-22 (movie), 147–48

The Caucasian Chalk Circle, 20

Coughlan, Robert, 30

CBC (Canadian Broadcasting Corporation), 240, 253

Cerebral Strip Mine, 319

   See also Upright Citizens Brigade (UCB)

Chase, Chevy, 206, 210, 225, 243, 257

Chicago, 13–14, 129–33, 206–7

   See also Second City Chicago

Chicago Daily News, 16, 17

Chicago Seven, 145–46

Chicago Tribune, 65, 146

Children's Theater, 99, 140, 294

Christiansen, Richard, 65

Citizen Gates, 343

Clark Theater, 71

Close, Del

   addictions of, 58–59, 66, 101, 170, 242, 250, 268

   auditions of, 41–42, 110

   Belushi and, 165, 303

   on Bill Murray, 171

   description of, 102, 111, 163, 325

   drug addiction of, 85–86, 87

   early life of, 4–5, 8, 11–12

   The Explainers, 141

   on Farley, 304–5

   father's suicide and, 58–59

   fired from Second City, 95, 242

   Halpern and, 283–86, 353–56

   on human discovery, 8, 74–75

   ImprovOlympic, xiii, 283, 290, 303, 330–31

   on improv's impermanence, xii, 85, 379

   improv workshops by, 80, 111–12, 120, 283–86

   as influence, 303

   Invocation, 269, 283–85

   on Jazz Freddy, 316–17

   on Kennedy's assassination, 93

   last party and death of, 353–56

   May and, 24, 52–53, 166

   in New York Compass, 58–59

   Patinkin and, 75, 85, 101–2

   on Radner and improv's prominence, 309–10

   recovery of, 255, 268–69

   Saturday Night Live and, 266

   on seeing Playwrights Theater Club, 22

   staged robbery by, 16

   in St. Louis Compass, 47–48, 49, 52

   in Story Theater, 149

   Truth in Comedy book, 330–31, 354

   unreleased improvised film and, 291–94

   work at Second City, 74, 163–65, 241–42

   See also Harolds (longform)

"Clowns," 313

The Clown Who Ran Away, 7

Club Paradise, 321

cocaine, 207, 239, 255, 258, 266, 268

Cochrane, Sally, 195

Coed Prison Sluts, 339–41

Cohen, Nathan, 177

Colbert, Stephen

   The Colbert Report, 364–65

   The Daily Show, 358–60

   early life and comedy of, 288–90, 298

   on failure and embarrassment, 312

   Good Morning America, 357–58

   in homecoming scene, 328–30

   immigration subcommittee appearance by, 368–69

   Iraq performance by, 367

   Second City and, 299–302

   at White House Correspondents' Dinner, 366–67

The Colbert Report, 364–65

Coltrane, John, 84

Columbia Pictures, 247, 265, 275, 276

Comedy Central, 364

comedy industry

   on Broadway, 39–40, 68–69, 74

   as democracy, xii–xiii, 366

in Hollywood, 109, 149–50
See also improv (improv comedy)
commedia dell'arte, xi, 33, 183, 187
Committee
  in L.A., 119
  players of, 273
  in San Francisco, 105–7
  workshops of, 111–14, 119–20
community, Paul Sills on, 12–13, 20, 43, 75,
  92, 104, 157
Compass Players
  devolution of, 42–44
  duet of May and Nichols in, 37–39
  establishment of, 28, 29–30
  Flicker on, 45–46
  in New York, 58–59
  Shepherd and Sills on method at, 32–34
  sketches and technique of, 30–32, 40–41,
    46–47
  in St. Louis, 47–53, 65
  See also specific players
Conservatory, 294–95
Contact (game), 6
Continental Divide, 267
Cooler Near the Lake, 146
Cort, Bud, 291, 293
Coven, Larry, 250
Crosby, John, 79
Crosscurrents, 283–85, 340
Cunningham, Dennis, 102, 128–29
Curtin, Jane, 225–26

The Daily Show, 357, 361–62, 364
Daley, Richard J., 119, 129, 130, 131
The Dana Carvey Show, 357
Dangerfield, Rodney, 258
Darden, Severn
  Compass Players and, 41, 45, 46, 58
  description of, 43
  Second City and, 60, 62, 74
Darling, Joan, 76, 78, 88, 89, 90
Daveikis, John, 204
Davis, Miles, 84
Davis, Rennie, 131
Davis, Tom, 238
Deconstruction (longform), 320, 333
Delany, Dana, 291, 292

De Maat, Martin, 294–95
Democratic National Convention, 128–33
Diller, Barry, 202, 219, 228
Dinello, Paul, 299
"The Dirtiest Sketch Show Ever," 352
Dock (nightclub), 39
Dolman, Bob, 205, 251, 260–61, 262, 267
Dolman, Nancy, 181, 184, 240–41
Dooley, Paul, 346
Dorff, Kevin, 316
"Doug," 328
Doumanian, Jean, 266
Downey, Jim, 236, 238
Doyle-Murray, Brian
  Caddyshack, 239, 256
  The National Lampoon Radio Hour, 206,
    208–9
  The National Lampoon Show, 212, 214
  Second City Chicago and, 144, 154,
    162–63, 171
  Second City Toronto and, 182, 183, 187,
    189
  in unreleased improvised film, 291
  Waiting for Guffman, 346
Dratch, Rachel, 316, 342
Dreyfuss, Richard, 273
Dr. Strangelove (film), 83, 97
Duke, Robin, 242, 251, 266
Duncan, Andrew, 43, 49, 60, 62, 64, 110

"East of Eatons," 241
Eastwood, Jayne, 182, 187, 188, 204
Ebersol, Dick, 225, 266
Ed (longform), 315–16
Eh?, 117
Elkins, Hilly, 150, 151
Enter Laughing, 100
Enterprise, 26, 28
Erickson, C. O., 322, 323
e.t.c. theater, 301, 302, 315, 327, 331, 337
Et Tu, Kohoutek, 193
Evans, Bill, 85
*An Evening with Mike Nichols and Elaine
  May*, 68–69, 100
Event, 57, 68
Excelsior and Other Outcries, 63–64
The Explainers, 141

Factory Theatre Lab, 184–85
failure, 94, 301–2, 312, 318, 378
Falk, Peter, 171, 174, 228–29
Family (ensemble), 318–21, 326–27
    See also Upright Citizens Brigade (UCB)
Fariña, Mimi, 124, 126
Farley, Chris
    addictions and death of, 310, 352–53
    early improv and humor of, 295–96,
        302–5
    early life and comedy of, 270–71
    "Motivation" (sketch), 310–11
    Saturday Night Live, 311–12
    Second City and, 299, 306
Feiffer, Jules
    cartoons by, 141, 172, 361
    The Explainers, 141
    on Gerald Ford, 225
    journalism by, 65, 132–33, 145
    Little Murders, 141–42
    on "Teenagers," 59
Feig, Paul, 371
Ferrell, Will, 370, 371
Fey, Tina
    Citizen Gates, 343
    description of, 325–26, 343
    early comedy influence and training of,
        279, 317, 320–21, 324–25, 337–38
    Second City and, 342–43
Fields, Bert, 224, 228
Finn, Pat, 302–4, 305, 316
Fire Hall. See Second City Toronto
"First Blow Job," 211
First Line/Last Line, 48, 56, 68–69, 122,
    153
Fish, Nancy, 119
Fisher, Jim, 138, 140, 155, 164
505 Club, 197, 204–5, 219
Flaherty, Joe
    on Belushi, 154, 155, 228
    on Bill Murray, 170
    on Candy, 186, 191
    on improv, 188
    The National Lampoon Radio Hour, 206,
        209–11
    The National Lampoon Show, 214
    "PTA," 146–47

SCTV, 230–36, 239, 250–51, 254, 260–61
    Second City and, 138–40, 177, 182–90
Flaherty, Paul, 252, 254
Flicker, Theodore J., 45, 47–53, 65, 88–90
    See also Premise Players
Flynn, Neil, 318
"Football Comes to the University of
    Chicago," 140
Ford, Gerald, 225
Forsberg, Jo, 99, 138, 168, 169, 294
The 40-Year-Old Virgin (movie), 371–73
The Forty-Year-Old Virgin (unreleased
    sketch), 313–14
43rd Parallel; or, Macabre and Mrs. Miller,
    165
Freeman, Al, Jr., 88
Friedberg, Martin Harvey, 119, 137
fuck, 93
"Funeral," 165

"The Game of Hurt," 31
Game Theater, 104–5, 127
Gardner, Pete, 315, 316
Gary Austin Workshop, 167–68
Gertz, Jami, 291
Get Smart, 110
Ghostbusters, 267, 275–79
Ghostbusters II, 307–8
Gianas, Tom, 328, 331–32
Ginsberg, Allen, 54
Global Studios, 234, 235
Global Village Theatre, 184, 185, 188, 203
Godspell, 179–82, 185, 187, 189
Goldberg, Dan, 244
Goodrow, Garry, 119
Gordon, Barbara, 35
Gordon, Bobbi, 43
Gordon, Brian, 183
Gordon, Mark, 43
Gordon, Max, 55–56
Gordon, Ruth, 39–41
Gottlieb, Carl, 119
The Graduate, 91–92, 109–10, 114–19, 121–24,
    126
Grant, Cary, 287
Greenberg, Ed, 114
Gregoropoulos, Noah, 316, 331

Grodin, Charles, 158, 159, 160
Grosbard, Ulu, 123
Gross, Mary, 266
Groundhog Day, 321–23
Groundlings, 167–68, 214–15, 356–57
Guest, Christopher, 142
  Little Murders, 142–43
  The National Lampoon Radio Hour, 206,
    208–9, 345
  opinion of *SCTV,* 344–45
  This Is Spinal Tap, 272–75, 345
  Waiting for Guffman, 344–50

Hackman, Gene, 77, 335
Halpern, Charna
  Close and, 283–86, 354–55
  Farley and, 303–4, 353
  on Fey and Poehler, 325–26, 327
  ImprovOlympic, xiii, 283, 290, 303, 330–31
  Truth in Comedy book, 330–31, 354
Hamilton, Rachel, 338
Hankin, Larry, 74, 76
Hanley, William, 115
Harolds (longform), 114, 119, 149, 166, 250,
  285–86
Harris, Barbara
  in Compass Players, 30, 32
  The Explainers, 141
  on improv, 84
  "Museum Piece," 71–73
  work at Second City, 62, 79
Harris, Sydney J., 16, 17
Hart and Lorne Terrific Hour, 189
Heard, Cordis, 128
The Heartbreak Kid, 158–60
Hefner, Hugh, 65
Helbig, Jack, 315, 320, 333
The Heliotrope Players' Production of
  Thornton Wilder's American Classic,
  Our Town, as Directed by d'Eric
  Blakemore; or, Cash Stations of the
  Cross, 315
Helms, Ed, 352
Henderson, Jo, 49
Hendrickson, Kathy, 309
Henry, Buck
  Get Smart, 110

Nichols and, 10, 110–11, 114–15, 147–48
in Premise Players, 78–80
Saturday Night Live, 238
heroin, 154, 268, 353
Hesseman, Howard, 106, 112, 119, 124–25
Heyman, Burt, 119, 137
Hi-Hat Lounge, 29
Hitchcock, Michael, 346
Hoffman, Abbie, 129, 132, 145
Hoffman, Dustin, 77, 117–19, 121–24, 263–66,
  296–98
Hoffman, Jackie, 313
Hoffman, Julius, 145
Holland, Tony, 291
Hollywood production process, 109,
  149–50
Hope, Bob, 55
"Horror" (sketch), 318
Howell, C. Thomas, 291
Hull House, 3–4
Humphrey, Hubert, 131, 132
Hutchins, Robert Maynard, 15

The Ice Harvest, 373
improv (improv comedy)
  Armandos, 332, 351
  ASSSSCAT 3000, 351–52
  British censorship of, 82–84
  Deconstruction, 320, 323
  as democracy, xii–xiii, 366
  Ed (longform), 315–16
  Event within, 57, 68
  first performance of, 26
  formal rules for, 46, 51, 65, 76
  Harolds, 114, 119, 149, 166, 250, 285–86
  invention of, xi, 30–35
  jazz and, 51–52, 84
  magic of, xi, 378–79
  play and games by Spolin, 3–7, 33
  premise of, 38, 65, 76–77
  vs. scenario play, 26, 31, 40–41
  slow comedy, 286, 304, 316, 363
  spot-improv, 47–51, 164
  See also comedy industry; *specific*
    companies and persons
improvisational music, 102–3, 113–14, 206–7,
  272–73

improvisational theater, xi
Improvisation for the Theater (Spolin),
    127–28, 290, 330
ImprovOlympic (iO), xiii, 283, 290, 303,
    330–31
Insana, Tino, 153, 192, 193, 194
Inside Vladimir, 327
Invocation, 269, 283–85
iO. *See* ImprovOlympic (iO)
Irwin, Bill, 291
Ishtar, 287, 296–98

Jacott, Carlos, 316
Jagodowski, T. J., 363–64
jazz, 51–52, 84–85, 206–7
    See also musical improvisation
Jazz Freddy, 315–17
    See also slow comedy
Jewison, Norman, 107–8
Joffe, Charles, 60
Johnson, Lyndon B., 124–26
Jolovitz, Jenna, 301, 334, 337, 342
Jolson-Colburn, Jeffrey, 266, 267
Jones, O-Lan, 291
Joseph, Jackie, 6
Josephine Forsberg's Players Workshop and
    Children's Theater, 294
Justice Is Done; or, Oh Cal Coolidge, 146

Kahn, Sheldon, 199–200, 202
Kampmann, Steven, 250
Kapelos, John, 249
Kash, Linda, 346
Kaz, Fred, 102, 193
Kazan, Elia, 14, 22, 40
Kazurinsky, Tim, 266
Kelly, Walt, 59
Kemper, Ellie, 352
Kemper, Victor, 172, 173, 201–2, 364
Kennedy, Jacqueline, 83
Kennedy, John F., 81, 89, 92–93
Kennedy, Robert, 82, 89, 127
Kennedy, Ted, 300
Kenney, Doug, 209, 239, 256
Key, Keegan-Michael, 360
Kitchen Rules, 51, 65, 76
Klausner, Julie, 352

Klein, Robert, 96
Knocked Up, 373
Koch, Howard, 150–51, 171–72
Koechner, Dave, 314, 316, 331, 350
Kolb, Mina, 62
Kubrick, Stanley, 83
"Ku Klux Klambake," 301
*Kuwait Until Dark; or, Bright Lights, Night
    Baseball*, 306

La Cage aux Folles, 335
    See also *The Birdcage*
Lake, Dawn, 346
Landis, John, 243–44
Lane, Nathan, 335–37
Lange, Jessica, 264
"Las Vegas," 193–94
Late Night with Conan O'Brien, 350, 351
Lavin, Linda, 141
LeCompte, Jo Ann, 88
Lees, Beatrice, 309
Lehman, Ernest, 109
Lemmings, 206, 207
Leonard, Kelly, 330, 331
Levine, Joseph E., 109
Levy, Eugene
    Cannibal Girls, 212
    improv style of, 195–96
    on O'Hara, 198
    as 1063 Avenue Road player, 179
    "Perry Como: Still Alive," 344
    SCTV, 230, 234, 236, 251
    Second City Toronto and, 182, 189, 220
    Waiting for Guffman, 344–47,
        349–50
Libera, Anne, 290, 299, 300, 328
Liebling, A. J., 13, 15
Life (magazine), 59
The Lily Tomlin Special, 214
Lindley, Audra, 160
Little Murders, 141–42
Live Bait Theater, 315–16
"Living Newspaper," 30–31, 78
Living Premise Players, 88–90
    See also Premise Players
Lois Kaz, 331
Lolita (film), 83

Lomax, Alan, 207
longforms
  Armandos, 332, 351
  ASSSSCAT 3000, 351–52
  Deconstruction, 320, 333
  Ed, 315–16
  Harolds, 114, 119, 149, 166, 250,
    285–86
  Movie, 320–21
  by Myerson, 112–13
  popularity of, 330, 331
  Wake, 354
love, 294–95
Luv, 104, 107

"Machine Gun Blackout," 319
Macmillan, Harold, 83–84
Mafia, 61, 71
Maguire, Roberta, 144, 145
Mailer, Norman, 69
Mamet, David, 97–98
Manchester, William, 31
The Man of Destiny, 20
Marsalis, Wynton, 206–7
Martin, Andrea
  Cannibal Girls, 212
  as Edith Prickley, 222–23
  as 1063 Avenue Road player, 179, 180, 181
  SCTV, 234, 251
  Second City Toronto and, 220, 222
Martin, Steve, 248, 308
Marx, Groucho, 59, 143
Marx Brothers, 31, 59, 183, 271
MASH, 147–48
Mason, James, 83
The Matchmaker, 39–41
Matheson, Tim, 243, 244
Mathieu, Bill
  as Committee's musical director, 113
  in Johnson sketch, 125
  music by, 64, 71, 113
  on music improv, 102–3
  residence of, 102
  at Second City, 62, 65
A Matter of Position, 86
Matthau, Walter, 150, 151, 201
Maxwell Street Market, Chicago, 206–7

May, Elaine
  The Birdcage, 335–37
  breakups and reunions with Nichols,
    86–87, 101, 201
  Close and, 42, 52–53, 166
  in Compass Players, 30, 34
  contract with Rollins, 54–56
  description of, 18, 27–28, 67, 151, 172
  early work with Nichols, 36–39
  *An Evening with Mike Nichols and Elaine
    May*, 68–69, 100
  final scene with Nichols, 374
  "The Game of Hurt," 31
  Ghostbusters II and, 307–8
  The Heartbreak Kid, 158–60
  Ishtar, 296–98
  JFK and, 81–82, 93
  litigation and, 158
  marriages of, 24, 68, 86, 99, 101, 228–29
  A Matter of Position, 86
  meeting Nichols, 17, 18–19
  Mikey and Nicky (see *Mikey and Nicky*)
  "Mother and Son," 57–58
  A New Leaf, 150–52, 158
  personal life and family of, 23–24, 37, 100
  seduction scene with Nichols, 22–23, 25
  "Teenagers," 38–39, 56, 59
  Tootsie, 264
May, Jeannie. *See* Berlin, Jeannie
May, Marvin, 24
Mazursky, Paul, 58, 213
McBrayer, Jack, 352
McKay, Adam
  Anchorman, 370–71
  ASSSSCAT 3000, 350–53
  early work of, 317–20
  Piñata Full of Bees, 332–35
  Second City and, 331
  See also Upright Citizens Brigade
    (UCB)
McKean, Michael, 142, 272–75
Meadows, Tim, 306
Meatballs, 244–47, 259, 279, 286
Meat Stop, 103
Metamorphoses, 149
Method acting technique, 14, 24, 27, 292,
  308

Michaels, Lorne
  casting by, 215, 311, 334–35
  description of, 184
  on early *Saturday Night Live* spirit,
    224–25
  at 505 Club, 205
  Hart and Lorne Terrific Hour, 189
  pitch for *Saturday Night*, 214,
    215–16
  Second City and, 249
  See also *Saturday Night Live* (*SNL*)
Michalski, Jeff, 312, 329
Mikey and Nicky
  creation and writing of, 27, 100, 158
  editing of, 198–202, 219–20, 223
  filming of, 171–76
  litigation on, 223–24, 228
  missing reels of, 228–29, 298
  previewing of, 229
Miller, Mike, 138
Miller, Tom, 176
Mirror (game), 6
Miss Julie (play), 16–18
Mob (the Mafia), 61, 71
Monroe, Marilyn, 81–82
Moranis, Rick, 251, 252, 253, 260, 262
Morris, Garrett, 225–26
Morrison, George, 308, 309
Morse, Robert, 40
"Mother and Son," 57–58
Motion Picture Daily, 67
"Motivation" (sketch), 311
Movie (longform), 320–21
Murray, Bill
  on Belushi's death, 269
  Caddyshack, 257
  early improv work of, 168–69,
    192–94
  early life and humor of, 160–62
  fame and travel of, 286–87, 373–74
  Ghostbusters, 275–79
  Groundhog Day, 321–24
  on Kennedy's assassination, 92–93
  "Las Vegas," 193–94
  Meatballs, 244–47, 259, 279, 286
  The National Lampoon Show, 214, 217
  "The New Guy," 237

  personality and interests of, 170–71,
    217–18, 259–60, 275–76
  Ramis and, 322–24, 370
  Reitman and, 216–17, 244–45
  Saturday Night Live, 236–37
  "Shower Mike," 237–38
  on Spolin workshop, 163
  Stripes, 247, 259, 279
  Tootsie, 265–66, 271–72
  unreleased improvised film by, 291–94
Murray, Brian. *See* Doyle-Murray, Brian
Murray, Joel, 302, 305, 306
"Museum Piece," 71–73
musical improvisation, 102–3, 113–14, 206–7,
    272–73
  See also jazz
Myerson, Alan, 75–76, 92, 105–7, 112–13,
    124–26
Myerson, Jessica, 119

Napier, Mick, 301, 339–43
Nation, 59
The National Lampoon Radio Hour, 206–11,
    345
National Lampoon's Animal House. See
    Animal House
The National Lampoon Show, 210–14,
    216–18
Nazi Germany, 9
NBC (National Broadcasting Corporation),
    216, 254–55
Neighbors, 266, 267
Nelson, Peter, 115
nerds, 313–14
New Actors Workshop, 308–9, 373
"The New Guy," 237
A New Leaf, 150–52, 158
Newman, Laraine, 214, 215, 225–26
New York Compass, 58–59
New Yorker, 13, 60
New York Herald Tribune, 79
New York Review of Books, 145
New York Times, 86, 142, 366, 373
New York Times Book Review, 59
Next Generation (ensemble), 137–41,
    144–47, 154
The Next Generation (revue), 144–46

Nichols, Mike
  Angels in America, 364
  Barefoot in the Park, 90–91
  The Birdcage, 335–37
  breakups and reunions with May, 86–87, 101, 201
  Buck Henry and, 10, 110–11, 114–15, 147–48
  in Compass Players, 34–36
  contract with Rollins, 54–56
  on Darden, 41
  description of, 10, 17, 21
  early life and family of, 8–10, 37, 57
  early work with May, 36–39
  An Evening with Mike Nichols and Elaine May, 68–69, 100
  final scene with May, 374
  on Gordon in *The Matchmaker*, 39–41
  The Graduate, 116–19, 121–24, 126
  on humor, 38–39
  JFK and, 81–82
  on language and behavior, 8–9, 10–11, 21–22, 73–74
  Luv, 104, 107
  on *MASH*, 147, 148
  A Matter of Position, 86
  meeting May, 17, 18–19
  "Mother and Son," 57–58
  in New York, 26–27, 32, 34
  on playing the Blue Angel, 56–57
  in Playwrights Theater Club, 22, 32
  repertory theater by, 126–27
  seduction scene with May, 22–23, 25
  Sills and, 103–4, 105, 148–49
  in St. Louis Compass, 50, 51–52
  "Teenagers," 38–39, 56, 59
  UCB and, 320
  at University of Chicago, 13–14, 15
  Who's Afraid of Virginia Woolf?, 104, 108–10
1964 High School Yearbook, 218
Not Enough Rope, 220

O'Brien, Conan, 351, 352
Odenkirk, Bob, 310–11
O'Donoghue, Michael, 209
The Office, 100
O'Hara, Catherine
  description of, 197–98
  on improv, 197
  as 1063 Avenue Road player, 179, 181
  SCTV, 230, 234, 251
  at Second City Toronto, 189, 221
  Waiting for Guffman, 345, 347, 348–49
O'Hara, Marcus, 203, 204
O'Keefe, Michael, 258
The OkStupid Show, 377–78
Old Wine in New Bottles, 332
Omnibus, 59
1063 Avenue Road, 179–81, 184
Orientation, 212
O'Rourke, P. J., 208
Osborn, Robert, 59
O'Toole, Peter, 83

Pally, Adam, 352
Paramount Pictures, 150–52, 171–72, 223–24, 228, 229
Pasquesi, Dave, 306, 363–64
Patinkin, Sheldon
  Close and, 75, 85, 101–2
  on May, 18, 27–28
  on Nichols, 17
  on 1950s culture and Compass, 31
  Not Enough Rope, 220
  Old Wine in New Bottles, 332
  SCTV, 231, 233, 236
  Second City and, 71, 94, 95–97, 119
  on University of Chicago, 15
Paulus, Diane, 308, 309
Payne, Dan, 153
Payne, Julie, 114
Penn, Arthur, 86
"The Perfect Master," 208
"Perry Como: Still Alive," 344
Peschkowsky, Mikhail Igor. *See* Nichols, Mike
Peters, Jon, 256
Petraeus, David, 367
Phantom-Black Rhino, 267
Picker, David, 172, 229
Piñata Full of Bees, 332–35
Pinter, Harold, 91, 97, 167
A Plague on Both Your Houses, 129–30
play behavior and improv games, 3–7, 33

Playboy, 65
Playwrights at Second City, 141, 220
Playwrights Theater Club, 19–21, 22, 24,
    25, 28
Poehler, Amy
    ASSSSCAT 3000, 350–53
    description of, 325–26
    early comedy influence and training of,
        321, 324–25
    in Family ensemble, 326–27
political cabaret, 78
Pollack, Sydney, 264, 265, 271–72, 291–94
Pomerantz, Hart, 189
Ponder, Nancy, 47–49
Posey, Parker, 346
Premise Players
    cancellation of, 87, 95
    establishment of, 65, 76–80
    touring company of, 82–84
    The Troublemaker, 110
    See also Living Premise Players; *specific
        players*
Premise Theater, 100
Price, Frank, 247, 276, 279
Prince, Stephen, 248
Production Code (Hollywood), 108–9
Proposition, 225
"PTA," 146–47

racism, 87, 88–89
Radcliffe, Rosemary, 195
Radner, Gilda
    cancer and death of, 296, 309
    description of, 181, 186–87
    improv style of, 196–97, 305
    The National Lampoon Radio Hour, 209,
        211
    as 1063 Avenue Road player, 177–78
    Saturday Night Live, 219, 225–26
Ramis, Harold
    Animal House, 231, 243, 248
    on Belushi, 152, 155, 249
    Bill Murray and, 171
    Caddyshack, 256–58
    Club Paradise, 321
    drugs and, 164, 373
    early life and humor of, 139, 143–44, 153

Ghostbusters, 276–79
Ghostbusters II, 307–8
Groundhog Day, 321–24
improv style of, 155–56
as influence, 370, 371–72
Meatballs, 245
Murray and, 322, 324, 370
The National Lampoon Radio Hour, 206,
    209–11, 213–14
The National Lampoon Show, 218
SCTV, 231–36, 239
Second City and, 140, 144, 146–47
Stripes, 247
The Razor's Edge, 259, 265, 275
Razowsky, David, 301–2, 306, 328–30
Redford, Robert, 116
Reed, Chris, 316
Reik, Theodor, 58
Reiner, Carl, 100, 107, 119, 273
Reiner, Rob, 119, 272–75
Reitman, Ivan
    Animal House, 231
    Ghostbusters, 276–79
    Meatballs, 244–47
    The National Lampoon Show, 216–18
    on Second City Toronto cast, 212, 213, 214
Reome, Kevin, 325
Rexroth, Kenneth, 59
"Ricardo and the Trained Amoeba," 195
Richmond, Jeff, 327, 352
Riordan, Irene, 105–6
Rivers, Joan, 75
Robbers and Cops, 100
Robbins, Jerome, 100
Roberts, Ian, 318
rock & roll, 273
Rogen, Seth, 372
Rollins, Jack, 54–56, 59–60
Roman, Rick, 317, 318, 319
Roos, Fred, 167
Rosato, Tony, 251, 266
Ross, Christopher, 106, 119
Ross, Katharine, 118, 123
Ross-Leming, Eugenie, 154, 155, 164, 378
Roth, Philip, 64
Rotter, Stephen, 297–98
Royale Theatre, 39–40

Rubin, Danny, 321, 322
Rubinfine, David, 68, 86, 99, 101, 228–29
*The Russians Are Coming, the Russians Are
    Coming,* 107–8
Ryan, Arthur N., 223
Ryerson, Ann, 193

Sahl, Mort, 55, 56
Sahlins, Bernie
    on Belushi, 153–54
    Close and, 85
    on comedy industry, 249–50
    SCTV, 230–36
    Second City Chicago and, 60, 62, 64, 94,
        137–41, 164
    Second City Toronto and, 182–83, 194
    selling of Second City by, 287–88
Salsberg, Gerry, 183, 187, 188
Sand, Paul
    The Clown Who Ran Away, 7
    The Explainers, 141
    on improv games, 6, 8
    music improv and, 103
    at Second City, 70, 74
Sands, Diana, 88–89
Sanz, Horatio, 319, 350–51
Saturday Evening Post, 59
Saturday Night Live (SNL)
    Blues Brothers, 248
    first show of, 224–27
    origin of, 214, 215–16
    reorganization of, 266–67
Saturday Night Live with Howard Cosell,
    231
Saturday Review, 59
Sawyer, Diane, 308, 366
scenario play, 26, 31, 40–41
Schiller, Tom, 224
Schlesinger, Arthur, Jr., 59
Schlosser, Herbert, 216
Schreiber, Avery, 74, 85
Schulman, Bruce J., 192
Schwartz, Stephen, 181, 182
Scoppa, Pete, 176
Scott, Pat, 51–52, 86
SCTV. See *Second City Television (SCTV)*
Seale, Bobby, 145

Second City Chicago
    Alexander and, 191–92, 287–88
    Children's Theater, 99, 140
    Conservatory, 294–95
    establishment of, 12, 60–64
    failures and Patinkin's reorganization of,
        94–97, 99, 119
    first shows and early success of, 64–66
    Next Generation players, 137–41, 144–47,
        154
    Playwrights Group, 141, 220
    second generation of, 74
    show after Kennedy's assassination, 93
    Sills's direction of, 60–66, 98–99
    touring company of, 99, 140, 170
    during Vietnam War era, 124–26,
        129–33
    workshops by Spolin at, 66, 74, 103
    See also specific cast and shows
Second City New York, 74, 79
Second City Television (SCTV), 230–36,
    239–40, 250–55, 260–63, 344–45
Second City Toronto
    establishment and casting of, 176–77, 182,
        187–91
    evolution of, 220–23
    management and first shows of, 194–98
    SCTV, 230–36, 239–40, 250–55, 260–63
    The Wizard of Ossington, 241
    See also specific cast and shows
Sedaris, Amy, 299, 312–13
Segal, George, 76, 78, 79
Sellers, Peter, 83, 97, 142
Session (improv group), 119, 273
"Seven Sealed Strawberries," 63
Shaffer, Paul, 179, 180
Shakespeare, William, 4, 5
Shaw, Bobbi, 273
Shearer, Harry, 272–75
Shepherd, Cybill, 158, 159
Shepherd, David
    Argo Off-Beat Room, 42
    Compass Players and, 29–31, 33–34, 39, 95
    Enterprise, 26, 28, 46
    Excelsior and Other Outcries, 63
    Flicker and, 45, 47, 49
    on player's weaknesses, 49

Shepherd, David (*cont.*)
  Playwrights Theater Club by, 19–21, 22, 25
  on scenario play, 26, 62
Shore, Howard, 207, 225
Short, Martin
  Colbert and, 367
  on improv, 220
  as 1063 Avenue Road player, 179, 180, 181
  Second City Toronto, 189–90, 240–41, 251
Short, Mike, 252
"Shower Mike," 237–38
Sills, Aretha, 128
Sills, Carol, 92, 102–3, 148, 309
Sills, Paul
  on community, 12–13, 20, 43, 75, 92, 104, 157
  Compass Players and, 28, 32, 53
  direction by, 98–99
  disenchantment of, 92, 95
  early life of, 5, 7–8
  establishment and early success of Second City, 60–66
  European tour of, 32–33
  Game Theater, 104–5, 127
  meeting Carol, 102–3
  memorial of, 373
  New Actors Workshop, 308–9, 373
  Nichols and, 103–4, 105, 148–49
  opinion of *The Daily Show*, 362
  Playwrights Theater Club by, 20–21, 22, 25
  Sills and Company, 290–91
  Story Theater, 127–29, 130, 149, 309
  Tonight theater group by, 13–14, 16, 20
Sills, William, 5
Sills and Company, 290–91
Silveira, Ruth, 114
Simmons, Matty, 212
Simon, Neil, 90, 158–59
Slate, Jenny, 352
Sloane, Joyce, 153, 163, 170, 250, 288, 360
slow comedy, 286, 304, 316, 363
  See also Jazz Freddy
Smigel, Robert, 311, 357
Smithberg, Madeleine, 357–58, 361
SNL. See *Saturday Night Live* (SNL)
Sontag, Susan, 15

Sound One, 297–98
Spolin, Viola
  book by, 127–28, 290, 330
  Compass Players and, 28
  description of, 6
  early life of, 3
  fired from Second City, 99
  immigrant work by, xi
  New Actors Workshop, 308–9, 373
  play and improv games by, 3–7
  Second City workshops by, 66, 74, 103
  Shepherd and, 327–28
spot-improv, 47–51, 164
Sprot, Bob, 221
Stack, Brian, 295, 296, 315, 316
Staahl, Jim, 191, 192
Steckler, Douglas, 170, 217, 260, 262, 268
The Steve Allen Show, 43, 58
Stevenson, Adlai, 59
Stewart, Jon, 362
Stewart, Mel, 119
Stiers, David Ogden, 120
St. Louis Compass, 47–53, 65
Story Theater, 127–29, 130, 149, 309
Strasberg, Lee, 22, 27, 32, 33, 57
A Streetcar Named Desire, 14
Stripes, 247, 259, 279
Stroth, Miles, 318
Students for a Democratic Society, 132
Sullavan, Margaret, 287
Sutherland, Donald, 243
Sylbert, Anthea, 151

Talley, Jill, 310
Tartikoff, Brandon, 254
Taylor, Elizabeth, 108
Tebelak, John-Michael, 181, 182
"Teenagers," 38–39, 56, 59
That Was the Week That Was (TW3), 110
Theaker, Deborah, 346
Theatre Regulation Act of 1843 (UK), 82–83
This Is Spinal Tap, 272–75, 345
Thomas, Dave
  on Aykroyd and Bromfield, 184
  on Candy, 233
  on *Godspell*, 182
  as 1063 Avenue Road player, 179

SCTV, 230, 234, 236, 251, 260–61
  at Second City Toronto, 220–22, 230, 233, 241–42
Thomas, Rick, 309–10
"Three Mad Rituals," 320
Time (magazine), 65
Time Dash, 286
Tippecanoe and Déjà Vu, 188
Tobolowsky, Stephen, 323–24
Tolan, Miriam, 316
Tomlin, Lily, 215
The Tonight Show (with Steve Allen), 110
Tonight theater group, 13–14, 16, 20
Tootsie, 263–66, 271–72
Toronto, 176–77, 182
  See also Second City Toronto
Transcendental Meditation, 283
Troobnick, Eugene, 62
The Troublemaker, 110
True Confessions, 148
Truth in Comedy (Halpern and Close), 330–31, 354
Turman, Larry, 91–92, 115
The TV Show, 273
Tynan, Kenneth, 84
The Typewriter, 20–21

United Talent Agency, 370
Universal Studios, 243
University of Chicago, 12–15
Upright Citizens Brigade (UCB), 317–20, 350–53, 377–78

Variety, 165
ventriloquist and dummy form, 79
Victim's Family. *See* Family (ensemble)
Vietnam War
  protest about, 129–33
  sketch on, 124–26
Village Vanguard, 55, 56
Village Voice, 65, 362
Virtual Reality, 319–20

Waiting for Godot, 308
Waiting for Guffman, 344–50
Wake, 354
Walsh, Matt, 312, 319, 350–53
Warner, Jack, 108
Watergate Tomorrow, Comedy Tonight, 191
Weaver, Sigourney, 278
We Made a Mesopotamia, Now You Clean It Up, 315
Wendt, George, 250
West, Bing, 367
West Compass Players, 153
Westminster Place Kitchen Rules. *See* Kitchen Rules
White House Correspondents' Dinner, 366–67
Whitley, Pat, 262
Who's Afraid of Virginia Woolf?, 104, 108–10
Whose Line Is It Anyway?, 317
Willard, Fred
  Little Murders, 141, 142–43
  on political comedy, 95
  at Second City, 96, 98
  This is Spinal Tap, 272, 274–75
  Waiting for Guffman, 345, 346, 347, 348
William Morris Agency, 95–96
Williams, Robin, 250, 268, 308, 335–37
Willingham, Calder, 115
Winstead, Lizz, 357
Winters, Jonathan, 107
Winters, Ralph, 258
The Wizard of Ossington, 241
"Wolverines," 227
Woolsey, Lynn, 367
Working Girl, 308
World Trade Center attacks (2001), 360

Yablans, Frank, 171, 201–2
yippies, 128–33
Young Actors Company, 5–7, 28

Zito, Johnny, 309